William P. Tolley

THE MEDIAEVAL MIND

THE
MEDIAEVAL MIND

A HISTORY OF THE DEVELOPMENT
OF THOUGHT AND EMOTION
IN THE MIDDLE AGES

BY

HENRY OSBORN TAYLOR

IN TWO VOLUMES

VOL. I

FOURTH EDITION

CAMBRIDGE, MASSACHUSETTS
HARVARD UNIVERSITY PRESS
1949

The Mediaeval Mind *was part of the author's bequest to Harvard College. This first issue to appear under the imprint of the Harvard University Press is the fifth printing of the fourth edition.*

PRINTED IN THE UNITED STATES OF AMERICA

TO

J. I. T.

PREFACE TO THE FOURTH EDITION

THE second edition of this book was carefully corrected and revised. The third (American) edition was reprinted from the second. Since then, for my fourth edition, I have altered a few statements and inserted some recent references, but without trying to include a full list of books and articles upon the Middle Ages, which have appeared in the last years. I have seen nothing, however, suggesting any material change in my attempt to portray the mediaeval culture or, as I have phrased it, the development of thought and emotion in the Middle Ages.

HENRY OSBORN TAYLOR.

NEW YORK, *March* 1925.

vii

PREFACE TO THE SECOND EDITION

WHEN through some years of happy labour one has written a book after his own plan, and has set forth in it the things which were to him interesting and valuable, there is no keener pleasure than to have others likewise find them so. The reception of *The Mediaeval Mind* has been very gratifying. My thanks are due to those reviewers who have praised it above its deserts, and to those whose salutary criticisms have been availed of for the present edition.

The book has been carefully reconsidered throughout, and some statements have been changed or amplified. A new chapter has been introduced upon the Towns and Guilds and the Crusades, regarded as phases of mediaeval growth. My translations from the Latin have been examined and the slips corrected. Although occasionally abridged, I have tried to keep them literal, and free from thoughts not in the original.

HENRY OSBORN TAYLOR.

NEW YORK, *January* 1914.

PREFACE TO THE FIRST EDITION

THE Middle Ages! They seem so far away; intellectually so preposterous, spiritually so strange. Bits of them
may touch our sympathy, please our taste; their window-
glass, their sculpture, certain of their stories, their romances,
—as if those straitened ages really were the time of
romance, which they were not, God knows, in the sense
commonly taken. Yet perhaps they were such intellectually, or at least spiritually. Their *terra*—not for them
incognita, though full of mystery and pall and vaguer
glory—was not the earth. It was the land of metaphysical
construction and the land of spiritual passion. There lay
their romance, thither pointed their veriest thinking, thither
drew their utter yearning.

Is it possible that the Middle Ages should speak to
us, as through a common humanity? Their mask is by
no means dumb: in full voice speaks the noble beauty
of Chartres Cathedral. Such mediaeval product, we hope,
is of the universal human, and therefore of us as well as
of the bygone craftsmen. Why it moves us, we are not
certain, being ignorant, perhaps, of the building's formative
and earnestly intended meaning. Do we care to get at
that ?   There is no way save by entering the mediaeval
depths, penetrating to the *rationale* of the Middle Ages,
learning the *doctrinale*, or *emotionale*, of the modes in which
they still present themselves so persuasively.

But if the pageant of those centuries charm our eyes
with forms that seem so full of meaning, why should we

stand indifferent to the harnessed processes of mediaeval thinking and the passion surging through the thought? Thought marshalled the great mediaeval procession, which moved to measures of pulsating and glorifying emotion. Shall we not press on, through knowledge, and search out its efficient causes, so that we too may feel the reality of the mediaeval argumentation, with the possible validity of mediaeval conclusions, and tread those channels of mediaeval passion which were cleared and deepened by the thought? This would be to reach human comradeship with mediaeval motives, no longer found too remote for our sympathy, or too fantastic or shallow for our understanding.

But where is the path through these footless mazes? Obviously, if we would attain, perhaps, no unified, but at least an orderly presentation of mediaeval intellectual and emotional development, we must avoid entanglements with manifold and not always relevant detail. We must not drift too far with studies of daily life, habits and dress, wars and raiding, crimes and brutalities, or trade and craft and agriculture. Nor will it be wise to keep too close to theology or within the lines of growth of secular and ecclesiastical institutions. Let the student be mindful of his purpose (which is my purpose in this book) to follow through the Middle Ages the development of intellectual energy and the growth of emotion. Holding this end in view, we, students all, shall not stray from our quest after those human qualities which impelled the strivings of mediaeval men and women, informed their imaginations, and moved them to love and tears and pity.

The plan and method by which I have endeavoured to realize this purpose in my book may be gathered from the Table of Contents and the First Chapter, which is introductory. These will obviate the need of sketching here the order of presentation of the successive or co-ordinated topics forming the subject-matter.

Yet one word as to the standpoint from which the book is written. An historian explains by the standards and limitations of the times to which his people belong. He judges—for he must also judge—by his own best wisdom. His sympathy cannot but reach out to those who lived up to their best understanding of life ; for who can do more ? Yet woe unto that man whose mind is closed, whose standards are material and base.

Not only shalt thou do what seems well to thee ; but thou shalt do right, with wisdom. History has laid some thousands of years of emphasis on this. Thou shalt not only be sincere, but thou shalt be righteous, and not iniquitous ; beneficent, and not malignant ; loving and lovable, and not hating and hateful. Thou shalt be a promoter of light, and not of darkness ; an illuminator, and not an obscurer. Not only shalt thou seek to choose aright, but at thy peril thou shalt so choose. " Unto him that hath shall be given "—nothing is said about sincerity. The fool, the maniac, is sincere ; the mainsprings of the good which we may commend lie deeper.

So, and at *his* peril likewise, must the historian judge. He cannot state the facts and sit aloof, impartial between good and ill, between success and failure, progress and retrogression, the soul's health and loveliness, and spiritual foulness and disease. He must love and hate, and at his peril love aright and hate what is truly hateful. And although his sympathies quiver to understand and feel as the man and woman before him, his sympathies must be controlled by wisdom.

Whatever may be one's beliefs, a realization of the power and import of the Christian Faith is needed for an understanding of the thoughts and feelings moving the men and women of the Middle Ages, and for a just appreciation of their aspirations and ideals. Perhaps the fittest standard to apply to them is one's own broadest conception of the Christian scheme, the Christian scheme whole and entire with the full life of Christ's Gospel. Every age has offered an interpretation of that Gospel and an attempt at fulfilment. Neither the interpretation of the Church Fathers, nor that of the Middle Ages satisfies us now. And by our further understanding of life and the Gospel of life, we criticize the judgment of mediaeval men. We have to sympathize with their best, and understand their lives out of their lives and the conditions in which they were passed. But we must judge according to our own best wisdom, and out of ourselves offer our comment and contribution.

HENRY OSBORN TAYLOR.

NEW YORK, *January* 1911.

CONTENTS

BOOK I

THE GROUNDWORK

CHAPTER XII

CHAPTER XIII

CHAPTER XIV

CHAPTER XV

BOOK I
THE GROUNDWORK

CHAPTER I

GENESIS OF THE MEDIAEVAL GENIUS

THE antique civilization of the Roman Empire was followed by that depression of decadence and barbarization which separates antiquity from the Middle Ages. Out of the confusion of this intervening period emerged the mediaeval peoples of western Europe. These, as knowledge increased with them, began to manifest spiritual traits having no clear counterpart in the ancient sources from which they drew the matter of their thought and contemplation.

The past which furnished the content of mediaeval thought was twofold, very dual, even carrying within itself the elements of irreconcilable conflict ; and yet with its opposing fronts seemingly confederated, if not made into one. Sprung from such warring elements, fashioned by all the interests of life in heaven as well as life on earth, the traits and faculties of mediaeval humanity were to make a motley company. Clearly each mediaeval century will offer a manifold of disparity and irrelationship, not to be brought to unity, any more than can be followed to the breast of one mighty wind-god the blasts that blow from every quarter over the waters of our own time. Nevertheless, each mediaeval century, and if one will, the entire Middle Ages, seen in distant perspective, presents a consistent picture, in which dominant mediaeval traits, retaining their due pre-eminence, may afford a just conception of the mediaeval genius.[1]

[1] The present work is not occupied with the brutalities of mediaeval life, nor with all the lower grades of ignorance and superstition abounding in the Middle Ages, and still existing, in a less degree, through parts of Spain and southern

I

While complex in themselves, and intricate in their interaction, the elements that were to form the spiritual constituency of the Middle Ages of western Europe may be disentangled and regarded separately. There was first the element of the antique, which was descended from the thought and knowledge current in Italy and the western provinces of the Roman Empire, where Latin was the common language. In those Roman times, this fund of thought and knowledge consisted of Greek metaphysics, physical science, and ethics, and also of much that the Latins had themselves evolved, especially in private law and political institutions.

Rome had borrowed her philosophy and the motives of her literature and art from Greece. At first, quite provincially, she drew as from a foreign source ; but as the great Republic extended her boundaries around the Mediterranean world, and brought under her levelling power the Hellenized or still Asiatic East, and Africa and Spain and Gaul as well, Greek thought, as the informing principle of knowledge, was diffused throughout all this Roman Empire, and ceased to be alien to the Latin West. Yet the peoples of the West did not become Hellenized, or change their speech for Greek. Latin held its own against its subtle rival, and continued to advance with power through the lands which had spoken other tongues before their Roman subjugation ; and it was the soul of Latium, and not the soul of Hellas, that imbued these lands with a new homogeneity of civic order. The Greek knowledge which spread through them was transmuted in Latin speech or writings ; while the great Latin authors who modelled Latin literature upon the Greek, and did so much to fill the Latin mind with Greek thoughts, recast their borrowings in their own style as well as language, and re-tempered the

France and Italy. Consequently I have not such things very actively in mind when speaking of the mediaeval genius. That phrase, and the like, in this book, will signify the more informed and constructive spirit of the mediaeval time

matter to accord with the Roman natures of themselves and their countrymen. Hence only through Latin paraphrase, and through transformation in the Latin classics, Greek thought reached the mediaeval peoples ; until the thirteenth century, when a better acquaintance was opened with the Greek sources, yet still through closer Latin translations, as will be seen.

Thus it was with the pagan antique as an element of mediaeval culture. Nor was it very different with the patristic, or Christian antique, element. For in the fourth and fifth centuries, the influence of pagan Greece on pagan Rome tended to repeat itself in the relations between the Greek and the Latin Fathers of the Church. The dogmatic formulation of Christianity was mainly the work of the former. Tertullian, a Latin, had indeed been an early and important contributor to the process. But, in general, the Latin Fathers were to approve and confirm the work of Athanasius and of his coadjutors and predecessors, who thought and wrote in Greek. Nevertheless, Augustine and other Latin Fathers ordered and made anew what had come from their elder brethren in the East, Latinizing it in form and temper as well as language. At the same time, they supplemented it with matter drawn from their own thinking. It was thus that patristic theology and the entire mass of Christianized knowledge and opinion came to the Middle Ages in a Latin medium.

A third and vaguest factor in the evolution of the mediaeval genius consisted in the diverse and manifold capacities of the mediaeval peoples : Italians whose ancestors had been very part of the antique ; inhabitants of Spain and Gaul who were descended from once Latinized provincials ; and lastly that widespread Teuton folk, whose forbears had barbarized and broken the Roman Empire in those centuries when a decadent civilization could no longer make Romans of barbarians. Moreover, the way in which Christianity was brought to the Teuton peoples and accepted by them, and the manner of their introduction to the pagan culture, reduced at last to following in the Christian train, did not cease for centuries to react upon the course of mediaeval development.

The distinguishing characteristics which make the Middle Ages a period in the history of western Europe were the result of the interaction of the elements of mediaeval development working together, and did not spring from the singular nature of any one of them. Accordingly, the proper beginning of the Middle Ages, so far as one may speak of a beginning, should lie in the time of the conjunction of these elements in a joint activity. That could not be before the barbaric disturbers of the Roman peace had settled down to life and progress under the action of Latin Christianity and the surviving antique culture. Nor may this beginning be placed before the time when Gregory the Great (d. 604) had refashioned Augustine, and much that was earlier, to the measure of the coming centuries ; nor before Boëthius (d. 523), Cassiodorus (d. 575), and Isidore of Seville (d. 636), had prepared the antique pabulum for the mediaeval stomach. All these men were intermediaries or transmitters, and belong to the epoch of transition from the antique and the patristic to the properly inceptive time, when new learners were beginning, in typically mediaeval ways, to rehandle the patristic material and what remained of the antique. Contemporary with those intermediaries, or following hard upon them, were the great missionaries or converters, who laboured to introduce Christianity, with the antique thought incorporated in it and the squalid survival of antique education sheltered in its train, to Teuton peoples in Gaul, England, and Rhenish Germany. Among these was the truculent Irishman, St. Columbanus (d. 615), founder of Luxeuil and Bobbio, whose disciple was St. Gall, and whose contemporary was St. Augustine of Canterbury, whom Gregory the Great sent to convert the Anglo-Saxons. A good century later, St. Winifried-Boniface is working to establish Christianity in Germany.[1] Thus it will not be easy to find a large and catholic beginning for the Middle Ages until the eighth century is reached, and we are come on what is called the Carolingian period.

Let us approach a little nearer, and consider the situation of western Europe with respect to antique culture and

[1] There will be much to say of all these men in later chapters.

Latin Christianity, in the centuries following the disruption of the Roman Empire. The broadest distinction is to be drawn between Italy and the lands north of the Alps. Under the Empire, there was an Italian people. However diverse may have been its ancient stocks, this people had long since become Latin in language, culture, sentiment and tradition. They were the heirs of the Greek, and the creators of the Roman literature, art, philosophy, and law. They were never to become barbarians, although they suffered decadence. Like all great peoples, they had shown a power to assimilate foreigners, which was not lost, but only degraded and diminished, in the fourth and fifth centuries, when Teutonic slaves, immigrants, invaders, seemed to be barbarizing the Latin order quite as much as it was Latinizing them. In these and the following times the culture of Italy sank lamentably low. Yet there was no break of civilization, but only a deep decline and then a re-emergence, in the course of which the Latin civilization had become Italian. For a lowered form of classical education had survived, and the better classes continued to be educated people according to the degraded standard and lessened intellectual energies of those times.[1]

Undoubtedly, in its decline this Latin civilization of Italy could no longer raise barbarians to the level of the Augustan age. Yet it still was making them over into the likeness of its own weakened children. The Visigoths broke into Italy, then, as we are told, passed into southern France ; other confused barbarians came and went, and then the Ostrogoths, with Theodoric at their head, an excellent but not very numerous folk. They stayed in Italy, and fought and died, or lived on, changing into indistinguishable Italians, save for flashes of yellow hair, appearing and re-appearing where the Goths had lived. And then the Lombards, crueller than the Goths, but better able to maintain their energies effective. Their numbers also were not great, compared with the Italians. And thereafter, in spite of their fierceness and the tenacity of their Germanic customs, the succeeding Lombard generations became imbued with the culture of Italy. They became North Italians, gravi-

---

[1] *Post*, Chapter XI.

tating to the towns of Lombardy, or perhaps, farther to the south, holding together in settlements of their own, or forming the nucleus of a hill-dwelling country nobility.

The Italian stock remained predominant over all the incomers of northern blood. It certainly needed no introduction to what had largely been its own creation, the Latin civilization. With weakened hands, it still held to the education, the culture, of its own past ; it still read its ancient literature, and imitated it in miserable verse. The incoming barbarians had hastened the land's intellectual downfall. But all the plagues of inroad and pestilence and famine, which intermittently devastated Italy from the fifth to the tenth century, left some squalid continuity of education. And those barbarian stocks which stayed in that home of the classics, became imbued with whatever culture existed around them, and tended gradually to coalesce with the Italians.

Evidently in its old home, where it merely had become decadent, this ancient culture would fill a rôle quite different from any specific influence which it might exert in a country where the Latin education was freshly introduced. In Italy, a general survival of Roman law and institution, custom and tradition, endured so far as these various elements of the Italian civilization had not been lost or dispossessed, or left high and dry above the receding tide of culture and intelligence. Christianity had been superimposed upon paganism ; and the Christian faith held thoughts incompatible with antique views of life. Teutonic customs were brought in, and the Lombard codes were enacted, working some specific supersession of the Roman law. The tone, the sentiment, the mind of the Italian people had altered from the patterns presented by Cicero, or Virgil, or Horace, or Tacitus. Nevertheless, the antique remained as the soil from which things grew, or as the somewhat turgid atmosphere breathed by living beings. It was not merely a form of education or vehicle of edifying knowledge, nor solely a literary standard. The common modes of the antique were there as well, its daily habits, its urbanity and its dross.

The relationship toward the antique held by the peoples

of the Iberian peninsula and the lands which eventually were to make France, was not quite the same as that held by the Italians. Spain, save in intractable mountain regions, had become a domicile of Latin culture before its people were converted to Christianity. Then it became a strong-hold of early Catholicism. Latin and Catholic Spain absorbed its Visigothic invaders, who in a few generations had appropriated the antique culture, and had turned from Arianism to the orthodoxy of their new home. Under Visigothic rule, the Spanish church became exceptionally authoritative, and its Latin and Catholic learning flourished at the beginning of the seventh century. These conditions gave way before the Moorish conquest, which was most complete in the most thoroughly Romanized portions of the land. Yet the permanent Latinization of the territory where Christianity continued, is borne witness to by the languages growing from the vulgar Latin dialects. The endurance of Latin culture is shown by the polished Latinity of Theodulphus, a Spanish Goth, who left his home at the invitation of Charlemagne, and died, the best Latin verse-maker of his time, as Bishop of Orleans in 821. Thus the education, culture, and languages of Spain were all from the antique. Yet the genius of the land was to be specific-ally Spanish rather than assimilated to any such deep-soiled paganism as underlay the ecclesiastical Christianization of Italy.

As for France, in the southern part which had been Provincia, the antique endured in laws and institutions, in architecture and in ways of life, to a degree second only to its dynamic continuity in Italy. And this in spite of the crude masses of Teutondom which poured into Provincia to be leavened by its culture. In northern France there were more barbarian folk and a less universally diffused Latinity. The Merovingian period swept most of the last away, leaving a fair field to be sown afresh with the Latin education of the Carolingian revival. Yet the inherited dis-cipline of obedience to the Roman order was not obliterated from the Gallic stock, and the lasting Latinization of Gaul endured in the Romance tongues, which were also to be impressed upon all German invaders. Franks, Burgundians, or Alemanni, who came in contact with the provincials, began to be affected by their language, their religion, their ways of living, and by whatever survival of letters there was among them. The Romance dialects were to triumph, were to become French ; and in the earliest extant pieces of this vernacular poetry, the effect of Latin verse-forms appears. Yet Franks and Burgundians were not Latinized in spirit ; and, in truth, the Gauls before them had only become good imitation Latins. At all events, from these mixed and intermediate conditions, a people were to emerge who were not German, nor altogether Latin, in spite of their Romance speech. Latin culture was not quite as a foreign influence upon these Gallo-Roman, Teutonically re-inspirited, incipient, French. Nor were they born and bred to it, like the Italians. The antique was not to dominate the French genius ; it was not to stem the growth of what was, so to speak, Gothic or northern or Teutonic. The glass-painting, the sculpture, the architecture of northern France were to become their own great French selves ; and while the literature was to hold to forms derived from the antique and the Romanesque, the spirit and the contents did not come from Italy.

The office of Latin culture in Germany and England was to be more definite and limited. Germany had never been subdued to the Roman order ; in Anglo-Saxon England, Roman civilization had been effaced by the Saxon conquest, which, like the Moorish conquest of Spain, was most complete in those parts of the land where the Roman influence had been strongest. In neither of these lands was there any antique atmosphere, or antique pagan substratum—save as the universal human soul is pagan ! Latinity came to Germans and Anglo-Saxons as a foreign culture, which was not to pertain to all men's daily living. It was matter for the educated, for the clergy. Its vehicle was a formal language, having no connection with the vernacular. And when the antique culture had obtained certain resting-places in England and Germany, the first benign labours of those Germans or Anglo-Saxons who had mastered the language consisted in the translation of edifying Latin matter into their own tongues. So Latinity in England and Germany was likely to remain a distinguishable influence. The Anglo-Saxons and the rest in England were to become Englishmen, the Germans were to remain Germans ; nor was either race ever to become Latinized, however deeply the educated people of these countries might imbibe Latinity, and exercise their intellects upon all that was contained in the antique metaphysics and natural science, literature and law.

Thus diverse were the situations of the young mediaeval peoples with respect to the antique store. There were like differences of situation in regard to Latin Christianity. It had been formed (from some points of view, one might say, created) by the civilized peoples of the Roman Empire who had been converted in the course of the original diffusion of the Faith. It was, in fact, the product of the conversion of the Roman Empire, and, in Italy and the Latin provinces, received its final fashioning and temper from the Latin Fathers. So from the Latin-speaking portions of the Empire came the system which was to be presented to the Teutonic heathen peoples of the north. They had neither made it nor grown up with it. It was brought to the Franks, to the Anglo-Saxons, and to the Germans east of the Rhine, as a new and foreign faith. And the import of the fact that it was introduced to them as an authoritative religion did not lessen as Christianity became a formative element in their natures.

One may say that an attitude of humble inferiority before Christianity and Latin culture was an initial condition of mediaeval development, having much to do with setting its future lines. In Italy, men looked back to what seemed even as a greater ancestral self, while in the minds of the northern peoples the ancient Empire represented all knowledge and the summit of human greatness. The formulated and ordered Latin Christianity evoked even deeper homage. Well it might, since besides the resistless Gospel (its source of life) it held the intelligence and the organizing power of Rome, which had passed into its own last creation, the Catholic Church. And when this Christianity, so mighty in itself and august through the prestige of Rome, was presented as under authority, its new converts might well be struck with awe.[1] It was such awe as this that acknowledged the claims of the Roman bishops, and made possible a Roman and Catholic Church—the most potent unifying influence of the Middle Ages.

Still more was the character of mediaeval progress set by the action and effect of these two forces. The Latin culture provided the means and method of elementary education, as well as the material for study ; while Latin Christianity, with transforming power, worked itself into the souls of the young mediaeval peoples. The two were assuredly the moulding forces of all mediaeval development ; and whatever sprang to life beyond the range of their action was not, properly speaking, mediaeval, even though seeing the light in the twelfth century.[2] Yet one should not think of these two great influences as entities, unchanging and utterly distinct from what must be called for simplicity's sake the native traits of the mediaeval peoples. The antique culture had never ceased to be part of the nature and faculties of Italians, and to some extent still made the inherited equipment of the Latinized or Latin-descended people of Spain and France. In the same lands also, Latin Christianity had attained its form. And even in England and Germany, Christianity and Latin culture would be distinct from the Teuton folk only at the first moment of presentation and acceptance. Thereupon the two would begin to enter into

---

[1] See *post*, Chapter IX., as to the manner of the coming of Augustine to England.

[2] The Icelandic Sagas, for example, were then brought into written form. They have a genius of their own ; they are realistic and without a trace of symbolism. They are wonderful expressions of the people among whom they were composed. *Post*, Chapter VIII. But, products of a remote island, they were unaffected by the moulding forces of mediaeval development, nor did they exert any influence in turn. The native traits of the mediaeval peoples were the great complementary factor in mediaeval progress—complementary, that is to say, to Latin Christianity and antique culture. Mediaeval characteristics sprang from the interaction of these elements ; they certainly did not spring from any such independent and severed growth of native Teuton quality as is evinced by the Sagas. One will look far, however, for another instance of such spiritual aloofness. For clear as are the different racial or national traits throughout the mediaeval period, they constantly appear in conjunction with other elements. They are discerned working beneath, possibly reacting against, and always affected by, the genius of the Middle Ages, to wit, the genius of the mutual interaction of the whole. Wolfram's very German *Parzival*, the old French *Chanson de Roland*, and above them all the *Divina Commedia*, are mediaeval. In these compositions in the vernacular, racial traits manifest themselves distinctly, and yet are affected by the mediaeval spirit.

and affect their new disciples, and would themselves change under the process of their own assimilation by these Teutonic natures.

Nevertheless, the Latin Christianity of the Fathers and the antique fund of sentiment and knowledge, through their self-conserving strength, affected men in constant ways. Under their action the peoples of western Europe, from the eighth to the thirteenth century, passed through a homogeneous growth, and evolved a spirit different from that of any other period of history—a spirit which stood in awe before its monitors divine and human, and deemed that knowledge was to be drawn from the storehouse of the past ; which seemed to rely on everything except its sin-crushed self, and trusted everything except its senses ; which in the actual looked for the ideal, in the concrete saw the symbol, in the earthly Church beheld the heavenly, and in fleshly joys discerned the devil's lures ; which lived in the unreconciled opposition between the lust and vain-glory of earth and the attainment of salvation ; which felt life's terror and its pitifulness, and its eternal hope ; around which waved concrete infinitudes, and over which flamed the terror of darkness and the Judgment Day.

II

Under the action of Latin Christianity and the antique culture the mediaeval genius developed, as it fused the constituents of its growth into temperament and power. It was not its destiny to produce an extension of knowledge or originate substantial novelties either of thought or imaginative conception. Its energies were rather to expend themselves in the creation of new forms—forms of apprehending and presenting what was (or might be) known from the old books, and all that from century to century was ever more plastically felt. This principle is most important for the true appreciation of the intellectual and emotional phenomena of the Middle Ages.

When a sublime religion is offered to capable but half-civilized peoples, and at the same time an acquaintance is opened to them with the education, the knowledge, the literature of a great civilization, they cannot create new forms or presentations of what they have received, until the same has been assimilated, and has become plastic in their minds, as it were, part of their faculty and feeling. Manifestly the northern peoples could not at once transmute the lofty and superabundant matter of Latin Christianity and its accompanying Latin culture, and present the same in new forms. Nor in truth could Italy, involved as she was in a disturbed decadence, wherein she seemed to be receding from an understanding of the nobler portions of her antique and Christian heritage, rather than progressing toward a vital use of one or the other. In Spain and France there was some decadence among Latinized provincials ; and the Teutonic conquerors were novices in both Christianity and Latinity. In these lands neither decadence nor the novelty of the matter was the sole embarrassment, but both combined to hinder creativeness, although the decadence was less obvious than in Italy, and the newness of the matter less utter than in Germany.

The ancient material was appropriated, and then re-expressed in new forms, through two general ways of transmutation, the intellectual and the emotional. Although patently distinguishable, these would usually work together, with one or the other dominating the joint progress.

Of the two, the intellectual is the easier to analyze. Thinking is necessarily dependent on the thinker, although it appear less intimately part of him than his emotions, and less expressive of his character. Accordingly, the mediaeval genius shows somewhat more palely in its intellectual productions, than in the more emotional phases of literature and art. Yet the former exemplify not only mediaeval capacities, but also the mediaeval intellectual temperament, or, as it were, the synthetic predisposition of the mediaeval mind. This temperament, this intellectual predisposition, became in general more marked through the centuries from the ninth to the twelfth. People could not go on generation after generation occupied with like topics of intellectual interest, reasoning upon them along certain lines of religious and ethical suggestion, without developing or intensifying some general type of intellectual temper.

From the Carolingian period onward, the men interested in knowledge learned the patristic theology, and, in gradually expanding compass, acquired antique logic and metaphysics, mathematics, natural science and jurisprudence. What they learned, they laboured to restate or expound. With each succeeding generation, the subjects of mediaeval study were made more closely part of the intelligence occupied with them ; because the matter had been considered for a longer time, and had been constantly restated and restudied in terms more nearly adapted to the comprehension of the men who were learning and restating it. At length mediaeval men made the antique and patristic material, or rather their understanding of it, dynamically their own. Their comprehension of it became part of their intellectual faculties, they could think for themselves in its terms, think almost originally and creatively, and could present as their own the matter of their thoughts in restatements, that is, in forms essentially new.

From century to century may be traced the process of restatement of patristic Christianity, with the antique material contained in it. The Christianity of the fifth century contained an amplitude of thought and learning. To the creative work of earlier and chiefly eastern men, the Latin intellect finally incorporate in Ambrose, Jerome, and Augustine had added its further great accomplishment and ordering. The sum of dogma was well-nigh made up ; the Trinity was established ; Christian learning had reached a compass beyond which it was not to pass for the next thousand years ; the doctrines as to the " sacred mysteries," as to the functions of the Church and its spiritual authority, existed in substance ; the principles of symbolism and allegory had been set ; the great mass of allegorical Scriptural interpretations had been devised ; the spiritual relationship of man to God's ordainment, to wit, the part to be played by the human will in man's salvation or damnation, had been reasoned out ; and man's need and love of God, his nothingness apart from the Source and King and End of Life, had been uttered in words which men still use. Evi-

dently succeeding generations of less illumination could not
add to this vast intellectual creation ; much indeed had to
be done before they could comprehend and make it theirs,
so as to use it as an element of their own thinking, or possess
it as an inspiration of passionate, imaginative reverie.

At the darkening close of the patristic period, Gregory
the Great was still partially creative in his barbarizing
handling of patristic themes.[1] After his death, for some
three centuries, theologians were to devote themselves to
mastering the great heritage from the Church Fathers. It
was still a time of racial antipathy and conflict. The
disparate elements of the mediaeval personality were as yet
unblended. How could the unformed intellect of such a
period grasp the patristic store of thought ? Still less
might this wavering human spirit, uncertain of itself and
unadjusted to novel and great conceptions, transform, and
so renew, them with fresh life. Scarcely any proper recasting of patristic doctrine will be found in the Carolingian
period, but merely a shuffling of the matter. There were
some exceptions, arising, as in the case of Eriugena, from
the extraordinary genius of this thinker ; or again from
the narrow controversial treatment of a matter argued with
rupturing detachment of patristic opinions from their
setting and balancing qualifications.[2] But the typical
works of the eighth and ninth centuries were commentaries
upon Scripture, consisting chiefly of excerpts from the
Fathers. The flower of them all was the compendious
Glossa Ordinaria of Walafrid Strabo, a pupil of the voluminous commentator Rabanus Maurus.[3]

Through the tenth and eleventh centuries, one finds no
great advance in the systematic restatement of Christian
doctrine.[4] Nevertheless, two hundred years of devotion
have been put upon it ; and statements of parts of it occur,
showing that the eleventh century has made progress over

[1] See *post*, Chapter V.
[2] The Predestination and Eucharistic controversies are examples ; *post*,
Chapter X.
[3] See *post*, Chapter X.
[4] The lack of originality in the first half of the tenth century is illustrated by
the Epitome of Gregory's *Moralia*, made by such an energetic person as Odo of
Cluny. It occupies four hundred columns in Migne's *Patrologia Latina*, 133
See *post*, Chapter XII.

the ninth in its thoughtful and vital appropriation of Latin
Christianity. A man like German Othloh has thought for
himself within its lines ;[1] Anselm of Canterbury has set
forth pieces of it with a depth of reflection and intimacy of
understanding which make his works creative ;[2] Peter
Damiani through intensity of feeling has become the
embodiment of Christian asceticism and the grace of Christian tears ;[3] and Hildebrand has established the mediaeval
papal church. Of a truth, the mediaeval man was adjusting
himself, and reaching his understanding of what the past had
given him.

The twelfth century presents a universal progress in
philosophic and theological thinking. It is the century of
Abaelard, of Hugo of St. Victor and St. Bernard, and of
Peter Lombard. The first of these penetrates into the
logical premises of systematic thought as no mediaeval man
had done before him ; St. Bernard moves the world through
his emotional and political comprehension of the Faith ;
Hugo of St. Victor offers a sacramental explanation of the
universe and man, based upon symbolism as the working
principle of creation ; and Peter Lombard makes or, at
least, typifies, the systematic advance, from the *Commentary*
to the *Books of Sentences,* in which he presents patristic
doctrine arranged according to the cardinal topics of the
Christian scheme. Here Abaelard's *Sic et non* had been a
precursor rather carping in its excessive clear-sightedness.

Thus, as a rule, each successive mediaeval period shows
a more organic restatement of the old material. Yet this
principle may be impeded or deflected, in its exemplifications,
by social turmoil and disaster, or even by the use of further
antique matter, demanding assimilation. For example,
upon the introduction of the complete works of Aristotle in
the thirteenth century, an enormous intellectual effort was
required for the mastery of their contents. They were not
mastered at once, or by all people who studied the
philosopher. So the works of Hugo of St. Victor, of the first
half of the twelfth century, are more original in their organic
restatement of less vast material than are the works of

---

[1] See *post,* Chapter XIII.   [2] See *post,* Chapter XI.
[3] See *post,* Chapter XVII.

Albertus Magnus, Aristotle's prodigious expounder, one hundred years later. But Thomas Aquinas accomplishes a final Catholic presentation of the whole enlarged material, patristic and antique.[1]

One may perceive three stages in this chief phase of mediaeval intellectual progress consisting in the appropriation of Latin Christianity : its first conning, its more vital appropriation, its re-expression, with added elements of thought. There were also three stages in the evolution of the outer forms of this same catholic mastery and re-expression of doctrine : first, the Scriptural *Commentary* ; secondly, the *Books of Sentences* ; and thirdly, the *Summa Theologiae*, of which Thomas Aquinas is the final definitive creator. The philosophical material used in its making was the substantial philosophy of Aristotle, mastered at length by this Christian Titan of the thirteenth century. In the *Summa*, regarded visibly, as well as more inwardly and essentially considered, the Latin Christianity of the Fathers received an organically new form.

Quite as impressive, more moving, and possibly more creative, than the intellectual recasting of the ancient patristic matter, were its emotional transformations. The sequence and character of mediaeval development is clearly seen in the evolution of new forms of emotional, and especially of poetic and plastic, expression. The intellectual transformation of the antique and more especially the patristic matter, was accompanied by currents of desire and aversion running with increasing definiteness and power. As patristic thought became more organically mediaeval, more intrinsically part of the intellectual faculties of men, it constituted with increasing incisiveness the suggestion and the rationale of emotional experiences, and set the lines accordingly of impassioned expression in devotional prose and verse, and in the more serious forms of art. Patristic theology, the authoritative statement of the Christian faith, contained men's furthest hopes and deepest fears set forth together with the divine Means by which those might be realized and these allayed. As generation after generation clung to this system as to the stay of their salvation, the intellectual

[1] These men will be fully considered later, Chapters XXXV.-XLI.

consideration of it became instinct with the emotions of desire and aversion, and with love and gratitude toward the suffering means and instruments which made salvation possible — the Crucified, the Weeping Mother, and the martyred or self-torturing saints. All these had suffered ; they were sublime objects for human compassion. Who could think upon them without tears ? Thus mediaeval religious thought became a well of emotion.

Emotion breaks its way to expression ; it feeds itself upon its expression, thereby increasing in resistlessness ; it even becomes identical with its expression. Surely it creates the modes of its expression, seeking continually the more facile, the more unimpeded, which is to say, the adequate and perfect form. Typical mediaeval emotion, which was religious, cast itself around the Gospel of Christ and the theology of the Fathers as studied and pondered on in the mediaeval centuries. Seeking fitting forms of expression, which are at once modes of relief and forms of added power, the passionate energy of the mediaeval genius constrained the intellectual faculties to unite with it in the production of these forms. They were to become more personal and original than any mere scholastic restatement of the patristic and antique thought. Yet the perfect form of the emotional expression was not quickly reached. It could not outrun the intelligent appropriation of Latin Christianity. Its media, moreover, as in the case of sculpture, might present retarding difficulties to be overcome before that means of presentation could be mastered. A sequence may be observed in the evolution of the forms of the mediaeval emotional expression of patristic Christianity. One of the first attained was impassioned devotional Latin prose, like that of Peter Damiani or St. Anselm of Canterbury.[1] But prose is a halting means of emotional expression. It is too circumstantial and too slow. Only in the chanted strophe, winged with the power of rhythm, can emotion pour out its unimpeded strength. But before the thought can be fused in verse, it must be plastic, molten indeed. Even then, the finished verse is not produced at once. The perfected mediaeval Latin strophe was a final form of religious

[1] See *post*, Chapter XXXII.

emotional expression, which was not attained until the twelfth century.[1]

Impassioned prose may be art ; the loftier forms of verse are surely art. And art is not spontaneous, but carefully intended ; no babbling of a child, but a mutual fitting of form and content, in which efficient unison the artist's intellect has worked. Such intellectual, such artistic endeavour, was evinced in the long development of mediaeval plastic art. The sculpture and the painted glass, which tell the Christian story in Chartres Cathedral, set forth the patristic and antique matter in forms expressive of the feeling and emotion which had gathered around the scheme of Latin Christianity. They were forms never to be outdone for appropriateness and power. Several centuries not only of spiritual growth, but of mechanical and artistic effort, had been needed for their perfecting.

In these and like emotional recastings, or indeed creations, patristic and antique elements were transformed and transfigured. And again, in fields non-religious and non-philosophical, through the evolution of the mediaeval mind and heart, novelties of sentiment and situation were introduced into antique themes of fiction ; new forms of romance, new phases of human love and devotion were evolved, in which (witness the poetry of chivalric love in Provençal and Old French) the energies of intellect and passion were curiously blended.[2] These represented a side of human growth not unrelated to the supreme mediaeval achievement, the vital appropriation and emotional humanizing of patristic Christianity. For that carried an impassioning of its teachings with love and tears, a fostering of them with devotion, an adorning of them with quivering fantasies, a translation of them into art, into poetry, into romance. With what wealth of love and terror, with what grandeur of imagination, with what power of mystery and symbolism, did the Middle Ages glorify their heritage, turning its precepts into spirit.

Of a surety the emotional is not to be separated from the intellectual recasting of Christianity. The greatest exponents of the one had their share in the other. Hugo of St.

Victor as well as St. Bernard were mighty agents of this spiritually passionate mode of apprehending Latin Christianity, and transfusing it with emotion, or reviving the Gospel elements in it. Here work, knowingly or instinctively, many men and women, Peter Damiani and St. Francis of Assisi, St. Hildegarde of Bingen and Mechthilde of Magdeburg, who, according to their diverse temperaments. overmasteringly and burningly loved Christ. With them the intellectual appropriation of dogmatic Christianity was subordinate.

Such men and women were poets and artists, even when they wrote no poetry, and did not carve or paint. For their lives were poems, unisons of overmastering thoughts and the emotions inspired by them. The life of Francis was a living poem. It was kin to the *Dies Irae*, the *Stabat Mater*, the hymns of Adam of St. Victor, and in a later time, the *Divina Commedia*. For all these poems, in their different ways, using Christian thought and feeling as symbols, created imaginative presentations of universal human moods, even as the lives of Francis and many a cloistered soul presented like moods in visible embodiment.

Such lives likewise close in with art. They poured themselves around the symbols of the human person of Christ and its sacrificial presence in the Eucharist ; they grasped the infinite and universal through these tangibilities. But the poems also sprang into being through a concrete realizing in mood, and a visualizing in narrative, of such symbols. And the same need of grasping the infinite and universal through symbols was the inspiration of mediaeval art : it built the cathedrals, painted their windows, filled their niches with statues, carving prophet types, carving the times and seasons of God's providence, carving the vices and virtues of the soul and its eternal destiny, and at the same time augmenting the Liturgy with symbolic words and acts. So saint and poet and artist-craftsman join in that appropriation of Christianity which was vivifying whatever had come from the Latin Fathers, by pondering upon it, loving it, living it, imagining it, and making it into poetry and art.

It is better not to generalize further, or attempt more specifically to characterize the mediaeval genius. As its

manifestations pass before our consideration, we shall see
the complexity of thought and life within the interplay of
the moulding forces of mediaeval development, as they
strove with each other or wrought in harmony, as they were
displayed in frightful contrasts between the brutalities of life
and the lofty, but not less real, strainings of the spirit, or
again in the opposition between inchoately variant ideals
and the endeavour for their more inclusive reconcilement.
Various phases of the mediaeval spirit were to unfold only
too diversely with popes, kings and knights, monks, nuns,
and heretics, satirists, troubadours and minnesingers ; in
emotional yearnings and intellectual ideals ; in the literature
of love and the literature of its suppression ; in mistress-
worship, and the worship of the Virgin and the passion-
flooded Christ of Canticles.   Sublimely will this spirit show
itself in the resistless apotheosis of symbolism, and in art
and poetry giving utterance to the mediaeval conceptions of
order and beauty.   Other of its phases will be evinced in
the striving of earnest souls for spiritual certitude ; in the
scholastic structure and accomplishment ; in the ways in
which men felt the spell of the Classics ; and everywhere
and universally in the mediaeval conflict between life's
fulness and the insistency of the soul's salvation.

CHAPTER II

THE LATINIZING OF THE WEST

THE intellectual and spiritual life of the partly Hellenized and at last Christianized, Roman Empire furnished the contents of the intellectual and spiritual development of the Middle Ages.[1] In Latin forms the Christian and antique elements passed to the mediaeval period. Their Latinization, their continuance, and their passing on, were due to the existence of the Empire as a political and social fact. Rome's equal government facilitated the transmission of Greek thought through the Mediterranean west ; Roman arms, Roman qualities conquered Spain and Gaul, subdued them to the Roman order, opened them to Graeco-Latin influences, also to Christianity. Indelibly Latinized in language and temper, Spain, Gaul, and Italy present first a homogeneity of culture and civic order, and then a common decadence and confusion. But decadence and confusion did not obliterate the ancient elements ; which painfully endured, passing down disfigured and bedimmed, to form the basis of mediaeval culture.

The all-important Latinization of western Europe began with the unification of Italy under Rome. This took five centuries of war. In central Italy, Marsians, Samnites, Umbrians, Etruscans, were slowly conquered ; and in the south Rome stood forth at last triumphant after the war against Tarentum and Pyrrhus of Epirus. With Rome's political domination, the Latin language also won its way to supremacy throughout the peninsula, being drasti-

---

[1] The term " spiritual " is here intended to signify the activities of the mind which are emotionalized with yearning or aversion, and therefore may be said to belong to the entire nature of man.

cally forced, along with Roman civic institutions, upon Tarentum and the other Greek communities of Magna Graecia.[1] Yet in revenge, from this time on, Greek medicine and manners, mythology, art, poetry, philosophy—Greek thought in every guise—entered the Latin pale.

At the time of which we speak, the third century before Christ, the northern boundaries of Italy were still the rivers Arno and, to the east, the Aesis, which flows into the Adriatic, near Ancona. North-west of the Arno, Ligurian highlanders held the mountain lands as far as Nice. North of the Aesis lay the valley of the Po. That great plain may have been occupied at an early time by Etruscan communities scattered through a Celtic population gradually settling to an agricultural life. Whatever may be the facts as to the existence of these earlier Celts, other and ruder Celtic tribes swarmed down from the Alps [2] about 400 B.C., spread through the Po Valley, pushing the Etruscans back into Etruria, and following them there to carry on the war. After this comes the well-known story of Roman interference, leading to Roman overthrow at the river Allia in 390, and the capture of the city by these " Gauls." The latter then retired northward, to occupy the Po Valley ; though bands of them settled as far south as the Aesis.

Time and again, Rome was to be reminded of the Celtic peril. Between the first and second Punic wars, the Celts, reinforced from beyond the Alps, attacked Etruria and threatened Rome. Defeating them, the Consuls pushed north to subdue the Po Valley (222 B.C.). South of the river the Celts were expelled, and their place was filled by Roman colonists. The fortress cities of Placentia (Piacenza) and Cremona were founded on the right and left banks of the Po, and south-east of them Mutina (Modena). The

---

[1] The history of the spread of Latin through Italy and the provinces is from the nature of the subject obscure. Budinsky's *Die Ausbreitung der lateinischer Sprache* (Berlin, 1881) is somewhat unsatisfactory. See also Meyer-Lübke, *Die lateinische Sprache in den romanischen Ländern* (Gröber's *Grundriss*, I², 451 sqq. ; F. G. Mohl, *Introduction à la chronologie du latin vulgaire* (1899). The statements in the text are very general, and ignore intentionally the many difficult questions as to what sort of Latin—dialectal, popular, or literary—was spread through the peninsula. See Mohl, *o.c.* § 33 *sqq.*

[2] Tradition says from Gaul, but the sifted evidence points to the Danube north of the later province of Noricum. See Bertrand and Reinach, *Les Celtes dans les vallées du Pô et du Danube* (Paris, 1894).

Flaminian road was extended across the Apennines to Fanum, and thence to Ariminum (Rimini), thus connecting the two Italian seas.

Hannibal's invasion of Italy brought fresh disturbance, and when the war with him was over, Rome set herself to the final subjugation of the Celts north of the Po. Upon their submission the Latinization of the whole valley began, and advanced apace ; but the evidence is scanty. Statius Caecilius, a comic Latin poet, was a manumitted Insubrian Celt who had been brought to Rome probably as a prisoner of war. He died in 168 B.C. Some generations after him, Cornelius Nepos was born in upper Italy, and Catullus at Verona ; Celtic blood may have flowed in their veins. In the meanwhile the whole region had been organized as Gallia Cisalpina, with its southern boundary fixed at the Rubicon, which flows near Rimini.

The Celts of northern Italy were the first palpably non-Italian people to adopt the Latin language. Second in time and thoroughness to their Latinization was that of Spain. Military reasons led to its conquest. Hamilcar's genius had created there a Carthaginian power, as a base for the invasion of Italy. This project, accomplished by Hamilcar's son, brought home to the Roman Senate the need to control the Spanish peninsula. The expulsion of the Carthaginians, which followed, did not give mastery over the land ; and two centuries of Roman persistence were required to subdue the indomitable Iberians.

So, in the end, Spain was conquered, and became a Latin country. Its tribal cantons were replaced with urban communities, and many Roman colonies were founded, to grow to prosperous cities. These were strongholds of Latin. Cordova became a very famous home of education and letters. Apparently the southern Spaniards had fully adopted the ways and speech of Rome before Strabo wrote his *Geography*, about A.D. 20. The change was slower in the mountains of Asturia, but quite rapid in the north-eastern region known as Nearer Spain, Hispania Citerior, as it was called. There, at the town of Osca (Huesca), Sertorius eighty years before Christ had established the first Latin school for the native Spanish youth.

The reign of Augustus, and especially his two years' sojourn in Spain (26 and 25 B.C.) brought quiet to the peninsula, and thereafter no part of the Empire enjoyed such unbroken peace. Of all lands outside of Italy, with the possible exception of Provincia, Spain became most completely Roman in its institutions, and most unequivo- cally Latin in its culture. It was the most populous of the European provinces ; [1] and no other held so many Roman citizens, or so many cities early endowed with Roman civic rights.[2] The great Augustan literature was the work of natives of Italy.[3] But in the Silver Age that followed, many of the chief Latin authors—the elder and younger Seneca, Lucan, Quintilian—were Spaniards. They were unquestioned representatives of Latin literature, with no provincial twang in their writings. Then, of Rome's emperors, Trajan was born in Spain, and Hadrian and Marcus Aurelius were of Spanish blood.

Perhaps even more completely Latinized was Narbonensis, commonly called Provincia. Its official name was drawn from the ancient town of Narbo (Narbonne), which in 118 B.C. was refounded as a Roman colony in partial accomplish- ment of the plans of Caius Gracchus. The boundaries of this colony touched those of the Greek city-state Massilia (Marseilles), whose rights were respected until it sided against Caesar in the Civil War. Save for the Massilian territory, which it later included, Provincia stretched from the eastern Pyrenees by the way of Nemausus (Nîmes) and the Arelate (Arles) north-easterly through the Rhone Valley, taking in Vienne and Valence in the country of the Allobroges, and then onward to the edge of Lake Geneva ; thence southerly along the Maritime Alps to the sea. Many of its towns owed their prosperity to Caesar. In his time the country west of the Rhone was already half Latin, and was filling

[1] See Beloch, *Bevölkerung der griechisch-römischen Welt*, p. 507 (Leipzig, 1886).

[2] Mommsen says that in Augustus's time fifty Spanish cities had the full privileges of Roman citizenship and fifty others the rights of Italian towns (*Roman Provinces*, i. 75, Eng. trans.). But this seems a mistake ; as the enumeration of Beloch, *Bevölkerung*, etc., p. 330, gives fifty in all, following the account of Pliny.

[3] Cicero, *Pro Archia*, 10, speaks slightingly of poets born at Cordova, but later, Latro of Cordova was Ovid's teacher.

up with men from Italy.[1] Two or three generations later,
Pliny dubbed it *Italia verius quam provincia*. At all events,
like northern Italy and Spain, Provincia, throughout its
length and breadth, had appropriated the Latin civilization
of Rome ; that civilization city-born and city-reared, solvent
of cantonal organization and tribal custom, destructive of
former ways of living and standards of conduct ; a civilization which was commercial as well as military in its means,
and urban in its ends ; which loved the life of the forum, the
theatre, the circus, the public bath, and seemed to gain its
finest essence from the instruction of the grammarian and
rhetorician. The language and literature of this civilization
were those of an imperial city, and were to be the language
and literature of the Latin city universal, in whatever western
land its walls might rise.

North of Provincia stretched the great territory reaching
from the Atlantic to the Rhine, and with its edges following
that river northerly, and again westerly to the sea. This
was Caesar's conquest, his *omnis Gallia*. The resistlessness
of Rome, her civic and military superiority over the western
peoples whom she conquered, may be grasped from the
record of Gallic subjugation by one in whom great Roman
qualities were united. Perhaps the deepest impression
received by the reader of those *Commentaries* is of the man
behind the book, Caesar himself. The Gallic War passes
before us as a presentation, or medium of realization, of that
all-compelling personality, with whom to consider was to
plan, and to resolve was to accomplish, without hesitation or
fear, by the force of mind. It is in the mirror of this man's
contempt for restless irresolution, for unsteadiness and
impotence, that Gallic qualities are shown, the reflection
undisturbed either by intolerance or sympathy. The Gauls
were always anxious for change, *mobiliter celeriterque* inflamed to war or revolution, says Caesar in his memorable
words ; and, like all men, they were by nature zealous for
liberty, hating the servile state—so it behoved Caesar
to distribute his legions with foresight in a certain

---

[1] The Roman law was used throughout Provincia. In this respect a line is
to be drawn between Provincia and the North. See *post*, Chapter XXXIV.,
II. and III.

crisis.[1] Thus, without shrug or smile, writes the greatest
of revolutionists who for himself was also seeking liberty
of action, freely and devisingly, not hurried by impatience
or any such planless restlessness as, for example, drove
Dumnorix the Aeduan to plot feebly, futilely, without plan
or policy, against fate, to wit Caesar—so he met his death.[2]

Instability appears as peculiarly characteristic of the
Gauls. They were not barbarians, but an ingenious folk,
quick-witted and loquacious.[3] Their domestic customs were
reasonable ; they had taxes and judicial tribunals ; their
religion held belief in immortality, and in other respects was
not below the paganism of Italy. It was directed by the
priestly caste of Druids, who possessed considerable knowledge, and used the Greek alphabet in writing. They also
presided at trials, and excommunicated suitors who would
not obey their judicial decrees.[4]

The country was divided into about ninety states
(*civitates*). Monarchies appear among them, but the greater
number were aristocracies torn with jealousy, and always in
alarm lest some noble's overweening influence upset the
government. The common people and poor debtors seem
scarcely to have counted. Factions existed in every state,
village, and even household, says Caesar,[5] headed by the
rival states of the Aedui and Sequani. Espousing, as he
professed to, the Aeduan cause, Caesar could always appear
as an ally of one faction. At the last a general confederacy
took up arms against him under the noble Auvernian,
Vercingetorix.[6] But the instability of his authority forced
the hand of this brilliant leader.

In fine, it would seem that the Gallic peoples had pro-

---

[1] *Bellum Gallicum*, iii. 10. Cf., generally, *Caesar's Conquest of Gaul*, T. R.
Holmes (2nd ed., Oxford, 1911).

[2] *Bellum Gallicum*, v. 6.

[3] Porcius Cato in his *Origines*, written a hundred years before Caesar crossed
the mountains, says that Gallia was devoted to the art of war and to eloquence
(*argute loqui*). Presumably the Gallia that Cato thus characterized as clever or
acute of speech, was Cisalpine Gaul, to wit, the north of Italy ; yet Caesar's
transalpine Gauls were both clever of speech and often the fools of their own arguments. Lucian, in his *Hercules* (No. 55, Dindorf's edition), has his " Celt "
argue that Hercules accomplished his deeds by the power of words.

[4] See, generally, Fustel de Coulanges, *Institutions politiques de l'ancienne
France*, vol. i. (*La Gaule romaine*).

[5] *Bellum Gallicum*, vi. 11, 12.

[6] Cf. Julian, *Vercingetorix* (2nd ed., Paris, 1902).

gressed in civilization as far as their limited political capacity
and self-control would allow. These were the limitations
set by the Gallic character. It is a Gallic custom, says
Caesar, to stop travellers, and insist upon their telling
what they know or have heard. In the towns the crowd
will throng around a merchant and make him tell where he
has come from and give them the news. Upon such hearsay the Gauls enter upon measures of the gravest importance.
The states which are deemed the best governed, he adds,
have a law that whenever any one has heard a report or
rumour of public moment, he shall communicate it to a
magistrate and to none else. The magistrates conceal or
divulge such news in their discretion. It is not permitted to
discuss public affairs save in an assembly.[1]

Apparently Caesar is not joking in these passages, which
speak of a statecraft based on gossip gathered in the streets,
carried straight to a magistrate, and neither discussed nor
divulged on the way ! Quite otherwise were Roman officials
to govern, when Caesar's great campaigns had subdued these
mercurial Gauls. It was after his death that Augustus
established the Roman order through the land. In those
famous *partes tres* of the *Commentaries* he settled it : Iberian
and Celtic Aquitania, Celtic Lugdunensis, and Celtic-Teuton
Belgica, making together the three Gauls. It is significant
that the emperor kept them as imperial provinces, still
needing military administration, while he handed over Provincia to the Senate.

Provincia had been Romanized in law and government
as the " Three Gauls " never were to be. Augustus followed
Caesar in respecting the tribal and cantonal divisions of the
latter, making only such changes as were necessary. Gallic
cities under the Empire show no great uniformity. Each
appears as the continuance of the local tribe, whose life and
politics were focussed in the town. The city (*civitas*) did
not end with the town walls, but included the surrounding
country and perhaps many villages. A number of these
cities preserved their ancient constitutions ; others conformed to the type of Roman colonies, whose constitutions
were modelled on those of Italian cities. Colonia Claudia

[1] *Bellum Gallicum,* iv. 5 ; vi. 20.

Agrippina (Cologne) is an example. But all the cities of the " Three Gauls " as well as those of Provincia, whatever their form of government, conducted their affairs with senate, magistrates and police of their choosing, had their municipal property, and controlled their internal finances. A diet was established for the " Three Gauls " at Lyons, to which the cities sent delegates. Whatever were its powers, its existence tended to foster a sense of common Gallic nationality. The Roman franchise, however, was but sparingly bestowed on individuals, and was not granted to any Gallic city (except Lyons) until the time of Claudius, himself born at Lyons. He refounded Cologne as a colony, granted the franchise to Trèves, and abolished the provisions forbidding Gauls to hold the imperial magistracies. With the reorganization of the Empire under Diocletian, Trèves became the capital not only of Gaul, but of Spain and Britain also.

Although there was thus no violent Romanization of Gaul, Roman civilization rapidly progressed under imperial fostering, and by virtue of its own energy. Roman roads traversed the country ; bridges spanned the rivers ; aqueducts were constructed ; cities grew, trade increased, agriculture improved, and the vine was introduced. At the time of Caesar's conquest, the quick-minded Gauls were prepared to profit from a superior civilization ; and under the mighty peace of Rome, men settled down to the blessings of safe living and law regularly enforced.

The spread of the Latin tongue and the finer elements of Latin culture followed the establishment of the Roman order. One Gallic city and then another adopted the new language according to its circumstances and situation. Of course the cities of Provincia took the lead, largely Italian as they were in population. On the other hand, Latin made slow progress among the hills of Auvergne. But further north, the Roman city of Lyons was Latin-tongued from its foundation. Thence to the remoter north and west and east, Latin spread by cities, the foci of affairs and provincial administration. The imperial government did not demand of its subjects that they should abandon their native speech, but required in Gaul, as elsewhere, the use of Latin in the transaction of official business. This compelled all to study Latin who had affairs

in law courts or with officials, or hoped to become magistrates.
Undoubtedly the rich and noble, especially in the towns,
learned Latin quickly, and it soon became the vehicle of
polite, as well as official, intercourse. It was also the
language of the schools attended by the noble Gallic youth.
But among the rural population, the native tongues continued indefinitely. Obviously one cannot assign any
specific time for the popular and general change from Celtic ;
but it appears to have very generally taken place before the
Frankish conquest.[1]

By that time, too, those who would naturally constitute
the educated classes, possessed a Latin education. First in
the cities of Provincia, Nîmes, Arles, Vienne, Fréjus, Aix in
Provence, then of course at Lyons and in Aquitaine, and
later through the cities of the north-east, Trèves, Mainz,
Cologne, and most laggingly through the north-west Belgic
lands lying over against the channel and the North Sea,
Latin education spread. Grammar and rhetoric were
taught, and the great Classics were explained and read, till
the Gauls doubtless felt themselves Roman in spirit as in
tongue.

Of course they were mistaken. To be sure the Gaul
was a citizen of the Empire, which not only represented
safety and civilization, but in fact was the entire civilized
world. He had no thought of revolting from that, any more
than from his daily habits or his daily food. Often he felt
himself sentimentally affected toward this universal symbol
of his welfare. He had Latin speech ; he had Roman
fashions ; he took his warm baths and his cold, enjoyed the
sports of the amphitheatre, studied Roman literature, and
talked of the *Respublica* and *Aurea Roma*. Yet he was,
after all, merely a Romanized inhabitant of Gaul. Roman
law and government, Latin education, and the colour of the

---

[1] There are a number of texts from the second to the fifth century which bear
on the matter. Taken altogether they are unsatisfying, if not blind. They have
been frequently discussed. See Gröber, *Grundriss der romanischen Philologie*,
i. 451 *sqq.* (2nd edition, 1904) ; Brunot, *Origines de la langue française*, which
is the Introduction to Petit de Julleville's *Histoire de la langue et de la
littérature française* (Paris, 1896) ; Bonnet, *Le Latin de Grégoire de Tours*, pp.
22-30 (Paris, 1890) ; Mommsen's *Provinces of the Roman Empire*, p. 108 *sqq.* of
English translation ; Fustel de Coulanges, *Institutions politiques*, vol. i. (*La Gaule
romaine*), pp. 125-135 (Paris, 1891) ; Roger, *L'Enseignement des lettres classiques
d'Ausone à Alcuin*, p. 24 *sqq.* (Paris, 1905).

Roman spirit had been imparted ; but the inworking, creative genius of Rome was not within her gift. or his capacity. The Gauls, however, are the chief example of a mediating people. Romanized and not made Roman, their epoch, their geographical situation, and their modified faculties, all made them intermediaries between the Roman and the Teuton.

If the Romanization of the " Three Gauls " was least thorough in Belgica, there was even less of it across the channel. Britain, as far north as the Clyde and Firth of Forth, was a Roman province for three or four hundred years. Latin was the language of the towns ; but probably never supplanted the Celtic in the country. The Romanization of the Britons, however, whether thorough or superficial, affected a people who were to be apparently submerged. They seem to have transmitted none of their Latin civilization to their Anglo-Saxon conquerors. Yet even the latter when they came to Britain were not quite untouched by Rome. They were familiar with Roman wares, if not with Roman ways ; and certain Latin words which are found in all Teutonic languages had doubtless entered Anglo-Saxon.[1] But this early Roman influence was slight, compared with that which afterwards came with Christianity. Nor did the Roman culture, before the introduction of Christianity, exert a deep effect on Germany, at least beyond the neighbourhood of the large Roman or Romanized towns like Cologne and Mainz. In many ways, indeed, the Germans were touched by Rome. Roman diplomacy, exciting tribe against tribe, was decimating them. Roman influences, and sojourn at Rome, had taught much to many German princes. Roman weapons, Roman utensils and wares of all kinds were used from the Danube to the Baltic. But all this did not Romanize the Germans, any more than the Latin words which had crept in Latinized their language.[2]

[1] Such words are, *e.g.*, wine, street, wall. See Toller, *History of the English Language* (Macmillan & Co., 1900), pp. 41, 42.
[2] See Paul, *Grundriss der germanischen Philologie*, Band i. pp. 305-315 (Strassburg, 1891).

CHAPTER III

GREEK PHILOSOPHY AS THE ANTECEDENT OF THE PATRISTIC APPREHENSION OF FACT

THE Latin West afforded the *milieu* in which the thoughts and sentiments of the antique and partly Christian world were held in Latin forms and preserved from obliteration during the fifth and succeeding centuries, until taken up by the currents of mingled decrepitude and callowness which marked the coming of the mediaeval time. Latin Christianity survived, and made its way across those stormy centuries to its mediaeval harbourage. The antique also was carried over, either in the ship of Latin Christianity, or in tenders freighted by certain Latin Christians who dealt in secular learning, though not in " unbroken packages." Those unbroken packages, to wit, the Latin classics, and after many centuries the Greek, also floated over. But in the early mediaeval times, men preferred the pagan matter rehashed, as in the *Etymologies* of Isidore.

The great ship of Christian doctrine not only bore bits of the pagan antique stowed here and there, but itself was built with many a plank of antique timber, and there were antique ingredients in its Christian freight ; in other words, the theology of the Church Fathers was partly made of Greek philosophy, and was put together in modes of Greek philosophic reasoning. The Fathers lived in the Roman Empire, or in what was left of it in the third, fourth, fifth, and sixth centuries. Many of them were born of pagan parents, and all received the common education in grammar, rhetoric, and literature, which were pagan and permeated with pagan philosophy. For philosophy was then the highest branch of education, and had become a source of

principles of conduct and " daily thoughts for daily needs."
Many of the Fathers in their pagan, or at least unsanctified
youth, had deeply studied it.

Philosophy held the sum of knowledge in the Empire,
and from it came the concepts in which all the Fathers
reasoned.   But the *Latin* Fathers, who were juristically and
rhetorically educated, might also reason through conceptions,
or in a terminology, taken from the Roman Law.   Nevertheless, in the rational process of formulating Christian
dogma, Greek philosophy was the overwhelmingly important
factor, because it furnished knowledge and the metaphysical
concepts, and because the greater number of Christian
theologians were Hellenic in spirit, and wrote Greek ; while
the Latins reset in Latin, and sometimes juristic, phrase what
their eastern brethren had evolved.[1]

Obviously, in order to appreciate the mental endowment
of the Middle Ages, it is essential to have cognizance of
patristic thought.   And in order to understand the mental
processes of the Fathers, their attitude toward knowledge
and their perception of fact, one must consider their intellectual environment ;   which was, of course, made up of
the store of knowledge and philosophic interests prevailing
in the Roman Empire.   So we have to gauge the intellectual
interests of the pagan world, first in the earlier times when
thinkers were bringing together knowledge and philosophic
concepts, and then in the later period when its accumulated
and somewhat altered thought made the actual environment
of the Church.

What race had ever a more genial appreciation of the
facts of nature and of mortal life, than the Greeks ?   The
older Greek philosophies had sprung from open and unprejudiced observation of the visible world.   They were physical
inquiries.   With Socrates philosophy turned, as it were, from

---

[1] A prime illustration is afforded by the Latin juristic word *persona* used in
the Creed.   The Latins had to render the three ὑποστάσεις of the Greeks ; and
" three somethings," *tria quaedam*, was too loose, as Augustine says (*De
Trinitate*, vii. 7-12).   The true and literal translation of ὑπόστασις would have
been *substantia* ; but that word had been taken to render οὐσία.   So the legal
word *persona* was employed in spite of its recognized unfitness.   Cf. Taylor,
Classical Heritage, etc., p. 116 *sqq.*

fact to truth, to a consideration of the validity of human understanding. Thereupon the Greek mind became entranced with its own creations. Man was the measure of all things, for the Sophists. More irrefragably and pregnantly, man became the measure of all things for Socrates and Plato. The aphorism might be discarded ; but its transcendental import was established in an imaginative dialectic whose correspondence to the divinest splendours of the human mind warranted its truth. With Platonists—and the world was always to be filled with them—perceptions of physical facts and the data of human life and history, were henceforth to constitute the outer actuality of a creation within the mind. Every observed fact is an apparent tangibility ; but its reality consists in its unison with the ultimate realities of rational conception. The apprehension of the fact must be made to conform to these. For this reason every fact has a secondary, nay, primary, because spiritual, meaning. Its true interpretation lies in that significance which accords with the mind's consistent system of conceptions, which present the fact as it must be thought, and therefore as it is ; it is the fact brought into right relationship with spiritual and ethical verity. Of course, methods of apprehending terrestrial and celestial phenomena as illustrations of ideally conceived principles, were unlikely to foster habits of close observation. The apparent facts of sense would probably be imaginatively treated if not transformed in the process of their apprehension. Nor, with respect to human story, would such methods draw fixed lines between the narration of what men are pleased to call the actual occurrence, and the shaping of a tale to meet the exigencies of argument or illustration.

All this is obvious in Plato. The *Timaeus* was his vision of the universe, in which physical facts became plastic material for the spirit's power to mould into the likeness of ideal conceptions. The creation of the universe is conformed to the structure of Platonic dialectic. If any meaning be certain through the words and imagery of this dialogue, it is that the world and all creatures which it contains derive such reality as they have from conformity to the thoughts or ideal patterns in the divine mind. Visible things are real only so far as they conform to those perfect conceptions. Moreover, the visible creation has another value, that of its ethical significance. Physical phenomena symbolize the conformity of humanity to its best ideal of conduct. Man may learn to regulate the lawless movements of his soul from the courses of the stars, the noblest of created gods.

Thus as to natural phenomena ; and likewise as to the human story, fact or fiction. The myth of the shadow-seers in the cave, with which the seventh book of the *Republic* opens, is just as illustratively and ideally true as that opening tale in the *Timaeus* of the ancient Athenian state, which fought for its own and others' freedom against the people of Atlantis—till the earthquake ended the old Athenian race, and the Atlantean continent was swallowed in the sea. This story has piqued curiosity for two thousand years. Was it tradition, or the creation of an artist dialect- ician ? In either case its ideal and edifying truth stood or fell, not by reason of conformity to any basic antecedent fact, but according to its harmony with the beautiful and good.

Plato's method of conceiving fact might be applied to man's thoughts of God, of the origin of the world and the courses of the stars ; also to the artistic manipulation of illustrative or edifying story. Matters, large, remote, and mysterious, admit of idealizing ways of apprehension. But it might seem idiocy, rather than idealism, to apply this method to the plain facts of common life, which may be handled and looked at all around—to which there is no mysterious other side, like the moon's, for ever turned away. Nevertheless the method and its motives drew men from careful observa- tion of nature, and would invest biography and history with interests promoting the ingenious application, rather than the close scrutiny, of fact.

Thus Platonism and its way of treating narrative could not but foster the allegorical interpretation of ancient tradition and literature, which was already in vogue in Plato's time. It mattered not that he would have nothing to do with the current allegories through which men moralized or rationalized the old tales of the doings of the gods. He was himself a weaver of the loveliest allegories when it

served his purpose. And after him the allegorical habit
entered into the interpretation of all ancient story. In the
course of time allegory will be applied by the Jew Philo of
Alexandria to the Pentateuch ; and one or two centuries
later it will play a great rôle in Christian polemics against
Jew and then against Manichean. It will become *par
excellence* the chief mode of patristic exegesis, and pass on
as a legacy of spiritual truth to the mediaeval church.

Aristotle strikes us as a man of different type from Plato.
Whether his intellectual interests were broader than his
teacher's is hardly for ordinary people to say. He certainly
was more actively interested in the investigation of nature.
Head of an actual school (as Plato had been), and assisted
by the co-operation of able men, he presents himself, with
what he accomplished, at least in threefold guise : as a
metaphysician and the perfecter, if not creator, of formal
logic ; as an observer of the facts of nature and the institutions and arts of men ; as a man of encyclopaedic learning.
These three phases of intellectual effort proportioned each
other in a mind of universal power and appetition. Yet it
has been thought that there was more metaphysics and
formal logic in Aristotle than was good for his natural
science.

The lost and extant writings which have been ascribed
to him, embraced a hundred and fifty titles and amounted
to four hundred books. Those which have been of universal
influence upon human inquiry suffice to illustrate the scope
of his labours. There were the treatises upon Logic and
first among them the *Categories* or classes of propositions,
and the *De interpretatione* on the constituent parts and kinds
of sentences. These two elementary treatises (the authorship of which has been questioned), were the only Aristotelian
writings generally used through the West until the latter
half of the twelfth century, when the remainder of the logical
treatises became known, to wit, the *Prior Analytics*, upon
the syllogism ; the *Posterior Analytics* upon logical demonstration ; the *Topics*, or demonstrations having probability ; and the *Sophistical Elenchi*, upon false conclusions
and their refutation. Together these constitute the *Organon*
or complete logical instrument, as it became known to the

latter half of the twelfth century, and as we possess it to-day.

The *Rhetoric* follows, not disconnected with the logical treatises. Then may be named the *Metaphysics*, and then the writings devoted to Nature, to wit, the *Physics, Concerning the Heavens, Concerning Genesis and Decay*, the *Meteorology*, the *Mechanical Problems*, the *History of Animals*, the *Anatomical descriptions*, the *De anima*, the *Parts of Animals*, the *Generation of Animals*. There was a Botany, which is lost. Finally, one names the great works on Ethics, Politics, and Poetry.

Every one is overwhelmed by the compass of the achievement of this intellect. As to the transcendent value of the works on Logic, Metaphysics, Psychology, Rhetoric, Ethics, Politics, and Poetry, the world of scholarship has long been practically at one. And to-day students of science are impressed by the intellectual power and the penetrating investigation represented by the writings on Natural History. Their author is commonly regarded as the founder of systematic Zoology. On the whole, perhaps one will not err in repeating what has been said hundreds of times, that the works ascribed to Aristotle, and which undoubtedly were produced by him or his co-labourers under his direction, represent the most prodigious intellectual achievement ever connected with any single name.

In the school of Aristotle, one phase or another of the master's activity would be likely to absorb the student's energy and fasten his entire attention. Aristotle's own pupil and successor was the admirable Theophrastus, a man of comprehensive attainment, who nevertheless devoted himself principally to carrying on his master's labours in botany, and other branches of natural science. A History of Physics was one of the most important of his works. Another pupil of Aristotle was Eudemus of Rhodes, who became a physicist and a historian of the three sciences of Geometry, Arithmetic, and Astronomy. He exhibits the learned activities thenceforth to characterize the Peripatetics. It would have been difficult to carry further the logic or metaphysics of the master. But his work in natural science might be supplemented, while the body of his writings offered a vast field for the labours of the commentator. And so, in fact, Peripatetic energies in the succeeding generations were divided between science and learning, the latter centring chiefly in historical and grammatical labours and the exposition of the master's writing.[1]

Aristotelianism was not to be the philosophy of the closing pre-Christian centuries, any more than it was to be the philosophy of the thousand years and more following the Crucifixion. During all that time, its logic held its own, and a number of its metaphysical principles were absorbed in other systems. But Aristotelianism as a system soon ceased to be in vogue, and by the sixth century was no longer known.

Yet one might find an echo of its spirit in all men who were seeking knowledge from the world of nature, from history and humane learning. There were always such ; and some famous examples may be drawn even from among the practical - minded Romans. One thinks at once of Cicero's splendid breadth of humane and literary interest. His friend Terentius Varro was a more encyclopaedic personality, and an eager student in all fields of knowledge. Although not an investigator of nature he wrote on agriculture, on navigation, on geometry, as well as the Latin tongue, and on Antiquities, divine and human, even on philosophy.[2]

Another lover of knowledge was the elder Pliny, who died from venturing too near to observe the eruption which destroyed Pompeii. He was an important functionary under the emperor Vespasian, just as Varro had held offices of authority in the time of the Republic. Pliny's *Historia naturalis* was an astounding compilation, intended to cover the whole plain of common and uncommon knowledge. The compiler neither observed for himself nor weighed the statements of others. His compilation is a happy harbourage for the preposterous as well as reasonable, where the traveller's tale of far-off wonders takes its place beside the testimony of Aristotle. All is fish that comes to the net

---

[1] On these Peripatetics see Zeller, *Philosophie der Griechen,* 3rd ed. vol. ii. pp. 506-946.

[2] See Boissier, *Étude sur M. T. Varron* (Paris, 1861).

of the good Pliny, though it be that wonderful *piscis*, the *Echinus*, which though but a cubit long has such tenacity of grip and purpose that it holds fast the largest galley, and with the resistance of its fins, renders impotent the efforts of a hundred rowers.   Fish for Pliny also are all the stories of antiquity, of dog-headed, one-legged, big-footed men, of the Pigmies and the Cranes, of the Phoenix and the Basilisk. He delights in the more intricate causality of nature's phenomena, and tells how the bowels of the field-mouse increase in number with the days of the moon, and the energy of the ant decreases as the orb of Venus wanes.[1]   But this credulous person was a marvel of curiosity and diligence, and we are all his debtors for an acquaintance with the hearsay opinions current in the antique world.

Varro and Pliny were encyclopaedists.   Yet before, as well as after them, the men possessed by the passion for knowledge of the natural world, were frequently devoted to some branch of inquiry, rather than encyclopaedic gleaners, or universal philosophers.   Hippocrates, Socrates's contemporary, had left a name rightly enduring as the greatest of physicians.   In the third century before Christ Euclid is a great mathematician, and Hipparchus and Archimedes have place for ever, the one among the great astronomers, the other among the great terrestrial physicists.   All these men represent reflection and theory, as well as investigation and experiment.   Leaping forward to the second century A.D., we find among others two great lovers of science.   Galen of Pergamos was a worthy follower, if not a peer, of the great physician of classic Greece ;   and Ptolemy of Alexandria emulated the Alexandrian Hipparchus, whose fame he revered, and whose labours (with his own) he transmitted to posterity.   Each of these men may be regarded as advancing some portion of the universal plan of Aristotle.

Another philosophy, Stoicism, had already reached a wide acceptance.   As for the causes of this, doubtless the decline of Greek civic freedom before the third century B.C., had tended to throw thoughtful men back upon their inner life ; and those who had lost their taste for the popular religion, needed a philosophy to live by.   Stoicism became especially

---

[1] *Hist. naturalis*, ii. 41.

popular among the Romans. It was ethics, a philosophy of practice rather than of knowledge. The Stoic looked out upon the world from the inner fortress of the human will. That guarded or rather constituted his well-being. He cared for such knowledge, call it instruction rather, as would make good the principle that human well-being lay in the rightly self-directing will. He did not seriously care for metaphysics, or for knowledge of the natural world, save as one or the other subserved the ends of his philosophy as a guide of life. Thus the Stoic physics, so important a part in the Stoic system, was inspired by utilitarian motives and deflected from unprejudiced observation by teleological considerations and reflections on the dispensations of Providence. Of course, some of the Stoics show a further range of intellectual interest ; Seneca, for example, who was a fine moralist and wrote beautiful essays upon the conduct of life. He, like a number of other people, composed a book of *Quaestiones naturales*, which was chiefly devoted to the weather, a subject always very close to man. But he was not a serious meteorologist. For him the interest of the fact lay rather in its use or in its moral bearing. After Seneca the Stoic interest in fact narrows still further, as with Epictetus and Marcus Aurelius.

Like things might be said of the school of Epicurus, a child of different colour, yet birthmate of the Stoa. For in that philosophy as in Stoicism, all knowledge beyond ethics had a subordinate rôle. As a Stoic or Epicurean, a man was not likely to contribute to the advance of any branch of science. Yet habits of eclectic thought and common curiosity, or call it love of knowledge, made many nominal members of these schools eager students and compilers from the works of others.

We have yet to speak of the system most representative of latter-day paganism, and of enormous import for the first thousand years of Christian thought. Neo-Platonism was the last great creation of Greek philosophy. More specifically, it was the noblest product of that latter-day paganism which was yearning somewhat distractedly, impelled by cravings which paganism could neither quench nor satisfy.

Spirit is; it is the Real. It makes the body, thereby presenting itself in sensible form ; it is not confined by body or dependent on body as its cause or necessary ground. In many ways men have expressed, and will express hereafter, the creative or causal antecedence of the spiritual principle. In many ways they have striven to establish this principle in God who is Spirit, or in the Absolute One. Many also have been the processes of individualization and diverse the mediatorial means, through which philosopher apostle, or Church Doctor has tried to bring this principle down to man, and conceive him as spirit manifesting an intelligible selfhood through the organs of sense. Platonism was a beautiful, if elusive, expression of this endeavour, and Neo-Platonism a very palpable although darkening statement of the same.

All men, except fools, have their irrational sides. Who does not believe what his reason shall labour in vain to justify ? Such belief may have its roots spread through generalizations broader than any specific rational processes of which the man is conscious. And a man is marked by the character of his supra-rational convictions, or beliefs or credulous conjectures. One thinks how Plato wove and coloured his dialectic, and angled with it, after those transcendencies that he well knew could never be so hooked and taken. His conviction—non-dialectical—of the supreme and beautiful reality of spirit led him on through all his arguments, some of which appear as playful, while others are very earnest.

Less elusive than Plato's was the supra-rationality of his distant disciple, the Egyptian Plotinus (died 270), creator of Neo-Platonism. With him the supra-rational represented an *élan*, a reaching beyond the clearly seen or clearly known, to the Spirit itself. He had a disciple Porphyry, like him-self a sage—and yet a different sage. Porphyry's supra-rationalities hungered for many things from which his rational nature turned askance. But he has a disciple, Iamblicus by name, whose rational nature not only ceases to protest, but of its free will prostitutes itself in the service of unreason.

The synthetic genius of Plotinus enabled him to weave

into his system valuable elements from Aristotle and the Stoics. But he was above all a Platonist. He presents the spiritual triad : the One, the Mind, the Soul. From the One comes the Mind, that is, the Nous, which embraces the totality of the knowable or intelligible, to wit, the Cosmos of Ideas. From that, come the Soul of the World and the souls of men. Matter, which is no-thing, gains form and partial reality when *informed* with soul. Plotinus's attitude toward knowledge of the concrete natural or historic fact, displays a transcendental indifference exceeding that of Plato. Perceptible facts with him are but half-real manifestations of the informing spirit. They were quite plastic, malleable, reducible. Moreover, thoughts of the evil of the multiple world of sense held for Plotinus and his followers a bitterness of ethical unreality which Plato was too great an Athenian to feel.

Dualistic ethics which find in matter the principle of unreality or evil, diminish the human interest in physical fact. The ethics of Plotinus consisted in purification and detachment from things of sense. This is asceticism. And Plotinus was an ascetic, not through endeavour, but from contempt. He did not struggle to renounce the world, but despised it with the spontaneity of a sublimated temperament. He seemed like a man ashamed of being in the body, Porphyry says of him. Nor did he wish to cure any contemptible bodily ailments, or wash his wretched body.

Plotinus's Absolute, the First or One, might not be grasped by reason. Yet to approach and contemplate It was the best for man. Life's crown was the ecstasy of the supra-rational and supra-intelligible vision of It. This Plotinean irrationality was lofty ; but it was too transcendent, too difficult, and too unrelated to the human heart, to satisfy other men. No fear but that his followers would bring it down to the level of *their* irrational tendencies.

The borrowed materials of this philosophy were made by its founder into a veritable system. It included, potentially at least, the popular beliefs, which, however, interested this metaphysical genius very little. But in those superstitious centuries, before as well as after him, these cruder elements were gathered and made much of by men of note. There was a tendency to contrast the spiritual and real with the manifold of material nonentity, and a cognate tendency to emphasize the opposition between the spiritual and good, and the material and evil, or between opposing spiritual principles. With less metaphysical people such opposition would take more entrancing shapes in the battles of gods and demons. Probably it would cause ascetic repression of the physical passions. Both tendencies had shown themselves before Plotinus came to build them into his system. Friend Plutarch, for instance, of Chaeroneia, was a man of pleasant temper and catholic curiosity. His philosophy was no great matter. He was gently credulous, and interested in anything marvellous and every imaginable god and demon. This good Greek was no ascetic, and yet had much to say of the strife between the good and evil principle. Like thoughts begat asceticism in men of a different temperament ; for instance in the once famous Apollonius of Tyana and others, who were called Neo-Pythagoreans, whatever that meant. Such men had also their irrationalities, which perhaps made up the major part of their natures. They did indeed belong to those centuries when Astrology flourished at the imperial Court,[1] and every mode of magic mystery drew its gaping votaries ; when men were ravenously drawing toward everything, except the plain concrete fact steadily viewed and quietly reasoned on.

But it was within the schools of Neo-Platonism, in the generations after Plotinus, that these tendencies flourished, beneath the shelter of his elastic principles. Here three kindred currents made a resistless stream : a transcendental, fact - compelling dialectic ; unveiled recognition of the supreme virtue of supra-rational convictions and experiences; and an asceticism which contemned matter and abhorred the things of sense. What more was needed to close the faculties of observation, befool the reason, and destroy knowledge in the end ?

Porphyry and Iamblicus show the turning of the tide. The first of these was a Tyrian, learned, intelligent, austere. His life extends from about the year 232 to the year 300

---

[1] From the reign of Augustus onward, Astrology flourished as never before. See Habler, *Astrologie im Alterthum*, p. 23 *sqq.* (Zwickau, 1879).

His famous *Introduction* to the *Categories* of Aristotle was a corner-stone of the early mediaeval knowledge of logic. He wrote a keenly rational work against the Christians, in which his critical acumen pointed out that the Book of Daniel was not composed before the reign of Antiochus Epiphanes. He did much to render intelligible the writings of his master Plotinus, and made a compend of Neo-Platonism in the form of *Sentences*. These survive, as well as his work on *Abstinence from Eating Flesh*, and other treatises, allegorical and philosophic.

He was to Plotinus as Soul, in the Neo-Platonic system, was to Mind—Soul which somehow was darkly, passionately tangled in the body of which it was the living principle. The individual soul of Porphyry wrestled with all the matters which the mind of Plotinus made slight account of. Plotinus lived aloof in a region of metaphysics warmed with occasional ecstasy. Porphyry, willy nilly, was drawn down to life, and suffered all the pain of keen mentality when limed and netted with the anxieties of common superstitions. He was forever groping in a murky atmosphere. He could not clear himself of credulity, deny and argue as he might. Nor could asceticism pacify his mind. Philosophically he followed Plotinus's teachings, and understood them too, which was a marvel. Many of his own, or possibly reflected, thoughts are excellent. No Christian could hold a more spiritual conception of sacrifice than Porphyry when thinking of the worship of the Mind—the Nous or Second God. Offer to it silence and chaste thought, which will unite us to it, and make us like itself. The perfect sacrifice is to disengage the soul from passions.[1] What could be finer? And again says Porphyry: The body is the soul's garment, to be laid aside; the wise man needs only God; evil spirits have no power over a pure soul. But, but, but—at his last statement Porphyry's confidence breaks. He is worried because it is so hard to know the good from evil demons; and the latter throng the temples, and must be exorcised before the true God will appear. This same man had said that God's true temple was the wise man's soul! Alas! Porphyry's nature reeks with contradictions. His letter to the Egyptian priest,

[1] *De abstinentia*, ii. 34.

Anebo, consists of sharply-put questions as to the validity
of any kind of theurgy or divination. How can men know
anything as to these things ? What reason to suppose that
this, that, or the other rite—all anxiously enumerated—is
rightly directed or has effect ? None ! none ! none ! such
is the answer expected by the questions.

But Porphyry's own soul answers otherwise. His works
—the *De abstinentia* for example—teem with detailed and
believing discussion of every kind of theurgic practice and
magic rite, whereby the divine and demonic natures may be
moved. He believed in oracles and sorcery. Vainly did
the more keenly intellectual side of his nature seek to hold
such matters at arm's length ; his other instincts hungered
for them, craved to touch and taste and handle, as the child
hankers for what is forbidden. There is angel-lore, but
far more devil-lore, in Porphyry, and below the earth the
demons have their realm, and at their head a demon-king.
Thus organized, these malformed devil-shapes torment the
lives of men, malignant deceivers, spiteful trippers up, as
they are.

Such a man beset by demons (which his intelligence
declares to have no power over him !), such a man, austere
and grim, would practise fanatically the asceticism recognized
so calmly by the system of Plotinus. With Porphyry,
strenuously, anxiously, the upper grades of virtue become
violent purification and detachment from things of sense.
Here he is in grim earnest.

It is wonderful that this man should have had a critical
sense of historic fact, as when he saw the comparatively late
date of the Book of Daniel. He could see the holes in
others' garments. But save for some such polemic purpose,
the bare, crude fact interests him little. He is an elaborate
fashioner of allegory, and would so interpret the fictions of
the poets. Plotinus, when it suited him, had played with
myths, like Plato. No such light hand, and scarcely concealed smile, has Porphyry. As for physical investigations,
they interest him no more seriously than they did his master,
and when he touches upon natural fact he is as credulous
as Pliny. " The Arabians," says he, " understand the speech
of crows, and the Tyrrhenians that of eagles ; and perhaps

we and all men would understand all living beings if a dragon licked our ears." [1]

These inner conflicts darkened Porphyry's life, and doubt-less made some of the motives which were turning his thoughts to suicide, when Plotinus showed him that this was not the true way of detachment. There was no conflict, but complete surrender, and happy abandonment in Iamblicus the Divine ($\theta\epsilon\hat{\iota}o\varsigma$) who when he prayed might be lifted ten cubits from the ground—so thought his disciples—and around whose theurgic fingers, dabbling in a magic basin of water, Cupids played and kissed each other. His life, told by the Neo-Platonic biographer, Eunapius, is as full of miracle as the contemporary Life of St. Antony by Athana-sius. Iamblicus floats before us a beautiful and marvel-lously garbed priest, a dweller in the recesses of temples. He frankly gave himself to theurgy, convinced that the Soul needs the aid of every superhuman being—hero, god, demon, angel.[2] He was credulous on principle. It is of first importance, he writes, that the devotee should not let the marvellous character of an occurrence arouse incredulity within him. He needs above all a " science " ($\epsilon\pi\iota\sigma\tau\acute{\eta}\mu\eta$) which shall teach him to disbelieve nothing as to the gods.[3] For the divine principle is essentially miraculous, and magic is the open door, yes, and the way up to it, the anagogic path.

All this and more besides is set forth in the De mysteriis, the chief composition of his school. It was the answer to that doubting letter of Porphyry to Anebo, and contains full proof and exposition of the occult art of moving god or demon. We all have an inborn knowledge ($\check{\epsilon}\mu\phi\upsilon\tau o\varsigma\ \gamma\nu\hat{\omega}\sigma\iota\varsigma$) [4] of the gods. But it is not thought or contemplation that unites us to them ; it is the power of the theurgic rite or cabalistic word, understood only by the gods. We cannot understand the reason of these acts and their effects.[5]

There is no lower depth. Plotinus's reason-surpassing

---

[1] De abstinentia, iii. 4.
[2] Porphyry before him had spoken of angels and archangels, which he had found in Jewish writings.
[3] For authorities cited, see Zeller, Gesch. der Phil. iii.³ p. 686.
[4] De mysteriis, i. 3.
[5] Ibid. ii. 3, 9.

vision of the One (which represents in him the principle of
irrationality) is at last brought down to the irrational act,
the occult magic deed or word. Truly the worshipper needs
his best credulity—which is bespoken by Iamblicus and by
this book. The work seems to argue, somewhat obscurely,
that the prayer or invocation or rite, does not actually draw
the god to us, but draws us toward the god, making our
wills fit to share in his. The writer of such a work is likely
to be confused in his statement of principles ; but will
expand more genially when expounding the natures of
demons, heroes, angels, and gods, and the effect of them
upon humanity. Perhaps the matter still seems dark ; but
the picturesque details are bright enough. For the writer
describes the manifestations and apparitions of these beings
—their ἐπιφανείαι and φάσματα. The apparitions of the
gods are μονοειδῆ, simple and uniform : those of the demons
are ποικίλα, that is, various and manifold ; those of the
angels are more simple than those of the demons, but
inferior to those of the gods. The archangels in their
apparitions are more like the gods ; while the ἄρχοντες, the
" governors," have variety and yet order. The gods as they
appear to men, are radiant with divine effulgence, the archangels terrible yet kind ; the demons are frightful, producing
perturbation and terror—on all of which the work enlarges.
Speaking more specifically of the effect of these apparitions
on the thaumaturgist, the writer says that visions of the
gods bring a mighty power, and divine love and joy ineffable ; the archangels bring steadfastness and power of
will and intellectual contemplation ; the angels bring
rational wisdom and truth and virtue. But the vision of
demons brings the desires of sense and the vigour to fulfil
them.

So low sank Neo-Platonism in pagan circles. Of course
it did not create this mass of superstitious fantasy. It merely
accepted it, and over every superstition flung the justification of its principles. In the process it changed from a
philosophy to a system of theurgic practice. The common
superstitions of the time, or their like, were old enough.
But now—and here was the portentous fact—they had
wound themselves into the natures of intellectual people ;

and Neo-Platonism represents the chief formal facilitation of this result.

A contemporary phenomenon, and perhaps the most popular of pagan cults in the third and fourth centuries, was the worship of Mithra, around which Neo-Platonism could throw its cloak as well as around any other form of pagan worship. Mithraism, a partially Hellenized growth from the old Mazdaean (even Indo-Iranian) faith, had been carried from one boundary of the Empire to the other, by soldiers or by merchants who had imbibed its doctrines in the East. It shot over the Empire like a flame. A warrior cult, the late pagan emperors gave it their adhesion. It was, in fine, the pagan Antaeus destined to succumb in the grasp of the Christian Hercules.

With it, or after it, came Manicheism, also from the East. This was quite as good a philosophy as the Neo-Platonism of Iamblicus. The system called after Manes was a crass dualism, containing fantastic and largely borrowed speculation as to the world and man. Satan was there and all his devils. He was the begetter of mankind, in Adam. But Satan himself, in previous struggles with good angels, had gained some elements of light ; and these passed into Adam's nature. Eve, however, is sensuality. After man's engendering, the strife begins between the good and evil spirits to control his lot. In ethics, of course, Manicheism was dualistic and ascetic, like Neo-Platonism, and also like the Christianity of the Eastern and Western Empire. Manicheism, unlike Mithraism, was not to succumb, but merely to retreat before Christianity. Again and again from the East, through the lower confines of the present Russia, through Hungary, it made advance. The Bogomiles were its children ; likewise the Cathari in the north of Italy, and the Albigenses of Provence.[1]

The insistence of the problem of evil and the drift to dualism were likewise marked in the Gnostic creeds, which consisted chiefly of Persian and Neo-Hellenic elements, but were affiliated with Christianity by the yearning for salvation and drawn to the Christian pale (though not within it) by the figure of the Saviour. The appeal of these oriental

[1] Cf. Döllinger, *Sektengeschichte.*

cults, speaking generally, was personal rather than civic. Careless of the State, they offered to the individual the means of purification from the defilements of matter and assured him of eternal bliss.[1]

Platonism, Stoicism, Neo-Platonism, Mithraism, Manicheism, and Gnosticism, these names, taken for simplicity's sake, serve to indicate the mind and temper of the educated world in which Christianity was spreading. Obviously the Christian Fathers' ways of thinking were given by all that made up their environment, their education, their second natures. They were men of their period, and as Christians their intellectual standards did not rise nor their understanding of fact alter, although their approvals and disapprovals might be changed. Their natures might be stimulated and uplifted by the Faith and its polemic ardours, and yet their manner of approaching and apprehending facts, *its* facts, for example, might continue substantially those of their pagan contemporaries or predecessors.

In the fourth century the leaders of the Church both in the East and West were greater men than contemporary pagan priests or philosophers or rhetoricians. For the strongest minds had enlisted on the Christian side, and a great cause inspired their highest energies with an efficient purpose. There is no comparison between Athanasius, Basil, Gregory Nazianzen, Gregory of Nyssa and Chrysostom in the East ; Ambrose, Jerome, and Augustine in the West ; and pagans, like Libanius, the favourite of the Emperor Julian, or even Julian himself, or Symmachus, the opponent of St. Ambrose in the cause of the pagan Altar of Victory. That was a lost cause, and the cause of paganism was becoming more and more broken, dissipated, uninspiring. Nevertheless, in spite of the superiority of the Christian doctors, in spite also of the mighty cause which marshalled their endeavours so efficiently, they present, both in their higher intelligence and their lower irrationalities, abundant likeness to the pagans.

It has appeared that metaphysical interests absorbed the attention of Plotinus, who has nevertheless his supreme irrationality atop of all. Porphyry also possessed a strong

---

[1] See Fr. Cumont, *Oriental Religions in Roman Paganism.*

reasoning nature, but was drawn irresistibly to all the things, gods, demons, divination and theurgy, of which one half of him disapproved. Plotinus, quite in accordance with his philosophic principles, has an easy contempt for physical life. With Porphyry this has become ardent asceticism. It was also remarked that Plotinus's system was a synthesis of much antecedent thought ; and that its receptivity was rendered extremely elastic by the Neo-Platonic principle that man's ultimate approach to God lay through ecstasy and not through reason. Herein, rather latent and not yet sorely taxed, was a broad justification of common beliefs and practices. To all these Iamblicus gladly opened the door. Rather than a philosopher, he was a priest, a thaumaturgist and magician. Finally, it is obvious that neither Iamblicus nor Porphyry nor Plotinus was primarily or even seriously interested in any clear objective knowledge of material facts. Plotinus merely noticed them casually in order to illustrate his principles, while Iamblicus looked to them for miracles.

Christianity as well as Neo-Platonism was an expression of the principle that life's primordial reality is spirit. And likewise with Christians, as with Neo-Platonists, phases of irrationality may be observed in ascending and descending order. At the summit the sublimest Christian supra-rationality, the love of God, uplifts itself. From that height the irrational conviction grades down to credulity pre-occupied with the demoniacal and miraculous. Fruitful comparisons may be drawn between Neo-Platonists and Christian doctors.

Origen (d. 253), very probably of Coptic descent, and the most brilliant genius of the Eastern Church, was by some fifteen years the senior of the Neo-Platonist. It is not certain that either of them directly influenced the other. In intellectual power the two were peers. Both were absorbed in the higher phases of their thought, but neither excluded the more popular beliefs from the system which he was occupied in constructing. Plotinus had no mind to shut the door against the beliefs of polytheism ; and Origen accepted on his part the demons and angels of current Christian credence.[1] In fact, he occupied himself with them more

---

[1] See Origen, *De principiis*, iii. 2.

than Plotinus did with the gods of the Hellenic pantheon
Of course Origen, like every other Christian doctor, had his
fundamental and saving irrationality in his acceptance of the
Christian revelation and the risen Christ.   This had already
taken its most drastic form in the *credo quia absurdum* of
Tertullian the Latin Father, who was twenty-five years his
senior.   Herein one observes the acceptance of the miraculous on principle.   That the great facts of the Christian creed
were beyond the proof or disproof of reason was a principle
definitely accepted by all the Fathers.

Further, since all Catholic Christians accepted the
Scriptures as revealed truth, they were obliged to accept
many things which their reason, unaided, might struggle
with in vain.   Here was a large opportunity, as to which
Christians would act according to their tempers, in
emphasizing and amplifying the authoritative or miraculous,
i.e. irrational, element.   And besides, outside even of these
Scriptural matters and their interpretations, there would be
the general question of the educated Christian's interest
in the miraculous.   Great mental power and devotion to
the construction of dogma by no means precluded a lively
interest in this, as may be seen in that very miraculous life
of St. Anthony, written probably by Athanasius himself.
This biography is more preoccupied with the demoniacal
and miraculous than Porphyry's *Life of Plotinus* ; indeed
in this respect it is not outdone by Eunapius's *Life of
Iamblicus.*   Turning to the Latin West, one may compare
with them that charming prototypal Vita Sancti, the *Life
of St. Martin* by Sulpicius Severus.[1]   A glance at these
writings shows a similarity of interest with Christian and
Neo-Platonist, and in both is found the same unquestioning
acceptance of the miraculous.

Thus one observes how the supernatural manifestation,
the miraculous event, was admitted and justified on principle
in both the Neo-Platonic and the Christian system.   In
both, moreover, metaphysical or symbolizing tendencies had
withdrawn attention from a close scrutiny of any fact,

[1] The Athanasian *Vita Antonii* is in Migne, *Patr. Graec.* 26, and trans. in
Nicene Fathers, second series, iv.   The *Vita S. Martini* is in Halm's ed. of Sulp.
Severus (Vienna, 1866), and in Migne, *Pat. Lat.* 20, and trans. in *Nicene Fathers,*
second series, xi.

observed, imagined, or reported. With both, the primary
value of historical or physical fact lay in its illumination
of general convictions or accepted principles. And with
both, the supernatural fact was the fact *par excellence*, in that
it was the direct manifestation of the divine or spiritual
power.

Iamblicus had announced that man must not be in-
credulous as to superhuman beings and their supernatural
doings. On the Christian side, there was no bit of popular
credence in miracle or magic mystery, or any notion as to
devils, angels, and departed saints, for which justification
could not be found in the writings of the great Doctors of
the Church. These learned and intellectual men evince
different degrees of interest in such matters ; but none
stands altogether aloof, or denies *in toto*. No evidence is
needed here. A broad illustration, however, lies in the
fact that before the fourth century the chief Christian rites
had become sacramental mysteries, necessarily miraculous
in their nature and their efficacy. This was true of Baptism ;
it was more stupendously true of the Eucharist. Mystically,
but none the less really, and above all inevitably, the bread
and wine have miraculously become the body and the
blood. The process, one may say, began with Origen ;
with Cyril of Jerusalem it is completed; Gregory of Nyssa
regards it as a continuation of the verity of the Incarnation,
and Chrysostom is with him.[1] One pauses to remark that
the relationship between the pagan and Christian mysteries
was not one of causal antecedence so much as one of
analogous growth. A pollen of terms and concepts blew
hither and thither, and effected a cross-fertilization of
vigorously growing plants. The life-sap of the Christian
mysteries, as with those of Mithra or the Gnostics, was
the passion for a symbolism of the unknown and the in-
expressible.

But one must not stop here. The whole Christian
Church, as well as Porphyry and Iamblicus, accepted
angels and devils, and recognized their intervention or
interference in human affairs. Then displacing the local

[1] See Harnack, *Dogmengeschichte*, ii. 413 *sqq.*, especially 432 *sqq.* Also Taylor,
Classical Heritage, pp. 94-97.

pagan divinities come the saints, and Mary above all. They
are honoured, they are worshipped. Only an Augustine
has some gentle warning to utter against carrying these
matters to excess.

In connection with all this, one may notice an illuminating point, or rather motive. In the third and fourth
centuries the common yearning of the Graeco-Roman world
was for an approach to God ; it was looking for the anagogic
path, the way up from man and multiplicity to unity and
God. An absorbing interest was taken in the means.
Neo-Platonism, the creature of this time, whatever else
it was, was mediatorial, a system of mediation between
man and the Absolute First Principle. Passing halfway
over from paganism to Christianity, the Celestial Hierarchy
of Pseudo-Dionysius is also essentially a system of mediation, which has many affinities (as well it might !) with the
system of Plotinus.[1] Within Catholic Christianity the great
work of Athanasius was to establish Christ's sole and all-
sufficient mediation. Catholicism was permanently set upon
the mediatorship of Christ, God and man, the one God-man
reconciling the nature which He had veritably, and not
seemingly, assumed, to the divine substance which He had
never ceased to be. Athanasius's struggle for this principle
was bitter and hard-pressed, because within Christianity as
well as without, men were demanding easier and more
tangible stages and means of mediation.

Of such, Catholic Christianity was to recognize a vast
multitude, perhaps not dogmatically as a necessary part of
itself ; but practically and universally. Angels, saints, the
Virgin over all, are mediators between man and God. This
began to be true at an early period, and was established
before the fourth century.[2] Moreover, every bit of rite
and mystery and miracle, as in paganism, so in Catholicism,
was essentially a means of mediation, a way of bringing

[1] In cap. iii. § 2 of the *Celestial Hierarchy*, Pseudo-Dionysius says that the
goal of his system is the becoming like to God and oneness with Him (ἡ πρὸς θεὸν
ἀφομοίωσίς τε καὶ ἕνωσις). He classifies his " celestial intelligences " even more
systematically than the *De mysteriis* of Iamblicus's school. His work is full of
Neo-Platonism. Cf. Vacherot, *Histoire de l'école d'Alexandrie*, iii. 24 sqq.

[2] The cult of the Virgin and the saints was of very early growth. See Lucius,
Die Anfänge des Heiligen Kults in der christlichen Kirche (ed. by Anrich, Tübingen,
1904).

the divine principle to bear on man and his affairs, and so of bringing man within the sphere of the divine efficiency.

Let us make some further Christian comparisons with our Neo-Platonic friends Plotinus, Porphyry, and Iamblicus. As we have adduced Origen, it would also be easy to find other parallels from the Eastern Church. But as the purpose is to mark the origin of the intellectual tendencies of the Western Middle Ages, we may at once draw examples from the Latin Fathers. For their views set the forms of mediaeval intellectual interests, and for centuries directed and even limited the mediaeval capacity for apprehending whatever it was given to the Middle Ages to set themselves to know. To pass thus from the East to the West is permissible, since the same pagan cults and modes of thought passed from one boundary of the Empire to the other. Plotinus himself lived and taught in Rome for the last twenty-five years of his life, and there wrote his *Enneads* in Greek. So on the Christian side, the Catholic Church throughout the East and West presents a solidarity of development, both as to dogma and organization, and also as to popular acceptances.

Let us train our attention upon some points of likeness between Plotinus and St. Augustine. The latter's teachings contain much Platonism; and with this greatest of Latin Fathers, who did not read much Greek, Platonism was inextricably mingled with Neo-Platonism. It is possible to search the works of Augustine and discover this, that, or the other statement reflecting Plato or Plotinus.[1] Yet their most interesting effect on Augustine will not be found in Platonic theorems consciously followed or abjured by the latter. Platonism was " in the air," at least was in the air breathed by an Augustine. He knew little of Plato's writings. But Plato had lived : his thoughts had influenced many generations, and in their diffusion had been modified, and had lost many a specific feature. Thereafter Plotinus had constructed Neo-Platonism ; that too had permeated the minds of many, itself loosened in the process. These views, these phases of thought and mood, were held or felt

---

[1] See, *e.g.*, Grandgeorge, *St. Augustin et le Néoplatonisme* (Paris, 1896). Or perhaps statements impregnated with the Manicheism which he had abjured.

by many men, who may not have known their source.
And Augustine was not only part of all this, but in mind
and temper was Platonically inclined.   Thus the most
important elements of Platonism and Neo-Platonism in
Augustine were his cognate spiritual mood and his attitude
toward the world of physical fact.

Note the personal affinity between Augustine and Plotinus.
Both are absorbed in the higher pointings of their thought ;
neither is much occupied with its left-handed relationships,
which, however, are by no means to be disowned.   The
minds and souls of both are set upon God the Spirit ; the
minds and eyes of both are closed to the knowledge of
the natural world.   Thus neither Plotinus nor Augustine
was much affected by the popular beliefs of Christianity
or paganism.   The former cared little for demon-lore or
divination, and was not seriously touched by polytheism.
No more was the latter affected by the worship of saints and
relics, or by other elements of Christian credulity, which
when brought to his attention pass from his mind as quickly
as his duties of Christian bishop will permit.

But it was *half* otherwise with Porphyry, and altogether
otherwise with Iamblicus.   The first of these was drawn,
repelled, and tortured by the common superstitions, especially
the magic and theurgy which made men gape ; but Iamblicus
gladly sported in these mottled currents.   On the Christian
side, Jerome might be compared with them, or a later man,
the last of the Latin Fathers, Gregory the Great.   Clear as
was the temporal wisdom of this great pope, and heavy as
were his duties during the troubled times of his pontificate
(590-604), still his mind was busy with the miraculous and
diabolic.   His mind and temperament have absorbed at least
the fruitage of prior superstitions, whether Christian or pagan
need not be decided.   He certainly was not influenced by
Iamblicus.   Nor need one look upon these phases of his
nature as specifically the result of the absorption of pagan
elements.   He and his forbears had but gone the path of
credulity and mortal blindness, thronged by both pagans and
Christians.   And so in Gregory the tendencies making for
intellectual obliquity do their perfect work.   His religious
dualism is strident ; his resultant asceticism is extreme ; and

finally the symbolical, the allegorical, habit has shut his mind to the perception of the literal (shall we say, actual) meaning, when engaged with Scripture, as his great Commentary on Job bears witness. The same tendencies, but usually in milder type, had shown themselves with Augustine, who, in these respects, stands to Gregory as Plotinus to Iamblicus. Augustine can push allegory to absurdity ; he can be ascetic ; he is dualistic. But all these things have not barbarized his mind, as they have Gregory's.[1] Similarly the elements, which in Plotinus's personality were held in innocuous abeyance, dominated the entire personality of Iamblicus and made him a high priest of folly.

Thus we have observed the phases of thought which set the intellectual conditions of the later pagan times, and affected the mental processes of the Latin Fathers. The matter may be summarized briefly in conclusion. Platonism had created an intellectual and intelligible world, wherein a dissolving dialectic turned the cognition of material phenomena into a reflection of the mind's ideals. This was more palpable in Neo-Platonism than it had been in Plato's system. Stoicism on the other hand represented a rule of life, the sanction of which was inner peace. Its working principle was the rightly directed action of the self-controlling will. Fundamentally ethical, it set itself to frame a corresponding conception of the universe. Platonism and Neo-Platonism found in material facts illustrations or symbols of ideal truths and principles of human life. Stoicism was interested in them as affording a foundation for ethics. None of these systems was seriously interested in facts apart from their symbolical exemplification of truth, or their bearing on the conduct of life ; and the same principles that affected the observation of nature were applied to the interpretation of myth, tradition, and history.

In the opening centuries of the Christian Era the world was becoming less self-reliant. It was tending to look to authority for its peace of mind. In religion men not only sought, as formerly, for superhuman aid, but were reaching outward for what their own rational self-control no longer gave. They needed not merely to be helped by the gods,

[1] On Gregory, see *post*, Chapter V.

but to be sustained and saved. Consequently, prodigious interest was taken in the means of bringing man to the divine, and obtaining the saving support which the gods alone could give. The philosophic thought of the time became palpably mediatorial. Neo-Platonism was a system of mediation between man and the Absolute First Principle ; and soon its lower phases became occupied with such palpable means as divination and oracles, magic and theurgy.

The human reason has always proved unable to effect this mediation between man and God. The higher Neo-Platonism presented as the furthest goal a supra-rational and ecstatic vision. This was its union with the divine. The lower Neo-Platonism turned this lofty supra-rationality into a principle of credulity more and more agape for fascinating or helpful miracles. Thus a constant looking for divine or demonic action became characteristic of the pagan intelligence.

The Gospel of Christ, in spreading throughout the pagan world, was certain to gather to itself the incidents of its apprehension by pagans, and take various forms, one of which was to become the dominant or Catholic. Conversely, Christians (and we have in mind the educated people) would retain their methods of thinking in spite of change in the contents of their thought. This would be true even of the great and learned Christian leaders, the Fathers of the Church. At the same time the Faith reinspired and redirected their energies. Yet (be it repeated for the sake of emphasis) their mental processes, their ways of apprehending and appreciating facts, would continue those of that paganism which in them had changed to Christianity.

Every phase of intellectual tendency just summarized as characteristic of the pagan world, entered the modes in which the Fathers of the Latin Church apprehended and built out their new religion. First of all, the attitude toward knowledge. No pagan philosophy, not Platonism or any system that came after it, had afforded an incentive for concentration of desire equal to that presented in the person and the precepts of Jesus. The desire of the Kingdom of Heaven was a master-motive such as no previous idealism had offered.   It would bring into conformity with itself not only all the practical considerations of life, but verily the whole human desire to know.   First it mastered the mind of Tertullian ; and in spite of variance and deviation it endured through the Middle Ages as the controlling principle of intellectual effort.   Its decree was this : the knowledge which men need and should desire is that which will help them to save and perfect their souls for the Kingdom of God.   Some would interpret this broadly, others narrowly ; some would actually be constrained by it, and others merely do it a polite obeisance.   But it was acknowledged by well-nigh all men, according to their individual tempers and the varying times in which they lived.

Platonism was an idealistic cosmos ; Stoicism a cosmos of subjective ethics and teleological conceptions of the physical world.   The furthest outcome of both might be represented by Augustine's cosmos of the soul and God. As for reasoning processes, inwardly inspired and then applied to the world of nature and history, Christianity combined the idealizing, fact-compelling ways of Platonic dialectic with the Stoical interest in moral edification.   And, more utterly than either Platonist or Stoic, the Christian Father lacked interest in knowledge of the concrete fact for its own sake.   His mental glance was even more oblique than theirs, fixed as it was upon the moral or spiritual— the anagogic—inference.   Of course he carried symbolism and allegory further than Stoic and Platonist had done, one reason being that he was impelled by the specific motive of harmonizing the Old Testament with the Gospel, and thereby proving the divine mission of Jesus.

Idealism might tend toward dualistic ethics, and issue in asceticism, as was the tendency in Stoicism and the open result with Plotinus and his disciples.   Such, with mightier power and firmer motive, was the outcome of Christian ethics, in monasticism.   Christianity was not a dualistic philosophy ; but neither was Stoicism nor Neo-Platonism. Yet, like them, it was burningly dualistic in its warfare against the world, the flesh, and the devil.

We turn to other but connected matters : salvation, mediatorship, theory and practice.   The need of salvation

made men Christians ; the God-man was the one and
sufficient mediator between man and God. Such was the
high dogma, established with toil and pain. And the
practice graded downward to mediatorial persons, acts, and
things, marvellous, manifold, and utterly analogous to their
pagan kin. The mediatorial persons were the Virgin and
the saints ; the sacraments were the magic mediatorial acts ;
the relic was the magic mediatorial thing. And, as with
Neo-Platonism, there was in Christianity a principle of supra-
rational belief in all these matters. At the top the revelation of Christ, and the high love of God which He inspired.
This was not set on reason, but above it. And, as with
Neo-Platonism, the supra-rational principle of Christianity
was led down through conduits of credulity, resembling those
we have become familiar with in our descent from Plotinus
to Iamblicus.

CHAPTER IV

INTELLECTUAL INTERESTS OF THE LATIN FATHERS

So it was that the intellectual conditions of the Roman Empire affected the attitude of the Church Fathers toward knowledge, and determined their ways of apprehending fact. There was, indeed, scarcely a spiritual tendency or way of thinking, in the surrounding paganism, that did not enter their mental processes and make part of their understanding of Christianity. On the other hand, the militant and polemic position of the Church in the Empire furnished new interests, opened new fields of effort, and produced new modes of intellectual energy. And every element emanating from the pagan environment was, on entering the Christian pale, reinspired by Christian necessities and brought into a working concord with the master-motive of the Faith.

Salvation was the master Christian motive. The Gospel of Christ was a gospel of salvation unto eternal life. It presented itself in the self-sacrifice of divine love, not without warnings touching its rejection. It was understood and accepted according to the capacities of those to whom it was offered, capacities which it should reinspire and direct anew, and yet not change essentially. The young Christian communities had to adjust their tempers to the new Faith. They also fell under the unconscious need of defining it, in order to satisfy their own intelligence and present it in a valid form to the minds of men as yet unconverted. Consequently, the new Gospel of Salvation drew the energies of Christian communities to the work of defining that which they had accepted, and of establishing its religious and rational validity. The intellectual interests of these communities were first unified by the master-motive of salvation, and then ordered and redirected according to the doctrinal and polemic exigencies of this new Faith precipitated into the Graeco-Roman world.

The intellectual interests of the Christian Fathers are not to be classified under categories of desire to know, for the sake of knowledge, but under categories of desire to be saved, and to that end possess knowledge in its saving forms. Their desire was less to know, than to know how— how to be saved and contribute to the salvation of others. Their need rightly to understand the Faith, define it and maintain it, was of such drastic power as to force into ancillary rôles every line of inquiry and intellectual effort. This need inspired those central intellectual labours of the Fathers which directly made for the Faith's dogmatic substantiation and ecclesiastical supremacy ; and then it mastered all provinces of education and inquiry which might seem to possess independent intellectual interest. They were either to be drawn to its support or discredited as irrelevant distractions.

This compelling Christian need did not, in fact, impress into its service the total sum of intellectual interests among Christians. Mortal curiosity survived, and the love of *belles lettres*. Yet its dominance was real. The Church Fathers were absorbed in the building up of Christian doctrine and ecclesiastical authority. The productions of Christian authorship through the first four centuries were entirely religious, so far as the extant works bear witness. This is true of both the Greek and the Latin Fathers, and affords a prodigious proof that the inspiration and the exigencies of the new religion had drawn into one spiritual vortex the energies and interests of Christian communities.

Some of the Fathers have left statements of their principles, coupled with more or less intimate accounts of their own spiritual attitude. Among the Eastern Christians Origen has already been referred to. With him Christianity was the sum of knowledge ; and his life's endeavour was to realize this view by co-ordinating all worthy forms of knowledge within the scheme of salvation through Christ. His mind was imbued with a vast desire to know. This he did not derive from Christianity. But his understanding of

Christianity gave him the schematic principle guiding h
inquiries.   His aim was to direct his labours with Christianit
as an end—τελικῶς εἰς χριστιανισμόν, as he says so pregnantly.   He would use Greek philosophy as a propaedeutic
for Christianity; he would seek from geometry and astronomy
what might serve to explain Scripture ;   and so with all
branches of learning.[1]

This was the expression of a mind of prodigious energy.
For more personal disclosures we may turn at once to the
Latin Fathers.   Hilary, Bishop of Poictiers (d. 367), was a
foremost Latin polemicist against the Arians in the middle
of the fourth century.   He was born a pagan ; and in the
introductory book to his chief work, the *De Trinitate*, he
tells how he turned, with all his intellect and higher aspirations, to the Faith.   Taking a noble view of human nature,
he makes bold to say that men usually spurn the sensual
and material, and yearn for a more worthy life.   Thus they
have reached patience, temperance, and other virtues, believing that death is not the end of all.   He himself, however, did not rest satisfied with the pagan religion or the
teachings of pagan philosophers ;   but he found doctrines to
his liking in the books of Moses, and then in the Gospel of
John.   It was clear to him that prophecy led up to the
revelation of Jesus Christ, and in that at length he gained a
safe harbour.   Thus Hilary explains that his better aspirations had led him on and upward to the Gospel ;   and when
he had reached that end and unification of spiritual yearning,
it was but natural that it should thenceforth hold the sum
of his intellectual interests.

A like result appears with greater power in Augustine.
His *Confessions* give the mode in which his spiritual progress
presented itself to him some time after he had become
a Catholic Christian.[2]   His whole life sets forth the same
theme, presenting the religious passion of the man drawing
into itself his energies and interests.   God and the Soul—
these two would he know, and these alone.   But these
alone indeed !   As if they did not embrace all life pointed
and updrawn toward its salvation.   God was the over-

---

[1] *Epistola ad Gregorium Thaumaturgum.*
[2] Cf. Boissier *Fin du paganisme.*

mastering object of intellectual interest and of passionate love. All knowledge should direct itself toward knowing Him. By grace, within God's light and love, was the Soul, knower and lover, expectant of eternal life. Nothing that was transient could be its chief good, or its good at all except so far as leading on to its chief good of salvation, life eternal in and through the Trinity. One may read Augustine's self - disclosures or the passages containing statements of the ultimate religious principles whereby he and all men should live, or one may proceed to examine his long life and the vast entire product of his labour. The result will be the same. His whole strength will be found devoted to the cause of Catholic Church and Faith ; and all his intellectual interests will be seen converging to that end. He writes nothing save with Catholic religious purpose ; and nothing in any of his writings had interest for the writer save as it bore upon that central aim. He may be engaged in a great work of ultimate Christian doctrine, as in his *De Trinitate* ; he may be involved in controversy with Manichean, with Donatist or Pelagian ; he may be offering pastoral instruction, as in his many letters ; he may survey, as in the *Civitas Dei*, the whole range of human life and human knowledge ; but never does his mind really bear away from its master-motive.

The justification for this centring of human interests and energies lay in the nature of the *summum bonum* for man. According to the principles of the *City of God*, eternal life is the supreme good and eternal death the supreme evil. Evidently no temporal satisfaction or happiness compares with the eternal. This is good logic ; but it is enforced with arguments drawn from the Christian temper, which viewed earth as a vale of tears. The deep Catholic pessimism toward mortal life is Augustine's in full measure : " Quis enim sufficit quantovis eloquentiae flumine, vitae hujus miserias explicare ? " Virtue itself, the best of mortal goods, does nothing here on earth but wage perpetual war with vices. Though man's life is and must be social, how filled is it with distress ! The saints are blessed with hope. And mortal good which has not that hope is a false joy and a great misery. For it lacks the real blessedness of the soul, which is the true wisdom that directs itself to the end where God shall be all in all in eternal certitude and perfect peace.   Here our peace is with God through faith ; and yet is rather a *solatium miseriae* than a *gaudium beatitudinis*, as it will be hereafter.   But the end of those who do not belong to the City of God will be *miseria sempiterna*, which is also called the second death, since the soul alienated from God cannot be said to live, nor that body be said to live which is enduring eternal pains.[1]   Augustine devotes a whole book, the twenty-first, to an exposition of the sempiternal, non-purgatorial, punishment of the damned, whom the compassionate intercession of the saints will not save, nor many other considerations which have been deemed eventually saving by the fondly lenient opinions of men. His views were as dark as those of Gregory the Great. Only imaginative elaboration was needed to expand them to the full compass of mediaeval fear.

Augustine brought all intellectual interests into the closure of the Christian Faith, or discredited whatever stubbornly remained without.   He did the same with ethics. For he transformed the virtues into accord with his Catholic conception of man's chief good.   That must consist in cleaving to what is most blessed to cleave to, which is God. To Him we can cleave only through *dilectio, amor,* and *charitas*.   Virtue which leads us to the *vita beata* is nothing but *summus amor Dei*.   So he defines the four cardinal virtues anew.   Temperance is love keeping itself whole and incorrupt for God ; fortitude is love easily bearing all things for God's sake ; justice is love serving God only, and for that reason rightly ruling in the other matters, which are subject to man ; and prudence is love well discriminating between what helps and what impedes as to God (*in deum*).[2] Conversely, the heathen virtues, as the heathen had in fact conceived them, were vices rather than virtues to Augustine. For they lacked knowledge of the true God, and therefore were affected with fundamental ignorance, and were also tainted with pride.[3]   Through his unique power of religious

---

[1] *Civ. Dei,* xix. caps. 49, 20, 27, 28.
[2] *De moribus Ecclesiae,* 14, 15 ; cf. *Epist.* 155, §§ 12, **13.**
[3] *Civ. Dei,* xix. 25.

perception, Augustine discerned the inconsistency between pagan ethics, and the Christian thoughts of divine grace moving the humbly and lovingly acceptant soul.

The treatise on Christian Doctrine clearly expresses Augustine's views as to the value of knowledge. He starts, in his usual way, from a fundamental principle, which is here the distinction between the use of something for a purpose and the enjoyment of something in and for itself. " To enjoy is to cleave fast in the love of a thing for its own sake. But to use is to employ a thing in obtaining what one loves." For an illustration he draws upon that Christian sentiment which from the first had made the Christian feel as a sojourner on earth.[1]

" It is as if we were sojourners unable to live happily away from our own country, and we wished to use the means of journeying by land and sea to end our misery and return to our fatherland, which is to be enjoyed. But the charm of the journey or the very movement of the vehicle delighting us, we are taken by a froward sweetness and become careless of reaching our own country whose sweetness would make us happy. Now if, journeying through this world, away from God, we wish to return to our own land where we may be happy, this world must be used, not enjoyed ; that the invisible things of God may be apprehended through those created things before our eyes, and we may gain the eternal and spiritual from the corporeal and temporal."

From this illustration Augustine leaps at once to his final inference that only the Trinity—Father, Son, and Holy Spirit—is to be enjoyed.[2] It follows as a corollary that the important knowledge for man is that which will bring him to God surely and for eternity. Such is knowledge of Holy Writ and its teachings. Other knowledge is valuable as it aids us to this.

Proceeding from this point of view, Augustine speaks more specifically. To understand Scripture one needs to know the words and also the things referred to. Knowledge of the latter is useful, because it sheds light on their figurative significance. For example, to know the serpent's habit of presenting its whole body to the assailant, in order

---

[1] See Clement of Rome, *Ep. to the Corinthians* (A.D. cir. 92), opening passage, and notes in Lightfoot's edition.
[2] *De doc. Chris.* i. 4, 5.

to protect its head, helps to understand our Lord's command
to be wise as serpents, and for the sake of our Head, which
is Christ, present our whole bodies to the persecutors. Again
the statement that the serpent rids itself of its skin by
squeezing through a narrow hole, accords with the Scriptural
injunction to imitate the serpent's wisdom, and put off the
old man that we may put on the new, and in a narrow place :
—Enter ye in at the strait gate, says the Lord.[1] The
writer gives a rule for deciding whether in any instance a
literal or figurative interpretation of Scripture should be
employed, a rule representing a phase of the idealizing way
of treating facts which began with Plato or before him, and
through many channels entered the practice of Christian
doctors. " Whatever in the divine word cannot properly
be referred to *morum honestas* or *fidei veritas* is to be
taken figuratively. The first pertains to love of God and
one's neighbour ; the second to knowing God and one's
neighbour." [2]

Augustine then refers to matters of human invention,
like the letters of the alphabet, which are useful to know.
History also is well, as it helps us to understand Scripture ;
and a knowledge of physical objects will help us to understand the Scriptural references. Likewise a moderate knowledge of rhetoric and dialectic enables one the better to understand and expound Scripture. Some men have made useful
vocabularies of the Scriptural Hebrew and Syriac words
and compends of history, which throw light on Scriptural
questions. So, to save Christians from needless labour, I
think it would be well if some one would make a general
description of unknown places, animals, plants and minerals,
and other things mentioned in Scripture ; and the same
might be done as to the *numbers* which Scripture uses.
These suggestions were curiously prophetic. Christians were
soon to produce just such compends, as will be seen when
noticing the labours of Isidore of Seville.[3] Augustine speaks
sometimes in scorn and sometimes in sorrow of those who
remain ignorant of God, and learn philosophies, or deem
that they achieve something great by curiously examining

---

[1] *De doc. Chris.* ii. 16.   [2] *De doc. Chris.* iii. cap. 10 *sqq.*
[3] *Post*, Chapter V.

into that universal mass of matter which we call the world.[1]

Augustine's word and his example sufficiently attest the fact that the Christian Faith constituted the primary intellectual interest with the Fathers. While not annihilating other activities of the mind, this dominant interest lowered their dignity by forcing them into a common subservience. Exerting its manifold energies in defining and building out the Faith, in protecting it from open attack or insidious corruption, it drew to its exigencies the whole strength of its votaries. There resulted the perfected organization of the Catholic Church and the production of a vast doctrinal literature. The latter may be characterized as constructive of dogma, theoretically interpretative of Scripture, and polemically directed against pagans, Jews, heretics or schismatics, as the case might be.

It was constructive of dogma through the intellectual necessity of apprehending the Faith in concepts and modes of reasoning accepted as valid by the Graeco-Roman world. In the dogmatic treatises emanating from the Hellenic East, the concepts and modes of reasoning were those of the later phases of Greek philosophy. Prominent examples are the *De principiis* of Origen or the *Orationes* of Athanasius against the Arians. For the Latin West, Tertullian's *Adversus Marcionem* or the treatises of Hilary and Augustine upon the Trinity serve for examples. The Western writings are distinguished from their Eastern kin by the entry of the juristic element, filling them with a mass of conceptions from the Roman Law.[2] They also develop a more searching psychology. In both of these respects, Tertullian and Augustine were the great creators.

Secondly, this literature, at least in theory, was interpretative or expository of Scripture. Undoubtedly Origen and Athanasius and Augustine approached the Faith with ideas formed from philosophical study and their own reflections ; and their metaphysical and allegorical treatment of Scripture texts elicited a significance different from the

---

[1] *De moribus Ecclesiae*, 21 ; *Confessions*, v. 7 ; x. 54-57.
[2] See Harnack, *Dogmengeschichte*, iii. 14 *sqq.* ; Taylor, *Classical Heritage*, p. 117 *sqq.*

meaning which we now should draw. Yet Christianity was an authoritatively revealed religion, and the letter of that revelation was Holy Scripture, to wit, the gradually formed canon of the Old and New Testaments. If the reasoning or conclusions which resulted in the Nicene Creed were not just what Scripture would seem to suggest, at all events they had to be and were confirmed by Scripture, interpreted, to be sure, under the stress of controversy and the influence of all that had gone into the intellectual natures of the Greek and Latin Fathers. And the patristic faculty of doctrinal exposition, that is, of reasoning constructively along the lines of Scriptural interpretation, was marvellous. Such a writing as Augustine's Anti-Pelagian *De spiritu et littera* is a striking example.

Moreover, the Faith, which is to say, the Scriptures rightly interpreted, contained the sum of knowledge needful for salvation, and indeed everything that men should seek to know. Therefore there was no question possessing valid claim upon human curiosity which the Scriptures, through their interpreters, might not be called upon to answer. For example, Augustine feels obliged to solve through Scriptural interpretation and inference such an apparently obscure question as that of the different degrees of knowledge of God possessed by demons and angels.[1] Indeed, many an un-answerable question had beset the ways by which Augustine himself and other doctors had reached their spiritual harbour-age in Catholic Christianity. They sought to confirm from Scripture *their* solutions of their own doubts. At all events, from Scripture they were obliged to answer other questioners seeking instruction or needing refutation.[2]

Thirdly, it is too well known to require more than a mere reminder, that dogmatic treatises commonly were con-troversial or polemic, directed against pagans or Jews, or Gnostics or Manicheans, or against Arians or Montanists

---

[1] *Civ. Dei*, ix. 21, 22 ; cf. *Civ. Dei*, xvi. 6-9.

[2] *Civ. Dei*, book xii., affords a discussion of such questions, *e.g.* why was man created when he was, and not before or afterwards. All these matters entered into the discussions of the mediaeval philosophers, Thomas Aquinas, for example.

Besides these dogmatic treatises, in which Scriptural texts were called upon at least for confirmation, the Fathers, Greek and Latin, composed an enormous mass of Biblical commentary, chiefly allegorical, following the chapter and verse of the canonical writings.

or Donatists.   Practically all Christian doctrine was of militant growth, advancing by argumentative denial and then by counter-formulation.

As already noticed at some length, the later phases of pagan philosophic inquiry had other motives besides the wish for knowledge.   These motives were connected with man's social welfare or his relations with supernatural powers.   The Stoical and Epicurean interest in knowledge had a practical incentive.   And Neo-Platonism was a philosophy of saving union with the divine, rather than an open-minded search for ultimate knowledge.   But no Hellenic or quasi-Romanized philosophy so drastically drew all subjects of speculation and inquiry within the purview and dominance of a single motive at once intellectual and emotional as the Christian Faith.

Naturally the surviving intellectual ardour of the Graeco-Roman world passed into the literature of Christian doctrine. For example, the Faith, with its master-motive of salvation, drew within its work of militant formulation and pertinent discussion that round of intellectual interest and energy which had issued in Neo-Platonism.   Likewise such ethical earnestness as had come down through Stoicism was drawn within the master Christian energy.   And so far as any interest survived in zoology, or physics or astronomy, it also was absorbed in curious Christian endeavours to educe an edifying conformity between the statements or references of Scripture and the round of phenomena of the natural world. Then history likewise passed from heathenism to the service of the Church, and became polemic narrative, or filled itself with edifying tales, mostly of miracles.

In fine, no branch of human inquiry or intellectual interest was left unsubjugated by the dominant motives of the Faith.   First of all, philosophy itself—the general inquiry for final knowledge—no longer had an independent existence.   It had none with Hilary, none with Ambrose, and none whatsoever with Augustine after he became a Catholic Christian.   Patristic philosophy consisted in the formulation of Christian doctrine, which in theory was an eliciting of the truth of Scripture.   It embodied the substantial results, or survivals if one will, of Greek philosophy, so far as it did not controvert and discard them.   As for the reasoning process, the dialectic whereby such results were reached, as distinguished from the results themselves, that also passed into doctrinal writings.   The great Christian Fathers were masters of it.   Augustine recognized it as a proper tool ; but like other tools its value was not in itself but in its usefulness. As a tool, dialectic, or logic as it has commonly been called, was to preserve a distinct, if not independent, existence. Aristotle had devoted to it a group of special treatises.[1] No one had anything to add to this Organon, or Aristotelian tool, which was to be preserved in Latin by the Boëthian translations.[2]   No attempt was made to supplant them with Christian treatises.

So it was with elementary education.   The grammarians, Servius, Priscianus, and probably Donatus, were pagans. As far as concerned grammatical and rhetorical studies, the Fathers had to admit that the best theory and examples were in pagan writings.   It also happened that the book which was to become the common text-book of the Seven Arts was by a pagan, of Neo-Platonic views.   This was the *De nuptiis Philologiae et Mercurii*, by Martianus Capella.[3] Possibly some good Christian of the time could have composed a worse book, or at least one somewhat more deflected from the natural objects of primary education. But the *De nuptiis* is astonishingly poor and dry.   The writer was an unintelligent compiler, who took his matter not from the original sources, but from compilers before him, Varro above all.   Capella talks of Eratosthenes, Hipparchus, Euclid, Ptolemy ; but if he had ever read them, it was to little profit.   Book VI., for example, is occupied with " Geometria."   The first part of it is simply geography ; then come nine pages [4] of geometry, consisting of definitions, with a few axioms ; and then, instead of following with theorems, the maid, who personifies " Geometria,"

---

[1] See *ante,* p. 37.   [2] See *post,* p. 92.

[3] The substance of Capella's book is framed in an allegorical narrative of the Marriage of Philology and Mercury.   For a nuptial gift, the groom presents the bride with seven maid-servants, symbolizing the Seven Liberal Arts—Grammar, Rhetoric, Dialectic, Arithmetic, Geometry, Astronomy, Music.   Cf. Taylor, *Classical Heritage, etc.,* p. 49 *sqq.*

[4] In Eyssenhardt's edition.

presents as a bridal offering the books of Euclid, amid great applause. Had she ever opened them, one queries. Book VII., "Arithmetica," is even worse. It begins with the current foolishness regarding the virtues and interesting qualities of the first ten numbers : "How shall I commemorate thee, O Seven, always to be revered, neither begotten like the other numbers, nor procreative, a virgin even as Minerva ? " Capella never is original. From Pythagoras on, the curiosities of numbers had interested the pagan mind.[1] These fantasies gained new power and application in the writings of the Fathers. For them, the numbers used in Scripture had prefigurative significance. Such notions came to Christianity from its environment, and then took on a new apologetic purpose. Here an intellect like Augustine's is no whit above its fellows. In arguing from Scripture numbers he is at his very obvious worst.[2] Fortunately the coming time was to have better treatises, like the *De arithmetica* of Boëthius, which was quite free from mysticism. But in Boëthius's time, as well as before and after him, it was the allegorical significance of numbers apologetically pointed that aroused deepest interest.

Astronomy makes one of Capella's seven *Artes*. His eighth book, a rather abject compilation, is devoted to it. His matter, of course, is not yet Christianized. But Christianity was to draw Astronomy into its service ; and the determination of the date of Easter and other Church festivals became the chief end of what survived of astronomical knowledge.

The patristic attitude toward cosmogony and natural science plainly appears in the *Hexaëmeron* of St. Ambrose.[3] This was a commentary on the first chapters of Genesis, or rather an argumentative exposition of the Scriptural account of the Creation, primarily directed against those who asserted that the world was uncreated and eternal. As one turns the leaves of this writing, it becomes clear that the interest of Ambrose is always religious, and that his soul is gazing

---

[1] On the symbolism of Numbers see Cantor, *Vorlesungen über Ges. der Mathematik*, 2nd ed. pp. 95, 96, 146, 156, 529, 531.

[2] See an extraordinary example taken from the treatise against Faustus, *post*, Chapter XXVIII. Also *De doc. Chris.* ii. 16 ; *De Trinitate*, iv. 4-6.

[3] Migne, *Pat. Lat.* 14, col. 123-273. Written cir. 389.

beyond the works of the Creation to another world. Physical phenomena have no laws for him except the will of God.

" To discuss the nature and position of the earth," says he, " does not help us in our hope of the life to come. It is enough to know what Scripture states, ' that He hung up the earth upon nothing ' (Job xxvi. 7). Why then argue whether He hung it up in air or upon the water, and raise a controversy as to how the thin air could sustain the earth ; or why, if upon the waters, the earth does not go crashing down to the bottom ? . . . Not because the earth is in the middle, as if suspended on even balance, but because the majesty of God constrains it by the law of His will, does it endure stable upon the unstable and the void."

The archbishop then explains that God did not fix the earth's stability as an artisan would, with compass and level, but as the Omnipotent, by the might of His command. If we would understand why the earth is unmoved, we must not try to measure creation as with a compass, but must look to the will of God : " voluntate Dei immobilis manet et stat in saeculum terra." And again Ambrose asks, Why argue as to the elements which make the heaven ? Why trouble oneself with these physical inquiries ? " Sufficeth for our salvation, not such disputation, but the verity of the precepts, not the acuteness of argument, but the mind's faith, so that rather than the creature, we may serve the Creator, who is God blessed forever." [1]

Thus with Ambrose, the whole creation springs from the immediate working of God's inscrutable will. It is all essentially a miracle, like those which He wrought in after times to aid or save men : they also were but operations of His will. God said *Fiat lux*, and there was light. Thus His will creates ; and nature is His work (*opus Dei natura est*). And God said, Let there be a firmament in the midst of the waters, and let it divide the waters from the waters ; and it was so. " Hear the word, *Fiat*. His will is the measure of things ; His word ends the work." The division of the waters above and beneath the firmament was a work of His will, just as He divided the waters of the Red Sea before the eyes of the Jews in order that those things might be believed which the Jews had not seen. He could have

[1] *Hex.* i. cap. 6.

saved them by another means.   The fiat of God is nature's
strength (*virtus*) and the substance of its endurance
(*diurnitatis substantia*) so long as He wishes it to continue
where He has appointed it.[1]

According to this reasoning, the miracle, except for its
infrequency, is in the same category with other occurrences.
Here Ambrose is fully supported by Augustine.   With the
latter, God is the source of all causation :   He is the cause of
usual as well as of extraordinary occurrences, *i.e.* miracles.
The exceptional or extraordinary character of certain
occurrences is what makes them miracles.[2]

Here are fundamental principles of patristic faith.   The
will of God is the one cause of all things.   It is unsearch-
able.   But we have been taught much regarding God's love
and compassionateness, and of His desire to edify and save
His people.   These qualities prompt His actions toward
them.   Therefore we may expect His acts to evince edifying
and saving purpose.   All the narratives of Scripture are for
our edification.   How many mighty saving acts do they
record, from the Creation, onward through the story of Israel,
to the birth and resurrection of Christ !   And surely God
still cares for His people.   Nor is there any reason to
suppose that He has ceased to edify and save them through
signs and wonders.   Shall we not still look for miracles
from His grace ?

Thus in the nature of Christianity, as a miraculously
founded and revealed religion, lay the ground for expecting
miracles, or, at least, for not deeming them unlikely to occur.
And from all sides the influences which had been obscuring
natural knowledge conspired to the same result.   We have
followed those influences in pagan circles from Plato on
through Neo-Platonism and other systems current in the first
centuries of the Christian era.   We have seen them obliterate
rational conceptions of nature's processes and destroy the
interest that impels to unbiassed investigation.   The character and exigencies of the Faith intensified the operation
of like tendencies among Christians.   Their eyes were lifted
from the earth.   They were not concerned with its transitory
things, soon to be consumed.   Their hope was fixed in the

_____
[1] *Hex.* ii. caps. 2, 3.   [2] Aug. *De Trinitate*, iii. 5-9.

assurance of their Faith ; their minds were set upon its
confirmation. They and their Faith seemed to have no use
for a knowledge of earth's phenomena save as bearing
illustrative or confirmatory testimony to the truth of
Scripture. Moreover, the militant exigencies of their
situation made them set excessive store on the miraculous
foundation and continuing confirmation of their religion.

For these reasons the eyes of the Fathers were closed to
the natural world, or at least their vision was affected with
an obliquity parallel to the needs of doctrine. Any veritable
physical or natural knowledge rapidly dwindled among them.
What remained continued to exist because explanatory of
Scripture and illustrative of spiritual allegories. To such
an intellectual temper nothing seems impossible, provided it
accord, or can be interpreted to accord, with doctrines elicited
from Scripture. Soon there will cease to exist any natural
knowledge sufficient to distinguish the normal and possible
from the impossible and miraculous. One may recall how
little knowledge of the physiology and habits of animals
was shown in Pliny's *Natural History*.[1] He had scarcely
an idea of what was physiologically possible. Personally,
he may or may not have believed that the bowels of the
field-mouse increase in number with the waxing of the
moon ; but he had no sufficiently clear appreciation of the
causes and relations of natural phenomena to know that
such an idea was absurd. It was almost an accident, whether
he believed it or not. It is safe to say that neither Ambrose
nor Jerome nor Augustine had any clearer understanding of
such things than Pliny. They had read far less about them,
and knew less than he. Pliny, at all events, had no motive
for understanding or presenting natural facts in any other
way than as he had read or been told about them, or perhaps
had noticed for himself. Augustine and Ambrose had a
motive. Their sole interest in natural fact lay in its confirmatory evidence of Scriptural truth. They were constantly impelled to understand facts in conformity with their
understanding of Scripture, and to accept or deny accordingly. Thus Augustine denies the existence of Antipodes,
men on the opposite side of the earth, who walk with their

---

[1] *Ante*, p. 39 *sqq.*

feet opposite to our own.[1]   That did not harmonize with his general conception of Scriptural cosmogony.

For the result, one can point to a concrete instance which is typical of much.   In patristic circles the knowledge of the animal kingdom came to be represented by the curious book called the *Physiologus*.   It was a series of descriptions of animals, probably based on stories current in Alexandria, and appears to have been put together in Greek early in the second century.   Internal evidence has led to the supposition that it emanated from Gnostic circles.   It soon came into common use among the Greek and Latin Fathers.   Origen draws from it by name.   In the West, to refer only to the fourth and fifth centuries, Ambrose seems to use it constantly, Jerome occasionally, and also Augustine.

Well known as these stories are, one or two examples may be given to recall their character : The Lion has three characteristics ; as he walks or runs he brushes his footprints with his tail, so that the hunters may not track him.   This signifies the secrecy of the Incarnation—of the Lion of the tribe of Judah.   Secondly, the Lion sleeps with his eyes open ; so slept the body of Christ upon the Cross, while His Godhead watched at the right hand of the Father.   Thirdly, the lioness brings forth her cub dead ; on the third day the father comes and roars in its face, and wakes it to life. This signifies our Lord's resurrection on the third day.

The Pelican is distinguished by its love for its young. As these begin to grow they strike at their parents' faces, and the parents strike back and kill them.   Then the parents take pity, and on the third day the mother comes and opens her side and lets the blood flow on the dead young ones, and they become alive again.   Thus God cast off mankind after the Fall, and delivered them over to death ; but He took pity on us, as a mother, for by the Crucifixion He awoke us with His blood to eternal life.

The *Unicorn* cannot be taken by hunters, because of his great strength, but lets himself be captured by a pure virgin.   So Christ, mightier than the heavenly powers, took on humanity in a virgin's womb.

The Phoenix lives in India, and when five hundred years

[1] *Civ. Dei*, xvi. 9.

old fills his wings with fragrant herbs and flies to Heliopolis, where he commits himself to the flames in the Temple of the Sun. From his ashes comes a worm, which the second day becomes a fledgling, and on the third a full-grown phoenix, who flies away to his old dwelling-place. The Phoenix is the symbol of Christ ; the two wings filled with sweet-smelling herbs are the Old and New Testaments, full of divine teaching.[1]

These examples illustrate the two general characteristics of the accounts in the *Physiologus* : they have the same legendary quality whether the animal is real or fabulous ; the subjects are chosen, and the accounts are shaped, by doctrinal considerations. Indeed, from the first the *Physiologus* seems to have been a selection of those animal stories which lent themselves most readily to theological application. It would be pointless to distinguish between the actual and fabulous in such a book ; nor did the minds of the readers make any such distinction. For Ambrose or Augustine the importance of the story lay in its doctrinal significance, or moral, which was quite careless of the truth of facts of which it was the " point." The facts were told as introductory argument.

The interest of the Fathers in physics and natural history bears analogy to their interest in history and biography. Looking back to classical times, one finds that historians were led by other motives than the mere endeavour to ascertain and state the facts. The Homeric Epos was the literary forerunner of the history which Herodotus wrote of the Persian Wars ; and the latter often was less interested in the closeness of his facts than in their aptness and rhetorical probability. Doubtless he followed legends when telling how Greek and Persian spoke or acted. But had not legend already sifted the chaff of irrelevancy from the story, leaving the grain of convincing fitness, which is also rhetorical probability ? Likewise Thucydides, in composing the

---

[1] For the sources of these accounts see Lauchert, *Ges. des Physiologus* (Strassburg, 1889), p. 4 *sqq.* ; also Goldstaub in *Philologus*, Supplement, Bd. viii. (1901) pp. 339-404. The wide use of this work is well known. It was soon translated into Ethiopian, Armenian, and Syrian ; into Latin not later than the beginning of the fifth century ; and subsequently, of course with many accretions, into the various languages of western mediaeval Europe. See Lauchert, *o.c.* p. 79 *sqq.*

History of the Peloponnesian War, that masterpiece of
reasoned statement, was not over-anxious as to accuracy of
actual word and fact reported.   He carefully inquired regarding the events, in some of which he had been an actor.   Often
he knew or ascertained what the chief speakers said in those
dramatic situations which kept arising in this war of neighbours.   Yet, instead of reporting actual words, he gives the
sentiments which, according to the laws of rhetorical probability, they must have uttered.   So he presents the
psychology and turning-point of the matter.

   This was true historical rhetoric ; the historian's art of
setting forth a situation veritably by presenting its intrinsic
necessities.   Xenophon's *Cyropaedia* went a step farther ; it
was a historical romance, which neither followed fact nor
proceeded according to the necessities of the actual situation.
But it did proceed according to moral proprieties, and so was
edifying and plausible.

   The classical Latin practice accorded with the Greek.
Cicero speaks of history as *opus oratorium*, that is, a work
having rhetorical and literary qualities.   It should set forth
the events and situations according to their inherent
necessities which constitute their rhetorical truth.   Then it
should possess the civic and social qualities of good oratory :
morals and public utility.   These are, in fact, the characteristics of the work of Sallust, Livy, and Tacitus.   None of
them troubled himself much over an accuracy of detail
irrelevant to his larger purpose.   Tacitus is interested in
memorable facts ; he would relate them in such form that
they might carry their lesson, and bear their part in the
education of the citizen, for whom it is salutary to study the
past.   He condemns, indeed, the historians of the Empire
who, under an evil emperor, lie from fear, and, upon his
death, lie from hate.   But such condemnation of immoral
lying does not forbid the shaping of a story according to
artistic probability and moral ends.   Some shaping and
adorning of fact might be allowed the historian, acting with
motives of public policy, or seeking to glorify or defend his
country.[1]   This quite accords with the view of Varro and
Cicero, that good policy should sometimes outweigh truth :

[1] Cf. Boissier, *Tacite* (Paris, 1903).

whether or not the accounts of the gods were true, it was well for the people to believe.

Thus the Fathers of the Church were accustomed to a historical tradition and practice in which facts were presented so as to conduce to worthy ends. Various motives lie back of human interest in truth. A knowledge of the world's origin, of man's creation, destiny, and relationship to God, may be sought for its own sake as the highest human good ; and yet it may be also sought for the sake of some ulterior and, to the seeker, more important end. With the Christian Fathers that more important end was salvation. To obtain a saving knowledge was the object of their most strenuous inquiries. Doubtless all men take some pleasure simply in knowing ; and, on the other hand, there are few among wisdom's most disinterested lovers that have not some thought of the connection between knowledge and the other goods of human life, to which it may conduce. Yet if seekers after knowledge be roughly divided into two classes, those who wish to know for the sake of knowing, and those who look to another end to which true knowledge is a means, then the Fathers of the Church fall in the latter class.

If truth be sought for the sake of something else, why may it not also be sacrificed ? A work of art is achieved by shaping the story for the drama's sake, and if we weave fiction to suit the end, why not weave fiction with fact, or, still better, *see* the fact in such guise as to suit the requirements of our purpose ? Many are the aspects and relationships of any fact ; its *actuality* is exhaustless.[1] In how many ways does a human life present itself ? What

[1] For example, what different truths can one speak afterwards of a social dinner of men and women at which he has sat. In the first place, there is the hostess, to whom he may say something pleasant and yet true. Then there is his congenial friend among the ladies present, to whom he will impart some intimate observations, also true. Thirdly, a club friend was at the dinner, and his ear shall be the receptacle of remarks on feminine traits illustrated by what was said and done there. Finally, there is himself, to whom in the watches of the night the dinner will present itself in its permanent values as an incident in human intercourse, which is so fascinating, so transitory, and so suggestive of topics of reflection. Here are four presentations ; and if there was a company of twelve, we might multiply four by that number and imagine forty-eight true, although inexhaustive, accounts of that dinner which has now joined the fading circle of events that are no more.

narrative could exhaust the actuality and significance of the assassination of Julius Caesar ?   Indeed, no fact has such narrow or compelling singleness of significance or actuality that all its truth can be put in any statement !   And again, who is it that can draw the line between reality and conviction ?

It is clear that the limited and special interest taken by the Church Fathers in physical and historic facts would affect their apprehension of them.   One may ask what was real to Plato in the world of physical phenomena ?   At all events, Christian Platonists, like Origen or Gregory of Nyssa,[1] saw the paramount reality of such phenomena in the spiritual ideas implicated and evinced by them.   The world's reality would thus be resolved into the world's moral or spiritual significance, and in that case its truth might be educed through moral and allegorical interpretation.   Of course, such an understanding of reality involves hosts of assumptions which were valid in the fourth century, but are not commonly accepted now ; and chief among them is this very assumption that the deepest meaning of ancient poets, and the Scriptures above all, is allegorical.

This is but a central illustration of what would determine the Fathers' conception of the truth of physical events. Again : the Creation was a great miracle ; its cause, the will of God.   The Cause of the Creation was spiritual, and spiritual was its purpose, to wit, the edification and salvation of God's people ; the building, preservation, and final consummation of the City of God.   Did not the deepest truth of the matter lie in this spiritual cause and purpose ?   And afterwards to what other end tended all human history ?   It was one long exemplification of the purpose of God through the ways of providence.   The conception of what constituted a fitting exemplification of that purpose would control the choice of facts and shape their presentation.   Then what was more natural than that events should exhibit this purpose, that it might be perceived by the people of God ?   It would clearly appear in saving interpositions or remarkable chronological coincidences. Such, even more palpably than the other links in the

[1] On Gregory of Nyssa, see Taylor, *Classical Heritage*, p. 125 *sqq.*

providential chain, were direct manifestations of the will of
God, and were miraculous because of their extraordinary
character.　History, made anew through these convictions,
became a demonstration of the truth of Christian doctrine—
in other words, *apologetic*.

The most universal and comprehensive example of this
was Augustine's *City of God*, already adverted to.　Its
subject was the ways of God with men.　It embraced
history, philosophy, and religion.　It was the final Christian
apology, and the conclusive proof of Christian doctrine
adversum paganos.　To this end Augustine unites the
manifold topics which he discusses ; and to this end his
apparent digressions eventually return, bearing their sheaves
of corroborative evidence.　In no province of inquiry does
his apologetic purpose appear with clearer power than in
his treatment of history, profane and sacred.[1]　Through
the centuries the currents of divine purpose are seen to draw
into their dual course the otherwise pointless eddyings of
human affairs.　Beneath the Providence of God, a revolving
succession of kingdoms fill out the destinies of the earthly
Commonwealth of war and rapine, until the red torrents
are pressed together into the terrestrial greatness of imperial
Rome.　No power of heathen gods effected this result, nor
all the falsities of pagan philosophy : but the will of the
one true Christian God.　The fortunes of the heavenly City
are traced through the prefigurative stories of antediluvian
and patriarchal times, and then on through the prophetic
history of the chosen people, until the end of prophecy
appears—Christ and the Catholic Church.

The *Civitas Dei* is the crowning example of the drastic
power with which the Church Fathers conformed the data
of human understanding into a substantiation of Catholic
Christianity.[2]　At the time of its composition, the Faith

---

[1] Chiefly in Books III. and XV.-XVIII.

[2] Like the *Civitas Dei*, the patristic writings devoted exclusively to history
were all frankly apologetic, yet following different manners according to the
temper and circumstances of the writer.　In the East, at the epoch of the formal
Christian triumph and the climax of the Arian dispute, lived Eusebius of Caesarea,
the most famous of the early Church historians.　He was learned, careful, capable
of weighing testimony, and possessed the faculty of presenting salient points.　He
does not dwell overmuch on miracles.　His apologetic tendencies appear in his
method of seeing and stating facts so as to uphold the truth of Christianity.　If

needed advocacy in the world. Alaric entered Rome in
410 ; and it was to meet the cry of those who would lay
that catastrophe at the Church's doors that Augustine began
the *Civitas Dei.* Soon after, an ardent young Spaniard
named Orosius came on pilgrimage to the great doctor at
Hippo, and finding favour in his eyes, was asked to write a
profane history proving the abundance of calamities which
had afflicted mankind before the time of Christ. So
Orosius devoted some years (417-418) to the compilation
of a universal chronicle, using Latin sources, and calling his
work *Seven Books of Histories " adversum paganos."* [1] Addressing Augustine in his prologue, he says :

> " Thou hast commanded me that as against the vain rhetoric
> of those who, aliens to God's Commonwealth, coming from country
> cross-roads and villages are called pagans, because they know
> earthly things, who seek not unto the future and ignore the past,
> yet cry down the present time as filled with evil, just because
> Christ is believed and God is worshipped ;—thou hast commanded
> that I should gather from histories and annals whatever mighty
> ills and miseries and terrors there have been from wars and
> pestilence, from famine, earthquake, and floods, from volcanic
> eruptions, from lightning or from hail, and also from monstrous
> crimes in the past centuries ; and that I should arrange and set
> forth the matter briefly in a book."

Orosius's story of the four great Empires—Babylonian,
Macedonian, African, and Roman—makes a red tale of
carnage. He deemed " that such things should be com-
memorated, in order that with the secret of God's ineffable
judgments partly laid open, those stupid murmurers at our
Christian times should understand that the one God
ordained the fortunes of Babylon in the beginning, and at
the end those of Rome ; understand also that it is through
His clemency that we live, although wretchedly because of

---

just then Christianity seemed no longer to demand an advocate, there was place
for a eulogist, and such was Eusebius in his *Church History* and fulsome *Life of
Constantine.* His *Church History* is translated by A. C. McGiffert, *Library of
Nicene Fathers,* second series, vol. i. (New York, 1890). It was translated into
Latin by Rufinus, friend and then enemy of St. Jerome.

[1] The best edition is Zangemeister's in the Vienna *Corpus scriptorum eccles.*
(1882). Orosius ignores the classic Greek historians, of whom he knew little or
nothing. Cf. Taylor, *Classical Heritage,* pp. 219-221.

our intemperance. Like was the origin of Babylon and Rome, and like their power, greatness, and their fortunes good and ill ; but unlike their destinies, since Babylon lost her kingdom and Rome keeps hers "; and Orosius refers to the clemency of the barbarian victors who as Christians spared Christians.[1]

At the opening of his seventh book he again presents his purpose and conclusions :

" I think enough evidence has been brought together, to prove that the one and true God, made known by the Christian Faith, created the world and His creature as He wished, and that He has ordered and directed it through many things, of which it has not seen the purpose, and has ordained it for one event, declared through One ; and likewise has made manifest His power and patience by arguments manifold. Whereat, I perceive, straitened and anxious minds have stumbled, to think of so much patience joined to so great power. For, if He was able to create the world, and establish its peace, and impart to it a knowledge of His worship and Himself, what was the need of so great and (as they say) so hurtful patience, exerted to the end that at last, through the errors, slaughters and the toils of men, there should result what might rather have arisen in the beginning by His virtue, which you preach ? To whom I can truly reply : the human race from the beginning was so created and appointed that living under religion with peace without labour, by the fruit of obedience it might merit eternity ; but it abused the Creator's goodness, turned liberty into wilful licence, and through disdain fell into forgetfulness ; now the patience of God is just and doubly just, operating that this disdain might not wholly ruin those whom He wished to spare, who might be reduced through labours ; and also so that He might always hold out guidance although to an ignorant creature, to whom if penitent He would mercifully restore the means of grace."

Such was the point of view and such the motives of this book, which was to be *par excellence* the source of ancient history for the Middle Ages. But, concerned chiefly with the Gentile nations, Orosius has few palpable miracles to tell. The miracle lies in God's *ineffabilis ordinatio* of events, and especially in marvellous chronological parallels shown in the histories of nations, for our edification. Likewise for mediaeval men these ineffable chronological correspondences

[1] *Hist.* ii. 3.

(which never existed in fact) were to be evidence of God's providential guidance of the world.

Some thirty years after Orosius wrote, a priest of Marseilles, Salvian by name, composed a different sort of treatise, with a like object of demonstrating the righteous validity of God's providential ordering of affairs, especially in those troubled times of barbarian invasion through which the Empire then was passing. The book declared its purpose in its title—*De gubernatione Dei*.[1] Its tenor is further elucidated by the title bestowed upon it by a contemporary : *De praesenti (Dei) judicio*. It is famous for the pictures (doubtless overwrought) which it gives of the low state of morals among the Roman provincials, and of the comparative decency of the barbarians.

These examples sufficiently indicate the broad apologetic purpose in the patristic writing of history. There was another class of composition, biographical rather than historical, the object of which was to give edifying examples of the grace of God working in holy men. The reference, of course, is to the *Vitae sanctorum* whose number from the fourth century onward becomes legion. They set forth the marvellous virtues of anchorites and their miracles. In the East, the prime example is the Athanasian Life of Anthony ; Jerome also wrote, in Latin, the lives of Anthony's fore-runner Paulus and of other saints. But for the Latin West the typical example was the Life of St. Martin of Tours, most popular of saints, by Sulpicius Severus.

To dub this class of compositions (and there are classes within classes here) uncritical, credulous, intentionally untruthful, is not warranted without a preliminary consideration of their purpose. That in general was to edify ; the writer is telling a moral tale, illustrative of God's grace in the instances of holy men. But the divine grace is the real matter ; the saint's life is but the example. God's grace exists ; it operates in this way. As to the illustrative details of its operation, why be over-anxious as to their correctness ? Only the *vita* must be interesting, to fix the reader's attention, and must be edifying, to improve him. These principles exerted sometimes a less, sometimes a

---

[1] Best edition that of Pauly, in Vienna *Corpus scrip. eccles.* (1883).

greater influence ; and accordingly, while perhaps none of
the *vitae* is without pious colouring, as a class they range
from fairly trustworthy biographies to vehicles of edifying
myth.[1]

Miracles are never lacking. The *vita* commonly was
drawn less from personal knowledge than from report or
tradition. Report grows, passing from mouth to mouth,
and is enlarged with illustrative incidents. Since no dis-
belief blocked the acceptance of miracles, their growth out-
stripped that of the other elements of the story, because they
interested the most people. Yet there was little originality,
and the *vitae* constantly reproduced like incidents. Especially, Biblical prototypes were followed, as one sees in the
Dialogi of Gregory the Great, telling of the career of St
Benedict of Nursia. The Pope finds that the great founder
of western monasticism performed many of the miracles
ascribed to Scriptural characters.[2] Herein we see the working of suggestion and imitation upon a " legend " ; but
Gregory found rather an additional wonder-striking feature,
that God not only had wrought miracles through Benedict,
but in His ineffable wisdom had chosen to conform the saint's
deeds to the pattern of Scriptural prototypes. And so, in
the *Vitae sanctorum*, the joinder of suggestion and the will to
believe literally worked marvels.

Usually the Fathers of the Church were as interested
in miracles as the uneducated laity. Ambrose, the great
Archbishop of Milan, writes a long letter to his sister

[1] An excellent statement of the nature and classes of the mediaeval *Vitae
sanctorum* is " Les Légendes hagiographiques," by Hipp. Delehaye, S.J., in
Revue des questions historiques, t. 74 (1903), pp. 56-122. An English translation
of this article has appeared as an independent volume.

[2] At Gregory's statement of the marvellous deeds of Benedict, his interlocutor,
the Deacon Peter, answers and exclaims : " Wonderful and astonishing is what
you relate. For in the water brought forth from the rock (*i.e.* by Benedict) I
see Moses, in the iron which returned from the bottom of the lake I see Elisha
(2 Kings vi. 6), in the running upon the water I see Peter, in the obedience of
the raven I see Elijah (1 Kings xvii. 6), and in his grief for his dead enemy I see
David (2 Sam. i. 11). That man, as I consider him, was full of the spirit of
all the just " (Gregorius Magnus, *Dialogi*, ii. 8. Quoted and expanded by Odo
of Cluny, Migne, *Pat. Lat.* 133, col. 724). The rest of the second book contains
other miracles like those told in the Bible. The Life of a later saint may also
follow earlier monastic types. Francis kisses the wounds of lepers, as Martin
of Tours had done. See Sulpicius Severus, *Vita S. Martini*. But often the
writer of a *vita* deliberately inserts miracles to make his story edifying, or enhance
the fame of his hero, perhaps in order to benefit the church where he is interred.

Marcellina upon finding the relics of certain martyrs, and the miracles wrought by this treasure-trove.[1] As for Jerome, of course, he is very open-minded, and none too careful in his own accounts. His passion for the relics of the saints appears in his polemic *Contra Vigilantium*. What interest, either in the writing or the hearing, would men have taken in a hermit desert life that was bare of miracles ? The desert and the forest solitude have always been full of wonders. In Jerome's Lives of Paulus and Hilarion, the romantic and picturesque elements consist exclusively in the miraculous. And again, how could any one devote himself to the cult of an almost contemporary saint or the worship of a martyr, and not find abundant miracles ? Sulpicius Severus wrote the *Vita* of St. Martin while the saint was still alive ; and there would have been no reason for the worship of St. Felix, carried on through years by Paulinus of Nola, if Felix's relics had not had saving power. It was to this charming tender of the dead, afterwards beatified as St. Paulinus of Nola,[2] that Augustine addressed his moderating treatise on these matters, entitled *De cura pro mortuis*. He can see no advantage in burying a body close to a martyr's tomb unless in order to stimulate the prayers of the living. How the martyrs help us surpasses my understanding, says the writer ; but it is known that they do help. Very few were as critical as the Bishop of Hippo ; and all men recognized the efficacy of prayers to the martyred saints, and the magic power of their relics.

Having said so much of the intellectual obliquities of the Church Fathers, it were well to dwell a moment on their power. Their inspiration was the Christian Faith, working within them and bending their strength to its call. Their mental energies conformed to their understanding of the Faith and their interpretation of its Scriptural presentation. Their achievement was Catholic Christianity consisting in the union of two complements, ecclesiastical organization and the complete and consistent organism of doctrine. Here, in fact, two living organisms were united as body and soul. Each was fitted to the other, and neither could have

---

[1] Ambrose, *Ep.* 22, *ad Marcellinam.*
[2] On Paulinus of Nola, see Taylor, *Classical Heritage*, pp. 272-276.

existed alone. In their union they were to prove unequalled in history for coherence and efficiency. Great then was the energy and intellectual power of the men who constructed Church and doctrine. Great was Paul; great was Tertullian; great were Origen, Athanasius, and the Greek Gregories. Great also were those Latin Fathers of the fourth and fifth centuries, Augustine their last and greatest, who finally completed Church and doctrine for transmission to the Middle Ages—the doctrine, however, destined to be re-adjusted as to emphasis, and barbarized in character by him whose mind at least is patristically re-creative, but whose soul is mediaeval, Gregorius Magnus.[1]

[1] As this chapter has been devoted to the intellectual interests of the Fathers, it should be supplemented by a consideration of the emotions and passions approved or rejected by them. But this matter may be considered more conveniently in connection with the development of mediaeval emotion, *post*, Chapter XV.

CHAPTER V

FOR the Latin West the creative patristic epoch closes with the death of Augustine. There follows a period marked by the cessation of intellectual originality. Men are engaged upon translations from the Greek ; they are busy commenting upon older writings or are expounding with a change of emphasis the systematic constructions of their predecessors. Epitomes and compendia appear, simplified and mechanical abstracts of the bare elements of inherited knowledge and current education. Compilations are made, put together of excerpts taken unshriven and unshorn into the compiler's writing. Knowledge is brought down to a more barbaric level. Yet temperament lingers for a while, and still appears in the results.

The representatives of this post-patristic period of translation, comment, and compendium, and of re-expression with temperamental change of emphasis, are the two contemporaries, Boëthius and Cassiodorus ; then Gregory the Great, who became pope soon after Cassiodorus closed his eyes at the age of ninety or more ; and, lastly, Isidore, Archbishop of Seville, who died in 636, twenty-two years after Gregory. All these were Latin bred, and belonged to the Roman world rather than to those new peoples whose barbarism was hastening the disruption of a decadent order, but whose recently converted zeal was soon to help on the further diffusion of Latin Christianity. They appear as transmitters of antique and patristic thought ; because, originating little, they put together matter congenial to their own lowering intellectual predilections, and therefore suitable as mental pabulum for times of mingled decadence and barbarism, and also for the following periods of mediaeval re-emergence which continued to hark back to the obvious and the easy.

Instead of *transmitters*, a word indicating function, one might call these men *intermediaries*, and so indicate their position as well as rôle. Both words, however, should be taken relatively. For all the Fathers heretofore considered were in some sense transmitters or intermediaries, even though creative in their work of systematizing, adding to, or otherwise transforming their matter. Yet one would not dub Augustine a transmitter, because he was far more of a remaker or creator. But Gregory the Great will appear a dark refashioner ; while Cassiodorus and Isidore are rather sheer transmitters or intermediaries, the last-named worthy destined to be the most popular of them all, through his unerring faculty of selecting for his compilations the foolish and the flat.

Among them, Boëthius alone was attached to the antique by affinity of sentiment and temper. Although doubtless a professing Christian, his sentiments were those of pagan philosophy. The *De consolatione philosophiae*, which comes to us as his very self, is a work of eclectic pagan moralizing, fused to a personal unity by the author's artistic and emotional nature, then deeply stirred by his imprisonment and peril.[1] He had enjoyed the favour of the great Ostrogoth, Theodoric, ruler of Italy, but now was fallen under suspicion, and had been put in prison, where he was executed in the year 525 at the age of forty-three. His book moves all readers by its controlled and noble pathos, rendered more appealing through the romantic interest surrounding its composition. It became *par excellence* the mediaeval source of such ethical precept and consolation as might be drawn from rational self-control and acquiescence in the ways of Providence. But at present we are concerned with the range of Boëthius's intellectual interests and his labours for the transmission of learning.

---

[1] See E. K. Rand, " On the Composition of Boëthius' Con. Phil.," *Harvard Classical Studies*, xv. ; also generally, Manitius, *Ges. der lateinischen Lit. des Mittelalters*, i. 22-36.

He was an antique-minded man, whose love of knowledge did not revolve around " salvation," the patristic focus of intellectual effort. Rather he was moved by an ardent wish to place before his Latin contemporaries what was best in the classic education and philosophy. He is first of all a translator from Greek to Latin, and, secondly, a helpful commentator on the works which he translates.

He was little over twenty years of age when he wrote his first work, the *De arithmetica*.[1] It was a free translation of the *Arithmetic* of Nichomachus, a Neo-Pythagorean who flourished about the year 100. Boëthius's work opens with a dedicatory *Praefatio* to his father-in-law Symmachus. In that and in the first chapter he evinces a broad conception of education, and shows that lovers of wisdom should not despise arithmetic, music, geometry and astronomy, the fourfold path or *quadrivium*, a word which he may have been the first to use in this sense.[2] With him arithmetic treats of quantity in and by itself ; music, of quantity related to measure ; geometry, of moveless and astronomy of moving quantity. He was a better Greek scholar than mathematician ; and his free translation ignores some of the finer points of Nichomachus's work, which would have impressed one better versed in mathematics.[3]

The young scholar followed up his maiden work with a treatise on Music, showing a knowledge of Greek harmonics. Then came a *De geometria*, in which the writer draws from Euclid as well as from the practical knowledge of Roman surveyors.[4] He composed or translated other works on elementary branches of education, as appears from a royal letter written by Cassiodorus in the name of Theodoric : " In your translations Pythagoras the musician, Ptolemy the astronomer, Nichomachus the arithmetician, Euclid the geometer are read by Italians, while Plato the theologian and Aristotle the logician dispute in Roman voice ; and you have given back the

---

[1] Migne, *Pat. Lat.* 63, col. 1079-1167. Also edited by Friedlein (Leipsic, 1867).

[2] I know of no earlier employment of the word to designate these four branches of study. But one might infer from Boëthius's youth at this time that he received it from a teacher.

[3] See Cantor, *Vorlesungen über die Ges. der Mathematik*, i. 537-540.

[4] See Cantor, *o.c.* i. 540-551.

mechanician Archimedes in Latin to the Sicilians." [1] Making
all allowance for politeness, this letter indicates the large
accomplishment of Boëthius, who was but twenty-five
years old when it was written. We turn to the com-
mentated Aristotelian translations which he now undertook.[2]
" Although the duties of the consular office [3] prevent the
bestowal of our time upon these studies, it still seems a
proper part of our care for the Republic to instruct its
citizens in the learning which is gained by the labours of
the lamp. Since the valour of a bygone time brought
dominion over other cities to this one Republic, I shall not
merit ill of my countrymen if I shall have instructed the
manners of our State with the arts of Greek wisdom." [4]
These sentences open the second book of Boëthius's translation of the *Categories* of Aristotle. His plan of work
enlarged, apparently, and grew more definite, as the years
passed, each adding its quota of accomplishment. At all
events, some time afterwards, when he may have been not
far from thirty-five, he speaks in the flush of an intellectual
anticipation which the many years of labour still to be
counted on seemed to justify :

" Labour ennobles the human race and completes it with the
fruits of genius ; but idleness deadens the mind. Not experience,
but ignorance, of labour turns us from it. For what man who
has made trial of labour has ever forsaken it ? And the power of
the mind lies in keeping the mind tense ; to unstring it is to ruin
it. My fixed intention, if the potent favour of the deity will so
grant, is (although others have laboured in this field, yet not with
satisfactory method) to translate into Latin every work of Aristotle that comes to my hand, and furnish it with a Latin commentary. Thus I may present, well ordered and illustrated with
the light of comment, whatever subtilty of logic's art, whatever
weight of moral experience, and whatever insight into natural
truth, may be gathered from Aristotle. And I mean to translate
all the dialogues of Plato, or reduce them in my commentary to

---

[1] Cassiodorus, *Ep. variae*, i. 45.

[2] Upon the dates of Boëthius's writings, see S. Brandt, " Entstehungszeit und
zeitliche Folge der Werke des Boëtius," *Philologus*, Band 62 (N.S. Bd. 16), 1903,
pp. 141 *sqq.* and 234 *sqq.*

[3] Social position, his own abilities, and the favour of Theodoric, obtained the
consulship for Boëthius in 510, when he was twenty-eight or -nine years old.

[4] Migne, *Pat. Lat.* 64, col. 201.

a Latin form. Having accomplished this, I shall not have despised the opinions of Aristotle and Plato if I evoke a certain
concord between them and show in how many things of importance for philosophy they agree—if only life and leisure last.
But now let us return to our subject." [1]

One sees a veritable love of intellectual labour and a
love of the resulting mental increment. It is distinctly the
antique, not the patristic, attitude towards interests of the
mind. In spite of his sixth-century way of writing, and
the mental fallings away indicated by it, Boëthius possessed
the old pagan spirit, and shows indeed how tastes might
differ in the sixth century. He never translated the whole
of Aristotle and Plato ; but he carried out his purpose to the
extent of rendering into Latin, with abundant comment, the
entire *Organon*, that is, all the logical writings of Aristotle.
First of all, and with elaborate explanation, he rendered
Porphyry's famous Introduction to the *Categories* of the
Master. Then the *Categories* themselves, likewise with
abundant explanation. Then Aristotle's *De interpretatione*,
in two editions, the first with simple comment suited to
beginners, the second with the best elaboration of formal
logic that he could devise or compile.[2] These elementary
portions of the *Organon*, as transmitted in the Boëthian
translations, made the logical discipline of the mediaeval
schools until the latter part of the twelfth century. He
translated also Aristotle's *Prior* and *Posterior Analytics*, the
Topics, and the *Sophistical Elenchi*. But such advanced
treatises were beyond the requirements of the early mediaeval
centuries. With the lessening of intellectual energy they
passed into oblivion, to re-emerge only when called for by
the livelier mental activities of a later time.[3]

The list of Boëthius's works is not yet exhausted, for
he wrote some minor logical treatises, and a voluminous
commentary on Cicero's *Topica*. He was also the author
of certain Christian theological tracts, themselves less
famous than the controversy which long has raged as to

[1] *In lib. de interpretatione*, ed. sec., Book II., Migne 64, col. 433.
[2] See *De inter*. ed. pr., I. ; ed. sec., III. and IV., Migne 64, col. 193, 487, 517.
[3] But it appears that the Latin versions of the *Analytics*, *Topics*, and *Elenchi*
in Migne 64 are not by Boëthius. Grabmann, *Ges. der schol. Methode*, I., 149 *sqq.*,
and II., 70 *sqq.*

their authorship.[1] They serve to prove his interest in Christian controversy as well as in pagan philosophy.

Boëthius's commentaries reproduced the comments of other commentators,[2] and he presents merely the logical processes of thought. But these, analyzed and tabulated, were just the parts of philosophy to be seized by a period whose lack of mental originality was rapidly lowering to a barbaric frame of mind. The logical works of Boëthius necessarily presented the method rather than the substance of philosophic truth. But their study would exercise the mind, and they were peculiarly adapted to serve as discipline for the coming centuries, which could not become progressive until they had mastered their antique inheritance, including this chief method of presenting the elemental forms of truth.

The " life and leisure " of Boëthius were cut off by his untimely death. Cassiodorus, although a year or two older, outlived him by half a century. He was born at Squillace, a Calabrian town which looks out south-easterly over the little gulf bearing the same name. His father, grandfather, and great-grandfather had been generals and high officials. He himself served for forty years under Theodoric and his successors, and at last became praetorian praefect, the chief office in the Gothic Roman kingdom.[3] Through his birth, his education, his long official career, and perhaps his pliancy, he belonged to both Goths and Romans, and like the great king whom he first served, stood for a policy of reconcilement and assimilation of the two peoples, and also for tolerance as between Arian and Catholic.

Some years after Theodoric's death, when the Gothic kingdom had passed through internecine struggles and seemed at last to have fallen before the skill of Belisarius, Cassiodorus forsook the troubles of the world. He retired to his birthplace Squillace, and there in propitious situations founded a pleasant cloister for coenobites and an austerer

---

[1] See A. Hildebrand, *Boëthius und seine Stellung zum Christentum* (Regensburg, 1885), and works therein referred to. The genuineness of four of these tracts seems finally shown by E. K. Rand, " Der dem Boëthius zugeschriebene Traktat de Fide Catholica " (Fleckeisen's *Jahrbuch*, 1901).

[2] See Prantl, *Ges. der. Logik*, i. 679 *sqq.*

[3] See his Life in Hodgkin's *Letters of Cassiodorus* ; also Roger, *Enseignement des lettres classiques d'Ausone à Alcuin*, pp. 175-187 (Paris, 1905).

hermitage for those who would lead lives of arduous seclusion. For himself, he chose the former. It was the year of grace 540, three years before the death of Benedict of Nursia. Cassiodorus was past sixty. In retiring from the world he followed the instinct of his time, yet temperately and with an increment of wisdom. For he was the first influential man to recognize the fitness of the cloister for the labours of the pious student and copyist. It is not too much to regard him as the inaugurator of the learned, compiling, commenting and transcribing functions of monasticism. Not only as a patron, but through his own works, he was here a leader. His writings composed after his retirement represent the intellectual interests of western monasticism in the last half of the sixth century. They indicate the round of study proper for monks ; just the grammar, the orthography, and other elementary branches which they might know ; just the history with which it behoved them to be acquainted ; and then, outbulking all the rest, those Scriptural studies to which they might well devote their lives for the sake of their own and others' souls.

In passing these writings in review, it is unnecessary to pause over the interesting collection of letters — *Variae epistolae* — which were the fruit of Cassiodorus's official life, before he shut the convent's outer door against the toils of office. He " edited " them near the close of his public career. Before that had ended he had made a wretched *Chronicon*, carelessly and none too honestly compiled. He had also written his Gothic History, a far better work. It survives only in the compend of the ignorant Jordanes, a fact the like of which will be found repeatedly recurring in the sixth and following centuries, when a barbaric mentality continually prefers the compend to the larger and better original, which demands greater effort from the reader. A little later Cassiodorus composed his *De anima*, a treatise on the nature, qualities, and destinies of the Soul. Although made at the request of friends, it indicated the turning of the statesman's interest to the matters occupying his latter years, during which his literary labours were guided by a paternal purpose. One may place it with the works coming from his pen in those thirty years of retirement, when study and composition were rather stimulated than disturbed by care of his convent and estates, the modicum of active occupation needed by an old man whose life had been passed in the management of State affairs. Its preface sets out the topical arrangement in a manner prophetic of scholastic methods :

" Let us first learn why it is called Anima ; secondly, its definition ; thirdly, its substantial quality ; fourthly, whether any form should be ascribed to it ; fifthly, what are its moral virtues ; sixthly, its natural powers (*virtutes naturales*) by which it holds the body together ; seventhly, as to its origin ; eighthly, where is its especial seat ; ninthly, as to the body's form ; tenthly, as to the properties of the souls of sinners ; eleventhly, as to those of the souls of the just ; and twelfthly, as to the resurrection." [1]

The short treatise which follows is neither original nor penetrating. It closes with an encomium on the number twelve, with praise of Christ and with a prayer.

Soon after Cassiodorus had installed himself in Vivarium, as he called his convent, from the fishponds and gardens surrounding it, he set himself to work to transcribe the Scriptures, and commenced a huge Commentary on the Psalms. But he interrupted these undertakings in 543 in order to write for his monks a syllabus of their sacred and secular education. The title of the work was *Institutiones divinarum et saecularium litterarum*.[2] In opening he refers to his failure to found a school of Christian teaching at Rome, on account of the wars. Partially to repair this want, he will compose an introduction to the study of Scripture and letters. It will not set out his own opinions, but those of former men. Through the expositions of the Fathers we ascend to divine Scripture, as by a ladder. The proper order is for the " tiros of Christ " first to learn the Psalms, and then proceed to study the rest of Scripture in carefully corrected codices. When the " soldiers of Christ " have completed the reading of Scripture, and fixed it in their minds by constant meditation, they will begin to recognize passages when cited, and be able to find them. They should also know the Latin commentators, and even the Greek, who have expounded the various books.

[1] Migne 70, col. 1281.　　　　[2] Migne 70, col. 1105-1219.

The first book of these *Institutiones* is strictly a guide to Scripture study, and in no way a commentary. For example, beginning with the " Octateuch," as making up the first " codex " of Scripture, Cassiodorus tells what Latin and what Greek Fathers have expounded it. He proceeds, briefly, in the same way with the rest of the Old and New Testaments. He mentions the Ecumenical Councils, which had passed upon Christian doctrine, and then refers to the division of Scripture by Jerome, by Augustine, and in the Septuagint. He states rules for preserving the purity of the text, exclaims over its ineffable value, and mentions famous doctrinal works, like Augustine's *De Trinitate* and the *De officiis* of Ambrose. He then recommends the study of Church historians and names the great ones, who while incidentally telling of secular events have shown that such hung not on chance nor on the power of the feeble gods, but solely on the Creator's will. Then he shortly characterizes the great Latin Doctors, Cyprian, Hilary, Ambrose, Jerome, and Augustine, and mentions a convenient collection of excerpts from the works of the last-named saint, made by a certain priest. Next he admonishes the student as to the careful reading of Scripture, and suggests convenient abbreviations for noting citations. He speaks of the desirability of knowing enough cosmography to understand when Scripture speaks of countries, towns, mountains, or rivers, and then reverts to the need of an acquaintance with the Seven Arts ; this secular wisdom, having been originally pilfered from Scripture, should now be called back to its true service. Those monks who lack intelligence for such studies may properly work in the fields and gardens which surround Vivarium (Columella and other writers on agriculture are to be found in the convent library), and the care of the sick is recommended to all. The second book of the *Institutiones* is a brief and unequal compend of the Seven Arts, in which Dialectic is treated at greatest length.

The remaining works of Cassiodorus appear as special aids to the student in carrying out the programme of the first book of the *Institutiones*. Such an aid was the bulky Commentary on the Psalms ; another such was the famous *Historia tripartita*, made of the Church histories of Socrates,

Sozomen, and Theodoret, translated by a friend of Cassiodorus, and crudely thrown together by himself into one
narrative. Finally, such another work was the compilation
upon Latin orthography which the good old man made for
his monks in his ninety-third year.

This long and useful life does not display the zeal for
knowledge for its own sake which marks the labours of
Boëthius. It is the Christian utilitarian view of knowledge
that Cassiodorus represents, and yet not narrowly, nor with
a trace of that intolerance of whatever did not bear directly
on salvation, which is to be found in Gregory. From
Boëthius's love of philosophy, and from the practical interest
of Cassiodorus in education, it is indeed a change to the
spiritual anxiousness and fear of hell besetting this great
pope.[1]

In appreciating a man's opinions and his mental clarity
or murkiness, one should consider his temperament and the
temper of his time. Gregory was constrained as well as
driven by temperamental yearnings and aversions, aggravated by the humour of the century that produced Benedict
of Nursia and was contemplating gloomily the Empire's ruin
and decay, now more acutely borne in upon the consciousness
of thoughtful people than in the age of Augustine. His
temper drew from prevailing moods, and in turn impressed
its spiritual incisiveness upon the influences which it
absorbed ; and his writings, so expressive of his own
temperament and all that fed it, were to work mightily
upon the minds and moods of men to come.

Born of a distinguished Roman family about the year
540, he was some thirty-five years old when Cassiodorus
died. His education was the best that Rome could give.
In spite of disclaimer on his part, rhetorical training shows
in the antithetic power of his style ; for example, in that
resounding sentence in the dedicatory letter prefixed to his
Moralia, wherein he would seem to be casting grammar to
the winds. Although quoted until threadbare, it is so

---

[1] Gregory's works are printed in Migne, *Patrologia Latina*, 75-79. His epistles
are also published in the *Monumenta Germaniae historica*. On Gregory, his life
and times, writings and doctrines, see F. H. Dudden, *Gregory the Great*, etc., 2 vols.
(Longmans, 1905) ; also E. G. Gardner, *The Dialogues of St. Gregory surnamed the
Great*.

illustrative as to justify citation : " Nam sicut hujus quoque
epistolae tenor enunciat, non metacismi collisionem fugio,
non barbarismi confusionem devito, situs motusque et prae-
positionum casus servare contemno, quia indignum vehe-
menter existimo, ut verba coelestis oraculi restringam sub
regulis Donati." [1] By no means will he flee the concussion
of the oft-repeated M, or avoid the confusing barbarism ; he
will despise the laws of place and case, because he deems it
utterly unfit to confine the words of the heavenly oracle
beneath the rules of Donatus. By all of which Gregory
means that he proposes to write freely, according to the
needs of his subject, and to disregard the artificial rules of
the somewhat emptied rhetoric, let us say, of Cassiodorus's
epistles.

In his early manhood naturally he was called to take
part in affairs, and was made *Praetor urbanus*. But soon
the prevalent feeling of the difficulty of serving God in the
world drove him to retirement. His father's palace on the
Coelian hill he changed to a convent, upon the site of which
now stands the Church of San Gregorio Magno ; and there
he became a monk. Passionately he loved the monk's life,
for which he was to long in vain through most of the years
to come. Soon he was dragged forth from the companionship of " Mary " to serve with " Martha." The toiling
papacy could not allow a man of his abilities to remain
hidden. He was harnessed to its active service, and sent as
the papal representative to the Imperial Court at Constantinople ; whence he returned, after several years, in 585.
Re-entering his monastery on the Coelian, he became its
abbot ; but was drawn out again, and made pope by acclama-
tion and insistency in the year 590. There is no need to
speak of the efficient and ceaseless activity of this pontiff,
whose body was never free from pain, nor his soul released
from longing for seclusion which only the grave was to bring.

Gregory's mind was less antique, and more barbarous and
mediaeval than Augustine's, whose doctrine he reproduced
with garbling changes of tone and emphasis. In the century
and a half between the two, the Roman institutions had
broken down, decadence had advanced, and the patristic

[1] Migne, *Pat. Lat.* 75, col. 516.

mind had passed from indifference to the laws of physical
phenomena to something like sheer barbaric ignorance of the
same.   Whatever in Ambrose, Jerome, or Augustine represented conviction or opinion, has in Gregory become mental
habit, spontaneity of acceptance, matter of course.   The
miraculous is with him a frame of mind ; and the allegorical
method of understanding Scripture is no longer intended,
not to say wilful, as with Augustine, but has become persistent unconscious habit.   Augustine desired to know God
and the Soul, and the true Christian doctrine with whatever
made for its substantiation.   He is conscious of closing his
mind to everything irrelevant to this.   Gregory's nature
has settled itself within this scheme of Christian knowledge which Augustine framed.   He has no intellectual
inclinations reaching out beyond.   He is not conscious of
closing his mind to extraneous knowledge.   His mental
habits and temperament are so perfectly adjusted to the
confines of this circle, that all beyond has ceased to exist
for him.

So with Gregory the patristic limitation of intellectual
interest, indifference to physical phenomena, and acceptance
of the miraculous are no longer merely thoughts and opinions
consciously entertained ; they make part of his nature.
There was nothing novel in his views regarding knowledge,
sacred and profane.   But there is a turbid force of temperament in his expressions.   In consequence, his vehement
words to Bishop Desiderius of Vienne [1] have been so taken
as to make the great pope a barbarizing idiot.   He exclaims
with horror at the report that the bishop is occupying himself
teaching grammar ; he is shocked that an episcopal mouth
should be singing praises of Jove, which are unfit for a lay
brother to utter.   But Gregory is not decrying here, any
more than in the sentence quoted from the letter prefixed
to his *Moralia*, a decent command of Latin.   He is merely
declaring with temperamental vehemence that to teach
grammar and poetry is not the proper function of a bishop
—the bishop in this case of a most important see.   Gregory
had no more taste for secular studies than Tertullian four
centuries before him.   For both, however, letters had their

[1] *Ep.* xi. 54 (Migne 77, col. 1171).

handmaidenly function, which they performed effectively in the instances of these two great rhetoricians.[1]

It is needless to say that the entire literary labour of Gregory was religious. His works, as in time, so in quality, are midway between those of Ambrose and Augustine and those of the Carolingian rearrangers of patristic opinion. Gregory, who laboured chiefly as a commentator upon Scripture, was not highly original in his thoughts, yet was no mere excerpter of patristic interpretations, like Rabanus Maurus or Walafrid Strabo, who belong to the ninth century.[2] In studying Scripture, he thought and interpreted in allegories. But he was also a man experienced in life's exigencies, and his religious admonishings were wise and searching. His prodigious Commentary upon Job has with reason been called Gregory's *Moralia*.[3] And as the moral advice and exhortation sprang from Gregory the bishop, so the allegorical interpretations largely were his own, or at least not borrowed and applied mechanically.

Gregory represents the patristic mind passing into a more barbarous stage. He delighted in miracles, and wrote his famous *Dialogues on the Lives and Miracles of the Italian Saints*[4] to solace the cares of his pontificate. The work exhibits a naïve acceptance of every kind of miracle, and presents the supple mediaeval devil in all his deceitful metamorphoses.[5]

---

[1] This is the view expressed in the *Commentary on Kings* ascribed to Gregory, but perhaps the work of a later hand. Thus, in the allegorical interpretation of I Kings (I Sam.) xiii. 20, " But all the Israelites went down to the Philistines, to sharpen every man his share, and his coulter, and his axe." Says the commentator (Migne, *Pat. Lat.* 79, col. 356) : We go down to the Philistines when we incline the mind to secular studies ; Christian simplicity is upon a height. Secular books are said to be in the plane since they have no celestial truths. God put secular knowledge in a plane before us that we should use it as a step to ascend to the heights of Scripture. So Moses first learned the wisdom of the Egyptians that he might be able to understand and expound the divine precepts ; Isaiah, most eloquent of the prophets, was *nobiliter instructus et urbanus* ; and Paul had sat at Gamaliel's feet before he was lifted to the height of the third heaven. One goes to the Philistines to sharpen his plow, because secular learning is needed as a training for Christian preaching.

[2] See *post*, Chapter X.

[3] Migne 75, 76.

[4] Migne 77, col. 149-430. The second book is devoted to Benedict of Nursia.

[5] For illustrations see Dudden, *o.c.* i. 321-366, and ii. 367-68. Gregory's interest in the miraculous shows also in his letters. The Empress Constantine had written requesting him to send her the head of St. Paul ! He replies (*Ep*

Quite in accord with Gregory's interest in these stories is his elaboration of certain points of doctrine, for example, the worship of the saints, whose intercession and supererogatory righteousness may be turned by prayer and worship to the devotee's benefit.   Thus he comments upon the eighth verse of the twenty-fourth chapter of Job :

" They are wet with the showers of the mountains, and embrace the rocks as a shelter.   The showers of the mountains are the words of the doctors.   Concerning which mountains it is said with the voice of the Church : ' I will lift up my eyes unto the hills.'   The showers of the mountains water these, for the streams of the holy fathers saturate.   We receive the ' shelter ' as a covering of good works, by which one is covered so that before the eyes of omnipotent God the filthiness of his perversity is concealed.   Wherefore it is written, ' Blessed are those whose iniquities are forgiven and whose sins are covered ' (Ps. xxxii. 1).   And under the name of stones whom do we understand except the strong men of the Church ?   To whom it is said through the first shepherd : ' Ye also as living stones are built up a spiritual house ' (1 Peter ii. 5).   So those who confide in no work of their own, run to the protection of the holy martyrs, and press with tears to their sacred bodies, pleading to obtain pardon through their intercession." [1]

Another point of Gregorian emphasis : no delict is remitted without punishment.[2] To complement which principle, Gregory develops the doctrine of penance in its three elements, *contritio, conversio mentis, satisfactio.*   Our whole life should be one long penitence and penance, and baptism of tears ; for our first baptism cannot wash out later sins, and cannot be repeated.   In the fourth book of the *Dialogi* he develops his cognate doctrine of Purgatory,[3] and amplifies upon the situation and character of hell.   These things are implicit in Augustine and existed before him : with Gregory they have become explicit, elaborated, and

iv. 30, *ad Constantinam Augustam*) in a wonderful letter on the terrors of such holy relics and their death-striking as well as healing powers, of which he gives instances. He says that sometimes he has sent a bit of St. Peter's chain or a few filings ; and when people come seeking those filings from the priest in attendance, sometimes they readily come off, and again no effort of the file can detach anything.
  [1] *Moralia* xvi. 51 (Migne 75, col. 1151).   Cf. Dudden, *o.c.* ii. 369-373.
  [2] *Mor.* ix. 34, 54 (Migne 75, col. 889).   Cf. Dudden, *o.c.* ii. 419-426.
  [3] *Dialogi,* iv. caps. 39, 55.

insisted on with recurrent emphasis. Thus Augustinianism
is altered in form and barbarized.[1]

Gregory is throughout prefigurative of the Middle Ages,
which he likewise prefigures in his greatness as a sovereign
bishop and a man of ecclesiastical affairs. He is energetic
and wise and temperate. The practical wisdom of the
Catholic Church is in him and in his rightly famed book of
Pastoral Rule. The temperance and wisdom of his letters
of instructions to Augustine of Canterbury are admirable.
The practical exigency seemed always to have the effect of
tempering any extreme opinion which apart from it he
might have expressed ; as one sees, for example, in those
letters to this apostle to the English, or in his letter to
Serenus, Bishop of Marseilles, who had been too violent as to
paintings and images. Gregory's stand is moderate and
reasonable. Likewise he opposes the use of force to convert
the Jews, although insisting firmly that no Jew may hold a
Christian slave.[2]

There has been occasion to remark that decadence tends
to join hands with barbarism on a common intellectual level.
Had Boëthius lived in a greater epoch, he might not have
been an adapter of an elementary arithmetic and geometry,
and his best years would not have been devoted to the
translation and illustration of logical treatises. Undoubtedly
his labours were needed by the times in which he lived and
by the centuries which followed them in spirit as well as
chronologically. He was the principal purveyor of the
strictly speaking intellectual grist of the early Middle Ages ;
and it was most apt that the great scholastic controversy as
to universals should have drawn its initial text from his
translation of Porphyry's Introduction to the *Categories* of
Aristotle.[3] Gregory, on the other hand, was a purveyor of
theology, the subject to which logic chiefly was to be applied.
He purveyed matter very much to the mediaeval taste ;
for example, his wise practical admonishments ; his elabora-

[1] A better Augustinianism speaks in Gregory's letter to Theoctista (*Ep.* vii. 26),
in which he says that there are two kinds of " compunction, the one which fears
eternal punishments, the other which sighs for the heavenly rewards, as the soul
thirsting after God is stung first by fear and then by love."

[2] *Ep.* iv. 21 ; vi. 32 ; ix. 6.

[3] See *post*, Chapter XXXVII. 1.

tion of such a doctrine as that of penance, so tangible that it could be handled, and felt with one's very fingers ; and, finally, his supreme intellectual endeavour, the allegorical trellising of Scripture, to which the Middle Ages were to devote their thoughts, and were to make warm and living with the love and yearning of their souls. The converging currents—decadence and barbarism—meet and join in Gregory's powerful personality. He embodies the intellectual decadence which has lost all independent wish for knowledge and has dropped the whole round of the mind's mortal interests ; which has seized upon the near, the tangible, and the ominous in theology till it has rooted religion in the fear of hell. All this may be viewed as a decadent abandonment of the more intellectual and spiritual complement to the brute facts of sin, penance, and hell barely escaped. But, on the other hand, it was also barbarization, and held the strength of barbaric narrowing of motives and the resistlessness of barbaric fear.

Such were the rôles of Boëthius and Gregory in the transmission of antique and patristic intellectual interests into the mediaeval time. Quite different was that of Gregory's younger contemporary, Isidore, the princely and vastly influential Bishop of Seville, the primary see in that land of Spain, which, however it might change dynasties, was destined never to be free from some kind of sacerdotal bondage. In Isidore's time, the kingdom of the Visigoths had recently turned from Arianism to Catholicism, and wore its new priestly yoke with ardour. Boëthius had provided a formal discipline and Gregory much substance already mediaevalized. But the whole ground-plan of Isidore's mind corresponded with the aptitudes and methods of the Carolingian period, which was to be the schoolday of the Middle Ages. By reason of his own habits of study, by reason of the quality of his mind, which led him to select the palpable, the foolish, and the mechanically correlated, by reason, in fine, of *his* mental faculties and interests, Isidore gathered and arranged in his treatises a conglomerate of knowledge, secular and sacred, exactly suited to the coming centuries.

In drawing from its spiritual heritage, an age takes what it cares for ; and if comparatively decadent or barbarized or childlike in its intellectual affinities, it will still manage to draw what is like itself. In that case, probably it will not draw directly from the great sources, but from intermediaries who have partially debased them. From these turbid compositions the still duller age will continue to select the obvious and the worse. This indicates the character of Isidore's work. His writings speak for themselves through their titles, and are so flat, so transparent, so palpably taken from the nearest authorities, that there is no call to analyze them. But their titles with some slight indication of their contents will show the excerpt character of Isidore's mental processes, and illustrate by anticipation the like qualities reappearing with the Carolingian doctors.

Isidore's *Quaestiones in vetus Testamentum* [1] is his chief work in the nature of a Scripture commentary. It is confined to those passages of the Old Testament which were deemed most pregnant with allegorical meaning. His Preface discloses his usual method of procedure : " We have taken certain of those incidents of the sacred history which were told or done figuratively, and are filled with mystic sacraments, and have woven them together in sequence in this little work ; and, collecting the opinions of the old churchmen, we have made a choice of flowers as from divers meadows ; and briefly presenting a few matters from so many, with some changes or additions, we offer them not only to studious but fastidious readers who detest prolixity." Every one may feel assured that he will be reading the interpretations of the Fathers, and not those of Isidore— " my voice is but their tongue." He states that his sources are Origen, Victorinus, Ambrose, Jerome, Augustine, Fulgentius, Cassian, and " Gregory so distinguished for his eloquence in our own time." The spirit of the mediaeval commentary is in this Preface. The phrase about " culling the opinions of the Fathers like flowers from divers meadows," will be repeated hundreds of times. Such a commentary is a thing of excerpts ; so it rests upon authority. The writer thus comforts both his reader and himself ; neither runs the

---

[1] Migne 83, col. 207-424. No reference need be made, of course, to the *False Decretals*, pseudonymously connected with Isidore's name ; they are later than his time.

peril of originality, and together they repose on the broad bosom of the Fathers.

Throughout his writings, Isidore commonly proceeds in this way, whether he says so or not. We may name first the casual works which represent separate parcels of his encyclopaedic gleanings, and then glance at his putting together of them, in his *Etymologiae*.[1] The muster opens with two books of Distinctions (*Differentiarum*). The first is concerned with the distinctions of like-sounding and like-meaning words. It is alphabetically arranged. The second is concerned with the distinctions of *things* : it begins with God and the Creation, and passes to the physical parts and spiritual traits of man. No need to say that it contains nothing that is Isidore's own. Now come the *Allegoriae quaedam sacrae Scripturae*, which give in chronological order the allegorical signification of all the important persons mentioned in the Old Testament and the New. It was one of the earliest hand-books of Scriptural allegories, and is a sheer bit of the Middle Ages in spirit and method. The substance, of course, is taken from the Fathers. Next, a little work, *De ortu et obitu Patrum*, states in short paragraphs the birthplace, span of life, place of sepulture, and noticeable traits of Scriptural personages.

There follows a collection of brief Isidorean prefaces to the books of Scripture. Then comes a curious book, which may have been suggested to the writer by the words of Augustine himself. This is the *Liber numerorum*, the book of the *numbers* occurring in the Scriptures. It tells the qualities and mystical significance of every number from one to sixteen, and of the chief ones between sixteen and sixty. These numbers were " most holy and most full of mysteries " to Augustine,[2] and Augustine is the man whom Isidore chiefly draws on in this treatise—Augustine at his very worst. One might search far for an apter instance of an ecclesiastical writer elaborately exploiting the most foolish statements that could possibly be found in the writings of a great predecessor.

---

[1] The *Etymologiae* is to be found in vol. 82 of Migne, col. 73-728 ; the other works fill vol. 83 of Migne.

[2] Aug. *Quaest. in Gen.* i. 152. See *ante*, p. 67.

Isidore composed a polemic treatise on the Catholic Faith against the Jews—*De fide Catholica contra Judaeos.* The good bishop had nothing to add to the patristic discussion of this weighty controversy. His book is filled with quotations from Scripture. It put the matter together in a way suited to his epoch and the coming centuries, and at an early time was translated into the German and other vernacular tongues. Three books of *Sententiae* follow, upon the contents of Christian doctrine—as to God, the world, evil, the angels, man, Christ and the Church. They consist of excerpts from the writings of Gregory the Great and earlier Church Fathers.[1] A more original work is the *De ecclesiasticis officiis*, upon the services of the Church and the orders of clergy and laity. It presents the liturgical practices and ecclesiastical regulations of Isidore's epoch.

Isidore seems to have put most pious feeling into a work called by him *Synonyma*, to which name was added the supplementary designation : *De lamentatione animae.* First the Soul pours out its lament in excruciating iteration, repeating the same commonplace of Christian piety in synonymous phrases. When its lengthy plaint is ended, Reason replies with admonitions synonymously reiterated in the same fashion.[2] This work combined a grammatical with a pious purpose, and became very popular through its doubly edifying nature, and because it strung together so many easy commonplaces of Christian piety. Isidore also drew up a *Regula* for monks, and a book on the Order of Creation has been ascribed to him. This completes the sum of his extant works upon religious topics, from which we pass to those of a secular character.

The first of these is the *De rerum natura*, written to

---

[1] Isidore's *Books of Sentences* present a topical arrangement of matters more or less closely pertinent to the Christian Faith, and thus may be regarded as a precursor of the *Sentences* of Peter Lombard (*post*, Chapter XXXV.). But Isidore's work is the merest compilation, and he does not marshal his extracts to prove or disprove a set proposition, and show the consensus of authority, like the Lombard. His chief source is Gregory's *Moralia*. Prosper of Aquitaine, a younger contemporary and disciple of Augustine, compiled from Augustine's works a book of Sentences, a still slighter affair than Isidore's (Migne, *Pat. Lat.* 51, col. 427-496).

[2] For example, Reason begins her reply thus : " Quaeso te, anima, obsecro te, deprecor te, imploro te, ne quid ultra leviter agas, ne quid inconsulte geras, ne temere aliquid facias," etc. (Migne 83, col. 845).

enlighten his king, Sisebut, " on the scheme (*ratio*) of the days and months, the bounds of the year and the change of seasons, the nature of the elements, the courses of the sun and moon and stars, and the signs of tempests and winds, the position of the earth, and the ebb and flow of the sea." Of all of which, continues Isidore, " we have made brief note, from the writings of the ancients (*veteribus viris*), and especially those who were of the Catholic Faith. For it is not a vain knowledge (*superstitiosa scientia*) to know the nature of these things, if we consider them according to sound and sober teaching." [1] So Isidore compiles a book of secular physical knowledge, the substance of which is taken from the *Hexaëmeron* of Ambrose and the works of other Fathers, and also from the lost *Prata* of pagan Suetonius.[2]

Of course Isidore busied himself also with history. He made a dismal universal *Chronicon*, and perhaps a History of the Kings of the Goths, through which stirs a breath of national pride ; and after the model of Jerome, he wrote a *De viris illustribus*, concerned with some fifty worthies of the Church flourishing between Jerome's time and his own.

Here we end the somewhat dry enumeration of the various works of Isidore outside of his famous " twenty books of Etymologies." This work has been aptly styled a *Konversationslexikon*—that excellent German word. It was named *Etymologiae*, because the author always gives the etymology of everything which he describes or defines. Indeed the tenth book contains only the etymological definitions of words alphabetically arranged. These etymologies follow the haphazard similarities of the words, and often are nonsensical. Sometimes they show a fantastic caprice indicating a mind steeped in allegorical interpretations, as, for example, when " *Amicus* is said to be, by derivation, *animi custos* ; also from *hamus*, that is, chain of love, whence we say *hami* or hooks because they hold." [3] This is not ignorance so much as fancy.

The *Etymologiae* were meant to cover the current know-

---

[1] *De rerum natura*, Praefatio (Migne 83, col. 963).
[2] See Prolegomena to Becker's edition.
[3] Migne 82, col. 367.

ledge of the time, doctrinal as well as secular. But the
latter predominates, as it would in a *Konversationslexikon*.
The general arrangement of the treatise is not alphabetical,
but topical. To indicate the sources of its contents would
be difficult as well as tedious. Isidore drew on many
previous authors and compilers : to Cassiodorus and Boëthius
he went for Rhetoric and Dialectic, and made frequent
trips to the *Prata* of Suetonius for natural knowledge—or
ignorance. In matters of doctrine he draws on the Church
Fathers ; and for his epitome of jurisprudence in the fifth
book, upon the Fathers from Tertullian on, and (probably)
upon some elementary book of legal Institutes.[1]   Glancing

---

[1] See Kübler, " Isidorus-Studien," *Hermes* xxv. (1890), 497, 518, and literature there cited.

An analysis of the *Etymologies* would be out of the question. But the captions
of the twenty books into which it is divided will indicate the range of Isidore's
intellectual interests and those of his time :

I. *De grammatica.*
II. *De rhetorica et dialectica.*
III. *De quatuor disciplinis mathematicis.* (Thus the first three books contain
the Trivium and Quadrivium.)
IV. *De medicina.* (A brief hand-book of medical terms.)
V. *De legibus et temporibus.* (The latter part describes the days, nights,
weeks, months, years, solstices and equinoxes. It is hard to guess why this was
put in the same book with Law.)
VI. *De libris et officiis ecclesiasticis.* (An account of the books of the Bible
and the services of the Church.)
VII. *De Deo, angelis et fidelium ordinibus.*
VIII. *De ecclesia et sectis diversis.*
IX. *De linguis, gentibus, regnis, etc.* (Concerning the various peoples of the
earth and their languages, and other matters.)
X. *Vocum certarum alphabetum.* (An etymological vocabulary of many
Latin words.)
XI. *De homine et portentis.* (The names and definitions of the various parts
of the human body, the ages of life, and prodigies and monsters.)
XII. *De animalibus.*
XIII. *De mundo et partibus.* (The universe and its parts—atoms, elements,
sky, thunder, winds, waters, etc.)
XIV. *De terra et partibus.* (Geographical.)
XV. *De aedificiis et agris.* (Cities, their public constructions, houses, temples,
and the fields.)
XVI. *De lapidibus et metallis.* (Stones, metals, and their qualities curious
and otherwise.)
XVII. *De rebus rusticis.* (Trees, herbs, etc.)
XVIII. *De bello et ludis.* (On war, weapons, armour ; on public games and
the theatre.)
XIX. *De navibus, aedificiis et vestibus.* (Ships, their parts and equipment ;
buildings and their decoration ; garments and their ornament.)
XX. *De penu et instrumentis domesticis et rusticis.* (On wines and provisions,
and their stores and receptacles.)

at the handling of topics in the *Etymologies* one feels it to
have been a huge collection of terms and definitions.   The
actual information conveyed is very slight.   Isidore is under
the spell of words.   Were they fetishes to him ? did they
carry moral potency ?   At all events the working of his
mind reflects the long-age dominance of grammar and
rhetoric in Roman education, which treated other topics
almost as illustrations of these chief branches.[1]

[1] The exaggerated growth of grammatical and rhetorical studies is curiously
shown by the mass of words invented to indicate the various kinds of tropes and
figures.   See the list in Bede, *De schematis* (Migne 90, col. 175 *sqq.*).

CHAPTER VI

THE BARBARIC DISRUPTION OF THE EMPIRE [1]

THE Latinizing of northern Italy, Spain, and Gaul was part of the expansion of Roman dominion. Throughout these lands, alien peoples submitted to the Roman order and acquired new traits from the training of its discipline. Voluntarily or under compulsion they exchanged their institutions and customs for those of Roman Italy, and their native tongues for Latin. The education and culture of the upper classes became identical with that gained in the schools about the Forum, and Roman literature was the literature which they studied and produced. In a greater or less degree their characters were Latinized, while their traditions were abandoned for those of Rome. Yet, although Romanized and Latinized, these peoples were not Roman. Their culture was acquired, their characters were changed, yet with old traits surviving. In character and faculties, as in geographical position, they were intermediate, and in rôle they were mediatorial. Much of what they had received, and what they had themselves become, they perforce transmitted to the ruder humanity which, as the Empire weakened, pressed in, serving, plundering, murdering, and finally amalgamating with these provincials. The surviving Latin culture passed to the mingled populations which were turning to inchoate Romance nations in Italy, Spain, and Gaul. Likewise Christianity, Romanized, paganized, barbarized, had been accepted through these countries. And now these mingled peoples, these inchoate Romance nations, were to accomplish a broader mediation in extending

---

[1] Cf. Hodgkin, *Italy and her Invaders*, 8 vols. ; Villari, *The Barbarian Invasions of Italy*, 2 vols.

the rudiments of Latin culture, along with the great new Religion, to the barbarous peoples beyond the Romance pale.

The mediating rôles of the Roman provincials began with their first subjection to Roman order. For barbarians were continually brought into the provinces as slaves or prisoners of war. Next, they entered to serve as auxiliary troops, coming especially from the wavering Teutonic outskirts of the Empire. And during that time of misrule and military anarchy which came between the death of Commodus (A.D. 192) and the accession of Diocletian (A.D. 284), Teutonic inroads threatened the imperial fabric. But, apart from palpable invasions, there was a constant increase in the Teutonic inflow from the close of the second century. More and more the Teutons tilled the fields ; more and more they filled the armies. They became officers of the army and officials of the Government. So long as the vigour of life and growth continued in the Latinized population of the Empire, and so long as the Roman law and order held, the assimilative power of Latin culture and Roman institutions was enormous ; the barbarians became Romanized. But when self-conserving strength and coercive energy waned with Romans and provincials, when the law's protection was no longer sure, and a dry rot infected civic institutions, then Roman civilization lost some of its transforming virtue. The barbarism of the Teutonic influx became more obstinate as the transmuting forces of civilization weakened. Evidently the decadent civilization of the Empire could no longer raise these barbarians to the level of its greater periods ; it could at most impress them with such culture and such order as it still possessed. Moreover, reacting upon these disturbed and infirm conditions, barbarism put forth a positive transforming energy, tending to barbarize the Empire, its government, its army, its inhabitants. The decay of Roman institutions and the grafting of Teutonic institutions upon Roman survivals were as universal as the mingling of races, tempers, and traditions. The course of events may briefly be reviewed.

In the third century the Goths began, by land and sea, to raid the eastern provinces of the undivided Roman

Empire; down the Danube they sailed, and out upon the Euxine ; then their plundering fleets spread through the eastern Mediterranean.   They were attacked, repulsed, overthrown, and slaughtered in hordes in the year 270.   Some of the survivors remained in bondage, some retired north beyond the Danube.   Aurelian gave up to them the province of Dacia, the latest conquest of the Empire, the first to be abandoned.   These Dacian settlers thenceforth appear as Visigoths.   For a century the Empire had no great trouble from them.   Dacia was the scene of the career of Ulfilas (b. 311, d. 380), the Arian apostle of the Goths.   They became Christian in part, and in part remained fiercely heathen.   About 372, harassed by the Huns, they pressed south to escape over the Danube.   Valens permitted them to cross ; then Roman treachery followed, answered by desperate Gothic raids in Thrace, till at last Valens was defeated and slain at Hadrianople in 378.

It was sixteen years after this that Theodosius the Great marched from the East to Italy to suppress Arbogast, the overweening Frank, who had cast out his weak master Valentinian.   The leader of the Visigothic auxiliaries was Alaric.   When the great emperor died, Alaric was proclaimed King of the Visigoths, and soon proceeded to ravage and conquer Greece.   Stilicho, son of a Vandal chief—one sees how all the high officers are Teutons—was the uncertain stay of Theodosius's weakling sons, Honorius and Arcadius. In 400 Alaric attempted to invade Italy, but was foiled by Stilicho, who five years later circumvented and destroyed another horde of Goths, both men and women, who had penetrated Italy to the Apennines.   In 408 Alaric made a second attempt to enter, and this time was successful, for Stilicho was dead.   Thrice he besieged Rome, capturing it in 410.   Then he died, his quick death to be a warning to Attila.   The new Gothic king, Ataulf, conceived the plan of uniting Romans and Goths in a renewed and strengthened kingdom.   But this task was not for him, and in two years he left Italy with his Visigoths to establish a kingdom in the south of Gaul.

Attila comes next upon the scene.   The eastern Empire had endured the oppression of this terrible Turanian, and

had paid him tribute for some years, before he decided to
march westward by a route north of the Alps, and attack
Gaul.   He penetrated to Orleans, which he besieged in vain.
Many nations were in the two armies that were now to
meet in battle on the " Catalaunian Plains."   On Attila's
side, besides his Huns, were subject Franks, Bructeri,
Thuringians, Burgundians, and the hosts of Gepidae and
Ostrogoths.   Opposed were the Roman forces, Bretons,
Burgundians, Alans, Saxons, Salian Franks, and the army of
the Visigoths.   Defeated, but not overthrown, the lion Hun
withdrew across the Rhine ; but the next spring, in 452, he
descended from the eastern Alps upon Aquileia and destroyed
it, and next sacked the cities of Venetia and the Po Valley
as far as Milan.   Then he passed eastward to the river
Mincio, where he was met by a Roman embassy, in which
Pope Leo was the most imposing figure.   Before this
embassy the Scourge of God withdrew, awed or persuaded,
or in superstitious fear.   The following year, upon Attila's
death, his realm broke up ; Gepidae and Goths beat the
Huns in battle, and again Teutons held sway in Central
Europe.

The fear of the Hun had hardly ceased when the Vandals
came from Africa, and leisurely plundered Rome.   They
were Teutons, perhaps kin to the Goths.   But theirs had
been a far migration.   At the opening of the fifth century
they had entered Gaul and fought the Franks, then passed
on to Spain, where they were broken by the Visigoths.   So
they crossed to Africa and founded a kingdom there, whence
they invaded Italy.   By this time, the middle of the fifth
century, the fighting and ruling energy in the western
Empire was barbarian.   The stocks had become mixed
through intermarriage and the confusion of wars and
frequent change of sides.   An illustrative figure is Count
Ricimer, whose father was a noble Suevian, while his mother
was a Visigothic princess.   He directed the Roman State
from 456 to 472, placing one after another of his Roman
puppets on the imperial throne.

In the famous year 476 the Roman army was made up
of barbarians, mainly drawn from lands now included in
Bohemia, Austria, and Hungary.   There were large con-

tingents of Rugii and Heruli, who had flocked in bands to Italy as adventurers. Such troops had the status of *foederati*, that is, barbarian auxiliaries or allies. Suddenly they demanded one-third of the lands of Italy.[1] Upon refusal of their demand, they made a king from among themselves, the Herulian Odoacer, and Romulus Augustulus flitted from the shadowy imperial throne. By reason of his dramatic name, rather than by any marked circumstance of his deposition, he has come to typify with historians the close of the line of western emperors.

The Herulian soldier-king or " Patrician," Odoacer, a nondescript transition personage, ruled twelve years. Then the nation of the Ostrogoths, which had learned much from the vicissitudes of fortune in the East, obtained the eastern emperor's sanction, and made its perilous way to the gates of Italy under the king, Theodoric. This invading people numbered perhaps two hundred thousand souls ; their fighting men were forty thousand. Odoacer was beaten on the river Isonzo ; he retreated to the line of the Adige, and was again defeated at Verona. After standing a long siege in Ravenna, he made terms with Theodoric, and was murdered by him.

The Goths were among the best of the barbarians, and Theodoric was the greatest of the Goths. The eastern emperors probably regarded him as their representative in Italy ; and he coined money only with the Emperor's image. But in fact he was a sovereign ; and, through his sovereignty over both Goths and Romans, from a Teutonic king he became an absolute monarch, even as his contemporary Clovis became, under analogous circumstances. He was a just despot, with his subjects' welfare at heart. The Goths received one-third of the Italian lands, in return for which their duty was to defend the whole. This third may have been that previously possessed by Odoacer's troops. Under Theodoric the relations between Goths and " Romans " were friendly. It was from the Code of Theodosius and other Roman sources that he drew the substance of his legislation,

---

[1] This demand was not so extraordinary in view of the common Roman custom in the provinces of billeting soldiers upon the inhabitants, with the right to one-third of the house and appurtenances.

the *Edictum* which about the year 510 he promulgated for
both Goths and Romans (*barbari Romanique*).[1] His aim—
and here the influence of his minister Cassiodorus appears—
was to harmonize the relations of the two peoples and
assimilate the ways of the Goths to those of their more
civilized neighbours.   But if his rule brought prosperity to
Italy, after his death came desolating wars between the
Goths under their noble kings, and Justinian's great generals,
Belisarius and Narses.   These wars ruined the Ostrogothic
nation.   Only some remnants were left to reascend the Alps
in 553.   Behind them Italy was a waste.

An imperial eastern Roman restoration followed.   It
was not to endure.   For already the able and savage
Lombard Alboin was making ready to lead down his army
of Lombards, Saxons, Gepidae and unassorted Teutons, and
perhaps Slavs.   No strength was left to oppose him in
plague-stricken Italy.   So the Lombard conquered easily,
and set up a kingdom which, united or divided under kings
and dukes, endured for two hundred years.   Then Charlemagne—his father Pippin had been before him—at the
entreaty of the Pope, invaded Italy with a host of mingled
Teuton tribes, and put an end to the Lombard kingdom,
but not to Lombard blood and Lombard traits.

The result of all these invasions was a progressive barbarization of Italy, which was not altogether unfortunate,
because fraught with some renewal of strength.   The Teutons
brought their customs ;   and at least one Teuton people, the
Lombards, maintained them masterfully.   The Ostrogoth,
Theodoric, had preserved the Italian municipal organization,
and had drawn his code for all from Roman sources.   But
the first Lombard Code, that of King Rothari, promulgated
about 643, ignored Roman law, and apparently the very
existence of Romans.   Though written in barbarous Latin,
it is Lombard through and through.   So, to a scarcely less
degree, is the Code of King Liutprand, promulgated about
725.[2]   Even then the Lombards looked upon themselves as
distinct from the " Romans."   Their laws were still those of
the Lombards, yet of Lombards settling down to urban life.

---

[1] Cf. *post*, Chapter XXXIV., II.
[2] On the Codes see Hodgkin, *o.c.* vol. vi.

Within Lombard territories the " Romans " were subjects. In Liutprand's Code they seem to be referred to under the name of *aldii* and *aldiae*, male and female persons, who were not slaves and yet not free.   Instead of surrendering one-third of the land, the Romans were obliged to furnish one-third of its produce.   Hence their Lombard masters were interested in keeping them fixed to the soil, perhaps in a state of serfdom.   Little is known as to the intermarriage of the stocks, or when the Lombards adopted a Latin speech.[1]

It is difficult, either in Italy or elsewhere, to follow the changes and reciprocal working of Roman and Teutonic institutions through these obscure centuries.   They wrought upon each other universally, and became what neither had been before.   The Roman State was there no longer ; where the names of its officials survived they stood for altered functions.   The Roman law prevailed within the dominions of the eastern Empire and the popes.   Everywhere the crass barbarian law and the pure Roman institution was passing away, or changing into something new.   In Italy another pregnant change was taking place, the passing of the functions of government to the bishops of Rome.   Its stages are marked by the names of great men upon whose shoulders fell the authority no longer held by a remote ruler.   Leo the Great heads the embassy which turns back the Hun ; a century and a half afterwards Gregory the Great leads the opposition to the Lombards, still somewhat unkempt savages. Thereafter each succeeding pope, in fact the papacy by necessity of its position and its aspirations, opposes the Lombards when they have ceased to be either savage or Arian.   It is an absent supporter that the papacy desires, and not a rival close at hand : Charlemagne, not Desiderius.

When the Visigoths under Ataulf left Italy they passed into southern Gaul, and there established themselves with Toulouse as the centre of the Visigothic kingdom.   They soon extended their rule to Spain, with the connivance of sundry Roman rulers.   Some time before them Vandals, Suevi and Alans, having crossed the Rhine into Gaul, had been drawn across the Pyrenees by half-traitorous invitations

---

[1] The Lombard language was still spoken in the time of Paulus Diaconus (eighth century).

of rival Roman governors. The Visigoths now attacked these peoples, with the result that the Suevi retreated to the north-west of the peninsula, and at length the restless Vandals accepted the invitation of the traitor Count Boniface, and crossed to Africa. Visigothic fortunes varied under an irregular succession of non-hereditary and occasionally murdered kings. Their kingdom reached its farthest limit in the reign of Euric (466-486), who extended its boundaries northward to the Loire and southward over nearly all of Spain.[1]

Under the Visigoths the lot of the Latinized provincials, who with their ancestors had long been Roman citizens, was not a hard one. The Roman system of quartering soldiers upon provincials, with a right to one-third of the house, afforded precedent for the manner of settlement of the Visigoths and other Teuton invaders after them. The Visigoths received two-thirds not only of the houses but also of the lands, which indeed were bare of cultivators. The municipal organization of the towns was left intact, and in general the nomenclature and structure of Roman officialdom were preserved. As the Romans were the more numerous and the cleverer, they regained their wealth and social consideration. In 506, Alaric II. promulgated his famous code, the *Lex Romana Visigothorum*, usually called the " Breviarium," for his Roman subjects. Although the next year Clovis broke down the Visigothic kingdom in Gaul, and confined it to narrow limits around Narbonne, this code remained in force, a lasting source of Roman law for the inhabitants of the south and west of Gaul.[2]

---

[1] Apollinaris Sidonius, *Ep.* i. 2 (trans. by Hodgkin, *o.c.* vol. ii. 352-358), gives a sketch of a Visigothic king, Theodoric II., son of him who fell in the battle against the Huns. He ascended the throne in 453, having accomplished the murder of his brother Thorismund. In 466, he was himself slain by his brother Euric. In the meanwhile he appears to have been a good half-barbaric, half-civilized king.

[2] See *post*, Chapter XXXIV., 11. For the Visigothic kingdom of Spain the great reigns were those of Leowigild (568-586) and his son Reccared (586-601). In Justinian's time the " Roman Empire " had again made good its rule over the south of Spain. Leowigild pushed the Empire back to a narrow strip of southern coast, where there were still important cities. Save for this, he conquered all Spain, finally mastering the Suevi in the north-west. His capital was Toledo. Great as was his power, it hardly sufficed to hold in check the overweening nobles and landowners. Under the declining Empire there had sprung up a system of clientage and protection, in which the Teutons found an obstacle to the establishment of monarchies. In Spain this system hastened the downfall of the Visigothic

Throughout Visigothic Spain there existed, in conflict if not in force, a complex mass of diverse laws and customs, written and unwritten, Roman, Gothic, ecclesiastical. Soon after the middle of the seventh century a general code was compiled for both Goths and Roman provincials, between whom marriages were formally sanctioned. This codification was the legal expression of a national unity, which however had no great political vigour. For what with its inheritance of intolerable taxation, of dwindling agriculture, of enfeebled institutions and social degeneracy, the Visigothic state fell an easy victim to the Arabs in 711. It had been subject to all manner of administrative abuse. In name the government was secular. But in fact the bishops of the great sees were all-powerful to clog, if not to administer, justice and the affairs of State within their domains ; the nobles abetted them in their misgovernment. So it came that instead of a united Government supported by a strong military power, there was divided misrule, and an army without discipline or valour. This misrule was also cruelly intolerant. The bitter persecution of the Jews, and the law that none but a Catholic should live in Spain, if not causes, were at least symptoms, of a fatal impotence, and prophetic of like measures taken by later rulers in that chosen land of religious persecution.[1]

---

kingdom. Another source of trouble for Leowigild, who was still an Arian, was the opposition of the powerful Catholic clergy. Reccared, his son, changed to the Catholic or " Roman " creed, and ended the schism between the throne and the bishops.

[1] The Spanish Roman Church, which controlled or thwarted the destinies of the doomed Visigothic kingdom, was foremost among the western churches in ability and learning. It had had its martyrs in the times of pagan persecution ; it had had its universally venerated Hosius, Bishop of Cordova and prominent at the Council of Nicaea ; it had its fiercely quelled heresies and schisms ; and it had an astounding number of councils, usually held at Toledo. Its bishops were princes. Leander, Bishop of Seville, had been a tribulation to the powerful, still Arian, King Leowigild, who was compelled to banish him. That king's son, Reccared, recalled him from banishment, to preside at the Council of Toledo in 589, when the Visigothic monarchy turned to Roman Catholicism. Leander was succeeded in his more than episcopal see by his younger brother Isidore (Bishop of Seville from 600 to 636). A princely prelate, Isidore was to have still wider and more lasting fame for sanctity and learning. The last encyclopaedic scholar belonging to the antique Christian world, he became one of the great masters of the Middle Ages (see *ante*, Chapter V.). The forger and compiler of the *False Decretals* in selecting the name of Isidore rather than another to clothe that collection with authority acted under the universal veneration felt for this great Spanish Churchman.

In Gaul, contact between Latinized provincials and Teutonic invaders produced interesting results. Mingled peoples came into being, whose polity and institutions were neither Roman nor Teutonic, and whose literature and intellectual achievement were to unite the racial qualities of both. The hybrid political and social phenomena of the Frankish period were engendered by a series of events which may be outlined as follows. The Franks, Salic and Ripuarian, were clustered in the region of the lower and middle Rhine. Like other Teutonic groups dwelling near the boundaries of the weakening Empire, they were alternately plunderers of Roman territory and auxiliaries in the imperial army, or its independent allies against Huns or Saxons or Alans. One Childeric, whose career opens in saga and ends in history, was king or hereditary leader of a part of the Salian Franks. This active man appears in frequent relations with Aegidius, the half-independent Roman ruler of that north-western portion of Gaul which was not held by Visigoths or Burgundians. If Childeric's forefathers had oftener been enemies than allies of the Empire, he was its ally, and perhaps commander of the forces which helped to preserve this outlying portion of its territory.

Aegidius died in 463, and the territories ruled by him passed to his son Syagrius practically as an independent kingdom. Childeric in the next eighteen years increased his power among the Salian Franks, and extended his territories through victories over other Teutonic groups. Upon his death in 481 his kingdom passed to his son Chlodoweg, or, as it is easier to call him, Clovis, then in his sixteenth year. The next five years were employed by this precocious genius of barbarian craft in strengthening his kingship among the Salians. At the age of twenty he attacked Syagrius, and overthrew his power at Soissons. The last Roman ruler of a part of Gaul fled to the Visigoths for refuge : their king delivered him to Clovis, who had him killed. So Clovis's realm was extended first to the Seine and then to the Loire. The Gallo-Romans were not driven out or dispossessed, but received a new master, who on his part treated them forbearingly and accepted them as subjects.

The royal domains of Syagrius perhaps were large enough to satisfy the cupidity of the victors.

Clovis was now king of Gallo-Romans as well as Salian Franks. Thus strengthened he could fight other Franks with success, and carry on a great war against the Alemanni to the south-east. At the " battle of Tolbiac," in which he finally overthrew these people, the heathen Frank invoked the Christian God (so tells Gregory of Tours), and vowed to accept the Faith if Christ gave him the victory. This is like the legend of Constantine at the battle of the Mulvian Bridge, nor is the probability of its essential truth lessened because of this resemblance. Both Roman emperor and Frankish king turned from heathenism to Christianity as to the stronger supernatural support. And if ever man received tenfold reward in this world from his faith it was this treacherous and bloody Frank.

Hitherto the Teuton tribes, Visigoths, Ostrogoths, Vandals, Burgundians who had accepted Christianity, were Arians by reason of the circumstances of their " conversion." On the other hand, the Romanized inhabitants of Italy, Spain, and Gaul were Catholics, and the influence of their Arian-hating clergy was enormous. Evidently when Clovis, under the influence of Catholic bishops and a Catholic wife, became a Catholic, the power of the Church and the sympathy of the laity would make his power irresistible. For the Catholic population was greatly in the majority, even in the countries held by Burgundian or Visigothic kings. The Burgundian rulers had half turned to Catholicism, and the Visigothic monarchy treated it with respect. Yet the Burgundian kings did not win the Church's confidence, nor did the Visigoths disarm its active hostility. With such ability as Clovis and his sons possessed, their conversion to Catholicism ensured victory over their rivals, and made a bond of friendship between them and their Gallo-Roman subjects.[1]

The extension of Clovis's kingdom, his overthrow of the Visigothic power, his partial conquest of the Burgundians, would have been even more rapid and decisive but for the opposing diplomacy of the great Arian ruler, Theodoric the

---

[1] Marriages between Romans and Franks were legalized as early as 497.

Ostrogoth, whose prestige and power even the bold Frank dared not defy. Moreover, the Burgundians stood well with their Roman subjects, whom they treated generously, and permitted to live under a code of Roman law. When it came to war between them and Clovis, the advantage rested with the latter ; but possibly the fear of Theodoric, or the pressure of war with the Alemanni, deferred the final conquest of the Burgundian kingdom for another generation.

In 507 Clovis attacked the Visigothic kingdom, and incorporated it with his dominions in the course of the next year. Whether or not he had cried out, in the words of Gregory of Tours, " it is a shame that these Arians should hold a part of Gaul ; let us attack them with God's help and take their land," at all events the war had a religious sanction, and its successful issue was facilitated by the Catholic clergy within the Visigothic territory. Clovis's career was now nearing its end. In his last years, by treachery, murder, and open war when needed, he made himself king of all the Franks, Ripuarian and Salian. The intense partisan sympathy of the Church for this its eldest royal Teuton son speaks in the words of Gregory of Tours, concluding his recital of these deeds of incomparable villainy : " Thus day by day God cast down his (Clovis's) enemies before him, because he did what was right in His eyes " !

The unresting sons and grandsons of Clovis not only conquered Burgundy, but extended their rule far to the east, into the heart of Germany, and Merovingians became masters of Thuringia and Bavaria. That such a realm should hold together was impossible. From Clovis to Charlemagne it was the regular practice to divide the realm at death among the ruler's sons, and for the ablest among them to pursue and slay the others, and so unite the realm again. Besides this principle of internecine conflict, differences of race and language and degrees of Latinization ensured eventual disruption.

Nothing passes away, and very little quite begins, but all things change ; and so the verity of social and political phenomena lies in the *becoming*, rather than in any temporary phase—as one may perceive in the Merovingian, later Carolingian, *regnum Francorum*. Therein Roman institutions survived either as decayed actualities or as names or effigies ; therein were conditions and even institutions which arose and were developed through the decay of previous institutions, through the weakening of the imperial peace and justice, the growth of abuses, and the need of the weak to put themselves under the protection of the nearest strong. This huge conglomerate of a government also held sturdy Teuton elements. There was the kingship and the strong body of personal followers, the latter an outgrowth of the *comitatus*, or rather of the needs of any barbaric chieftaincy. There was *wergeld*, not so much exclusively a Teutonic institution, as belonging to a rough society which sees the need of checking feuds, and finds the means in a system of compensation to the injured person or his kin, who would otherwise make reprisals ; there was also *Sippe*, the rights and duties of kin among themselves, and of the kinship as a corporate unit toward the world without ; and therein, in general, was continuance of the warrior spirit of the Franks and other Teutons, of their social ways and mode of dress, of their methods of warfare and their thoughts of barbaric hardihood.

These elements, and much more besides, were in process of mutual interplay and amalgamation. Childeric had been king of some of the Salian Franks, and had allied himself with the last fragment of the Roman Empire in Gaul. Clovis, his son, is greater : he makes himself king of more Franks, and becomes the head of the Roman-Frankish combination by overthrowing Syagrius and taking his place as lord of the Gallo-Romans. As towards them he becomes even as Syagrius and the emperors before him, absolute ruler, *princeps*. This authority enhanced the dignity of Clovis's kingship over his own Franks and the Alemanni, and his personal power increased with each new conquest. He became a novel sort of monarch, combining heterogeneous prerogatives. Hence his sovereignty and that of his successors was not a simple development of Teutonic kingship, nor was it a continuation of Roman imperial or proconsular rule, but rather a new composite evolution. Some of its contradictions and anomalies were symbolized by Clovis's acceptance of the title of Consul and stamping the effigies of the eastern emperors upon his coins—as if they held any power in the *regnum Francorum* ! As between Gallo-Romans and Franks, the headship had gone over to the latter ; yet there was neither hatred on the one side nor oppression from the other. A common catholicism and many similarities of condition promoted mutual sympathy and union. For example, through the decay of the imperial power, oppression had increased, and the common Gallo-Roman people were compelled to place themselves under the patronage of powerful personages who could give them the protection which they could no longer look for from the Government. So relationships of personal dependence developed, not essentially dissimilar from those subsisting between the Franks and their kings, when the kings were mere leaders of small tribes or war bands. But the vastness of the Salian realm impaired the personal relationship between king and subjects, and again the latter, Frankish or Gallo-Roman, needed nearer protectors, and found them in neighbouring great proprietors and functionaries, Frankish or Gallo-Roman as the case might be.[1]

Through all the turmoil of the Merovingian period, there was doubtless individual injustice and hardship everywhere, but no racial tyranny. The Gallo-Roman kept his language and property, and continued to live under the Roman law. He was not inferior to the Frank, except that the latter was entitled to a higher *wergeld* for personal injury, which, how-ever, soon was equalized. The Frank also lived under his own law, Salic or Ripuarian. But the general mingling of peoples in the end made it impossible to distinguish the law personally applicable ; and thereupon, both as to Franks and Gallo-Romans, the territorial law superseded the law of race.[2] And when, after two centuries, the Merovingian kingdom, through change of dynasty, became the Caro-lingian, political discrepancies between Frank and Gallo-Roman had passed away. Yet this huge colossus of a realm with its shoulders of iron and its feet of clay, still included enough disparities of race and land, language and institution, to ensure its dissolution.

---

[1] See Flach, *Les Origines de l'ancienne France*, vol. i. chap. i. *sqq.* (Paris, 1886).
[2] See *post*, Chapter XXXIV., II.

CHAPTER VII

THE CELTIC STRAIN IN GAUL AND IRELAND

THE northern races who were to form part of the currents of mediaeval life are grouped under the names of Celts and Teutons.[1] The chief sections of the former, dwelling in northern Italy and Gaul and Spain, were Latinized and then Christianized long before the mediaeval period, and themselves helped to create the patristic and even the antique side of the mediaeval patrimony. Their rôle was largely mediatorial, and geographically, as well as in their

[1] The physiological criterion of a race is consanguinity. But unfortunately racial lineage soon loses itself in obscurity. Moreover, during periods as to which we have some knowledge, no race has continued pure from alien admixture ; and every people that has taken part in the world's advance has been acted upon by foreign influences from its prehistoric beginnings throughout the entire course of its history. Indeed, foreign suggestions and contact with other peoples appear essential to tribal or national progress. For the historian there exists no pure and unmixed race, and even the conception of one becomes self-contradictory. To him a race is a group of people, presumably related in some way by blood, who appear to transmit from generation to generation a common heritage of culture and like physical and spiritual traits. He observes that the transmitted characteristics of such a group may weaken or dissipate before foreign influence, and much more as the group scatters among other people ; or again he sees its distinguishing traits becoming clearer as the members draw to a closer national unity under the action of a common physical environment, common institutions, and a common speech. The historian will not accept as conclusive any single kind of evidence regarding race. He may attach weight to complexion, stature, and shape of skull, and yet find their interpretation quite perplexing when compared with other evidence, historical or linguistic. He will consider customs and implements, and yet remember that customs may be borrowed, and implements are often of foreign pattern. Language affords him the most enticing criterion, but one of the most deceptive. It is a matter of observation that when two peoples of different tongues meet together, they may mingle their blood through marriage, combine their customs, and adopt each other's utensils and ornaments ; but the two languages will not structurally unite : one will supplant the other. The language may thus be more single in source than the people speaking it ; though, conversely, people of the same race, by reason of special circumstances, may not speak the same tongue. Hence linguistic unity is not conclusive evidence of unity of race.

time of receiving Latin culture, they were intermediaries between the classic sources and the Teutons, who also were to drink of these magic draughts, but not so deeply as to be transformed to Latin peoples. The rôle of the Teutons in the mediaeval evolution was to accept Christianity and learn something of the pagan antique, and then to react upon what they had received and change it in their natures.

Central Europe seems to have been the early home alike of Celts and Teutons. Thence successive migratory groups appear to have passed westwardly and southerly. Both races spoke Aryan tongues, and according to the earliest notices of classic writers resembled each other physically— large, blue-eyed, with yellow or tawny hair. The more penetrating accounts of Caesar and Tacitus disclose their distinctive racial traits, which contrast still more clearly in the remains of the early Celtic (Irish) and Teutonic litera- tures. Whatever were the ethnological affinities between Celt and Teuton, and however imperceptibly these races may have shaded into each other, for example, in northern France and Belgium, their characters were different, and their opposing racial traits have never ceased to display themselves in the literature as well as in the political and social history of western Europe.

The time and the manner of the Celtic occupation of Gaul and Spain remain obscure.[1] It took place long before the turmoils of the second century B.C., when the Teutonic tribes began to assert themselves, probably in the north of the present Germany, and to press south-westwardly upon Celtic neighbours on both sides of the Rhine. Some of them pushed on towards lands held by the Belgae, and then passed southward toward Aquitania, drawing Belgic and Celtic peoples with them. Afterwards turning eastwardly they invaded the Roman Provincia in southern Gaul, and through their victories threatened the great Republic. This

---

[1] As to the Celts in Gaul and elsewhere, and the early non-Celtic population of Gaul, see A. Bertrand, *La Gaule avant les Gaulois* (Paris, 1891) ; *La Religion des Gaulois* (Paris, 1897) ; *Les Celtes dans les vallées du Pô et du Danube* (in con- junction with S. Reinach) ; D'Arbois de Jubainville, *Les Premiers Habitants de l'Europe* (second edition, Paris, 1894) ; Fustel de Coulanges, *Institutions politiques de l'ancienne France* (Paris, 1891) ; Karl Müllenhoff, *Deutsche Altertumskunde*, Bde. I. and II. ; Zupitza, " Kelten und Gallier," *Zeitschrift für keltische Philologie*, 1902.

was the peril of the Cimbri and Teutones, which Marius quelled by the waters of the Durance and then among the hills of Piedmont. The invasion did not change the ethnology of Gaul, which, however, was not altogether Celtic in Caesar's time. The opening sentences of his *Commentaries* indicate anything but racial unity. The Roman province was mainly Ligurian in blood. West of the province, between the Pyrenees and the Garonne, were the " Aquitani," chiefly of Iberian stock. The Celtae, whose western boundary was the ocean, reached from the Garonne as far north as the Seine, and eastwardly across the centre of Gaul to the head waters of the Rhine. North of them were the Belgae, extending from the Seine and the British Channel to the lower Rhine. These Belgae also apparently were Celts, and yet, as their lands touched those of the Germans on the Rhine, they naturally show Teutonic affinities, and some of their tribes contained strains of Teuton blood. But it is not blood alone that makes the race ; and Gaul, with its dominant Celtic element, was making Gauls out of all these peoples. At all events a common likeness may be discerned in the picture of Gallic traits which Caesar gives.[1]

Gallic civilization had then advanced as far as the native political incapacity of the Gauls would permit. Quick-witted and intelligent, they were to gain from Rome the discipline they needed. Once accustomed to the enforcement of a stable order, their finer qualities responded by a ready acceptance of the benefits of civilization and a rapid appropriation of Latin culture. Not a sentence of the Gallic literature survives. But that this people were endowed with eloquence and possessed of a sense of form, was to be shown by works in their adopted tongue.[2] Romanized and Latinized, they were converted to Christianity and then renewed with fresh Teutonic blood. So they enter upon the

[1] See *ante*, Chapter II.

[2] The Latin literature produced by their descendants in the fourth century is usually good in form, whatever other qualities it lack. This statement applies to the works of the nominally Christian, but really pagan, rhetorician and poet, Ausonius, born in 310, at Bordeaux, of mingled Aquitanian and Aeduan blood ; likewise to the poems of Paulinus of Nola, born at the same town, in 353, and to the prose of Sulpicius Severus, also born in Aquitaine a little after. In the fifth century, Avitus, an Auvernian, Bishop of Vienne, and Apollinaris Sidonius continue the Gallo-Latin strain in literature.

CHAP. VII   CELTIC STRAINS   127

mediaeval period ; and when, after the millennial year, the
voices of the Middle Ages cease simply to utter the barbaric
or echo the antique, it becomes clear that nowhere is there
a happier balance of intellectual faculty and emotional
capacity than in these peoples of mingled stock who long
had dwelt in the country which we know as France.

Since the Celts of Gaul have left no witness of themselves
in Gallic institutions or literature, it is necessary to turn to
Ireland for clearer evidence of Celtic qualities. There one
may see what might come of a predominantly Celtic people
who lacked the lesson of Roman conquest and the discipline
of Roman order. The early history of the Irish, their
presentation of themselves in imaginative literature, their
attainment in learning and accomplishment in art, are not
unlike what might have been expected from Caesar's Gauls
under similar conditions of comparative isolation. Irish
history displays the social turmoil and barbarism resulting
from insular aggravation of the Celtic weaknesses noticeable
in Caesar's sketch ; and the same are carried to burlesque
excess in the old Irish literature. On the other hand, Irish
qualities of temperament and mind bear such fair fruit in
literature and art as might be imagined springing from the
Gallic stem but for the Roman graft.[1]

No trustworthy story can be put together from the myth,
tradition, and conscious fiction which record the unpro-

[1] Without hazarding a discussion of the origin of the Irish, of their proportion
of Celtic blood, or their exact relation to the Celts of the Continent, it may in a
general way· be said, that Ireland and Great Britain were inhabited by a prehistoric and pre-Celtic people. The Celts came from the Continent, conquered
them, and probably intermarried with them. The Celtic inflow may have begun
in the sixth century before Christ, and perhaps continued until shortly before
Caesar's time. Evidences of language point to a dual Celtic stock, Goidelic and
Brythonic. It may be surmised that the former was the first to arrive. The
Celtic dialect spoken by them is now represented by the Gaelic of Ireland, Man,
and Scotland. The Brythonic is still represented by the speech of Wales and
the Armoric dialects of Brittany. This was the language of the Britons who
fought with Caesar, and were subdued by later Roman generals. After the
Roman time they were either pressed back into Wales and Cornwall by Angles,
Jutes, and Saxons, or were absorbed among these conquering Teutons. Probably
Caesar was correct in asserting the close affinity of the Britons with the Belgic
tribes of the Continent. See the opening chapters of Rhys and Brynmor-Jones's
Welsh People ; also Rhys's *Early Britain* (London, 1882) ; Zupitza, " Kelten und
Gallier," *Zeitschrift fur keltische Phil.*, 1902 ; T. H. Huxley, " On some Fixed
Points in British Ethnology," *Contemporary Review* for 1871, reprinted in *Essays*
(Appleton's, 1894) ; Ripley, *Races of Europe*, chap. xii. (New York, 1899).

gressive turbulence of pre-Christian Ireland.   But the Irish
character and capacities are clearly mirrored in this enormous
Gaelic literature.   Truculence and vanity pervade it, and a
passion for hyperbole.   A weak sense of fact and a lack of
steady rational purpose are also conspicuous.   It is as
ferocious as may be.   Yet, withal, it keeps the charm of the
Irish temperament.   Its pathos is moving, even lovely.
Some of the poetry has a mystic sensuousness ; the lines
fall on the ear like the lapping of ripples on an unseen shore ;
the imagery has a fantastic and romantic beauty, and the
reader is wafted along on waves of temperament and feeling.[1]

Whatever themes sprang from the pagan age, probably
nothing was written down before the Christian time, when
Christian matter might be foisted into the pagan story.
The sagas belonging to the so-called Ulster Cycle afford the
best illustration of early Irish traits.[2]   They reflect a society

[1] The Irish art of illumination presents analogies to the literature. The
finesse of design and execution in the *Book of Kells* (seventh century) is astonishing.
Equally marvellous was the work of Irish goldsmiths.   Both arts doubtless made
use of designs common upon the Continent, and may even have drawn suggestions
from Byzantine or late Roman patterns.   Nevertheless, illumination and the
goldsmith's art in Ireland are characteristically Irish and the very climax of
barbaric fashions.   Their forms pointed to nothing further.   These astounding
spirals, meanders, and interlacings, combined with utterly fantastic and impossible
drawings of the human form, required essential modification before they were
suited to form part of that organic development of mediaeval art which followed
its earlier imitative periods.

Irish illumination was carried by Columba to Iona, and spread thence through
many monasteries in the northern part of Britain.   It was imitated in the Anglo-
Saxon monasteries of Northumbria, and from them passed with Alcuin to the
Court of Charlemagne.   Through these transplantings the Irish art was changed,
under the hands of men conversant with Byzantine and later Roman art.   The
influence of the art also worked outward from Irish monasteries upon the
Continent, St. Gall, for example.   The Irish goldsmith's art likewise passed into
Saxon England, into Carolingian France, and into Scandinavia.   See J. H.
Middleton, *Illuminated Manuscripts* (Cambridge Univ. Press, 1892), and the
different view as to the sources of Irish illuminating art in Muntz, *Études
iconographiques* (Paris, 1887) ;   also Kraus, *Geschichte der christlichen Kunst*, i.
607-619 ;   Margaret Stokes, *Early Christian Art in Ireland* (South Kensington
Museum Art Hand-Books, 1894), vol. i. p. 32 *sqq.*, and vol. ii. pp. 73, 78 ; Sophus
Müller, *Nordische Altertumskunde*, vol. ii. chap. xiv. (Strassburg, 1898).

[2] The classification of ancient Irish literature is largely the work of O'Curry,
Lectures on the Manuscript Materials of Ancient Irish History (Dublin, 1861,
2nd ed., 1878).   See also D. Hyde, *A Literary History of Ireland*, chaps. xxi.-xxix.
(London, 1899) ;   D'Arbois de Jubainville, *Introduction à l'étude de la littérature
celtique*, chap. préliminaire (Paris, 1883).   The tales of the Ulster Cycle, in the
main, antedate the coming of the Norsemen in the eighth century ; but the later
redactions seem to reflect Norse customs ; see Pflugk-Hartung, in *Revue celtique,*
t. xiii. (1892), p. 170 *sqq.*

apparently at the " Homeric " stage of development, though the Irish heroes suffer in comparison with the Greek by reason of the immeasurable inferiority of these Gaelic Sagas to the *Iliad* and *Odyssey*.   There is the same custom of fighting from chariots, the same tried charioteer, the hero's closest friend, and the same unstable relationship between the chieftains and the king.[1]

The Achilles of the Ulster Cycle is Cuchulain.   The Tain Bo Cuailgne (Englished rather improperly as the " Cattle-raid of Cooley ") is the long and famous Saga that brings his glory to its height.[2]   Other Sagas tell of his mysterious birth, his youthful deeds, his wooing, his various feats, and then the moving, fateful story of his death.   Loved by many women, cherished by heroes, beautiful in face and form, possessed of strength, agility, and skill in arms beyond belief, uncontrolled, chivalric, his battle-ardour unquenchable, he is a brilliant epic hero.   But his story is weakened by hyperbole.   Even to-day we know how sword-strokes and spear-thrust kill.   So do great narrators, who likewise realize the literary power of truth.   Through the *Iliad* there is no combat between heroes where spear and sword do not pierce and kill as they do in fact.   So in the Sagas of the Norse, the man falls before the mortal blow.   But in the Ulster Cycle, day after day, two heroes may mangle each other in every impossible and fantastic way, beyond the bounds of the faintest shadow of verisimilitude.[3]   In

[1] This comparison with Homeric society might be extended so as to include the Celts of Britain and Gaul. Close affinities appear between the Gauls and the personages of the Ulster Cycle. Several of its Sagas have to do with the " hero's portion " awarded to the bravest warrior at the feast, a source of much pleasant trouble. Posidonius, writing in the time of Cicero, mentions the same custom among the Celts of Gaul (Didot-Müller, *Fragmenta hist. Graec.* t. iii. p. 260, col. 1 ; D'Arbois de Jubainville, *Introduction*, etc., pp. 297, 298).

[2] Probably first written down in the seventh century. Some of the Cuchulain Sagas are rendered by D'Arbois de Jubainville, *Épopée celtique* ; they are given popularly in E. Hull's Cuchulain Saga (D. Nutt, London, 1898). Also to some extent in Hyde's *Lit. Hist., etc.*

[3] See the famous Battle of the Ford between Cuchulain and Ferdiad (Hyde, *Lit. Hist. of Ireland*, pp. 328-334). A more burlesque hyperbole is that of the three caldrons of cold water prepared for Cuchulain to cool his battle-heat ; when he was plunged in the first, it boiled ; plunged into the second, no one could hold his hand in it ; but in the third, the water became tepid (D'Arbois de Jubainville, *Épopée celtique*, p. 204).

this weakness of hyperbole the Irish Sagas are outdone only by the monstrous doings of the epics of India.

Besides hyperbole, Irish tales display another weakness, which is not unpleasing, although an element of failure both in the people and their literature. This is the quality of non-arrival. Some old tales evince it in the unsteadfast purpose of the narrative, the hero quite forgetting the initial motive of his action. In the *Voyage of Maeldun*, for instance, a son sets out upon the ocean to seek his father's murderers, a motive which is lost sight of amid the marvels of the voyage.[1] As may be imagined, qualities of vanity, truculence, irrationality, hyperbole, and non-arrival or lack of sequence, frequently impart an air of *bouffe* to the Irish Sagas, making them humorous beyond the intention of their composers.[2]

Yet true heroic notes are to be heard.[3] And however rare the tales which have not the makings of a brawl on every page, these truculent Sagas sometimes speak with power and pathos, and sweetly present the loveliness of nature or the charms of women ; all in a manner happily indicative of the impressionable Irish temperament. Examples are the moving tales of *The Children of Usnach* and the *Pursuit of Diarmuid and Grainne*.[4] They bring to

[1] Certain interpolated Christian chapters at the end tell how Maeldun is led to forgive the murderers—an idea certainly foreign to the original pagan story, which may perhaps have had its own ending. The tale is translated in P. W. Joyce, *Old Celtic Romances* (London, 1894), and by F. Lot in D'Arbois de Jubainville's *Épopée celtique*, pp. 449-500.

[2] Perhaps no one of the Ulster Sagas exhibits these qualities more amusingly than *The Feast of Bricriu*, a tale in which contention for the " hero's portion " is the leading motive. Its *personae* are the men and women who constantly appear and reappear throughout this cycle. In this Saga they act and speak admirably in character, and some of the descriptions bring the very man before our eyes. It is translated by George Henderson, Vol. II. Irish Texts Society (London, 1899), and also by D'Arbois de Jubainville in his *Épopée celtique* (Paris, 1892).

[3] For example, in a historical Saga the great King Brian speaks, fighting against the Norsemen : " O God . . . retreat becomes us not, and I myself know I shall not leave this place alive ; and what would it profit me if I did ? For Aibhell of Grey Crag came to me last night, and told me that I should be killed this day."

[4] " Deirdre, or the Fate of the Sons of Usnach," is rendered in E. Hull's *Cuchulain Saga*; Hyde, *Lit. Hist.*, chap. xxv., and D'Arbois de Jubainville, *Épopée celtique*, pp. 217-319. *The Pursuit of Diarmuid and Grainne* was edited by O'Duffy for the Society for the Preservation of the Irish Language (Dublin, Gill and Son, 1895), and less completely in Joyce's *Old Celtic Romances* (London, 1894).

mind the Tristram story, which grew up among a kindred
people. The first of them only belongs to the Ulster Cycle.
Both are stories of a beautiful and headstrong maiden
betrothed to an old king. Each maid rebels against union
with an old man ; each falls in love with a young hero, and,
unabashed, asks him to flee with her. In the former tale
the heroine's charms win the hero, while in the latter he is
overcome by the violent insistence of a woman not to be
gainsaid. In both stories love brings the hero to his death.

The Irish genius also showed an aptitude for lyric expression, and at an early period developed elaborate modes
of rhymed and alliterative verse.[1] Peculiarly beautiful
are the poems descriptive of nature [2] and those reflecting
the Gaelic belief in a future life. A charming description
of Elysium is offered by *The Voyage of Bran*, a Saga of the
Otherworld, dating from the seventh century. Its verse
portions preponderate, the prose serving as their frame.[3]
But it opens in prose, telling how one day, walking near his
stronghold, Bran heard sweet music behind him, and as
often as he turned the music was still behind him. He fell
asleep at last from the sweetness of the strains. When he
awoke, he found by him a branch silvery with white blossoms.
He took it to his home, where was seen a woman who sang :

> " A branch of the apple-tree from Emain I bring ;
>   Twigs of white silver are on it,
>   Crystal boughs with blossoms.
>   There is a distant isle,
>   Around which sea-horses (waves) glisten : "

And the woman sings on, picturing " Mag Mell of many
flowers," and of the host ever rowing thither from across
the sea ; till at last Bran and his people set forth in their
boat and row on and on, till they are welcomed by sweet
women with music and wine in island-fields of flowers and
bird-song. There is no sad strain in the music from this
Gaelic land beyond the grave.

[1] Cf. Hyde, *o.c.*, chaps. xxi., xxxvi.
[2] For examples see Kuno Meyer, *Selections from Ancient Irish Poetry* (Constable,
1911).
[3] *The Voyage of Bran*, edited and translated by Kuno Meyer, with essays on
the *Celtic Otherworld*, by Alfred Nutt (2 vols., David Nutt, London, 1895). A
Saga usually is prose interspersed with lyric verses at critical points of the story.

Irish traits observed in poem and Saga are reflected in accounts of not improbable events, and exemplified in Christian saints ; for the Irish did not change their spots upon conversion. How Christianity failed to affect the manners of the ancient Irish is illustrated in the story of the Cursing of Tara, where tradition says the high-kings of Ireland held sway. The account is scarcely historical ; yet Tara existed, and fell to decay in the sixth century.[1] Its cursing was on this wise. King Dermot was high-king of Ireland. His laws were obeyed throughout the land, and over its length and breadth marched his spear-bearer asserting the royal authority, and holding the king's spear across his body before him. Every town and castle must open wide enough to let this spear pass, carried crosswise. The spear-bearer comes to the strong house of Aedh. He finds the outer palisade breached to let the spear through, but not the inner house. The bearer demands that it be torn open. " Order it so as to please thyself," quoth Aedh, as he smote off his head.

King Dermot sent his men to lay waste to Aedh's land and seize his person. Aedh flees, and at last takes refuge with St. Ruadhan. The king again sends messengers, but they are foiled, till he comes himself, seizes the outlaw, and carries him off to hang him at Tara. Thereupon St. Ruadhan seeks St. Brendan of Birr and others. They proceed to Tara and demand the prisoner. The king answers that the Church cannot protect lawbreakers. So all the clergy rang their bells and chanted psalms against the king before Tara, and fasted on him (in order that their imprecations might be more potent), and he fasted on them. King and clergy fasted on each other, till one night the clergy made a show of eating in sight of the town, but passed the meat and ale beneath their cowls. So the king was tricked into taking meat ; and an evil dream came to him, by which he knew the clergy would succeed in destroying his kingdom.

In the morning the king went and said to the clergy : " Ill have ye done to undo my kingdom, because I main-

---

[1] On Tara, see Index in O'Curry's *Manners and Customs of the Ancient Irish* ; also Hyde, *Literary History*, pp. 126-130. For this story, see O'Grady, *Silva Gaedelica*, pp. 77-88 (London, 1892) ; Hyde, pp. 226-232.

CELTIC STRAINS

tained the righteous cause. Be thy diocese, Ruadhan, the first one ruined, and may thy monks desert thee."

Said the saint : " May thy kingdom droop speedily."

Said the king : " Thy see shall be empty, and swine shall root up thy churchyards."

Said the saint : " Tara shall be desolate, and therein shall no dwelling be for ever."

It was the custom of ancient bards to utter an imprecation or " satire " against those offending them.[1] The irate fasting and cursing by the Irish clergy was a thinly Christianized continuation of the same Irish habit, inspired by the same Irish temper. There was no chasm between the pagan bards and the Christian clergy, who loved the Sagas and preserved them. They had also their predecessors in the Druids, who had performed the functions of diviners, magicians, priests, and teachers, which were assumed by the clergy in the fifth and sixth centuries.[2] Doubtless many of the Druids became monks.

Christianity came to the Irish as a new ardour, effacing none of their characteristics. Irish monks and Irish saints were as irascible as Irish bards and Saga heroes. The Irish temper lived on in St. Columba of Iona and St. Columbanus of Luxeuil and Bobbio. Both of these men left Ireland to spread monastic Christianity, and also because, as Irishmen, they loved to rove, like their forefathers. Christianity furnished this Irish propensity with a definite aim in the mission-passion to convert the heathen. It likewise brought the ascetic hermit-passion, which drove these travel-loving islanders over the sea in search of solitude ; and so a yearning came on Irish monks to sail forth to some distant isle and gain within the seclusion of the sea a hermitage beyond the reach of man. There are many stories of these explorers. They sailed along the Hebrides, they settled on the Shetland Islands, they reached the Faroes, and even brought back news of Iceland. But before the seventh century closed, their sea hermitages

[1] See D'Arbois de Jubainville, *Introduction à la litt. celtique*, pp. 259-271 (Paris, 1883).
[2] See D'Arbois de Jubainville, *Introduction*, etc., p. 129 *sqq.* ; Bertrand, *La Religion des Gaulois*, chap. xx. (Paris, 1897). Also O'Curry, *o.c. passim.*

were harried by Norsemen who were sailing upon quite different ventures. From an opposite direction they too had reached the Shetlands and the Hebrides, and had pushed on farther south among the islands off the west coast of Scotland. So there come sorry tales of monks fleeing from one island to another. These harryings and flights had gone on for a century and more before the Vikings landed in Ireland, apparently for the first time, in 795.[1] There followed two centuries of fierce struggle with the invaders, during which much besides blows was exchanged. Vikings and Irish learned from each other; Norse strains passed into Irish literature, and conversely the Norse story-tellers probably obtained the Saga form of composition.

The rôle of the Irish in the diffusion of Christianity with its accompaniment of Latin culture will be noted hereafter, and a sketch of the unquestionably Irish saint Columbanus will be given in illustration. A few paragraphs on his almost namesake of Iona, whose career hardly extended beyond Celtic circles, may fitly close the present chapter on the Celtic genius. In him is seen the truculent Irishman and the clan-abbot of royal birth, violent, dominating by his impetuosity and the strident fervour of his voice; also the saint, devoted, loving, to his followers. Colum,[2] surnamed Cille, " of the church," from his incessant devotions,

---

[1] For this whole story see H. Zimmer, " Über die frühesten Berührungen der Iren mit den Nordgermanen," *Sitzungsbericht der Preussischen Akad.*, 1891 (1), pp. 279-317.

[2] For the life of Saint Columba the chief source is the *Vita* by Adamnan, his eighth successor as abbot of Iona. It contains well-drawn sketches of the saint and much that is marvellous and incredible. It was edited with elaborate notes by Dr. W. Reeves, for the Irish Archaeological Society, in 1857. His work, rearranged and with a translation of the *Vita*, was republished as Vol. VI. of *The Historians of Scotland* (Edinburgh, 1874); it has also been edited by J. T. Fowler (Oxford, 1894). The *Vita* may also be found in Migne, *Patrologia Latina*, 88, col. 725-776. Bede, *Ecc. Hist.* iii. 4, refers to Columba. The Gaelic life from the *Book of Lismore* is published, with a translation by M. Stokes, *Anecdota Oxoniensia* (Oxford, Clarendon Press, 1890). The Bodleian Eulogy, *i.e.* the *Amra Choluim chille*, was published, with translation by M. Stokes, in *Revue celtique*, t. xx. (1899); as to its date, see *Rev. celtique*, t. xvii. p. 41. Another (later) Gaelic life has been published by R. Henebry in the *Zeitschrift für celtische Philologie*, 1901, and later. There is an interesting article on the hymns ascribed to Columba in *Blackwood's Magazine* for September 1899. See also Cuissard, *Rev. celtique*, t. v. p. 207. The hymns themselves are in Dr. Todd's *Liber Hymnorum*. Montalembert's *Monks of the West*, book ix. (vol. iii. Eng. trans.), gives a long, readable, and uncritical account of " St. Columba, the Apostle of Caledonia."

and by his Latin name known as Columba, was born at
Gartan, Donegal, in the extreme north-west of Ireland,
about the year 520. His family was chief in that part of the
country, and through both his parents he was descended
from kings. He does not belong to those early Irish saints
represented by Patrick and his storied coadjutors of both
sexes, whose missionary activities were not constrained
within any ascetic rule ; but to the later generation who
lived in those monastic communities which were so very
typically Irish.[1]

Columba appears to have passed his youth wandering
from one monastery to another, and his manhood in founding
them. But so strong a nature could not hold aloof from the
wars of his clan, which belonged to the northern branch of
the Hy-neill race, then maintaining its independence against
the southern branch. The head of the latter was that very
King Dermot (usually called Diarmaid or Diarmuid) against
whom St. Ruadhan [2] and the clergy fasted and rang their

[1] The Irish monastery was ordered as an Irish clan, and indeed might be a
clan monastically ordered. At the head was an abbot, not elected by the monks,
but usually appointed by the preceding abbot from his own family, as an Irish
king appointed his successor. The monks ordinarily belonged to the abbot's clan.
They lived in an assemblage of huts. Some devoted themselves to contemplation,
prayer, and writing ; more to manual labour. There were recluses among
them. Besides the monks other members of the clan living near the " monastery "
owed it duties and were entitled to its protection and spiritual ministration.
The abbot might be an ordained priest ; he rarely was a bishop, though he had
bishops under him who at his bidding performed such episcopal functions as that
of ordination. But he was the ruler, lay as well as spiritual. Not infrequently
he also was a king. Although there was no common ordering of Irish monasteries,
a head monastery might bear rule over its daughter foundations, as did Columba's
primal monastery of Iona over those in Ireland or Northern Britain which owed
their origin to him. Irish monasteries might march with their clan on military
expeditions, or carry on a war of monastery against monastery. " A.D. 763. A
battle was fought at Argamoyn, between the fraternities of Clonmacnois and
Durrow, where Dermod Duff, son of Donnell, was killed with 200 men of the
fraternity of Durrow. Bresal, son of Murchadh, with the fraternity of Clonmacnois,
was victor " (Ancient Annals). This entry is not alone, for there is another one
of the year 816, in which a " fraternity of Columcille " seems to have been worsted
in battle, and then to have gone " to Tara to curse " the reigning king. See
Reeve's Adamnan's Life of Columba, p. 255. Of course Irish armies felt no qualms
at sacking the monasteries and slaying the monks of another kingdom. The
sanctuaries of Clonmacnois, Kildare, Clonard, Armagh were plundered as readily
by " Christian " Irishmen as by heathen Danes. In the ninth century, Phelim,
King of Munster, was an abbot and a bishop too ; but he sacked the sacred places
of Ulster and killed their monks and clergy. See G. T. Stokes, Ireland and the
Celtic Church ; Killen, Eccl. Hist. of Ireland, vol. i. p. 145 sqq.

[2] The title of saint is regularly given to the higher clergy of this period in Ireland.

bells. Columba appears to have had no part in the cursing of Tara. But Dermot was the king against whom the wars of his family were waged, and all the traditions point to the saint as their instigator. The account given by Keating, the seventeenth century historian of Gaelic Ireland, is curious.[1]

" Diarmuid . . . King of Ireland, made the Feast of Tara, and a nobleman was killed at that feast by Curran, son of Aodh ; wherefore Diarmuid killed him in revenge for that, because he committed murder at the Feast of Tara, against the law and the sanctuary of the feast ; and before Curran was put to death he fled to the protection of Colum-Cille, and notwithstanding the protection of Colum-Cille he was killed by Diarmuid. And from that it arose that Colum-Cille mustered the Clanna Neill of the North, because his own protection and the protection of the sons of Earc was violated. Whereupon the battle of Cul Dreimhne was gained over Diarmuid and over the Connaughtmen, so that they were defeated through the prayer of Colum-Cille."

Keating adds that another book relates another cause of this battle, to wit :

". . . the false judgment which Diarmuid gave against Colum-Cille when he wrote the gospel out of the book of Finnian without his knowledge.[2] Finnian said that it was to himself belonged the son-book which was written from his book, and they both selected Diarmuid as judge between them. This is the decision that Diarmuid made : that to every book belongs its son-book, as to every cow belongs her calf."

Less consistent is the tradition that Columba left Ireland because of the sentence passed upon him by certain of his fellow-saints, as penance for the bloodshed which he had occasioned. Indeed, for his motives one need hardly look beyond the desire to spread the Gospel, and the passion of the Irish monk *peregrinam ducere vitam*. Reaching the west of Scotland, Columba was granted that rugged little island then called Hy, but Iova afterwards, and now Iona. This was in 563, and he continued abbot of Hy until his

---

[1] " *The History of Ireland by Geoffrey Keating* " *in the original Gaelic with an English translation, by Comyn and Dineen* (Irish Texts Society. David Nutt, London, 1902-1908).

[2] This means that he copied a manuscript belonging to Finnian.

death in 597. Not that he stayed there all these years, for he moved about ceaselessly, founding churches among the Picts and Scots. Some thirty foundations are attributed to him, besides his thirty odd in Ireland.

Adamnan's *Vita* largely consists of stories of the saint's miracles and prophecies and the interpositions of Providence in his behalf. It nevertheless gives a consistent picture of this man of powerful frame and mighty voice, restless and unrestrained, ascetically tempered, working always for the spread of his religion. We see him compelling men to set sail with him despite the tempest, or again rushing into " the green glass water up to his knees " to curse a plunderer in the name of Christ. " He was not a gentle hero," says an old Gaelic Eulogy. Yet if somewhat quick to curse, he was still readier to bless, and if he could be masterful, his life had its own humility. " Surely it was great lowliness in Colomb Cille that he himself used to take off his monks' sandals and wash their feet for them. He often used to carry his portion of corn on his back to the mill, and grind it and bring it home to his house. He never used to put linen or wool against his skin. His side used to come against the bare mould." [1]

So this impetuous life passes before our eyes filled with adventure, touched with romance, its colours heightened through tradition. As it draws to its close the love in it seems to exceed the wrath ; and thus it ends : as the old man was resting himself the day before his death, seated by the barn of the monastery, the white work-horse came and laid its head against his breast. Late the same night, reclining on his stone bed he spoke his last words, enjoining peace and charity among the monks. Rising before dawn, he entered the church alone, knelt beside the altar, and there he died.[2]—His memory still hangs the peace of God and man over the Island of Iona.

[1] The Life of Colomb Cille from the *Book of Lismore*.　　　[2] Adamnan.

CHAPTER VIII

TEUTON QUALITIES : ANGLO-SAXON, GERMAN, NORSE

THERE were intellectual as well as emotional differences between the Celts and Teutons. A certain hard rationality and grasp of fact mark the mentality of the latter. On land or sea they view the situation, realize its opportunities, their own strength, and the opposing odds : with definite and persistent purpose they move, they fight, they labour. The quality of purposefulness becomes clearer as they emerge from the forest obscurity of their origins into the open light of history. To a definite goal of conquest and settlement Theodoric led the Ostrogoths from Moesia westward, and fought his way into Italy. With persistent purposefulness Clovis and his Merovingian successors intrigued and fought. Among Anglo-Saxon pirates the aim of plunder quickly grew to that of conquest. And in times which were to follow, there was purpose in every voyage and battle of the Vikings. The Teutons disclose more strength and persistency of desire than the Celts. Their feelings were slower, less impulsive ; also less quickly diverted, more unswerving, even fiercer in their strength. The general characteristic of Teutonic emotion is its close connection with some motive grounded in rational purpose.

Caesar's short sketch of the Germans [1] gives the impression of barbarous peoples, numerous, brave, overweening. They had not reached the agricultural stage, but were devoted to war and hunting. There were no Druids among

---

[1] *B.G.* iv. 1-3 ; vi. 21-28. For convenience I use the word *Teuton* as the general term and *German* as relating to the Teutons of the lands still known as German. But with reference to the times of Caesar and Tacitus the latter word must be taken generally.

them. Their bodies were inured to hardship. They lived
in robust independence, and were subject to their chiefs
only in war. Their fiercest folk, the Suevi, from boyhood
would submit neither to labour nor discipline, that their
strength and spirit might be unchecked. It was deemed
shameful for a youth to have to do with women before his
twentieth year.

The Roman world knew more about these Germans by
the year A.D. 99 when Tacitus composed his *Germania*.
They had scarcely yet turned to agriculture. Respect for
women appears clearly. These barbarians are most reluctant
to give their maidens as hostages ; they listen to their
women's voices and deem that there is something holy and
prophetic in their nature. Upon marriage, oxen, a horse,
and shield and lance make up the husband's *morgengabe* to
his bride : she is to have part in her husband's valour.
Fornication and adultery are rare, the adulteress is ruthlessly
punished ; men and maidens marry late. The men of the
tribe decide important matters, which, however, the chiefs
have previously discussed apart. The people sit down
armed ; the priests proclaim silence ; the king or war-
leader is listened to, and the assembly is swayed by his
persuasion and repute. They dissent with murmurs, or
assent brandishing their spears. There is thus participation by the tribe, and yet deference to reputation. This
description discloses Teutonic freedom as different from
Celtic political unrestraint. Tacitus also speaks of the
Germanic *Comitatus*, consisting of a chief and a band of
youths drawn together by his repute, who fight by his side
and are disgraced if they survive him dead upon the field.
In time of peace they may seek another leader from a tribe
at war ; for the Germans are impatient of peace and toil,
and slothful except when fighting or hunting. They had
further traits and customs which are barbaric rather than
specifically Teutonic : cruelty and faithlessness toward
enemies, feuds, *wergeld*, drinking bouts, gambling, slavery,
absence of testaments.

Between the time of Tacitus and the fifth century many
changes came over the Teuton tribes. Early tribal names
vanished, while a regrouping into larger and apparently

more mobile aggregates took place. The obscure revolutions occurring in Central Europe in the second, third, and fourth centuries do not indicate social progress, but rather retrogression from an almost agricultural state toward stages of migratory unrest.[1] We have already noted the fortunes of those tribes that helped to barbarize and disrupt the Roman Empire, and lost themselves among the Romance populations of Italy, Gaul, and Spain. We are here concerned with those that preserved their native speech and qualities, and as Teuton peoples became contributories to the currents of mediaeval evolution.

I

When the excellent Apollinaris Sidonius, writing in the middle of the fifth century to a young friend about to enter the Roman naval service off the coasts of Gaul, characterized the Saxon pirates as the fiercest and most treacherous of foes, whose way is to dash upon their prey amid the tempest, and for whom shipwreck is a school, he spoke truly, and also illustrated the difference that lies in point of view.[2] Fierce they were, and hardy seamen, likewise treacherous in Roman eyes, and insatiate plunderers. From the side of the sea they represented the barbarian disorder threatening the world. The Roman was scarcely interested in the fact that these men kept troth among themselves with energy and sacrifice of life. The Saxons, Angles, Jutes, whose homes ashore lay between the Weser and the Elbe and through Sleswig, Holstein, and Denmark, possessed interesting qualities before they landed in Britain, where under novel circumstances they were to develop their character and institutions with a rapidity that soon raised them above the condition of their kin who had stayed at home. Bands of them had touched Britain before the year 411, when the Roman legions were withdrawn. But it was only with the landing of Hengest and Horsa in 449 that they began to

---

[1] These views are set forth brilliantly, but with exaggeration, by Fustel de Coulanges, in *L'Invasion germanique*, vol. ii. of his *Institutions politiques*, etc. (revised edition, Paris, 1891).

[2] Apoll. Sid. *Epist.* viii. 6 (Migne, *Pat. Lat.* 58, col. 697).

come in conquering force. The Anglo-Saxon conquest of
the island went on for two centuries. Information regarding it is of the scantiest ; but the Britons seem to have
been submerged or driven westward. There is at least no
evidence of any friendly mingling of the races. The invaders
accepted neither Christianity nor Roman culture from the
conquered, and Britain became a heathen England.

While these Teuton peoples were driving through their
conquest and also fighting fiercely with each other, their
characters and institutions were becoming distinctively
Anglo-Saxon. Under stress of ceaseless war, military leaders
became hereditary kings, whose powers, at least in intervals
of peace, were controlled by the Witan or Council of the
Wise, and limited by the jurisdiction of the Hundred Court.
Likewise the temporary ties of the Teutonic *Comitatus*
became permanent in the body of king's companions (thegns,
thanes), whose influence was destined to supplant that of
the eorls, the older nobility of blood. The *Comitatus*
principle pervades Anglo-Saxon history as well as literature ;
it runs through the *Beowulf* epic ; Anglo-Saxon Biblical
versifiers transfer it to the followers of Abraham and the
disciples of Christ ; and every child knows the story of
Lilla, faithful thegn, who flung himself between his
Northumbrian king, Edwin, and the sword of the assassin
—the latter sent by a West Saxon king and doubtless one
of *his* faithful thegns. Their law consisted mainly in the
graded *wergeld* for homicide, in an elaborate tariff of compensation for personal injuries, and in penalties for cattle-
raiding. Beyond the matter of theft, property law was
still unwritten custom, and contract law did not exist.
The rules of procedure, for instance in the Hundred Court,
were elaborate, as is usual in a primitive society where the
substantial rights are simple, and the important thing is to
induce the parties to submit to an adjudication. Similar
Teutonic customs obtained elsewhere. But the course of
their development in Saxon England displays an ever clearer
recognition of fundamental principles of English law :
justice is public ; the parties immediately concerned must
bring the case to court and there conduct it according to
rules of procedure ; the court of freemen hear and determine,

but do not extend the inquiry beyond the evidence adduced before them ; to interpret and declare the law is the function of the court, not of the king and his officers.[1]

During these first centuries in England, the Anglo-Saxon endowment of character and faculty becomes clearly shown in events and expressed in literature. A battle-loving people whose joy in fight flashes from their " shield-play " and " sword-game " epithets, even as their fondness for seafaring is seen in such phrases as " wave-floater," " foam-necked," " like a swan " breasting the " swan-road " of the sea. But their sword-games and wave-floatings had purpose, a quality that became large and steady as generation after generation, unstopped by fortress, forest, or river, pushed on the conquest of England. When that conquest had been completed, and these Saxons were in turn hard pressed by their Danish kin more lately sailing from the north, their courage still could not be overborne. It is reflected in the overweening mood of *Maldon*, the poem which is also called *The Death of Byrhtnoth*. The cold grey scene lies in the north of England. The Viking invaders demand rings of gold ; Byrhtnoth, the Alderman of the East Saxons, retorts scornfully. So the fight begins with arrows and spear throwings across the black water. The Saxons hold the ford. The Sea-wolves cannot force it. They call for leave to cross. In his overmood Byrhtnoth answers : " To you this is yielded : come straightway to us ; God only wots who shall hold fast the place of battle." In the bitter end when Byrhtnoth is killed, still speaks his thane : " Mind shall the harder be, heart the keener, mood the greater, as our might lessens. Here lies our Elder hewn to death. I am old ; I will not go hence. I think to lay me down by the side of my lord."

The spiritual gifts of the Anglo-Saxons are discernible in their language, which so adequately could render the Bible [2] and the phraseology of the Seven Liberal Arts.

---

[1] See Pollock and Maitland, *History of English Law* ; and Pollock, *English Law before the Norman Conquest, Law Quarterly Review.*

[2] The ancient Anglo-Saxon version is Anglo-Saxon through and through. The considerable store of Latin (or Greek) words retained by the " authorized " English version (for example, Scripture, Testament, Genesis, Exodus, etc., prophet, evangelist, religion, conversion, adoption, temptation, redemption

Its terms were somewhat more concrete and physical than
the Latin, but readily lent themselves to figurative meanings.
More palpably the poetry with its reflection upon life shows
the endowment of the race. Its elegiac mood is marked.
In an old poem is heard the voice of one who sails with
hapless care the exile's way, and must forego his dear lord's
gifts : in sleep he kisses him, and again lays hands and head
upon those knees, as in times past. Then wakes the friend-
less man, and sees the ocean's waves, the gulls spreading
their wings, rime and snow falling. More impersonal is
the heavy tone of a meditative fragment over the ruins,
apparently, of a Roman city :

> " Wondrous is this wall-stone,
> fates have broken it,
> have burst the stronghold,
> roofs are fallen,
> towers tottering,
> hoar gate-towers despoiled,
> shattered the battlements,
> riven, fallen.
>
>   .   .   .   .   ;
>
> Earth's grasp holdeth
> the mighty workmen
> worn away, done for,
> in the hard grip of the grave." [1]

But the noblest presentation of character in pagan Anglo-
Saxon poetry is afforded by the epic poem of *Beowulf*, which
tells the story of a Geatic hero who sets out for Denmark
to slay a monster, accomplishes the feat, is nobly rewarded
by the Danish king, and returns to rule his own people justly
for fifty winters, when his valiant and beneficent life ends
in a last victorious conflict with a hoard-guarding dragon.
The myth and tradition were not peculiarly Anglo-Saxon ;
but the finally recast and finished work, noble in diction,
sentiment, and action, expresses the highest ethics of Anglo-

---

salvation and damnation) were all translated into sheer Anglo-Saxon. See
Toller, *Outlines of the History of the English Language* (Macmillan & Co., 1900),
pp. 90-101. Some hundreds of years before, Ulfilas's fourth century Gothic
translation had shown a Teutonic tongue capable of rendering the thought of
the Pauline epistles.

[1] Cf. generally, R. W. Chambers, *Widsith* (Cambridge, 1913), and W. F. Ker,
English Literature Medieval (London, 1913).

Saxon heathendom. Beowulf does what he ought to do, heroically ; and finds satisfaction and reward. He does not seek his pleasure, though that comes with gold and mead-drinking ; consciousness of deeds done bravely and the assurance of fame sweeten death at last.[1]

A century or more after the composition of this poem, there lived an Anglo-Saxon whose aims were spiritualized through Christianity, whose vigorous mind was broadened by such knowledge and philosophy as his epoch had gathered from antique sources, and whose energies were trained in generalship and the office of a king. He presents a life intrinsically good and true, manifesting itself in warfare against heathen barbarism and in endeavour to rule his people righteously and enlarge their knowledge. Many of the qualities and activities of Alfred had no place in the life of Beowulf. Yet the heathen hero and the Christian king were hewn from the same rock of Saxon manhood. Alfred's life was established upon principles of right conduct generically the same as those of the poem. But Christianity, experience, contact with learned men, and education through books, had informed him of man's spiritual nature, and taught him that human welfare depends on knowledge and intent and will. Accordingly, his beneficence does not stop with the armed safe-guarding of his realm, but seeks to compass the instruction of those who should have knowledge in order the better to guide the faith and conduct of the people. " He seems to me a very foolish man and inexcusable, who will not increase his knowledge the while that he is in this world, and always wish and will that he may come to the everlasting life where nothing shall be dark or unknown." [2]

II

In spite of the general Teutonic traits and customs which the Germans east and west of the Rhine possessed in common

[1] See the " Beowulf " translated in Gummere's *Oldest English Epic* (Macmillan, 1909).
[2] This is the closing sentence of Alfred's *Blossoms*, culled from divers sources. Hereafter (Chapter IX.) when speaking of the introduction of antique and Christian culture there will be occasion to note more specifically what Alfred accomplished in his attempt to increase knowledge throughout his kingdom.

with the Anglo-Saxons, distinct qualities appear in the one and the other from the moment of our nearer acquaintance with their separate history and literature. So scanty, however, are the literary remains of German heathendom that recourse must be had to Christian productions to discover, for example, that with the Germans the sentiment of home and its dear relationships [1] is as marked as the Anglo-Saxon's elegiac meditative mood. Language bears its witness to the spiritual endowment of both peoples. The German dialects along the Rhine were rich in abstract nouns ending in *ung* and *keit* and *schaft* and *tum*.[2]

There remains one piece of untouched German heathenism, the *Hildebrandslied*, which dates from the end of the eighth century, and may possibly be the sole survivor of a collection of German poems made at Charlemagne's command.[3] It is a tale of single combat between a father and son, the counterpart of which is found in the Persian, Irish, and Norse literatures. Such an incident might be diversely rendered ; armies might watch their champions engage, or the combat might occur unwitnessed in some mountain gorge ; it might be described pathetically or in warrior mood, and the heroes might fight in ignorance, or one of them know well, who was the man confronting him. In German, this story is a part of that huge mass of legend which grew up around the memory of the terrible Hun Attila, and transformed him to the Atli of Norse literature, and to the worthy King Etzel of the *Nibelungenlied*, at whose Court the flower of Burgundian chivalry went down in that fierce feud in which Etzel had little part. Among his vassal kings appears the mighty exile Dietrich of Bern, who in the *Nibelungen* reluctantly overcomes the last of the Burgundian heroes. This Dietrich is none other than Theodoric the Ostrogoth, transformed in legend and represented as driven from his kingdom of Italy by Odoacer, and for the time forced to take refuge with

---

[1] See *e.g.* in Otfried's *Evangelienbuch, post*, p. 203.

[2] For example : *skidunga* (Scheidung), *saligheit* (Seligkeit), *fiantscaft* (Feindschaft), *heidantuom* (Heidentum). By the eighth century the High German of the Bavarians and Alemanni began to separate from the Low German of the lower Rhine, spoken by Saxons and certain of the Franks. The greater part of the Frankish tribes, and the Thuringians, occupied intermediate sections of country and spoke dialects midway between Low German and High.

[3] Text in Piper's *Die älteste Literatur* (Deutsche National Lit.).

Etzel; for the legend was not troubled by the fact that
Attila was dead before Theodoric was born. Bern is the
name given to Verona, and legend saw Theodoric's castle
in that most beautiful of Roman amphitheatres, where the
traveller still may sit and meditate on many things. It is
told also that Theodoric recovered his kingdom in the
legendary Rabenschlacht fought by Ravenna's walls. Old
Hildebrand was his master-at-arms, who had fled with him.
In the *Nibelungen* it is he that cuts down Kriemhild, Etzel's
queen, before the monarch's eyes; for he could not endure
that a woman's hand had slain Gunther and Hagen, whom,
exhausted at last, Dietrich's strength had set before her
helpless and bound. And now, after years of absence, he
has recrossed the mountains with his king come to claim his
kingdom, and before the armies he challenges the champion
of the opposing host. Here the Old German poem, which
is called the *Hildebrandslied*, takes up the story :

"Hildebrand spoke, the wiser man, and asked as to the other's
father—'Or tell me of what race art thou; 'twill be enough;
every one in the realm is known to me.'
"Hadubrand spoke, Hildebrand's son : 'Our people, the old
and knowing of them, tell me Hildebrand was my father's name ;
mine is Hadubrand. Aforetime he fled to the east, from Otacher's
hate, fled with Dietrich and his knights. He left wife to mourn,
and ungrown child. Dietrich's need called him. He was always
in the front ; fighting was dear to him. I do not believe he is
alive.'
"'God forbid, from heaven above, that thou shouldst wage
fight with so near kin.' He took from his arm the ring given by
the king, lord of the Huns. 'Lo! I give it thee graciously.'
"Hadubrand spoke : 'With spear alone a man receives gift,
point against point. Too cunning art thou, old Hun. Beguiling
me with words thou wouldst thrust me with thy spear. Thou art
so old—thou hast a trick in store. Seafaring men have told me
Hildebrand is dead.'
"Hildebrand spoke : 'O mighty God, a drear fate happens.
Sixty summers and winters, ever placed by men among the spear-
men, I have so borne myself that bane got I never. Now shall
my own child smite me with the sword, or I be his death.' "

There is a break here in the poem ; but the uncontrolled son evidently taunted the father with cowardice.
The old warrior cries :

" ' Be he the vilest of all the East people who now would refuse thee the fight thou hankerest after.　Happen it and show which of us must give up his armour.' "

The end fails, but probably the son was slain.

Stubborn and grim appears the Old German character. Point to point shall foes exchange gifts.　Such also was the way when a lord made reward ; on the spear's point presenting the arm-ring to him who had served, he accepting it in like fashion, each on his guard perhaps.　The *Hildebrandslied* exhibits other qualities of the German spirit, for instance its bluntness and lack of tact ; even its clumsiness is evinced in the seventy lines of the poem, which although broken is not a fragment, but a short poem—a ballad graceless and shapeless because of its stiff unvarying lines.

In a later poem, which gives the story of Walter of Aquitaine, the same set and stubborn mood appears, although lightened by rough banter.　This legend existed in Old German as well as Anglo - Saxon.　In the tenth century, Ekkehart, a monk of St. Gall, freely altering and adding to the tale, made of it the small Latin epic which is extant.[1]　Monk as he was, he tells a spirited story in his rugged hexameters.　He had studied classic authors to good purpose ; and his poem of Walter fleeing with his love Hildegund from the Hunnish Court (for the all-pervasive Attila is here also) is vivid, diversified, well-constructed— qualities which may not have been in the story till he remodelled it.　Its leading incidents still present German traits.　Walter and Hildegund carry off a treasure in their flight ; and it is to get this treasure that Gunther urges Hagen (for they are here too) to attack the fugitive.　This is Teutonic.　It was for plunder that Teuton tribes fought their bravest fights from the time of Alaric and Genseric to the Viking age, and the hoard has a great part in Teutonic story.　In the *Waltarius* Gunther's driving avarice, Walter's

---

[1] On the Waltari poem, see Ebert, *Allgemeine Gesch. der Literatur des Mittelalters*, Bd. iii. 264-276 ; also K. Strecker, " Probleme in der Walthariusforschung," *Neue Jahrbücher für klass. Altertumsgesch. und Deutsche Literatur*, 2te Jahrgang (Leipzig, 1899), pp. 573-594, 629-645.　The author is called Ekkehart I. (d. 973), being the first of the celebrated monks bearing that name at St. Gall.　The poem is edited by Peiper (Berlin, 1873), by Scheffel and Holder (Stuttgart, 1874), and by Althof (Leipzig, 1896) ; it is translated into German by San Marte (Magdeburg, 1853), and by Althof (Leipzig, 1902).

stubborn defence of his gold are Teutonic. The humour and the banter are more distinctly German, and nobly German is the relationship of trust and honour between Walter and the maiden who is fleeing with him. Yet the story does not revolve around the woman in it, but rather around the shrewdly got and bravely guarded treasure.

German traits obvious in the *Hildebrandslied*, and strong through the Latin of the *Waltarius*, evince themselves in the epic of the *Nibelungenlied* and in the *Kudrun*, often called its companion piece. The former holds the strength of German manhood and the power of German hate, with the edged energy of speech accompanying it. In the latter, German womanhood is at its best. Both poems, in their extant form, belong to the middle or latter part of the twelfth century, and are not unaffected by influences which were not native German.

The *Nibelungenlied* is but dimly reminiscent of any bygone love between Siegfried and Brunhilde, and carries within its own narrative a sufficient explanation of Brun hilde's jealous anger and Siegfried's death. Kriemhild is left to nurse the wrath which shall never cease to devise vengeance for her husband's murderers. Years afterwards, Hagen warns Gunther, about to accept Etzel's invitation, that Kriemhild is *lancraeche* (long vengeful). The course of that vengeance is told with power ; for the constructive soul of a race contributed to this Volksepos. The actors in the tragedy are strikingly drawn and contrasted, and are lifted in true epic fashion above the common stature by intensity of feeling and the power of will to realize through unswerving action the promptings of their natures. The fatefulness of the tale is true to tragic reality, in which the far results of an ill deed involve the innocent with the guilty.

A comparison of the poem with the *Hildebrandslied* shows that the sense of the pathetic had deepened in the intervening centuries. There is scarcely any pathos in the earlier composition, although its subject is the fatal combat between father and son. But the *Nibelungen*, with a fiercer hate, can set forth the heroic pathos of the lot of one, who, struggling between fealties, is driven on to dishonour and to death. This is the pathos of the death of Rüdiger, who had

received the Burgundians in his castle on their way to Etzel's
Court, had exchanged gifts with them, and betrothed his
daughter to the youngest of the three kings. He was as
unsuspecting as Etzel of Kriemhild's plot. But in the end
Kriemhild forces him, on his fealty as liegeman, to outrage
his heart and honour, and attack those whom he had sheltered
and guided onward—to their death.

Not much love in this tale, only hate insatiable. But
the greatness of hate may show the passional power of the
hating soul. The centuries have raised to high relief the
elemental Teutonic qualities of hate, greed, courage and
devotion, and human personality has enlarged with the
heightened power of will. The reader is affected with
admiration and sympathy. First he is drawn to Siegfried's
bright morning courage, his noble masterfulness — his
character appears touched with the ideals of chivalry.[1]
After his death the interest turns to Kriemhild planning for
revenge. It may be that sympathy is repelled as her hate
draws within its tide so much of guiltlessness and honour ;
and as the doomed Nibelungen heroes show themselves
haughty, strong-handed, and stout-hearted to the end, he
cheers them on, and most heartily that grim, consistent
Hagen in whom the old German troth and treachery for
troth's sake are incarnate.

The *Kudrun*[2] is a happier story, ending in weddings
instead of death. There was no licentiousness or infidelity
between man and wife in the *Nibelungen*, and through all
its hate and horror no outrage is done to woman's honour.
That may be taken as the leading theme of the *Kudrun*.
An ardent wooer, to be sure, may seize and carry off the
heroine, and his father drag her by the hair on her refusal to
wed his son ; but her honour, and the honour of all women

---

[1] The description of Siegfried's love for Kriemhild is just touched by the
chivalric love, which exists in Wolfram's *Parzival*, in Gottfried's *Tristan*, and of
course in their French models. See *post*, Chapter XXIV. For example, as he
first sees her who was to be to him " beide lieb und leit," he becomes " bleich
unde rôt " ; and at her greeting, his spirit is lifted up : " dô wart im von dem
gruoze vil wol gehoehét der muot." And the scene is laid in May (*Nibelungenlied*, Aventiure V., stanzas 284, 285, 292, 295).

[2] A convenient edition of the *Kudrun* is Pfeiffer's in *Deutsche Klassiker des
Mittelalters* (Leipzig, 1880). Under the name of *Gudrun* it is translated into
modern German by Simrock, and into English by M. P. Nichols (Boston, 1899).

in the poem, is respected and maintained. The ideal of womanhood is noble throughout : an old king thus bids farewell to his daughter on setting forth to be married " You shall so wear your crown that I and your mother may never hear that any one hates you.   Rich as you are, it would mar your fame to give any occasion for blame." [1]

A mediaeval epic may tell of the fortunes of several generations, and the *Kudrun* devotes a number of books to the heroine's ancestors, making a half-savage narrative, in which one feels a conflict between ancient barbarities and a newer and more courtly order. When the venturesome wooing and wedded fortune of Kudrun's mother have been told, the poem turns to its chief heroine, who grows to stately maidenhood, and becomes betrothed to a young king, Herwig. A rejected wooer, the " Norman " Prince Hartmuth, by a sudden descent upon the land in the absence of its defenders, carries off Kudrun and her women by force of arms, and the king, her father, is killed in an abortive attempt to recapture her. In Hartmuth's castle by the sea Kudrun spends bitter years waiting for deliverance. His sister, Ortrun, is kind to her, but his mother, Gerlint, treats her shamefully. The maiden is steadfast. Between her and Hartmuth stands a double barrier : his father had killed hers ; she was betrothed to Herwig. Hartmuth repels his wicked mother's advice to force her to his will. In his absence on a foray Gerlint compels Kudrun to do unfitting tasks. Hartmuth, returning, asks her : " Kudrun, fair lady, how has it been with you while I and my knights were away ? "

" Here I have been forced to serve, to your sin and my

---

[1] *Kudrun*, viii. 558. Whatever may have been the facts of German life in the Middle Ages, the literature shows respect for marriage and woman's virtue. This remark applies not only to those works of the Middle High German tongue which are occupied with themes of Teutonic origin, but also to those—Wolfram's *Parzival*, for example—whose foreign themes do not force the poet to magnify adulterous love. When, however, that is the theme of the story, the German writer, as in Gottfried's *Tristan*, does not fail to do it justice.

Willmans, in his *Leben und Dichtung Walthers von der Vogelweide* (Bonn, 1882), note 1a on page 328, cites a number of passages from Middle High German works on the serious regard for marriage held by the Germans. Even the German minnesingers sometimes felt the contradiction between the broken marriage vow and the ennobling nature of chivalric love. See Willmans, *ibid.* p. 102 and note 7.

shame," [1] answers Kudrun—a great answer, in its truth and self-control.

After an interval of kind treatment the old " she-wolf " Gerlint sets Kudrun with her faithful Hildeburg to washing clothes in the sea. It is winter ; their garments are mean, their feet are naked. They see a boat approaching, in which are Kudrun's brother Ortwin, and Herwig her betrothed, who had come before their host as spies. A recognition follows ; Herwig is for carrying them off ; Ortwin forbids it. " With open force they were taken ; my hand shall not steal them back " ; dear as Kudrun is, he can take her only *nâch êren* (as becomes his honour). When they have gone, Kudrun throws the clothes to be washed into the sea. " No more will I wash for Gerlint ; two kings have kissed me and held me in their arms."

Kudrun returns to the castle, which soon is stormed. She saves Hartmuth and his sister from the slaughter, and all sail home, where the thought is now of wedding festivals.

Kudrun is married to Herwig ; at her advice Ortwin weds Ortrun, and then she thinks of Hartmuth's plight, and asks her friend Hildeburg whether she will have him for a husband. Hildeburg consents. Kudrun commands that Hartmuth be brought, and bids him be seated by the side of her dear friend " who had washed clothes along with her ! "

" Queen, you would reproach me with that. I grieved at the shame they put on you. It was kept from me."

" I cannot let it pass. I must speak with you alone, Hartmuth."

" God grant she means well with me," thought he. She took him aside and spoke : " If you will do as I bid, you will part with your troubles."

Hartmuth answered : " I know you are so noble that your behest can be only honourable and good. I can find nothing in my heart to keep me from doing your bidding gladly, Queen." [2] The high quality of speech between these two will rarely be outdone.

There is directness and troth in all these German poems. Troth is an ideal which must carry truth within it. The more thoughtful and reflecting German spirit will evince

---

[1] *Kudrun*, xx. 1013.   [2] *Kudrun*, xxx. 1632 *sqq.*

loyalty to truth itself as an ideal. Wolfram's poem of *Parzival* has this ; and by virtue of this same ideal, Walter von der Vogelweide's judgments upon life and emperors and popes are whole and steady, unveiling the sham, condemning the lie and defying the liar.[1] In them dawns the spirit of Luther and the German Reformation, with its love of truth stronger than its love of art.

III

Chronologically these last illustrations of German traits belong to the mediaeval time ; and in fact the *Nibelungenlied* and *Kudrun,* and much more Wolfram's *Parzival* and Walter's poems, are mediaeval, because to some extent affected by that interplay of influences which made the mediaeval genius.[2] On the other hand, the almost contemporaneous Norse Sagas and the somewhat older Eddic poems exhibit Teutonic traits in their northern integrity. For the Norse period of free and independent growth continued long after the distinctive barbarism of other Teutons had become mediaevalized. There resulted under the strenuous conditions of Norse life that unique heightening of energy which is manifested in the deeds of the Viking age and reflected in Norse literature.[3]

This time of extreme activity opens in the eighth century, toward the end of which Viking ravagers began to harry

[1] As to the *Parzival,* and Walter's poems, see *post,* Chapters XXV., XXVII.
[2] *Ante,* Chapter I.
[3] It is not known when Teutons first entered Denmark and the Scandinavian peninsula. Although non-Teutonic populations may have preceded them, the archaeological remains do not point clearly to a succession of races, while they do indicate ages of stone, bronze, and iron (Sophus Müller, *Nordische Altertums-kunde*). The bronze ages began in the Northlands a thousand years or more before Christ. In course of time, beautiful bronze weapons show what skill the race acquired in working metals not found in Scandinavia, but perhaps brought there in exchange for the amber of the Baltic shores. The use of iron (native to Scandinavia) begins about 500 B.C. A progressive facility in its treatment is evinced down to the Christian Era. Then a foreign influence appears—Rome. For Roman wares entered these countries where the legionaries never set foot, and native handicraft copied Roman models until the fourth century, when northern styles reassert themselves. The Scandinavians themselves were unaffected by Roman wares ; but after the fifth century they began to profit from their intercourse with Anglo-Saxons and Irish.

the British Isles.　St. Cuthbert's holy island of Lindisfarne
was sacked in 793, and similar raids multiplied with portentous rapidity.　The coasts of Ireland and Great Britain,
and the islands lying about them, were well plundered
while the ninth century was young.　In Ireland permanent
conquests were made near Dublin, at Waterford, and
Limerick.　The second half of this century witnesses the
great Danish Viking invasion of England.　On the Continent the Vikings worried the skirts of the Carolingian
colossus, and the Lowlands suffered before Charlemagne
was in his grave.　After his death the trouble began in
earnest.　Not only the coasts were ravaged, but the river
towns trembled, on the Elbe, the Rhine, the Somme, the
Seine, the Loire.　Paris foiled or succumbed to more than
one fierce siege.　About the middle of the ninth century the
Vikings began to winter where they had plundered in the
summer.

The north was ruled by chiefs and petty kings until
Harold Fairhair overcame the chiefs of Norway and made
himself supreme about the year 870.　But he established
his power only after great sea-fights, and many of the
conquered, choosing exile rather than submission, took
refuge in the Orkneys, the Faroes, and other islands.　Harold
pursued with his fleets, and forced them to further flight.
It was this exodus from the islands and from Norway in the
last years of the ninth century that gave Iceland the greater
part of its population.　Thither also came other bold spirits
from the Norse holdings in Ireland.

While these events were happening in the west, the
Scandinavians had not failed to push easterly.　Some
settled in Russia, by the Gulf of Finland, others along the
south shore of the Baltic between the Vistula and Oder.
So their holdings in the tenth century encircled the north of
Europe ; for besides Sleswig, Denmark, and Scandinavia,
they held the coast of Holland, also Normandy, where Rollo
came in 912.　Of insular domain, they held Iceland, parts
of Scotland, and the islands north and west of it, some bits
of Ireland, and much of England.　Moreover, Scandinavians
filled the Varangian corps of the Byzantine emperors, and
old Runic inscriptions are found on marbles at Athens.

Their narrow barks traversed the eastern Mediterranean [1] long before Norman Roger and Norman Robert conquered Sicily and southern Italy. Such reach of conquest shows them to have been moved by no passion for adventure. Their fierce valour was part of their great capacity for the strategy of war. As pirates, as invaders, as settlers, they dared and fought and fended for a purpose—to get what they wanted, and to hold it fast. When they had mastered the foe and conquered his land, they settled down, in England and Normandy and Sicily.

Such genius for fighting was in accord with shrewdness and industry in peace. The Vikings laboured, whether in Norway or in Iceland. In the *Edda* the freeman learns to break oxen, till the ground, timber houses, build barns, make carts and ploughs.[2] So a tenth-century Viking king may be found in the field directing the cutting and stacking of his corn and the gathering of it into barns. They were also traders and even money-lenders. The Icelanders, whom we know so intimately from the Sagas, went regularly upon voyages of trade or piracy before settling down to farm and wife. Sharp of speech, efficient in affairs, and often adepts in the law, they eagerly took part in the meetings of the Althing and its settlement of suits. If such settlement was rejected, private war or the *holmgang* (an appointed single combat on a small island) was the regular recourse. But it was murder to kill in the night or without previous notice. Nothing should be said behind an enemy's back that the speaker would not make good ; and every man must keep his plighted word.

Much of the Norse wisdom consists in a shrewd wariness. Contempt for the chattering fool runs through the *Edda*.[3]

---

[1] It is said that some twenty-five thousand Arabian coins, mostly of the Viking periods, have been found in Sweden.

[2] See Vigfusson and Powell, *Corpus poeticum Boreale*, i. 238.

[3] There is much controversy as to the date (the Viking Age ?) and place of origin (Norway, the Western Isles, or Iceland ?) of the older Eddic poems ; also as to the presence of Christian elements. The last are denied by Müllenhoff (*Deutsche Altertumskunde*, Bd. v., 1891) and others ; while Bugge finds them throughout the whole Viking mythology (*Home of the Eddic Poems*. London, D. Nutt, 1899), and Chr. Bang has endeavoured to prove that the *Voluspa*, the chief Eddic mythological poem, was an imitation of the Christian Sibyl's oracles (*Christiania Videnskabsselskabs Forhanlinger*, 1879, No. 9 ; Müllenhoff, *o.c.* Bd. v. p. 3 *sqq.*). Similar views are held in Vigfusson and Powell's *Corpus poeticum Boreale* (i.

Let a man be chary of speech and in action unflinching.
Eddic poetry is full of action ; even its didactic pieces are
dramatic.   The *Edda* is as hard as steel.   In the mythological pieces the action has the ruthlessness of the elements,
while the stories of conduct show elemental passions working
in elemental strength.   The men and women are not rounded
and complete ; but certain disengaged motives are raised to
the titanic and thrown out with power.   Neither present
anguish, nor death surely foreseen, checks the course of
vengeance for broken faith in those famous Eddic lays of
Atli, of Sigurd and Sigrifa, Helgi and Sigrun, Brynhild and
Gudrun, out of which the Volsunga Saga was subsequently
put together, and to which the *Nibelungenlied* is kin.   They
seem to carry the same story, with change of names and
incidents.   Always the hero's fate is netted by woman's
vengeance and the curse of the Hoard.   But still the women
feel most ; the men strike, or are struck.   Hard and cold
grey, with hidden fire, was the temper of these people.
Their love was not over-tender, and yet stronger than death :
cries Brynhild's ghost riding hellward, " Men and women
will always be born to live in woe.   We two, Sigurd and I,
shall never part again."   And the power of such love speaks
in the deed and word of Sigrun, who answers the ghostly
call of slain Helgi from his barrow, and enters it to cast her
arms about him there : " I am as glad to meet thee as are
the greedy hawks of Odin when they scent the slain.   I will
kiss thee, my dead king, ere thou cast off thy bloody coat.
Thy hair, my Helgi, is thick with rime, thy body is drenched
with gory dew, dead-cold are thy hands."

The characters which appear in large grey traits in the
Edda, come nearer to us in the Icelandic Sagas.   The *Edda*
has something of a far, unearthly gloom ; the Saga the light
of day.   Saga-folk are extraordinarily individual ; men and
women are portrayed, body and soul, with homely, telling

ci.-cvii. and 427).   These scholars find Celtic influences in the Eddic poems.
The whole controversy is still far from settlement.
    As for English translations of the *Edda*, that by B. Thorpe (*Edda Saemundar*)
is difficult to obtain.   Those of the *Corpus poeticum Boreale* are literal ; but the
rendering of the mythological poems is shaped to the theory of Christian influence.   The best translation is *The Poetic Edda* by H. A. Bellows, with an
introduction and notes.   Two vols. in one.   (New York, American Scandinavian
Foundation, 1923.)

realism. Nevertheless, within a fuller round of human trait, Eddic qualities endure. There is the same clear purpose and the strong resolve, and still the deed keeps pace with the intent.[1]

The period which the Sagas would delineate commences when the Norse chiefs sail to Iceland with kith and kin and following to be rid of Harold Fairhair, and lasts for a century or more on through the time of King Olaf Tryggvason who, shield over head, sprang into the sea in the year 1000, and the life of that other Olaf, none too rightly called the Saint, who in 1030 perished in battle fighting against overwhelming odds. Following hard upon this heroic time comes the age of telling of it, telling of it at the midsummer Althing, telling of it at Yuletide feasts, and otherwise through the long winter nights in Iceland. These tellings are the Sagas in process of creation ; for a Saga is essentially a tale told by word of mouth to listeners. Thus pass another hundred years of careful telling, memorizing, and retelling of these tales, kept close to the old incidents and deeds, yet ever with a higher truth intruding. They are becoming true

---

[1] The best account of the Sagas, in English, is the Prolegomena to Vigfusson's edition of the Sturlunga Saga (Clarendon Press, 1878). Dasent's Introduction to his translation of the Njáls Saga (Edinburgh, 1861) is instructive as to the conditions of life in Iceland in the early times. W. P. Ker's *Epic and Romance* (Macmillan & Co., 1897) has elaborate literary criticism upon the Sagas. The following is Vigfusson's : " The Saga proper is a kind of prose Epic. It has its fixed laws, its set phrases, its regular epithets and terms of expression, and though there is, as in all high literary form, an endless diversity of interest and style, yet there are also bounds which are never over-stepped, confining the Saga as closely as the employment and restrictions of verse could do. It will be best to take as the type the smaller Icelandic Saga, from which indeed all the later forms of composition have sprung. This is, in its original form, the story of the life of an Icelandic gentleman, living some time in the tenth or eleventh centuries. It will tell first of his kin, going back to the settler from whom he sprung, then of his youth and early promise before he left his father's house to set forth on that foreign career which was the fitting education of the young Northern chief. These *wander-jahre* passed in trading voyages and pirate cruises, or in the service of one of the Scandinavian kings, as poet or henchman, the hero returns to Iceland a proved man, and the main part of the story thus preluded begins. It recounts in fuller detail and in order of time his friendships and his enmities, his exploits and re-nown, and finally his death ; usually concluding with the revenge taken for him by his kinsmen, which fitly winds up the whole. This tale is told in an earnest straightforward way, as by a man talking, in short simple sentences, changing when the interest grows into the historic present, with here and there an ' aside ' of explanation put in. . . . The whole composition, grouped around a single man and a single place, is so well balanced and so naturally unfolded piece by piece that the great art shown therein often at first escapes the reader."

to reality itself, in concrete types, and not simply narratives
of facts actually occurring—if indeed facts ever occur in
any such unequivocal singleness of actuality and with such
compelling singleness of meaning, that one man shall not
read them in one way and another otherwise. And the
more imaginative reading may be the truer.

This century of Saga-growth in memory and word of
mouth came to an end, and men began to write them down.
For still another hundred years (beginning about 1140) this
process lasted. In its nature it was something of a remodelling. As oral tales to be listened to, the Sagas had
come to these scribe-authors, and as such the latter wrote
them down, yet with such modification as would be involved
in writing out for mind and eye and ear that which the ear
had heard and the memory retained. In some instances
the scribe-author set himself the more ambitious task of
casting certain tales together in a single, yet composite story.
Such is the Njála, greatest of all Sagas ; it may have been
written about the year 1220.[1]

As representative of the Norse personality, the Sagas,

[1] The Story of Burnt Njal (Njáls Saga or Njála), trans. by Dasent (2 vols.
Edinburgh, 1861). A prose narrative interspersed with occasional lyric verses
is the form which the Icelandic Sagas have in common with the Irish. In view
of the mutual intercourse and undoubted mingling of Norse and Celtic blood both
in Ireland and Iceland, it is probable that the Norse Saga-form was taken from
the Irish. But, except in the Laxdæla Saga (trans. by Mrs. Press in the Temple
Classics, Dent, 1899), one seems to find no Celtic strain. The Sagas are the
prose complement of the poetic *Edda*. Both are Norse absolutely : fruit of one
spirit, part of one literature, a possession of one people. As to racial purity of
blood in their authors and fashioners, or in the men of whom the tales are told,
that is another matter. Who shall say that Celtic blood and inherited Celtic
gifts of expression were not the leaven of this Norse literature ? But whatever
entered into it and helped to create it, became Norse just as vitally as, ages
before, every foreign suggestion adopted by a certain gifted Mediterranean race
was Hellenized, and became Greek. In Iceland, in the Orkneys and the Faroes,
Viking conditions, the Viking spirit, and Norse blood, dominated, assimilating,
transforming and doubtless using whatever talents and capacities came within the
vortex of Viking life. See generally W. A. Craigie, *The Icelandic Sagas* (1913).
    It may be added that there is merely an accidental likeness between the Saga
and the Cantefable. In the Saga the verses are the utterances of the heroes
when specially moved. One may make a verse as a short death-song when his
death is imminent, or as a gibe on an enemy, whom he is about to attack. In the
Cantefable—*Aucassin and Nicolette*, for example—the verses are a lyric summary
of the parts of the narrative following them, and are not spoken by the *dramatis
personae*. The Cantefable (but not the Sagas) perhaps may be traced back to
such a work as Boëthius's *De consolatione*, which at least is identical in form,
or Capella's *De nuptiis Philologiae et Mercurii*. The *De planctu naturae* of Alanus
de Insulis (*post*, Chapter XXXIII. 1) plainly shows such antecedents.

like all national literature, bear a twofold testimony : that of their own literary qualities, and that of the characters which they portray.   In the first place, a Saga is absolute narrative : it relates deeds, incidents, and sayings, in the manner and order in which they would strike the eye and ear of the listener, did the matter pass before him.   The narrator offers no analysis of motives ; he inserts no reflections upon characters and situations.   He does not even relate the incidents from the vantage-ground of a full knowledge of them, but from the point of view of each instant's impression upon the participants or onlookers. The result is an objective and vivid presentation of the story.   Next, the Sagas are economical of incident as well as language.   That incident is told which the story needs for the presentation of the hero's career ; those circumstances are given which the incident needs in order that its significance may be perceived ; such sayings of the actors are related as reveal most in fewest words.   There is nothing more extraordinary in these stories than the significance of the small incident, and the extent of revelation carried by a terse remark.

For example, in the Gisli Saga, Gisli has gone out in the winter night to the house of his brother Thorkel, with whom he is on good terms, and there has slain Thorkel's wife's brother in his bed.   In the darkness and confusion he escapes unrecognized, gets back to his own house and into bed, where he lies as if asleep.   At daybreak the dead man's friends come packing to Gisli's farm :

" Now they come to the farm, Thorkel and Eyjolf, and go up to the shut-bed where Gisli and his wife slept ; but Thorkel, Gisli's brother, stepped up first on to the floor, and stands at the side of the bed, and sees Gisli's shoes lying all frozen and snowy.   He kicked them under the foot-board, so that no other man should see them." [1]

This little incident of the shoes not only shows how near was Gisli to detection and death, but also discloses the way in which Thorkel meant to act and did act toward his brother : to wit, shield him so long as it might be done without exposing himself.

[1] Story of Gisli the outlaw, trans. by Dasent, chap. ix. (Edinburgh, 1866).

Another illustration. The Njáls Saga opens with a sketch of the girl Hallgerda, so drawn that it presages most of the trouble in the story. There were two well-to-do brothers, Hauskuld and Hrut :

" It happened once that Hauskuld bade his friends to a feast, and his brother Hrut was there, and sat next to him. Hauskuld had a daughter named Hallgerda, who was playing on the floor with some other girls. She was fair of face and tall of growth, and her hair was as soft as silk ; it was so long, too, that it came down to her waist. Hauskuld called out to her, ' Come hither to me, daughter.' So she went up to him, and he took her by the chin and kissed her ; after that she went away. Then Hauskuld said to Hrut, ' What dost thou think of this maiden ? Is she not fair ? ' Hrut held his peace. Hauskuld said the same thing to him a second time, and then Hrut answered, ' Fair enough is this maid, and many will smart for it ; but this I know not, whence thief's eyes have come into our race.' Then Hauskuld was wroth, and for a time the brothers saw little of each other." [1]

The picture of Hallgerda will never leave the reader's mind throughout the story, of which she is the evil genius. It is after she has caused the death of her first husband and is sought by a second, that she is sent for by her father to ask what her mind may be :

" Then they sent for Hallgerda, and she came thither, and two women with her. She had on a cloak of rich blue woof, and under it a scarlet kirtle, and a silver girdle round her waist ; but her hair came down on both sides of her bosom, and she had turned the locks up under her girdle. She sat down between Hrut and her father, and she greeted them all with kind words, and spoke well and boldly, and asked what was the news. After that she ceased speaking."

This is the woman that the girl has grown to be ; and she is still at the beginning of her mischief. Such narrative art discloses both in the tale-teller and the audience an intelligence which sees the essential fact and is impatient of encumbrance. It is the same intelligence that made these Vikings so efficient in war, and in peace quick to seize cogent means.

Truthfulness is another quality of the Sagas. Indeed their respect for historical or biographical fact sometimes

[1] The Story of Burnt Njal, chap. i., trans. by Dasent.

hindered the evolution of a perfect story. They hesitated to omit or alter well-remembered incidents. Nevertheless a certain remodelling came, as generation after generation of narrators made the incidents more striking and the characters more marked, and, under the exigencies of story-telling, omitted details which, although actual, were irrelevant to the current of the story. The disadvantages from truthfulness were slight, compared with the admirable artistic qualities preserved by it. It kept the stories true to reality, excluding unreality, exaggeration, absurdity. Hence these Sagas are convincing : no reader can withhold belief. They contain no incredible incidents. On occasions they tell of portents, prescience, and second sight, but not so as to raise a smile. They relate a very few encounters with trolls —the hideous, unlaid, still embodied dead. But those accounts conform to the hard-wrung superstitions of a people not given to credulity. So they are real. The reality of Grettir's night-wrestling with Glam, the troll, is hardly to be matched.[1] Truthfulness likewise characterizes their heroes : no man lies about his deeds, and no man's word is doubted.

While the Saga-folk include no cowards or men of petty manners, there is still great diversity of character among them. Some are lazy and some industrious, some quarrel-some and some good-natured, some dangerous, some forbear-ing, gloomy or cheerful, open-minded or biassed, shrewd or stupid, generous or avaricious. Such contrasts of character abound both in the Sagas of Icelandic life and those which handle the broader matter of history. One may note in the *Heimskringla* [2] of the Kings of Norway the contrasted char-acters of the kings Olaf Tryggvason and St. Olaf. The latter appears as a hard-working, canny ruler, a lover of

---

[1] The Story of Grettir the Strong (Grettis Saga), chaps. 32-35, trans. by Magnusson and Morris (London, 1869). See also *ibid.* chaps. 65, 66. These accounts are analogous to the story of Beowulf's fights with Grendel and his dam ; but are more convincing.

[2] The stories of the Kings of Norway, called the *Round World* (Heimskringla), by Snorri Sturluson, done into English by Magnusson and Morris (London, 1893). Snorri Sturluson (b. 1178, d. 1241) composed or put together the *Heims-kringla* from earlier writings, chiefly those of Ari the Historian (b. 1067, d. 1148), " a man of truthfulness, wisdom, and good memory," who wrote largely from oral accounts.

order, a legislator and enforcer of the laws ; in person, short, thick-set, carrying his head a little bent. A Viking had he been, and was a fighter, till he fell in his last great battle undaunted by odds.

But the other Olaf, Norway's darling hero, is epic : tall, golden-haired, peerless from his boyhood, beloved and hated. His marvellous physical masteries are told, his cliff-climbing, his walking on the sweeping oars keeping three war-axes tossing in the air. He smote well with either hand and cast two spears at once. He was the gladdest and game-somest of men, kind and lowly-hearted, eager in all matters, bountiful of gifts, glorious of attire, before all men for high heart in battle, and grimmest of all men in his wrath ; marvellous great pains he laid upon his foes. " No man durst gainsay him, and all the land was christened whereso-ever he came." Five short years made up his reign. At the end, neither he was broken nor his power. But a plot, moved by the hatred of a spurned heathen queen, delivered him to unequal combat with his enemies, the Kings of Denmark and Sweden, and Eric the great Viking Earl.

Olaf is sailing home from Wendland. The hostile fleet crouches behind an island. Sundry of Olaf's ships pass by. Then the kings spy a great ship sailing—that will be Olaf's *Long Worm* they say ; Eric says no. Anon come four ships, and a great dragon amid them—the *Long Worm* ? not yet. At last she comes, greatest and bravest of all, and Olaf in her, standing on the poop, with gilded shield and golden helm and a red kirtle over his mail coat. His men bade to sail on, and not fight so great a host ; but Olaf said, " Never have I fled from battle." So Olaf's ships are lashed in line, at the centre the *Long Worm*, its prow forward of the others because of her greater length. Olaf would have it thus in spite of the " windy weather in the bows " predicted by her captain. The enemies' ships close around them. Olaf's grapplings are too much for the Danes ; they draw back. Their places are taken by the ships of Sweden. They fare no better. At last Earl Eric lays fast his iron-beaks to Olaf's ships ; Danes and Swedes take courage and return. It is hand to hand now, the ships laid aboard of each other.

At last all of Olaf's ships are cleared of men and cut adrift, save the *Long Worm*. There fight Olaf's chosen, mad with battle. Einar, Olaf's strong bowman, from the *Worm* aft in the main hold, shot at Earl Eric ; one arrow pierced the tiller by his head, the second flew beneath his arm. Says the Earl to Finn, his bowman, " Shoot me yonder big man." Finn shot, and the arrow struck full upon Einar's bow as he was drawing it the third time, and it broke in the middle.

" What broke there so loud ? " said Olaf.

" Norway, king, from thine hands," answered Einar.

" No such crash as that," said the king ; " take my bow and shoot."

But the foeman's strength was overpowering. Olaf's men were cut down amidships. They hardly held the poop and bow. Earl Eric leads the boarders. The ship is full of foes. Olaf will not be taken. He leaps overboard. About the ship swarm boats to seize him ; but he threw his shield over his head and sank quickly in the sea.

The private Sagas construct in powerful lines the characters of the heroes from the stories of their lives. A great example is the Saga of Egil,[1] whose father was a Norse chief who had sailed to Iceland, where Egil was born. As a child he was moody, intractible, and dangerous, and once killed an older lad who had got the better of him at ball playing. There was no great love between him and his father. When he was twelve years old his father used him roughly. He entered the great hall and walked up to his father's steward and slew him. Then he went to his seat. After that, father and son said little to each other. The boy was bent on going cruising with his older brother, Thorolf. The father yields, and Egil goes a-harrying. Fierce is his course in Norway, where they come. On the sea his vessel bears him from deed to deed of blood and daring. His strength won him booty and reward ; he won a friend too, Arinbjorn, and there was always troth between them.

Thorolf and Egil took service with King Athelstane, who was threatened with attack from the King of the Scots.

[1] The Story of Egil Skallagrimson, trans. by W. C. Green (London, 1893).

The brothers led the Vikings in Athelstane's force. In the battle Thorolf loses his life ; but Egil hears the shout when Thorolf falls. His furious valour wins the day for Athelstane. After the fight he buries his brother and sings staves over his grave.

" Then went Egil and those about him to seek King Athelstan, and at once went before the king, where he sat at the drinking. There was much noise of merriment. And when the king saw that Egil was come in, he bade the lower bench be cleared for them, and that Egil should sit in the high seat facing the king. Egil sat down there, and cast his shield before his feet. He had his helm on his head, and laid his sword across his knees ; and now and again he half drew it, and then clashed it back into the sheath. He sat upright, but with head bent forward. Egil was large-featured, broad of forehead, with large eye-brows, a nose not long but very thick, lips wide and long, chin exceeding broad, as was all about the jaws ; thick-necked was he, and big-shouldered beyond other men, hard-featured, and grim when angry. He would not drink now, though the horn was borne to him, but alternately twitched his brows up and down. King Athelstan sat in the upper high-seat. He too laid his sword across his knees. When they had sat there for a time, then the king drew his sword from the sheath, and took from his arm a gold ring large and good, and placing it upon the sword-point he stood up, and went across the floor, and reached it over the fire to Egil. Egil stood up and drew his sword, and went across the floor. He stuck the sword-point within the round of the ring, and drew it to him ; then he went back to his place. The king sate him again in his high-seat. But when Egil was set down, he drew the ring on his arm, and then his brows went back to their place. He now laid down sword and helm, took the horn that they bare to him, and drank it off. Then sang he :

> ' Mailed monarch, god of battle,
> Maketh the tinkling circlet
> Hang, his own arm forsaking,
>   On hawk-trod wrist of mine.
> I bear on arm brand-wielding
> Bracelet of red gold gladly.
> War-falcon's feeder meetly
>   Findeth such meed of praise.'

" Thereafter Egil drank his share, and talked with others. Presently the king caused to be borne in two chests ; two men bare each. Both were full of silver. The king said : ' These chests, Egil, thou shalt have, and, if thou comest to Iceland, shalt carry this money to thy father ; as payment for a son I send it to

him : but some of the money thou shalt divide among such kinsmen of thyself and Thorolf as thou thinkest most honourable.
But thou shalt take here payment for a brother with me, land or
chattels, which thou wilt.   And if thou wilt abide with me long,
then will I give thee honour and dignity such as thyself mayst
name.'

" Egil took the money, and thanked the king for his gifts and
friendly words.   Thenceforward Egil began to be cheerful : and
then he sang :

> ' In sorrow sadly drooping
>   Sank my brows close-knitted ;
> Then found I one who furrows
>   Of forehead could smooth.
> Fierce-frowning cliffs that shaded
> My face a king hath lifted
> With gleam of golden armlet :
>   Gloom leaveth my eyes.' "

Like many of his kind in Iceland and Norway, this fierce
man was a poet.   Once he saved his life by a poem, and
he had made poems as gifts.   It was when the old Viking's
life was drawing to its close at his home in Iceland that
he composed his most moving lay.   His beautiful beloved
son was drowned.   After the burial Egil rode home, went
to his bed-closet, lay down and shut himself in, none daring
to speak to him.   There he lay, silent, for a day and night.
At last his daughter knocks and speaks ; he opens.   She
enters and beguiles him with her devotion.   After a while
the old man takes food.   And at last she prevails on him
to make a poem on his son's death, and assuage his grief.
So the song begins, and at length rises clear and strong—
perhaps the most heart-breaking of all old Norse poems.[1]

In the portrayal of contrasted characters no other Saga
can equal the great Njála, a Saga large and complex, and
doubtless composite ; for it seems put together out of three
stories, in all of which figured the just Njal, although he is
the chief personage in only one of them.   The story, with
its multitude of personages and threefold subject-matter,
lacks unity perhaps.   Yet the different parts of the Saga

---

[1] These poems are in the Saga, and will be found translated in Mr. Green's
edition.   They are also edited with prose translations in *C.P.B.*, vol. i. pp. 266-
280.   With Egil one may compare the still more truculent, but very different
Grettir, hero of the Grettis Saga.   The Story of Grettir the Strong, trans. by
Magnusson and Morris (2nd ed., London, 1869).

successively hold the attention. In the first part, the incomparable Gunnar is the hero ; in the second, Njal and his sons engage our interest in their varied characters and common fate. These are great narratives. The third part is perhaps epigonic, excellent and yet an aftermath. Only a reading of this Saga can bring any realization of its power of narrative and character delineation. Its chief personages are as clear as the day. One can almost see the sunlight of Gunnar's open brow, and certainly can feel his manly heart. The foil against which he is set off is his friend Njal, equally good, utterly different : unwarlike, wise in counsel, a great lawyer, truthful, just, shrewd and foreseeing. Hallgerda of the long silken hair is Gunnar's wife ; she has caused the deaths of two husbands already, and will yet prove Gunnar's bane. Little time passes before she is the enemy of Njal's high-minded spouse, Bergthora. Then Hallgerda beginning, Bergthora following quick, the two push on their quarrel, instigating in counter-vengeance alternate manslayings, each one a little nearer to the heart and honour of Gunnar and Njal. Yet their friendship is unshaken. For every killing the one atones with the other ; and the same blood-money passes to and fro between them.

Gunnar's friendship with the pacific Njal and his warlike sons endured till Gunnar's death. That came from enmities first stirred by the thieving of Hallgerda's thieving thrall. She had ordered it, and in shame Gunnar gave her a slap in the face, the sole act of irritation recorded of this generous, forbearing, peerless Viking, who once remarked : " I would like to know whether I am by so much the less brisk and bold than other men, because I think more of killing men than they ? " At a meeting of the Althing he was badgered by his ill-wishers into entering his stallion for a horse-fight, a kind of contest usually ending in a man-fight. Skarphedinn, the most masterful of Njal's sons, offered to handle Gunnar's horse for him :

" Wilt thou that I drive thy horse, kinsman Gunnar ? "

" I will not have that," says Gunnar.

" It wouldn't be amiss, though," says Skarphedinn ; " we are hot-headed on both sides."

" Ye would say or do little," says Gunnar, " before a

quarrel would spring up ; but with me it will take longer, though it will be all the same in the end."

Naturally the contest ends in trouble. Gunnar's beaten and enraged opponent seizes his weapons, but is stopped by bystanders. " This crowd wearies me," said Skarphedinn ; " it is far more manly that men should fight it out with weapons." Gunnar remained quiet, the best swordsman and bowman of them all. But his enemies fatuously pushed on the quarrel ; once they rode over him working in the field. So at last he fought, and killed many of them. Then came the suits for slaying, at the Althing. Njal is Gunnar's counsellor, and atonements are made : Gunnar is to go abroad for three winters, and unless he goes, he may be slain by the kinsmen of those he has killed. Gunnar said nothing. Njal adjured him solemnly to go on that journey : " Thou wilt come back with great glory, and live to be an old man, and no man here will then tread on thy heel ; but if thou dost not fare away, and so breakest thy atonement, then thou wilt be slain here in the land, and that is ill knowing for those who are thy friends."

Gunnar said he had no mind to break the atonement, and rode home. A ship is made ready, and Gunnar's gear is brought down. He rides around and bids farewell to his friends, thanking them for the help they had given him, and returns to his house. The next day he embraces the members of his household, leaps into the saddle, and rides away. But as he is riding down to the sea, his horse trips and throws him. He springs from the ground, and says with his face to the Lithe, his home : " Fair is the Lithe : so fair that it has never seemed to me so fair ; the cornfields are white to harvest, and the home mead is mown ; and now I will ride back home, and not fare abroad at all."

So he turns back—to his fate. The following summer at the Althing, his enemies give notice of his outlawry. Njal rides to Gunnar's home, tells him of it, and offers his sons' aid, to come and dwell with him : " they will lay down their lives for thy life."

" I will not," says Gunnar, " that thy sons should be slain for my sake, and thou hast a right to look for other things from me."

Njal rode to his home, while Gunnar's enemies gathered and moved secretly to his house. His hound, struck down with an axe, gives a great howl and expires. Gunnar awoke in his hall, and said : " Thou hast been sorely treated, Sam, my fosterling, and this warning is so meant that our two deaths will not be far apart." Single-handed, the beset chieftain maintains himself within, killing two of his enemies and wounding eight. At last, wounded, and with his bow-string cut, he turns to his wife Hallgerda : " Give me two locks of thy hair, and do thou and my mother twist them into a bowstring for me."

" Does aught lie on it ? " she says.

" My life lies on it," he said ; " for they will never come to close quarters with me if I can keep them off with my bow."

" Well," she says, " now I will call to thy mind that slap on the face which thou gavest me ; and I care never a whit whether thou holdest out a long while or a short."

Then Gunnar sang a stave, and said, " Every one has something to boast of, and I will ask thee no more for this." He fought on till spent with wounds, and at last they killed him.

Here the Njála may be left with its good men and true and its evil plotters, all so differently shown. It has still to tell the story and fate of Njal's unbending sons, of Njal himself and his high-tempered dame, who will abide with her spouse in their burning house, which enemies have surrounded and set on fire to destroy those sons. Njal himself was offered safety if he would come out, but he would not.

Perhaps we have been beguiled by their unique literary qualities into dwelling overlong upon the Sagas. These Norse compositions belong to the Middle Ages only in time ; for they were uninfluenced either by Christianity or the antique culture, the formative elements of mediaeval development. They are interesting in their aloofness, and also important for our mediaeval theme, because they were the ultimate as well as the most admirable expression of the native Teutonic genius as yet integral, but destined to have mighty part in the composite course of mediaeval growth

More specifically they are the voice of that falcon race which came from the Norseland to stock England with fresh strains of Danish blood, to conquer Normandy, and give new courage to the Celtic-German-Frenchmen, and thence went on to bring its hardihood, war cunning, and keen statecraft to southern Italy and Sicily. In all these countries the Norse nature, supple and pliant, accepted the gifts of new experience, and in return imparted strength of purpose to peoples with whom the Norsemen mingled in marriage as well as war.

This chapter has shown Teutonic faculties still integral and unmodified by Latin Christian influence. Their participation in the processes of mediaeval development will be seen as Anglo-Saxons and Germans become converted to Latin Christianity, and apply themselves to the study of the profane Latinity, to which it opened the way.

CHAPTER IX

THE BRINGING OF CHRISTIANITY AND ANTIQUE KNOWLEDGE TO THE NORTHERN PEOPLES

THE northern peoples, Celts and Teutons for the most part as they are called, came into contact with Roman civilization as the great Republic brought Gaul and Britain under its rule. Since Rome was still pagan when these lands were made provinces, an unchristianized Latinity was grafted upon their predominantly Celtic populations. The second stage, as it were, of this contact between Rome and the north, is represented by that influx of barbarians, mostly Teutonic, which, in both senses of the word, *quickened* the disruption of the Empire in the fourth and following centuries. The religion called after the name of Christ had then been accepted ; and invading Goths, Franks, Burgundians, Lombards, and the rest, were introduced to a somewhat Christianized Latindom. Indeed, in the Latin-Christian combination, the Christian element was becoming dominant, and was soon to be the chief means of extending the antique culture. For Christianity, with Latinity in its train, was to project itself outward to subjugate heathen Anglo-Saxons in England, Frisians in the Low Countries, and the unkempt Teutondom which roved east of the Rhine, and was ever pressing southward over the boundaries of former provinces now reverting to unrest. In past times the assimilating energy of Roman civilization had united western Europe in a common social order. Henceforth Christianity was to be the prime amalgamator, while the survivals of Roman institutions and the remnants of antique culture were to assist in secondary rôles. With Charles Martel, with Pippin, and with Charlemagne, Latin Christianity is the symbol of civilized order, while heathendom and savagery are identical.

I

The conversion of the northern peoples, and their incidental introduction to profane knowledge, wrought upon them deeply ; while their own qualities and the conditions of their lives affected their understanding of what they received and their attitude toward the new religion. Obviously the dissemination of Christianity among rude peoples would be unlike that first spreading of the Gospel through the Empire, in the course of which it had been transformed to Greek and Latin Christianity. Italy, Spain, and Gaul made the western region of this primary diffusion of the Faith. Of a distinctly missionary character were the further labours which resulted in the conversion of the fresh masses of Teutons who were breaking into the Roman pale, or were still moving restlessly beyond it. Moreover, between the time of the first diffusion of Christianity within the Empire and that of its missionary extension beyond those now decayed and fallen boundaries, it had been formulated dogmatically, and given ecclesiastical embodiment in a Catholic church into which had passed the conquering and organizing genius of Rome. This finished system was presented to simple peoples, sanctioned by the authority and dowered with the surviving culture of the civilized world. It offered them mightier supernatural aid, nobler knowledge, and a better ordering of life than they had known. The manner and authority of its presentation hastened its acceptance, and also determined the attitude toward it of the new converts and their children for generations. Theirs was to be the attitude of ignorance before recognized wisdom, and that of a docility which revered the manner and form as well as the substance of its lesson. The development of mediaeval Europe was affected by the mode and circumstances of this secondary propagation of Christianity. For

centuries the northern peoples were to be held in tutelage
to the form and constitution of that which they had received ·
they continued to revere the patristic sources of Christian
doctrines, and to look with awe upon the profane culture
accompanying them.

Thus, as under authority, Christianity came to the
Teutonic peoples, even to those who, like the Goths, were
converted to the Arian creed.   Likewise the orthodox belief
was brought to the Celtic Britons and Irish as a superior
religion associated with superior culture.   But the qualities
or circumstances of these western Celts reacted more freely
upon their form of faith, because Ireland and Britain were
the fringe of the world, and Christianity was hardly fixed in
dogma and ritual when the conversion at least of Britain
began.

Certain phrases of Tertullian indicate that Christianity
had made some progress among the Britons by the beginning
of the third century.   For the next hundred years nothing
is known of the British Church, save that it did not suffer
from the persecution under Diocletian in 304, and ten years
afterwards was represented by three bishops at the Council
of Arles.   It was orthodox, accepting the creed of Nicaea
(A.D. 325) and the date of Easter there fixed.   The fourth
century seems to have been the period of its prosperity.
It was affiliated with the Church of Gaul ; nor did these
relations cease at once when the Roman legions were withdrawn from Britain in 410.   But not many decades later
the Saxon invasion began to cut off Britain from the Christian
world.   After a while certain divergences appear in rite and
custom, though not in doctrine.   They seem not to have been
serious when Gildas wrote in 550.   Yet when Augustine
came, fifty years later, the Britons celebrated Easter at a
different date from that observed by the Roman Catholic
Church ; for they followed the old computation which
Rome had used before adopting the better method of
Alexandria.   Also the mode of baptism and the tonsure
differed from the Roman.

At the close of the sixth century the British Church
existed chiefly in Wales, whither the Britons had retreated
before the Saxons.   Formerly there had been no unwilling-

ness to follow the Church of Rome. But now a long period
had elapsed, during which Britain had been left to its mis-
fortunes. The Britons had been raided and harassed ; their
country invaded ; and at last they had been driven from
the greater portion of their land. How they hated those
Saxon conquerors ! And forsooth a Roman mission appears
to convert those damned and hateful heathen, and a somewhat haughty summons issues to the expelled or down-
trodden people to abandon their own Christian usages for
those of the Roman communion, and then join this Roman
mission in its saving work among those Saxons whom the
Britons had met only at the spear's point. Love of ancient
and familiar customs soured to obstinacy in the face of such
demands ; a sweeping rejection was returned. Yet to
conform to Roman usages and join with Augustine in his
mission to the Saxons, was the only way in which the
dwindling British Church could link itself to the Christian
world, and save its people from exterminating wars. By
refusing, it committed suicide.

A refusal to conform, although no refusal to undertake
missions to the Saxons, came from the Irish-Scottish Church.
As Ireland had never been drawn within the Roman world,
its conversion was later than that of Britain. Yet there
would seem to have been Christians in Ireland before 431 ;
for in that year, according to an older record quoted by
Bede, Palladius, the first bishop (*primus episcopus*), was sent
by Celestine the Roman pontiff " ad Scottos in Christum
credentes." [1] The mission of Palladius does not appear to
have been acceptable to the Irish. Some accounts have
confused his story with that of Patrick, the " Apostle of
Ireland," whose apostolic glory has not been overthrown by
criticism. The more authentic accounts, and above all his
own *Confession*, go far to explain Patrick's success. His
early manhood, passed as a slave in Antrim, gave him
understanding of the Irish ; and doubtless his was a great
missionary capacity and zeal. The natural approach to
such a people was through their tribal kings, and Patrick

---

[1] Bede, *Hist. Ecc.* i. 13. Moreover, the chief partisan of Pelagius (a Briton)
was Coelestinus, an Irishman whose restless activity falls in the thirty years
preceding the mission of Palladius.

appears to have made his prime onslaught upon Druidical heathendom at Tara, the abode of the high king of Ireland. The earliest accounts do not refer to any authority from Rome. Patrick seems to have acted from spontaneous inspiration ; and a like independence characterizes the monastic Christianity which sprang up in Ireland and over-leapt the water to Iona, to Christianize Scotland as well as northern Anglo-Saxon heathendom.[1]

Irish monasticism was an ascetically ordered continuance of Irish society. If, like other early western monasticism, it derived suggestions from Syria or Egypt, it was far more the product of Irish temperament, customs, and conditions. One may also find a potent source in the monastic communities alleged to have existed in Ireland in the days of the Druids. Doubtless many members of that caste became Christian monks.

The noblest passion of Irish monastic Christianity was to *peregrinare* for the sake of Christ, and spread the Faith among the heathen ; the most interesting episodes of its history are the wanderings and missionary labours and foundations of its leaders. The careers of Columba and Columbanus afford grandiose examples. Something has been said of the former. The monastery which he founded on the Island of Iona was the Faith's fountainhead for Scotland and the Saxon north of England in the sixth and seventh centuries. About the time of Columba's birth, men from Dalriada on the north coast of Ireland crossed the water to found another Dalriada in the present Argyleshire, and transfer the name of Scotia (Ireland) to Scotland. When Columba landed at Iona, these settlers were hard pressed by the heathen Picts under King Brude or Bridius. Accompanied by two Pictish Christians, he penetrated to Brude's dwelling, near the modern Inverness, converted that monarch in 565, and averted the overthrow of Dalriada. For the next thirty years Columba and his monks did not cease from their labours ; numbers of monasteries were founded, daughters of Iona ; and great parts of Scotland became Christian at least in name. The supreme authority

---

[1] On Patrick, see Bury, *The Life of St. Patrick and his Place in History* (London, 1905).

was the Abbot of Iona with his council of monks ; " bishops " performed their functions under him.   Early in the seventh century, St. Aidan was ordained bishop in Iona and sent to convert the Anglo-Saxons of Northumberland.   The story of the Irish Church in the north is one of effective mission work, but unsuccessful organization, wherein it was inferior to the Roman Church.   Its representatives suffered defeat at the Synod of Whitby in 664.   Fifty years afterward Iona gave up its separate usages and accepted the Roman Easter.[1]

The missionary labours of the Irish were not confined to Great Britain, but extended far and wide through the west of Europe.   In the sixth and seventh centuries, Irish monasteries were founded in Austrasia and Burgundy, Italy, Switzerland, Bavaria ; they were established among Frisians, Saxons, Alemanni.   And as centres of Latin education as well as Christianity, the names of Bobbio and St. Gall will occur to every one.   Of these, the first directly and the second through a disciple were due to Columbanus.   With him we enter the larger avenues of Irish missions to the heathen, the semi-heathen, and the lax, and upon the question of their efficacy in the preservation of Latin education throughout the rent and driven fragments of the western Roman Empire.   The story of Columban's life is illuminating and amusing.[2]

---

[1] As for the Irish Church in Ireland, there were many differences in usage between it and the Church of Rome.   In the matters of Easter and the tonsure the southern Irish were won over to the Roman customs before the middle of the seventh century, and after that the Roman Easter made its way to acceptance through the island.   Yet still the Irish appear to have used their own Liturgy, and to have shown little repugnance to the marriage of priests.   The organization of the churches remained monastic rather than diocesan or episcopal, in spite of the fact that " bishops," apparently with parochial functions, existed in great numbers.   Hereditary customs governed the succession of the great abbots, as at Armagh, until the time of St. Malachy, a contemporary of St. Bernard. See St. Bernard's *Life of Malachy*, chap. x., Migne 182, col. 1086, cited by Killen, *o.c.* vol. i. p. 173.   The exertions of Gregory VII. and Lanfranc, Archbishop of Canterbury, did much to bring the Irish Church into obedience to Rome.   Various Irish synods in the twelfth century completed a proper diocesan system.   Cf. Killen, *Eccl. Hist. of Ireland*, vol. i. pp. 162-222 ; also the article in the *Encyclopaedia Britannica* on the history of Ireland by Quiggin and Bagwell.

[2] The works of St. Columbanus or Columban, usually called of Luxeuil, are printed in Migne's *Patrologia Latina*, 80, col. 209-296.   The chief source of knowledge of his life is the *Vita* by Jonas his disciple : Migne, *Pat. Lat.* 87, col. 1009-1046. It has been translated by D. C. Munro, in vol. ii. No. 7 (series of 1895) of *Translations, etc.*, published by University of Pennsylvania (Phila. 1897).   See also Montalembert, *Monks of the West*, book vii. (vol. ii. of English translation).

He was born in Leinster. While yet a boy he felt the
conflict between fleshly lusts and that counter-ascetic passion
which throughout the Christian world was drawing thousands
into monasteries. Asceticism, with desire for knowledge,
won the victory, and the youth entered the monastery of
Bangor, in the extreme north-east of Ireland. There he
passed years of labour, study, and self-mortification. At
length the pilgrim mission-passion came upon him (*coepit
peregrinationem desiderare*) and his importunity overcame
the abbot's reluctance to let him depart. Twelve disciples
are said to have followed him across the water to the shores
of Britain. There they hesitated in anxious doubt, till it
was decided to cross to Gaul.

This was about the year 590. Columban's austere and
commanding form, his fearlessness, his quick and fiery
tongue, impressed the people among whom he came.
Reports of his holiness spread ; multitudes sought his
blessing. He traversed the country, preaching and setting
his own stern example, until he reached the land of the
Burgundians, where Gontran, a grandson of Clovis, reigned.
Well received by this ruler, Columban established himself in
an old castle. His disciples grew in numbers, and after a
while Gontran granted him an extensive Roman structure
called Luxovium (Luxeuil) situated at the confines of the
Burgundian and Austrasian kingdoms. Columban converted this into a monastery, and it soon included many
noble Franks and Burgundians among its monks. For them
he composed a monastic *regula*, stern and cruel in its penalties
of many stripes imposed for trivial faults. " Whoever may
wish to know his strenuousness (*strenuitatem*) will find it in
his precepts," writes the monk Jonas, who had lived under
him.

The strenuousness of this masterful and overbearing
man was displayed in his controversy with the Gallican
clergy, upon whom he tried to impose the Easter day
observed by the Celtic Church in the British Isles. In his
letter to the Gallican synod, he points out their errors, and
lectures them on their Christian duties, asking pardon at the
end for his loquacity and presumption. Years afterwards,
entering upon another controversy, he wrote an extra-

ordinary letter to Pope Boniface IV. The superscription is
Hibernian : " To the most beautiful head of all the churches
of entire Europe, the most sweet pope, the most high
president, the most reverent investigator : O marvellous !
mirum dictu ! nova res ! rara avis !—that the lowest to the
loftiest, the clown to the polite, the stammerer to the prince
of eloquence, the stranger to the son of the house, the last
to the first, that the Wood-pigeon (Palumbus) should dare
to write to Father Boniface ! " Whereupon this Wood-
pigeon writes a long letter in which belligerent expostulation
alternates with self-debasement. He dubs himself "garrulus,
presumptuosus, homunculus vilissimae qualitatis," who caps
his impudence by writing unrequested. He implores pardon
for his harsh and too biting speech, while he deplores—to
him who sat thereon—the *infamia* of Peter's Seat, and shrills
to the Pope to watch : " Vigila itaque, quaeso, papa, vigila ;
et iterum dico : vigila " ; and he marvels at the Pope's
lethal sleep.

One who thus berated pope and clergy might be cen-
sorious of princes. Gontran died. After various dynastic
troubles, the Burgundian land came under the rule nominally
of young Theuderic, but actually of his imperious grand-
mother, the famous Brunhilde. In order that no queen-
wife's power should supplant her own, she encouraged her
grandson to content himself with mistresses. The youth
stood in awe of the stern old figure ruling at Luxeuil, who
more than once reproved him for not wedding a lawful
queen. It happened one day when Columban was at
Brunhilde's residence that she brought out Theuderic's
various sons for him to bless. " Never shall sceptre be held
by this brothel-brood," said he.

Henceforth it was war between these two : Theuderic
was the pivot of the storm ; the one worked upon his fears,
the other played upon his lusts. Brunhilde prevailed. She
incited the king to insist that Luxeuil be made open to all,
and with his retinue to push his way into the monastery.
The saint withstood him fiercely, and prophesied his ruin.
The king drew back ; the saint followed, heaping reproaches
on him, till the young king said with some self-restraint :
" You hope to win the crown of martyrdom through me.

But I am not a lunatic, to commit such a crime. I have a better plan : since you won't fall in with the ways of men of the world, you shall go back by the road you came."

So the king sent his retainers to seize the stubborn saint. They took him as a prisoner to Besançon. He escaped, and hurried back to Luxeuil. Again the king sent, this time a count with soldiers, to drive him from the land. They feared the sacrilege of laying hands on the old man. In the church, surrounded by his monks praying and singing psalms, he awaited them. " O man of God," cried the count, " we beseech thee to obey the royal command, and take thy way to the place from which thou camest." " Nay, I will rather please my Creator, by abiding here," returned the saint. The count retired, leaving a few rough soldiers to carry out the king's will. These, still fearing to use violence, begged the saint to take pity on them, unjustly burdened with this evil task—to disobey their orders meant their death. The saint reiterates his determination to abide, till they fall on their knees, cling to his robe, and with groans implore his pardon for the crime they must execute.

From pity the saint yields at last, and a company of the king's men make ready and escort him from the kingdom westward toward Brittany. Many miracles mark the journey. They reach the Loire, and embark on it. Proceeding down the river they come to Tours, where the saint asks to be allowed to land and worship at St. Martin's shrine. The leader bids the rowers keep the middle of the stream and row on. But the boat resistlessly made its way to the landing-place. Columban passed the night at the shrine, and the next day was hospitably entertained by the bishop, who inquired why he was returning to his native land. " The dog Theuderic has driven me from my brethren," answered the saint. At last Nantes was reached near the mouth of the Loire, where the vessel was waiting to carry the exile back to Ireland. Columban wrote a letter to his monks, in which he poured forth his love to them with much advice as to their future conduct. The letter is filled with grief—suppressed lest it unman his beloved children. " While I write, the messenger comes to say that the ship is ready to bear me, unwilling, to my country. But there is no guard to prevent my escape, and these people even seem to wish it."

The letter ends, but not the story. Columban did not sail for Ireland. Jonas says that the vessel was miraculously impeded, and that then Columban was permitted to go whither he would. So the dauntless old man travelled back from the sea, and went to the Neustrian Court, the people along the way bringing him their children to bless. He did not rest in Neustria, for the desire was upon him to preach to the heathen. Making his way to the Rhine, he embarked near Mainz, ascended the river, and at last established himself, with his disciples, upon the lake of Constance. There they preached to the heathen, and threw their idols into the lake. He had the thought to preach to the Wends, but this was not to be.

The time soon came when all Austrasia fell into the hands of Brunhilde and Theuderic, and Columbanus decided to cross over into northern Italy, breaking out in anger at his disciple Gall, who was too sick to go with him. With other disciples he made the arduous journey, and reached the land of the Lombards. King Agilulf made him a gift of Bobbio, lying in a gorge of the Apennines near Genoa, and there he founded the monastery which long was to be a stronghold of letters. For himself, his career was well-nigh run ; he retired to a solitary spot on the banks of the river Trebbia, where he passed away, being, apparently, some seventy years of age.

It may seem surprising that this strenuous ascetic should occasionally have occupied a leisure hour writing Latin poems in imitation of the antique. There still exists such an effusion to a friend :

> " Accipe, quaeso,
> Nunc bipedali
> Condita versu
> Carminulorum
> Munera parva."

The verses consist mainly of classic allusions and advice of an antique rather than a Christian flavour : the wise will

cease to add coin to coin, and will despise wealth, but not
the pastime of such verse as the

> " Inclyta Vates
> Nomine Sappho "

was wont to make. " Now, dear Fedolius, quit learned
numbers and accept our squibs—*frivola nostra.* I have
dictated them oppressed with pain and old age : Vive, vale,
laetus, tristisque memento senectae." The last is a pagan
reminiscence, which the saint's Christian soul may not have
deeply felt. But the poem shows the saint's classic training,
which probably was exceptional. For there is no evidence
of like knowledge in any Irishman before him ; and after
his time, in the seventh century, or the eighth, Latin education in Ireland was confined to a few monastic centres. A
small minority studied the profanities, sometimes because
they liked them, but oftener as the means of proficiency in
sacred learning.

The Irish had cleverness, facility, ardour, and energy.
They did much for the dissemination of Christianity and
letters. Their deficiency was lack of organization ; and
they had but little capacity for ordered discipline humbly
and obediently accepted from others. Consequently, when
the period of evangelization was past in western Europe,
and organization was needed, with united and persistent
effort for order, the Irish ceased to lead or even to keep pace
with those to whom once they had brought the Gospel. In
Anglo-Saxon England and on the Carolingian continent
they became strains of influence handed on. This was the
fortune which overtook them as illuminators of manuscripts
and preservers of knowledge. Their emotional traits, moreover, entered the larger currents of mediaeval feeling and
imagination. Strains of the Irish, or of a kindred Celtic
temperament passed on into such " Breton " matters as the
Tristan story, wherein love is passion unrestrained, and is
more distinctly out of relationship with ethical considerations than, for example, the equally adulterous tale of
Lancelot and Guinevere.[1]

[1] The article of H. Zimmer, " Uber die Bedeutung des irischen Elements für
die mittelalterliche Cu'tur," *Preussische Jahrbücher,* Bd. 59, 1887, presents an
interesting summary of the Irish influence. His views, and still more those of

II.

The Saxon invasions of the fifth and sixth centuries drove Christianity and letters from the land where the semi-Romanized Britons and their church had flourished. To reconvert and instruct anew a relapsed heathen country was the task which Gregory the Great laid on the willing Augustine. The story of that famous mission (A.D. 597) need not be told ; [1] but we may note the manner of the presentation of Christianity to the heathen Saxons, and the temper of its reception. Most impressive was this bringing of the Faith. Augustine and his band of monks came as a stately embassy from Rome, the traditionary centre of imperial and spiritual power. Their coming was a solemn call to the English to associate themselves with all that was most august and authoritative in heaven and earth. According to Bede, Augustine sent a messenger to Ethelbert, the Kentish king, to announce that he had come from Rome bearing the best of messages, and would assure to such as hearkened, eternal joys in heaven and dominion without end with the living and true God. To Ethelbert, whose kingdom lay at the edge of the great world, the message came from this world's sovereign pontiff, who in some awful way represented its almighty God, and had authority to admit to His kingdom. He was not ignorant of what lay within the hand of Rome to give. His wife was a Catholic Christian, daughter of a Frankish king, and had her own ministering bishop. Doubtless the queen had spoken with her lord. Still Ethelbert feared the spell-craft of this awe-inspiring embassy, and would meet Augustine only under

---

Ozanam in *Civilisation chrétienne chez les Francs*, chap. v., should be controlled by the detailed discussion in Roger's *L'Enseignement des lettres classiques d'Ausone à Alcuin* (Paris, 1905), chaps. vi. vii. and viii.   See also G. T. Stokes, *Ireland and the Celtic Church*, Lect. XI. (London, 1892, 3rd ed.); D'Arbois de Jubainville, *Introduction à l'étude de la littérature celtique*, livre ii. chap. ix. ; F. J. H. Jenkinson, *The Hisperica Famina* (Cambridge and New York, 1909).   Obviously it is un-justifiable (though it has been done) to regard the scholarship of gifted Irishmen who lived on the Continent in the ninth century (Sedulius Scotus, Eriugena, etc.) as evidence of scholarship in Ireland in the sixth, seventh, or eighth century. We do not know where these later men obtained their knowledge; there is little reason to suppose that they got it in Ireland.

[1] See the narrative in Green's *History of the English People*.

the open sky. Augustine came to the meeting, a silver cross borne before him as a banner, and the pictured image of Christ, his monks singing litanies and loudly supplicating their Lord for the king's and their own salvation. Knowledge, authority, supernatural power, were represented here. And how could the king fail to be struck by the nobility of Augustine's Gospel message, by its clear assurance, its love and terror,[1] so overwhelming and convincing, so far outsoaring Ethelbert's heathen religion ? To be sure, in Christian love and forgiveness lay some reversal of Saxon morality, for instance of the duty of revenge. But this was not prominent in the Christianity of the day ; and experience was to show that only in isolated instances did this teaching impede the acceptance of the Gospel.[2]

Ethelbert spoke these missionaries fair ; accorded them a habitation in Canterbury with the privilege of celebrating their Christian rites and preaching to his people. There they abode, zealous in vigils and fastings, and preaching the word of life. Certain heathen men were converted, then the king, and then his folk in multitudes—the usual way. Under the direction of Gregory, Augustine proceeded with that combination of insistence, dignity, and tolerance, so well understood in the Roman Church. There was insistence upon the main doctrines and requirements of the Faith—upon the Roman Easter day and baptism, as against the practices of the British Church. Tolerance was shown respecting heathen fanes and sacrificial feastings ; the fanes should be reconsecrated as Christian churches ; the feasts should be continued in honour of the true God.[3]

Besides zeal and knowledge and authority, miracles advanced Augustine's enterprise. To eliminate by any sweeping negation the miraculous element from the causes

---

[1] There is no positive evidence that Augustine painted the terrors of the Day of Judgment in his first preaching. But it was a chief part of the mediaeval Gospel, and never absent from the soul of Augustine's master, Gregory. The latter set it forth vividly in his letter to Ethelbert after his baptism (Bede, *Hist. Ecc.* i. 32).

[2] Bede, *Hist. Ecc.* iii. 22, tells how a certain noble gesith slew his king from exasperation with the latter's practice of forgiving his enemies, instead of requiting them, according to the principles of heathen morality.

[3] Bede, *Hist. Ecc.* i. 30. Well known are the picturesque scenes surrounding the long controversy as to Easter between the Roman clergy and the British and Irish. The matter bulks hugely in Bede's book, as it did in his mind.

of success of such a mission is to close our eyes to the situation. All men expected miracles ; Gregory who sent Augustine was infatuated with them. Augustine performed them, or believed he did, and others believed it too. Throughout these centuries, and indeed late into the mediaeval period, the power and habit of working miracles constituted sainthood in the hermit or the monk, thereby singled out as the special instrument of God's will or the Virgin's kindness. Of course miracles were ascribed to the great missionary apostles like Augustine or Boniface ; and this conviction brought many conversions.

Among the heathen English about to be converted, there was diversity of view and mood as to the Faith. They stood in awe of these newcomers from Rome, fearing their spell-craft. From their old religion they had sought earthly victory and prosperity ; and some had found it of uncertain aid. " See, king, how this matter stands," says Coifi, at the Northumbrian Witenagemot held by Edwin to decide as to the new religion : " I have learned of a certainty that there is no virtue or utility whatever in that religion which we have been following. None of your thanes has slaved in the worship of our gods more zealously than I. Yet many have had greater rewards and dignities from you, and in every way have prospered more. Were the gods worth anything, they would wish rather to aid me, who have been so zealous in serving them. So if these new teachings are better and stronger, let us accept them at once." [1] Coifi expressed the common motives of converts of all nations from the time of Constantine. No better thought of Christian expediency had inspired Gregory of Tours's story of Clovis's career ; and Bede in no way condemns Coifi's *verba prudentiae*, as he terms them. Naturally in times of adversity such converts were quick to abandon their new religion, proved ineffectual.[2]

Among these Angles of Northumberland, however, finer souls were looking for light and certitude. Such a one was that thane who followed Coifi with the wonderful illustration of man's mortal need of enlightenment, the thane for whom life was as the swallow flying through the warmed and

---

[1] Bede ii. 13. [2] *E.g.* as in Bede iii. 1.

lighted hall, from the dark cold into the dark cold : " So this life of men comes into sight for a little ; we are ignorant of what shall follow or what may have preceded. If this new doctrine offers anything more certain, I think we should follow it." The heathen poetry had given varied voice to this contemplative melancholy so wont to dwell on life's untoward changes ; and there was ghostly evidence of the other world before the coming of the Roman monks. Now, as those monks came with authority from the traditionary home of ghostly lore, why question their knowledge of the life beyond the grave ? Many Anglo-Saxons were prepared to fix their gaze upon a life to come and to let their fancies fill with visions of the great last severance unto heaven and hell. When once impressed by the monastic Christianity [1] of the Roman, or the Irish, mission, they were quick to throw themselves into the ascetic life which most surely opened heaven's doors. So many a noble thane became an anchorite or a monk, many a noble dame became a nun; and Saxon kings forsook their kingdoms for the cloister : " Cenred, who for some time had reigned most nobly in Mercia, still more nobly abandoned his sceptre. For he came to Rome, and there was tonsured and made a monk at the church of the Apostles, and continued in prayers and fastings and almsgiving until his last day." [2]

As might be expected, the re-expression of Christianity in Anglo-Saxon writings was martial and emotional. A martial tone pervades the epic paraphrases of Scripture, the Anglo-Saxon *Genesis* for example. On the other hand, adaptations of devotional Latin compositions [3] evince a realization of Christian feeling and prevalent ascetic sentiments. The " elegiac " Anglo-Saxon feeling seems to reach its height in a more original composition, the *Christ* of Cynewulf, while the emotional fervour coming with Christianity is disclosed in Bede's account of the inspiration which fell upon the cowherd Cædmon, in St. Hilda's monastery

---

[1] One may bear in mind that practically all active proselytizing Christianity of the period was of a monastic type.

[2] A D. 709. *Hist. Ecc.* v. 19, where another instance is also given ; and see *ibid.* v. 7.

[3] See the pieces in Thorpe's *Codex Exoniensis, e.g.* the " Supplication," p. 452.

of Whitby, to sing the story of creation.[1] A pervasive monastic atmosphere also surrounds the visions of hell and purgatory, which were to continue so typically characteristic of monastic Christianity.[2]

What knowledge, sacred and profane, came to the Anglo-Saxons with Christianity ? Quite properly learned were Augustine and the other organizers of the English Church. Two generations after him, the Greek monk Theodore was sent by the Pope to become Archbishop of Canterbury, complete Augustine's work, and instruct the English monks and clergy. Theodore was accompanied by his friend Hadrian, as learned as himself. Their labours finally established Roman Christianity in England. The two drew about them a band of students, and formed at Canterbury a school of sacred learning, where liberal studies were conducted by these foreigners with a knowledge and intelligence novel in Great Britain. In the north, Benedict Biscop, a Northumbrian, promoted the ends of Roman Catholicism and learning by establishing the monasteries of Wearmouth and Jarrow under the monastic *regula* of St. Benedict of Nursia, as modified by the practices of continental monasteries in the seventh century. He had been in Italy, and brought thence many books. It was among these books that Bede grew up at Jarrow.

Thus strong currents of Roman ecclesiasticism and liberal knowledge reached England. On the other hand, Irish monastic Christianity had already made its entry in the south-western part of Great Britain, and with greater strength established itself in the north, converting multitudes to the Faith and instructing such as would learn. The Irish teaching had been eagerly received by those groups of Anglo-Saxons who henceforth were to prosecute their studies with the aid of the further knowledge and discipline brought from the Continent by Theodore. Some of them had even journeyed to Ireland to study.

From this dual source was drawn the education of

---

[1] *Ecc. Hist.* iv. 22.

[2] Bede, *Hist. Ecc.* iii. 19 ; v. 12, 13, 14. Of these the most famous is the vision of Fursa, an Irishman ; but others were had by Northumbrians. Plummer, in his edition of Bede, vol. ii. p. 294, gives a list of such visions in the Middle Ages.

Aldhelm. He was born in Wessex about the year 650, and
was nephew of the powerful King Ini. He became abbot
of Malmesbury in 675. An Irish monk was his first teacher ;
his second, the learned Hadrian. From the two he received
a broader education than any Anglo-Saxon had possessed
before him. Always holding in view the perfecting of his
sacred knowledge, he studied grammar and kindred topics,
produced treatises himself, and as a Catholic student and
teacher was a true forerunner of the greatest scholar among
his younger contemporaries, Bede.[1]

Bede the Venerable, and we may add the still beloved,
was Aldhelm's junior by some twenty-five years. He was
born in 673 and died in 735. He passed his whole life
reading, teaching, and writing in the Cloister of Jarrow near
where he was born, and not far from where, beneath the
" Galilee " of Durham Cathedral, his bones have long re-
posed. Behind him was the double tradition of learning,
the Irish and the Graeco-Roman. Through a long life of
pious study, Bede drew into his mind, and incorporated in
his writings, practically the total sum of knowledge then
accessible in western Europe. He stands between the great
Latin transmitters (Boëthius, Cassiodorus, Gregory and
Isidore) and the epoch known as the Carolingian. He was
himself a transmitter of knowledge to that later time. If
in spirit, race, epoch and circumstances, Aldhelm was Bede's
direct forerunner, Bede had also a notable predecessor in
Isidore. The writings of the Spanish bishop contributed
substance and suggestions of plan and method to the Anglo-
Saxon monk, whose works embrace practically the same
series of topics as Isidore's, whose intellectual interests also,
and attitude toward the Church Fathers, appear the same.
But Bede was the more genial personality, and could not
help imbuing his compositions with something from his
own temperament. Even in his Commentaries upon the
books of Scripture, which were made up principally of
borrowed allegorical interpretations, there is common sense
and some endeavour to present the actual meaning and

[1] On Aldhelm see Ebert, *Allegemeine Ges. der Lit. des Mittelalters* ; and Roger,
L'Enseignement des lettres classiques, etc., p. 288 *sqq.* ; also Leslie Stephen in
Dict. Nat. Biog., and R. Ehwald, " Aldhelm von Malmesbury," *Königl. Akad. zu
Erfurt*, N.F. xxxiii. (1907).

situation.[1] But he disclaimed originality, as he says in the
preface to his Commentary on the Hexaemeron, addressed
to Bishop Acca of Hexham :

" Concerning the beginning of Genesis where the creation of
the world is described, many have said much, and have left to
posterity monuments of their talents.   Among these, as far as our
feebleness can learn, we may distinguish Basil of Caesarea (whom
Eustathius translated from Greek to Latin), Ambrose of Milan,
and Augustine, Bishop of Hippo.   Of whom the first-named in
nine books, the second following his footprints in six books, the
third in twelve books and also in two others directed against the
Manichaeans, shed floods of salutary doctrine for their readers ;
and in them the promise of the Truth was fulfilled : ' Whoso
believeth in me, as the Scripture saith, out of his belly shall flow
rivers of living water. . . .'   But since these works are so great
that only the rich may own them, and so profound that they may
be fathomed only by the learned, your holiness has seen fit to lay
on us the task of plucking from them all, as from the sweetest
wide-flowering fields of paradise, what might seem to meet the
needs of weaklings." [2]

Bede was also a lovely story-teller.   His literary charm
and power appear in his Life of St. Cuthbert, and still more
in his ever - famous *Ecclesiastical History of the English
People*, so warm with love of mankind, and presenting so
wonderful a series of dramatic stories animate with vital
motive and the colour of incident and circumstance.   Midway between the spontaneous genius of this work and the
copied Scripture Commentary, stand Bede's grammatical,
metrical, and scientific compositions, compiled with studious
zeal.   They evince a broad interest in scholarship and in
nature.   Still, neither material nor method was original.
For instance, his *De rerum natura* took its plan and much
of its substance from Isidore's work of the same name.
Bede has, however, inserted further matter and made his
work less of a mere shell of words than Isidore's.   For he

---

[1] This is noticeable in his Commentary on the Gospel of John, Migne, *Pat.
Lat.* 92, col. 633 *sqq.*
[2] Migne, *Pat. Lat.* 91, col. 9.   In another prefatory epistle to the same bishop
Acca, Bede intimates that he has abridged the language of the Fathers : he says
it is inconvenient always to put their names in the text.   Instead he has inscribed
the proper initials of each Father in the margin opposite to whatever he may
have taken from him (*In Lucae Evangelium expositio*, Migne 92, col. 304).

is interested in connecting natural occurrences with their
causes, stating, for example, that the tides depend on the
moon.[1] In this work as in his other *opera didascalica*, like
the *De temporum ratione* and his learned *De arte metrica*,[2]
he shows himself a more intelligent student than his Spanish
predecessor. Yet he drew everything from some written
source.

One need not wonder at the voluminousness of Bede's
literary productions.[3] Many of the writings emanating
from monasteries are transcriptions rather than compositions.
The circumstance that books, *i.e.* manuscripts, were rare and
costly was an impelling motive. Isidore and Bede made
systematic compilations for general use. They and their
congeners would also make extracts from manuscripts, of
which they might have but the loan, or from unique codices
in order to preserve the contents. Such notes or excerpts
might have the value of a treatise, and might be preserved
and in turn transcribed as a distinct work. Yet whether
made by a Bede or by a lesser man, they represent mainly
the labour of a copyist.

Bede's writings were all in Latin, and were intended
for the instruction of monks. They played a most important
rôle in the transmission of learning, sacred and profane, in
Latin form. For its still more popular diffusion, translations into the vernacular might be demanded. Such at all
events were made of Scripture ; and perhaps a century and
a half after Bede's death, the translation of edifying Latin
books was undertaken by the best of Saxon kings. King
Alfred was born in 849 and closed his eyes in 901 In the
midst of other royal labours he set himself the task of
placing before his people, or at least his clergy, Anglo-
Saxon versions of some of the then most highly regarded
volumes of instruction. The wise *Pastoral Care* of Gregory
the Great ; his *Dialogues*, less wise according to our views ;
the *Histories* of Orosius [4] and Bede ; and that philosophic

[1] Migne 90, col. 258 ; *ibid.* col. 422. I have not observed this statement
in Isidore.

[2] All of these are in t. 90 of Migne.

[3] His writings fill about five volumes (90-95) in Migne's *Patrol. Latina.* A
list may be found in the article " Bede " in the *Dictionary of National Biography.*
Beda der Ehrwürdige, by Karl Werner (Vienna, 1881), is a good monograph.

[4] *Ante*, p. 82 *sqq.*

vade mecum of the Middle Ages, the *De consolatione philosophiae* of Boëthius. Of these, Alfred translated the *Pastoral Care* and the *De consolatione*, also Orosius ; the other works appear to have been translated at his direction.[1] Alfred's translations contain his own reflections and other matter not in the originals. In rendering Orosius, he rewrote the geographical introduction, inserted a description of Germany and accounts of northern Europe given by two of his Norse liegemen, Ohthere and Wulfstan. The alertness of his mind is shown by this insertion of the latest geographical knowledge. Other and more personal passages will disclose his purpose, and illustrate the manner in which his Christianized intelligence worked upon trains of thought suggested perhaps by the Latin writing before him.

Alfred's often-quoted preface to Gregory's *Pastoral Care* tells his reasons for undertaking its translation, and sets forth the condition of England. He speaks of the " wise men there formerly were throughout England, both of sacred and secular orders," and of their zeal in learning and teaching and serving God ; and how foreigners came to the land in search of wisdom and instruction. But " when I came to the throne," so general was the decay of learning in England " that there were very few on this side of the Humber who could understand their rituals in English, or translate a letter from Latin into English ; and I believe there were not many beyond the Humber. . . . Thanks be to God Almighty that we have any teachers among us now." Alfred therefore commands the bishop, to whom he is now sending the copy, to disengage himself as often as possible from worldly matters, and apply the Christian wisdom God has given him. " I remembered also how I saw, before it had been all ravaged and burnt, how the churches throughout the whole of England stood filled with treasures and books, and there was also a great multitude of God's

[1] *The Works of King Alfred the Great* are translated from Anglo-Saxon in the Jubilee edition of Giles (2 vols. London, 1858). The *Pastoral Care* and the *Orosius* are translated by Henry Sweet in the publications of the Early English Text Society. W. J. Sedgefield's translation of Alfred's version of the *Consolations of Boëthius* is very convenient from the italicizing of the portions added by Alfred to Boëthius's original. The extracts given in the following pages have been taken from these editions.

servants, but they had very little knowledge of books, for
they could not understand anything of them because they
were not written in their own language." It therefore
seemed wise to me " to translate some books which are
most needful for all men to know, into the language which
we can all understand, and . . . that all the youth now in
England of free men, who are rich enough to be able to
devote themselves to it, be set to learn so long as they are
not fit for any other occupation, until that they are well
able to read English writing : and let those be afterwards
taught more in the Latin language who are to continue
learning and be promoted to a higher rank."

In the *De consolatione* of Boëthius, the antique pagan
thought, softened with human sympathy, and in need of
such comfort and assurance as was offered by the Faith,
is found occupied with questions (like that of free-will)
prominent in Christianity. The book presented meditations which were so consonant with Christian views that its
Christian readers from Alfred to Dante mistook them for
Christian sentiments, and added further meanings naturally
occurring to the Christian soul. Alfred's reflections in his
version of the *De consolatione* are very personal to Saxon
Alfred and show how he took his life and kingly office .

" O Philosophy, thou knowest that I never greatly delighted
in covetousness and the possession of earthly power, nor longed
for this authority "—so far Boëthius,[1] and now Alfred himself :
" but I desired instruments and materials to carry out the work
I was set to do, which was that I should virtuously and fittingly
administer the authority committed unto me. Now no man,
as thou knowest, can get full play for his natural gifts, nor conduct
and administer government, unless he hath fit tools, and the raw
material to work upon. By material I mean that which is
necessary to the exercise of natural powers ; thus a king's raw
material and instruments of rule are a well-peopled land, and he
must have men of prayer, men of war, and men of work. As
thou knowest, without these tools no king may display his special
talent. Further, for his materials he must have means of support
for the three classes above spoken of, which are his instruments ;

---

[1] Boëthius's words, which Alfred here paraphrases and supplements, are as
follows : " Tum ego, scis, inquam, ipsa minimum nobis ambitionem mortalium
rerum fuisse dominatam ; sed materiam gerendis rebus optavimus, quo ne virtus
tacita consenesceret " (*De consol. phil.* ii. prosa 7).

and these means are land to dwell in, gifts, weapons, meat, ale, clothing, and what else soever the three classes need. Without these means he cannot keep his tools in order, and without these tools he cannot perform any of the tasks entrusted to him. [I have desired material for the exercise of government that my talents and my power might not be forgotten and hidden away [1]] for every good gift and every power soon groweth old and is no more heard of, if Wisdom be not in them. Without Wisdom no faculty can be fully brought out, for whatsoever is done unwisely can never be accounted as skill. To be brief, I may say that it has ever been my desire to live honourably while I was alive, and after my death to leave to them that should come after me my memory in good works."

The last sentence needs no comment. But those preceding it will be illuminated by another passage inserted by Alfred :

" Therefore it is that a man never by his authority attains to virtue and excellence, but by reason of his virtue and excellence he attains to authority and power. No man is better for his power, but for his skill he is good, if he is good, and for his skill he is worthy of power, if he is worthy of it. Study Wisdom then, and, when ye have learned it, contemn it not, for I tell you that by its means ye may without fail attain to power, yea, even though not desiring it."

Perhaps from the teaching of his own life Alfred knew, as well as Boëthius, the toil and sadness of power : " Though their false hope and imagination lead fools to believe that power and wealth are the highest good, yet it is quite otherwise." And again, speaking of friendship, he says that Nature unites friends in love, " but by means of these worldly goods and the wealth of this life we oftener make foes than friends," which doubtless Alfred had discovered, as well as Marcus Aurelius. Perhaps the Saxon king knew wherein lay peace, as he makes Wisdom say : " When I rise aloft with these my servants, we look down upon the storms of this world, even as the eagle does when he soars in stormy weather above the clouds, where no storm can harm him." The king was thinking of man's peace with God.[2]

[1] The substance of this bracketed clause is in Boëthius—the last words quoted in the preceding note.

[2] Towards the close of his life Alfred gathered some thoughts from Augustine's *Soliloquies* and from other writings, with which he mingled reflections of his own. He called the book *Blossoms*. He says in his preface : " I gathered me then

III

Christianity came to the cities of Provincia and the chief Roman colonies of Gaul (Lyons, Trèves, Cologne) in the course of the original dissemination of the Faith. There were Roman, Greek, or Syrian Christians in these towns before the end of the second century. Early Gallic Christianity spoke Greek and Latin, and its rather slow advance was due partly to the tenacity of Celtic speech even in the cities ; while outside of them heathen speech and practices were scarcely touched. Through Gaul and along the Rhine, the country in the main continued heathen in religion, and Celtic or Germanic in speech, during the fifth century.[1] The complete Latinizing of Gaul and the conversion of its rural population proceeded from the urban churches, and from the labours and miracles of anchorites and monks. In contrast with the decay of the municipal governments, the urban churches continued living institutions. Their bishops usually were men of energy. The episcopal office was elective, yet likely to remain in the same influential family, and the bishop, the leading man in the town, might be its virtual ruler. He represented Christianity and Latin culture, and when Roman officials yielded to Teutonic conquerors, the bishop was left as the spokesman of the

staves and props, and bars, and helves for each of my tools, and boughs ; and for each of the works that I could work, I took the fairest trees, so far as I might carry them away. Nor did I ever bring any burden home without longing to bring home the whole wood, if that might be ; for in every tree I saw something of which I had need at home. Wherefore I exhort every one who is strong, and has many wains, that he direct his steps to the same wood where I cut the props. Let him there get him others, and load his wains with fair twigs, that he may weave thereof many a goodly wain, and set up many a noble house, and build many a pleasant town, and dwell therein in mirth and ease, both winter and summer, as I could never do hitherto. But He who taught me to love that wood, He may cause me to dwell more easily, both in this transitory dwelling . . . and also in the eternal home which He has promised us " (Translation borrowed from *The Life and Time of Alfred the Great*, by C. Plummer, Clarendon Press, 1902). These metaphors represent Alfred's way of putting what Isidore or Bede or Alcuin meant when they spoke in their prefaces of searching through the pantries of the Fathers or culling the sweetest flowers from the patristic meadows. See *e.g. ante*, Chapter V. and *post*, Chapter X.

[1] Far into the Frankish period there were many heathen in northern Gaul and along the Rhine : Hauck, *Kirchengeschichte Deutschlands*, I. Kap. i. (second edition, Leipzig, 1898). Cf. Vacandard, " L'Idolatrie en Gaule au VI⁰ et au VII⁰ siècles," *Rev. des questions historiques*, 65 (1899), 424-454.

Gallo-Roman population. Thus the Gallic churches, far from succumbing before the barbarian invasions, rescued and appropriated the derelict functions of government. and emerged aggrandized from the political and racial revolution. In the year 400 the city of Trèves was Latin in speech and Roman in government ; in the year 500 the Roman government had been overthrown, and a German-speaking population predominated in what was left of the city, but the church went on unchanged in constitution and in language.

There was constant intercourse between Teutons and Romans along the northern boundaries of the Empire. In the Danube regions many of the former were converted. The Goths, through the labours of Ulfilas and others in the fourth century, became Arian Christians ; their conversion was of moment to themselves and others, but destiny severed the continuity of its import for history. In the provinces of Rhaetia, Vindelicia, and Noricum there were Christians, some of them Teutons, as early as the time of Constantine. For the next century, when disruption of the Empire was in full progress, the Life of St. Severinus by Eugippius, his disciple, gives the picture.[1] Bits and fragments of Roman government endured ; letters were not quite quenched ; but Alemanni and Rugii moved as they would, marauding, besieging, and destroying. Everywhere there was uncertainty and confusion, and yet civilized Roman provincials still clung to a driven life. Through this mountain land, the monk Severinus went here and there, barefoot even in ice and snow, austere, commanding. He encouraged the townspeople to maintain decency and courage ; he turned the barbarians from ruthlessness. Clear-seeing, capable, his energies shielded the land. He was an ascetic who took nothing for himself, and won men to the Faith by this guarantee of disinterestedness. So he shepherded his harrowed flocks, and more than once averted their destruction. But his arm was too feeble ; after his death even his cell was plundered, while the confusion swept on.

Such were fifth-century conditions on the northern boundary of what had been the Empire, conditions amid

---

[1] *Mon. Germ. hist. Auctores antiquissimi*, tom. i. Cf. Ebert, *Ges. der Lit. des Mittelalters*, i. 452 *sqq.*

which the culture and doctrine germane to Christianity went down, although the Faith still glimmered here and there. Farther to the west, the Burgundians had gained a domicile in a land sparsely tenanted by Roman and Catholic provincials. Here on the left bank of the Rhine, in the neighbourhood of Worms, this people accepted the Christianity which they found. Afterwards, in the year 430, their heathen kin on the right bank were baptized as a people ; for they hoped, through aid from fellow-Christians, to ward off the destruction threatening from the Huns. Yet five years later they were overthrown by those savage riders— an overthrow out of which was to rise the *Nibelungenlied.* The Burgundian remnants found a new home by the Rhone.

The Christianity of Burgundians and Goths was subject to the vicissitudes of their fortunes. The permanent conversion to Catholicism of the great masses of the Germans commenced somewhat later, when the turmoil of fifth-century migration was settling into contests for homes destined to prove more lasting. Its beginning may be dated from the baptism of Clovis as a Catholic on Christmas Day in the year 496. His retainers followed him into the consecrated water. By reason of the king's genius for war and politics, this event was the beginning of the final triumph of Catholicism.[1]

The baptism of Clovis and his followers was typical of early Teutonic conversions. King and tribal following acted as a unit. Christ gave victory ; He was the mightier God : such was the crude form of the motive. Its larger scope was grasped by the far-seeing king. Believing in supernatural aid, he desired it from the mightiest source, which, he was persuaded, was the Christian God. It was to be obtained by such homage to Christ as heretofore the king had paid to Wuotan. Any doubt as to the sincerity of his belief presupposes a point of view impossible for a fifth-century barbarian. But to this sincere expectation of Christ's aid, to be gained through baptism, Clovis joined careful consideration of the political situation. Catholic Christianity was the religion of the Gallo-Roman population forming the

[1] Cf. *ante*, Chapter VI.

greater part of the Frankish king's subjects. He knew of
Arian peoples ; probably attempts had been made to draw
him to their side. They constituted the great Teutonic
powers at the time ; for Theodoric was the monarch of Italy,
and Arian Teutons ruled in southern France, in Spain, and
Africa. Nevertheless, it was of paramount importance for
the establishment of his kingdom that there should be no
schism between the Franks and the Gallo-Roman people
who exceeded them in number and in wealth and culture.
Catholic influences surrounded Clovis ; Catholic interests
represented the wealth and prosperity of his dominions, and
when he decided to be baptized he did not waver between
the Catholic and the Arian belief. Thus the king attached
to himself the civilized population of his realm. A common
Catholic faith quickly obliterated racial antagonism within
its boundaries and gained him the support of Catholic church
and people in the kingdoms of his Arian rivals.

So under Clovis and his successors the Gallic Church
became the Frankish Church, and flourished exceedingly.
Tithes were paid it, and gifts were made by princes and
nobles. Its lands increased, carrying their dependent
population, until the Church became the largest landholder
in the Merovingian realm. It was governed by Roman law,
but the clergy were subject to the penal jurisdiction of the
king.[1] It was he that summoned councils, although he did
not vote and left ecclesiastical matters to the bishops, who
were his liegemen and appointees.[2] They recognized the
king's virtually unlimited authority, which they patterned
on the absolute power of the Roman Emperors and the
prerogatives of David and Solomon. In fine, the Merovingian Church was a national church, subject to the king.
Until the seventh century it was quite independent of the
Bishop of Rome.[3]

It is common knowledge—especially vivid with readers

---

[1] In those of its lands which were granted immunity from public burdens,
the Church gradually acquired a jurisdiction by reason of its right to exact
penalties, which elsewhere fell to the king.

[2] The synod of 549 declared (ineffectually) for the election of bishops, to be
followed by royal confirmation.

[3] Hauck, *Kirchenges. Deutschlands*, Bd. I. Buch. ii. Kap. ii. ; Möller, *Kirchengeschichte*, Bd. II. p. 52 *sqq.* (2nd ed., Leipzig, 1893).

of the famous *Historia Francorum* of Gregory of Tours—
that, ethically viewed, the conduct of the Merovingian house
was cruel, treacherous, and abominable ; and likewise the
conduct of their vassals.   Frankish kings and nobles appear
as men no longer bound by the ethics of the heathenism
which they had forsworn, and as yet untouched by the
moral precepts of the Christian code.   Not Christianity,
however, but contact with decadent civilization, and rapid
increase of power and wealth, had loosened their heathen
standards.   Merovingian history leaves a unique impression
of a line of rulers and dependents among whom mercy and
truth and chastity were unknown.   The elements of sixth-
century Christianity which the Franks made their own were
its rites, its magic, and its miracles, and its expectation of
the aid of a God and His saints duly solicited.   Here the
customs of heathenism were a preparation, or themselves
passed into Frankish Christianity.   Nevertheless, the general
character of Christian observances—baptism, the mass,
prayer, the sign of the cross, the rites at marriage, sickness,
and death—could not fail to impress a certain tone and
demeanour upon the people, and impart some sense of human
sinfulness.   The general conviction that patent and outrageous crime would bring divine vengeance gained point
and power from the terrific doctrine of the Day of Wrath,
and the system of penances imposed by the clergy proved
an excellent discipline with these rough Christians.   Many
bishops and priests were little better than the nobles, yet
the Church preserved Christian belief and did something to
improve morality.   Everywhere the monk was the most
striking object-lesson, with his austerities, his terror-stricken
sense of sinfulness, and conviction of the peril of the world.
No martial, grasping bishop, no dissolute and treacherous
priest denied that the monk's was the ideal Christian life ;
and the laity stood in awe, or expectation, of the wonder-
working power of his asceticism.   Indeed monasticism was
becoming popular, and the Merovingian period witnessed
the foundation of numberless cloisters.

   In the fifth and through part of the sixth century the
Gallic monastery of Lerins, on an island in the Mediterranean,
near Fréjus, was a chief source of ascetic and Christian

influence for Gaul. Its monks took their precepts from
Syria and Egypt, and some of the zeal of St. Martin of
Tours had fallen on their shoulders. As the energy of this
community declined, Columban's monastery at Luxeuil
succeeded to the work. The example of Columbanus, his
precepts and severe monastic discipline, proved a source of
ascetic and missionary zeal. With him or following in his
steps came other Irishmen ; and heathen German lands soon
looked upon the walls of many an Irish monastery. But
Columbanus failed, and all the Irish failed, in obedience,
order, and effective organization. His own monastic *regula*,
with all its rigour, contained no provisions for the government of the monasteries. Without due ordering, bands of
monks dwelling in heathen communities would waver in their
practices and even show a lack of doctrinal stability. Sooner
or later they were certain to become confused in habit and
contaminated with the manners of the surrounding people.
These Irish monasteries omitted to educate a native priesthood to perpetuate their Christian teaching. The best of
them, St. Gall (founded by Columbanus's disciple Gallus),
might be a citadel of culture, and convert the people about
it, through the talents and character of its founder and his
successors. But other monasteries, farther to the east, were
tainted with heathen practices. In fine, it was not for the
Irish to convert the great heathen German land, or effect a
lasting reform of existing churches there or in Gaul.

The labours of Anglo-Saxons were fraught with more
enduring results. Through their abilities and zeal, their
faculty of organization and capacity of submitting to
authority, through their consequent harmony with Rome
and the support given them by the Frankish monarchy,
these Anglo-Saxons converted many German tribes, established permanent churches among them, reorganized the
heterogeneous Christianity which they found in certain
German lands, and were a moving factor in the reform of the
Frankish Church. The most striking features of their work
on the Continent were diocesan organization, the training of
a native clergy, the establishment of monasteries under the
Benedictine constitution, union with Rome, obedience to
her commands, strenuous conformity to her law, and in-

sistence on like conformity in others. Their presentation
of Christianity was orthodox, regular, and authoritative.

Some of these features appear in the work of the Saxon
Willibrord among the Frisians, but are more largely illustrated in the career of St. Boniface-Winfried. Willibrord
moved under the authority of Rome ; the varying fortunes
of his labours were connected with the enterprises of Pippin
of Heristal, the father of Charles Martel. They advanced
with the power of that Frankish potentate. But after his
death, during the strife between Neustria and Austrasia, the
heathen Frisian king Radbod drove back Christianity as
he enlarged his dominion at the expense of the divided
Franks. Later, Charles Martel conquered him, and the
Frankish power reached (718) to the Zuyder Zee. Under
its protection Willibrord at last founded the bishopric of
Utrecht (734). He succeeded in educating a native clergy ;
and his labours had lasting result among the Frisians who
were subject to the Franks, but not among the free Frisians
and the Danes.

Evidently there was no sharp geographical boundary
between Christianity and heathendom. Throughout broad
territories, Christian and heathen practices mingled. This
was true of the Frisian land. It was true in greater range
and complexity of the still wider fields of Boniface's career.
This able man surrendered his high station in his native
Wessex in order to serve Christ more perfectly as a missionary monk among the heathen. He went first to Frisia
and worked with Willibrord, yet refused to be his bishop-
coadjutor and successor, because planning to carry Christianity into Germany.

His life strikingly exemplifies Anglo-Saxon faculties
working under the directing power of Rome among heathen
and partly Christian peoples. On his first visit to Rome he
became imbued with the principles, and learned the ritual,
of the Roman Church. He returned to enter into relations
with Charles Martel, and to labour in Hesse and Thuringia,
and again with Willibrord in Frisia. Not long afterwards,
at his own solicitation, Gregory II. called him back to
Rome (722), where he fed his passion for punctilious conformity by binding himself formally to obey the Pope,

follow the practices of the Roman Church, and have no fellowship with bishops whose ways conflicted with them. Gregory made him bishop over Thuringia and Hesse, and sent him back there to reform Christian and heathen communities. Thus Gregory created a bishop within the bounds of the Frankish kingdom—an unprecedented act. Nevertheless, Charles, to whom Boniface came with a letter from Gregory, received him favourably and furnished him with a safe conduct, only exacting a recognition of his own authority.

Boniface set forth upon his mission. In Hesse he cut down the ancient heathen oak, and made a chapel of its timber ; he preached and he organized—the land was not altogether heathen. Then he proceeded to Thuringia. That also was a partly Christian land ; many Irish-Scottish preachers were labouring or dwelling there. Boniface set his face against their irregularities as firmly as against heathenism. Again he dominated and reorganized, yet continued unfailing in energetic preaching to the heathen. Gregory watched closely and zealously co-operated.

On the death of the second Gregory in 731, the third Gregory succeeded to the papacy and continued his predecessor's support of the Anglo-Saxon apostle, making him archbishop with authority to ordain bishops. Many Anglo-Saxons, both men and holy women, came to aid their countryman, and brought their education and their nobler views of life to form centres of Christian culture in the German lands. Cloisters for nuns, cloisters for monks were founded. The year 744 witnessed the foundation of Fulda by Sturm under the direction of Boniface, and destined to be the very apple of his eye and the monastic model for Germany. It was placed under the authority of Rome, with the consent of Pippin, who then ruled. The reorganization rather than the conversion of Bavaria was Boniface's next achievement. The land long before had been partially Romanized, and now was nominally Christian. Here again Boniface acted as representative of the Pope, and not of Charles, although Bavaria was part of the Frankish empire.

The year 738 brought Boniface to Rome for the third time. He was now yearning to leave the fields already tilled, and go as missionary to the heathen Saxons. But Gregory sent him back to complete the reorganization of the Bavarian Church, and to this large field of action he added also Alemannia with its diocesan centre at Speyer. Here he came in conflict with Frankish bishops, firm in their secular irregularities. Yet again he prevailed, reorganized the churches, and placed them under the authority of Rome. Evidently the two Gregories had in large measure turned the energies of Boniface from the mission-field to the labours of reform.

On the death of Charles in 741 (and in the same year died Gregory, to be succeeded by the lukewarm Zacharias) his sons Carloman and Pippin succeeded to his power. The following year Carloman in German-speaking Austrasia called a council of his church (*Concilium Germanicum primum*) under the primacy of Boniface. Its decrees confirmed the reforms for which the latter had struggled :

" We Carloman, Duke and Prince of the Franks, in the year 742 of the Incarnation, on the 21st of April, upon the advice of the servants of God, the bishops and priests of our realm, have assembled them to take counsel how God's law and the Church's discipline (fallen to ruin under former princes) may be restored, and the Christian folk led to salvation, instead of perishing deceived by false priests. We have set up bishops in the cities, and have set over them as archbishop Bonifatius, the legate of St. Peter."

The council decreed that yearly synods should be held, that the possessions taken from the Church should be restored, and the false priests deprived of their emoluments and forced to do penance. The clergy were forbidden to bear arms, go to war, or hunt. Every priest should give yearly account of his stewardship to his bishop. Bishops, supported by the count in the diocese, should suppress heathen practices. Punishments were set for the fleshly sins of monks and nuns and clergy, and for the priestly offences of wearing secular garb or harbouring women. The Benedictine rule was appointed for monasteries. It was easier to make these decrees than carry them out against the opposition of such martial bishops as those of Mainz and Trèves, whose support was necessary to Carloman's government ; and military conditions rendered the restoration of Church lands impracticable. Yet the word was spoken, and something was done.

The next year in Neustria Pippin instituted like reforms. He was aided by Boniface, although the latter held no ecclesiastical office there. In 747 Carloman abdicated and retired to a monastery ; [1] and Pippin became sole ruler, and at last formally king, anointed by Boniface under the direction of the Pope in 752. After this, Boniface, withdrawing from the direction of the Church, turned once more to satisfy his heart's desire by going on a mission among the heathen Frisians, where he crowned a great life with a martyr's death.

Thus authoritatively, supported by Rome and the Frankish monarchy, Christianity was presented to the Germans. It carried suggestions of a better order and some knowledge of Latin letters. The extension of Roman Catholic Christianity was the aim of Boniface first and last and always. But a Latin education was needed by the clergy to enable them to understand and set forth this somewhat elaborated and learned scheme of salvation. Boniface and his coadjutors had no aversion to the literary means by which a serviceable Latin knowledge was to be obtained, and their missionary and reorganizing labours necessarily worked some diffusion of Latinity.

---

[1] Carloman went at first to Rome, and built a monastery, in which he lived for a while. But here his *contemptum regni terreni* brought him more renown than his monk's soul could endure. So, with a single companion, he fled, and came unmarked and in abject guise to Monte Cassino. He announced himself as a murderer seeking to do penance, and was received on probation. At the end of a year he took the vows of a monk. It happened that he was put to help in the kitchen, where he worked humbly but none too dexterously, and was chidden and struck by the cook for his clumsiness. At which he said with placid countenance, " May the Lord forgive thee, brother, and Carloman." This occurring for the third time, his follower fell on the cook and beat him. When the uproar had subsided, and an investigation was called before the brethren, the follower said in explanation, that he could not hold back, seeing the vilest of the vile strike the noblest of all. The brethren seemed contemptuous, till the follower proclaimed that this monk was Carloman, once King of the Franks, who had relinquished his kingdom for the love of Christ. At this the terrified monks rose from their seats and flung themselves at Carloman's feet, imploring pardon, and pleading their ignorance. But Carloman, rolling on the ground before them (*in terram provolutus*) denied it all with tears, and said he was not Carloman, but a common murderer. Nevertheless, thenceforth, recognized by all, he was treated with great reverence (*Regino, Chronicon*, Migne, *Pat. Lat.* 132, col. 45).

The Frankish secular power which had supported Boniface, advanced to violent action when Charlemagne's sword bloodily constrained the Saxons to accept his rule and Christianity, the two inseverable objects which he tirelessly pursued. Nor could this ruler stay his mighty hand from the government of the Church within his realm. With his power to appoint bishops, he might, if he chose, control its councils. But apparently he chose to rule the Church directly; and his, and his predecessors' and successors' Capitularies (rather than Conciliar decrees) contain the chief ecclesiastical legislation for the Frankish realm.

In its temporalities and secular action the Church was the greatest and richest of all subjects; it possessed the rights of lay vassals and was affected with like duties.[1] But in ritual, doctrine, language and affiliation, the Frankish Church made part of the Roman Catholic Church. It used the Roman liturgy and the Latin tongue. The ordering of the clergy was Roman, and the regulation of the monasteries was Romanized by the adoption of the Benedictine *regula*. Within the Church Rome had triumphed. Prelates were vassals of the king who had now become Emperor; and the great corporate Church was subject to him. Nevertheless, this great corporate institution was Roman rather than Gallic or Frankish or German. It was Teuton only in those elements which represented ecclesiastical abuses, for example, the remaining irregularities of various kinds, the lay and martial habits of prelates, and even their appointment by the monarch. These were the elements which the Church in its logical Roman evolution was to eliminate. Charlemagne himself, as well as his lesser successors, strove just as zealously to bring the people into obedience to the Church as into obedience to the lay rulers. While the Carolingian rule was strong, its power was exerted on behalf of ecclesiastical

---

[1] For example, immunity (from governmental taxation and visitation) might attach to the lands of bishops and abbots, as it might to the lands of a lay potentate. On the other hand, the lands of bishops and abbots owed the Government such temporal aid in war and peace as would have attached to them in the hands of laymen. Such dignitaries had high secular rank. The king did not interfere with the appointment and control of the lower clergy by their lords, the bishops and abbots, any more than he did with the domestic or administrative appointments of great lay functionaries within their households or jurisdictions.

authority and discipline ; and when the royal administration
weakened after Charlemagne's death, the Church was not
slow to revolt against its temporal subjection to the royal
power.

But the Church, in spite of Latin and Roman affinities,
strove also to come near the German peoples and speak to
them in their own tongues. This is borne witness to by
the many translations from Latin into Frankish, Saxon,
or Alemannish dialects, made by the clergy. Christianity
deeply affected the German language. Many of its words
received German form, and the new thoughts forced old
terms to take on novel and more spiritual meanings. To be
sure, these German dialects were there before Christianity
came, and the capacities of the Germans acquired in heathen
times are attested by the sufficiency of their language to
express Christian thought. Likewise the German character
was there, and proved its range and quality by the very
transformation of which it showed itself capable under
Christianity. And just as Christianity was given expression
in the German language, which retained many of its former
qualities, so many fundamental traits of German character
remained in the converted people. Yet so earnestly did the
Germans turn to Christianity, and such draughts of its spirit
did they draw into their nature, that the early Germanic
re-expression of it is sincere, heartfelt, and moving, and
illumined with understanding of the Faith.

These qualities may be observed in the series of Christian
documents in the German tongues commencing in the first
years of Charlemagne's reign. They consist of baptismal
confessions of belief, the first of which (cir. 769) was composed for heathen Saxons just converted by the sword, and
of catechisms presenting the elements of Christian precept
and dogma. The earliest of the latter (cir. 789), coming
from the monastery at Weissenburg in Alsace, contains
the Lord's Prayer, with explanations, an enumeration of
the deadly sins according to the fifth chapter of the Epistle
to the Galatians, the Apostles' Creed and the Athanasian.
Further, one finds among these documents a translation of
the *De fide Catholica* of Isidore of Seville, and of the Benedictine *regula* ; also Charlemagne's *Exhortatio ad plebem*

Christianam, which was an admonition to the people to learn the Creed and the Lord's Prayer. There are likewise general confessions of sins. Less dependent on a Latin original is the so-called *Muspilli*, a spirited description in alliterative verse of the last times and the Day of Judgment.

German qualities, however, express themselves more fully in two Gospel versions, the first the famous Saxon *Heliand* (cir. 835), (which follows Tatian's " Harmony ") ; the second the somewhat later *Evangelienbuch* of Otfrid the Frank. They were both composed in alliterative verse, though Otfrid also made use of rhyme.[1] The martial, Teutonic ring of the former is well known. Christ is the king, the disciples are His thanes whose duty is to stand by their lord to the death ; He rewards them with the promised riches of heaven, excelling the earthly goods bestowed by other kings. In the " betrayal " they close around their Lord, saying : " Were it thy will, mighty Lord of ours, that we should set upon them with the spear, gladly would we strike and die for our Lord." Out broke the wrath of the " ready swordsman " (*snel suerdthegan*) [2] Simon Peter ; he could not speak for anguish to think that his lord should be bound. Angrily strode the bold knight before his lord, drew his weapon, the sword by his side, and smote the nearest foe with might of hands. Before his fury and the spurting blood the people fled fearing the sword's bite.

The *Heliand* has also gentler qualities, as when it calls the infant Christ the *fridubarn* (peace-child), and pictures Mary watching over her " little man." But German love of wife and child and home speak more clearly in Otfrid's book. Although a learned monk, his pride of Frankish race rings in his oft-quoted reasons for writing *theotisce*, *i.e.* in German : why shall not the Franks sing God's praise in Frankish

---

[1] There are numerous editions of the *Heliand* : by Sievers (1878), by Rückert (1876). Very complete is Heyne's third edition (Paderborn, 1883). Portions of it are given, with modern German interlinear translation, in Piper's *Die älteste Literatur* (Deutsche Nat. Lit.), pp. 164-186. Otfrid's book is elaborately edited by Piper (2nd edition with notes and glossary, Freiburg i. B., 1882). See also Piper's *Die älteste Literatur*, where portions of the work are given with modern German interlinear translation. Compare Ebert, *Literatur des Mittelalters*, iii. 100-117.

[2] The *Heliand* uses the epic phrases of popular poetry ; they reappear three centuries later in the *Nibelungenlied*.

tongue ? Forcible and logical it is, although not bound by grammar's rules. Yes, why should the Franks be incapable ? they are brave as Romans or Greeks ; they are as good in field and wood ; wide power is theirs, and ready are they with the sword. They are rich, and possess a good land, with honour. They can guard their own ; what people is their equal in battle ? Diligent are they also in the Word of God. Otfrid is quite moving in his sympathetic sense of the sorrow of the Last Judgment, when the mother from child shall be parted, the father from son, the lord from his faithful thane, friend from friend—all human kind. Deep is the mystic love and yearning with which he realizes Heaven as one's own land : there is life without death, light without darkness, the angels and eternal bliss. We have left it—that must we bewail always, banished to a strange land, poor misled orphans. The antithesis between the *fremidemo lant* (*fremdes land*) of earth, and the *heimat*, the *eigan lant* of heaven, which is home, real home, is the key note strongly felt and movingly expressed.

BOOK II

THE EARLY MIDDLE AGES

CHAPTER X

CAROLINGIAN PERIOD : THE FIRST STAGE IN THE
APPROPRIATION OF THE PATRISTIC AND ANTIQUE

WITH the conversion of Teuton peoples and their introduction to the Latin culture accompanying the new religion,
the factors of mediaeval development came at last into conjunction.   The mediaeval development was to issue from
their combined action, rather than from the singular nature
of any one of them.[1]   Taking up the introductory theme
concerning the meeting of these forces, we followed the
Latinizing of the West resulting from the expansion of the
Roman Republic, which represents the political and social
preparation of the field.   Then we considered the antique
pagan gospel of philosophy and letters, which had quickened
this Latin civilization and was to form the spiritual environment of patristic Christianity.   Next in order we observed
the intellectual interests of the Latin Fathers, and then
turned to the great Latin transmitters of the somewhat
amalgamated antique and patristic material — Boëthius,
Cassiodorus, Gregory the Great, and Isidore of Seville—
who gathered what they might, and did much to reduce
the same to decadent forms, suited to the barbaric understanding.   Then the course of the barbaric disruption of
the Empire was reviewed ; and this led to a consideration
of the qualities and circumstances of the Celts and Teutons,
both those who to all appearances had been Latinized, and
those who took active part in the barbarization and disruption of the Roman order.   And finally we closed these

[1] *Ante*, Chapter I.

introductory, though essential, chapters by tracing the ways in which Christianity, with the now humbled and degraded antique culture, was presented to this renewed and largely Teutonic barbarism.

Having now reached the epoch of conjunction of the various elements of the mediaeval evolution, it lies before us to consider the first stage in the action of true mediaeval conditions upon the two chief spiritual forces, the first stage, in other words, of the mediaeval appropriation of the patristic and antique material. The period is what is called Carlovingian or Carolingian, after the great ruler Charlemagne. Intellectually considered, it may be said to have begun when Charles palpably evinced his interest in sacred and liberal studies by calling Alcuin and other scholars to his Court about the year 781. Let us note the political and social situation.

The Merovingian kingdom created by Clovis and his house has been spoken of.[1] One may properly refer to it in the singular, although frequently, instead of one, there were several kingdoms, since upon the death of a Merovingian monarch his realm was divided among his sons. But no true son of the house could leave the others unconquered or unmurdered ; and therefore if the Merovingian kingdom constantly was divided, it also tended to coalesce again, coerced to unity. Constituted both of Roman and Teutonic elements, it operated as a mediating power between Latin Christendom and barbaric heathendom. Its energies were great, and were not waning when its royal house was passing into insignificance before the power of the nobles and the chief personage among them who had become the *major domus* (" Mayor of the palace ") and virtual ruler. Moreover, experience, contact with Latin civilization, membership in the Roman Catholic Church, were informing the Merovingian energies. They were becoming just a little less barbarous and a little more instructed ; in fine, were changing from Merovingian to Carolingian.

In the latter part of the seventh century, Pippin, called " of Heristal," ruled as *major domus* (as one or more of his ancestors before him) in Austrasia, the eastern Frankish

[1] *Ante*, Chapter VI.

kingdom. Many were his wars, especially with the Neustrian or western Frankish kingdom, under its *major domus*, Ebroin. This somewhat unconquerable man at last was murdered, and one of the two Merovingian kings being murdered likewise, Pippin about the year 688 became *princeps regiminis ac major domus* for the now united realm. From this date the Merovingians are but shadow kings, whose names are not worth recording. Pippin's rule marks the advent of his house to virtual sovereignty, and also the passing of the preponderance of power from Neustria to Austrasia. These two facts became clear after Pippin's death (714), when his redoubtable son Charles in a five years' struggle against great odds made himself sole *major domus*, and with his Austrasians overwhelmed the Neustrian army. Thenceforth this Charles, called Martel the Hammer, mightily prevailed, smiting Saxons, Bavarians, and Alemanni, and, after much warfare in the south with Saracens, at last vindicated the Cross against the Crescent at Tours in 732. Nine years longer he was to reign, increasing his power to the end, and supporting the establishment of Catholicism in Frisia, by the Anglo-Saxon Willibrord, and in heathen German lands by St. Boniface.[1] He died in 741, dividing what virtually was his realm between his sons Carloman and Pippin : the former receiving Austrasia, Alemannia, Thuringia ; the latter, Neustria, Burgundy, Provence.

These two sons valiantly took up their task, reforming the Church under the inspiration of Boniface, and ruling their domains without conflict with each other until 747, when Carloman retired and became a monk, leaving the entire realm to Pippin. The latter in 751 at Soissons, with universal approval and the consent of the Pope, was crowned king, and anointed by the hand of Boniface. This able sovereign pursued the course of his father and grandfather on still larger scale ; aiding the popes and reducing the Lombard power in Italy, carrying on wars around the borders of his realm, bringing Aquitania to full submission, and expelling the Saracens from Narbonne and other fortress towns. In 768 he died, again

---

[1] *Ante*, Chapter IX.

dividing his vast realm between his two sons Carloman and Charles.

These bore each other little love ; but fortunately the former died (771) before an open breach occurred. So Charles was left to rule alone, and prove himself, all things considered, the greatest of mediaeval sovereigns. Having fought his many wars of conquest and subjugation against Saracens, Saxons, Avars, Bavarians, Slavs, Danes, Lombards ; having conquered much of Italy and freed the Pope from neighbouring domination ; having been crowned and anointed emperor in the year 800 ; having opened new roads for commerce and forbidden lawless tolls ; having regulated measures, weights, and coinage ; having christianized with iron hand much stubborn heathen folk ; having restored letters, uplifted the church, and administered his vast realm with never-failing energy, he died in 814—just one hundred years after the time when his grandfather Charles was left to fight so doughtily for life and power.

Poetry and history have conspired to raise the fame of Charlemagne. In more than one *chanson de geste*, the old French *épopée* has put his name where that of Pippin, Charles Martel, or perhaps that of some Merovingian should have been.[1] Sober history has not thus falsified its matter, and yet has over-dramatized the incidents of its hero's reign. For example, every schoolboy has been told of the embassy to Charlemagne from Harun al Raschid, Caliph of Bagdad. But not so many schoolboys know that Pippin had sent an embassy to a previous caliph, which was courteously entertained for three years in Bagdad ;[2] and Pippin, like his son, received embassies from the Greek emperor. The careers of Charles Martel and Pippin have not been ignored ; and yet historical convention has focused its attention and its phrases upon " the age of Charlemagne." One should not forget that this exceedingly great man stood upon the shoulders of the great men to whose achievement he succeeded.

---

[1] *E.g.* Charles Martel and Pippin drove the Saracens from Narbonne—not Charlemagne, to whom these *chansons* ascribe the deed : Pippin regulated the coinage, as well as Charlemagne.

[2] The dates are 801 and 765.

Neither politically, socially, intellectually, nor geographically [1] was there discontinuity or break or sudden change between the Merovingian and the Carolingian periods.[2] The character of the monarchy was scarcely affected by the substitution of the house of Pippin of Heristal for the house of Clovis. The baleful custom of dividing the realm upon a monarch's death survived ; but Fortune rendered it innocuous through one strong century, during which (719-814) the realm was free from internecine war, while the tossing streams of humanity were driven onward by three great successive rulers.

The Carolingian, like the Merovingian, realm included many different peoples who were destined never to become one nation ; and the whole Carolingian system of government virtually had existed in the Merovingian period. Before, as well as after, the dynastic change, the government throughout the realm was administered by *Counts*. Likewise the famous *missi dominici*, or royal legates, are found in Merovingian times ; but they were employed more effectively by Charles Martel, Pippin, and, finally, by Charlemagne, who enlarged their sphere of action. He elaborately defined their functions in a famous Capitulary of the year 802. It was set forth that the emperor had chosen these legates from among his best and greatest (*ex optimatibus suis*), and had authorized them to receive the new oaths of allegiance, and supervise the observance of the laws, the execution of justice, the maintenance of the military and fiscal rights of the emperor. They were given power to see that the permanent functionaries (the counts and their subordinates) duly administered the law as written

[1] Historical atlases usually devote a double map to the Empire of Charlemagne, and little side-maps to the Merovingian realm, which included vast German territories, and for a time extended into Italy.

[2] A part of the serious historian's task is to get rid of " epochs " and " renaissances "—Carolingian, Twelfth Century, or Italian. For such there should be substituted a conception of historical continuity, with result properly arising from conditions. Of course, one must have convenient terms, like " periods," etc., and they are legitimate ; for the Carolingian period did differ in degree from the Merovingian, and the twelfth century from the eleventh. But it would be well to eliminate " renaissance." It seems to have been applied to the culture of the *quattrocento*, etc., in Italy sixty or seventy years ago (1845 is the earliest instance in Murray's *Dictionary* of this use of the word), and carries more false notions than can be contradicted in a summer's day.

or recognized. The *missi* had jurisdiction over ecclesiastical as well as lay officials ; and many of them were entrusted with special powers and duties in the particular instance.

Thus Charlemagne developed the functions of these ancient officers. Likewise his Court and royal council, the synods and assemblies of his reign, the military service, modes of holding land, methods of collecting revenue, were not greatly changed from Merovingian prototypes. Yet the old institutions had been renewed and bettered. A vast misjoined and unrelated realm was galvanized into temporary unity. And, most impressive and portentous thing of all, an *Empire*—the *Holy* Roman Empire—was resurrected for a time in fact and verity : the same was destined to endure in endeavour and contemplation.

So there was no break politically or socially between the Carolingian Empire and its antecedents, which had made it possible. Likewise there was no discontinuity spiritually and intellectually between the earlier time and that epoch which begins with Charlemagne's first endeavours to restore knowledge, and extends through the ninth and, if one will, even the tenth century.[1] Western Europe (except Scandinavia) had become nominally Christian, and had been made acquainted with Latin education to the extent indicated in the preceding chapter, the purpose of which was to tell how Christianity and the antique culture were brought to the northern peoples. The present chapter, on the other hand, seeks to describe how the eighth and ninth centuries proceeded to learn and consider and react upon this newly introduced Christianity and antique culture, out of which the spiritual destinies of the Middle Ages were to be forged. The task of Carolingian scholars was to learn what had been brought to them. They scarcely excelled even the later intermediaries through whom this knowledge had been

[1] The architecture, sculpture, and painting of the Carolingian time continued the Christian antique or Byzantine styles. Church interiors were commonly painted, a custom coming from early Christian mosaic and fresco decoration. Charlemagne's Capitularies provided for the renovation of the churches, including their decorations. No large sculpture has survived ; but we see that there was little artistic originality either in the illumination of manuscripts or in ivory carving. The royal chapel at Aix was built on the model of St. Vitale at Ravenna, and its columns appear to have been taken from existing structures and brought to Aix.

transmitted. One need not look among them for better scholarship than was possessed by Bede, who died in 735, the birth year of Alcuin who drew so much from him, and was to be the chief luminary of the Palace School of Charlemagne. Charlemagne's exertions and example caused a revival of sacred and profane studies through the region of the present France and Rhenish Germany. His primary motive was the purification and extension of Catholic Christianity.[1] For this, Charles Martel and Pippin (with his brother Carloman) had done much, as their support of Boniface testifies. But Charlemagne's efforts went beyond those of his predecessors. More clearly than they he understood the need of education, and he was himself intensely interested in knowledge. His open-minded love of knowledge was shown in all that the Palace School became under his inspiration and Alcuin's directorship. There young princes and nobles received a primary education in Latin letters, and learned to breathe an atmosphere of intellectual curiosity. Stimulating questions were asked, sometimes by Charles himself, and answers were given by the scholars whom he had drawn together.

Charlemagne was primarily a ruler in the largest sense, conqueror, statesman, law-giver, one who realized the needs of the time, and met or forestalled them. His monarchy with its powers inherited, as well as radiating from his own personality, provided an imperial government for western Europe. The chief activities of this ruler and his epoch were practical, to wit, political and military. In laws, in institutions, and in deeds, he and his Empire represent creativeness and progress ; although, to be sure, that conglomerate empire of his had itself to fall in pieces before there could take place a more lasting and national evolution of States. And, of course, Carolingian political creativeness

---

[1] Charlemagne's famous open letters of general admonition, *de litteris colendis* and *de emendatione librorum*, and his *admonitio generalis* for the instruction of his legates (*missi*), show that the fundamental purpose of his exhortations was to advance the true understanding of Scripture : " ut facilius et rectius divinarum scripturarum mysteria valeatis penetrare." To this end he seeks to improve the Latin education of monks and clergy ; and to this end he would have the texts of Scripture emended and a proper liturgy provided ; and, as touching the last, he refers to the efforts of his father Pippin before him. The best edition of these documents is by Boretius in the *Monumenta Germaniae historica*.

included the conservation of existing social, political, and, above all, ecclesiastical, institutions. In fine, this period was creative and progressive in its practical energies. The factors were the pressing needs and palpable opportunities, which were met or availed of. And to the same effective treatment of problems ecclesiastical and doctrinal was due the modicum of originality in the Carolingian literature. Aside from this, the period's intellectual accomplishment, in religious as well as secular studies, shows a diligent learning and imitation of pagan letters, and a rehandling and arrangement of the work of the Church Fathers and their immediate successors. Its efforts were spent in rearranging the heritage of Christian teaching, or in endeavours to acquire the transmitted antique culture and imitate the antique in phrase and metre. The combined task, or occupation, absorbed the minds of scholars. The whole period was at school, where it needed to be : at school to the Church Fathers, at school to the transmitters of antique culture. Its task was one of adjustment of its materials to itself, and of itself to its materials.[1]

The restoration of studies marking the life-time of Charlemagne and the decades following his death did not extend to Italy. Rather that land where letters might decay but never ceased, furnished a number of the scholars who contributed to the northern revival. Nor did it extend to Anglo-Saxon England, where Bede had taught and whence Alcuin had come. The revival radiated, one may say, from the Palace School attached to the Court, which had its least intermittent domicile at Aix-la-Chapelle. It extended to the chief monastic centres of Gaul and Germany, and to cathedral schools where such existed. From many lands scholars were drawn by that great hand so generous in giving, so mighty to protect. Some came on invitation more or less compelling, and many of their own free will. The first and most famous of them all was the Anglo-Saxon, Alcuin of York.[2] Charles first saw him at Parma in the year 781, and ever after kept him in his service as his most trusted teacher and director

[1] For an interesting estimate of the time, see G. Monod, *Études critiques sur les sources de l'histoire carolingienne. Bib. de l'École des Hautes Études* (1898).
[2] On Alcuin, see Manitius, *Ges. der lat. Lit. des Mittelalters*, i. pp. 273-288.

of studies. Love of home drew Alcuin back, once at least, to England. In 796 Charles permitted him to leave the Court, and entrusted him with the re-establishment of the Abbey of St. Martin at Tours and its schools. There he lived and laboured till his death in 804.

Another scholar was Peter of Pisa, a grammarian, who seems to have shared with Alcuin the honourable task of instructing the king. Of greater note was Paulus Diaconus, who, like Alcuin himself, was to sigh for the pious or scholarly quiet which the seething, half-barbarous, and loose-mannered Court did not afford. Paulus at last gained Charles's consent to retire to Monte Cassino. He was of the Lombard race, like another favourite of Charles, Paulinus of Aquileia. From Spain, apparently, came Theodulphus, by descent a Goth, and reputed the most elegant Latin versifier of his time. Charles made him Bishop of Orleans. A little later, Einhart the Frank appears, who was to be the emperor's secretary and biographer. Likewise came certain sons of Erin, among them such a problematic poet as he who styled himself " Hibernicus Exul "—not the first or last of his line !

These belonged to the generation about the emperor. Belonging to the next generation, and for the most part pupils of the older men, were Abbot Smaragdus, grammarian and didactic writer ; the German, Rabanus Maurus, Abbot of Fulda and, against his will, Archbishop of Mainz, an encyclopaedic excerpter and educator, *primus praeceptor Germaniae* ; his pupil was Walafrid Strabo, the cleverest putter-together of the excerpt commentary, and a pleasing poet. In Lorraine at the same time flourished the Irishman, Sedulius Scotus, and in the West that ardent classical scholar, Servatus Lupus, Abbot of Ferrières, and Agobard, Bishop of Lyons, a man practical and hard-headed, with whom one may couple Claudius, Bishop of Turin, the opponent of relic-worship. One might also mention those theological controversialists, Radbertus Paschasius and Ratramnus, Hincmar, the great Archbishop of Rheims, and Gottschalk, the unhappy monk, ever recalcitrant ; at the end John Scotus Eriugena should stand, the somewhat too intellectual Neo-Platonic Irishman, translator of Pseudo-

Dionysius, and announcer of various rationalizing propositions for which men were to look on him askance.

There will be occasion to speak more particularly of a
number of these men. They were all scholars, and interested
in the maintenance of elementary Latin education as well as
in theology. They wished to write good Latin, and sometimes tried for a classical standard, as Einhart did in his
Vita Caroli. Few of them refrained from verse, for they
were addicted to metrical compositions made of borrowed
classic phrase and often of reflected classic sentiment, sometimes prettily composed, but usually insipid, and in the
mass, which was great, exceptionally uninspired. Such
metrical effort, quite as much as Einhart's consciously
classicizing Latin prose, represents a survival of the antique
excited to recrudescence in forms which, if they were not
classical, at least had not become anything else. Stylistically and perhaps temperamentally, it represented the ending
of what had nearly passed away, rather than the beginning
of the more organic development which was to come.[1]

Among these men, Alcuin and Rabanus broadly represent
at once the intellectual interests of the period and the
first stage in the process of the mediaeval appropriation of
the patristic and antique material. The affectionate and
sympathetic personality of the former [2] appears throughout
his voluminous correspondence with Charles and others,
which shows, among other matters, the interest of the
time in elementary points of Latinity, and the alertness
of the mind of the great king, who put so many questions
to his genial instructor upon grammar, astronomy, and such
like knowledge. An examination of the works of Alcuin
will indicate the range and character of the educational and
more usual intellectual interests of the epoch. In fact, they
are outlined in a simple fashion suited to youthful minds in
his treatise upon Grammar.[3] Its opening colloquy presents

[1] As to the stylistic qualities of Carolingian prose and metre see *post*, Chapters
XXXII., XXXIII.

[2] Alcuin's works are printed conveniently in tomes 100 and 101 of Migne's
Patrologia Latina. Extracts are given, *post*, Chapter XXXII., to indicate the
place of Carolingian prose in the development of mediaeval Latin styles.

[3] Printed in Migne 101, col. 849-902. Alcuin adopted for his *Grammar* the
dialogue form frequent in Anglo-Saxon literature ; and from his time the question

a sort of programme and justification of elementary secular studies.

"We have heard you saying," begins Discipulus, "that philosophy is the teacher (*magistra*) of all virtues, and that she alone of secular riches has never left the possessor miserable. Lend a hand, good Master,"—and the pupil becomes self-deprecatory. "Flint has fire within, which comes out only when struck ; so the light of knowledge exists by nature in human minds, but a teacher is needed to knock it out."

"It is easy," responds the Master, "to show you wisdom's path, if only you will pursue it for the sake of God, for the sake of the soul's purity and to learn the truth, and also for its own sake, and not for human praise and honour."

We confess, answers little Discipulus, that we love happiness, but know not whether it can exist in this world. And the dialogue rambles on in discursive comment upon the superiority of the lasting over the transitory, with some feeble echoing of notes from Boëthius's *De consolatione.* There is talk to show that man, a rational animal, the image of his Creator, and immortal in his better part, should seek what is truly of himself, and not what is alien, the abiding and not the fugitive. In fine, one should adorn the soul, which is eternal, with wisdom, the soul's true lasting dignity. There is some coy demurring over the steepness of the way ; but the pupil is ardent, and the Master confident that with the aid of Divine Grace they will ascend the seven grades of philosophy, by which philosophers have gained honour brighter than that of kings, and the holy doctors and defenders of our Catholic Faith have triumphed over all heresiarchs. "Through these paths, dearest son, let your youth run its daily course, until its completed years and strengthened mind shall attain to the heights of the Holy Scriptures upon which you and your like shall become armed defenders of the Faith and invincible assertors of its truth." This means, of course, that the Liberal Arts are the proper preparation for the study of Scripture, that is, theology. But Alcuin's discourse seems to tarry with those

and answer of *Discipulus* and *Magister* will not cease their cicada chime in didactic Latin writings.

studies as if detained by some love of them for their own sake.

The body of this treatise is in form a disputation between two youthful pupils, a Frank and a Saxon. A *Magister* makes a third interlocutor, and sets the subject of the argument. These *personae* discuss letters and syllables in definitions taken from Donatus, Priscian, or Isidore ; and whenever Alcuin permits any one of them to stray from the words of those authorities, the language shows at once his own confused ideas regarding the parts of speech. He uses terms without adequately comprehending them, and thus affords one of the myriad examples of how, under decadent or barbarized conditions, phrases may outlive an intelligent understanding of their meaning. " Grammar," says the *Magister*, when solicited to define it, " is the science of letters, and the guardian of correct speech and writing. It rests on nature, reason, authority, and custom." " In how many species is it divided ? " " In twenty-six : words, letters, syllables, clauses, dictions, speeches, definitions, feet, accent, punctuation, signs, spelling, analogies, etymologies, glosses, differences, barbarism, solecism, faults, metaplasm, schemata, tropes, prose, metre, fables and histories." [1] The actual treatise does not cover these twenty-six topics, but confines itself to the division of grammar commonly called Etymology.

Though the mental processes of an individual preserve a working harmony, some of them appear more rational than others. Such disparities may be glaring in men who enter upon the learning of a higher civilization without proper pilotage. How are they to discriminate between the valuable and the foolish ? The common sense, which they apply to familiar matters, contrasts with their childlike lucubrations upon novel topics of education or philosophy. And if that higher culture to which such pupils are introduced be in part decadent, it will itself contain disparities between the stronger thinking held in the surviving writings of a prior time and the later degeneracies which are declining to the level, it may be, of these new learners.

[1] Migne 101, col. 857. See Mullinger, *Schools of Charles the Great*, p. 76 (an excellent book), and West's *Alcuin*, chap. v. (New York, 1892).

There would naturally be disparities in the mental processes of an Anglo-Saxon like Alcuin introduced to the debris of Latin education and the writings of the Fathers ; and his state would typify the character of the studies at the Palace School of Charlemagne and at monastic schools through his northern realm. This newly stimulated scholarship held the same disparities that appear in the writings of Alcuin. He may seem to be adapting his teaching to barbaric needs, but it is evident that his matter accords with his own intellectual tastes, as, for example, when he introduces into his educational writings the habit of riddling in metaphors, so dear to the Anglo-Saxon.[1] The sound but very elementary portions of his teaching were needed by the ignorance of his scholars. For instance, no information regarding Latin orthography could come amiss in the eighth century. And Alcuin in his treatise on that subject [2] took many words commonly misspelled and contrasted them with those which sounded like them, but were quite different in meaning and derivation. One should not, for example, confuse *habeo* with *abeo* ; or *bibo* and *vivo*. Such warnings were valuable. The use of the vulgar Romance-forms of Latin spoken through a large part of Charles's dominions implied no knowledge of correct Latinity. Even among the clergy, there was almost universal ignorance of Latin orthography and grammar.

As a companion to his *Grammar* and *Orthography*, Alcuin composed a *De rhetorica et virtutibus*,[3] in the form of a dialogue between Charles and himself. The king desired such instruction to equip him for the civil disputes (*civiles quaestiones*) which were brought before him from all parts of his realm. And Alcuin proceeded to furnish him with a compend of the *scientia bene dicendi*, which is Rhetoric. This crude epitome was based chiefly on Cicero's *De inventione*, but indicates a use of other of his oratorical writings, and has bits here and there which apparently have filtered

---

[1] As in his *Disputatio Pippini* (the son of Charlemagne), Migne 101, col. 975-980, which is just a series of didactic riddles : What is a letter ? The guardian of history. What is a word ? The betrayer of the mind. What generates language ? The tongue. What is the tongue ? The whip of the air—and so forth.

[2] *De orthographia*, Migne 101, col. 902-919.

[3] Migne 101, col. 919-950. Mullinger, *o.c.* pp. 83-85.

through from the *Rhetoric* of Aristotle. Some illustrations are taken from Scripture. The work is most successful in showing the difference between Cicero and Alcuin. The genius, the spirit, the art of the great orator's treatises are lost ; a naked skeleton of statement remains. We have words, terms, definitions, even rules ; and Alcuin is not conscious that beyond them there is the living spirit of discourse.

A more complete descent from substance to a clatter of words and definitions is exhibited by Alcuin's *De dialectica*.[1] In logical studies *facilis descensus* ! Others had illustrated this before him. His treatise is again a dialogue, with Charlemagne for questioner. Opening with the stock definitions and divisions of philosophy, it arrives at logic, which is composed (as Isidore and Cassiodorus said) of dialectic and rhetoric, " the shut and open fist," a simile which had come down from Varro. Says Charles : " What are the *species* of dialectic ? " Answers Alcuin : " Five principal ones : Isagogae, categories, forms of syllogisms and definitions, topics, periermeniae." What a classification ! Introductions, categories, syllogisms, topics, *De interpretatione*-s ! It is not a classification but in reality an enumeration of the treatises which had served as sources for those men from whom Alcuin drew ! Evidently this excerpter is not really thinking in the terms and categories of his subject. His work shows no intelligence beyond Isidore's, from whose *Etymologies* it is largely taken. And the genius of our author for metaphysics may be perceived from the definition which he offers Charles of substance— *substantia* or *usia* (*i.e.* οὐσία) : it is that which is discerned by corporeal sense ; while *accidens* is that which changes frequently and is apprehended by the mind. *Substantia* is the underlying, the *subjacens*, in which the *accidentia* are said to be.[2] One observes the crassness of these statements

There are illustrations of the knowledge and methods shown in the educational writings of the man who, next to Charles himself, was the guiding spirit of the intellectual revival. No mention has been made of those of his works that were representative of the chief intellectual labour of

[1] Migne 101, col. 951-976.   [2] Migne 101, col. 956.

the period—that of exploiting the Patristic material.   Here
Alcuin contributed a compend of Augustine's doctrines on
the Trinity,[1] and a book on the Vices and Virtues, drawn
chiefly from Augustine's sermons.[2] Like most of his
learned contemporaries, he also compiled Commentaries
upon Scripture, the method of which is prettily told in a
prefatory epistle placed by him before his Commentary on
the Gospel of John, and addressed to two pious women :

" Devoutly searching the pantries of the holy Fathers, I let you
taste whatever I have been able to find in them.   Nor did I deem
it fitting to cull the blossoms from any meadow of my own, but
with humble heart and head bowed low, to search through the
flowering fields of many Fathers, and thus safely satisfy your
pious pleasure.   First of all I seek the suffrage of Saint Augustine,
who laboured with such zeal upon this Gospel ; then I draw
something from the tracts of the most holy doctor Saint Ambrose ;
nor have I neglected the homilies of Father Gregory the pope,
or those of the blessed Bede, nor, in fact, the works of others of
the holy Fathers.   I have cited their interpretations as I found
them, preferring to use their meanings and their words, than trust
to my own presumption." [3]

In the next generation, a most industrious compiler of
such Commentaries was Alcuin's pupil, Rabanus Maurus.[4]

[1] Migne 101, col. 11-56.   [2] Migne 101, col. 613-638.
[3] Migne 100, col. 737, 744.
[4] An important person.   He was born at Mainz about 776.   Placed as a child
in the convent of Fulda, his talents and learning caused him to be sent at the
age of twenty-one to Alcuin at Tours for further instruction.   After Alcuin's
death in 804, Rabanus returned to Fulda and was made Principal of the monastery
school.   In 822 he was elected Abbot.   His labours gained for him the title of
Primus praeceptor Germaniae.   Resigning in 842, he withdrew to devote himself
to literary labours ; but he was soon drawn from his retreat and made Archbishop
of Mainz.   He died in 856.   While archbishop, and also while abbot, Rabanus
with spiteful zeal prosecuted that rebellious monk, the high-born Saxon Gottschalk,
who, among other faults, held too harsh views upon Predestination.   His works
are published in Migne, *Pat. Lat.* 107-112.
    Rabanus has left huge Commentaries upon the books of the Old and New
Testaments, in which he and his pupils gathered the opinions of the Fathers.
He also added such needful comment of his own as his " exiguity " of mind permitted (Praef. to *Com. in Lib. Judicum*, Migne 108, col. 1110).   His Commentaries
were superseded by the *Glossa ordinaria* (Migne 113 and 114) of his own pupil,
Walafrid Strabo, which was systematically put together from Rabanus and those
upon whom he drew.   It was smoothly done, and the writer knew how to eliminate
obscurity and prolixity, and in fact make his work such that it naturally became
the Commentary in widest use for centuries.   The dominant interest of these
commentators is in the allegorical significance of Scripture, as we shall see (Chapter
XXVIII.).   On Rabanus and Walafrid, see Ebert, *Allge. Gesch. der Lit. des
Mittelalters*, ii. 120-166.

More deeply learned than his master, his conception of the purposes of study has not changed essentially. Like Alcuin, he sets forth a proper intellectual programme for the instruction of the clergy : " The foundation, the state, and the perfection, of wisdom is knowledge of the Holy Scriptures." The Seven Arts are the ancillary *disciplinae* ; the first three constitute that grammatical, rhetorical, and logical training which is needed for an understanding of the holy texts and their interpretation. Likewise arithmetic and the rest of the quadrivium have place in the cleric's education. A knowledge of pagan philosophy need not be avoided : " The philosophers, especially the Platonists, if perchance they have spoken truths accordant with our faith, are not to be shunned, but their truths appropriated, as from unjust possessors." [1] And Rabanus continues with the never-failing metaphor of Moses despoiling the Egyptians.

Raban, however, had somewhat larger thoughts of education than his master. For example, he takes a broader view of grammar, which he regards as the *scientia* of inter-preting the poets and historians, and the *ratio* of correct speech and writing.[2] Likewise he treats *Dialectica* more seriously. With him it is the " *disciplina* of rational investigation, of defining and discussing, and distinguishing the true from the false. It is therefore the *disciplina disciplinarum*. It teaches how to teach and how to learn ; in this same study, reason itself demonstrates what it is and what it wills. This art alone knows how to know, and is willing and able to make knowers. Reasoning in it, we learn what we are, and whence, and also to know Creator and creature ; through it we trace truth and detect falsity, we argue and discover what is consequent and what incon-sequent, what is contrary to the nature of things, what is true, what is probable, and what is intrinsically false in disputations. Wherefore the clergy ought to know this noble art, and have its laws in constant meditation, so that subtly they may discern the wiles of heretics, and confute their poisoned sayings with the conclusions of the syllogism."[3]

This somewhat extravagant but not novel view of logic's

---

[1] *De cleric. inst.* iii. 26 (Migne 107, col. 404).
[2] *Ibid.* iii. 18.   [3] *Ibid.* iii. 20 (Migne 107, col. 397).

function was prophetic of the coming scholastic reliance
upon it as the means and instrument of truth. Rabanus
had no hesitancy in commending this edged tool to his
pupils. But the operations of his mind were predominantly
Carolingian, which is to say that ninety-nine per cent of the
contents of his *opera* consist of material extracted from
prior writers. His Commentaries upon Scripture outbulk
all his other works taken together, and are compiled in
this manner. So is his encyclopaedic compilation, *De
universo libri XXII.*,[1] two books more than in Isidore's
Etymologies, from which he chiefly drew ; but he changed
the arrangement, and devoted a larger part of his parchment
to religious topics ; and he added further matter gleaned
from the Church Fathers, from whom he had drawn his
Commentaries. This further matter consisted of the
mystical interpretations of things, which he subjoined to
their " natural " explanations. He says, in his Praefatio,
addressed to King Louis :

" Much is set forth in this work concerning the natures of things
and the meanings of words, and also as to the mystical signification of things. Accordingly I have arranged my matter so that
the reader may find the historical and mystical explanations of
each thing set together—*continuatim positam* ; and may be able
to satisfy his desire to know both significations."

These allegorical elaborations accorded with the habits of
this compiler of allegorical comment upon Scripture.[2]

Rabanus was a full Teutonic personality, a massive
scholar for his time, untiring in labour and intrinsically
honest. Except when involved in the foolishness of the
mystic qualities of numbers, or following the will-o'-wisps
of allegory, he evinces much sound wisdom. He abhors
the pretence of teaching what one has not first diligently
learned ; and his good sense is shown in his admonition to
teachers to use words which their pupils or audience will
understand. His views upon profane knowledge were
liberal : one should use the treasured experience and
accumulated wisdom of the ancients, for that is still the

---

[1] Migne 111, col. 9-614.
[2] Raban's excruciating *De laudibus sanctae crucis* shows what he could do as
a virtuoso in allegorical mystification (Migne 107, col. 137-294).

mainstay of human society ; but one should shun their vain
as well as pernicious idolatries and superstitions.[1] Let us
by all means preserve their sound educational learning and
the elements of their philosophy which accord with the
verities of Christian doctrine. Raban also realized the
sublimity of the study of Astronomy, which he deemed " a
worthy argument for the religious and a torment for the
curious. If pursued with chaste and sober mind, it floods
our thoughts with immense love. How admirable to mount
the heavens in spirit, and with inquiring reason consider
that whole celestial fabric, and from every side gather in
the mind's reflective heights what those vast recesses veil." [2]
He then rebukes the folly of those who vainly would draw
auguries from the stars.[3]

Raban's mental activities were commonly constrained
by the need felt by him and his pious contemporaries to
master the works of the Latin Fathers. Perhaps more than
any other one man (though here his pupil Walafrid Strabo
made a skilful second) he contributed to what necessarily
was the first stage in this mediaeval achievement of appropriating patristic Christianity, to wit, the preliminary task
of rearranging the doctrinal expositions of the Fathers
conveniently, and for the most part in Commentaries
following verse and chapter of the canonical books of
Scripture. But, like many of his contemporaries, Raban,
when compelled by controversial exigencies, would think
for himself if the situation could not be met with matter
taken from a Father. Accordingly, individual and personal
views are vigorously put in some of his writings, as in his
Liber de oblatione puerorum,[4] directed against the attempt of
the interesting Saxon, Gottschalk, to free himself from the
vows made by those who dedicated him in boyhood as an
oblatus at the monastery of Fulda, of which Raban was
abbot. Raban's tract maintained that the monastic vows
made upon such dedication of children could not be broken
by the latter on reaching years of discretion.

This same Gottschalk was the centre of the storm,

---

[1] *De cleric. inst.* iii. 16 (Migne 107, col. 392).
[2] *De cleric. inst.* iii. 25 (Migne 107, col. 403).
[3] Compare his *De magicis artibus*, Migne 110, col. 1095 *sqq.*
[4] Migne 107, col. 419 *sqq.*

which he indeed blew up, over Predestination ; and again Raban was his fierce opponent.   This controversy, with that relating to the Eucharist, will serve to illustrate the doctrinal interests of the time, and also to exemplify the quasi-originality of its controversial productions.

Of course Predestination and the Eucharist had been exhaustively discussed by the Latin Fathers.   No man of the ninth century could really add anything to the arguments touching the former set forth in the works of Augustine and his Pelagian adversaries.   And the substance of the discussion as to the eucharistic Body and Blood of Christ had permeated countless tomes, both Greek and Latin, from the time of Irenaeus, Bishop of Lyons (d. 202) ; and yet neither as to the impossible topic of Predestination, nor as to the distinctly Christian mystery of the Eucharist, had the Latin Church authoritatively and finally fixed doctrine in dogma or put together the arguments.   The ninth century with its lack of elastic thinking, and its greater need of tangible authority, was compelled by its mental limitations to attempt in each of these matters to drag a definite conclusion from out of its entourage of argument, and strip it of its decently veiling obscurities.   Thereupon, and with its justifying and balanced foundation of reasons and considerations knocked from under, the conclusion had to sustain itself in mid air, just at the level of the common eye.

Such, obviously, was the result of the Eucharistic or Paschal controversy.   The symbol, all indecision brushed away, hardened into the tangible miraculous reality. Radbertus, Abbot of Corbie, who was so rightly named Paschasius, was the chief agent in the process.   His method of procedure, just as the result which he obtained, was what the time required.   The method was almost a bit of creation in itself : he put the matter in a separate monograph, *De corpore et sanguine Domini*,[1] the first work exclusively devoted to the subject.   This was needed as a matter of arrangement and presentation.   Men could not endure to look here and thither among many books on many subjects, for arguments one way and the other.   That was too distraught.   There was call for a compendium, a manual

[1] Migne 120, col. 1267-1350.

of the matter ; and in providing it Paschasius was a master mechanic for his time. Inevitably the discussion and the conclusion took on a new definiteness. It is impossible to glean and gather arguments and matter from all sides, and bring them together into a single composition, without making the thesis more organic, tangible, definite. Thus Paschasius presented the scattered, wavering discussion—the victorious side of it—as a clear dogma reached at last. And whatever qualification of counter-doctrine there was in his grouped arguments, there was none in the conclusion ; and the definite conclusion was what men wanted.

And practically for the whole western Church, clergy and laity, the conclusion was but one, and accorded with what was already the current acceptance of the matter. Radbert's arguments embraced the spiritual realism of Augustine, according to which the ultra reality of the Eucharistic elements consisted in the *virtus sacramenti*, that is in their miraculous and real, but invisible, transformation into the veritable substance of Christ's veritable body. This took place through priestly consecration, and existed only for believers. For the brute to eat the elements was nothing more than to consume other similar natural substances. For the misbeliever it was not so simple. He indeed ate not Christ's body, but his own *judicium*, his own deeper damnation. Here lay the terror, which made more anxious, more poignant, the believer's hope, that he was faithful and humbled, and was eating the veritable Christ-body to his sure salvation. For the Eucharist could not fail, though the partaker might.

Out of all of this emerged the one clear thing, the point, the practical conclusion, which was transubstantiation, though the word was not yet made. Here it is in Paschasius ; says he : " That body and blood veritably come into existence (*fiat*) by the consecration of the Mystery, no one doubts who believes the divine words ; hence Truth says, ' For my flesh verily is food, and my blood verily is drink ' (John vi. 55). And that it should be clearer to the disciples who did not rightly understand of what flesh he spoke, or of what blood, he added, to make this plain, ' Whoso eateth my flesh, and drinketh my blood, abideth in me and I in him ' (*ibid*. 56). Therefore, if it is veritably food, it is veritable flesh ; and if it is veritably drink, it also is veritable blood. Otherwise how could he have said, ' The bread which I will give is my flesh for the life of the world ' (*ibid*. 52) ? "

Could anything be more positive and simplified ? At first sight it is a marvel how Paschasius, even though treading in the steps of so many who had gone before, could give a literal interpretation to words which Christ seems to have used as figuratively as when He said, " I am the vine, ye are the branches." A marvel indeed, when we think that Paschasius and all of his generation, as well as those who went before, had abandoned themselves to the most wonderful and far-fetched allegorical interpretations of every historical and literal statement in the Scriptures. And this same Paschasius, and all the rest too, do not hesitate to interpret and explain by allegory the significance of every accompanying act and circumstance of the mass. This might seem the climax of the marvel, but it is a step toward explaining it. For the literal interpretation of the phrases which Paschasius quotes was followed for the sake of the more absolute miracle, the deeper mystery, the fuller florescence of encompassing allegorical meaning. Only thus could be brought about the transformation of the palpable symbol into the miraculous reality ; and only *then* could that bread and wine be what Cyril of Alexandria and others, five hundred years before Paschasius, had called it : " the drug of immortality." Only through the miraculous and real identity of the elements of the Eucharist with the body and blood of Christ could they save the souls of the partakers.

In partial disagreement with these hard and fast conclusions, Ratramnus, also of Corbie,[1] and others might still try to veil the matter, with utterances capable of more equivocal meaning ; might try to make it all more dim, and therefore more possibly reasonable. That was not what the Carolingian time, or the centuries to come, wanted ; but rather the definite tangible statement, which they could grasp as readily as they could see and touch the elements

[1] Ratramnus, *De corpore*, etc. (Migne 121, col. 125-170).

before their eyes. In disenveloping the question and conclusion from every wavering consideration and veiling ambiguity, the Carolingian period was creative in this Paschal controversy. New propositions were not devised ; but the old, such of them as fitted, were put together and given the unity and force of a projectile.

It was the same and yet different with the Predestination strife. Gottschalk, who raised the storm, stated doctrines of Augustine. But he set them out naked and alone, with nothing else as counterpoise, as Augustine had not done. Thus to draw a single doctrine out from the totality of a man's work and the demonstrative suggestiveness of all the rest of his teachings, whether that man be Paul or Augustine, is to present it so as to make it something else. For thereby it is left naked and alone, and unadjusted with the connected and mitigating considerations yielded by the rest of the man's opinions. Such a procedure is a garbling, at least in spirit. It is almost like quoting the first half of a sentence and leaving off everything following the author's " but " in the middle of it.

At all events the hard and fast, complete and twin (*gemina*) divine predestination, unto hell as well as heaven, was too unmitigated for the Carolingian Church. This doctrine, and his own intractable temper, immured the unhappy announcer of it in a monastic dungeon till he died. It was monstrous, as monstrous as transubstantiation, for example ! But transubstantiation saved ; and while the Church could stand the doctrine of the election of the Elect to salvation, it revolted from the counter-inference, of the election of the damned to hell, which contradicted too drastically the sweet and lovely teaching that Christ died for all. The theologians of one and more generations were drawn into the strife, which was to have a less definitive result than the Paschal controversy. Even to-day the adjustment of human free - will with omnipotent fore-knowledge has not been made quite clear.[1]

There was one man who was drawn into the Predestination strife, although for him it lacked cardinal import. For

[1] On the Carolingian controversies upon Predestination and the Eucharist see Harnack, *Dogmengeschichte*, vol. iii. chap. vi.

the Neo-Platonic principles of John Scotus Eriugena scarcely permitted him to see in evil more than non-existence, and led him to trace all phases of reality downward from the primal Source. His intellectual attitude, interests, and faculties were exceptional, and yet nevertheless partook of the characteristics of his time, out of which not even an Eriugena could lift himself. He was an Irishman, who came to the Court of Charles the Bald on invitation, and for many years, until his orthodoxy became too suspect, was the head of the Palace School. He may have died about the year 877.

Eriugena was in the first place a man of learning, widely read in the works of the Greek Fathers. From the *Celestial Hierarchy* of Pseudo-Dionysius and other sources, he had absorbed huge draughts of Neo-Platonism. One must not think of him always as an original thinker. A large part of his literary labours correspond with those of contemporaries. He was a translator of the works of Pseudo-Dionysius, for he knew Greek. Then he composed or compiled Commentaries upon those writings. He cared supremely for the fruits of those faculties with which he was pre-eminently endowed. He, the man of acquisitive powers, loved learning ; and he, the man with a faculty of constructive reason, loved rational truth and the labour of its systematic and syllogistic presentation. He ascribed primal validity to what was true by force of logic, and in his soul set reason above authority. Certain of his contemporaries, with a discernment springing from repugnance, perceived his self-reliant intellectual mood. The same ground underlay their detestation, which centuries after underlay St. Bernard's for Abaelard. That Abaelard should deem himself to be something ! here was the root of the saint's abhorrence. And, similarly, good Deacon Florus of Lyons wrote a vituperative polemic quite as much against the man Eriugena as against his detestable views of Predestination. Eriugena, forsooth, would be disputing with human argument, which he draws from philosophy, and for which he would be accountable to none. He proffers no authority from the Fathers, " as if daring to define with his own presumption what should be held and followed." [1] Such was not the way that Carolingian Churchmen liked to argue, but rather with attested sentences from Augustine or Gregory. Manifestly Eriugena was not one of them.

Had his works been earlier understood, they would have been earlier condemned. But people did not realize what sort of Neo-Platonic, pantheistic and emanational, principles this Irishman from over the sea was setting forth. St. Denis, the great saint who was becoming St. Denis of France, had been authoritatively (and most preposterously) identified with Dionysius the Areopagite who heard Paul preach, and, according to the growing legend, won a martyr's crown not far from Paris. This was set forth in his Life by Abbot Hilduin ; [2] this was confirmed by Hincmar, the great Archbishop of Rheims, who said, closing his discussion of the matter : " veritas saepius agitata magis splendescit in lucem ! " [3] Eriugena seemed to be a translator of his holy writings, and might be regarded as a setter forth of his exceptionally resplendent truths. He could use the Fathers' language too. So in his book on Predestination he quotes Augustine as saying, Philosophy, which is the study of wisdom, is not other than religion.[4] But he was not going to keep meaning what Augustine meant. He slowly extends his talons in the following sentences which do *not* stand at the *beginning* of his great work *De divisione naturae*.

Says the Magister, for the work is in dialogue form :
" You are aware, I suppose, that what is prior by nature is of greater dignity than what is prior in time."

Answers Discipulus : " This is known to almost all."

Continues Magister : " We learn that reason is prior by nature, but authority prior in time. For although nature was created at the same moment with time, authority did not begin with the beginning of time and nature. But reason sprang with nature and time from the beginning of things."

Discipulus clenches the matter : " Reason itself teaches

---

[1] Migne 119, col. 102. Florus called his tract " Libellus Flori adversus cuiusdam vanissimi hominis, qui cognominatur Joannes, ineptias et errores de praedestinatione," etc. Florus was a contemporary of Eriugena.

[2] Migne 106.

[3] Hincmar, *Ep.* 23 (Migne 126, col. 153).   [4] Migne 122, col. 357.

this. Authority sometimes proceeds from reason ; but reason never from authority. For all authority which is not approved by true reason seems weak. But true reason, since it is stablished in its own strength, needs to be strengthened by the assent of no authority." [1]

No doubt of the talons here ! Reason superior to authority—is it not also prior to faith ? Eriugena does not press that reversal of the Christian position. But his *De divisione naturae* was a reasoned construction, although of course the materials were not his own. It was no loosely compiled encyclopaedia, such as Isidore or Bede or Rabanus would have presented under such a title. It did not describe every object in nature known to the writer ; but it discussed Nature metaphysically, and presented its lengthy exposition as a long argument in linked syllogistic form. Yet it respected its borrowed materials, and preserved their characteristics — with the exception of Scripture, which Eriugena recognized as supreme authority ! That he interpreted figuratively of course ; so had every one else done. But he differed from other commentators and from the Church Fathers, in degree if not in kind For his interpretation was a systematic moulding of Scriptural phrase to suit his system He transformed the meaning with as clear a purpose as once Philo of Alexandria had done. The pre-Christian Jew changed the Pentateuch—holding fast, of course, to its authority !—into a Platonic philosophy ; and so, likewise by figurative interpretations, Eriugena turned Scripture into a semi-Christianized Neo-Platonic scheme.[2] The logical nature of the man was strong within him, so strong, indeed, that in its working it could not but present all topics as component parts of a syllogistic and systematized philosophy.[3] If he borrowed his materials, he also made them his own with power He appears as the one

---

[1] *De div. nat.* i. 69 (Migne 122, col. 513).

[2] One may say that the work of Eriugena in presenting Christianity transformed in substance as well as form, stood to the work of such a one as Thomas Aquinas as the work of the Gnostics in the second century had stood toward the dogmatic formulation of Christianity by the Fathers of the Church. With the Church Fathers as with Thomas, there was earnest endeavour to preserve the substance of Christianity, though presenting it in a changed form. This cannot be said of either the Gnostics or Eriugena.

[3] See Prantl, *Ges. der Logik*, ii. 20-36.

man of his time that really could build with the material received from the past.

Beyond the range of these acute theological polemics which we have been considering, the pressing exigencies of political or ecclesiastical controversy might cause a capable man to think for himself even in the ninth century. Such a man was Claudius, Bishop of Turin, the foe of image and relic worship, and of other superstitions too crass for one who was a follower of Augustine.[1] And another such a one even more palpably was Agobard, Archbishop of Lyons (d. 840), a brave and energetic man, clear-seeing and enlightened, and incessantly occupied with questions of living interest, to which his nature responded more quickly than to theologic lore. Absorbed in the affairs of his diocese, of the Church at large, and of the Empire, he expresses views which he has made his own. Practical issues, operating upon his mind, evoked a personal originality of treatment His writings are clear illustrations of the originality which actual issues aroused in the Carolingian epoch. They were directed against common superstitions and degraded religious opinion, or against the Jews whose aggressive prosperity in the south of France disturbed him ; or they were political. In fine, they were the fruit of the living issue. For example, his so-often-cited pamphlet, " Against the silly opinion of the crowd as to hail and thunder,"[2] was doubtless called forth by the intolerable conditions stated in the first sentence :

" In these parts almost all men, noble and common, city folk and country folk, old and young, think that hail storms and thunder can be brought about at the pleasure of men. People say when they hear thunder and see lightning ' Aura levatitia est.' When asked what aura levatitia may be, some are ashamed or conscience-stricken, while others, with the boldness of ignorance, assert that the air is raised (levata) by the incantations of men called Tempestarii, and so is called ' raised air.' "

Agobard does not marshal physical explanations against this folly, but texts of Scripture showing that God alone can raise and lay the storms. Perhaps he thought such texts

---

[1] Claudius died about 830. His works are in tome 104 of Migne.
[2] Migne 104, col. 147-158.

the best arguments for those who needed any. The manner
of the writing is reasonable, and the reader perceives that
the clear - headed archbishop, apart from his Scriptural
arguments, deemed these notions ridiculous, as well as
harmful.[1]

In like spirit Agobard argued against trials by combat
and ordeal. Undoubtedly, God might thus announce His
righteous judgment, but one should not expect to elicit it in
modes so opposed to justice and Scripture ; again, he cites
many texts while also considering the matter rationally.[2]
On the other hand, his book against image-worship is made
up of extracts from Augustine and other Church authorities.
There was no call for originality here, when the subject
seemed to have been so exhaustively and authoritatively
treated.[3]

One cannot follow Agobard so comfortably in his ran-
corous tracts against the Jews. Doubtless this subject
also presented itself to him as an exigency requiring handling, and he was just in his contention that heathen slaves
belonging to Jews might be converted and baptized, and
then should not be given back to their former masters, but
a money equivalent be made instead. The question was
important from its frequency. Yet one would be loath to
approve his arguments, unoriginal as they are. He gives
currency to the common slanders against the Jews, and then
at great length cites passages from the Church Fathers, to
show in what detestation they held that people. Then he
sets forth the abominable opinions of the hated race, and
ransacks Scripture to prove that the Jews are therein
authoritatively and incontestably condemned.[4]

[1] Compare Agobard's Ep. ad Bartholomaeum (Migne 104, col. 179).
[2] Liber contra judicium Dei (Migne 104, col. 250-268). Here the powerful
Hincmar, Archbishop of Rheims, is emphatically on the opposite side, and argues
lengthily in support of the judicium aquae frigidae, in Epist. 26, Migne 126, col. 161.
Hincmar (cir. 806-882) was a man of imposing eminence. He was a great ecclesiastical statesman. The compass and character of his writings is what might be
expected from such an archiepiscopal man of affairs. They include edifying
tracts for the use of the king, an authoritative Life of St. Remi, and writings
theological, political, and controversial. As the writer was not a profound
thinker, his works have mainly that originality which was impressed upon them
by the nature of whatever exigency called them forth. They are contained in
Migne 125, 126.
[3] Liber de imaginibus sanctorum (Migne 104, col. 199-226).
[4] These writings are also in vol. 104 of Migne.

The years of Agobard's maturity belong to the troubled time which came with the accession of the incompetent Louis, in 814, to the throne of his father Charlemagne. In the contentions and wars that followed, Agobard proved himself an apt political partisan and writer. His political tracts, notwithstanding their constant citation of Scripture, are his own, and evince an originality evoked by the situation which they were written to influence.

Something of the originality which the pressing political exigency imparted to these tracts of Agobard might be transmitted to such history as was occupied with contemporary events. As long as the historian was a mere excerpting chronicler extracting his dry summaries from the writings of former men, his work would not rouse him to independence of conception or presentation. That would have come with criticism upon the old authorities. But criticism had scarcely begun to murmur among the Carolingians, too absorbed with the task of grasping their inherited material to weigh it, and too overawed by the authority of the past to question the truth of its transmitted statements. Excerpts, however, could not be made to tell the stirring events of the period in which the Carolingian historian lived. He would have to set forth his own perception and understanding of them, and in manner and language which to a less or greater extent were his own : to a less extent with those feebly beginning Annals, or Year-books, which set down the occurrences of cloister life or the larger happenings of which the report penetrated from the outer world ; [1] to a greater extent, however, with a more veritable history of some topic of living and coherent interest. In the latter case the writer must present his conception of events, and therewith something of himself.[2]

---

[1] See Wattenbach, *Deutschlands Geschichtsquellen*, i. 130-142 (5th ed.). Writings known as *Annales* drew their origin from the notes made by monks upon the margin of their calendars. These notes were put together the following year, and subsequently might be revised, perhaps by some person of larger view and literary skill. Thus the Annals found in the cloister of Lorsch are supposed to have been rewritten in part by Einhart.

[2] There were two great earlier examples of such histories : one was the *Historia Francorum* of Gregory of Tours, the author of which was of distinguished Roman descent, born in 540 and dying in 594 ; the other was Bede's *Church History of the English People*, which was completed shortly before its author's death in 735.

An example of this necessitated originality in the writing of contemporary history is the work of Count Nithard. He was the son of Charlemagne's daughter Bertha and of Angilbert, the emperor's counsellor and lifelong friend. His parents were not man and wife, because Charles would not let his daughters marry, from reasons of policy ; but the relationship between them was open, and apparently approved by the lady's sire. Angilbert studied in the Palace School with Charlemagne, and became himself a writer of Latin verse. He was often his sovereign's ambassador, and continued active in affairs until his closing years, when he became the lay-abbot of a rich monastery in Picardy, and received his emperor and virtual father-in-law as his guest. He died the same year with Charles.

Like his father, Nithard was educated at the Palace School, perhaps with his cousin who was to become Charles the Bald. His loyalty continued staunch to that king, whose tried confidant he became. He was a diplomatist and a military leader in the wars following the death of Louis the Pious ; and he felt impelled to present from his side the story of the strife among the sons of Louis, in " four books of histories " as they grew to be.[1] Involved with his king in that same hurricane (*eodem turbine*) he describes those stormy times which they were fighting out together even while he was writing. This man of action could not but present himself, his views, his temperament, in narrating the events he moved in. Throughout, one perceives the pen of the participant, in this case an honest partisan of his king, and the enemy of those whose conduct had given the divided realm over to rapine. So the vigorous narrative of this noble Frank partakes of the originality which inheres in the writings of men of action when their literary faculty is sufficient to enable them to put themselves into their compositions.

Engaged, as we have been, with the intellectual or

In individuality and picturesqueness of narrative, these two works surpass all the historical writings of the Carolingian time.

[1] In *Mon. Germ. Hist. Scrip.* ii. ; also Migne, vol. 116, col. 45-76 ; trans. in German in *Geschichtsschreiber der deutschen Vorzeit* (Leipzig). See also Wattenbach, *Deutschlands Geschichtsquellen*, i., and Ebert, *Ges. der Litt.* ii. 370 *sqq.*

scholarly interests of the Carolingian period, we should not forget how slender in numbers were the men who promoted them, and how few were the places where they throve. There was the central group of open-minded laymen and Churchmen about the palace school, or following the Court in its journeyings, which were far and swift. Then there were monastic or episcopal centres of education as at Tours, or Rheims, or Fulda. The scholars carried from the schools their precious modicum of knowledge, and passed on through life as educated men living in the world, or dwelt as learned compilers, reading in the cloister. But scant were the rays of their enlightening influence amidst that period's vast encompassing ignorance.

To have classified the Carolingian intellectual interests according to topics would have been misleading, since that would have introduced a fictitious element of individual preference and aptitude, as if the Carolingian scholar of his spontaneous volition occupied himself with mathematical studies rather than grammar, or with astronomy rather than theology. In general, all was a matter of reading and learning from such books as Isidore's *Origines*, which handled all topics indiscriminately, or from Bede, or from the works of Augustine or Gregory, in which every topic did but form part of the encyclopaedic presentation of the relationship between the soul and God, and the soul's way to salvation.

What then did these men care for ? Naturally, first of all, for the elements of their primary education, their studies in the Seven Arts. They did what they might with Grammar and Rhetoric, and with Dialectic, which sometimes was Rhetoric and formal Logic joined. Logic, for those who studied it seriously, was beginning to form an important mental discipline. The four branches of the quadrivium were pursued more casually. Knowledge of arithmetic, geometry, music, and astronomy (one may throw in medicine as a fifth) was as it might be in the individual instance— always rudimentary, and usually rather less than more.

All of this, however, and it was not very much, was but the preparation, if the man was to be earnest in his pursuit of wisdom. Wisdom lay chiefly in Theology, to wit, the whole saving contents of Scripture as understood and interpreted by Gregory and Augustine. There was little mortal knowledge which this range of Scriptural interpreta tion might not include. It compassed such knowledge of the physical world as would enable one to understand the work of Creation set forth in Genesis ; it embraced all that could be known of man, of his physical nature, and assuredly of his spiritual part. Here Christian truth might call on the better pagan philosophy for illustration and rational corroboration, so far as that did corroborate. When it did not, it was pernicious falsity.

So Christian piety viewed the matter. But the pious commonly have their temporal fancies, sweet as stolen fruit. These Carolingian scholars, the man in orders and the man without, studied the Latin poets, historians, and orators. Among them were ardent humanists like Servatus Lupus ;[1] who loved the classics for their human message. And in their imaginative or poetic moods, as they followed classic metre, so they reproduced classic phrase and sentiment in their verses. The men who made such—it might be Alcuin, or Theodulphus, or Walafrid Strabo — chose what they would as the subject of their poems ; but the presentation took form and phrase from Virgil and other old poets. The antique influence so strong in the Carolingian period, included much more than matters of elegant culture, like poetry and art, or even rhetoric and grammar. It held the accumulated experience in law and institution, which still made part of the basis of civic life. Rabanus Maurus recognized it thus broadly. And, thus largely taken, the antique survives in the Carolingian time as a co-ordinate dominant, with Latin Christianity. Neither, as yet, was affected by the solvent processes of transmutation into new human faculty and power. None the less, this same antique survival was destined to pass into modes and forms belonging quite as much to the Middle Ages as to antiquity ; and, thus recast, it was to become a broadening and informing element in the mediaeval personality.

---

[1] His letters show sympathetic knowledge of Livy, Sallust, Caesar, Cicero, Virgil, Martial and other classics. They are printed in Migne, *Pat. Lat.*, t. 119. A sketch of Lupus is given by Mullinger, *Schools of Charles the Great*, chap. iv.

Likewise with the patristic Christianity which had been transmitted to the Carolingian time, to be then and there not only conned and studied, but also rearranged by these painful students, so that they and their successors might the better comprehend it. It was not for them to change the patristic forms organically, by converting them into the modes of mediaeval understanding of the same. These would be devised, or rather achieved, by later men, living in centuries when the patristic heritage of doctrine, long held and cherished, had permeated the whole spiritual natures of mediaeval men and women, and had been itself transmuted in what it had transformed.[1]

[1] S. Hellmann in his *Sedulius Scottus (Quellen, etc., zur latein. Philol.*, Munich, 1906), gives a critical text of Sedulius' politico-ecclesiastical tract, *De rectoribus Christianis,* and discusses Carolingian political writing.

CHAPTER XI

MENTAL ASPECTS OF THE ELEVENTH CENTURY : ITALY

I. From Charlemagne to Hildebrand.
II. The Human Situation.
III. The Italian Continuity of Antique Culture.
IV. Italy's Intellectual Piety : Peter Damiani and
St. Anselm.

I

The Empire of Charlemagne could not last. Two obvious causes, among others, were enough to prevent it. No single government (save when temporarily energized by some extraordinary ruler) could control such enormous and widely separated regions, which included much of the present Germany and Austria, the greater part of Italy, France, and the Low Countries. Large portions of this Empire were almost trackless, and nowhere were there good roads and means of transportation. Then, as the second cause, within these diverse and ununited lands dwelt or moved many peoples differing from each other in blood and language, in conditions of life and degrees of civilization or barbarism. No power existed that could either hold them in subjection or make them into proper constituents of an Empire.[1]

There were other, more particular, causes of dissolution : the Frankish custom of partitioning the realm brought war between Louis the Pious and his sons, and then among the

[1] In both these respects a contrary condition had made possible the endurance of the Roman Empire. Its territories in the main were civilized, and were traversed by the best of roads, while many of them lay about that ancient common highway of peoples, the Mediterranean. Then the whole Empire was leavened, and one part made capable of understanding another, by the Graeco-Roman culture.

latter ; no scion of the Carolingian house was equal to the situation ; under the ensuing turbulence, the royal power weakened, and local protection, or oppression, took its place ; constant war exhausted the strength of the Empire, and particularly of Austrasia, while from without Norsemen, Slavs, and Saracens were attacking, invading, plundering everywhere.   These marauders still were heathen, or obstinate followers of the Prophet ; while Christianity was the bond of unity and empire.   Charlemagne and his strong predecessors had been able thus to view and use the Church ; but the weaker successors, beginning with Louis the Pious, too eager for the Church's aid and condonation, found their subservience as a reed that broke and pierced the hand.

These causes quickly brought about the Empire's actual dissolution.   On the other hand, a potent conception had been revived in western Europe.   Louis the Pious, himself made emperor in Charlemagne's lifetime, associated his eldest son with him as co-emperor, and made his two younger sons kings, hoping thus to preserve the Empire's unity.   If that unity forthwith became a name, it was a name to conjure with ; and the corresponding imperial fact was to be again made actual by the first Saxon Otto, a man worthy to reach back across the years and clasp the hand of the great Charles.

That intervening century and a half preceding the year 962 when Otto was crowned emperor, carried political and social changes.   To the West, in the old Neustrian kingdom which was to form the nucleus of mediaeval France, the Carolingian line ran out in degenerates surnamed the Pious, the Bald, the Stammerer, the Simple, and the Fat.   The Counts of Paris, Odo, Robert, Hugh the Great, and, finally, Hugh Capet, playing something like the old rôle of the palace mayors, were becoming the actual rulers, although not till 987 was the last-named Hugh formally elected and anointed king.

Other great houses also had arisen through the land of France, which was very far from being under the power of the last Carolingians or the first Capetians.   The year 911 saw the treaty between Norman Rollo and Charles the Simple, and may be taken to symbolize the settling down of Norsemen from freebooters to denizens, with a change of faith. Rollo received the land between the Epte and the sea, to the borders of Brittany, along with temporary privileges, granted by the same Simple Charles, of sack and plunder over the latter. But a generation later the valiant Count Alan of the Twisted Beard drove out the plunderers, and established the feudal duchy long to bear the name of Brittany. Likewise, aided by the need of protection against invading plunderers, feudal principalities were formed in Flanders, Champagne, Burgundy, Aquitaine, Languedoc.

At the time when Hugh Capet drew near his royal destiny, his brother was Duke of Burgundy, the Dukes of Normandy and Aquitaine were his brothers-in-law, and Adalberon, Archbishop of Rheims, was his partisan. As a king elected by his peers, his royal rights were only such as sprang from the feudal homage and fidelity which they tendered him. Yet he, with the clergy, deemed that his consecration by the Church gave him the prerogatives of Frankish sovereigns, which were patterned on those of Roman emperors and Old Testament kings. It was to be the long endeavour of the Capetian line to make good these higher claims against the counter-assumptions of feudal vassals, who individually might be stronger than the king.[1]

Austrasia, the eastern Frankish kingdom, formed the centre of those portions of the Carolingian Empire which were to remain German. Throughout these lands, as in the West, feudal disintegration was progressing. The great territorial divisions were set by differences of race or *stamm*. Saxons, Franks, Bavarians, Suabians, had never been one people. In the tenth century each of these *stamms*, with the land it dwelt in, made a dukedom ; and there were besides marks or frontier lordships, each under its mark-grave, upon whom lay the duty of repelling outer foes. These divisions, fixed in differences of law, language, and blood, were destined to prevent the formation of a strong kingdom like that of France.

Yet what was to prove a veritable German royalty

---

[1] Within his hereditary domain, Hugh had the powers of other feudal lords ; but this domain, instead of expanding, tended to shrink under the reigns of the Capetians of the eleventh century.

sprang from the ducal Saxon house. Upon the failure of
the German Carolingian branch in 911, Conrad, Duke of
Franconia, was elected king, the Saxons and Suabians consenting. After struggling a few years, mainly against the
power of the Saxon duke Henry, Conrad at his death in 918
pronounced in favour of his stronger rival. Thereupon
Henry, called by later legend " The Fowler," became king,
and having maintained his royal authority against recal-
citrants, and fought successfully with Hungarians and
Bohemians, he died in 936, naming his son Otto as his
successor.

The latter's reign was to be a long and great one. He
was consecrated at Aix-la-Chapelle in Charlemagne's basilica,
thus at the outset showing what and whom he had in mind.
Then and thereafter all manner of internal opposition had
to be suppressed. His own competing brothers were, first
of all, to be put down ; and with them the Dukes of Bavaria,
Franconia, and Lorraine, whom Otto conquered and replaced with men connected with him by ties of blood or
marriage. Far to the West he made his power felt, settling
affairs between Louis and Hugh the Great. Hungarians and
Slavs attacked his realm in vain. New *marks* were established to hold them in check, and new bishoprics were
founded, fonts of missionary Christianity and fortresses of
defence.

Thereupon Otto looked southward, over the Alps. To
say that Italy was sick with turmoil and corruption, and
exposed to the attack of every foe, is to give but the negative
and least interesting side. She held more of civilized life
and of education than any northern land ; she differed from
the north in her politics and institutions. Feudalism was
not so universal there, nor so deeply rooted, as in the north ;
although the Roman barons, who made and unmade popes,
represented it ; and in many regions, as later among the
Normans in the south, there was to be a feudal land-holding
nobility. But in Italy, it was the city, whether under civic
or episcopal government, or in a despot's grip, that took the
lead, and was to keep the life of the peninsula predominantly
urban, as it had been in the Roman time.

Tenth-century Italy contained enough claimants to the

royal, even the imperial, title.   Rome reeked with faction ;
and the papal power was nearly snuffed out.   Pope followed
pope, to reign or be dragged from his throne—eight of them
between 896 and 904.   Then began at Rome the domination
of the notorious, but virile, Theodora and her daughter
Marozia, makers and perhaps mistresses of popes, and leaders
in feudal violence.   Marozia married a certain valiant
Alberic, " markgrave of Camerino " and forerunner of many
a later Italian soldier and tyrant of fortune.   When he fell,
she married again, and overthrew Pope John X., who had
got the better of her first husband.   In 931 she made her son
pope as John XI.   For yet a third husband she took a certain
King Hugo, a Burgundian ; but another son of hers, a
second Alberic, roused the city, drove him out, and proclaimed himself " Prince and Senator of all the Romans."

It was in this Italy that Otto intervened, in 951, drawn
perhaps by the wrongs of Queen Adelaide, widow of Hugo's
son, Lothaire, a landless king, since Markgrave Berengar had
ousted him from his Italian holdings.   This Berengar now
persecuted and imprisoned the queen-widow.   She escaped ;
Otto descended from the Alps, and married her ; Lombardy
submitted ; Berengar fled.   This time Otto did not advance
to Rome, being impeded by many things—Alberic's refusal
to admit him, and behind his back in Germany the rebellion
of his own son Liudolf aided by the Archbishop of Mainz,
and later by those whom Otto left in Italy to represent him
as he hurried north.   These were straitened times for the
king, and the Hungarians poured over the boundaries to
take advantage of the confusion.   But Otto's star triumphed
over both rebels and Hungarians—a bloody star for the
latter, as the plains of Lech might testify, where they were
so handled that they never ravaged German lands again.

Otto's power now reached its zenith.   He reordered the
German dukedoms, filled the archbishoprics with faithful
servants, bound the German clergy to himself with gifts
and new foundations, and ruled them like another Charlemagne.   It was his time to become emperor, an emperor like
Charlemagne, and not like later weaklings.   In 961 he again
entered Italy, to be greeted with universal acclaim as by
men longing for a deliverer.   He was crowned king in Pavia ;

the levies of the once more hostile Berengar dispersed before him.   In February 962 he was anointed emperor at Rome by John XII., son of that second Alberic who had refused to open the gates, but whose debauched son had called for aid upon the mighty German.   Once more the Holy Roman Empire of the Germans was refounded to endure a while with power, and continue a titular existence for eight centuries.

The power of the first Otto was so overwhelming that the papacy could not escape the temporary subjection which its vile state deserved.   And the Empire was its honest patron, for the good of both.   So on through the reigns of Otto II., who died in 983, aged twenty-eight, and his son Otto III., who died in 1002, at the age of twenty-two, a dreamer and would-be universal potentate.   Then came the practical-minded rule of the second Henry (1002–1024), who still aided and humbly ruled the Church.   Conrad II., of Franconia, followed, faithful to the imperial tradition.[1] He was succeeded in 1039 by his son Henry III., beneficent and prosperous, if not far-seeing, who again cared for both Church and State, and imperially constrained the papacy, itself impotent in the grip of the Roman barons and the Counts of Tusculum.   Henry did not hesitate to clear away at once three rival popes (1046) and name a German, Clement II.   It was this worthy man, but still more another German, his successor, Leo IX. (1049–1054), who lifted the papacy from its Italian mire, and launched it full on its course toward an absolute spiritual supremacy that was to carry the temporal control of kings and princes.   But the man already at the helm was a certain deacon Hildebrand, who was destined to guide the papal policy through the reigns of successive popes until he himself was hailed as Gregory VII. (1073–1085).[2]

With Hildebrand's pontificate, which in truth began before he sat in Peter's chair, the reforming spirits among

---

[1] In Conrad's reign " Burgundy," comprising most of the eastern and southern regions of France, and with Lyons and Marseilles, as well as Basle and Geneva within its boundaries, was added to the Empire.

[2] Papal elections were freed from lay control, and a great step made toward the emancipation of the entire Church, by the decree of Nicholas II. in 1059, by which the election of the popes was committed to the conclave of cardinals.

the clergy, aroused to his keen policy, set themselves to the uplifting of their order. In all countries the Church, heavy with its possessions, seemed about to become feudal and secular. Bishops and abbots were appointed by kings and the great feudatories, and were by them *invested* with their lands as fiefs, for which the clerical appointee did homage, and undertook to perform feudal duties. Church fiefs failed to become hereditary only because bishops and abbots could not marry ; yet in fact great numbers of the lower clergy lived in a state of marriage or " concubinage." Evidently the celibacy of the clergy was a vital issue in Church reform ; and so were investitures and the matter of simony. Under mediaeval conditions, the most open form of this " heresy " called after Simon Magus, was the large gift from the new incumbent to his feudal lord who had invested him with abbey or bishopric. Such simony was not wrong from the feudal point of view, and might properly represent the duty of bishop or abbot to his lord.

Obviously, for the reform and emancipation of the Church, and in order that it should become a world-power, and not remain a semi-secular local institution in each land, it was necessary that the three closely connected corruptions of simony, lay investitures, and clerical concubinage should be destroyed. The papacy addressed itself to this enormous task under the leadership of Hildebrand.[1] In his pontificate the struggle with the supreme representative of secular power, to wit, the Empire, came to a head touching investitures. Gregory's secular opponent was Henry IV., of tragic and unseemly fame ; for whom the conflict proved to be the road by which he reached Canossa, dragged by the Pope's anathema, and also driven to this shame by a rebellious Germany (1076, 1077). Henry was conquered, although a revulsion of the long-swaying war drove Gregory from Rome, to die an exile for the cause which he deemed that of righteousness.

Between the papacy and the secular power represented in this struggle by the Empire, a peaceful co-equality could not exist. The superiority of the spiritual and eternal over

---

[1] For the matter of clerical celibacy, and the part played by monasticism in these reforms, see *post*, Chapter XVI.

the carnal and temporal had to be vindicated ; and in terms admitting neither limit nor condition, Hildebrand maintained the Church's universal jurisdiction upon earth. The authority granted by Christ to Peter and his successors, the popes, was absolute for eternity. Should it not include the passing moment of mortal life, important only because determining man's eternal lot ? The divine grant was made without qualification or exception *in saeculo* as well as for the life to come. If spiritual men are under the Pope's jurisdiction, shall he not also constrain secular folk from their wickedness ? [1] Were kings excepted when the Lord said, Thou art Peter ? [2] Nay ; the salvation of souls demands that the Pope shall have full authority *in terra* to suppress the waves of pride with the arms of humility. The *dictatus papae* of the year 1075 make the Pope the head of the Christian world : the Roman Church was founded by God alone ; the Roman pontiff alone by right is called *universal* ; he alone may use the imperial insignia ; his feet alone shall be kissed by all princes ; he may depose emperors and release subjects from fealty ; and he can be judged by no man.[3]

In the century and a half following Gregory's reign the papacy well-nigh attained the realization of the claims made by this great upbuilder of its power.[4] Constantine's forged donation was outdone in fact ; and the furthest hopes of Leo I. and the first, second, and third Gregories were more than realized.

II

One might liken the Carolingian period to a vessel at her dock, taking on her cargo, casks of antique culture and

---

[1] Gregory VII., *Ep.* iv. 2 (Migne 148, col. 455).

[2] *Ep.* viii. 21 (Migne 148, col. 594).

[3] Migne 148, col. 407, 408, and in Jaffé, *Regesta Pontificum*. The *Dictatus* is thought by many to have been composed by Cardinal Deusdedit a few years later. Cf. *post*, Chapter XXXIV., iv.

[4] As between the Empire and the Papacy the particular struggle over investitures was adjusted by the Concordat of Worms (1122), by which the Church should choose her bishops ; but the elections were to be held in the presence of the king, who conferred, by special investiture, the temporal fiefs and privileges. For translations of Gregory's Letters and other matter, see J. H. Robinson's *Readings in European History*, i. 274-293.

huge crates of patristic theology. Then western Europe in
the eleventh century would be the same vessel getting under
way, well started on the mediaeval ocean.

This would be one way of putting the matter. A closer
simile already used is the likening of the Carolingian period
to the lusty schoolboy learning his lessons, thinking very
little for himself. By the eleventh century he will have
left school, though still impressionable, still with much to
learn ; but he has begun to turn his conned lessons over in
his mind, and to think a little in the terms of what he has
acquired—has even begun to select therefrom tentatively,
and still under the mastery of the whole. He perceives the
charm of the antique culture, of the humanly inspiring
literature, so exhaustless in its profane fascinations ; he is
realizing the spiritual import of the patristic share of his
instruction, and already feels the power of emotion which
lay implicit in the Latin formulation of the Christian Faith.
Withal he is beginning to evolve an individuality of his own.

Speaking more explicitly, it should be said that instead
of one such hopeful youth there are several, or rather groups
of them, differing widely from each other. The forefathers
of certain of these groups were civilized and educated men,
at home in the antique and patristic curriculum with which
our youths are supposed to have been busy. The forefathers of other groups were rustics, or rude herdsmen and
hunters, hard-hitting warriors, who once had served, but
more latterly had rather lorded it over, the cultivated
forbears of the others. Still, again, the forefathers of other
numerous groups had been partly cultivated and partly rude.
Evidently these groups of youths are diverse in blood and
in ancestral traits ; evidently also the antique and patristic
curriculum is quite a new thing to some of them, while
others had it at their fathers' knees.

Our different youthful groups represent Italians,
Germans, and the inhabitants of France and the British
Isles. One may safely speak of the ninth-century Germans
as schoolboys just brought face to face with Christianity
and the antique culture. So with the Saxon stock in
England. The propriety is not so clear as to the Italians ;
for they are not newly introduced to these matters. Yet

their household affairs have been disturbed, and they themselves have slackened in their study. So they too have much to learn anew, and may be regarded as truants, dirtied and muddied, and perhaps refreshed, by the scrambles of their time of truancy, and now returning to lessons which they have pretty well forgotten.

Obviously, in considering the intellectual condition of western Europe in the tenth and eleventh centuries, it will be convenient to regard each country in turn : and, besides, a geographical is more appropriate than a topical arrangement, because there was still little choice of one branch of discipline rather than another. The majority still were conning indiscriminately what had come from the past, studying heterogeneous matters in the same books, the same forlorn compendia. They read the *Etymologies* of Isidore or the corresponding works of Bede, and followed as of course the Trivium and Quadrivium. In sacred learning they might read the Scriptural Commentaries of Rabanus Maurus or Walafrid Strabo, or study the works of Augustine. This was still the supreme study, and all else, properly viewed, was ancillary to it. Nevertheless, as between sacred study and profane literature, an even violent divergence of choice existed. Everywhere there were men who loved the profanities in themselves, and some who felt that for their souls' sake they must abjure them.

For further diverging lines of preference, one should wait for the twelfth century. Many men will then be found absorbed in religious study, while others cultivate logic and metaphysics, with the desire to know more active in them than the fear of hell. Still others will study " grammar " and the classics, or, again, with conscious specializing choice, devote their energies to the civil or the canon law. In later chapters, and mainly with reference to this culminating mediaeval time which includes the twelfth, the thirteenth, and at least, for Dante's sake, the first part of the fourteenth, century, we shall review these various branches of intellectual endeavour in topical order. But for the earlier time which still enshrouds us, we pass from land to land as on a tour of intellectual inspection.

III

We start with Italy.   There was no break between her
antique civilization and her mediaeval development, but
only a period of depression and decay.   Notwithstanding
the change from paganism to Christianity and the influx
of barbarians, both a race-continuity and a continuity of
culture persisted.   The Italian stock maintained its numerical
preponderance, as well as the power of transforming newcomers to the likeness of itself.   The natural qualities of
the country, and the existence of cities and antique constructions, assisted in the Italianizing of Goth, Lombard,
German, Norman.   Latin civic reminiscence, tradition,
custom, permeated society, and prevented the growth of
feudalism.   Italy remained urban, and continued to reflect
the ancient time.   " Consuls " and " tribunes " long survived
the passing of their antique functions, and the fame endured
of antique heroes, mythical and historical.   Florence
honoured Mars and Caesar ; Padua had Antenor, Cremona
Hercules.   Such names remained veritably eponymous.
Other cities claimed the birthplace of Pliny, of Ovid, of
Virgil.   An altar might no longer be dedicated to a pagan
hero, yet the town would preserve his name upon monuments, would adorn his fancied tomb, stamp his effigy on
coins or keep it in the communal seal.   Of course the
figments of the Trojan Saga were current through the land,
which, however divided, was conscious of itself as Italy.   *Te
Italia plorabit* writes an eleventh-century Pisan poet of a
young Pisan noble fallen in Africa.

In Italy, as in no other country, the currents of antique
education, disturbed yet unbroken, carried clear across that
long period of invasions, catastrophes, and reconstructions,
which began with the time of Alaric.   Under the later
pagan emperors, and under Constantine and his successors,
the private schools of grammar and rhetoric had tended to
decline.   There were fewer pupils with inclination and
ability to pay.   So the emperors established municipal
schools in the towns of Italy and the provinces.   The towns
tried to shirk the burden, and the teachers, whose pay came

tardily, had to look to private pupils for support.   In Italy
there was always some demand for instruction in grammar
and law.   The supply rose and fell with the happier or the
more devastated condition of the land.   Theodoric the
Ostrogoth re-established municipal schools through his
dominion.   After him further troubles came, for example
from the Lombards, until they too became gentled by
Italian conditions, and their kings and nobles sought to
encourage and acquire the education and culture which
their coming had disturbed.   In the seventh and eighth
centuries the grade of instruction was very low ; but there
is evidence of the unintermitted existence of lay schools,
private or municipal, in all the important towns, from the
eighth century to the tenth, the eleventh, and so on and on.
These did not give religious instruction, but taught grammar
and the classic literature, law and the art of drawing
documents and writing letters.   The former branches of
study appear singularly profane in Italy.   The literature
exemplifying the principles of grammar was pagan and
classical, and the fictitious themes on which the pupils
exercised their eloquence continued such as might have
been orated on in the time of Quintilian.   Intellectually
the instruction was poverty-stricken, but the point to note
is, that in Italy there never ceased to be schools conducted
by laymen for laymen, where instruction in matters profane
and secular was imparted and received for the sake of its
profane and secular value, without regard to its utility for
the saving of souls.   There was no barbaric contempt for
letters, nor did the laity fear them as a spiritual peril.
Gerbert before the year 1000 had found Italy the field for
the purchase of books ;[1] and about 1028 Wipo, a native
of Burgundy and chaplain of the emperor Conrad II.,
contrasts the ignorance of Germany with Italy, where " the
entire youth (*tota juventus*) is sent to sweat in the schools " ;[2]
and about the middle of the twelfth century, Otto of Freising
suggests a like contrast between the Italy and Germany of
his time.[3]

[1] See *post*, Chapter XII., 1. The copying of manuscripts was a lucrative profession in Italy.
[2] Tetralogus, Pertz, *Mon. Germ. scriptores*, xi. 251.
[3] The clerical schools were no less important than the lay, but less distinctive

In Italy the study of grammar, with all that it included, was established in tradition, and also was regarded as a necessary preparation for the study both of law and medicine. Even in the eleventh century these professions were followed by men who were " grammarians," a term to be taken to mean for the early Middle Ages the profession of letters. In the eleventh century, a lawyer or notary in Italy (where there were always such, and some study of law and legal forms) needed education in a Latinity different from the vulgar Latin which was turning into Italian. A little later, Irnerius, the founder of the Bologna school, was a teacher of " grammar " before he became a teacher of law.[1] As for medicine, that appears always to have been cultivated at least in southern Italy ; and a knowledge of grammar, even of logic, was required for its study.[2]

The survival of medical knowledge in Italy did not, in means and manner, differ from the survival of the rest of the antique culture. Some acquaintance had continued with the works of Galen and other ancient physicians ; but more use was made of compendia, the matter of which may

because their fellows existed north of the Alps. Cathedral schools may be obscurely traced back to the fifth century ; and there were schools under the direction of the parish priests. In them aspirants for the priesthood were educated, receiving some Latin and some doctrinal instruction. So the cathedral and parochial schools helped to preserve the elements of antique education ; but they present no such open cultivation of letters for their own profane sake as may be found in the schools of lay grammarians. The monastic schools are better known. From the ninth century they usually consisted of an outer school (schola exterior) for the laity and youths who wished to become secular priests, and an inner school (interior) for those desiring to become monks. At different times the monastery schools of Bobbio, Farfa, and other places rose to fame, but Monte Cassino outshone them all.

As to the schools and culture of Italy during the early Middle Ages, see Ozanam, Les Écoles en Italie aux temps barbares (in his Documents inédits, etc., and printed elsewhere) ; Giesebrecht, De literarum studiis apud Italos, etc. (translated into Italian by C. Pascal, Florence, 1895, under the title L' Istruzione in Italia nei primi secoli del Medio-Evo) ; G. Salvioli, L' Istruzione publica in Italia nei secoli VIII., IX., X. (Florence, 1898) ; Novati, L' Influsso del pensiero latino sopra la civiltà italiana del Medio-Evo (2nd ed., Milan, 1899).

[1] See post, Chapter XXXIV., III.

[2] At Salerno, according to the Constitution of Frederick II., three years' preliminary study of the scientia logicalis was demanded, because " numquam sciri potest scientia medicinae nisi de scientia logicali aliquid praesciatur " (cited by Novati, L' Influsso del pensiero latino, etc., p. 220). Just as Law and Medical Schools in the United States may require a college diploma from applicants for admission.

have been taken from Galen, but was larded with current superstitions regarding disease. Such compendia began to appear in the fifth century, and through these and other channels a considerable medical knowledge found its way to a congenial home in Salerno. There are references to this town as a medical community as early as the ninth century. By the eleventh, it was famous for its medicine. About the year 1060 a certain Constantine seems to have brought there novel and stimulating medical knowledge which he had gained in Africa from Arabian (ultimately Greek) sources. Nevertheless, translations from the Arabic seem scarcely to have exerted much influence upon medicine for yet another hundred years.[1]

Thus in Italy the antique education never stopped, antique reminiscence and tradition never passed away, and the literary matter of the pagan past never faded from the consciousness of the more educated among the laity and clergy. Some understanding of the classic literature, as well as a daily absorption of the antique from its survival in habits, laws, and institutions, made part of the capacities and temperament of Italians. Grammarians, lawyers, doctors, monks even, might think and produce under the influence of that which never had quite fallen from the life of Italy. And just as the ancient ways of civic life and styles of building became rude and impoverished, and yet passed on without any abrupt break into the tenth and the eleventh centuries, so was it with the literature of Italy, or at least with those productions which were sheer literature, and not deflected from traditional modes of expression by any definite business or by the distorting sentiments of Christian asceticism. This literature proper was likely to take the form of verse in the eleventh century. A practical matter would be put in prose ; but the effervescence of the soul, or the intended literary effort, would fall into rhyme or resort to metre.

We have an example of the former in those often-cited

---

[1] On Constantine see Wüstenfeld, " Übersetzungen arabischer Werke," etc. *Abhand. Göttingen Gesellschaft*, vol. 22 (1877), pp. 10-20, and p. 55 *sqq.* Also on the Salerno school, Meyer-Steinegg und Sudhoff, *Geschichte der Medicin*, pp. 199 *sqq.* (1921).

tenth-century verses exhorting the watchers on the walls of
Modena :

> " O tu qui servas armis ista moenia,
> Noli dormire, moneo, sed vigila.
> Dum Hector vigil extitit in Troia,
> Non eam cepit fraudulenta Graecia.

> " Vigili voce avis anser candida
> Fugavit Gallos ex arce Romulea."

The antique reminiscence fills this jingle, as it does the
sensuous

> " O admirabile Veneris ydolum
> Cuius materiae nichil est frivolum :
> Archos te protegat, qui stellas et polum
> Fecit et maria condidit et solum." [1]

And so on from century to century.   At the end of the
eleventh, a Pisan poet celebrates Pisa's victory over Saracens
in Africa :

> " Inclytorum Pisanorum scripturus historiam,
> Antiquorum Romanorum renovo memoriam,
> Nam ostendit modo Pisa laudem admirabilem,
> Quam olim recepit Roma vincendo Carthaginem."

For an eleventh-century example of more literary verse,
one may turn to the metres of Alphanus, a noble Salernian,
lover of letters, pilgrim traveller, archbishop of his native
town, and monk of Monte Cassino, the parent Benedictine
monastery, which had been the cultured retreat of Paulus
Diaconus in the time of Charlemagne.   It was destroyed
by the Saracens in 884.   Learning languished in the
calamitous decades which followed.   But the convent was
rebuilt, and some care for learning recommences there under
the abbot Theobald (1022-1035).   The monastery's troubles
were not over ; but it re-entered upon prosperity under the
energetic rule of the German Richer (1038-1055).[2]   Shortly

---

[1] *Traube,* " O Roma nobilis," *Abhand. philos.-philol. Classe Bayer. Akad.* Bd.
19, p. 301.   This poem probably belongs to the tenth century.   " Archos " is
mediaeval Greek for " The Lord."

[2] The *Rationes dictandi,* a much-used book on the art of composing letters,
comes from the hand of one Alberic, who was a monk at Monte Cassino in the
middle of the eleventh century.   He died a cardinal in 1088.   The *ars dictaminis*
related either to drawing legal documents or composing letters.   See *post,* Chapter
XXXI., II.

after his death two close friends were received among its monks, Alphanus and Desiderius. The latter was of princely Lombard stock, from Beneventum. He met Alphanus at Salerno, and there they became friends. Afterwards both saw something of the world and experienced its perils Desiderius was born to be monk, abbot, and at last pope (Victor III.) against his will. Alphanus, always a man of letters, was drawn by his friend to monastic life. Long after, when Archbishop of Salerno, he gave a refuge and a tomb to the outworn Hildebrand.

The rebuilding and adorning of Monte Cassino by Desiderius with the aid of Greek artists is a notable episode in the history of art.[1] Under the long rule of this great abbot (1058-1087) the monastery reached the summit of its repute and influence. It was the home of theology and ecclesiastical policy. There law and medicine were studied. Likewise " grammar " and classic literature, the latter not too broadly, as would appear from the list of manuscripts copied under Desiderius—Virgil, Ovid, Terence, Seneca, Cicero's *De natura deorum*. But then there was the whole host of early Christian poets, historians, and theologians. Naturally, Christian studies were dominant within those walls.

Alphanus did not spend many of his years there. But his loyalty to the great monastery never failed, nor his intercourse with its abbot and monks. He has left an enthusiastic poem descriptive of the place and the splendour of its building.[2] A general and interesting feature of his poetry is the naturalness of its classical reminiscence and its feeling for the past, which is even translated into the poet's sentiments toward his contemporaries and toward life. In his metrical verses *ad Hildebrandum archidiaconum Romanum*, his stirring praise of that statesman is imbued with pagan sentiment.

" How great the glory which so often comes to those defending the republic, has not escaped thy knowledge, Hildebrand. The Via Sacra and the Via Latina recall the same, and the lofty crown

---

[1] See E. Bertaux, *L'Art dans l'Italie méridionale*, i. 155 *sqq.* (Paris, 1904).
[2] The poems of Alphanus are in Migne, *Pat. Lat.* 147, col. 1219-1268.

of the Capitol, that mighty seat of empire. . . . The hidden poison
of envy implants its infirmity in wretched affairs, and brings overthrow only to such.   That thou shouldst be envied, and not envy,
beseems thy skill. . . . How great the power of the anathema !
Whatever Marius and Julius wrought with the slaughter of
soldiers, thou dost with thy small voice. . . . What more does
Rome owe to the Scipios and the other Quirites than to thee ? "

Perhaps the glyconic metre of this poem was too
much for Alphanus.   His awkward constructions, however,
constantly reflect classic phrases.   And how naturally his
mind reproduced the old pagan—or fundamental human—
views of life, appears again in his admiring sapphics to
Romuald, chief among Salerno's lawyers :

> " Dulcis orator, vehemens gravisque,
> Inter omnes causidicos perennem
> Gloriam juris tibi, Romualde,
>   Prestitit usus."

Further stanzas follow on Romuald's wealth, station,
and mundane felicity.   Then comes the sudden turn, and
Romuald is praised for having spurned them all :

> " Cumque sic felix, ut in orbe sidus
> Fulseris, mundum roseo jacentem
>   Flore sprevisti. . . . "

Apparently Romuald had become a monk :

> " Rite fecisti, potiore vita
>   Perfruiturus." [1]

This turn of sentiment curiously accorded with the poet's
own fortune and way of life ; for Alphanus, with all his
love of antique letters, was also a monk and an ascetic, of
whom a contemporary chronicler tells that in Lent he ate
but twice a week and never slept on a bed.   Yet monk, and
occasional ascetic, as he was, the ordinary antique-descended
education and inherited strains of antique feeling made the
substratum of his nature, and this although he could inveigh
against the philosophic and grammatical studies flourishing

---

[1] " Ad Romualdum causidicum," printed in Ozanam, *Doc. inédits*, p. 259.

in a neighbouring monastery, and advise one of its studious
youths to turn from such :

> " Si, Transmunde, mihi credis, amice,
> His uti studiis desine tandem ;
> Fac cures monachi scire professum,
> Ut vere sapiens esse puteris." [1]

Eleventh-century Italian "versificatores" were interested
in a variety of things. Some of them gave the story of a
saint's or bishop's life, or were occupied with an ecclesiastic
theme. Others sang the fierce struggle between rival cities,
or some victory over Saracens, or made an idyl of very
human love with mythological appurtenances. The verse-
forms either followed the antique metres or were accentual
deflections from them with the new added element of rhyme ;
the ways of expression copied antique phrase and simile,
except when the matter and sentiment of the poem compelled
another choice. In that case the Latin becomes freer, more
mediaeval, ruder, if one will ; and still antique turns of
expression and bits of sentences show how naturally it came
to these men to construct their verses out of ancient phrases.
Yet borrowed phrases and the constraint of metre impeded
spontaneity, and these feeble versifiers could hardly create
in modes of the antique. A fresher spirit breathes in certain
anonymous poems, which have broken with metre, while they
give voice to sentiments quite after the feeling of the old
Italian paganism. In one of these, from Ivrea, the poet
meets a nymph by the banks of the Po, and in leonine
elegiacs bespeaks her love, with all the paraphernalia of
antique reference, assuring her that his verse shall make her
immortal, a perfectly pagan sentiment—or affectation :

> " Sum sum sum vates, musarum servo penates,
> Subpeditante Clio queque futura scio.
> Me minus extollo, quamvis mihi cedit Apollo,
> Invidet et cedit, scire Minerva dedit.
> Laude mea vivit mihi se dare queque cupivit,
> Immortalis erit, ni mea Musa perit." [2]

---

[1] Printed in Giesebrecht, *De lit. stud.*, etc.
[2] Printed by Dummler in *Anselm der Peripatetiker*, pp. 94-102. See also the
rhyming colloquy between Helen and Ganymede, of the twelfth century, printed
in Ozanam, *Documents inédits, etc.*, p. 19.

It is obvious that in the tenth and eleventh centuries there were Italians whose sentiments and intellectual interests were profane, humanistic in a word.   These men might even be high ecclesiastics, like Liutprand, Bishop of Cremona (d. 972).[1] He was of Lombard stock, and yet a genuine Italian, bred in an atmosphere of classical reminiscence and contemporary gossip and misdeed.   Politically, at least, the Italy of John XII. was not so much better than its pope ; and the *Antapodosis* of Liutprand goes along in its easy, and often dramatic way, telling of crime and perfidy, and showing scant horror.   It was a general history of the historian's times, written while in exile in Germany ; for Liutprand had been driven out of Italy by King Berengar, whom he had once served.   He hated Berengar and his wife, and although well received at the Court of the great Otto, he did not love his place of exile.[2]

In exile Liutprand wrote his book to requite Berengar. The work had also a broader purpose, yet one just as consolatory to the writer.   It should acknowledge and show the justice of the divine judgments exemplified in history. Herein lay a fuller, although less Italian, consolation for his exile than in Berengar's requital.   Liutprand keeps in mind Boëthius and his *De consolatione*, and regards his own work as a Consolation of History, as that of Boëthius was a Consolation of Philosophy.   The paths of Liutprand's Consolation are as broad as the justice and power of the Trinity, " which casts down these for their wicked deeds and raises up those for their merits' sake." [3]

Quite explicitly he explains the title and reason of his work at the opening of its third book :

" Since it will show the deeds of famous men, why call it Antapodosis ?   I reply : Its object is to set forth and cry aloud the acts of this Berengar who at this moment does not reign but tyrannize in Italy, and of his wife Willa, who for the boundlessness of her tyranny should be called a second Jezebel, and Lamia for her insatiate rapines.   Me and my house, my family and kin, have

---

[1] On Liutprand see Ebert, *Ges. der Lit.* iii. 414-427 ; Molinier, *Sources de l'histoire de France*, i. 274.   His works are in the *Monumenta Ger.*, also in 136 of Migne.   The *Antapodosis* and *Embassy to Constantinople* are translated into German in the *Geschichtsschreiber der deutschen Vorzeit.*

[2] See *Antapod.* vi. 1 (Migne 136, col. 893).

[3] *Antapod.* i. 1 (Migne 136, col. 791).

they harassed with so many javelins of lies, so many spoliations, so many essays of wickedness, that neither tongue nor pen can avail to set them forth.   May then these pages be to them an antapodosis, that is retribution, to make their wickedness naked before men living and unborn.   None the less may it prove an antapodosis for the benefits conferred on me by holy and happy men." [1]

Liutprand's narrative is breezy and interspersed with ribald tales.   The writer meant to amuse his readers and himself.   These literary qualities give picturesqueness to his well-known *Embassy to Constantinople*, where he was sent by Otto the Great, for purposes of peace and to ask the hand of the Byzantine princess for Otto II.   The highly coloured ceremonial life of thè Greek Court, the chicane and contemptuous treatment met with, the spirited words of Liutprand, and the rancour of this same thwarted envoy, all appear vividly in his report. [2]

There were also many laymen occupied with Latin studies.   Such a one was Gunzo of Novara, a curiously vain grammarian of the second half of the tenth century. According to his own story, the fame of his learning incited Otto the Great to implore his presence in Germany.   So he condescended to cross the Alps, with all his books, perhaps in the year 965.   On his way he stopped with the monks of St. Gall, themselves proud of their learning, and perhaps jealous of the southern scholar.   As the weary Gunzo was lifted, half frozen, from his horse at the convent door, and the brethren stood about, a young monk caught at a slip in grammar, and made a skit on him—because, forsooth, he had used an accusative when it should have been an ablative.

Gunzo neither forgave nor forgot.   Passing on to the rival congregation of Reichenau, he composed a long and angry epistle of pedantic excuse and satirical invective, addressed to his former hosts. [3]   In it he parades his wide knowledge of classic authors, justifies what the monks of St. Gall had presumed to mock as a ridiculous barbarism, and closes with a prayer for them in hexameters.   His letter contains the interesting avowal, that, although the monk of

[1] Migne 136, col. 837.
[2] *Legatio Constantinopolitana* (Migne 136, col. 909-937).
[3] Migne, *Pat. Lat.* 136, col. 1283-1302.

St. Gall had wrongly deemed him ignorant of grammar, his
Latin sometimes was impeded by the " usu nostrae vulgaris
linguae, quae latinitati vicina est." So a slip would be due
not to unfamiliarity with Latin, but to an excessive colloquial
familiarity with the vulgar tongue which had scarcely ceased
to be Latin—an excuse no German monk could have given.
It is amusing to see an Italian grammarian of this early
period enter the lists to defend his reputation and assuage
his wounded vanity. Later, such learned battles became
frequent.[1]

Gunzo died as the tenth century closed. Other Italians
of his time and after him crossed the Alps to learn and
teach and play the orator. From the early eleventh century
comes a satirical sketch of one. The subject was a certain
Benedict, Prior of the Abbey of St. Michael of Chiusa, and
nephew of its abbot—therefore doubtless born to wealth and
position. At all events as a youth he had moved about for
nine years " per multa loca in Longobardia et Francia
propter grammaticam," spending the huge sum of two
thousand gold soldi. His pride was unmeasured. " I have
two houses full of books ; there is no book on the earth that
I do not possess. I study them every day. I can discourse
on letters. There is no instruction to be had in Aquitaine,
and but little in Francia. Lombardy, where I learned most,
is the cradle of knowledge." So the satire makes Benedict
speak of himself. Then it makes a monk sketch Benedict's
sojourn at a convent in Angoulême : " He knows more than
any man I ever saw. We have heard his chatter the whole
day. *O quam loquax est !* He is never tired. Wherever
he may be, standing, sitting, walking, lying, words pour from
his mouth like water from the Tigris. He orders the whole
convent about as if he were Abbot. Monks, laity, clergy,
do nothing without his nod. A multitude of the people,
knights too, were always hastening to hear him, as the goal
of their desires. Untired, hurling words the entire day he
sends them off worn out. And they depart, saying : Never
have we seen sic eloquentem grammaticum." [2]

[1] See Ebert, *Allgem. Ges.* iii. 370, etc. ; Novati, *L' Influsso del pensiero latino,*
etc., p. 31 *sqq.* ; and Migne, *Pat. Lat.* 136.
[2] See Novati, *L' Influsso, etc.*, pp. 188-191. The passage is from the vituperative polemic of a certain Ademarus (Migne, *Pat. Lat.* 141, col. 107-108).

Another of these early wandering Italian humanists won
kinder notice, a certain Lombard Guido, who died where
he was teaching in Auxerre, in 1095, and was lamented in
leonine hexameters : " Alas, famous man, so abounding, so
diligent, so praised, so venerated through many lands—

" Filius Italiae, sed alumnus Philosophiae.

Let Gaul grieve, and thou Philosophy who nourished him :
Grieve Grammar, thou. With his death the words of Plato
died, the work of Cicero is blotted out, Maro is silent and
the muse of Naso stops her song." [1]

A final instance to close our examples. In the middle
of the eleventh century flourished Anselm the Peripatetic,
a rhetorician and humanist of Besate (near Milan). In his
Rhetorimachia he tells of a dream in which he finds himself in Heaven, surrounded and embraced by saintly souls.
Their spiritual kisses were still on his lips when three
virgins of another ilk appear, to reproach him with forsaking them. These are Dialectic and Rhetoric and Grammar
—we have met them before ! Now the embraces of the
saints seem cold ! and to the protests of the blessed throng
that Anselm is theirs, the virgins make reply that he is
altogether their own fosterling. Anselm gives up the saints
and departs with the three.[2] This was his humanistic choice.

This rather pleasant dream discloses the conflict between
Letters and the call of piety, which might harass the learned
and the holy in Italy. Distrust of the enticements of pagan
letters might transform itself to diabolic visions. Such a
tale comes from the neighbourhood of Ravenna, in the late
tenth century. It is of one Vilgard, a grammarian, who
became infatuated with the great pagan poets, till their
figures waved through his dreams and he heard their thanks
and assurances that he should participate in their glory.
He foolishly began to teach matters contrary to the Faith,
and in the end was condemned as a heretic. Others were
infected with his opinions, and perished by the sword and fire.[3]

[1] Dümmler, " Gedichte aus Abdinghof," in *Neues Archiv*, **v.** 1 (1876), p. 181
(cited by Novati, p. 19ː).
[2] Dümmler, *Anselm der Peripatetiker*, p. 36 *sqq.* ; cf. Hauréau, *Singularités
historiques*, p. 179 *sqq.*
[3] The account is from Radolphus Glaber, *Historiarum libri*, ii. 12.

Evidently Vilgard's profane studies made him a heretic. But, ordinarily, the Italians with their antique descended temperament were not troubled in the observance and the expression of their Faith by the paganism of their intellectual tastes. Such tastes did not produce open heretics in Italy in the eleventh century any more than in the fifteenth. A pagan disposition seldom prevented an Italian from being a good Catholic.

Yet the monastic spirit in Italy, as elsewhere, in the eleventh century defied and condemned the pagan literature, and in fact all Latin studies beyond the elements of grammar. The protest of the monk or hermit might represent his individual ignorance of classic literature ; or, as in the case of Peter Damiani, the ascetic soul is horrified at the seductive nature of the pagan sweets which it knows too well. Peter indeed could say in his sonorous Latin : " Olim mihi Tullius dulcescebat, blandiebantur carmina poetarum, philosophi verbis aureis insplendebant, et Sirenes usque in exitium dulces meum incantaverunt intellectum." [1]   So a few decades after Peter's death, Rangerius, Bishop of Lucca, writes the life of an episcopal predecessor in elegiacs which show considerable knowledge of grammar and prosody ; and yet he protests against liberal studies—philosophy, astronomy, grammar—with pithy commonplace :

" Et nos ergo scholas non spectamus inanes

Scire Deum satis est, quo nulla scientia maior." [2]

So with the Italians the antique never was an influence brought from without, but always an element of their temperament and faculties. We have not seen that they recast it into novel and interesting forms in the eleventh century ; yet they used it familiarly as something of their own, being quite at home with it. As one may imagine some grand old Roman garden, planned and constructed by

---

[1] On Damiani's views of classical studies, see *Opusc.* xi., *Liber qui dicitur Dominus vobiscum,* cap. i. (Migne 145, col. 232) ; *Opusc.* xlv., *De sancta simplicitate* (*ibid.* col. 695) ; *Opusc.* lviii., *De vera felicitate et sapientia* (*ibid.* col. 831).   For the life and works of this interesting man see *post,* p. 262 *sqq.,* and *post,* Chapter XVII. Cf. also J. A. Endres, *Petrus Damiani und die weltliche Wissenschaft* (Baeumker's *Beiträge,* 1910).

[2] *Vita Anselmi,* 1247 (cited by Ronca, p. 227).

rich and talented ancestors, and still remaining as a home and heritage to descendants whose wealth and capacities have shrunken. The garden is somewhat ruinous, and fallen to decay ; yet these sons are still at home in it, their daily steps pursue its ancient avenues ; they still recline upon the marble seats by the fountains where perhaps scant water runs. Fauns and satyrs—ears gone and noses broken— with even an occasional god, still haunt the courts and sylvan paths, while everywhere, above and about these lazy sons, the lights still chase the shadows, and anon the shadows darken the green and yellow flashes. Perhaps nothing in the garden has become so subtly in and of the race as this play of light and shade. And when the Italian genius shall revive again, and children's children find themselves with power, still within this ancient garden the great vernacular poems will be composed ; great paintings will be painted in its light and shade and under the influence of its formal beauties ; and Italian buildings will never escape the power of the ruined structures found therein.

IV

In the tenth and eleventh centuries, as remarked already, studiously inclined people made no particular selection of one study rather than another. But men discriminated sharply between religious devotion and all profane pursuits. Energies which were regarded as religious might have a political-ecclesiastical character, and be devoted to the purification and upbuilding of the Church ; or they might be intellectual and aloof ; or ascetic and emotional. All three modes might exist together in religious-minded men ; but usually one form would dominate, and mark the man's individuality. Hildebrand, for example, was a monk, fervent and ascetic ; but his strength was devoted to the discipline of the clergy and the elevation of the papal power.   In the great Hildebrandine Church which was his more than any other man's creation, the organizing and political genius of Rome re-emerges, and Rome becomes again the seat of Empire.[1]

---

[1] Another great politico-ecclesiastical Italian was Lanfranc (cir. 1005-1089), whose life was almost exactly contemporaneous with that of Hildebrand. He was

Eminent examples of Italians who illustrate the ascetic-emotional and the intellectual mode of religious devotion are the two very different saints, Peter Damiani and Anselm. The former, to whom we shall again refer when considering the ideals of the hermit life, was born in Ravenna not long after the year 1000. His parents, who were poor, seem to have thought him an unwelcome addition to their already burdensome family. His was a hard lot until he reached the age of ten, when his elder brother Damianus was made an archpresbyter in Ravenna and took Peter to live with him, to educate the gifted boy. From his brother's house the youth proceeded in search of further instruction, first to Faenza, then to Parma. He became proficient in the secular knowledge comprised in the Seven Liberal Arts, and soon began to teach. A growing reputation brought many pupils, who paid such fees that Peter had amassed considerable property when he decided upon a change of life. For some years he had been fearful of the world, and he now turned from secular to religious studies. He put on hair-cloth underneath the gentler garb in which he was seen of men, and became earnest in vigils, fasts, and prayers. In the night-time he quelled the lusts of the flesh by immersing himself in flowing water ; he overcame the temptations of avarice and pride by lavishly giving to the poor, and tending them at his own table. Still he felt unsafe, and yearned to escape the dangers of worldly living. A number of hermits dwelt in a community known as the Hermitage of the Holy Cross of Fonte Avellana, near Faenza ; Peter became one of them shortly before his thirtieth year. They lived ascetically, two in a cell together, spending their time in watching, fasting, and prayer : thus they fought the Evil

---

born in high station at Pavia, and educated in letters and the law. Seized with the desire to be a monk, he left his home and passed through France, sojourning on his way, until he came to the convent of Bec in Normandy, in the year 1042. A man of practical ability and a great teacher, it was he that made the monastery great. Men, lay and clerical, noble and base, came thronging to hear him : Anselm came and Ives of Chartres, both future saints, and one who afterwards as Pope Alexander II. rose before Lanfranc, then Archbishop of Canterbury, and said : " Thus I honour, not the Archbishop of Canterbury, but the master of the school of Bec, at whose feet I sat with other pupils." William the Conqueror made Lanfranc Primate of England and prince-ruler of the land in the Conqueror's absence.

One. Damiani was not satisfied merely with following the austerities practised at Fonte Avellana. Quickly he surpassed all his fellows, except a certain mail-clad Dominic, whose scourgings he could not equal. His chief asceticism lay in the temper of his soul.

From this congenial community (the hermits had made him their prior) Damiani was drawn forth to serve the Church more actively, sorely against his will, and was made Cardinal-Bishop of Ostia by Pope Stephen IX. in 1058. It was indeed the hand of Hildebrand, already directing the papal policy, that had fastened on this unwilling yet serviceable tool. Peter feared and also looked askance upon the relentless spirit, whom he called Sanctus Satanas, not deeming him to be altogether of the kingdom of heaven. He deprecates his censure upon one occasion : " I humbly beg that my Saint Satan may not rage so cruelly against me, and that his worshipful pride may not destroy me with long scourgings ; rather straightway, may it, appeased, quiet to a calm around his servant. In this same letter, which is addressed to the two conspiring souls, Pope Alexander II. and Archdeacon Hildebrand, he sarcastically likens them to the Wind and the Sun of Aesop's fable, who contended as to which could the sooner strip the Traveller of his cloak.[1] Peter's tongue was sharp enough, and apt to indulge in epigram :

> " Wilt thou live in Rome, cry aloud :
> The Pope's lord more than the Lord Pope I obey."

And another squib he writes on Hildebrand :

> " Papam rite colo, sed te prostratus adoro ;
> Tu facis hunc dominum, te facit iste deum." [2]

It was, however, for his own soul that Damiani feared, while in the service of the Curia. To Desiderius, Abbot of Monte Cassino, he exclaims : " He errs, Father, errs indeed, who imagines he can be a monk and at the same time zealously serve the Curia. Ill he bargains, who presumes to

---

[1] *Petri Damiani Ep.* i. xvi. (Migne 144, col. 236). Damiani's works are contained in Migne 144 and 145. Alexander II. was pope from 1061 to 1073, when he was succeeded by Hildebrand.
[2] Migne, *Pat. Lat.* 145, col. 961, 967.

desert the cloister, that he may take up the warfare of the world." [1]

Albeit against his will, Damiani became a soldier of the Church in the fields of her secular militancy against the world. He was sent on more than one important mission— to Milan, to crush the married priests and establish the Pope's authority, or to Mainz, there to quell a rebellious archbishop and a youthful German king. Such missions and others he might accomplish with holy strenuousness ; his more spontaneous zeal, however, was set upon the task of cleansing the immoralities of monks and clergy. In spite of his enforced relations with the powers of the world, he was a fiery reforming ascetic, a scourge of his time's wickedness, rather than a statesman of the Church. His writings were a vent for the outcries of his horror-stricken soul. The corruption of the clergy filled his nostrils : they were rotten, like the loin-cloth of Jeremiah, hidden by the Euphrates ; their bellies were full of drunkenness and lust.[2] As for the apostolic see :

> " Heu ! sedes apostolica,
> Orbis olim gloria,
> Nunc, proh dolor ! efficeris
> Officina Simonis." [3]

These, with other verses written in tears, relate to schisms of pope and antipope which so often rent the papacy in Peter's lifetime.[4] He never ceased to cry out against monks

[1] *Opusculum*, xxxvi. (Migne 145, col. 595). It is also bad to be an abbot, as Damiani shows in plaintive and almost humorous verses :

> " Nullus pene abbas modo
> Valet esse monachus,
> Dum diversum et nocivum
> Sustinet negotium :
> Et, quod velit sustinere,
> Velut iniquus patitur
>
> " Spiritaliter abbatem
> Volunt fratres vivere,
> Et per causas saeculares
> Cogunt illum pergere ;
> Per tam itaque diversa
> Quis valet incedere ? "
>
> *De abbatum miseria rhythmus*
> (Migne, *Pat. Lat.* 145, col. 972).

[2] Lib. v. Ep. iv. ; cf. Jer. xiii.
[3] Ep. iv. 11 (Migne, *Pat. Lat.* 144, col. 313).
[4] He died in 1072, a year before Hildebrand was made pope.

and clergy, denouncing their simony and avarice, their luxury, intemperance and vile unchastity, their viciousness of every kind. Such denunciations fill his letters, while many of his other writings chiefly consist of them.[1] They culminate in his horrible *Liber Gomorrhianus*, which was issued with the approval of one pope, to be suppressed by another as too unspeakable.

Naturally over so foul a world, flame and lower the terrors of the Day of Judgment. For Damiani it was near at hand. He writes to a certain judge :

" Therefore, lord and father, now while the world smiles for thee, while thy body glows in health, while the prosperity of earth allures, think upon those things which are to come. Deem whatever is transitory to be but as the illusion of a dream. And that terrible day of the last Judgment keep ever present to thy sight, and brood with quaking bowels over the sudden coming of such majesty—nor think it to be far off ! "[2]

Beware of penitence postponed !

" O how full of grief and dole is that late unfruitful repentance, when the sinful soul, beginning to be loosed from its dungeon of flesh, looks behind it, and then directs its gaze into the future. It sees behind it that little stadium of mortal life, already traversed ; it sees before it the range of endless aeons. That flown moment which it has lived it perceives to be an instant ; it contemplates the infinite length of time to come."[3]

From Damiani's stricken thoughts upon the wickedness of the age, we may turn to the more personal disclosures of one who wrote himself *Petrus peccator monachus*. There is one tell-tale letter of confession to his brother Damianus, whom he loved and revered :

" To my lord Damianus, my best loved brother,—Peter, sinner and monk, his servant and son.

" I would not have it hid from thee, my sweetest father in Christ, that my mind is cast down with sadness while it contemplates its own exit which is so near. For I count my length of years, I note that my head is streaked with grey, and observe that in whatever assemblage I find myself nearly all are younger

---

[1] *Opusc.* xvii., *De coelibatu* ; *Opusc.* xviii., *Contra intemperantes clericos* ; *Opusc.* xxii., *Contra clericos aulicos*, etc.

[2] Lib. iv. Ep. 5 (Migne, *Pat. Lat.* 144, col. 300).

[3] Lib. v. Ep. 3 (Migne 144, col. 343).

than myself.   When I consider this, I ponder upon death alone,
I meditate upon my tomb ; I do not withdraw the eyes of my
mind from my tomb.   Nor is my unhappy mind content to limit
its fear and its consideration to the death of the body ; for it
is at once haled to judgment, and meditates with terror upon
what it may be reproached with and what may be its defence.
Wretched me ! with what fountains of tears must I lament ! I who
have done every evil, and through my long life have fulfilled
scarce one commandment of the divine law.   For what evil have
not I, miserable man, committed ?   Where are the vices, where
are the crimes in which I am not implicated ; I confess my life
has fallen in a lake of misery ; my soul is taken in its iniquities.
Pride, lust, anger, impatience, malice, envy, gluttony, drunkenness, concupiscence, robbery, lying, perjury, idle talking, scurrility,
ignorance, negligence, and other pests have overthrown me, and
all the vices like ravening beasts have devoured my soul.   My
heart and my lips are defiled.   I am contaminate in sight, hearing,
taste, smell, and touch.   And in every way, in cogitation, in
speech or action, I am lost.   All these evils have I done ; and
alas ! alas ! I have brought forth no fruit meet for repentance.

   " One pernicious fault, among others, I bewail : scurrility
has been my besetting sin ; it has never really left me.   For
howsoever I have fought against this monster, and broken the
wicked teeth of this beast with the hammer of austerity, and at
times repelled it, I have never won the full victory.   When, in the
ways of spiritual gladness, I wish to show myself cheerful to the
brethren, I drop into words of vanity ; and when as it were dis-
creetly for the sake of brotherly love, I think to throw off my
severity, then indiscreetly my tongue unbridled utters foolishness.
If the Lord said : ' Blessed are they that mourn, for they shall
be comforted,' what judgment hangs over those who not only
are slack at weeping, but act like buffoons with laughter and vain
giggling.   Consolation is due to those who weep, not to those who
rejoice ; what consolation may be expected from that future
Judge by those who now give way to foolish mirth and vain
jocularity ?   If the Truth says : ' Woe unto ye who laugh now,
for ye shall mourn and weep,' what shall they say upon that
awful day of judgment who not only laugh themselves, but with
scurrilities drag laughter from their listeners ? "

   The penitent saint then shows from Scripture how that
our hearts ought to be vessels of tears, and concludes with
casting himself at the feet of his beloved " father " in entreaty
that he would interpose the shield of his holy prayers between
his petitioner and that monster, and exorcise its serpentine
poison, and also that he would ever pour forth prayers

to God, and beseech the divine mercy in behalf of all the other vices confessed in this letter.[1]

A strange confession this—or, indeed, is it strange? This cowled Peter Damiani who passes from community to community, seeing more keenly than others may, denouncing, execrating every vice existent or imagined, who wears haircloth, goes barefoot, lives on bread and water, scourges himself with daily flagellations, urging others to do likewise, —this Peter Damiani is yet unable quite to scourge out the human nature from him, and evidently cannot always refrain from that jocularity and *inepta laetitia* for which the Abbess Hildegard also saw sundry souls in hell.[2] Perhaps, with Peter, revulsions from the strain of austerity took the form of sudden laughter. His imagination was fine, his wit too quick for his soul's safety. His confession was no matter of mock humility, nor did he deem laughter vulgar or in bad taste. He feared to imperil his soul through it. Of course, in accusing himself of other, and as we should think more serious crimes—drunkenness, robbery, perjury—Peter was merely carrying to an extreme the monkish conventions of self-vilification.

If it appears from this letter that Damiani had been unable quite to scourge his wit out of him, another letter, to a young countess, will show more touchingly that he had been unable quite to fast out of him his human heart.

" To Guilla, most illustrious countess, Peter, monk and sinner, [sends] the instancy of prayer.

" Since of a thing out of which issues conflict it is better to have ignorance without cost, than with dear-bought forgetting wage hard war, we prudently accord to young women, whose aspect we fear, audience by letter. Certainly I, who now am an old man, may safely look upon the seared and wrinkled visage of a blear-eyed crone. Yet from sight of the more comely and adorned I guard my eyes like boys from fire. Alas my wretched heart which cannot hold Scriptural mysteries read through a hundred times, and will not lose the memory of a form seen but once ! There where the divine law has not remained, no oblivion blurs vanity's image. But of this another time. Here I have

[1] Lib. v. Ep. 2 (Migne 144, col. 340). Damiani's *Rhythmus poenitentis monachi* (Migne, *Pat. Lat.* 145, col. 971) expresses the passionate remorse of a sinful monk.
[2] *Post*, Chapter XX.

not to write of what is hurtful to me but of what may be salutary for thee."

Peter then continues with excellent advice for the young noblewoman, exhorting her to deeds of mercy and kindness, and warning her against the enjoyment of revenues wrung from the poor.[1] Indeed Damiani's writings contain much that still is wise. His advice to the great and noble of the world was admirable,[2] and though couched in austere phrase, it demanded what many men feel bound to fulfil in the twentieth century. His little work on Almsgiving [3] contains sentences which might be spoken to-day. He has been pointing out that no one can be exercising the ascetic virtues all the time : no one can be always praying and fasting, washing feet and subjecting the body to pain. Some people, moreover, shun such self-castigation. But one can always be benevolent ; and, though fearing to afflict the body, can stretch forth his hand in charity : " Those then who are rich are bidden to be dispensers rather than possessors. They ought not to regard what they have as their own : for they did not receive this transitory wealth in order to revel in luxury, or turn it to their private uses, but that they should administer it so long as they continue in their stewardship. Whoever gives to the poor does not distribute his own but restores another's." [4]

This sounds modern—it also sounds like Seneca.[5] Yet Damiani was no modern man, nor was he antique, but very fearful of the classics. Having been a rhetorician and grammarian, when he became a hermit-monk he made

---

[1] Lib. vii. Ep. 18 (Migne 144, col. 458).

[2] Much is contained in the eighth book of his letters. The third letter of this book is addressed to a nobleman who did not treat his mother as Peter would have had him. The whole family situation is given in two sentences : " But you may say : ' My mother exasperates me often, and with her rasping words worries me and my wife. We cannot endure such reproaches, nor tolerate the burden of her severity and interference.' But for this, your reward will be the richer, if you return gentleness for contumely, and mollify her with humility when you are sprinkled with the salt of her abuse " (Migne, *Pat. Lat.* 144, col. 467). Some sentences from this letter are given *post*, Chapter XXXII., as examples of Latin style.

The next letter is addressed to the same nobleman and his wife on the death of their son. It gently points out to them that his migration to the *coelestia regna*, where among the angels he has put on the garment of immortality, is cause for joy.

[3] *Opusc.* ix., *De eleemosyna* (Migne 145, col. 207 *sqq.*).

[4] *Opusc.* ix., *De eleemosyna*, cap. i.

[5] Seneca, *De vita beata*, 20.

Christ his grammar (*mea grammatica Christus est*).[1] Horror-
stricken at the world, and writhing under his own contamination, he cast body and soul into the ascetic life. That was
the harbour of escape from the carnal temptations which
threatened the soul's hope of pardon from the Judge at the
Last Day. Therefore Peter is fierce in execration of all
lapses from the hermit-life, so rapturously praised with its
contrition, its penitence, and tears. His ascetic rhap-
sodies, with which, as a poet might, he delighted or
relieved his soul, are eloquent illustrations of the monastic
ideal.[2]

Other men in Italy less intelligent than Damiani, but
equally picturesque, were held by like ascetic and emotional
obsession. Intellectual interest, however, in theology was
less prominent, because the Italian concern with religion was
either emotional or ecclesiastical, which is to say, political
The philosophic or dialectical treatment of the Faith was to
run its course north of the Alps ; and those men of Italian
birth—Anselm, Peter Lombard, Bonaventura, and Aquinas
—who contributed to Christian thought, early left their
native land, and accomplished their careers under intellectual
conditions which did not obtain in Italy. Nevertheless,
Anselm and Bonaventura at least did not lose their Italian
qualities ; and it is as representative of what might come
out of Italy in the eleventh century that the former may
detain us here.

The story of Anselm is told well and lovingly by his
companion Eadmer.[3] His life, although it was drawn within
the currents of affairs, remained intellectual and aloof, a
meditation upon God. It opens with a dream of climbing
the mountain to God's palace-seat. For Anselm's boyhood
was passed at Aosta, within the shadows of the Graian
Alps.[4] Surely the heaven rested upon them. Might he
not then go up to the hall where God, above in the heaven,
as the boy's mother taught, ruled and held all ?

---

[1] Lib. viii. Ep. 8 (Migne, *Pat. Lat.* 144, col. 476). Cf. *ante*, p. 261.

[2] Extracts will be given *post*, Chapter XVII., together with Damiani's remarkable Life of Romuald.

[3] Migne 158, col. 50 *sqq.*

[4] Anselm was born in 1033 and died in 1109. His works are in Migne 158, 159.
See also Domet de Vorges, *S. Anselme* (Les grands Philosophes, 1901).

' So one night it seemed he must ascend to the summit of the mountains, and go to the hall of the great King. In the plain at the first slopes, he saw women, the servants of the King, reaping grain carelessly and idly. He would accuse them to their Lord. He went up across the summit and came to the King's hall. He found Him there alone with His seneschal, for it was autumn and He had sent His servants to gather the harvest. The Lord called the boy as he entered ; and he went and sat at His feet. The Lord asked kindly (*jucunda affabilitate*) whence he came and what he wished. He replied just as he knew the thing to be (*juxta quod rem esse sciebat*). Then, at the Lord's command, the Seneschal brought him bread of the whitest, and he was there refreshed in His presence. In the morning he verily believed that he had been in Heaven and had been refreshed with the bread of the Lord."

A pious mother had been the boy's first teacher. Others taught him Letters, till he became proficient, and beloved by those who knew him. He wished to be made a monk, but a neighbouring abbot refused his request, fearing the displeasure of Anselm's father, of whom the biographer has nothing good to say. The youth fell sick, but with returning health the joy of living drew his mind from study and his pious purpose. Love for his mother held him from over-indulgence in pastimes. She died, and with this sheet-anchor lost, Anselm's ship was near to drifting out on the world's slippery flood. Here the impossible temper of the father wrought as God's providence, and Anselm, unable to stay with him, left his home, and set out across Mount Senis attended by one clericus. For three years he moved through Burgundy and Francia, till Lanfranc's repute drew him to Bec. Day and night he studied beneath that master, and also taught. The desire to be a monk returned ; and he began to direct his purpose toward pleasing God and spurning the world.

But where ? At either Cluny or Bec he feared to lose the fruit of his studies ; for at Cluny there was the strictness of the rule,[1] and at Bec Lanfranc's eminent learning would " make mine of little value." Anselm says that he was not yet subdued, nor had the contempt of the world become strong in him   Then the thought came : " Is this to be a monk to wish to be set before others and magnified above

[1] " Districtio ordinis," *Vita*, i. 6. This indicates that liberal studies were not favoured in Cluny at this time, cir. 1060.

them ? Nay,—become a monk where, for the sake of God,
you will be put after all and be held viler than all. And
where can this be ? Surely at Bec. I shall be of no weight
while he is here, whose wisdom and repute are enough for all.
Here then is my rest, here God alone will be my purpose,
here the single love of Him will be my thought, and
here the constant remembrance of Him will be a happy
consolation."

Scripture bade him : Do all things with counsel. Whom
but Lanfranc should he consult ? So he laid three plans
before him—to become a monk, a hermit, or (his father
being dead) for the sake of God administer his patrimony
for the poor. Lanfranc persuaded Anselm to refer the
decision to the venerable Archbishop of Rouen. Together
they went to him, and such, says the biographer, was
Anselm's reverence for Lanfranc, that on the way, passing
through the wood near Bec, had Lanfranc bade him stay in
that wood, he would not have left it all his days.

The archbishop decided for the monastic life. So
Anselm took the vows of a monk at Bec, being twenty-
seven years of age. Lanfranc was then Prior, but soon left
to become Abbot of St. Stephen's at Caen.[1] Made Prior in
his place, Anselm devoted himself in gentleness and wisdom
to the care of the monks and to meditation upon God and
the divine truths. He was especially considerate of the
younger monks, whose waywardness he guided and whose
love he won. The envy of cavillers was stilled. Yet the
business of office harassed one whose thoughts dwelled more
gladly in the blue heaven with God. Again he sought the
counsel of the archbishop ; for Herluin, the first Abbot and
founder of Bec, still lived on, old and unlettered, and
apparently no great fount of wisdom. The archbishop
commanded him *per sanctam obedientiam* not to renounce his
office, nor refuse if called to a higher one. So, sad but
resolute, he returned to the convent, and resumed his
burdens in such wise as to be held by all as a loved father.
It was at this period that he wrote several treatises upon the
high doctrinal themes which filled his thoughts. Gradually

---

[1] In a convent where there is an abbot, the prior is the officer directly under
him.

his mind settled to the search after some single proof of that which is believed concerning God—that He exists, and is eternal, unchanging, omnipotent, just, and pitying, and is truth and goodness. This thing caused him great difficulty. Not only it kept him from food and drink and sleep, but what weighed upon him more, it interfered with his devotion to God's service. Reflecting thus, and unable to reach a valid conclusion, he decided that such speculation was a temptation of the devil, and tried to drive it from his thoughts. But the more he struggled, the more it beset him. And one night, at the time of the nocturnal vigils, the grace of God shed light in his heart, and the argument was clear to his mind, and filled his inmost being with an immense jubilation. All the more now was he confirmed in the love of God and the contempt of the world, of which one night he had a vision as of a torrent filled with obscene filth, and carrying in its flood the countless host of people of the world, while apart and aloof from its slime rose the sweet cloister, with its walls of silver, surrounded by silvery herbage, all delectable beyond conception.

In the year 1078 old Herluin died. Anselm long had guided the convent, and with one voice the brethren chose him Abbot. He reasoned and argued, but could not dissuade them, and in his anxiety he knew not what to do. Some days passed. He had recourse to entreaties ; with tears he flung himself prostrate before them all, praying and protesting in the name of God, and beseeching them, if they had any bowels of compassion, to permit him to remain free from this great burden. But they only cast themselves upon the earth, and prayed that he would rather commiserate them, and not disregard the convent's good. At length he yielded, for the command of the archbishop came to his mind. Such a scene occurs often in monastic history. None the less is it moving when the participants are in earnest, as Anselm was, and his monks.

So Anselm's life opened ; so it sought counsel, gathered strength, and centred to its purpose, pursuing as its goal the thought of God. Anselm had love and gentleness for his fellows ; he drew their love and reverence. Yet, aloof, he lived within his spirit. Did he open its hidden places even

to Lanfranc ?   Although one who in his humility always
desired counsel, perhaps neither Lanfranc nor Eadmer, the
friend whom the Pope gave him for an adviser, knew the
meditations of his heart.   We at all events should discern
little of them by following the outer story of his life.   It
might even be fruitless to sail with him across the Channel
to visit Lanfranc, now Primate of England.   The biographer
has little that is important to tell of the converse between
the two, although quite rightly impressed at the meeting
between him who was pre-eminent in *auctoritas* and *scientia*
and him who excelled in *sanctitas* and *sapientia Dei*.[1]   Nor
would it enlighten us to follow Anselm's archiepiscopal
career, save so far as to realize that he who lives in the
thought of God will fear no brutal earthly majesty, such as
that of William Rufus, to admonish whom Anselm once more
crossed the Channel after Lanfranc's death.   Whatever this
despoiler of bishoprics then thought, he fell sick afterwards,
and, being terrified, named Anselm archbishop, this being in
the year 1093.   One may imagine the unison between them !
and how little the Red King's ways would turn the enskied
steadfastness of Anselm's soul.   But the king had the power,
and could keep the archbishop in trouble and in peril.
Anselm asked and asked again for leave to go to Rome, and
the king refused.   After more than one stormy scene—the
storm being always on the Red King's part—Anselm made
it plain that he would obey God rather than man in the
matter.   At the very last he went in to the king and his
Court, and seating himself quietly at the king's right he
said : " I, my lord, shall go, as I have determined.   But
first, if you do not decline it, I will give you my blessing."
So the king acquiesced.

The archbishop went first to Canterbury, to comfort
and strengthen his monks, and spoke to them assembled
together :

" Dearly beloved brothers and sons, I am, as you know, about
to leave this kingdom.   The contention with our lord the king
as to Christian discipline, has reached this pass that I must either

---

[1] In the *Vita*, i. 30, Anselm and Lanfranc discuss the title of a certain beatified
Aelfegus to veneration as a saint.

do what is contrary to God and my own honour, or leave the realm.
Gladly I go, hoping through the mercy of God that my journey
may advance the Church's liberty hereafter.   I am moved to
pity you, upon whom greater tribulations will come in my absence.
Even with me here you have not been unoppressed, yet I think
I have given you more peace than you have had since the death
of our Father Lanfranc.   I think those who molest you will rage
the more with me away.   You, however, are not undisciplined
in the school of the Lord.   Nevertheless I will say something,
because, since you have come together within the close of this
monastery to fight for God, you should always have before your
eyes how you should fight.

   " All retainers do not fight in the same way either for an earthly
prince, or for God whose are all things that are.   The angels
established in eternal beatitude wait upon Him.   He has also
men who serve Him for earthly benefits, like hired knights.   He
has also some who, cleaving to His will, contend to reach the
kingdom of heaven, which they have forfeited through Adam's
fault.   Observe the knights who are in God's pay.   Many you
see leading a secular life and cleaving to the household of God
for the good things which they gain in His service.   But when,
by God's judgment, trial comes to them, and disaster, they fly
from His love and accuse Him of injustice.   We monks—would
that we were such as not to be like them !   For those who cannot
stand to their professed purpose unless they have all things comfortable, and do not wish to suffer destitution for God, how shall
they not be held like to these ?   And shall such be heirs of the
kingdom of heaven ?   Faithfully I say, No, never, unless they
repent.

   " He who truly contends toward recovering the kingdom of
life, strives to cleave to God through all ; no adversity draws him
from God's service, no pleasure lures him from the love of Him.
Per dura et aspera he treads the way of His commands, and from
hope of the reward to come, his heart is aflame with the ardour
of love, and sings with the Psalmist, Great is the glory of the Lord.
Which glory he tastes in this pilgrimage, and tasting, he desires,
and desiring, salutes as from afar.   Supported by the hope of
attaining, he is consoled amid the perils of the world and gladly
sings, Great is the glory of the Lord.   Know that this one will
in no way be defrauded of that glory of the Lord, since all that
is in him serves the Lord, and is directed to winning this reward.
But I see that there is no need to say to you another word.   My
·brothers, since we are separated now in grief, I beseech you so
to strive that hereafter we may be united joyfully before God.
Be ye those who truly wish to be made heirs of God."

The clarity and gentle love of this high argument is Anselm.   Now the story follows of Anselm and Eadmer and another monk travelling on, sometimes unknown, sometimes acclaimed, through France to Italy and Rome.   Anselm's face inspired reverence in those who did not know him, and the peace of his countenance attracted even Saracens.   Had he been born and bred in England, he might have managed better with the Red King.   He never got an English point of view, but remained a Churchman with Italian-Hilde-brandine convictions.   Of course, two policies were clashing then in England, where it happened that there was on one side an able and rapacious tyrant, while the other was represented by a man with the countenance and temperament of an angel.   But we may leave Anselm now in Italy, where he is beyond the Red King's molestation, and turn to his writings.

Their choice and treatment of subject was partly guided by the needs of his pupils and friends at Bec and elsewhere in Normandy or Francia or England.   For he wrote much at their solicitation ; and the theological problems of which solutions were requested, suggest the intellectual temper of those regions, rather than of Italy.   In a way Anselm's works, treating of separate and selected Christian questions, are a proper continuation of those composed by northern theologians in the ninth century on Predestination and the Eucharist.[1]   Only Anselm's were not evoked by the exigency of actual controversy as much as by the insistency of the eleventh-century mind, and the need it felt of some ad-justment regarding certain problems.   Anselm's theological and philosophic consciousness is clear and confident.   His faculties are formative and creative, quite different from the compiling instincts of Alcuin or Rabanus.   The matter of his argument has become his own ; it has been remade in his thinking, and is presented as from himself--and God. He no longer conceives himself as one searching through the " pantries " of the Fathers or culling the choice flowers of their " meadows."   He will set forth the matter as God has deigned to disclose it to him.   In the *Cur Deus homo* he begins by saying that he has been urged by many, verbally

[1] *Ante*, Chapter X.

and by letter, to consider the reasons why God became man and suffered, and then, assenting, says : " Although, from the holy Fathers on, what should suffice has been said, yet concerning this question I will endeavour to set forth for my inquirers what God shall deign to disclose to me." [1]

Certain works of Anselm, the *Monologion*, for instance (as demanded by its topic), present the dry and the formal method of reasoning which was to make its chief home in France ; others, like the *Proslogion*, seem to be Italian in a certain beautiful emotionalism. The feeling is very lofty, even lifted out of the human, very skyey, even. The *Proslogion*, the *Meditationes*, do not throb with the red blood of Augustine's *Confessions*, the writing which influenced them most. The quality of their feeling suggests rather Dante's *Paradiso* ; and sometimes with Anselm a sense of formal beauty and perfection seems to disclose the mind of Italy. Moreover, Anselm's Latin style appears Italian. It is elastic, even apparently idiomatic, and varies with the temper and character of his different works. Throughout, it shows in Latin the fluency and simple word-order natural to an author whose *vulgaris eloquentia* was even closer to Latin in the time of Anselm than when Dante wrote.

So Anselm's writings were intimately part of their author, and very part of his life-long meditation upon God. Led by the solicitations of others, as well as impelled by the needs of his own faculties and nature, he takes up one Christian problem after another, and sets forth his understanding of it with his conclusion. He is devout, an absolute believer ; and he is wonderfully metaphysical. He is a beautiful, a sublimated, and idealizing reasoner, convinced that a divine reality must exist in correspondence with his thought, which projects itself aloft to evoke from the blue an answering reality. The inspiration, the radiating point of Anselm's intellectual interest, is clearly given—to understand that which he first believes. It is a spontaneous intellectual interest, not altogether springing from a desire to know how to be saved. It does not seek to understand in order to believe ; but seeks the happiness of knowing

[1] *Cur Deus homo*, i. 1 (Migne, *Pat. Lat.* 158, col. 361).

and understanding that which it believes and loves.   Listen
to some sentences from the opening of the *Proslogion* :

" Come now, mannikin, flee thy occupations for a little, and
hide from the confusion of thy cares.   Be vacant a little while
for God, and for a little rest in Him. . . . Now, O Lord my God,
teach my heart where and how to seek thee, where and how to
find thee.   Lord, Lord, illuminate us ; show us thyself.   Pity
us labouring toward thee, impotent without thee. . . . Teach
me to seek thee, and show thyself to my search ; for I cannot
seek thee unless thou dost teach, nor find thee unless thou dost
show thyself. . . . I make no attempt, Lord, to penetrate thy
depths, for my intellect has no such reach ; but I desire to understand some measure of thy truth, which my heart believes and
loves.   I do not seek to know in order that I may believe ; but
I believe, that I may know.   For I believe this also, that unless
I shall have believed, I shall not understand." [1]

So Anselm is first a believer, then a theologian ; and
his reason devotes itself to the elucidation of his faith.
Faith prescribes his intellectual interests, and sets their
bounds.   His thought does not occupy itself with matters
beyond.   But it takes a pure intellectual delight in reasoning
upon the God which his faith presents and his heart cleaves
to.   The motive is the intellectual and loving delight
which his mind takes in this pursuit.   His faith was
sure and undisturbed, and ample for his salvation.   His
intellect, affected by no motive beyond its own strength
and joy, delights in reasoning upon the matter of his
faith.[2]

We may still linger for a moment to observe how closely
part of Anselm's nature was his proof of the existence of

[1] In the *Cur Deus homo*, i. 2, Anselm has his approved disciple state the same
point of view : " As the right order prescribes that we should believe the pro-
fundities of the Christian Faith, before presuming to discuss them rationally, so
it seems to me neglect if after we are confirmed in faith we do not study to understand what we believe.   Wherefore, since by the prevenient grace of God, I deem
myself to hold the faith of our redemption, so that even if I could by no reason
comprehend what I believe, there is nothing that could pluck me from it, I ask
from thee, as many ask, that thou wouldst set forth to me, as thou knowest it,
by what necessity and reason, God, being omnipotent, should have assumed the
humility and weakness of human nature for its restoration."

[2] There is indeed an early treatise, *De grammatico* (Migne 158, col. 561-581),
in which Anselm seems to abandon himself to dialectic concerned with an academic
topic.   The question is whether *grammaticus*, a grammarian, is to be subsumed
under the category of substance or quality ; dialectically is a grammarian a
man or an incident ?

God.[1] It sprang directly from his saintly soul and the compelling idealism of his reason. In the *Monologion* Anselm ranged his many arguments concerning the nature and attributes of the *summum bonum* which is God. Its chain of inductions failed to satisfy him and his pupils. So he set his mind to seek a sole and unconditioned proof (as Eadmer states in the *Vita*) of God's existence and the attributes which faith ascribes to Him. Anselm says the same in the Preface to the *Proslogion* :

" Considering that the prior work was woven out of a concatenation of many arguments, I set to seek within myself (*mecum*) whether I might not discover one argument which needed nothing else than itself alone for its proof ; and which by itself might suffice to show that God truly exists, and that He is the *summum bonum* needing nothing else, but needed by all things in order that they may exist and have well-being (*ut sint et bene sint*) ; and whatever we believe concerning the divine substance."

The famous proof which at length flashed upon him is substantially this : By very definition the word *God* means the greatest conceivable being. This conception exists even in the atheist's mind, for he knows what is meant by the words, the absolutely greatest. But the greatest cannot be in the intellect alone, for then conceivably there would be a greater which would exist in reality as well. And since, by definition, God is the absolutely greatest, He must exist in reality as well as in the mind.[2] Carrying out the scholia to this argument, Anselm then proves that God possesses the various attributes ascribed to Him by the Christian Faith.

That from a definition one may not infer the existence of the thing defined, was pointed out by a certain monk Gaunilo almost as soon as the *Proslogion* appeared. Anselm answered him that the argument applied only to the greatest conceivable being. Since that time Anselm's proof has been upheld and disproved many times. It was at all events a great dialectic leap ; but likely one may not with such a bound cross the chasm from definition to existence—

---

[1] Cf. Kaulich, *Ges. der scholastischen Philosophie*, i. 293-332 ; Hauréau, *Histoire de la philosophie scholastique*, i. 242-288 ; Stöckl, *Philosophie des Mittelalters*, i. 151-208 ; De Wulf, *History of Medieval Philosophy*, 3rd ed. (Longmans, 1909), p. 162 *sqq.*, and authorities.

[2] The *locus classicus* is *Proslogion*, cap. 2.

at least one will be less bold to try when he realizes that this chasm is there. Temperamentally, at least, this proof was the summit of Anselm's idealism : he could not but conceive things to exist in correspondence to the demands of his conceptions. He never made another so palpable leap from conception to conviction as in this proof of God's existence ; yet his theology proceeded through like processes of thought. For example, he is sure of God's omnipotence, and also sure that God can do nothing which would detract from the perfection of His nature : God cannot lie : " For it does not follow, if God wills to lie that it is just to lie ; but rather that He is not God. For only that will can will to lie in which truth is corrupted, or rather which is corrupted by forsaking truth. Therefore when one says ' if God wills to lie,' he says in substance, ' if God is of such a nature as to will to lie.' " [1]

Anselm's other famous work was the *Cur Deus homo,* upon the problem why God became man to redeem mankind. It was connected with his view of sin, and the fall of the angels, as set forth chiefly in his dialogue *De casu Diaboli.* One may note certain cardinal points in his exposition : Man could be redeemed only by God ; for he would have been the bond-servant of whoever redeemed him, and to have been the servant of any one except God would not have restored him to the dignity which would have been his had he not sinned.[2] Or again : The devil had no rights over man, which he lost by unjustly slaying God. For man was not the devil's, nor does the devil belong to himself but to God.[3] Evidently Anselm frees himself from the conception of any ranson paid to the devil, or any trickery put on him—thoughts which had lowered current views of the Atonement. Anselm's arguments (which are too large, and too interwoven with his views upon connected subjects, to be done justice to by any casual statement) are free from degrading foolishness. His reasonings were deeply felt, as one may see in his *Meditationes,* where thought and feeling mutually support and enhance each other. So he recalls Augustine, the great model and predecessor whom he followed and revered. And still the feeling in Anselm's

---

[1] *Cur Deus homo,* i. 12.   [2] *Ibid.* i. 5.   [3] *Ibid.* i. 7.

Meditationes, as in the *Proslogion*, is somewhat sublimated and lifted above human heart-throbs. Perhaps it may seem rhetorical, and intentionally stimulated in order to edify. Even in the *Meditationes* upon the humanity and passion of Jesus, Anselm is not very close to the quivering tenderness of St. Bernard, and very far from the impulsive and passionate love of Francis of Assisi. One thinks that his feelings rarely distorted his countenance or wet it with tears.[1]

---

[1] Examples of Anselm's prose are given *post*, Chapter XXXII. On Anselm's position in scholasticism and his scholastic method, see Grabmann, *Ges. der scholastischen Methode*, Bd. I. p. 265 *sqq*. (1909–).

CHAPTER XII

MENTAL ASPECTS OF THE ELEVENTH CENTURY : FRANCE

I. GERBERT.
II. ODILO OF CLUNY.
III. FULBERT AND THE SCHOOL OF CHARTRES ; TRIVIUM
    AND QUADRIVIUM.
IV. BERENGAR OF TOURS, ROSCELLIN, AND THE COMING
    TIME.

I

IT appeared in the last chapter that Anselm's choice of topic was not uninfluenced by his northern domicile at Bec in Normandy, from which, one may add, it was no far cry to the monastery (Marmoutier) of Anselm's sharp critic Gaunilo. These places lay within the confines of central and northern France, the home of the most originative mediaeval development. For this region, the renewed studies of the Carolingian period were the proper antecedents of the efforts of the eleventh century. The topics of study still remained substantially the same ; yet the later time represents a further stage in the appropriation of the antique and patristic material, and its productions show the genius of the authors more clearly than Carolingian writings, which were taken piecemeal from patristic sources or made of borrowed antique phrase.

The difference is seen in the personality and writings of Gerbert of Aurillac,[1] the man who with such intellectual

---

[1] On Gerbert see *Lettres de Gerbert publiées avec une introduction, etc.*, par Julien Havet (Paris : Picard, 1889 ; I have cited them according to this edition) ; *Œuvres de Gerbert*, ed. by Olleris (Clermont and Paris, 1867) ; also in Migne, *Pat. Lat.* 139 ; Richerus, *Historiarum libri IV.* (especially lib. iii. cap. 55 *sqq.*) ; *Mon. Germ. script.* iii. 561 *sqq.* ; Migne, *Pat. Lat.* 138, col. 17 *sqq.* Also Picavet, *Gerbert, un pape philosophe* (Paris : Leroux, 1897) ; Cantor, *Ges. der Mathematik,* i. 728-751 (Leipzig, 1880) ; Prantl, *Ges. der Logik,* ii. 53-57 (Leipzig, 1861).

catholicity opens the story of this period. One will be struck with the apparently arid crudity of his intellectual processes. Crude they were, and of necessity ; arid they were not, being an unavoidable stage in the progress of mediaeval thinking. Yet it is a touch of fate's irony that such an interesting personality should have been afflicted with them. For Gerbert was the redeeming intellect of the last part of the tenth century. The cravings of his mind compassed the intellectual predilections of his contemporaries. Secular and by no means priestly they appear in him ; and it is clear that religious motives did not dominate this extraordinary individual who was reared among monks, became Abbot of Bobbio, Archbishop of Rheims, Archbishop of Ravenna, and pope at last.

He appears to have been born shortly before the year 950. From the ignorance in which we are left as to his parents and the exact place of his birth in Aquitaine, it may be inferred that his origin was humble. While still a boy he was received into the Benedictine monastery of St. Geraldus at Aurillac in Auvergne. There he studied grammar (in the extended mediaeval sense), under a monk named Raymund, and grew to love the classics. A loyal affectionateness was a life-long trait of Gerbert, and more than one letter in after life bears witness to the love which he never ceased to feel for the monks of Aurillac among whom his youthful years were passed, and especially for this brother Raymund from whom he received his first instruction.

Raymund afterwards became abbot of the convent. But it was his predecessor, Gerald, who had received the boy Gerbert, and was still to do something of moment in directing his career. A certain duke of the Spanish March came on a pilgrimage to Aurillac ; and Gerald besought him to take Gerbert back with him to Spain for such further instruction as the convent did not afford. The duke departed, taking Gerbert, and placed him under the tuition of the Bishop of Vich, a town near Barcelona. Here he studied mathematics. The tradition that he travelled through Spain and learned from the Arabs lacks probability. But in the course of time the duke and bishop set

forth to pray for sundry material objects at the fountain-
head of Catholicism, and took their *protégé* with them to
Rome.

In Rome, Gerbert's destiny advanced apace. His
patrons, doubtless proud of their young scholar, introduced
him to the Pope, John XIII., who also was impressed by
Gerbert's personality and learning. John told his own
protector, the great Otto, and informed him of Gerbert's
ability to teach mathematics ; and the two kept Gerbert in
Rome, when the Spanish duke and bishop returned to their
country. Gerbert began to teach, and either at this time or
later had among his pupils the young Augustus, Otto II.
But he was more anxious to study logic than to teach
mathematics, even under imperial favour. He persuaded
the old emperor to let him go to Rheims with a certain
archdeacon from that place, who was skilled in the science
which he lacked. The emperor dismissed him, with a
liberal hand. In his new home Gerbert rapidly mastered
logic, and impressed all with his genius. He won the love
of the archbishop, Adalberon, who soon set the now triply
accomplished scholar at the head of the episcopal school.
Gerbert's education was complete, in letters, in mathematics
including music, and in logic. Thenceforth for ten years
(972-982), the happiest of his life, he studied and also
taught the whole range of academic knowledge.

Fortune, not altogether kind, bestowed on Gerbert the
favour of three emperors. The graciousness of the first
Otto had enabled him to proceed to Rheims. The second
Otto listened to his teaching, admired the teacher, and early
in the year 983 made him Abbot and Count of Bobbio.
Long afterwards the third Otto made him Archbishop of
Ravenna, and then pope.

Bobbio, the chief foundation of Columbanus, situated not
far from Genoa, was powerful and rich ; but its vast
possessions, scattered throughout Italy, had been squandered
by worthless abbots or seized by lawless nobles. The new
count-abbot, eager to fulfil the ecclesiastical and feudal
functions of his position, strove to reclaim the monastery's
property and bring back its monks to decency and learning.
In vain. Now, as more than once in Gerbert's later life,

brute circumstances proved too strong.   Otto died.   Gerbert was unsupported.   He struggled and wrote many letters which serve to set forth the situation for us, though they did not win the battle for their writer :

"According to the largeness of my mind, my lord (Otto II.) has enriched me with most ample honours.   For what part of Italy does not hold the possessions of the blessed Columbanus ? So should this be, from the generosity and benevolence of our Caesar.   Fortune, indeed, ordains it otherwise.   Forsooth according to the largeness of my mind she has loaded me with most ample store of enemies.   For what part of Italy has not my enemies ?   My strength is unequal to the strength of Italy ! There is peace on this condition : if I, despoiled, submit, they cease to strike ; intractable in my vested rights, they attack with the sword.   When they do not strike with the sword, they thrust with javelins of words." [1]

Within a year Gerbert gave up the struggle at Bobbio, and returned to Rheims to resume his duties as head of the school, and secretary and intimate adviser of Adalberon.   Politically the time was one of uncertainty and turmoil.   The Carolingian house was crumbling, and the house of Capet was scheming and struggling on to a royalty scarcely more considerable.   In Germany intrigue and revolt threatened the rights of the child Otto III.   Archbishop Adalberon, guided by Gerbert, was a powerful factor in the dynastic change in France ; and the two were zealous for Otto.   Throughout these troubles Gerbert constantly appears, directing projected measures and divining courses of events, yet somehow, in spite of his unmatched intelligence, failing to control them.

Time passed, and Adalberon died at the beginning of the year 989.   His successor, Arnulf, a scion of the falling Carolingian house, was subsequently unseated for treason to the new-sprung house of Capet.   In 991 Gerbert himself was made archbishop.   But although seeming to reach his longed-for goal, troubles redoubled on his head.   There was rage at the choice of one so lowly born for the princely dignity.   The storm gathered around the new archbishop, and the See of Rome was moved to interfere, which it did gladly, since at Rome Gerbert was hated for the reproaches

[1] *Ep.* 12.

cast upon its ignorance and corruption by bishops at the
council which elected him and deposed his predecessor.   In
that deposition and election Rome had not acquiesced ; and
we read the words of the papal legate :

" The acts of your synod against Arnulf, or rather against the
Roman Church, astound me with their insults and blasphemies.
Truly is the word of the Gospel fulfilled in you, ' There shall be
many anti-Christs.' . . . Your anti-Christs say that Rome is as a
temple of idols, an image of stone.   Because the vicars of Peter
and their disciples will not have as master Plato, Virgil, Terence or
the rest of the herd of Philosophers, ye say they are not worthy to
be door-keepers—because they have no part in such song." [1]

The battle went against Gerbert.   Interdicted from
his archiepiscopal functions, he left France for the Court
of Otto III., where his intellect at once dominated the
aspirations of the young monarch.   Otto and Gerbert went
together to Italy, and the emperor made his friend
Archbishop of Ravenna.   The next year, 999, Gregory V.
died, and the archbishop became Pope Sylvester II.   For
three short years the glorious young imperial dreamer and
his peerless counsellor planned and wrought for a great
united Empire and Papacy on earth.   Then death took first
the emperor and soon afterwards the pope-philosopher.

Gerbert was the first mind of his time, its greatest
teacher, its most eager learner, and most universal scholar.
His pregnant letters reflect a finished man who has mastered
his acquired knowledge and transformed it into power.
They also evince the authorship of one who had uniquely
profited from the power and spirit of the great minds of the
pagan past, had imbibed their sense of form and pertinency,
and with them had become self-contained and self-controlled,
master of himself and of all that had entered in and made
him what he was.   Notice how the personality of the writer,
with his capacities, tastes, and temperament, is unfolded
before us in a letter to a close friend, abbot of a monastery
at Tours :

" Since you hold my memory in honour, and in virtue of
relationship declare great friendship, I deem that I shall be happy
for your opinion, if only I am one who in the judgment of so great

----
[1] *Mon. Germ. scriptores.* iii. 686.

a man is found worthy to be loved. But since I am not one who, with Panetius, would sometimes separate the good from the useful, but rather with Tully would mingle it with everything useful, I wish these best and holiest friendships never to be void of reciprocal utility. And as morality and the art of speech are not to be severed from philosophy, I have always joined the study of speaking well with the study of living well. For although by itself living well may be nobler than speaking well, and may suffice without its fellow for one absolved from the direction of affairs ; yet for us, busied with the State, both are needed. For it is of the greatest utility to speak appositely when persuading, and with mild discourse check the fury of angry men. In preparing for such business, I am eagerly collecting a library ; and as formerly at Rome and elsewhere in Italy, so likewise in Germany and Belgium, I have obtained copyists and manuscripts with a mass of money, and the help of friends in those parts. Permit me likewise to beg of you also to promote this end. We will append at the end of this letter a list of those writers we wish copied. We have sent for your disposal parchment for the scribes and money to defray the cost, not unmindful of your goodness. Finally, lest by saying more we should abuse epistolary *convenances*, the cause of so much trouble is contempt of faithless fortune ; a contempt which not nature alone has given to us—as to many men—but careful study. Consequently when at leisure and when busied in affairs, we teach what we know, and learn where we are ignorant." [1]

Gerbert's letters are concise, even elliptical to the verge of obscurity. He discloses himself in a few words to his old friend Raymund at the monastery of Aurillac : " With what love we are bound to you, the Latins know and also the barbarians,[2] who share the fruit of our studies. Their vows demand your presence. Amid public cares philosophy is the sole solace ; and from her study we have often been the gainer, when in this stormy time we have thus broken the attack of fortune raging grievously against others or ourselves. . . ." [3]

Save for the language, one might fancy Cicero speaking to some friend, and not the future pope of the year 1000 to a monk. The sentiment is quite antique. And Gerbert not only uses antique phrase but is touched, like many a

[1] *Ep.* 44.
[2] Presumably Gerbert's German-speaking scholars are meant.
[3] *Ep.* 45, *Raimundo monacho.*

mediaeval man, with the antique spirit.   In another letter
he writes of friendship, and queries whether the divinity has
given anything better to mortals.   He refers to his prospects,
and remarks :   " sed involvit mundum caeca fortuna," and
he is not certain whither it will cast him.[1]

Doubtless such antique sentiments were a matter of
mood with Gerbert ; he can readily express others of a
Christian colour, and turn again to still other topics very
readily, as in the following letter—a curious one.   It is to a
monk :

" Think not, sweetest brother, that it is through my fault I lack
my brethren's society.   After leaving thee, I had to undertake
many journeys in the business of my father Columbanus.[2]   The
ambitions of the powers, the hard and wretched times, turn right
to wrong.   No one keeps faith.   Yet since I know that all things
hang on the decree of God, who changes both hearts and the
kingdoms of the sons of men, I patiently await the end of things.
I admonish and exhort thee, brother, to do the same.   In the
meanwhile one thing I beg, which may be accomplished without
danger or loss to thee, and will make me thy friend forever.   Thou
knowest with what zeal I gather books everywhere, and thou
knowest how many scribes there are in Italy, in town and country.
Come then, quietly procure me copies of Manlius's (Boëthius)
De astrologia, Victorinus's *Rhetoric*, Demosthenes's *Optalmicus*.[3]
I promise thee, brother, and will keep my word, to preserve a
sacred silence as to thy praiseworthy compliance, and will remit
twofold whatever thou dost demand.   Let this much be known
to the man, and the pay too, and cheer us more frequently with
a letter ; and have no fear that knowledge will come to any one
of any matter thou mayest confide to our good faith."[4]

When he wrote this letter, about the year 988, Gerbert
was dangerously deep in politics, and great was the power of
this low-born titular Abbot of Bobbio, head of the school at
Rheims and secretary to the archbishop.   The tortuous
statecraft and startling many-sidedness of this " scholar in
politics " must have disturbed his contemporaries, and may
have roused the suspicions from which grew the stories, told
by future men, that this scholar, statesman, and philosopher-

[1] *Ep. 46, ad Geraldum Abbatem.*
[2] *I.e.* on the affairs of the monastery of Bobbio.
[3] A Greek doctor of Augustus's time, who wrote on the diseases of the eye.
[4] *Ep.* 130.

pope was a magician who had learned from forbidden sources much that should be veiled. Withal, however, one may deem that the most veritable inner bit of Gerbert was his love of knowledge and of antique literature, and that the letters disclosing this are the subtlest revelation of the man who was ever transmuting his well-guarded knowledge into himself and his most personal moods.

" For there is nothing more noble for us in human affairs than a knowledge of the most distinguished men ; and may it be displayed in volumes upon volumes multiplied. Go on then, as you have begun, and bring the streams of Cicero to one who thirsts. Let M. Tullius thrust himself into the midst of the anxieties which have enveloped us since the betrayal of our city, so that in the happy eyes of men we are held unhappy through our sentence. What things are of the world we have sought, we have found, we have accomplished, and, as I will say, we have become chief among the wicked. Lend aid, father, in order that divinity, expelled by the multitude of sinners, bent by thy prayers, may return, may visit us, may dwell with us—and if possible, may we who mourn the absence of the blessed father Adalberon, be rejoiced by thy presence." [1]

So Gerbert wrote from Rheims, himself a chief intriguer in a city full of treason.

Gerbert was a power making for letters. The best scholars sat at his feet ; he was an inspiration at the Courts of the second and third Ottos, who loved learning and died so young ; and the great school of Chartres, under the headship of his pupil Fulbert, was the direct heir to his instruction. At Rheims, where he taught so many years, he left to others the elementary instruction in Latin. A pupil, Richer, who wrote his history, speaks of courses in rhetoric and literature, to which he introduced his pupils after instructing them in logic :

" When he wished to lead them on from such studies to rhetoric, he put in practice his opinion that one cannot attain the art of oratory without a previous knowledge of the modes of diction which are to be learned from the poets. So he brought forward those with whom he thought his pupils should be conversant. He read and explained the poets Virgil, Statius, and Terence, the satirists Juvenal and Persius and Horace, also Lucan

---

[1] *Ep.* 167 (in Migne, *Ep.* 174).

the historiographer. Familiarized with these, and practised in their locutions, he taught his pupils rhetoric. After they were instructed in this art, he brought up a sophist, to practise them in disputation, so that practised in this art as well, they might seem to argue artlessly, which he deemed the height of oratory." [1]

So Gerbert used the classic poets in teaching rhetoric, and doubtless the great prose writers too, with whom he was familiar. Following Cicero's precept that the orator should be a proficient reasoner, he prepared his young rhetoricians by a course in logic, and completed their discipline with exercises in disputation.

Richer also speaks of Gerbert's epoch-making mathematical knowledge.[2] In arithmetic he improved the current methods of computation; in geometry he taught the traditional methods of measurement descended from the Roman surveyors, and compiled a work from Boëthius and other sources. For astronomy he made spheres and other instruments, and in music his teaching was the best obtainable. In none of these provinces was he an original inventor; nor did he exhaust the knowledge had by men before him. He was, however, the embodiment of mediaeval progress, in that he drew intelligently upon the sources within his reach, and then taught with understanding and enthusiasm. Richer's praise is unstinted:

" He began with arithmetic ; then taught music, of which there had long been ignorance in Gaul. . . . With what pains he set forth the method of astronomy, it may be well to state, so that the reader may perceive the sagacity and skill of this great man. This difficult subject he explained by means of admirable instruments. First he illustrated the world's sphere by one of solid wood, the greater by the less. He fixed it obliquely as to the horizon with two poles, and near the upper pole set the northern constellations, and by the lower one those of the south. He determined its position by means of the circle called by the Greeks *orizon* and by the Latins *limitans*, because it divides the constellations which are seen from those which are not. By his sphere thus fixed, he demonstrated the rising and setting of the stars, and taught his disciples to recognize them. And at night he followed their courses and marked the place of their rising and setting upon the different regions of his model."

---

[1] Richer, *Hist.* iii. 47, 48.
[2] Several of his compositions are extant.

The historian passes on to tell how Gerbert with ingenious devices showed on his sphere the imaginary circles called parallels, and on another the movements of the planets, and on still another marked the constellations of the heavens, so that even a beginner, upon having one constellation pointed out, could find the others.[1]

In the province of philosophy, Gerbert's labours extended little beyond formal logic, philosophy's instrument. He could do no more than understand and apply as much of Boëthius's rendering of the Aristotelian *Organon* as he was acquainted with. Yet he appears to have used more of the Boëthian writings than any man before him, or for a hundred and fifty years after his death. Richer gives the list. Beyond this evidence, curious testimony is borne to the nature of Gerbert's dialectic by Richer's account of a notable debate. The year was 980, when the fame of the brilliant young *scholasticus* of Rheims had spread through Gaul and penetrated Germany. A certain master of repute at Magdeburg, named Otric, sent one of his pupils to report on Gerbert's teaching, and especially as to his method of laying out the divisions of philosophy as " the science of things divine and human." The pupil returned with notes of Gerbert's classification, in which, by error or intention, it was made to appear that he subordinated physics to mathematics, as species to genus, whereas, in truth, he made them of equal rank. Otric thought to catch him tripping, and so managed that a disputation was held between them at a time when Adalberon and Gerbert were in Italy with the Emperor Otto II. It took place in Ravenna. The emperor, then nineteen years of age, presided, there being present many masters and dignitaries of the Church. Holding in his hand a tablet of Gerbert's alleged division of the sciences, His Majesty opened the debate :

" Meditation and discussion, as I think, make for the betterment of human knowledge, and questions from the wise rouse our thoughtfulness. Thus knowledge of things is drawn forth by the learned, or discovered by them and committed to books, which remain to our great good. We also may be incited by certain objects which draw the mind to a surer understanding. Observe

---

[1] Richer, *Hist.* iii. 48-53.

now, that I am turning over this tablet inscribed with the divisions of philosophy. Let all consider it carefully, and each say what he thinks. If it be complete, let it be confirmed by your approbation. If imperfect, let it be rejected or corrected.

" Then Otric, taking it before them all, said that it was arranged by Gerbert, and had been taken down from his lectures. He handed it to the Lord Augustus, who read it through, and presented it to Gerbert. The latter, carefully examining it, approved in part, and in part condemned, asserting that the scheme had not been arranged thus by him. Asked by Augustus to correct it, he said : ' Since, O great Caesar Augustus, I see thee more potent than all these, I will, as is fitting, obey thy behest. Nor shall I be concerned at the spite of the malevolent, by whose instigation the very correct division of philosophy recently set forth so lucidly by me, has been vitiated by the substitution of a species. I say then, that mathematics, physics, and theology are to be placed as equals under one genus. The genus likewise has equal share in them. Nor is it possible that one and the same species, in one and the same respect, should be co-ordinate with another species and also be put under it as species under a genus.' "

Then in answer to a demand from Otric for a more explicit statement of his classification, he said there could be no objection to dividing philosophy according to Vitruvius (Victorinus) and Boëthius ; " for philosophy is the genus, of which the species are the practical and the theoretical : under the practical, as species again, come *dispensativa, distributiva* and *civilis* ; under the theoretical fall *phisica naturalis, mathematica intelligibilis,* and *theologia intellectibilis.*"

Otric then wonders that Gerbert put mathematics immediately after physics, omitting physiology. To which Gerbert replies that physiology stands to physics as philology to philosophy, of which it is part. Otric changes his attack to a flank movement, and asks Gerbert what is the *causa* of philosophy. Gerbert asks whether he means the cause by which, or the cause for which, it is devised (*inventa*). Otric replies the latter. " Then," says Gerbert, " since you make your question clear, I say that philosophy was devised that from it we might understand things divine and human." " But why use so many words," says Otric, " to designate the cause of one thing ? " " Because one word may not suffice to designate a cause. Plato uses three to designate the cause of the creation of the world, to wit, the *bona Dei voluntas.* He could not have said *voluntas* simply." " But," says Otric, " he could have said more concisely *Dei voluntas,* for God's will is always good, which he would not deny."

" Here I do not contradict you," says Gerbert, " but consider : since God alone is good in himself, and every creature is good only by participation, the word *bona* is added to express the quality peculiar to His nature alone. However this may be, still one word will not always designate a cause. What is the cause of shadow ? Can you put that in one word ? I say, the cause of shadow is a body interposed to light. It is not ' body ' nor even ' body interposed.' I don't deny that the causes of many things can be stated in one word, as the genera of substance, quantity, or quality, which are the causes of species. Others cannot be expressed so simply, as *rationale ad mortale.*"

This enigmatic phrase electrifies Otric, who cries : " You put the mortal under the rational ? Who does not know that the rational is confined to God, angels, and mankind, while the mortal embraces everything mortal, a limitless mass ? "

" To which Gerbert : ' If, following Porphyry and Boëthius, you make a careful division of substance, carrying it down to individuals, you will have the rational broader than the mortal as may readily be shown. Since substance, admittedly the most general genus, may be divided into subordinate genera and species down to individuals, it is to be seen whether all these subordinates may be expressed by a single word. Clearly, some are designated with one word, as *corpus,* others with several, as *animatum sensibile.* With like reason, the subordinate, which is *animal rationale,* may be predicated of the subject that is *animal rationale mortale.* Not that *rationale* may be predicated of what is mortal simply ; but *rationale,* I say, joined to *animal* is predicated of *mortale* joined to *animal rationale.'*

" At this, Augustus with a nod ended the argument, since it had lasted nearly the whole day, and the audience were fatigued with the prolix and unbroken disputation. He splendidly rewarded Gerbert, who set out for Gaul with Adalberon." [1]

Evidently Richer's account gives merely the captions of this disputation. There was not the slightest originality in any of the propositions stated by the disputants ; everything is taken from Porphyry and Boëthius and the current Latin translation of Plato's *Timaeus.* Yet the whole affair, the

[1] Richer, *Hist.* iii. cap. 55-65.

selection of the questions, the nature of the answers, the limitation of the matter to the bare poles of logical palestrics, is most illustrative of the mentality and intellectual interests of the late tenth century. The growth of the mediaeval intellect lay unavoidably through such courses of discipline. And just as early mediaeval Latin had to save itself from barbarism by cleaving to grammar, so the best intellect of this early period grasped at logic not only as the most obviously needed discipline and guide, but also with imperfect consciousness that this discipline and means did not contain the goal and plenitude of substantial knowledge. Grammar was then not simply a means but an end in the study of letters, and so was logic unconsciously. In the one case and the other, the palpable need of the *disciplina* and its difficulties kept the student from realizing that the instrument was but an instrument.

Moreover, upon Gerbert's time pressed the specific need to consider just such questions as the disputation affords a sample of. An enormous mass of theology, philosophy, and science awaited mastering, the heritage from a greater past, antique and patristic. Perhaps a true instinct guided Gerbert and his contemporaries to problems of classification and method as a primary essential task. Had the Middle Ages been a period when knowledge, however crude, was perforce advancing through experience, investigation, and discovery, the problems of classification and method would not have presented themselves as preliminary. But mediaeval development lay through the study of what former men had won from nature or received from God. This was preserved in books which had to be studied and mastered. Hence classifications of knowledge were essential aids or sorely needed guides. With a true instinct the Middle Ages first of all looked within this mass of knowledge for guides to its mazes, seeking a plan or scheme by the aid of which universal knowledge might be unravelled, and then reconstructed in forms corresponding to even larger verities.[1]

---

[1] See *post*, Chapter XXXVI. If one should hesitate to find a phase of the veritable Gerbert in Richer's report of the disputation with Otric, one .nay turn to Gerbert's own philosophic or logical *Libellus—de rationali et ratione uti* (Migne

II

The decades on either side of the year 1000 were cramped and dull.   In Burgundy, to be sure, the energies of Cluny,[1] under its great abbots, were rousing the monastic world to a sense of religious and disciplinary decency.   This reform, however, took little interest in culture.   The monks of Cluny were commonly instructed in the rudiments of the Seven Arts.   They had a little mathematics ; bits of crude physical knowledge had unavoidably come to them ; and just as unavoidably had they made use of extracts from the pagan poets in studying Latinity.[2] But they did not follow letters for their own sake, nor knowledge because they loved it and felt that love a holy one.   Monastic principles hardly justified such a love, and Cluny's abbots had enough to do in bringing the monastic world to decency, without dallying with inapplicable knowledge or the charms of pagan poetry.

Religious reforms in the ninth century had helped letters in the cathedral and monastic schools of Gaul.   The latter soon fell back to ignorance ; but among the cathedral schools, Chartres and Rheims and Laon continued to flourish. A moral ordering of life increases thoughtfulness and may stimulate study.   Hence, in the latter part of the tenth century, the Cluniac reforms, like the earlier reforming movements, affected letters favourably in the monasteries.

139, col. 159-168).   It is addressed to Otto II., and the opening paragraph recalls to the emperor the disputation which we have been following.   The *Libellus* is naturally more coherent than the disputation, in which Otric's questions seem intended rather to trip his adversary than to lead a topic on to its proper end. It is devoted, however, to a problem exactly analogous to the point taken by Otric, that the term rational was not as broad as the term mortal.   For the *Libellus* discusses whether the use of reason (*ratione uti*) can be predicated of the rational being (*rationale*).   The concept of the predicate should be the broader one, but here it might seem less broad, since all reasonable beings do not exercise reason. The discussion closely resembles the dispute in the character of the intellectual interests disclosed, and its arguments are not more original than those employed against Otric.   Disputation and *Libellus* alike represent necessary endeavours of the mind, which has reached a certain stage of tuition and development, to adjust itself with problems of logical order and method.

[1] *Post*, Chapter XVI.

[2] Cf. Sackür, *Die Cluniacenser*, ii. 330 *sqq.* ; Pfister, *Études sur le règne de Robert le Pieux*, p. 2 *sqq.* (the latter takes an extreme view).

Here and there an exceptional man created an exceptional situation. Such a one was Abbo, Abbot of St. Benedict's at Fleury on the Loire, who died the year after Gerbert. He was fortunate in his excellent pupil and biographer, Aimoin, who ascribes to him as liberal sentiments toward study as were consistent with a stern monasticism :

" He admonished his hearers that having cast out the thorns of sin, they should sow the little gardens of their hearts with the spices of the divine virtues.   The battle lay against the vices of the flesh, and it was for them to consider what arms they should oppose to its delights.   To complete their armament, after the vows of prayer, and the manly strife of fastings, he deemed that the study of letters would advantage them, and especially the exercise of composition.   Indeed he himself, the studious man, scarcely let pass a moment when he was not reading, writing, or dictating." [1]

It is curious to observe the unavoidable influence of a crude Latin education upon the most strenuous of these reforming monks.   In 994 Odilo became Abbot of Cluny. After a most notable and effective rule of more than half a century, he died just as the year 1049 began.   The closing scenes are typically illustrative of the passing of an early mediaeval saint.   The dying abbot preaches and comforts his monks, gives his blessing, adores the Cross, repels the devil :

" I warn thee, enemy of the human race, turn from me thy plots and hidden wiles, for by me is the Cross of the Lord, which I always adore : the Cross my refuge, my way and virtue ; the Cross, unconquerable banner, the invincible weapon.   The Cross repels every evil, and puts darkness to flight.   Through this divine Cross I approach my journey ; the Cross is my life—death to thee, Enemy ! "

The next day, " in the presence of all, the Creed is read for a shield of faith against the deceptions of malignant

---

[1] Aimoin's *Vita Abbonis*, cap. 7 (Migne, *Pat. Lat.* 139, col. 393).   The same volume contains most of Abbo's extant writings, and those of Aimoin.   On Abbo see Sackür, *Die Cluniacenser*, ii. 345 *sqq.*

An incredibly large number of students are said to have attended Abbo's lectures.   His studies and teaching lay mainly in astronomy, mathematics, chronology, and grammar.   The pupil Aimoin cultivated history and biography, compiling a History of the Francs and a History of the miracles of St. Benedict, the latter a theme worthy of the tenth century.   One leaves it with a sigh of relief, so barren was it save for its feat of gestation in giving birth to Gerbert.

spirits and the attacks of evil thoughts ; Augustine is
brought in to expound, intently listened to, and discussed." [1]

For Odilo, the Cross is a divine, not to say magic, safe-
guard. His prayer and imprecation have something of the
nature of an uttered spell. No antique zephyrs seem to
blow in this atmosphere of faith and fear, in which he passed
his life and performed his miracles before and after death.
Nevertheless the antique might mould his phrases, and
perhaps unconsciously affect his ethical conceptions. He
wrote a Life of a former abbot of Cluny, ascribing to him the
four *cardinales disciplinas,* in which he strove to perfect
himself " in order that through *prudentia* he might assure the
welfare of himself and those in his charge ; that through
temperantia (which by another name is called *modestia*), by
a proper measure of a just discretion, he might modestly
discharge the spiritual business entrusted to him ; that
through *fortitudo* he might resist and conquer the devil and
his vices ; and that through *justitia,* which permeates all
virtues and seasons them, he might live soberly and piously
and justly, fight the good fight and finish his course." [2]

Thus the antique virtues shape Odilo's thoughts, as seven
hundred years before him the point of view and reasoning
of Ambrose's *De officiis ministrorum* were set by Cicero's
De officiis.[3] The same classically touched phrases, if not
conceptions, pass on to Odilo's pupil and biographer, the
monk Jotsaldus, to whom we owe our description of Odilo's
last moments. He ascribes the four cardinal virtues to his
hero, and then defines them from the antique standpoint,
but with Christian turns of thought :

" The philosophers define Prudence as the search for truth and
the thirst for fuller knowledge. In which virtue Odilo was so
distinguished that neither by day nor night did he cease from the
search for truth. The Book of the divine contemplation was
always in his hands, and ceaselessly he spoke of Scripture for the
edification of all, and prayer ever followed reading.

" Justice, as the philosophers say, is that which renders each

---

[1] Jotsaldus, *Vita Odilonis* (Migne 142. col. 1037).

[2] Odilo, *Vita Maioli* (Migne 142, col. 951).

[3] See Taylor, *Classical Heritage of the Middle Ages,* p. 74 *sqq.* One may compare
the influence of Cicero's *De amicitia* on the *De amicitia Christiana* of Peter of Blois
(cir. 1200), Migne 207, col. 871-898.

his due, lays no claim to what is another's, and neglects self-advantage, so as to maintain what is equitable for all." [To illustrate this virtue in Odilo, the biographer gives instances of his charity, by which one observes the Christian turn taken by the conception.]

" Fortitude is to hold the mind above the dread of danger, to fear nothing save the base, and bravely bear adversity and prosperity. Supported by this virtue, it is difficult to say how brave he was in repelling the plots of enemies and how patient in enduring them. You might observe in him this very privilege of patience ; to those who injured him, as another David he repaid the grace of benefit, and toward those who hated him, he preserved a stronger benevolence." [Again the Christian turn of thought.]

" Temperance, last in the catalogue of the aforesaid virtues, according to its definition maintains moderation and order in whatever is to be said or done. Here he was so mighty as to hold to moderation and observe propriety (*ordinem*) in all his actions and commands, and show a wonderful discretion. Following the blessed Jerome, he tempered fasting to the golden mean, according to the weakness or strength of the body, thus avoiding fanaticism and preserving continency. Neither elegance nor squalor was noticeable in his dress. He tempered gravity of conduct with gaiety of countenance. He was severe in the correction of vice as the occasion demanded, gracious in pardoning, in both balancing an impartial scale." [1]

III

A friend of Odilo was Gerbert's pupil Fulbert, Bishop of Chartres from 1006 to 1028. His name is joined forever with that chief cathedral school of early mediaeval France, which he so firmly and so broadly re-established as to earn a founder's fame. It will be interesting to notice its range of studies. Chartres was an ancient home of letters. Caesar [2] speaks of the land of the Carnuti as the centre of Druidism in Gaul ; and under the Empire, liberal studies quickly sprang up in the Gallo-Roman city. They did not quite cease even in Merovingian times, and revived with the Carolingian revival. Thenceforth they were pursued continuously at the convent school of St. Peter, if not at the school attached to the cathedral. For some years before he was made bishop, the grave and kindly Fulbert had been

---

[1] *Vita Odilonis*, chaps. vi.-xiii. (Migne 142, col. 909 *sqq.*).
[2] *Bellum Gallicum*, vi. 13.

the head of this cathedral school, where he did not cease
to teach until his death. As bishop, widely esteemed and
influential, he rebuilt the cathedral, aided by the kings of
France and Denmark, the dukes of Aquitaine and Normandy,
the counts of Champagne and Blois. His vast crypt still
endures, a shadowy goal for thousands of pilgrim knees, and
an ample support for the great edifice above it. Admiring
tradition has ascribed to him even this glory of a later
time.

From near and far, pious students came to benefit by
the instruction of the school, of which Fulbert was the head
and inspiration. Their intercourse was intimate with their
" Venerable Socrates " in the small school buildings near the
cathedral. From the accounts, we can almost see him
moving among them, stopping to correct one here, or looking over the shoulder of another engaged upon a geometric
figure, and putting some new problem. Among the pupils
there might be rivalry, quarrels, breaches of decorum ; but
there was the master, ever grave and steadfast, always ready
to encourage with his sympathy, but prepared also to
reprove, either silently by withdrawing his confidence, or in
words, as when he forbade an instructor to joke when
explaining Donatus : " spectaculum factus es omnibus ; cave."

Some of these scholars became men of sanctity and
renown—Berengar of Tours gained an unhappy fame. A
fellow-student wrote to him in later years addressing him as
foster-brother :

" I have called thee foster-brother because of that sweetest
common life led by us while youths in the Academy of Chartres
under our venerable Socrates. Well we proved his saving doctrine
and holy living, and now that he is with God we should hope to be
aided by his prayers. Surely he is mindful of us, cherishing us
even more than when he moved a pilgrim in the body of this death,
and drew us to him by vows and tacit prayer, entreating us in
those evening colloquies (*vespertina colloquia*) in the garden by the
chapel, that we should tread the royal way, and cleave to the
footprints of the holy fathers." [1]

The cathedral school included youths receiving their first
lessons, as well as older scholars and instructors. They

[1] Migne 143, col. 1290.

lived together under rules, and together celebrated the services of the cathedral, chanting the matins, the hours, and the mass. The Trivium and Quadrivium made the basis of their studies. Text-books and courses were already some centuries old.

The first branch of the Trivium was Grammar, which included literature by way of illustration ; and he who held the chair had the title of *grammaticus*. For the beginners, *Donatus* was the text-book, and *Priscianus* for the more advanced.[1] Nor was Martianus Capella neglected. The student annotated these works with citations from the *Etymologies* of Isidore. Divers mnemotechnic processes assisted him to commit the contents to memory. The grammatical course included the writing of compositions in prose and verse, according to rule, and the reading of classic authors. For their school verses in metre the pupils used Bede's *De arte metrica*, an encyclopaedia of metrical forms. They also wrote accentual and rhymed Latin verse. Of profane authors the Library appears to have contained Livy, Valerius Maximus, Virgil, Ovid, Horace, Statius, Servius the commentator on Virgil ; and of writers who were Christian Classics in the Middle Ages, Orosius, Gregory of Tours, Fortunatus, Sedulius, Arator, Prudentius, and Boëthius, the last named being the most important single source of early mediaeval education. Rhetoric, the second branch of the Trivium, bore that vague relationship to grammar which it bears in modern parlance. The rules of the rhetoricians were learned ; the works of profane or Christian orators were read and imitated. This study left its mark on mediaeval sermons and *Vitae Sanctorum*.

As for the third branch, Dialectic, Fulbert's pupils studied the logical treatises in general use in the earlier Middle Ages : to wit, the *Categories* and the *De interpretatione* of Aristotle, and Porphyry's *Introduction*, all in the Latin of Boëthius. For works which might be regarded as commentaries upon these, the school had at its disposal the *Categories* ascribed to Augustine and Apuleius's *De interpretatione*, Cicero's *Topica*, and Boëthius's discussion of definition, division, and categorical and hypothetical

---

[1] For a description of these works, see *post*, Chapter XXXI. II.

syllogisms—the logical writings expounded by Gerbert at Rheims.   The school had likewise Gerbert's own *Libellus de ratione uti* and Boëthius's *De consolatione*, that chief ethical compend for the early Middle Ages ;   also the writings of Eriugena, and Dionysius the Areopagite in Eriugena's translation.   Whether or not it possessed the current Latin version of Plato's *Timaeus*, Fulbert and Berengar at all events refer to Plato in terms of eulogy.

Passing to the Quadrivium, we find that Fulbert had studied its four branches under Gerbert.   In Arithmetic the students used the treatise of Boëthius, and also the Abacus, a table of vertical columns, with Roman numerals at the top to indicate the order of units, tens, and hundreds according to the decimal system.   In Geometry the students likewise fell back upon Boëthius.   Astronomy, the third branch of the Quadrivium, had for its practical object the computation of the Church's calendar.   The pupils learned the signs of the Zodiac and were instructed in the method of finding the stars by the *Astrolabius*, a sphere (such as Gerbert had constructed) representing the constellations, and turning upon a tube as an axis, which served to fix the polar star.   Music, the fourth branch of the Quadrivium, was zealously cultivated.   For its theory, the treatise of Boëthius was studied ;   and Fulbert and his scholars did much to advance the music of the liturgy, composing texts and airs for organ chanting.

In addition to the Quadrivium, medicine was taught. The students learned receipts and processes handed down by tradition and commonly ascribed to Hippocrates.   For more convenient memorizing, Fulbert cast them into verse. Such " medicine " was not founded on observation ;   and a mediaeval scholar-copyist would as naturally transcribe a medical receipt-book as any other work coming within the range of his stylus.   One may remember that in the early Middle Ages the relic was the common means of cure.

The seven *Artes* of the Trivium and Quadrivium were the handmaids of Theology ;   and Fulbert gave elaborate instruction in this Christian queen of the sciences, expounding the Scriptures, explaining the Liturgy, and taking up the controversies of the time.   As a part of this sacred science, the students apparently were taught something of Canon and Roman law and of Charlemagne's Capitularies.[1]

IV

The Chartres Quadrivium represents the extreme compass of mathematical and physical studies in France in the eleventh century, when slight interest was taken in physical science—a phrase far too grand to designate the crass traditional views of nature which prevailed. Indifference to natural knowledge was the most palpable intellectual defect of Ambrose and Augustine, and the most portentous. The coming centuries, which were to look upon their writings as universal guides to living and knowing, found therein no incentive to observe or study the natural world. Of course the Carolingian period evolved out of itself no such desire ;[2] nor did the eleventh century. At the best, the general understanding of physical fact remained that which had been handed down. It was gleaned from the books commonly read, the *Physiologus* or the edifying stories of miracles in the myriad *Vitae Sanctorum*, quite as much as from the scant information given in Isidore's *Origines*, Bede's *Liber de temporibus*, or the *De universo* of Rabanus Maurus.

So much for natural science. In historical writing the quality of composition rarely rose above that of the tenth century.[3] No sign of critical acumen had appeared, and the writers of the period show but a narrow local interest. There was no France, but everywhere a parcelling of the land into small sections of misrule, between which travel was difficult and dangerous. The chroniclers confine their attention, as doubtless their knowledge also was confined, to the region where they lived. To lift history over these narrow barriers, there was needed the renewal of the royal

---

[1] The substance of this sketch of the school of Chartres is taken chiefly from the Abbé Clerval's exhaustive study, " Les Écoles de Chartres au moyen âge," *Mémoires de la Société archéologique d'Eure-et-Loir*, xi., 1895. For the later fortunes of this school see *post*, Chapter XXXI.

[2] Unless possibly in the mind of Eriugena.

[3] The Histories of Gerbert's pupil Richer are somewhat better, and show an imitation of Sallust.

power, which came with the century's close, and the stimulus to curiosity springing from the Crusades.[1]

In fine, the eleventh century was crude and inchoate, preparatory to the intellectual activity and the unleashed energies of life which mark the opening of the twelfth. Yet the mediaeval mind was assimilating and appropriating dynamically its lessons from the Fathers, as well as those portions of the antique heritage of thought which, so far, it had felt a need of. Difficult problems were stated, but in ways presenting, as it were, the apices of alternatives too narrow to hold truth, which lies less frequently in warring opposites than in an inclusive and discriminating conciliation. This century, especially when we fix our attention upon France, appears as the threshold of mediaeval thinking, the immediate antecedent to mediaeval formulations of philosophic and theological conviction. The controversies and the different mental tendencies which thereafter were to move through such large and often diverging courses, drew their origin from still prior times. With the coming of the eleventh century they had been sturdily cradled, and seemed safe from the danger of dying in infancy. Thence on through the twelfth century, through the thirteenth, the climacteric of mediaeval thought, opinions and convictions are set in multitudes of propositions, relating to many provinces of human meditation.

These masses of propositions, convictions, opinions, philosophic and religious, constitute the religious philosophy of the Middle Ages—scholasticism as it commonly is called. Hereafter [2] it will be necessary to consider that large matter in its continuity of development, with its roots or antecedents stretching back through the eleventh century to the Carolingian period, and beyond. Mediaeval thinkers will then be seen to fall into two classes, very roughly speaking, the one tending to set authority above reason, and the other tending to set reason above authority. Both classes appear in the ninth century, represented respectively by Rabanus Maurus and Eriugena. In the eleventh they are also evident. St. Anselm, who came from Italy, is the most

---

[1] Cf. Molinier, *Les Sources de l'histoire de France*, v., lxix.
[2] *Post*, Chapters XXXV.-XLIII.

admirable representative of the first class, being in heart and mind a theologian whose philosophy revolved entire around his faith. Of him we have spoken ; and here may mention in contrast with him two Frenchmen, Berengar of Tours and Roscellinus. In place and time they come within the scope of the present chapter ; nor were their mental processes such as to attach them to a later period. By temperament, and in somewhat confused expression, they set reason above authority, save that of Scripture as they understood it.

Berengar was born, apparently at Tours, and of wealthy parents, just as the tenth century closed. After studying under his uncle, the Treasurer of St. Martin, he came to Chartres, where Fulbert was bishop. Judging from a general consensus of expression from men who became his opponents, but had been his fellow-pupils, he quickly aroused attention by his talents, and anxiety or enmity by his pride and the self-confident assertion of his opinions. He would neither accept with good grace the admonitions of those about him, nor follow the authority of the Fathers. He was said to have despised even the great grammarians and logicians, Priscian, Donatus, and Boëthius. Why err with everybody if everybody errs, he asked. He appears as a vain man eager for admiration. The report comes down that he imitated Fulbert's manner in lecturing, first covering his visage with a hood so as to seem in deep meditation, and then speaking in a gentle, plaintive voice. From Chartres he passed to Angers, where he filled the office of archdeacon, and thence he returned to Tours, was placed over the Church schools of St. Martin's, and in the course of time began to lecture on the Eucharist. This was between the years 1030 and 1040.

That a man's fortunes and fame are linked to a certain doctrine or controversy may be an accident of environment. Berengar chose to adduce and partly follow the teachings of Eriugena, whose fame was great, but whose orthodoxy was tainted. The nature of the Eucharist lent itself to dispute, and from the time of Ratramnus, Radbertus, and Eriugena, it was common for theologians to try their hand on it, if only in order to demonstrate their adherence to the extreme

doctrines accepted by the Church.   These were not the
doctrines of Eriugena, nor were they held by Berengar, who
would not bring himself to admit an absolute substantial
change in the bread and wine.   Possibly his convictions
were less irrational than the dominant doctrine.   Yet he
appears to have asserted them, not because he had a clearer
mind than others, but by reason of his more self-assertive
and combative temperament.   He was not an original
thinker, but a controversial and turgid reasoner, who
naturally enough was forced into all kinds of tergiversation
in order to escape condemnation as a heretic.   His self-
assertiveness settled on the most obvious theological
dispute of the time, and his self-esteem maintained the
superiority of his own reason over the authorities adduced
by his adversaries.   Of course he never impugned the
authority of Scripture, but relied on it to substantiate his
views, merely asserting that a reasonable interpretation was
better than a foolish one.   Throughout the controversy, one
may observe that Berengar's understanding of fact kept
somewhat closer than that of his opponents to the tangible
realities of sense.   But a difference of intellectual temperament lay at the bottom of his dissent ; and had not the
Eucharist presented itself as the readiest topic of dispute,
he would doubtless have fallen upon some other question.
As it was, his arguments gained adherents, the dominant
view being repellent to independent minds.   Still, it won the
day, and Berengar was condemned by more than one
council, and forced into all manner of equivocal retractions,
by which at least he saved his life, and died in extreme old
age.

It may be that a larger relative import attributed by
Berengar and also Roscellin to the tangibilities of sense-
perception, led the latter at the close of the century to put
forth views on the nature of universals which have given
him a shadowy repute as the father of nominalism.   The
Eucharistic controversy pertained primarily to Christian
dogmatics.   That regarding universals, or general ideas,
pertains to philosophy, and, from the standpoint of formal
logic, lies at the foundation of consistent thinking.   So
closely does it make part of the development of scholasticism

that its discussion had best be postponed ; merely assuming for the present that Roscellin's thinking upon the topic to which his name is attached was not superior in method and analysis to Berengar's upon the Eucharist.

One cannot escape the conclusion that intellectually the eleventh century in France was crude. The mediaeval intellect was still but imperfectly developed ; its manifestations had not reached the zenith of their energy. Yet doub less the mental development of mankind proceeds at a more uniform rate than would appear from the brilliant phenomena which crowd the eras of apparent culmination, in contrast with the previous dulness. The profounder constancy of growth may be discerned by scrutinizing those dumb courses of gestation, from which spring the marvels of the great epoch. The opening of the twelfth century was to inaugurate a brilliant intellectual era in France. The efficient preparation stretched back into the latter half of the eleventh, whose Catholic progress heralded a period of awakening. The Church already was striving to accomplish its own reordering and regeneration, free itself from things that drag and hinder, from lay investiture and simony, abominations through which feudal depotentiating principles had intruded into the ecclesiastic body ; free itself likewise from clerical marriage and concubinage, which kept the clergy from being altogether clergy, and weighted the Church with the claims of half-spurious priests' offspring. In France the reform of the monks comes first, impelled by Cluny ; and when Cluny herself becomes less zealous, because too great and rich, the spirit of soldiery against sin reincarnates itself in the Grand-Chartreuse, in Citeaux and Clairvaux. The reform of the secular clergy follows, with Hildebrand the veritable master ; for the Church was passing from prelacy to papacy, and the Pope was becoming a true monarch, instead of nominal head of an episcopal aristocracy.

The perfected organization and unceasing purification of the Church made one part of the general progress of the period. Another consisted in the disengaging of the greater powers from out the indiscriminate anarchy of feudalism, and the advance of the French monarchy, under Louis the

Sixth,[1] toward effective sovereignty, all making for a surer law and order throughout France.   Then through the eleventh and twelfth centuries came the struggle of the people, out of serfdom into some control over their own persons and fortunes.   Everywhere the population increased; old cities grew apace, and a multitude of new ones came into existence.   Economic evolution progressed, advancing with the affranchisement of industry, the organization of guilds, the growth of trade, the opening of new markets, fairs, and freer avenues of commerce.   Architecture with new civic resources was pushing on through Romanesque toward Gothic, while the affiliated arts of sculpture and painting were becoming more expressive.   The Crusades began, and did their work of spreading knowledge through the Occident, carrying foreign ideas and institutions across provincial barriers.   They could not have taken place had it not been for the freeing of social forces during the half century preceding their inception in the year 1096.[2]

Thus humanity was universally bestirring itself throughout the land we know as France.   Such a bestirring could not fail to crown itself with a mightier winging of the spirit through the higher provinces of thought.   This was to show itself among saints and doctors of the Church in their philosophies and theologies of the mind and heart ; with like power it was to show itself among those hardier rationalists who with difficulty and misgivings, or under hard compulsion, still kept themselves within the Church's pale.   It showed itself too with heretics who let themselves be burned rather than surrender their outlawed convictions. It was also to show itself through things beautiful, in the strivings of art toward the perfect symbolical presentation of what the soul cherished or abhorred ; and show itself too in the literature of the common tongues as well as the literature of the time-honoured Latin.   In fine, it was to show itself, through every heightened faculty and appetition of the universally striving and desirous soul of man, in a larger, bolder understanding and appreciation of life.

[1] Born 1078 ; king from 1108 to 1137.
[2] See *post*, Chapter XIV.

CHAPTER XIII

MENTAL ASPECTS OF THE ELEVENTH CENTURY:
GERMANY ; ENGLAND ; CONCLUSION

I. German Appropriation of Christianity and Antique Culture.
II. Othloh's Spiritual Conflict.
III. England ; Closing Comparisons.

I

In the Germans of the eleventh century one notes a strong sense of German selfhood, supplemented by a consciousness that Latin culture is a foreign matter, introduced as a thing of great value which it were exceeding well for them to make their own. They are even conscious of having been converted to Latin Christianity, which on their part they are imbuing with German thoughts and feeling. They are not Romance people ; they have never spoken Latin ; it has never been and will never be their speech. They will master what they can of the antique education which has been brought to them. But even as it was no part of their forefathers' lives, so it will never penetrate their own personalities, so as to make them the spiritual descendants of any antique Latin or Latinized people. They have never been and never will be Latinized ; but will remain forever Germans.

Consequently the appropriation of the Latin culture in Germany is a labour of translation : first a palpable labour of translation from the Latin language into the German tongue, and secondly, and for always, a more subtle kind of translation of the antique influence into a German understanding of the same, and gradually into informing principles

made use of by a strong and advancing racial genius.   The
German genius will be enlarged and developed through these
foreign elements, but it will never cease to use the Latin
culture as a means of informing and developing itself.

No need to say that these strong statements apply to
the Germans in their home north of the Alps and east of
the Rhine ; not to those who left the Fatherland, and in the
course of generations became Italians, for example.   Moreover, general phrases must always be taken subject to
qualification and rounding of the corners.   No people can
absorb a foreign influence without in some degree being
made over into the likeness of what they are receiving, and
to that extent ceasing to be their unmitigated selves.   In
general, however, while Latin Christianity and the antique
culture both were brought to Germany from abroad, the
Germans were converted or transformed only by the former,
and merely took and used the latter—a true statement this,
so far as one may separate these two great mingled factors
of mediaeval progress.

Evidently those Germans of the opening mediaeval
centuries who did most to advance the civilization of their
people were essentially introducers of foreign culture.   This
was manifestly true of the missionaries (chief among whom
was the Anglo-Saxon Boniface) who brought Christianity to
Germany.   It was true both as to the Christian and the
secular learning of Rabanus Maurus, who was born at Mainz,
a very German.[1]   With all his Latin learning he kept his
interest in his mother tongue, and always realized that his
people spoke German and not Latin.   He encouraged
preaching in German ; and with the aid of his favourite
pupil, Walafrid, he prepared German glosses and Latin-
German glossaries for Scripture.

Before Rabanus's death popular translations of the Gospels had appeared, imbued with the Germanic spirit.   The
Heliand and Otfrid's *Evangelienbuch* are the best known of
these.[2]   Then, extending through the last part of the tenth
and the first part of the eleventh century we note the labours
of that most diligent of translators, Notker the German,
a monk of St. Gall, and member of the Ekkehart family,

---

[1] *Ante*, p. 221 *sqq.*   [2] *Ante*, p. 203 *sqq.*

which gave so many excellent abbots to that cloister. He died in 1022. Like Bede, Rabanus, and many other Teutonic scholars, he was an encyclopaedia of the knowledge afforded by his time. He was the head of a school of German translators. His own translations covered part of Boëthius's *De consolatione,* Virgil's *Bucolics,* Terence's *Andria,* Martianus Capella's *De nuptiis,* Aristotle's *Categories* and *De interpretatione,* an arithmetic, a rhetoric, Job, and the Psalms. He was a teacher all his life, and a German always, loving his mother tongue, and occupying himself with its grammar and word forms. His method of translation was to give the Latin sentence, with a close German rendering, accompanied by an occasional explanation of the matter, also in German.[1] All the while, this foreign learning was being mastered gallantly in the leading cloisters, Fulda, St. Gall, Reichenau, Hersfeld, and others. Within their walls this Latin culture was studied and mastered, as one with resolve and perseverance masters that to which he is not born.

Besides those who laboured as translators, other earnest fosterers of learning in Germany appear as introducers of the same. Bruno, youngest brother of Otto I., is distinguished in this rôle. He promoted letters in his archiepiscopal diocese of Cologne. From many lands learned men came to him, Liutprand and Ratherius among others. Otto himself loved learning, and drew foreign scholars to his Court, one of whom was that conceited Gunzo, already spoken of.[2]

---

[1] On Notker see Piper, *Die älteste Litteratur* (Deutsche Nat. Lit.), pp. 337-340.

[2] *Ante,* Chapter XI., where something was said of Liutprand also. Ratherius was a restless intriguer and pamphleteer, a sort of stormy petrel, who was born in 890 near Liège. In the course of his career he was once bishop of that northern city, and three times bishop of Verona, where he died, an old man of angry soul and bitter tongue. Two years and more had he passed in a dungeon at Pavia—a sharpening experience for one already given overmuch to hate. There he compiled his rather dreary six books of *Praeloquia* (Migne 136, col. 145-344), preparatory discourses, perhaps precursive of another work, but at all events containing moral instruction for all orders of society. It was in the nature of a compilation, and yet touched with a strain of personal plaint, which sometimes makes itself clearly audible in words that show this work to have been its author's prison *consolatio*: "Think what anguish impelled me to it, what calamity, what necessity showed me these paths of authorship. Dread of forgetting was my first reason for writing. Buried under all sorts of the rubbish of wickedness, surrounded by the darkness of evil, and distracted with the clamours of affairs, I feared that I should forget, and was delighted to find how much I could remember. Books were lacking, and friends to talk with, while sorrow gnawed the soul; so I used this book of mine as a friend to chat with, and was comforted by it as by a com-

Schools moved with the emperor (*scholae translatitiae*) also with Bruno, who though archbishop, duke, and burdened with affairs, took the time to teach. A passage in his Life by Ruotger shows the education and accomplishments of this most worthy prince of the Church and land :

"Then as soon as he learned the first rudiments of the grammatic art, as we have heard from himself, often pondering upon this to the glory of the omnipotent God he began to read the poet Prudentius, at the instance of his master. This poet, as he is catholic in faith and argument, eminent for eloquence and truth, and most elegant in the variety of his works and metres, with so great sweetness quickly pleased the palate of his heart, that at once, with greater avidity than can be expressed, he drank up not only the knowledge of the outer word, but even the marrow of the innermost meaning and purest nectar, if I may so say. Afterwards there was no branch of liberal study in all Greek or Latin eloquence, that escaped the quickness of his genius. Nor indeed, as often happens, did the multitude of riches, or the insistency of clamouring crowds, nor any disgust otherwise coming over him, ever turn his mind from this noble employment of leisure. . . . Often he seated himself as a learned arbiter in the midst of the most learned Greek and Latin doctors, when they argued on the sublimity of philosophy or upon the subtility of any discipline flourishing within her, and gave satisfaction to the disputants, amid universal plaudits, than which he cared for nothing less." [1]

One may read between these awkward lines that all this learning was something to which Bruno had been introduced at school. Another short passage shows how new and strange this Latin culture seemed, and how he approached it with a timorous seriousness natural to one who did not well understand what it all meant :

"The buffoonery and mimic talk in comedies and tragedies, which cause such laughter when recited by a number of people, he would always read seriously ; he took small count of the matter, but chiefly of authority, in literary compositions." [2]

Such an attitude would have been impossible for an

---

panion. Nor did I worry, asking who will read it ; since I knew me for its reader, and as its lover, if it had none other " (*Praeloq.* vi. 26 ; Migne 136, col. 342). On Ratherius see Ebert, *Ges. der Lit.* iii. 375 *sqq.*

[1] *Vita Brunonis*, caps. 4, 6.   [2] *Vita Brunonis*, cap. 8.

Italian cradled amid Latin or quasi-Latin speech and reminiscence.

The most curious if not original literary phenomenon of the time of Bruno and his great brother was the nun Hrotsvitha of Gandersheim, a Saxon cloister supported by the royal Saxon house. The Abbess was a niece of the Emperor, and it was she who introduced Hrotsvitha to the Latin Classics, after the completion of her elementary studies under another *magistra*, likewise an inmate of the convent. The account bears witness to the taste for Latin reading among this group of noble Saxon dames. Hrotsvitha soon surpassed the rest, at least in productivity, and became a prolific authoress. She composed a number of sacred *legendae*, in leonine or rhymed hexameters.[1] One of them gave the legend of the Virgin, as drawn from the Apocryphal Gospel of Matthew. She also wrote several *Passiones* or accounts of the martyrdoms of saints, and the story of the Fall and Repentance of Theophilus, the oldest poetic version of a compact with the devil. Quite different in topic was the Deeds of Otto I. (*De gestis Oddonis I. imperatoris*), written between 962 and 967, likewise in leonine hexameters. It told the fortunes of the Saxon house as well as the career of its greatest member.

Possibly more interesting were six moral dramas written in formal imitation of the *Comedies* of Terence. As an antidote to the poison of the latter, they were to celebrate the virtue of holy virgins in this same kind of composition which had flaunted the adulteries of lascivious women—so, the preface explains. Again, Hrotsvitha's sources were *legenda*, in which Christian chastity, martyred though it be, triumphs with no uncertain note of victory.[2] These pious imitations of the impious Terence do not appear to have been imitated by other mediaeval writers : they exerted no influence upon the later development of the Mystery Play. They remain as evidence of the writer's courage, and of the studies of certain denizens of the cloister at Gandersheim.

Besides this convent for high-born women, and such

---

[1] Cf. *post*, Chapter XXXIII. III.

[2] On Hrotsvitha and her works see Ebert, *Allgem. Ges. der Lit.* iii. 285-329. H. J. W. Tillyard and Christopher St. John have made translations of her plays.

monasteries as Fulda and St. Gall, an interesting centre of introduced learning was Hildesheim, fortunate in its bishops, who made it an oasis of culture in the north. Otwin, bishop in 954, supplied its school with books from Italy. Some years after him came that great hearty man, Bernward, of princely birth, who began his clerical career at an early age, and was made bishop in 992. For thirty years he ruled his see with admirable piety, energy, and judgment ; qualities which he likewise showed in affairs of State. He was a diligent student of Latin letters, one " who conned not only the books in the monastery, but others in divers places, from which he formed a goodly library of codices of the divines and also the philosophers." [1] His was a master's faculty and a master-hand, itself skilfully fashioning ; for not only did he build the beautiful cloister church of St. Michael at Hildesheim, and cause it to be sumptuously adorned, but he himself carved and painted, and set gems. Some of the excellent works of his hand remain to-day. His biographer tells of that munificence and untiring zeal which rendered Hildesheim beautiful, as one still may see. Yet, throughout, Bernward appears as consciously studying and gathering and bringing to his beloved church an art from afar and a learning which was not of his own people. The bronze work on the Bernward column in Hildesheim is thought to suggest an influence of Trajan's column, while the doors of Bernward's church unquestionably follow those of St. Sabina on the Aventine. This shows how Bernward noticed and learned and copied during his stay at Rome in the year 1001, when Otto III. was imperator and Gerbert was pope.

Bernward's successor, Godehard, continued the good work. One of his letters closes with a quick appeal for books : " Mittite nobis librum Horatii et epistolas Tullii." [2] Belonging to the same generation was Froumundus (fl. cir. 1040), a monk of Tegernsee, where Godehard had been abbot before becoming bishop of Hildesheim. He was a sturdy German lover of the classics—very German. At one

---

[1] *Vita Bernwardi*, 6 (Migne 140, col. 397), by Thangmar, who was Bernward's teacher and outlived him to write his Life.

[2] Migne 141, col. 1229.

time he writes for a copy of Horace, apparently to complete
his own, and at another for a copy of Statius ; other letters
refer to Juvenal and Persius.[1] His ardour for study is as
apparent as the fact that he is learning a literature to which
he was not born. His turgid hexameters sweat with effort
to master the foreign language and metre. People would
have made a priest of him ; not he :

" Cogere me certant, fatear, quod sim sapiens vir,"

and a good grin seems to escape him :

" Discere decrevi libros, aliosque docere :

from such work no difficulty shall repel me ; be it my reward to be
co-operator (*synergus*) with what almighty God grants to flourish
in this time of Christ, or in the time of yore." [2]

The spirit is grand, the literary result awful. With
diligence, the studious *élite* of Germany applied themselves
to Latin letters. And in the course of time tremendous
scholars were to rise among them. But the Latin culture
remained a thing of study ; its foreign tongue was never as
their own ; and in the eleventh century, at least, they used
it with a painful effort that is apparent in their writings
and the Germanisms abounding in them. There may come
one like Lambert of Hersfeld, the famous annalist of the
Hildebrandine epoch, who with exceptional gifts gains a
good mastery of Latin, and writes with a conscious approach
to quasi-classical correctness. The place of his birth and the
sources of his education are unknown. He was thirty years
old, and doubtless had obtained his excellent training in
Latin, when he took the cowl in the cloister of Hersfeld
in 1058. But the next year he made a pilgrimage to
Jerusalem, and afterwards other journeys. He wrote his
Annals [3] in his later years, laying down his pen in 1077,
when he had brought the Emperor to Canossa. His was a
practised hand, and his style the evident result of much

---

[1] See Froumundus, *Ep.* 9, 11, 13 (Migne 141, col. 1288 *sqq.*). A number of
his poems are published by F. Seiler, *Zeitschrift für deutsche Philologie*, Bd. 14,
pp. 406-442.
[2] Migne 141, col. 1292. I am not sure that I have caught Froumund's meaning.
[3] *Mon. Ger. Scriptores*, v. 134 *sqq.* (Migne, *Pat. Lat.* 146, col. 1027 *sqq.*).

study of the classics. His work remains the best piece of Latin from an eleventh-century German.

Among German scholars of the period, one can find no more charming creature than Hermann Contractus, the lame or paralytic. His father, a Suabian count, brought the little cripple to the convent of Reichenau. It was in the year 1020. Hermann was seven years old. There he studied and taught, and loved his fellows, till his death thirty-four years later. His mind was as strong as his body was weak. He could not rise from the movable seat on which his attendant placed him, and could scarcely sit up. He enunciated with difficulty ; his words were scarcely intelligible. But his learning was encyclopaedic, his sympathies were broad : " Homo revera sine querela nihil humani a se alienum putavit," says a loving pupil who sketched his life. Evil was foreign to his nature. Affectionate, cheerful, happy, his sweet and engaging personality drew all men's love, while his learning attracted pupils from afar.

" At length, after he had been labouring for ten days in a grievous pleurisy, God's mercy saw fit to free his holy soul from prison. I who was his familiar above the rest," says the biographer, " came to his couch at dawn of day, and asked him whether he was not feeling a little better. ' Do not ask me,' he replied, ' but rather listen to what I have to tell you. I shall die very soon and shall not recover : so to thee and all my friends I commend my sinful soul. This whole night I have been rapt in ecstasy. With such complete memory as we have for the Lord's Prayer, I seemed to be reading over and over Cicero's *Hortensius*, and likewise to be scanning the substance and very written pages of what I intended to write Concerning the Vices—just as if I had it already written. I am so stirred and lifted by this reading, that the earth and all pertaining to it and this mortal life are despicable and tedious ; while the future everlasting world and the eternal life have become such an unspeakable desire and joy, that all these transitory circumstances are inane—nothing at all. It wearies me to live.' " [1]

Was not this a scholar's vision ? The German dwarf cares for the *Hortensius* even as Augustine, from whose *Confessions* doubtless came the recommendation of this

[1] *Vita Hermanni* (Migne 143, col. 29).

classic. The barbarous Latin of the *Vita* is so uncouth and
unformed as to convey no certain grammatical meaning.
One can only sense it. The biographer cannot write Latin
correctly, nor write it glibly and ungrammatically, like a
man born to a Latinesque speech. Hermann's own Latin
is but little better. It approaches neither fluency nor style.
But the scholar ardour was his, and his works remain—a
long chronicle, a treatise on the Astrolabe, and one on
Music ; also, perhaps, a poem in leonine elegiacs, " The
Dispute of the Sheep and the Flax," which goes on for several
hundred lines till one comes to a welcome *caetera desunt.*[1]

Thus, with a heavy-footed Teutonic diligence, the
Germans studied the Trivium and Quadrivium. They
sweated at Latin grammar, reading also the literature or the
stock passages. Their ignorance of natural science was no
denser than that of peoples west of the Rhine or south of
the Alps. Many of them went to learn at Chartres or
Paris. Within the mapped-out scheme of knowledge, there
was too much for them to master to admit of their devising
new provinces of study. They could not but continue for
many decades translators of the foreign matter into their
German tongue or German selves. In the twelfth and
thirteenth centuries they will be translators of the French
and Provençal literatures.

Even before the eleventh century, Germans were at work
at Logic—one recalls Gerbert's opponent Otric ; [2] and some
of them were engaged with dialectic and philosophy.
William, Abbot of Hirschau, crudely anticipated Anselm in
attempting a syllogistic proof of God's existence.[3] He died
in 1091, and once had been a monk in the convent of St.
Emmeram at Ratisbon in Bavaria, where he may have
known a certain monk named Othloh, who has left a unique
disclosure of himself. One is sufficiently informed as to
what the Germans and other people studied in the eleventh
century ; but this man has revealed the spiritual conflict
out of which he hardly brought his soul's peace.

---

[1] The writings of Hermannus Contractus are in Migne, *Pat. Lat.* 143. The
poem is reprinted from Du Meril's *Poésies populaires* ; a more complete text is in
Bd. XI. of the *Zeitschrift für deutsches Altertum.*
[2] *Ante*, p. 291 *sqq.*   [3] Prantl, *Ges. Logik*, ii. 83.

I[1]

Nothing is so fascinating in the life of a holy man as the struggle and crisis through which his convictions are established and his peace attained. How diverse has been this strife—with Buddha, with Augustine, with Luther, or Ignatius Loyola. Its heroes fall into two companies : in one of them the man attains through his own thought and resolution ; in the other he casts himself on God, and it may be that devils and angels carry on the fight, of which his soul is the battle-ground and prize. Nevertheless, the man himself holds the scales of victory ; the choice is his, and it is he who at last goes over to the devil or accepts the grace of God. This conflict, in which God is felt to aid, is still for men ; only its forms and setting change. Therefore the struggle and the tears, through which souls have won their wisdom and their peace, never cease to move us. Othloh, like many another mediaeval scholar, was disturbed over the sinful pleasure derived from Tully and Virgil, Naso and Lucan. But his soul's chief turmoil came from the doubts that sprang from his human sympathies and from moral grounds—can the Bible be true and God omnipotent when sin and misery abound ? The struggle through which he became assured was the supreme experience of his life : it fixed his thoughts ; his writings were its fruit ; they reflect the struggle and the struggler, and present a psychological tableau of a mediaeval German soul.

He was born in the bishopric of Freising in Bavaria not long after the year 1000, and spent his youth in the monastic schools of Tegernsee and Hersfeld. His scholarship was made evident to men about him through his skill in copying texts in a beautiful script, ornamented with illuminations. In the year 1032 he took the monk's vows in the monastery of St. Emmeram at Ratisbon, which had been founded long before in honour of this sainted Frankish missionary bishop, who had met a martyr's death in Bavaria in the late Merovingian period. The annals of the monastery are extant. When the Ottos were emperors, grammatical and theological studies flourished there, especially under a

certain capable Wolfgang, who died as Bishop of Ratisbon in
994, and whose life Othloh wrote. The latter, on becoming
a monk, received charge of the monastery school, which he
continued to direct for thirty years.[1] Then he left, because
some of the young monks had turned the Abbot against him;
but after some years spent mainly at the monastery of Fulda,
he returned to St. Emmeram's in 1063, where he died an
old man ten or fifteen years later. From his youth he had
been subject to illness, even to fits of swooning, and, writing
in the evening of his days, he speaks of his many bodily
infirmities.

As Othloh looked back over his life, his soul's crisis
seemed to have been reached soon after he was made a
monk. The wisdom brought through it came as the
answer to those questionings which made up the diabolic
side of that great experience. Othloh describes it in his
Book concerning the Temptations of a certain Monk:

" There was a sinful clerk, who, having often been corrected by
the Lord, at last turned to the monastic life. In the monastery
where he was made a monk he found many sorts of men, some of
whom were given over to the reading of secular works, while some
read Holy Scripture. He resolved to imitate the latter. The
more earnest he was in this, the more was he molested by temptations of the devil ; but committing himself to the grace of God,
he persevered ; and when, after a long while, he was delivered,
and thought over what he had suffered, it seemed that others
might be edified by his temptations, as well as by the passages
of Holy Scripture which had come to him through divine inspiration. So he began to write as follows : I wish to tell the delusions
of Satan which I endured sleeping and waking. His deceits first
confounded me with doubt as to whether I was not rash in taking
the vow perilous of the monastic life, without consulting parents
or friends, when Scripture bids us ' do all things with counsel.'
Diabolic illusion, as if sympathizing and counselling with me,
brought these and like thoughts. When, the grace of God resisting him, the Tempter failed to have his way with me here,
he tried to make me despair because of my many sins. ' Do you
think,' said he, ' that such a wretch can expect mercy from God
the Judge, when it is written, Scarcely shall a righteous man be
saved ? ' So he overwhelmed me, till I could no nothing but

[1] Cf. Endres, " Othloh's von St. Emmeram Verhältnis zu den freien Kunsten,"
Philos. Jahrbuch, 1904.

weep, and tears were my bread day and night. I protest, from
my innermost heart, that save through the grace of God alone,
no one can overcome such delusions.

"When the Weaver of wiles failed to cause me utterly to
despair, he tried with other arguments of guile to lead me to
blaspheme the divine justice, suggesting thoughts, as if condoling
with my misery : ' O most unhappy youth, whose grief no man
deigns to consider—but men are not to blame, for they do not
know your trouble. God alone knows, and since He can do all
things, why does He not aid you in tribulation, when for love of
Him you have surrendered the world and now endure this agony ?
Have done with impossible prayers and foolish grief. The
injustice of that Potentate will not permit all to perish.' These
delusions were connected with what I now wish to mention :
Often I was awakened by some imaginary signal, and would
hasten to the oratory before the time of morning prayer ; also,
and for a number of years, though I slept at night as a man
sound in body, when the hour came to rise, my limbs were numb,
and only with uncertain trembling step could I reach the Church.

" One delusion and temptation must be spoken of, which I
hardly know how to describe, as I never read or heard of anything
like it. By the stress of my many temptations I was driven—
though by God's grace I was never utterly torn from faith and
hope of heavenly aid—to doubt as to Holy Scripture and the
essence of God himself. In the struggle with the other temptations there was some respite, and a refuge of hope remained.
In this I knew no alleviation, and when formerly I had been
strengthened by the sacred book and had fought against the darts
of death with the arms of faith and hope, now, shut round with
doubt and mental blindness, I doubted whether there was truth
in Holy Scripture and whether God was omnipotent. This broke
over me with such violence as to leave me neither strength of
body nor strength of mind, and I could not see or hear. Then
sometimes it was as if a voice was whispering close to my ear :
' Why such vain labourings ? Can you not, most foolish of
mortals, prove by your own experience that the testimony of
Scripture is without sense or reason ? Do you not see that what
the divine book says is the reverse of what the lives and habits
of mankind approve ? Those many thousands who neither.
know nor care to know its doctrine, do you think they err ? '
Troubled, I would urge, as if against some one questioning and
objecting : ' How then is there such agreement among all the
divinely inspired writings when they speak of God the Founder
and of obedience to His commands ? ' Then words of this kind
would be suggested in reply : ' Fool, the Scriptures on which
you rely for knowledge of God and religion speak double words ;

for the men who wrote them lived as men live now. You know
how all men speak well and piously, and act otherwise, as advantage or frailty prompts. From which you may learn how the
authors of the ancient writings wrote good and religious sayings,
and did not live accordingly. Understand then, that all the
books of the divine law were so written that they have an outer
surface of piety and virtue, but quite another inner meaning.
All of which is proved by Paul's saying, The letter killeth ; the
spirit, that is the meaning, maketh to live. So you see how
perilous it is to follow the precepts of these books. Likewise
should one think concerning the essence of God. And besides,
if there existed any person or power of an omnipotent God there
would not be this apparent confusion in everything,—nor would
you yourself have had all these doubts which trouble you.' "

The last diabolically insidious suggestion was just the
one to bring despair to the unaided reason seeking faith.
Othloh's soul was passing through the depths ; but the path
now ascends, and rapidly :

" I was assaulted with an incredible number of these delusions,
and so strange and unheard of were they that I feared to speak of
them to any of the brothers. At last I threw myself upon the
ground groaning in bitterness, and, collecting the forces of my
mind, I cried with my lips and from my heart : ' O if thou art
some one, Almighty, and if thou art everywhere, as I have read
so often in so many books, now, I pray, show me whom thou art
and what thou canst do, delivering me quickly from these perils ;
I can bear this strife no more.' I did not have to wait ; the grace
of God scattered the whole cloud of doubt, and such a light of
knowledge poured into my heart that I have never since had to
endure the darkness of deadly doubt. I began to understand
what I had scarcely perceived before. Then the grace of knowledge was so increased that I could no longer hide it. I was urged
by ineffable impulse to undertake some work of gratitude for the
glory of God, and it seemed that this new ardour should be devoted to composition. So I wrote what I have written concerning
those diabolic delusions which sprang from my sins, and then
it seemed reasonable to tell of the divine inspiration by which
my mind was enabled to repel them ; so that he who reads these
delusions may at the same time know the workings of the divine
aid, and not ascribe to me a victory which was never mine, or,
thinking that aid was lacking in my temptation, fear lest it fail
in his. I remember how often, especially on rising in the mornings,
it was as if there was some one rising with me and walking with
me, who mutely warned, or gently persuaded me to amend faults

which it may be only the day before 1 was ignorantlv committing
and deeming of no consequence.

" When surrounded by such inspirations I would enter the
Church and bow down in prayer—God knows that I do not lie—
it seemed as if some one besought me with like earnestness of
prayer, saying : ' As that has been granted which you asked of
me, it will be precious to me if you will obey my entreaties.   Do
you not continue in those vices which I have often begged you
to abandon ? are you not proud and carnal, neglectful of God's
service, hating whom you should not hate, although the Scripture
says, Every one who hates his brother is a murderer ?   Where
now is the patience and constancy and that perfection which you
promised God, if He would deliver you from perils and make you
a monk ?   God has done as you asked, why do you delay to pay
your vow ?   You have asked Him to set you in a place where
you would have a store of books.   Lo, you have been heard ;
you have books—from which you may learn of life eternal.
Why do you dissipate your mind in vanities and do not hasten
to take the desired gift ?   You have also asked to be tried, and
tried you have been in temptation, and delivered.   Yet you are
still a man unfit for peace or war, since when the battle is far off
you are ready for it, and when it approaches you flee.   Which
of the holy fathers that you have read of in the Old or New
Testament was so dear to me that I did not seek to try him in the
furnace of tribulation ?   Blessed are those who suffer persecution
for righteousness' sake.   Steep and narrow is the way ; no one is
crowned who has not striven lawfully.   When you have read
these, and many more passages of Scripture, why if you desire a
crown of life eternal, do you wish to suffer no tribulation for your
sins ? ' "

Then the Spirit of God, with many admonishings, shows
Othloh how easy had been his lot and how needful to him
were his temptations, even the very carnal temptations of the
flesh, which Othloh suffered in common with all monks.
And he is bid to consider their reason and order :

" First you were tried with lighter trials, that gradually you
might gain strength for the weightier ; as you progressed you
ascribed to your own strength what was wrought by my grace.
Wherefore I subjected you to the final temptation, from which
you will emerge the more certain of my grace the less you trust
in your merits."

The " warring opposites " of Othloh's spiritual struggle
were, on the one side, evil thoughts and delusions from the

devil, and, on the other, the strength and enlightenment imparted by the grace of God. The nearer the crisis comes, the clearer are the devil's whisperings and the warnings of the instructing voice. Othloh's part in it was his choice and acceptance of the divine counsellor. This conflict never faded from his mind. He has much to say of the visions[1] in which parts of his enlightenment had come. Once reading Lucan in the monastery, he swooned, and in his swoon was beaten with many stripes by a man of terrible and threatening countenance. By this he was led to abandon profane reading and other worldly vanities. These visionary floggings left him feeble and ill in body. They were the approaches to his great spiritual conflict. His "fourth vision" is in and of the crisis. This monk, immersed in spiritual struggles, had also his opinions regarding the government of the monastery, and for a time refused obedience to the abbot's irregular rulings, and spoke harshly of him:

"For this I did penance before the abbot but not before God, against whom I had greatly sinned; and after a few days I fell sick. This sickness was from God, since I have always begged of His mercy, that for any sin committed I might suffer sickness or tribulation, and so it has come to me. On this occasion, when weakness had for some days kept me in the infirmary, one evening as it was growing dark I thought I should feel better if I rose and sat by my cot. Immediately the house appeared to be filled with flame and smoke. Horror-stricken, my wonted trust in God all scattered, I started, tottering, towards the cot of the lay brother in charge, but, ashamed, I turned back and went to the cot of a brother who was sick; he was asleep. Then I sank exhausted on my cot, thinking how to escape the horror of that vision of smoke. I had no doubt that the smoke was the work of evil spirits, who, from its midst, would try to torment me. As I gradually saw that it was not physical, but of the spirit, and that there was no one to help me, as all were asleep, I began to sing certain psalms, and, singing, went out and entered the nearest church, of St. Gallus, and fell down before the altar. At once, for my sins, strength of mind and body left me, and I perceived that my lips were held together by evil spirits, so that I could not move them, to sing a psalm. I tried till I was weary to open them with my hands.

"Leaving that church, crawling rather than walking I gained

---

[1] *Liber visionum.*

the great church of St. Emmeram, where I hoped for some alleviation of my agony.   But it was as before ; I could barely utter a
few words of prayer.   So I painfully made my way back to my
bed, hoping, from sheer weariness, to get some sleep.   But none
came, and, turn as I would, still I saw the vision of smoke.
Suddenly—was I asleep or awake ?—I seemed to be in a field well
known to me, surrounded by a crowd of demons mocking me with
shrieks of laughter.   The louder they laughed, the sadder I was,
seeing them gathered to destroy me.   When they saw that I
would not laugh, they became enraged, crying, ' So ! you won't
laugh and be merry with us !   Since you choose melancholy
you shall have enough.'   Then flying about me, with blows from
all sides, they whirled me round and round with them over vast
spaces of earth, till I thought to die.   Suffering unspeakably, I
was at length set down on the top of a peak which scarcely held
me ; no eye could fathom its abyss.   Vainly I looked for a descent,
and the demons kept flying about me, saying : ' Where now is
your hope in God !   And where is that God of yours !   Don't
you know that neither God is, as men say, nor is there any power
in Him which can prevail against us ?   One proof of this is that
you have no help, and there is no one who can deliver you from
our hands.   Choose now ; for unless you join with us you shall
be cast into the abyss.'   In this strait, scarcely consenting or
resisting, I faintly remembered that I had once believed and read
that God was everywhere, and so I looked around to see whether
He would not send some aid.   Now when the demons kept insisting that I should choose, and when I was well-nigh put to
it to promise what they wished, a man suddenly appeared, and,
standing by me, said : ' Do not do it ; all that these cheats say is
false.   Abide firm in that faith which you had in God.   He knows
all that you suffer, and permits it for your good.'   Then he
vanished, and the demons returned, flying about me, and saying :
' Miserable man, would you trust one who came to deceive you ?
Why, he dared not wait till we came !   Come now, yield yourself
to our power.'
  " Uttering these words with fury, they snatched me up, and
whirled me, sorely beaten, across plains and deserts, over heights
and precipices, and set me on a yet more dreadful peak, hurling at
me abuse and threats, to make me do their will.   And, as before,
I was near succumbing, and was looking around for some aid from
God, when that same man again stood near, and heartened me.
' Do not yield ; let your heart be comforted against its besiegers.'
And I replied : ' Lord, I can no longer bear these perils.   Stay
with me, and aid, lest when you go away they torment me still
more grievously.'   To which he said :   Their threats cannot
prevail so long as you persevere in faith and hope in the Lord.

Be comforted ; the sharper the strife, the quicker will it end. If with constancy you wage the Lord's battles, you shall have eternal rewards in the future, and in this world you shall be famous.'

"Then he vanished the second time, and the demons, who dared do nothing in his presence, raged and mocked more savagely, and kept me in anguish, until, the divine grace effecting it, the convent bell rang for early prayer. I heard it as I lay in bed, and gradually gaining my senses, I was conscious that I was living, and I no longer saw the vision of smoke. With gratitude I remembered what the man in my vision told me that my trial would soon be over. After this, though for many days I lay sick in body and soul, my spiritual temptations began to lessen ; and I have learned that without the Grace of God I am, and always shall be, a thing of naught."

The struggle through which faith and peace came to Othloh became the fountain-head of his wisdom ; it fixed the point of view from which he judged life, and set the categories in which he ordered his knowledge ; it directed his thoughts and imparted purpose and unity to his writings. His gratitude to God incited him to write in order that others might share in the light and wisdom which God's grace had granted him ; and his writings chiefly enlarge upon those questions which the victory in his spiritual conflict had solved. I will refrain from drawing further from them, although they seem to me the most interesting works of a pious and doctrinal nature emanating from any German of this still crude and inchoate intellectual period.[1]

III

From the point of view of the development of mediaeval intellectual interests in the eleventh century, England has little that is distinctive to offer. The firm rule of Canute (1016–1035) brought some reinstatement of order, after the times of struggle between Dane and Saxon. But his son, Hardicanute, was a savage. The reign of Edward the Confessor (1042–1066) followed. It wears a halo because it was the end of the old order, which henceforth was to be a memory. Then came the revolution of the Norman Conquest.

[1] Othloh's works are all in tome 146 of Migne's *Patrologia Latina.*

Letters did not thrive amid these storms.   At the beginning
of the period, Dunstan is the sole name of note, as one who
fostered letters in the monasteries where his energies were
bringing discipline.   English piety and learning looked
then, as it had looked before and was for centuries to look,
to the Continent.   And Dunstan promoted letters by calling
to his assistance Abbo of St. Fleury, of whom something
has been said.[1]

In Dunstan's time Saxon men were still translating
Scripture into their tongue—paraphrasing it rather, with a
change of spirit.   Such translations were needed in Anglo-
Saxon England, as in Germany.   But after the Conquest
the introduction of Norman-French tended to lessen at
least the consciousness of such a need.   That language, as
compared with Anglo-Saxon, came so much nearer to Latin
as to reduce the chasm between the learned tongue and the
vernacular.   The Normans had (at least in speech) been
Gallicized, and yet had kept many Norse traits.   England
likewise took on a Gallic veneering as Norman-French
became the language of the Court and the new nobility.
But the people continued to speak English.   The degree of
foreign influence upon their thought and manners may be
gauged by the proportion of foreign idiom penetrating the
English language ; and the fact that English remained
essentially and structurally English proves the same for
England racially.   In spite of the introduction of foreign
elements, people and language endured and became more
and more distinctively English.

In the island before the Conquest, the round of studies
had been the same as on the Continent ; and that event
brought no change.   The studies might improve, but would
have no novel source to draw upon.   And in this period
of racial turmoil and revolution, it was unlikely that the
Anglo-Saxon temperament would present itself as clearly as
aforetime in the Saxon poem of *Beowulf* or the personality
of the Saxon Alfred, or in the Saxon *Genesis* and the
writings of Cynewulf.[2]   In a word, the eleventh century
in England was specifically the period when the old
traits were becoming obscure, and no distinct modifica-

---

[1] *Ante*, Chapter XII. II.   [2] *Ante*, Chapters VIII., IX.

tions had been evolved in correspondence with the new conditions. Consequently, for presentations of the intellectual genius of the English people, one has to wait until the next century, the time of John of Salisbury and other English minds. Even such will be found receiving their training and their knowledge in France and Italy. England was still intellectually as well as politically under foreign domination.

In every way it has been borne in upon us how radically the conditions and faculties of men differed in England, Germany, France, and Italy in the eleventh century. Very different were their intellectual qualities, and different also was the measure of their attainment to a palpable mediaeval character, which in Italy was not that of the ancient Latins, in France was not that of the Gallic provincials, and in England and Germany was not altogether that of the original Celtic and Teutonic stocks. Neither in the eleventh century nor afterwards was there an obliteration of race traits ; yet the mediaeval modification tended constantly to evoke a general uniformity of intellectual interest and accepted view.

There exists a certain ancient *Chronicon Venetum* written by a Venetian diplomat and man of affairs called John the Deacon, who died apparently soon after 1008.[1] He was the chaplain of the Doge, Peter Urseolus, and the doge's ambassador to the emperors Otto III. and Henry II. The earlier parts of his *Chronicon* were taken from Paulus Diaconus and others ; the later are his own, and form a facile narrative, which makes no pretence to philosophic insight and has nothing to say either of miracles or God's Christian providence. Its interests are quite secular. John writes his Latin, glib, clear, and unclassical, just as he might talk his Venetian speech, his *vulgaris eloquentia*. There is no effort, no struggle with the medium of expression, but a pervasive quality of familiarity with his story and with the language he tells it in. These characteristics, it is safe to say, are not to be found, to a like degree,

---

[1] Printed in Migne, *Pat. Lat.* 139, col. 871 *sqq.* and elsewhere. For editions see Wattenbach, *Deutschlands Geschichtsquellen*, 6th ed. i. 485.

in the work of any contemporary writer north of the Alps.

The man and his story, in fine, however mediocre they may be, have arrived : they are not struggling or apparently tending anywhither. The writing suggests no capacity in the writer as yet unreached, nor any imperfect blending of disparate elements in his education. One should not generalize too broadly from the qualities exemplified in this work ; yet they indicate that the people to which the writer belonged were possessed of a certain entirety of development, in which the component elements of culture and antecedent human growth and decadence were blended in accord. This old *Chronicon* affords an illustration of the fact that the transition and early mediaeval centuries had brought little to Italy that was new or foreign, little that was not in the blood, and little to disturb the continuity of Italian culture and character which moved along without break, whether in ascending or descending curves.

Yet evidently the eleventh-century Italian is no longer a Latin of the Empire. For one thing, he is more individualistic. Formerly the prodigious power of Roman government united citizens and subject peoples, and impressed a human uniformity upon them. The surplus energies of the Latin race were then absorbed in the functions of the *Respublica*, or were at least directed along common channels. That great unification had long been broken ; and the smaller units had reasserted themselves—the civic units of town or district, and the individual units of human beings upon whom no longer pressed the conforming influence of one great government.

In imperial times cities formed the subordinate units of the *Respublica* ; the Roman, like the Greek civilization, was essentially urban. This condition remained. The civilization of Italy in the eleventh century was still urban, but was now more distinctly the civilization of small closely compacted bodies, which were no longer united. For the most part, the life, the thought, of Italy was in the towns ; it remained predominantly humanistic, taken up with men and their mortal affairs, their joys and hates, and all that is developed by much daily intercourse with fellows. Thus the intellect of Italy continued secular, interesting itself in mortal life, and not so much occupied with theology and the life beyond the grave. This is as true of the intellectual energies of the Roman papacy as it is of the mental activities of the towns which served or opposed it, according to their politics.

On the other hand, the intense emotional nature of the Italians was apt to be religious, and given to despair and tears and ecstasy ; its love welled up and flung itself around its object, without the mediating offices of reason. If reflection came, it was love's ardent musing, rather than religious ratiocination. One does not forget that the Italians who became scholastic theologians or philosophers left Italy, and subjected themselves to northern spiritual influences at Paris or elsewhere. Their greatest were Anselm, Peter Lombard, Bonaventura, Thomas Aquinas. None of these remained through life altogether Italian.

Thus, with Italians, religion meant either the papal government and the daily conventions of observance and minor mental habits, all very secular ; or it meant that which was a thing of ecstasy and not of thought—generally speaking, of course. The mediaeval Italian (in the eleventh century only to a slightly less degree than in the twelfth or thirteenth) is, typically speaking, a man of urban human interests and affairs, a politician, a trader, a doctor, a man of law or letters, an artist, or a poet. If really religious, his religion is an emotion, and is not occupied with dogma, nor interested in doctrinal correctness or reform. Such a religious character may, according to individual temper, result in a Romuald [1] or a Peter Damiani ; its perfected ideal is Francis of Assisi.

Things were already different in the country now called France. No need to repeat what has been said as to the lesser strength and somewhat broken continuity of the antique there, as compared with Italy. Yet there was a sufficient power of antique influence and descent to keep the language Romanesque, and the forms of its literature partly set by antique tradition. But the spirit was not Latin

[1] *Post*, Chapter XVII.

Perhaps it had but seemed such with the Gallic provincials. At all events, the incoming Franks and other Germans brought a Teutonic infusion and reinspiration that forever kept France from being or becoming a northern Italy.

Neither was the spirit urban. To be sure, much of the energy of French thought awoke and did its work in towns; and Paris was to become the intellectual centre. But the stress of French life was not so surely in the towns, nor men's minds so characteristically urban as in Italy, and by no means so predominantly humanistic. Even in the eleventh century the lofty range of French thought, of French intellectual interests, is apparent; for it embraces the problems of philosophy and theology, and does not find its boundary and limit in phenomenal or mortal life. Gerbert is almost too universal an intellect to offer as a fair example. Yet all that he cared for is more than represented by somewhat younger men taken together; for Gerbert did not fully represent the interests of religious thought in France. His was the humanism and the thirst for all the round of knowledge included in the Seven Arts. But he scarcely reached out beyond logic to philosophy; and theology did not trouble him. Both philosophy and theology, however, made part of the intellectual interests of France; for there were Berengar and Roscellinus, Gaunilo and St. Anselm, and the wrangling of many disputatious, although overwhelmingly orthodox, councils of French Churchmen. Paris also, with its great schools of theology and philosophy, looms on the horizon. The intellectual matter is but inchoate, yet universally germinating, in the eleventh century.

Thus intellectual qualities of mediaeval France appear inceptively. The French mediaeval temperament needs perhaps another century for its clear development. Both as to temperament and intellectual interests, a line will have to be drawn between the south and north; between the land of the *langue d'oc*, the Roman law, the troubadour, and the easy, irreligious, gay society which jumped the life to come; and the land of the various old French dialects (among which that of the Isle de France will win to dominance), the land of philosophy and theology, the land of Gothic architecture and religion, the hearth of the crusades against the

Saracen or the Albigensian heretic ; the land of the most distinctive mediaeval thought and strongest intellectual development.

In the Germany and the England of the eleventh century there is less of interest from this point of view. England had scarcely become her mediaeval self ; the time was one of desperate struggle, or, at most, of tumultuous settling down and shaking together. As for Germany, it was surely German then, and not a medley of Saxon, Dane, and Norman-French. The people were talking in their German tongues. German song and German epos were already heard in forms which were not to be cast aside, but retained and developed ; of course the influence of the French poetry was not yet. The Germans were still living their own sturdy and half-barbarous life. Those who loved knowledge had turned with earnest purpose to the Latin culture ; they were studying Latin and logic, and, as we have said, translating it into their German tongue or temperament. But the lessons were not fully mastered—not yet transformed into German mediaeval intellectual capacity. And in this respect, at least, the German will become more entirely his Germanic mediaeval self in another century, when he has more faculty of using the store of foreign knowledge in combination with his strongly felt and honestly considered Christianity.

CHAPTER XIV

PHASES OF MEDIAEVAL GROWTH

I. THE CRUSADES.
II. TOWNS AND GUILDS.

I

THE Crusades may profitably be regarded as a phase in the mediaeval development, and at the same time as a chapter in the long story of the effect of the Orient upon the West. Eastern influences have always been complex, and historians have found difficulty in distinguishing their fruit from much that was more properly the product of the native and progressive energies of Europe. When and where do they begin? It is only our ignorance that would commence with the Phoenicians and their western voyages, or with the Greeks living under oriental influences on the islands or the coasts of Asia Minor. The data are subtile, intricate, ubiquitous, indistinguishable, especially from the time when Hellenism with its oriental elements becomes the informing spirit of taste and knowledge for the Latins. Christianity enters, also from the East, not Greek in origin, but passing westward through Hellenic media. If afterwards under the barbarization of the West, Hellenism seems to sink away, one knows that it had become very part of that Roman Christian civilization which was being barbarized. Through the following centuries the West according to its opportunities and capacities still draws from the East, styles of architecture for example, as at Ravenna, or at Lyons, or at Aix-la-Chapelle where the only surviving building of the Carolingian period is a replica of the Byzantine Church of St. Vitale at

Ravenna. Through the earlier Middle Ages Byzantine currents never ceased to affect church building and decoration, and in the twelfth century the great Byzantine mosaics bloom anew in Norman Sicily, while Venice rises from her lagoons half Byzantine, if still Italian.[1]

With the advance of life and wealth and industry and thought in the twelfth and thirteenth centuries the West became more efficiently receptive, and the currents from the East seem to take on new vigour; trade routes were thronged, cities were springing up along them, people were journeying farther, mental as well as physical horizons were expanding. Along those new routes, and into those new-grown cities, more wares were passing ; which also meant that more wares from the East were being carried westward in Genoese, Pisan, and Venetian bottoms, to where the land and river transport opened northerly and westerly through France, Germany, and the Low Countries. This is also the very time of those hostile counter-movements from West to East, known as the Crusades ; which resulted in some transient European advance on Asia, and then in greatly increased intercourse between the West and the Greek and Moslem East, with mutual assimilation of views and habits at the borders where Moslem and western Christian populations met and stained each other. A returning Asiatic invasion followed, destined for centuries to oppress the eastern half of Europe and wrest enormous territories from Christianity.

In their inception the Crusades were holy wars for the recovery of the Holy Land : they never entirely lost the religious motive. One must, however, be on guard against attaching too fine a meaning to the words " holy " and " religious." There always had been wars, and wars of conquest. With whom should wars be waged if not with hostile aliens of different faith ? Was the war against Attila in the fifth century other than a holy war against heathen ? And the wars of Charles Martel and Charlemagne, whether with Arabs toward the south, or with Saxons on the north and east, were they not holy wars, either to drive back the heathen, or conquer them and bring them within the pale of Frankish domination ? Con-

[1] Cf. C. Diehl, *Manuel d'art byzantin*, pp. 668-691 (Paris, 1910).

version by the sword was an essential part of this subjugation. When at the close of the eleventh century the heathen were not so close at hand in western Europe, the West began a series of distant holy wars. They were a result of all the conditions of the time, an expression of the social situation. The religious motive led, was indeed the torch which fired the whole train of feudal, economic, fanatical combustibles. All sorts of people joined ; the impecunious and the criminal ; the religious and the adventurous, surplus younger sons and great feudal lords and princes whose territories would have been the better for the master's hand at home. Many a fief was pledged to equip the baron and his men on this far war which would yield him adventure and the joy of battle, win him eastern lands and slaves and plunder, and bring him salvation when he fell.

Jerusalem was won and held for eighty years (1099–1181). And when it was lost, the " Franks," as the East called them, with Venetians and Genoese who had aided in the business, still held the line of trading towns along the coast of Syria, while the sea-power and commercial marine also remained in Christian hands. More Crusaders from the West launched themselves upon the Moslem. With some the fiercest motive was still to win Jerusalem—a holy motive in that holiest of mediaeval kings, St. Louis, who died at Tunis on his second Crusade. Yet politics and commerce had gradually become dominant with Crusaders ; and the conduct of the enterprises became more completely lay. From the time of Urban II.'s great preaching at Clermont in 1095 the popes had not ceased to urge the holy war ; and the furtherance of these enterprises had provided opportunity for their interference in the affairs of king and count and baron throughout Christian lands. Incitements, promises, threats, and excommunications, employed for this holy end, strengthened the powers of the papacy. Yet the control of the Crusades at length passed from papal hands. Innocent III., perhaps the most powerful of all the popes, failed to retain it. The Venetians beat him : in opposition to his will, in the face of his excommunications, they turned the crusading force against the island of Zara for their private ends ; and then Venetians, Frenchmen, Flemings united in

the capture of—Constantinople ! And the pope acquiesced.[1]
This was in 1204. Some twenty-five years later the excommunicated Emperor Frederic II. obtained Jerusalem,
with many commercial advantages, by treaty from the
Saracens ; and while he was entering the Holy City, the
soldiers of Pope Gregory IX. were invading his dominions in
Italy.

So the management of the Crusades, even as their
motives and results, became political and commercial. At
all events their effects on western Europe pertained entirely
to this world—unless the increase of the papal power be
deemed an other-worldly fact. One may imagine what
sudden expansion of Mediterranean shipping was evoked
by the repeated call to transport and victual and support
armies upon armies from the West. If men and horses
sometimes went by land (commonly to their destruction)
supplies were still transported from Marseilles or Genoa or
Venice. Only such powerful maritime republics could cope
with these emergencies and profit by them.

Yet those Italian maritime republics were rapidly rising
in power and prosperity irrespective of the opportunity for
trade-expansion brought by the Crusades. Indeed, viewing
the industrial advance, the growth of cities, the increase
in wealth as well as knowledge, marking the twelfth and
thirteenth centuries, one is tempted to regard not only the
Crusades themselves, but even their effect upon the West,
as very part of these progressive conditions. It was not the
paynim East that sent its wares, customs, knowledge, to
the West ; the West came and got what the East had to
offer, acting as discoverer, appropriator, and carrier of these
matters. Asia has rarely sent its wares to Europe ; Europe
has ever gone to fetch them.

So indeed one will hesitate to regard the Crusades as the
cause of an advance in European civilization. Here as
always it is safer to speak of the conditions and the many
causes making for such an advance. Viewed in their results
the Crusades were partially successful attempts on the part
of a feudal society to conquer and colonize : they represent

[1] See the whole story admirably told by A. Luchaire, *Innocent III.. la
question d'Orient* (Paris, 1907).

also the rising commercial energies of western Europe, expanding through the eastern Mediterranean and the surrounding lands, then pushing backwards more vigorously through the west, along old routes or new, planting fresh cities, feeding the growth of old ones and through exchange of wares increasing the effective wealth of every land. In turn, conquest, colonization, trade expansion, with stimulated cupidity and curiosity, led to an increase of knowledge of the earth and its peoples. If the Arabs contributed from their (borrowed) stores of astronomy, mathematics, and medicine, still larger was the passive role held by the Orient in the advance of European culture. Through the Crusades the western peoples came in contact with a civilization different from their own ; new fields of study were suggested, the oriental languages for example ; from which of course many words passed into the western tongues, just as new plants and fruits and hand-made wares passed westward,— but in European bottoms. The Crusades also did not fail to inspire literature. The *Historia transmarina* of William of Tyre [1] is second to no other history in the Middle Ages ; the *Cycle of the Crusades* enriched the store of narrative poetry, while ever and anon the soul of lyric genius was moved by longing for that far holy enterprise whose symbol was the Cross. [2]

II

Towns and guilds in the Middle Ages were the creatures of the mediaeval faculty of industrial association. Their growth represents the means as well as measure of the civic and industrial advance which swept, with constantly enlarging currents, from the opening of the twelfth century on through the thirteenth and into the fourteenth, till checked by the Hundred Years' War between France and England and the coming of the Black Death. The need of privileged exemption from the exactions of the feudal lord

---

[1] Migne, *Patrologia Latina*, tome 201.

[2] See *post*, p. 553 *sqq.*; also the Crusader's song of Hartmann von Aue, *post*, p. 365, or the yearning of Walter von der Vogelweide, *post*, Chapter XXVII. The article by Ernest Barker on the Crusades in the eleventh edition of the *Encyclopaedia Britannica* is excellent.

was the basic *raison d'être* of the town in France, England, Germany, if not in Italy. The guild was the closer protective association of merchants or craftsmen. With the twelfth century both the one and the other seem to spring into being.[1] Their quick development was due to contemporary conditions ; and one gains scant explanation of these chief manifestations of the industrial energies of the twelfth and thirteenth centuries by attempting to explore their antecedents.

In ways complex and obscure beyond the possibility of exposition, that intricate ensemble of personal protection (or oppression) and dependency known as the feudal system established itself, apparently destroying and superseding the civic institutions of the Roman Empire. In France, Germany, England, where the old site and decaying walls still held some huddled denizens, hardly a vestige of municipal organization remained to differentiate the status of these denizens from other serfs or freemen of the land. In the twelfth century the population of the old urban centres increased ; and many new towns of moderate size arose. The industrial class which stocked them, increasing with growing trade and improving handicraft, needed personal freedom and protection for the fruits of industry. Associated effort was the means by which these traders and artisans were to attain this end. Such protective association took the forms of towns and guilds, advancing toward municipal independence or corporate coherency. This came about in many different ways ; and even within the

[1] A. Luchaire, in his Introduction to *Les Communes françaises* (1890), speaks thus : " En France, comme dans la plupart des régions de l'Europe féodale, les institutions populaires se sont développées assez tardivement. Sauf de rares exceptions, le peuple urbain et rural n'a pas d'histoire avant le début du XII⁰ siècle. C'est alors seulement que les actes d'affranchissement, les concessions de libertés, les chartes de commune deviennent assez nombreux pour forcer l'attention des classes privilégiées et leur apprendre que la couche inférieure de la société, surgissant des bas-fonds du servage, demande sa place au soleil, ose même aspirer à l'existence politique. Mais si le peuple n'entre en scène qu'après l'Église et la noblesse, il se dédommage rapidement du temps perdu. Le XII⁰ et le XIII⁰ siècle ont vu se produire ce mouvement merveilleux d'émancipation qui donna la liberté aux serfs, créa les bourgeoisies privilégiées et les communes indépendantes, fit sortir de terre les villes neuves et les bastides, affranchit les corporations de marchands et d'ouvriers, en un mot plaça du premier coup, à côté de la royauté, de la féodalité et de l'Église, une quatrième force sociale destinée à absorber un jour les trois autres."

same country at the same time there were stages and varieties of urban organization. The corporate existence of the town was based on privileged exemption ;[1] industrial monopoly was its aim and the aim of any merchant guild or craft guilds within it.

Let us imagine a feudal seignory at some time prior to the twelfth century, somewhere say in the heart of the present France. It covers many miles of territory. Probably there is a central stronghold of the lord. Within or around it may be groups of men, or families, engaged in some sort of productive labour, perhaps combined with trade. Many of them may be serfs, or if freemen there will still be scant restriction on the lord's seignorial rights as against their persons and over the ground they occupy. All these people, few or many, grouped or scattered, do not form a town or commune, for they possess no corporate privileges : as a body they have not won from their lord any general surrender of his ordinary seignorial rights,—his taxes fixed or arbitrary, his annual rents, his share in the crops or cattle, his rights over trade and the holding of markets and fairs, over the exercise of the crafts, and to tolls innumerable from those who would travel by road or river, or cross a bridge, or carry merchandise to or from a

---

[1] This seems true for the regions comprised under the present names of England, France, and Germany, as may be seen from the following citations from English, French, and German authorities speaking of the towns in their respective lands. " The history of constitutional progress in any town is . . . the history of the particular steps by which the inhabitants secured immunity from various disabilities." W. Cunningham, *English Industry and Commerce*, p. 211, vol. i. 5th ed. (1910).

" A l'état individuel, le vilain, même affranchi, reste impuissant et annihilé dans le seigneurie où il est fixé. Il ne commence à compter que lorsqu'il fait partie d'une *communauté*. La communauté populaire, à son tour, ne devient une force sociale que lorsqu'elle est *privilégiée*, et que la collection de ses habitants, formant corps, échappe (en partie du moins) à l'exploitation seigneuriale, qui est le droit commun. Elle arrive enfin à la dignité de puissance politique, lorsqu'elle devient *ville libre*, c'est-à-dire lorsque ses habitants, liés entre eux par une association assermentée, constituent collectivement une *seigneurie* et entrent à ce titre dans la hiérarchie féodale." A. Luchaire, *Manuel des institutions françaises*, p. 353 (1892).

G. von Below, in *Das ältere deutsche Städtwesen und Bürgertum* (1905), in the opening pages explains that the distinguishing marks of a town are the possession of a market, a fortified wall, special town jurisdiction, independence in town matters, municipal organization, privileges (not enjoyed by the country) in taxation and military service, and freedom from tolls. Privilege (*Vorrecht*) enters all these features, and thus distinguishes the town.

town. There were also the so-called " banalities," which required the people to use the forge, the mill, the press of the lord, paying for the service ; also rights of forced entertainment, and finally very lucrative rights over the administration of justice and the freely levied fines, which were the usual punishments. Still further oppressive rights existed over serfs and the land they tilled.[1]

In various ways and degrees of completeness, bringing one stage or another of corporate freedom, some of these groups of men bound together by occupation, interest, or oath, obtained privileges of exemption. The usual act of consummation was the granting of the charter, giving the townsmen corporate existence as a town, with free jurisdiction over their acts and delicts as townsmen, and such immunity from the seignorial rights of their former master that they became a political or, if one will, feudal entity, a seignory, a corporate lordship, almost as their former master was himself a lord.[2] Thus the formation of a town represented emergence from serfdom or subjection, and the establishment of reciprocal obligations of lord and vassal. Such manner of coming into existence admits little direct heirship of Roman municipal institutions, and makes the mediaeval town a mediaeval creation.

The above statements apply but lamely to the towns of Italy. True, their constitutions were not developed out of Roman municipal institutions. And yet, being Italian, they were the heirs of the great *hereditas jacens* of Roman Italy. That had been predominantly urban ; and as Italian civilization reasserted itself after its period of degeneracy and confusion it also showed itself urban, and proceeded to prove its power by attacking intrusive Germanic feudal elements, destroying some, accepting some, and in general effecting a compulsory transmuting of them into turbulent constituents of city life. The cities of Italy evinced a more various and complex life within their walls than contemporary northern towns, because they included a greater variety of human elements. Undoubtedly the conditions of

[1] See A. Luchaire, *Manuel des institutions françaises* (1892), pp. 294 *sqq.* and especially pp. 335-351.

[2] Cf. Luchaire, *o.c.*, p. 402. But the town would remain a vassal of a lord, or of the king. Its lord usually was himself a vassal of a higher feudal dignitary.

growth of the towns in England, France, and Germany varied to some extent within each country. More essentially variegating factors affected the growth of towns in Italy, racial differences for example, renewed invasions from without, the bodily presence of the papacy, a great variety of circumstance and situation ; also a more manifold genius for city life quickened these diverse conditions.

Moreover there had been a general continuity of city life in Italy with which the North had nothing to compare. In Gothic, Lombard, Frankish times the Italian towns were squalid and harassed. But there they were, in Lombardy for example, where Milan could show a continuous existence scarcely second to that of Rome. The towns were storm-swept islands in a surging sea ; and in such islands the bishop was likely to be the rock of refuge. The population consisted of the Italian stocks rather than of the invading German. The Germans brought Feudalism in the making, and small and great they formed a somewhat anti-urban or at least anti-civic class, until they too were drawn within the dominating civic currents of Italy. The growth of city freedom was usually to consist in immunity from the domination of the Emperor or other royal ruler, and next from the rule of the bishop himself. The latter might be the Emperor's representative ; but he frequently was the episcopal nucleus of town administration, to which municipal immunities had been attached. Growth in civic freedom also lay in gaining mastery over the recalcitrant anti-civic class, who as feudal nobles held strongholds without the city or within. These with their followers in course of time were made into an upper class, *capitani* and *valvassori*, as they were called, in distinction from the industrial *popolo*. If they were disturbing elements they also added greatly to the variety of life and faculty within the city walls. Italian towns (our eyes are rather fixed on northern Italy) reached organization as communes generally in the eleventh century.

Everywhere the mediaeval town included a number of industrial groups, which sometimes had been organized in societies before the town had obtained a charter or otherwise become a commune. Florence, for example, did not formally become a commune until the end of the eleventh

century ; but there is evidence that the *arti* were organized
before then, and had indeed conducted the government of
the virtual city.   Thus Florence seems to arise out of their
federation.   Usually an Italian town harked back to unhealed
animosities and hostile divisions, which had been brought
to some sort of warring co-existence within its walls.   Opposing factions and industrial groups were apt to consider
themselves first.   Their animosities were a barrier to civic
sentiment which, on the other hand, was fostered by the
hatred and fear of other towns or powers.

The obscure origins of these industrial groups (we shall
soon be calling them guilds) were vague, unintended, casual :
definite assertions are likely to misstate such poor little
unformed facts.   In northern lands the Guild Merchant
was the first to reach significance.   In England, where it was
of great moment, it admitted members of the crafts which
were gradually forming into guilds.   Its English history
begins with the security and increase of trade brought by
the Norman Conquest.   At first a private society, it became
an important privilege of the town and even part of its
government in the twelfth century.[1]   Its function was
to regulate the town's trade monopoly, but its activities
might extend to the control of every industry.   Organized
mediaeval trade and craft rested on monopoly.[2]   The
creation of craft guilds entitled to monopolize the making
and selling of their wares, would seem to have weakened the
Guild Merchant in England ;   and during the fourteenth
century this general organization controlling a monopoly of
trade tended to separate into special trade and craft organiza-
tions, each controlling the monopoly by its branch.[3]

The craft guilds (German *Zunft* or *Amt*, French *métier*)
appear later than the Merchant Guild.   Some would find

[1] In France in certain instances (*e.g.* that of St. Omer), the commune apparently
grows out of the Merchant Guild.   " Il est hors de doute que les privilèges com-
merciaux accordés, dès le Xe et le XIe siècle, aux sociétés de marchands, ont été,
sur bien des points, l'origine des libertés postérieurement obtenues par les villes
où s'étaient formées ces associations.   Le gilde marchande fut souvent, en effet,
le ressort principal de la révolution communale et devint la commune elle-même
par la simple extension du lien qui la constituait."   Luchaire, *Manuel*, etc., p. 359.

[2] " Les hommes du moyen âge ne connaissaient le travail industriel que sous
le forme d'un privilège collectif, constituant un monopole en faveur du corps qui
en était investi."   Luchaire, *Manuel*, etc., p. 360.

[3] Cf. C. Gross, *The Gild Merchant* (Oxford, 1890).

their origin in groups of manorial workmen gradually acquiring freedom and organization ;[1] and others, for the towns of Italy and even those of France, would see in them continuations of the Roman *collegia* or schools of workmen ; while again, presumably for the north, they have been thought to revert to ancient heathen functions or associations. One may remark that the natural tendency of men to associate will apply itself to any interest they have in common, especially where that interest can best be served through common action : moreover mediaeval society in all its parts rested upon claimed and accorded privilege. So the men of each industry meeting together as was natural, gradually organized themselves into craft guilds, to be composed of master workmen and apprentices when these societies became fully developed in the thirteenth century. In each town they monopolized the exercise of their trade or craft. They also concerned themselves with the moral and religious conduct of members, with the regulation of their hours of labour and the quality of the product. They became extremely numerous in certain large centres, such as Paris, where they were minutely specialized.

Let us trace a little further the fortunes of the towns. In general their development was to conform to the rôle of industrial segregations within a predominantly feudal world. Divergences arose from the different political and social conditions in England and France and Germany and Italy ; also from the particular situation of each town and the genius for city life distinguishing the towns by race and country or from one another individually. Everywhere their ends had been reached under the dominant and often selfish leadership of the upper class within them, however that class may be named or constituted, *e.g.* the merchants, the patricians, the rich, the *grandi*. Gradually, by insistence, by riots, by revolts, and the strength of numbers, the lesser

---

[1] Luchaire, *Manuel*, etc., p. 361 *sqq.* There might be grouping and association of the serf or free workmen on an estate ; but it would be naturally in the towns that a corporate development would take place. *E.g.* at Chartres, about the mansions of the Count and bishop, artisans soon planted themselves, first as serfs, but with their condition improving gradually. Their numbers increase ; each trade has its quarter, butchers, saddlers, money-changers, jewellers. Levasseur, *Hist. des classes ouvrières*, etc., i. p. 264.

trades and crafts gained an important or dominant share in the city government. The time of this revolution was the thirteenth and fourteenth centuries.[1]

In the next stage, the political and municipal liberties of the towns declined or were destroyed, but from the action of very different agencies. In France the larger number of towns had been industrially enfranchised, but never constituted political entities. Those which did become free self-governing communes, chiefly in the north, found their freedom of small avail against the expanding power of the French monarchy in the thirteenth century. Sometimes the lower orders sought the royal intervention against the oppressive upper class, even as the intervention of the Counts of Flanders might be sought in towns within their feudal territories. There was frequent trouble in the towns of northern France and Flanders, and their political and financial affairs were fatally mismanaged.[2] Yet the liberties which these free communes lost, the *bourgeoisie* were in part to regain in the administration of the national government ; and this loss of liberties on the part of the communes did not prevent the economic and social progress of the industrial classes in towns which never had attained a like unstable independence.[3]

In England there was no such destruction of municipal liberties as came upon the Communes of northern France ; but in the progressive reign of Edward I., through the action of parliaments in which the towns were represented, their franchises were gradually transmuted into law common to the realm ; and the close protective ordinances of particular towns tended to widen into more national economic policies.[4]

---

[1] Venice affords the particular exception, in her complicated course towards a formal commercial oligarchy ; and England is the national anomaly, for, from the fourteenth century, the government of English towns tended rather to centre in smaller and more strictly closed groups. See C. Gross, *The Gild Merchant*.

[2] " La commune a été une institution assez éphémère. En tant que seigneurie réellement indépendante, elle n'a guère duré plus de deux siècles. Les excès des communiers, leur mauvaise administration financière, leurs divisions intestines, l'hostilité de l'Église, la protection onéreuse du haut suzerain et surtout du roi : telles ont été les causes immédiates de cette décadence rapide." A. Luchaire, *Les Communes françaises*, p. 288 (1890).

[3] Cf. Luchaire, *o.c.*, p. 292.

[4] Cf. Cunningham, *English Industry and Commerce*, 5th ed., 1910, vol. i. p. 261 *sqq.*

In Germany town privileges had been won through the exertions of the larger merchants, who with other people of consequence constituted a circle of leading families within the town and conducted town affairs. For a while these patrician administrations proceeded satisfactorily ; but during the fourteenth century, discontent permeated the lesser orders of tradesmen and craftsmen, who by this time were organized in guilds and able to make their numbers felt in town affairs. Thereupon in a large proportion of German towns, the process of democratization advanced, either peaceably or with violence, until the lower orders had their will. Often the craft guilds became the ruling element in town administration. The towns retained their liberties and political influence for a long period through the weakness of the imperial government and its conflicts with the princes, and those of the latter with each other. They constantly enhanced their power through the formation of leagues for commercial or military purposes, and were the *foyer* for the development of administrative and commercial law through that politically divided land.[1]

In Italy, from Rome northward, we find parts of the same story with interesting differences. During the twelfth and thirteenth centuries, the heroic age of the Italian Communes, very generally the exclusive town administration was wrested from the upper class, and the craft guilds became powerful in town affairs. But the towns were not to preserve their liberties ; for the fourteenth century opens the well-known story of the capture by successful *condottieri*, or by dynastic families, of the liberties of one after another of the north Italian towns. Venice is the well-known and most peculiar exception. But the story of the anomalous and fitful commune of Rome is also of curious interest. During the twelfth and thirteenth centuries when for good or ill the papacy awed Europe, the popes, even Innocent III., were often fugitives from Rome ! And the power of the

[1] The mediaeval town, says Karl Lamprecht, vol. iv. p. 206 of his *Deutsche Geschichte*, was a closed economic body, which sought to fill its own needs by its own products, and tended toward a protective policy. But prohibitive protection was avoided in Germany through city leagues, which made commercial intercourse possible among their members. In the course of the fourteenth century the territorial powers were persuaded to fall in with the policy of the towns.

popes over their own city was finally established at the closing
of the great schism in the reign of Martin V. (1417–1431),
a time when the liberties of so many Italian towns had
fallen captive to local tyrannies, and also a time when the
universal papal power was broken, and the popes were about
to become local dynasts.[1]

In the twelfth and thirteenth centuries the towns of
England, France, and Germany were sheer industrial centres,
and the townspeople were taken up with trade and handicraft. They had scant intellectual interests, but were very
practically religious or superstitious, with dashes of coarse
scepticism. Their thoughts did not represent the intellectually and spiritually best in the world, did not touch the
higher reaches of the saint, the theologian-philosopher, or
the romantic poet. In fine, town life in the Middle Ages
did not contribute to what was loftiest in mediaeval thinking,
or to what has proved most appealing in mediaeval romance,
or was most sublimely or most subtly beautiful in mediaeval
art, or even to what still may seem to have been most
intimate and precious in mediaeval life. Hugo of St. Victor,
Thomas Aquinas, or Bonaventura did not draw the substance
of their meditations from the town, nor did they need the
experiences of its promiscuous human intercourse to move
them to the expression of their best. In romance, Lancelot
and Guinevere, Tristan and Iseult, or if one will, the endless
garrulity of a Bénoît de St. More, had no dependence on the
town. Art, which is skilful craft, is connected with industrial
training, and perhaps the town's financial contribution
might be needed for the building and decoration of a
cathedral. But the inspiring thought and plan and meaning
of the structure had more to do with cloistered meditations ;
nor did the manifold intricacy of symbolic meaning guiding
the sculpture and glass painting, spring from the daily jog
and stir of concrete unsymbolic incidents which furnish
thoughts for townsfolk. To be sure, certain genial details
of decoration, like the representation of the crafts, were
city-born ; but they were of little significance in the building's scheme, just as the little span of mortal business is a

---

[1] This story is told by Pasquale Villari in the article on " The Roman Republic
in the Middle Ages," *Encyclopaedia Britannica*, vol. xxiii. p. 660 *sqq.*

slight thing in the vista of the soul's endless bliss or misery. One need not look beyond the range of these instances for evidence of the fact that the most precious, the most typical and original elements of mediaeval life drew little inspiration from the towns.

But again this view does not apply to Italy, where the matter of chief interest is the story of the towns, whether under aristocracies, democracies, or despotisms. Within them worked the strength of Italy for statecraft, art, culture, and the freeing of the human spirit. Italian civilization, the Italian habit of life, was urban ; and whatever thought or feeling or romance grew up in mediaeval Italy, could be found within the towns, and had its share if not its source in city life. Did not the *Divina Commedia* draw its human setting from the life and strife of towns and in towns attain to its inspired being ? But more especially Italian humanism was to be the fruit of towns, even as the Greek and Latin classics were ; and from city life, rather than from seclusion, the Italian humanists were to learn to understand them. The greater part of these humanists, especially as the Middle Ages close, were town-bred scholars, who perhaps might seek for a while a quiet retreat for their studies or to indulge that taste for country - life which is so unmistakably a city-child. Petrarch's literary delight in the solitude of Vaucluse or the quiet of Aqua was as city-bred and self-conscious as the pastoral poetry of the Alexandrian Theocritus.

CHAPTER XV

THE GROWTH OF MEDIAEVAL EMOTION

I. THE PATRISTIC CHART OF PASSION.
II. EMOTIONALIZING OF LATIN CHRISTIANITY.

THE characteristic passions of a period represent the emotionalized thoughts of multitudes of men and women. Mediaeval emotional development followed prevailing ideas, opinions, convictions, especially those of mediaeval Christianity. Its most impressive phases conformed to the tenets of the system which the Middle Ages had received from the Church Fathers, and represented the complement of passion arising from the long acceptance of the same. One may observe, first, the process of exclusion, inclusion, and enhancement, through which the Fathers formed a certain synthesis of emotion from the matter of their faith and the circumstances of their environment ; and, secondly, the further growth of emotion in the Middle Ages.

I

In the centuries immediately preceding and following the Christian era there took place a remarkable growth of the pathetic or emotional element in Greek and Roman literature. Yet during the same period Stoicism, the most respected system of philosophy, kept its face as stone, and would not recognize the ethical value of emotion in human life.[1] But the emotional elements of paganism, which were stretching out their hands like the shades by Acheron, were

[1] Cf. Taylor, *Ancient Ideals*, chaps. xv., xvi. ; *Classical Heritage*, chaps. ii., iii.

not to be restrained by philosophic admonition, or Virgilian *desine fata deum flecti sperare precando*.   And though the Stoic could not consent to Juvenal's avowal that the sense of tears is the best part of us, Neo-Platonism soon was to uphold the sublimated emotion of a vision transcending reason as the highest good for man.   Rational self-control was disintegrating in the Neo - Platonic dialectic, which pointed beyond reason to ecstasy.   That ecstasy, however, was to be super-sensual, and indeed came only to those who had long suppressed all cravings of the flesh.   This ascetic emotionalism of the Neo-Platonic *summum bonum* was strikingly analogous to the ideal of Christian living pressing to domination in the patristic period.

No need to say that the Gospel of Jesus was addressed to the heart as well as to the mind ; and for times to come the Saviour on the Cross and at its foot the weeping Mother were to rouse floods of tears over human sin, which caused the divine sacrifice.   The words *Jesus wept* heralded a new dispensation under which the heart should quicken and the mind should guide through reaches of humanity unknown to paganism.   This Christian expansion of the spirit did not, however, address itself to human relationships, but uplifted itself to God, its upward impulse spurning mortal loves.   In its mortal bearings the Christian spirit was more ascetic than Neo-Platonism, and its *élan* of emotion might have been as sublimated in quality as the Neo-Platonic, but for the greater reality of love and terror in the God toward whom it yearned with tears of contrition, love, and fear.

Another strain very different from Neo-Platonism con-tributed to the sum of Christian emotion.   This was Judaism, which recently had shown the fury of its energy in de-fence of Jerusalem against the legions of Titus.   Christians imbibed its force of feeling from the books of the Old Testament.   The passion of those writings was not as the humanly directed passions of the Greeks.   Israel's desire and aversion, her scorn and hatred, her devotion and her love, hung on Jehovah.   " Do I not hate them, O Jehovah, that hate thee ? "   This cry of the Psalmist is as Elijah's " Take the prophets of Baal ; let not one of them escape." Jewish wrath was a righteous intolerance, which would

neither endure idolatrous Gentiles nor suffer idolaters in
Israel.   Moses is enraged by the sight of the people dancing
before the golden calf ; and Isaiah's scorn hisses over those
daughters of Israel who have turned from Jehovah's ways
of decorum : " Because the daughters of Zion are haughty,
and walk with stretched forth necks, and wanton eyes,
mincing as they go, and making a tinkling with their feet ;
therefore Jehovah will smite with a scab the crown of the
head of the daughters of Zion, and Jehovah will lay bare
their secret parts."

Did a like scorn and anger find harbourage in Him who
likened the Pharisees to whitened sepulchres, and with a
scourge of small cords drove the money-changers from His
Father's house ?   At all events a kindred hate found an
enduring home in the religion of Tertullian and Athanasius,
and in the great Church that persecuted the Montanists at
Augustine's entreaty, and thereafter poured its fury upon
Jew and Saracen and heretic for a thousand years.

Jehovah was also a great heart of love, loving His
people along the ways of every sweet relationship understood
by man.   " When Israel was a child, then I loved him, and
out of Egypt called my son hither."   " Can a woman forget
her sucking child, so as not to yearn upon the son of her
womb ?   Yea, these may forget, yet will I not forget thee."
Again, Jehovah is the husband, and Israel the sinning wife
whom He will not put away.[1]   Israel's responding love
answers : " My soul waits on God—My heart and flesh cry
aloud to the living God—Like as the hart panteth for
the water-brooks " !   Such passages throb obedience to
Deuteronomy's great command, which Jesus said was the
sum of the Law and the Prophets.   No need to say that
the Christian's love of God had its emotional antecedent in
Psalmist and Prophet.   Jehovah's purifying wrath of love
also passed over to the Christian words, " As many as I
love, I reprove and chasten."   And " the fear of the Lord,
which is the beginning of wisdom," found its climax in
the Christian terror of the Judgment Day.

The Old Testament has its instances of human love :
Isaac and Rebekah, Jacob and Rachel.   There is Jacob's

[1] Hosea, i.-iii.

love of Joseph and Benjamin, and Joseph's love, which yearned upon his brethren who had sold him to the Egyptians. The most loving man of all is David, with his love of Jonathan, " wonderful and passing the love of women," unforgotten in the king's old age, when he asks, " Is there yet any living of the house of Saul, that I may show him kindness for Jonathan's sake ? " To a later time belongs the Song of Songs. Beautiful, orientally sensuous, too glowing perhaps for western taste, is this utterance of unchecked passion. And its fortune has been the most wonderful that ever fell to a love poem. It became the epithalamion of the Christian soul married to Christ, an epithalamion which was to be enlarged with passionate thought by doctor, monk, and saint, through the Christian centuries. The first to construe it as the bridal of the Soul was one who, by an act more irrevocable than a monastic vow, put from him mortal bridals—Origen, the greatest thinker of the Eastern Church. Thus the passion of the Hebrew woman for the lover that was to her as a bundle of myrrh lying between her breasts, was lifted, still full of desire, to the love of the God-man, by those of sterile flesh and fruitful souls.

Christianity was not eclecticism, which, for lack of principles of its own, borrows whatever may seem good. But it made a synthetic adoption of what could be included under the dominance of its own motives, that is, could be made to accord with its criterion of Salvation. What sort of synthesis could it make of the passions and emotions of the Graeco-Roman-Oriental-Jewish world ? That which was achieved by the close of the patristic period, and was to be passionately approved by the Middle Ages, proceeded partly in the way of exclusion, and partly by adding a quality of boundlessness to the emotional elements admitted.

With the first conversions to the new religion, arose the problem : What human feelings, what loves and interests of this world, shall the believer recognize as according with his faith, and as offering no obstacle to the love of God and the attainment of eternal life ? A practical answer was given by the growth of an indeterminate asceticism within the Christian communities, which in the fourth century went

forth with power, and peopled the desert with anchorites
and monks.

Ascetic suggestions came from many sources to the
early Christians. Stoicism was ascetic in tendency ; Neo-
Platonism ascetic in principle, holding that the soul should
be purged from contamination with things of sense. Throughout Egypt asceticism was rife in circles interested in the
conflict of Set and his evil host with Horus seeking
vengeance for Osiris slain ; and we know that some of the
earliest Christian hermits had been recluses devoted to the
cult of Serapis. In Syria dwelt communities of Jewish
Essenes, living continently like monks. Nevertheless, whatever may have been the effects of such examples, monasticism
developed from within Christianity, and was not the fruit of
influences from without.

The Lord had said, " My kingdom is not of this world " ;
and soon enough there came antagonism between the early
Churches and the Roman Empire. The Church was in
a state of conflict. It behoved the Christian to keep
his loins girded : why should he hamper himself with
ephemeral domestic ties, when the coming of the Lord
was at hand ? Moreover, the Christian warfare to the
death was not merely with political tyranny, but against
fleshly lusts. Such convictions, in men and women desirous
of purifying the soul from the cravings of sense, might bring
the thought that even lawful marriage was not as holy as
the virgin state. The Christian's ascetic abnegation had
as a further motive the love of Christ and the desire to help
on His kingdom and attain to it, the motive of sacrifice for
the sake of the Kingdom of Heaven ; for which one man
must be burned, another must give up his goods, and a third
renounce his heart's love. Ascetic acts are also a natural
accompaniment of penitence : the sinner, with fear of hell before him, seeks to undergo temporal in order to avoid eternal
pain ; or, better, stung by love of the Crucified, his heart
cries for flagellation. When St. Martin came to die he
would lie only upon ashes : " I have sinned if I leave you a
different example." [1] A similar strain of religious conviction
is rendered in Jerome's " You are too pleasure-loving, brother,

[1] Sulpicius Severus, *Epist.* iii.

if you wish to rejoice in this world and hereafter to reign with Christ." [1]

So currents of ascetic living early began in Christian circles ; and before long the difficulty of leading lives of self-mortification within the community was manifest. It was easier to withdraw : ascetics must become anchorites, " they who have withdrawn." Here was reason why the movement should betake itself to the desert. But the solitary life is so difficult, that association for mutual aid will soon ensue ; and then regulations will be needed for these newly-formed ascetic groups. So anchorites tended to become coenobites ; monasticism has begun.

In both its hermit and coenobitic phases, monasticism began in the East, in Syria and the Thebaid. It was accepted by the Latin West, and there became impressed with Roman qualities of order, regularity, and obedience. The precepts of the eastern monks were collected and arranged by Cassian, a native of Gaul, in his *Institutes* and *Conlocations*, between the years 419 and 428. And about a century afterwards, western monasticism received its type-form in the *Regula* of St. Benedict of Nursia (d. 543), which was approved by the authority of Gregory the Great (d. 604).[2]

By the close of the patristic period, monasticism had

---

[1] These words occur in Jerome's famous letter (*Ep.* xiv.), in which he exhorts the wavering Heliodorus to sever all ties and affections : " Do not mind the entreaties of those dependent on you, come to the desert and fight for Christ's name. If they believe in Christ, they will encourage you ; if they do not,—let the dead bury their dead. A monk cannot be perfect in his own land ; not to wish to be perfect is a sin ; leave all, and come to the desert. The desert loves the naked. O desert, blooming with the flowers of Christ ! O solitude, whence are brought the stones of the city of the Great King ! O wilderness, rejoicing close to God ! What would you, brother, in the world,—you that are greater than the world ? How long are the shades of roofs to oppress you ? How long the dungeon of a city's smoke ? Believe me, I see more of light ! Do you fear poverty ? Christ called the poor ' blessed.' Are you terrified at labour ? No athlete without sweat is crowned. Do you think of food ? Faith fears not hunger. Do you dread the naked ground for limbs consumed with fasts ? The Lord lies with you. Does the infinite vastness of the desert fright you ? In the mind walk abroad in Paradise. Does your skin roughen without baths ? Who is once washed in Christ needs not to wash again. And in a word, hear the apostle answering : The sufferings of the present time are not to be compared with the glory to come which shall be revealed in us ! "

[2] In my *Classical Heritage*, pp. 136-197, I have given an account of the origins of monasticism, and of its distinctive western features. There I have also set out the Rule of Benedict, with sketches of the early monastic character.

become the most highly applauded practical interpretation
of Christianity.   Its precepts represented the requirements
of the Christian criterion of Salvation applied to earthly life.
Like all great systems which have widely prevailed and long
endured, it was not negation, but substitution.   If it condemned usual modes of pleasure, this was because of their
incompatibility with the life it inculcated.   The *Regula* of
Benedict set forth a manner of life replete with positive
demands.   Its purpose was to prescribe for those who had
taken monastic vows that way of living, that daily round of
occupation, that constant mode of thought and temper,
which should make a perfected Christian, that is, a perfect
monk.   And so broad and spiritually interwoven were its
precepts that one of them could hardly be obeyed without
fulfilling all.   Read, for example, the beautiful seventh
chapter upon the twelve grades of humility, and it will become evident that whoever achieves this virtue will gain all
the rest : he will always have the fear of God before his eyes,
the terror of hell and the hope of heaven ; he will cut off the
desires of the flesh ; he will do, not his own will, but the
Lord's ; since Christ obeyed His Father unto death, he will
render absolute obedience to his superior, obeying readily and
cheerfully even when unjustly blamed ; in confession he will
conceal no evil thought ; he will deem himself vilest of all,
and will do nothing save what the *regula* of the monastery
or the example of the elders prescribes ; he will keep from
laughter and from speech, except when questioned, and then
he will speak gently and humbly, and with gravity, in few
words ; he will stand and walk with inclined head and looks
bent on the ground, feeling himself unworthy to lift up his
eyes to heaven : through these stairs of humility he will
reach that perfect love of God which banishes fear, and will
no longer need the fear of hell, as he will do right from habit
and through the love of Christ.

Having thus pointed out the way of righteousness,
Benedict's *regula* gives minute precepts for the monk's
conduct and occupation through each hour of the day and
night.   No time, no circumstance shall be left unguarded,
or unoccupied with those acts which lead to God.   Wise
was this great prototypal *regula* in that its abundance of

positive precepts kept the monk busy with righteousness, so
that he might have no leisure for sin.   Its prohibitions are
comparatively unemphatic, and the monk is guided along
the paths of righteousness rather than forbidden to go astray

Thus monk and nun were consecrated to a calling which
should contain their whole desire, as it certainly demanded
their whole strength.   Was the monk a celibate because
carnal marriage was denied him ?   Rather he was wedded
to Christ.   If this is allegory, it is also close to literal truth.
" Thou shalt love the Lord thy God with all thy heart, and
with all thy soul, and with all thy mind."   Is not love the
better part of marriage ?   And how if the Lord thy God has
been a gracious loving figure here on earth, who loved thee
humanly as well as divinely, and died for thee at last ?   Will
not the complete love required by the commandment become
very ardent, very heart-filling ?   Shalt thou not always yearn
to see Him, fall at His feet, confess thy unworthiness, and
touch His garment ?   Is there any end to the compass of
thy loving Him, and musing upon Him, and dwelling in His
presence ?   Dost thou not live with Him in a closer communion than the sunderances of mortality permit among
men, or between men and women ?   And if it be thou art a
nun, art thou not as close to Him in tears and washing of
those blessed feet, as ever was that other woman, who had
been a sinner ?   Thou shalt keep thy virginity for Him as
for a bridegroom.[1]

But the great commandment to love the Lord thy
God has an adjunct—" and thy neighbour as thyself."   *As
thyself*—how does the monk love himself ?   why, unto Christ
and his own salvation.   He does not love his sinful pleasures,
nor those matters of earth which might not be sins, had he
not realized how they conflicted with his scheme of life.
His love for a fellow could not recognize those pleasures

---

[1] Cyprian said in the third century, addressing himself to Christian virgins:
" Dominus vester et caput Christus est ad instar ad vicem masculi " (*De habitu
virginum*, 22).   To realize how near to the full human relationship was this
wedded love of Christ, one should read the commentaries and sermons upon
Canticles.   Those of a later time—St. Bernard's, for example—are the best,
because they sum up so much that had been gathering fervour through the
centuries.   One might look further to those mediaeval instances that break
through mysticism to a sensuousness in which the man Christ becomes an almost
too concrete husband for ecstatic women.   See *post*, Chapter XX.

which he himself had cast away.   He must love his fellow,
like himself, unto the saving, not the undoing, of him—be
his true lover, not his enemy.   This vital principle of
Christian love had to recast pagan passion and direct the
affections to an immortal goal.   Under it these reached a
new absoluteness.   The Christian lover should always be
ready to give his life for his friend's salvation, as for his own.
So love's offices gained enlargement and an infinity of new
relationship, because directed toward eternal life.[1]

Unquestionably in the monk's eyes passionate love
between the sexes was mainly lust.   Within the bonds of
marriage it was not mortal sin ; but the virgin state was the
best.   Here, as we shall see, life was to claim its own and
free its currents.   Monasticism did not stop the human race,
or keep men from loving women.   Such love would assert
itself ; and ardent natures who felt its power were to find in
themselves a love and passion somewhat novel, somewhat
raised, somewhat enlarged.   In the end the love between
man and woman drew new inspiration and energy from the
enhancement of all the rest of love, which came with
Christianity.

Evidently the great office of Christian love in a heathen
period was to convert idolaters to the Faith.   So it had
been from the days of Paul.   Rapidly Christianity spread
through all parts of the Roman Empire.   Then the Faith
pressed beyond those crumbling boundaries into the barbarian
world.   Hereupon, with Gregory the Great and his successors,
it became clear that the great pope is always a missionary
pope, sending out such Christian embassies as Gregory sent
to the Anglo-Saxon kingdoms.

If conversion was a chief office of Christian love, the

[1] The whole Christian love, first the love of God and then the love of man,
is felt and set forth by Augustine.   "Thou hast made us toward thee, and
unquiet is our heart until it rests in thee. . . . That is the blessed life to rejoice
toward thee, concerning thee and because of thee. . . . Give me thyself, my God.
. . . All my plenty which is not my God is need."   With his love of God his love
for man accords.   "This is true love, that cleaving to truth we may live aright ;
and for that reason we contemn all mortal things except the love of men, whereby
we wish them to live aright.   Thus can we profitably be prepared even to die for
our brethren, as the Lord Jesus Christ taught us by His example. . . . It is love
which unites good angels and servants of God in the bond of holiness, joins us to
them and them to us, and subjoins all unto God."   These passages are from the
Confessions and from the *De Trinitate*.

great object of Christian wrath was unbelief. That existed
within and without Christendom : within in forms of heresy,
without in the practices of heathenism. Christian wrath
was moved by whatever opposed the true faith. The
Christian should discriminate : hate the sin, and love the
sinner unto his betterment. But it was so easy, so human,
from hating the sin to hate the obdurate sinner who could
not be saved and could but harm the Church. One need
not recount how the disputes of the Athanasian time
regarding the nature of Christ came to express themselves
in curses ; nor how the Christian sword began its slaughter
of heretic and heathen. Persecution seemed justified in
reason ; it was very logical ; broad reasons of Christian
statecraft seemed to make for it ; and often a righteous
zeal wielded the weapon. It had moreover its apparent
sanction in Jehovah's destroying wrath against idolaters
within and without the tribes of Israel.

So the two opposites of love and wrath laid aside
some of their grossness, and gained new height and compass
in the Christian soul. A like change came over other
emotions. As life lifted itself to further heights of holiness,
and hitherto unseen depths of evil yawned, there came a
new power of pity and novel revulsions of aversion. The
pagan pity for life's mortality, which filled Virgil's heart,
could not but take on change. There was no more
mortality, but eternal joy and pain. Souls which had so
unavailingly stretched forth their hands to fate, had now
been given wings of faith. Yet death gained blacker terror
from the Christian Hell, the newly-assured alternative of
the Christian Heaven. The great Christian pity did not
touch the mortal ebbing of the breath ; that should be
a triumphant birth. But an enormous and terror-stricken
pity was evoked by sin, and the thought of the immortal
soul hanging over an eternal hell. And since all human
actions were connected with the man's eternal lot, they
became invested with a new import. So the Christian's
compassion would deepen, his sympathy become more
intense, although no longer stirred by everything that had
moved his pagan self. With him fear was raised to a new
intensity by other terrors than had driven the blood from

pagan cheeks. His sense of joy was deepened also ; for
a joy hitherto unrealized came from his new love of God
and the God-man, from the assurance of his salvation, and
the thought of loved human relationships never to end.
So Christian joy might have an absoluteness which it
never had under the pause-giving mortal limitations of
paganism.

Within the compass of pagan joyfulness there had been
no deeper passion than the love of beauty. That had its
sensuous phases, and its far blue heights, where Plato saw
the beauty of order, justice, and proportion. For the
Christian, the beauty of the flesh became a veil through
which he looked for the beauty of the soul. If a face
testified to the beauty of holiness within, it was fair. Better
the pale, drawn visages of monk and nun than the red lip
too quickly smiling. Feeling as well as thought should be
adjusted to these sentiments. Yet Plato's realization of
intellectual beauty found home within the Christian thoughts
of God and holiness, indeed helped to construct them.
This is clear with the Fathers. In the East, Gregory of
Nyssa's passion for divine beauty was Platonism set in
Christian phrase ; in the West, Augustine reached his
thoughts of beauty through considerations which came to him
from Greek philosophy.[1] " Love is of the beautiful," said
Plato ; " Do we love ought else ? " says Augustine. Both
men shape their thoughts of beauty after their best ideals of
perfection. Augustine's burn upward to the beauty of a
God as loving as He is omnipotent ; Plato's had been more
abstract. Augustine's Platonism shows the highest Greek
thoughts of beauty and goodness changed into attributes of
a personal God, who could be loved because He was loving.

In these ways the loftier Christian souls suppressed, or
transformed and greatened, the emotions of their natures.
It was thus with those possessed of a faith that brought
the whole of life within its dominance. There were many
such. Yet the multitude of Christians ranged downward
from such great obsession, through all stages of human
half-heartedness and frailty, to the state of those whose
Christianity was but a name, or but a magic rite. Always

[1] Cf. *Classical Heritage*, p. 123 *sqq.*

preponderant in numbers, and often in influence and power, these nominal and fetichistic Christians would keep alive the loves and hates, the interests and tastes, the approvals and disapprovals, of paganism or barbaric heathenism, as the case might be.

II

The patristic synthesis of emotion passed on entire and authoritative to the Middle Ages. It exercised enormous influence (usually in the way of compulsion, but sometimes in the way of repulsion) upon emotional phenomena both of a religious and a secular nature. Yet it was merely the foundation, or the first stage, of mediaeval emotional development. The subsequent stages were dependent on the conditions under which mediaeval attitudes of mind arose, very dependent upon the maturing and blending of the native traits of inchoate mediaeval peoples and upon their appropriation of Latin Christianity and the antique education.

The northern races had been introduced to a novel religion and to modes of thought considerably above them. Their old conceptions were discredited, their feelings somewhat distraught. Emotionally as well as intellectually they were confused. Turbid feelings, arising from ideas not fully mastered, had to clarify and adjust themselves. From the sixth to the eleventh century the crude mediaeval stocks, tangled but not blended, strange to the religion and culture which held their destinies, were not possessed of clear and dominant emotions that could create their own forms of expression. They could not think and feel as they would when their new acquirements had mellowed into faculty and temperament, and unities of character had once more emerged.

Christianity and Latin culture were operative everywhere, and everywhere tended to produce a uniform development. Yet the peoples affected by these common influences were kept unlike each other through varieties of environment and a diversity of racial traits which still showed clearly as the centuries passed. In consequence.

the emotional development of these different peoples remained marked by racial characteristics, while also becoming mediaeval under the action of common influences.   It
proceeded in two parallel and partially mingling streams :
the one of the religious life, the other of earth's desires.
They may be observed in turn.

Augustine represents the sum of doctrine and emotion
contained in the Latin Christianity of the fifth century.
However imperfectly others might comprehend his thought
or feel the power of his grandly reasoned love of God, he
established this love for time to come as the centre and
the bound of Christian righteousness : " Virtus non est nisi
diligere quod diligendum est." [1]   He drew within this principle the array of dogma and precept constituting Latin
Christianity.   On the other hand, the practical embodiment
of the patristic synthesis of human interests and emotions
was monasticism, with its lines set by the Rule of Benedict.

Pope Gregory the Great [2] refashioned Augustine's
teachings, and placed the seal of his approval upon
Benedictine monasticism as the perfect way of Christian
living.   His mind was darkened with the new ignorance
and intellectual debasement which had come in the century
and a half separating him from Augustine ; and his soul
was filled with the fantastic terrors which were to constitute
so large a part of the religion of the Middle Ages.   Devil
lore, relic worship, miracles, permeate his consciousness of
life.   The soul's ceaseless business is so to keep itself
that it may at last escape the sentence of the awful Judge.
Love and terror struggle fearfully in Gregory.   Christ's
death had shown God's love ; and yet the Dies Irae
impends.   No delict is wiped out without penitence and
punishme⁻t, in this life or afterwards—let it be in Purgatory
and not in Hell !

The centuries following Gregory's death rearranged the
contents of Latin Christianity, including Gregory's teachings, to suit their own intellectual capacities.   This (Carolingian) period of rearrangement and painful learning, as it
was unoriginative intellectually, was likewise unproductive
of Christian emotion.   Occasionally from far-off converts,

---

[1] Augustine, *Epp.* 155, c. 13.   [2] *Ante*, Chapter V.

who are not troubled overmuch with learning, come utterances of simple feeling for the Faith (one thinks of Bede's story of Cædmon) ; and the Teuton spirit, warlike as well as intimate and sentimental, enters the vernacular interpretation of Christianity.[1] The Christian message could not be understood at all without a stirring of the convert's nature : some quickening of emotion would ensue. This did not imply a development of emotion corresponding to the credences of Latin Christianity, to which so many people had been newly introduced. That system had to be more vitally appropriated before it could arouse the emotional counterpart of its tenets, and run its course in modes of mediaeval religious passion.

Accordingly one will look in vain among the Carolingian scholars for that torrential feeling which becomes articulate in the eleventh century. They were excerpting and re-arranging patristic Christianity to suit their own capacities. They could not use it as a basis for further thinking ; nor, on the other hand, had it become for them the ground of religious feeling. Undoubtedly, Alcuin and Rabanus Maurus and Walafrid Strabo were pious Christians, taking their Faith devoutly. But such religious emotion as was theirs, was reflected rather than spontaneous. Alcuin, as well as Gregory the Great, realizes the opposition between heaven and the *vana delectibilia* [2] of this world. But Alcuin's words have lost the horror-stricken quality of Gregory ; neither do they carry the floods of tears which like thoughts bring to Peter Damiani in the eleventh century. Odo, Abbot of Cluny in the middle of the tenth century, has something of Gregory's heavy horror ; but even in him the gift of tears is not yet loosed.[3]

From the eleventh century onward, the gathering religious feeling pours itself out in passionate utterances ; and in this new emotionalizing of Latin Christianity lay the chief religious office of the Middle Ages, wherein they went far beyond the patristic authors of their faith. The Fathers of the Latin Church from Tertullian to Gregory the Great had been occupied with doctrine and ecclesiastical organization.

[1] *Ante*, Chapter IX.

[2] Alcuin, *Ep.* 40 (Migne, *Pat. Lat.* 100, col. 201).

[3] Cf. Odo's *Collationes*, in Migne 133, and Chapter XII. ii., *ante*. Gregory was Odo's favourite author.

This dual achievement was the work of the constructive mind of the Latin West, following, of course, what had been accomplished by the Greek Fathers. It stood forth mainly as the creation of those human faculties which are grouped under the name of intellect. Patristic Latin Christianity hardly presents itself as the product of the whole man. Its principles were not as yet fully humanized, made matter of the heart, and imbued with love and fear and pity : this creature of the intellect had yet to receive a soul.

It is true that Augustine had an enormous love of God. It was fervently felt ; it was powerfully reasoned ; it impassioned his thought. Yet it did not contain that tender love of the divinely human Christ which trembles in the words of Bernard and makes the life of Francis a lyric poem. St. Jerome also had even an hysterically emotional nature ; Tertullian at the beginning of the patristic period was no placid soul, nor Gregory the Great at its close. But it does not follow that Latin Christianity was as yet emotionalized, or that it had become a matter of the heart because it was accepted by the mind. Its dogmas and constructive principles were still too new ; the energies of men had been spent in devising and establishing them. Not yet had they been pondered over for generation after generation, and hallowed through time ; they had not yet become part of human life, cherished in men's hopes, fondled in their affections, frozen in their fears, trembled before and loved.

What was absent from the formation of Latin Christianity constituted the conditions of its gradual appropriation by the Middle Ages. It had come to them from a greater past, sanctioned by the saints who now reigned above. Through the centuries, men had come to understand it, and had made it their own with power. Through generations its commands and promises, its threats and rewards, had been feared and loved. Its persons, symbols, and sacraments had become animate with human quality and were endeared with intimate incident and association. Every one had been born to it, had been suckled upon it, had adored it in child-hood, youth, and age : it filled all life ; with hope or menace it overhung the closing hour.

The Middle Ages have been given credit for dry theologies and sublimated metaphysics. Less frequently have they been credited with their great achievement, the imbuing of patristic Christianity with the human elements of love and fear and pity. Yet their religious phenomena clearly display this emotionalizing of transmitted theological elements. Chapters which are to follow will illustrate it from the lives of many saints of different temperaments. As wide apart as life will be the phases of its manifestations The tears of Peter Damiani are not like the love of the God-man in St. Bernard ; St. Francis's love of Christ and love of man is again different and new ; and the mystic thought-shot visions of a Hildegard of Bingen are as blue to crimson when compared with the sense-passion for the Bridegroom of a Mechthild of Magdeburg. Even as illustrated in these so different natures, it will still appear that the emotional humanizing of Latin Christianity in the Middle Ages shaped itself to the tenets of the system formulated by the Church Fathers. It was an emotionalizing of that system, quite as much as a direct appropriation of the Gospel-heart of Christ. Christ and the heart of Christ were with the mediaeval saints ; and yet the emotions as well as thoughts through which they turned to Him received their form from patristic Christianity.

Religious art plainly tells the story. Let one call to mind the character of its achievements in the fourth, fifth, and sixth centuries. That was the period following the recognition of Christianity as the religion of the Roman Empire. Everywhere basilicas arose.[1] Some of them may be seen in Rome, in Ravenna, in Constantinople. They still contain many of the mural mosaics which were their glory. Numberless artists laboured in the composition of those stately church decorations. There was a need, unprecedented and never afterwards paralleled, of creative composition. Spacious surfaces were to be covered with prefigurative scenes from the Old Testament, with scenes from the life of Christ on earth, and representations of His

---

[1] Before Constantine's reign there had been few Christian basilicas ; Christian art was sepulchral, drawing upon the galleries of the Catacombs, in meagre and monotonous designs, the symbols of the soul's deliverance from death. These designs were antique in style and poor in execution.

apocalyptic triumph in the Resurrection. They had all to
be composed without aid from previous designs, for there
were none. The artists had need to be as constructive as
the Church Fathers, who through the same period were
perfecting the formulation of the Faith. They succeeded
grandly, setting forth the subjects they were told to execute,
in noble, balanced, and decorative compositions, which
presented the facts and tenets of the Faith strikingly and
correctly. Stylistically, these great church mosaics belonged
to antique art. What did they lack ? Merely the human,
veritably tragic, qualities of love and fear and pity, which
had not yet come. Like the dogmatic system, this mosaic
presentation was too recently composed. Its subjects were
not yet humanized through centuries of contemplation,
reverence, and love.[1]

Many of the early compositions, repeated from century
to century, in time were humanized and transformed with
feeling. But this was not in the seventh, eighth, and ninth
centuries, when art was but a decadent and barbarized
survival of the antique Christian manner, nor in the tenth
and eleventh. One may note also that the mediaeval
expression of Christian emotion was beginning in religious
literature. This came with fulness in the twelfth century,
and along with it the emotionalizing, the veritable humanizing, of religious art began. Yet the artists of western
Europe still lacked the skill requisite for delicate execution.
A marked advance came in the thirteenth and fourteenth
centuries. That was the great period of Gothic architecture ;
and in the sculpture on the French cathedrals, stone seems
to live and feel. The prophetic figures from the Old
Testament, the scenes of man's redemption and final
judgment, are humanized with love and terror. Moreover,
the sculptor surrounds them with the myriad subsidiary
detail of mortal life and changing beauty, showing how
closely they are knit to every human love and interest.

In Italy a like story is told in a different manner. There
is sculpture, but there also is mosaic, and above all there is
and will be fresco. Before the end of the thirteenth century,
Giotto was busy with his new dramatic art ; no need to tell

---

[1] See Taylor, *Classical Heritage*, chap. x. sec. 2.

what power of human feeling filled the works of that chief of painters and his school. The hard materials of the mosaicist were also made to render emotion. If one will note the mosaics along the nave in Santa Maria Maggiore, belonging to the fifth century, and then turn to the mosaics of the Coronation of the Virgin in the apse, or cross the Tiber and look at those in the lower zone of the apse of Santa Maria in Trastevere, which tell the Virgin's story, he will see the change which was bringing love and sweetness into the stiff mosaic medium. Torriti executed the former in 1295 ; and the latter with their gentler feeling were made by Giotto's pupil, Cavallini, in 1351. The art is still as correct and true and orthodox as in the fifth century. It conforms to Latin Christianity in the choice of topics and the manner of presenting them, and drapes its human emotions around conceptions which the patristic period formed and delivered to the Middle Ages. Thus, in full measure, it has taken to itself the emotional qualities of the mediaeval transformation of Latin Christianity, and is filled with a love and tears and pity, which were not in the old Christian mosaics.

Quite analogous to the emotionalizing of Christian art is the example afforded by the evolution of the Latin hymn. The earliest extant Latin hymns are those of St. Ambrose, written in iambic dimeters. Antique in phrase as in metre, they are also trenchantly correct in doctrine, as behoved the compositions of the great Archbishop of Milan who commanded the forces of orthodoxy in the Arian conflict. They were sung in anxious seasons. Yet these dignified and noble hymns are no emotional outpour either of anxiety or adoration. Such feeling as they carry lies in their strength of trust in God and in the power of conviction of their stately orthodoxy.

Between the death of Ambrose and the tenth century, Latin hymns gradually substituted accent in the place of metrical quantity, as the dominant principle of their rhythm. With this partial change there seems to come increase of feeling. The

> " Jesu nostra redemptio,
> Amor et desiderium,"

of the seventh century is different from the

"Te diligat castus amor,
Te mens adoret sobria"

of Ambrose.[1] And the famous pilgrim chant of the tenth century, " O Roma nobilis, orbis et domina," has the strength of long-deepening emotion.[2]

These hymns have but dropped the constraint of metre. Religious passion had not yet proved its creative power, and the new verse-forms with their mighty rhyme, fit to voice the accumulated emotions of the Liturgy, were not in existence. The eleventh and twelfth centuries witnessed the strophic evolution of the Latin hymn, in which feeling, joined with art, at last perfected line and stanza and the passionate phrases filling them.[3] Yet nothing could be more orthodox than the Latin hymn throughout its course of development. Its function was liturgical. It was correct in doctrinal expressions, and followed in every way the authoritative teachings of the Church ; its symbolism was derived from the works of learned doctors ; and its feeling took form from the tenets of Latin Christianity.   The *Dies Irae* and the *Stabat Mater* yield evidence of this.[4]

From the religious phases of mediaeval emotion, one may pass to modes of feeling which were secular and human. The antecedents were again the racial traits of the peoples who were to become mediaeval ; the formative influences still are Christianity and the profane antique culture.   The racial traits show clearest in vernacular compositions, some of which may carry fervent feeling, such as enkindles the Crusader's song of *Hartmann von Aue* :

[1] See *Classical Heritage*, p. 267, and cf. *ibid*. chap. ix. sec. 1.
[2] See *post*, Chapter XXXIII. II.
[3] The account of the evolution of the hymn from the prose sequence is given *post*, Chapter XXXIII. III.
[4] Further illustrations of the mediaeval emotionalizing of Latin Christianity could be made from the history of certain Christian conceptions, angels for example: —the Old and New Testaments and the Apocrypha contain the revelation of their functions ; next, their natures are defined in the works of the Fathers and the *Celestial Hierarchy* of Pseudo-Dionysius the Areopagite.   The matter is gone over at great length, and their nature and functions logically perfected, by the school- men of the twelfth and thirteenth centuries. But, all the while, religious feeling, popular credences, and the imagination of poet and artist went on investing with beauty and loveliness these guardian spirits who carried out God's care of man. Thus angels became the realities they were felt to be.

" Min fröude wart nie sorgelos
  Unz an die tage
Daz ich mir Kristes bluomen kos
  Die ich hie trage.
Die kundent eine sumerzît,
  Die alsô gar
In suezer augenweide lît ;
  Got helfe uns dar.

" Mich hât diu werlt also gewent (gewöhnt),
  Daz mir der muot
Sich z'einer mâze nâch ir sent :
  Dêst mir nu guot.
Got hat vil wol ze mir getân,
  Als ez nu stât,
Daz ich der sorgen bin erlân
  Diu manegen hât
Gebunden an den fuoz,
  Daz er belîben muoz
Swenn' ich in Kristes schar
  Mit frouden wünneclichen var." [1]

The secular emotional development was connected with
the religious. It was stimulated by the deepening of
emotional capacity caused by Christianity, and was not
unrelated to the Christian love of God, the place of which
was taken, in secular mediaeval passion, by an idealizing,
but carnal, love of woman ; and instead of the terror-
stricken piety which accompanied the Christian's love for
his Maker and his Judge, the heart was glad and the temper
open to every joy, while also subject to the fears and hates
which spring up among men of mortal passions.

In the romantic and utter abandonment required of its
votaries, this earthly love may well have drawn suggestion

[1] Hartmann belongs to that great group of courtly German poets whose lives
surround the year 1200. He was the translator of Chrètien de Troye's *Erec*
and *Ivain*. See Bech's *Hartmann von Aue* (Deutsche Klassiker). The verses
quoted can hardly be rendered ; but the meaning is as follows :

" My joys were never free from care until the day which showed me the flowers
of Christ which I wear here (*i.e.* the Crusader's cross). They herald a summer-time
leading to sweet pastures of delight. God help us thither ! The world has treated
me so that my spirit yearns therefor ;—well for me ! God has been good to me,
so that I am released from cares which tie the feet of many, chaining them here,
while I in Christ's band with blissful joys fare on."

These lines carry that same yearning of the simple soul for heaven, *its home*,
which was expressed, some centuries before, in Otfried's *Evangelienbuch* (*ante*,
Chapter IX.). The words and their connotations (*augenweide, wünneclich*) are
utterly German. Yet the author lived in a literary atmosphere of translation from
the French.

from that boundless love of God which had superseded the Greek precept of " nothing in excess," teaching instead that no limit should be set on what was absolutely good. The principle of love unrestrained was thus inaugurated, and did not always turn to God. Ardent natures who felt love's power, might hold it as the supreme arbiter and law of life, and the giver of strength and virtue. These thoughts will shape the tale of Lancelot and myriad poems besides. They also may be found incarnate in the living instance : the heart of Heloïse held a passion for her human master which she recognized as her highest law. It was such a passion as she would hardly have conceived but for the existence of like categories of devotion to the Christian God. Not in her nature alone, but through many Christian generations whereof she was the fruit, there had gone on a continual enhancement of capacities of feeling, for which she was a greater woman when she grew to womanhood and felt its passion. Through such heightening of her powers of loving, and through the suggestiveness of the Christian love of God, she could conceive and feel a like absolute devotion to a man.[1]

There were, moreover, partially humanized stages in which the love of God was affiliated with loves of mortal hue. Many a mediaeval woman felt a passionate love for the spiritual Bridegroom. Its expression, its suggestions, its training, might transmit power and passion to the love of very mortal men : while from the worship of the Blessed Virgin expressions of passionate devotion might pass over into poems telling man's love of woman. And what reaches of passion might not the Song of Songs suggest, although that imagined bridal of the Soul was never deemed a song of human love ? [2]

[1] Post, Chapter XXVI.

[2] The makers of love poems borrowed expressions from poems to the Virgin. Cf. Wilmanns, Leben und Dichtung Walter's Von der Vogelweide, p. 179. Touches of mortal passion sometimes appear in the adoration of men for the Blessed Virgin. See Caesar of Heisterbach, vii. 32 and 50, and viii. 58. Of course, many suggestions were drawn also from the antique literature. See post, Chapter XXXIII. iv. The subject of courtly and romantic love will come up properly for treatment in Chapter XXIV.

BOOK III

THE IDEAL AND THE ACTUAL: THE SAINTS

CHAPTER XVI

THE REFORMS OF MONASTICISM

MEDIAEVAL EXTREMES ; BENEDICT OF ANIANE ; CLUNY ; CITEAUX'S
CHARTA CHARITATIS ; THE VITA CONTEMPLATIVA ACCEPTS
THE VITA ACTIVA.

THE present Book and the following will set forth the
higher manifestations of the religious energies of the Middle
Ages, and then the counter ideals which knights and ladies
delighted to contemplate, and sometimes strove to reach.
In religious as well as mundane life, ideals admired and
striven for constitute human facts, make part of the human
story, quite as veritably as the spotted actuality everywhere
in evidence. The tale of piety is to be gathered from those
efforts of the religious purpose which almost attain their
ideal ; while as a comment on them, and a foil and contrast,
the deflections of human frailty may be observed. Likewise
the full reality of chivalry lies in its ideals, supplemented by
the illuminating contrast of failure and oppression, making
what we may call its actuality. The emotional element,
reviewed in the last chapter, will for the time be dominant.

Practice always drops below the ethical standards of a
period. The contrast appears in the history of Greece and
Rome. Yet in neither Greece nor Rome could there exist
the abysms of contradiction which disclose themselves after
the conversion of western Europe to the religion of Christ.
And for the following reasons. Greek and Roman standards were finite ; they regarded only the mortal happiness
of the individual and the terrestrial welfare of the State.
To Greek thought the indefinite or limitless was as the

monstrous and unformed ; and therefore abhorrent to the classic ideals of perfection. Again, Greek and Roman standards demanded only what Greek and Roman humanity could fulfil in the mortal life of earth. But the Christian ideal of conduct assumes the universal imperfection and infinite perfectibility of man. It has constant regard to immortality, and eternity is needed for its fulfilment. Moreover, whether or not Christ's Gospel set forth any inherent antagonism between the fulness of mortal life and the sure attainment of heaven, its historical interpretations have never effected a complete reconcilement. They have always presented a conflict between the finite and the eternal, unconceived and unsuspected by the pagan ethics of Greece and Rome.

This conflict dawned in the Apostolic Age. During the patristic period it worked itself out to a formulated opposition between the world and the City of God. Of this, monasticism was the chief expression. Nevertheless, pagan principle and feeling lived on in the reasonings and characters of the Church Fathers. The Roman qualities in Ambrose, the general survival of antique greatness in Augustine, preserved them from the rhetorical hysteria of Jerome and the exaggeration of phrase which affects the writings of Gregory the Great.[1] With the decadence preceding, and the confusion following, the Carolingian period, antique qualities passed away ; and when men began again to think and feel constructively, there remained no antique poise to restrain the strife of those mighty opposites—the joys of life and the terrors of the Judgment Day.

This conflict, inherent in mediaeval Christianity, was in part a struggle between temporal desires which many men approved, and their renunciation for eternal joy. From this point of view it was a conflict of ideals, though, to be sure, life's common cravings were on one side, and often unideally turned the scale. We are not immediately concerned, however, with this conflict of ideals ; but with the contrasts

---

[1] One will bear in mind that much mediaeval phraseology goes back to the Fathers. For example, in monkish vilification of woman there is no phrase more common than *janua diaboli*, and it was Tertullian's, who died in the first part of the third century.

presented between the actual and the ideal, between conduct and the principles which should have controlled it. The opposition between this life and eternity is mentioned in order to make clear the tremendous demands of the Christian ethical ideal, and the unlikelihood of its fulfilment by mediaeval humanity. So one may perceive a reason why the Middle Ages were to show such extremes of contrast between principles and practices. The standards recognized as holiest countered the natural lives of men ; and for that reason could be lived up to only under transient spiritual enthusiasm or by exceptional people. Monasticism held the highest ideals of Christian living, and its story illustrates the continual falling away of conduct from the recognized ideal.

Without regard to the contrast between the ideal and the actual, the Middle Ages were a period of extremes—of extreme humility and love as well as cruelty and hate. Such extremes may be traceable to a certain unlimited quality in Christian principles, according to which no man could have too much humility or Christian love, or could too strenuously combat the enemies of Christ. To be sure, an all-proportioning principle of conduct lay in man's love of God, answering to God's love which encompassed all His creatures. But such proportionment is difficult for simple minds, and many of the extremes which meet us in the Middle Ages were directly due to the simplicity with which mediaeval men and women carried out such Christian precepts as they were taken with, in disregard of all else that commonly balances and conventionalizes human lives.

For this reason also the Middle Ages are picturesque and poetic. Nothing could be more picturesque and more like a poem than the simple absoluteness with which St. Francis interpreted and lived out his Lord's principle of love, and made universal application of his Lord's injunction to the rich young man, to go and sell his goods and give to the poor, and then come follow Him. This particular solution of the problem of God's service was taken by Francis, and by many another, as of general application, and was literally carried out ; just as Francis with exquisite simplicity carried out other precepts of his Lord in a way that would be foolishness were it not so beautiful.

There was no contrast between conduct and principle in the life of Francis ; and in other men conduct might agree with such principles as they understood. Many a rustic layman, many a good knight, fulfilled the standards of his calling. Many a parish priest did his whole duty, as he conceived it. And many a monk and nun lived up to their monastic *regula,* if indeed never satisfying the inner yearning of the soul unquenchably striving for perfection. Indeed, for the monk ever to have been satisfied with him-self would have meant a fall from humility to vainglory.

The precepts of the Gospel were for every man and woman. Nevertheless, the same rules of living did not apply to all. In this regard, mediaeval society falls into the two general divisions of clergy and laity, meaning by the former all persons making special profession of religion or engaged in the service of the Church.[1] This would include anchorites and monks (also the *conversi*[2] or lay-brethren) and the secular clergy from the rank of bishop downward. To such (excepting seculars below the grade of sub-deacon) the rule of celibacy applied, as well as other ascetic precepts dependent on the vows they had taken or the regulations under which they lived. Conversely, certain rules like those relating to the conduct of man and wife would touch the laity alone.

A general similarity of principle pervaded the rules of conduct applying to all orders of the clergy, secular and regular.[3] Yet there was a difference in the severity of the rules and the stringency of their application. The mediaeval code of religious ethics applied in its utter strenuousness only to monks and nuns. They alone had seriously under-taken to obey the Gospel precept, *estote perfecti* ; and they alone could be regarded as living the life of complete Christian militancy against the world, the flesh, and the devil. The trials, that is to say the temptations, of this

[1] For the different meanings of the term *clericus* see Du Cange, *Glossarium,* under that word.

[2] For the meanings of this term also see Du Cange, *Glossarium,* under that word.

[3] Regular clergy are the monks, who live under a *regula.*

warfare could be fully known only to the monk. " Tentatio,"
says Caesar of Heisterbach, " est militia," *i.e.* warfare ; it is
possible only for those who live humanly and rationally,
after the spirit, which is to say, as monks ; " the seculars
(*i.e.* the laity or possibly the clergy who were not monks) and
the carnal (*i.e.* the laity) who walk according to the flesh, are
improperly said to be tempted ; for as soon as they feel
the temptation they consent, or resist lukewarmly, like the
horse and the mule who have no understanding." [1]

We have spoken of the inception of monasticism, and
of its early motives,[2] which included the fear of hell, the
love of Christ, and the conviction of the antagonism between
pleasure and that service which opens heaven's gates.   Such
sentiments were likely to develop and expand.   The fear
of hell might be inflamed and made visible by the same
imagination that festered over the carnality of pleasure ;
the heart could impassion and extend the love of Christ
through humanity's full capacity for loving what was holiest
and most lovable ; and the mind could attain to an over-
mastering conviction of the incompatibility of pleasure with
absolute devotion.   Through the Middle Ages these motives
developed and grew together, until they made a mode of
life, and fashioned human characters into accord with it.
Century after century the lives of thousands fulfilled the
monastic spirit, and often so perfectly as to belie humanity's
repute for frailty.   Their virtues shunned encomium.
Record was made of those whose mind and energy organized
and wrought, or whose piety and love of God burned so
hotly that others were enkindled.   But legion upon legion
of tacit lives are registered only in the Book with seven
seals.

Monastic abuses have usually spoken more loudly than
monastic regularity.   In Christian monasticism there is an
energy of renovation which constantly cries against corruption.   Its invective reaches us from all the mediaeval
centuries ; while monastic regularity has more commonly
been unreported.   It is well to bear this in mind when

[1] *Dialogus miraculorum,* ed. J. Strange, iv. i. (Cologne, 1851). Of course
Caesar was a monk.
[2] *Ante,* Chapter XV.

reading of monastic vice. It always existed, and judging from the fiery denunciations which it awakened, it was often widely prevalent. In fact, the monastic life required such love of God or fear of hell, such renunciation of this world, its ambitions, its lusts and its lures, that monks were likely to fall below the prescribed standards, and then quickly into all manner of sin, from lack of the restraints, or outlets, of secular life.

Consequently the most patent history of monasticism is the history of its attempts to reform and renew itself. Its heroes come before us as reformers or refounders, whose endeavour is to reinstitute the perfect way, impassion men anew to follow it, by added precepts discipline them for its long ascents, and so occupy them in the practice of its virtues that all distracting impulses may perish. Their apparent endeavour (at least until the day of Francis of Assisi) is to renew a life from which their contemporaries have fallen away. And yet through all there was unconscious innovation and progress.

The greater part of the fervent piety of the Middle Ages dwelt in cloisters, when not drawn forth unwillingly to serve the Lord in the world. Mediaeval saints were, or yearned to be, monks or nuns. Consequently monastic reforms, as well as attempts to raise the condition of the secular clergy, emanated from within monasticism. Its own rules of living had been set from within by Benedict of Nursia, and others who were monks. There was much irregularity at first ; but the seventh and eighth centuries witnessed the conflict between different types of monastic organization, and then the general victory of the Benedictine *regula*. This was also a victory for monastic reform ; for moral looseness, accompanied by heathenish irregularities, easily penetrated cloisters when not protected by a common and authoritative rule. As it was, the energy of Benedictine uniformity seemed exhausted in the contest.

But a Benedictine refounder arose. This was the high-born Witiza of Aquitaine, the ascetic virtuosity of whose early life had won him repute. Assuming the name of Benedict, he established a monastery on the bank of the little Aniane, in Aquitaine, in the year 779. His foundation flourished in righteousness and increased in numbers, till it drew the attention of Alcuin and Charlemagne to its abbot. Benedict was given the task of reforming the monasteries of Aquitaine. Afterwards Louis the Pious extended his authority; till in 817 a reforming synod, over which he presided, was held at Aix, and the king's authority was attached to its decrees. All Frankish monasteries were therein commanded to observe the *regula* of Benedict of Nursia, with many further precepts set by him of Aniane, aggravating the severity of the older rule; for example, by enforcing a more rigid silence among the monks when at labour, and restricting their intercourse with the laity. Great stress was laid upon the labours of the field. There was little novelty in the work of this reorganizer, with his consistent ascetic contempt for profane literature. His labours were typical of those of many a monastic reformer after him, who likewise sought to re-establish the strictness of the old Benedictine rule, and in fact added to its austerities.

The next example of reform is Cluny, founded in the year 910. Its cloister discipline followed the *regula* of Benedict with the additions decreed by the synod of Aix. Under Odo (d. 942) Majolus (d. 994) and Odilo (d. 1048) it rose to unprecedented power and influence. Mainly because of the winning and commanding qualities of its abbots, it received the support of kings and popes; its authority and privileges were increased, until it became the head of more than three hundred cloisters distributed through France, Italy, Germany, and Spain. In ecclesiastical policy it stood for decency and reform, but without giving extreme support to either emperor or pope. Balance and temperance characterized its career. It was a monastic organization which by precept and example, and by the wide supervising powers it received from the papacy and from temporal authorities, promoted regularity and propriety of life among monks, and also among the secular clergy. The "reforms of Cluny" do not represent any specific intensifying of monastic principles, but rather the general endeavour of the better elements in Burgundian and French monasticism to overcome the crass secularization of the Church, within and without the cloister. Cluny's influence told generally against monastic degradation, rather than in favour of any special ascetic or ecclesiastic policy. The prevailing simony, the clerical concubinage, the rough and warlike ways of bishops and abbots were all corruptions standing in the way of any monastic or ecclesiastical improvement ; and Cluny opposed them, in moderation however, and with considerable acquiescence in the apparently necessary conditions of the time.[1]

After the comparative strictness of its first abbots, Cluny's discipline moderated almost to laxity ; and the interests of the rich and magnificent monastery became elegant and somewhat secular. It still maintained monastic decencies while not going beyond their demands. Its face was no longer set against comfortable living, nor against art and letters. And the time came when fervent spirits demanded a more uncompromising attack upon the world and the flesh.

Such came from Citeaux (near Dijon), where a few monks founded a struggling monastery in 1098. Its fortunes were small and feeble until the time of its third abbot, the Englishman, Stephen Harding (1109–1134), whose genius set the lines of Citeaux's larger destinies. Her great period began when, shortly after Harding's entrance on his abbacy, there arrived a band of well-born youths, led by one Bernard. Then of a truth the cloister burned with ardour. Its numbers grew, and Bernard was sent with a Cistercian band to found a daughter monastery at Clairvaux (1115).

Like Stephen Harding, Bernard was an ascetic, and the Cistercian Order represents a stern tightening of the reins which Cluny left lying somewhat slackly upon the backs of her stall-fed monks.[2] Controversies arose between the Cluniac Benedictines and the Cistercian Benedictines insisting on a stricter rule. Bernard himself entered into heated controversy with that great temperate personality of the twelfth century, Peter the Venerable, Cluny's revered lord.

The original *regula* of Benedict provided an admirable

---

[1] See Sackur, *Die Cluniacenser*, etc., *passim*, and Bd. II. 464 (Halle, 1892).

[2] On the differences between Cluny and Citeaux see Vacandard, *Vie de St Bernard*, chap. iv. (2nd ed., Paris, 1897), and Zöckler, *Askese und Mönchtum*, 2nd ed. pp. 406-415 (Frankfurt a. M., 1897).

constitution for the single monastery, but no plan for the supervision of one monastery by another. The mediaeval advance in monastic organization consisted in the authoritative supervision of subordinate or " daughter " foundations by the superior or primal monastery of the Order. The Abbot of Cluny exercised such authority over Cluniac foundations, as well as over monasteries which, at the instance of the secular lord of the land, had been reorganized by Cluny.

The Cistercian Order represents a less monarchical, or more decentralized subordination, on a plan similar to the feudal principle of sub-infeudation, whereby the holder of the fief owed his duties to his immediate lord, who in turn owed duties to his own lord, still above him. Thus in the Cistercian Order the visitatorial authority over each foundation was vested in the immediate mother abbey, rather than in the primal abbey of Citeaux, from which the intervening mother abbey had gone forth.

This plan was formulated by Stephen Harding's *Charta Charitatis*,[1] the charter of the Cistercian Order and a monument of constructive genius. Apparently mindful of the various privileges recognized by the feudal system, it begins by renouncing on the part of the superior monastery all claim to temporal emolument from the daughter foundations : " Nullam terrenae commoditatis seu rerum temporalium exactionem imponimus." " But for love's sake (*gratia charitatis*) we desire to retain the care of their souls ; so that should they swerve from the holy way and the observance of the Holy Rule, they may through our solicitude return to rectitude of life."

Then follows the command that all Cistercian foundations obey implicitly the *regula* of Benedict, as understood and practised at Citeaux, and that all follow the customs of Citeaux, and the same forms of chant and prayer and service (for we receive their monks in our cloister, and they ours), " so that without discordant actions we may live by one love, one rule, and like practices (*una charitate, una regula, similibusque vivamus moribus*)." A short sentence follows, forbidding all monasteries and individual monks to accept

---

[1] Migne, *Pat. Lat.* 166, col. 1377-1384.

from any source any privilege inconsistent with the customs of the Order.

So the *Charta* enjoined a uniformity of discipline. Wise and temperate provision was made for the enforcement of the same when necessary by the immediate parent monastery of the delinquent foundation. " Whenever the Abbot of Citeaux comes to a monastery to visit it, its abbot shall make way for him, and he shall there hold the office of abbot. Yet let him not presume to order or conduct affairs against the wishes of its abbot and the brethren. But if he sees that the precepts of the *Regula* or of our Order are transgressed, let him seek to correct the brethren with the advice and in the presence of the abbot. If the abbot be absent, he may still proceed." Once a year the Abbot of Citeaux, in person or through one of his co-abbots, must visit all the monasteries (coenobia) which he has founded, and if more often, the brethren should the more rejoice. Likewise must the four primary abbots of La Ferté, Pontigny, Clairvaux, and Morimond, together visit Citeaux once a year, at such time as they may choose, except that set for the annual meeting of the general Chapter. At Citeaux also, let any visiting abbot be treated as if he were abbot there.

" Whenever any of our churches (monasteries) by God's grace so increases that it is able to found another brotherhood, let the same relationship (*definitio*) obtain between them which obtains between us and our *cofratres*, except that they may not hold an annual Chapter ; but rather let all abbots come without fail every year to the annual Chapter at Citeaux.

" At which Chapter let them take measures for the safety of their souls ; if in the observance of the holy *Regula* or the Order, anything should be amended or supplemented, let them ordain it ; let them re-establish the bond of peace and love among themselves."

The annual Chapter is also given authority to correct any abbot and settle controversies between abbots ; but when an abbot appears unworthy of his charge, and the Chapter has not acted, it is the duty of the abbot of his mother church to admonish him, and, upon his obduracy, summon other abbots and move for his deposition. Thus the *Charta Charitatis* apportioned authority among the abbots of the Order, providing, as it were, a mutual power of enforcement in which every abbot had part. One notices also that the *Charta* is neither monarchical nor democratic, but aristocratic ; for the abbots (not the Abbot of Citeaux alone) manage and control the Order, and without any representation of the monks at the annual Chapter.[1] The *Charta Charitatis* seems a spiritual mirror of the feudal system.

Mediaeval monasticism, whether cloistered or sent forth into the world, was predominantly coenobitic or communal. Yet through the Middle Ages the anchorite or hermit way of life was not unrepresented. Both monk and hermit existed from the beginning of Christian monasticism ; they recognized the same purpose, but employed different means to achieve it. For their common aim was to merit the kingdom of heaven through the suppression of sense-desires and devotion to spiritual righteousness. But the communal system recognized the social nature of man, his essential weakness in isolation, and his inability to satisfy his bodily wants by himself. Thus admitting the human need of fellowship and correction, it deemed that man's spiritual progress could be best advanced in a way of life which took account of these facts. On the other hand, anchoritism looked rather to man's self-sufficiency alone with God— and the devil. It held that man could best conquer his carnal nature in solitude, and in solitude best meditate upon his soul and God. The society of one's fellows, even though they be like-minded, is a distraction and a hindrance. Obviously, the devoted temper has its variants ; and some 'souls will draw from solitude that strength which others gain from support and sympathy.

Both the coenobitic and the hermit life were, from the time of their inception, phases of the *vita contemplativa*. Yet more active duties had constantly been recognized, until at last monasticism, in an ardour of love for fellow-men, broke from the cloister and went abroad in the steps of Francis and Dominic. Even this active and uncloistered monasticism drew its strength from its hidden meditation,

[1] In fact, paragraph 15 provides that at the Chapter accusations against an abbot shall be brought only by an abbot.

and, strengthened from within itself, entered upon the *vita activa*, and practised among men the virtues which it had acquired through contemplation and the quiet discipline of the cloister. So if we people of the world would have understanding of the matter, we must never forget that at its source and in its essence the monastic life is a *vita contemplativa*, whether the monastic man, as a member of a fervent community, be sustained through the support of his brethren and the counsel or command of his superior, or whether, as an anchorite, he seclude himself in solitude. And the essence of this *vita contemplativa* is not to do or act, but to contemplate, meditate upon God and the human soul. By one line of ancestry it is a descendant of Aristotle's βίος θεωρητικός. But its mightier parent was the Saviour's manifestation of God's love of man and man's love of God. From this source came the emotional elements (and they were the predominant and overwhelming) of the Christian *vita contemplativa*, its terror and despair, its tears and hope, and its yearning love. Through these any Hellenic calm was transformed to storm-tossed Christian ecstasy.

Monastic quietism might at any time be drafted into Christian militancy. In the crises of the Church, or when there was call to go forth and convert the heathen or the carnal, both monk and hermit became zealots in the world. Yet important and frequent as these active functions were, they were not commanded by the Benedictine *regula*, either in its original form or in its many modifications, Cluniac, Cistercian, or Carthusian ; hence they were not treated as part of the monastic life. There was to come a change. The *vita contemplativa* was to take to itself the *vita activa* as a regular and not an occasional function of perfect Christian piety. An evangelization of monasticism, according to the more active spirit of the Gospel, was at hand. The monastic ideal was to become humane and actively loving. In principle and theory, as well as practice, Christian piety was no longer to find its entire end and aim in contemplation, in asceticism, in purity : it was *regularly* henceforth to occupy itself with a loving beneficence among men.

Some of the ardent beginnings of this movement did not receive the sanction of the Church. The Poor of Lyons, the

Humbled Folk (*Humiliati*) of Lombardy, the Beghards of Liége, were pronounced to be heretics. Predominantly lay and ecclesiastically somewhat bizarre, they were scarcely monks. Yet these irregular evangelists of the latter part of the twelfth century were forerunners of that chief evangelizer of Monasticism, Francis of Assisi.[1]

The life of Francis, as all men know, fulfilled the current demands of monasticism. He lived and taught obedience, chastity, humility, and a more absolute poverty than had been before conceived. With respect to the first three virtues, it was only through his loving way of living them that Francis set anything new before his brethren. As for the last, it may be said that monks had always been forbidden to own property ; only the monastery or the Order might. Francis's absolute acceptance of poverty comes to us as inspired by the command of Christ to the rich young man : Go and sell all, and give to the poor, and then come follow me. But had no Christian soul read this before and accepted it absolutely ? The Athanasian Life of St. Anthony,

---

[1] It is interesting to observe how much of Stephen of Bourbon's description of the Poor of Lyons applies to Franciscan beginnings, and how much more of it would have applied had not St. Francis possessed the gift of obedience among his other virtues. Stephen was a Dominican of the first half of the thirteenth century, and himself an inquisitor. Thus he describes these misled people : " The Waldenses are called after the author of this heresy, whose name was Waldensis. They are also called the Poor of Lyons, because there they first professed poverty. Likewise they call themselves the Poor in Spirit, because the Lord says : ' Blessed are the poor in spirit. . . .' Waldensis, who lived in Lyons, was a man of wealth, but of little education. Hearing the Gospels, and curious to understand their meaning, he bargained with two priests that they should make a translation in the vulgar tongue. This they did, with other books of the Bible and many precepts from the writings of the saints. When this townsman had read the Gospel till he knew it by heart, he set out to follow apostolic perfection, just as the Apostles themselves. So, selling all his goods, in contempt of the world, he tossed his money like dirt to the poor. Then he presumed to usurp the office of the Apostles, and preached the Gospels in the open streets. He led many men and women to do the same, exercising them in the Gospels. He also sent them to preach in the neighbouring villages. These ignorant men and women running through villages, entering houses, and preaching in the open places as well as the churches, drew others to the same ways."

Up to this point we are close to the Franciscans. But now the Archbishop of Lyons forbids these ignorant irregular evangelists to preach. Their leader answers for them, that they must obey God rather than man, and Scripture says to preach the Gospel to every creature. Thus they fell into disobedience, contumacy, and incurred excommunication, says Stephen (*Anecdotes, etc., d'Étienne de Bourbon*, edited by Lecoy de la Marche (Soc. de l'Histoire de France, Paris, 1877), cap. 342).

at the very beginning of Christian monasticism, has the same account ; he too gave up all he had on reading this passage. But then he fled to the desert, while Francis, when he had given up all, opened his arms to mankind. In accordance with his brotherly and social evangelization of monasticism, Francis modified certain of its practices. He removed restrictions upon intercourse among the brethren, and took away the barriers, save those of holiness, between the brethren and the world. Then he lifted the veil of silence from the brethren's lips. They should thence-forth speak freely, in love of God and man. So monasticism stepped forth, at last uncloistered, upon its course of love and teaching in the world.

In spite of the temperamental differences between Francis and Dominic, and in spite of the different tasks which they set before their Orders, the analogy between Franciscans and Dominicans was fundamental ; for the latter, as well as the former, regularly undertook to evoke the *vita activa* from the *vita contemplativa*. The Dominicans were to preach and teach true Christian doctrine, and as veritable *Domini canes* destroy the wolves of heresy menacing the Christian fold.

Dominic received from Pope Honorius III., in 1217, the confirmation of his Order, as an Order of Canons according to the *Regula* supposed to have been taught by Augustine. The Preaching Friars were never cloistered by their *regula*, any more than were the Minorites. Two or three years later, Dominic added, or emphasized anew, the principle of voluntary poverty, not only in the individuals but in the Order as a corporate whole. Whencesoever he derived this idea—whether from the Franciscans, or because it was rife among men—at all events it was not his originally ; for Dominic had accepted at an earlier period the one-sixth of the revenues of the Bishop of Toulouse. This he now renounced, and instead accepted voluntary poverty.

It was not given to Dominic to love as Francis loved. Nor was he an incarnate poem. But it was in the spirit of Christian devotion that he undertook and laid upon his Order the performance of active duties in the world, especi-ally of preaching true doctrines for the salvation of souls. Dominic took no personal part in the Albigensian bloodshedding ; and he was not the founder of the Inquisition, although his Order was so soon to be identified with it.   He was a theologian, a teacher, and an ardent preacher ; a devoted man, given to tears.   Almost the only words we have from him are those of his Testament : " Caritatem habete, humilitatem servate, paupertatem voluntariam possedete." [1]

[1] The rôle of Franciscans and Dominicans in the spread of philosophic knowledge in the thirteenth century will be considered *post*, Chapter **XXXVIII.** Chapter **XIX.**, *post*, is devoted to the personal qualities of Francis.

CHAPTER XVII

THE HERMIT TEMPER

PETER DAMIANI ; ROMUALD ; DOMINICUS LORICATUS ; BRUNO AND GUIGO, CARTHUSIANS

To contemplate goodness in God, and strain toward it in yearning love, is the method of the Christian *vita contemplativa*. In this way the recluse cultivates humility, patience, purity, and love, and perfects his soul for heaven. And herein, in that it is more undistracted and more undisturbed, lies the superiority of the solitary life over the coenobitic.

Yet this conceived superiority is but the reason and the conscious motive for the solitary life. The call to it is felt as well as intellectually accepted. It is temperament that makes the recluse ; his reasons are but his justification. In solitude he lives the reaches of his life ; from solitude he draws his utmost bliss. To leave it involves the torture of separation, and then all the petty pains of unhappy labour and distasteful intercourse with men. " Whoever would reach the summit of perfection should keep within the cloister of his seclusion, cherish spiritual leisure, and shudder at traversing the world, as if he were about to plunge into a sea of blood. For the world is so filthy with vices, that any holy mind is befouled even by thinking about it." [1]

Here speaks the hermit temper, by the mouth of a supreme exponent. If Hildebrand, who compelled all men to his purposes, kept Peter Damiani in the world, that ascetic soul did not cease to yearn for the hermit life. His skilful pen served it untiringly. Its temper, its merits, and its grounds, appear with unique clarity in the writings

[1] Peter Damiani, *De contemptu saeculi*, cap. 32 (Migne 145, col. 287).

of him who, sore against his will, was the Cardinal-Bishop of Ostia.[1]

" The solitary life is the school of celestial doctrine and the divine arts (*artes divinae*)," says Damiani, meaning every word. " For there God is the whole that is learned. He is also the way by which one advances, through which one attains knowledge of the highest truth." [2] To obtain its benefits, it must be led assiduously and without break or wandering abroad among men : " Habit makes his cell sweet to the monk, but roving makes it seem horrible. . . . The unbroken hermit life is a cooling refreshment (*refrigerium*) ; but, if interrupted, it seems a torment. Through continued seclusion the soul is illuminated, vices are uncovered, and whatever of himself had been hidden from the man, is disclosed." [3]

Peter argues that the hermit life is free from temptations (!) and offers every aid to victory.

" The wise man, bent on safeguarding his salvation, watches always to destroy his vices ; he girds his loins—and his belly— with the girdle of perfect mortification. Truly that takes place when the itching palate is suppressed, when the pert tongue is held in silence, the ear is shut off from evil-speaking and the eye from unpermitted sights ; when the hand is held from cruel striking, and the foot from vainly roving ; when the heart is withstood, that it may not envy another's felicity, nor through avarice covet what is not its own, nor through anger sever itself from fraternal love, nor vaunt itself arrogantly above its fellows, nor yield to the ticklings of lust, nor immoderately sink itself in grief or abandon itself wantonly to joy. Since, then, the human mind has not the power to remain entirely empty, and unoccupied with the love of something, it is girt around with a wall of the virtues.

" In this way, then, our mind begins to be at rest in its Author and to taste the sweetness of that intimacy. At once it rejects whatever it deems contrary to the divine law, shrinks from what does not agree with the rule of supernal righteousness. Hence true mortification is born ; hence it comes that man bearing the Cross of his Redeemer seems dead to the world. No longer he delights in silly fables, nor is content to waste his time with idle talk. But he is free for psalms and hymns and spiritual songs ;

---

[1] On Damiani, see *ante*, Chapter XI. iv.
[2] Peter Damiani, *Opusc.* xi., *Dominus vobiscum*, cap. 19 (Migne 145, col. 246).
[3] Peter Damiani, *De contemptu saeculi*, cap. 25 (Migne 145, col. 278).

he seeks seclusion, he longs for a hiding-place ; he regards the cloister as a shop for talkers, a public forum, and rejoices in nooks and pries out corners ; and that he may the more freely attend to the contemplation of his Creator, so far as he may he declines colloquy with men." [1]

" In fine," says Damiani, in another chapter, " our entire conversion, and renunciation of the world, aims at nothing else than rest. This rest is won through the man's prior discipline in the toils of strife, in order that when the tumult of disturbance ceases, his mind, through the grace of contemplation, may be translated to explore the face of truth. But since one attains to this rest only through labour and conflict, how can one reach it who has not gone down into the strife ? By what right can one enter the halls of the King who has not traversed the arena before the doors ? " [2]

" It further behoves each brother who with his whole heart has abandoned the world, to unlearn and forget forever whatever is injurious. He should not be disputatious as to cookery, nor clever in the petty matters of the town ; nor an adept in rhetoric's jinglings, or in jokes or word play. He should love fasts and cherish penury ; he should flee the sight of man, restrain himself under the censorship of silence, withdraw from affairs, keep his mouth from idle talk, and seek the hiding-place of his soul, and in such hiding be on fire to see the face of his Creator. Let him pant for tears, and implore God for them by daily prayer." [3]

---

[1] Peter Damiani, De perfectione monachi, caps. 2, 3 (Migne 145, col. 294).

[2] De perfectione monachi, cap. 8 (Migne 145, col. 303).

[3] De perf. mon. cap. 12 (Migne 145, col. 307). For such as have feeling for these matters, I give these further extracts from the same De perf. mon. cap. 12. " For the dew of tears cleanses the soul from every stain and makes fruitful the meadows of our hearts so that they bring forth the sprouts of virtue. For often as under an icy frost the wretched soul sheds its foliage, and, grace departing, it is left to itself barren and stripped of its shortlived blossoms. But anon tears given by the Tester of hearts burst forth, and this same soul is loosed from the cold of its slothful torpor, and is clothed again with the renewed blossom of its virtues, as a tree in spring kindled by the south wind.

" Tears, moreover, which are from God, with confidence approach the tribunal of divine hearing, and quickly obtaining what they ask, assure us of the remission of our sins. Tears are intermediaries in concluding peace between God and men ; they are the truthful and the very wisest (doctissimae) teachers in the dubiousness of human ignorance. For when we are in doubt whether something may be pleasing to God, we can reach no better certitude than through prayer, weeping truthfully. We need never again hesitate as to what our mind has decided on under such conditions.

" Tears," continues Damiani, " washed the noisomeness of her guilt from the Magdalen, saved the Apostle who denied his Lord, restored King David after deadly sin, added three years to Hezekiah's life, preserved inviolate the chastity of Judith, and won for her the head of Holophernes. Why mention the centurion Cornelius, why mention Susanna ? indeed were I to tell all the deeds of tears,

With this last sentence Damiani makes his transition to the emotional side of the Christian *vita contemplativa*. He will now pour himself out in a rhapsody of praise of tears, which purify and refresh the soul, and open it to the love of God.

" From the fire of divine love rises the grace of contrition (*gratia compunctionis*), . . . and again from the contrition of tears (*ex compunctione lacrymarum*) the ardour of celestial yearning is increased. The one hangs from the other, and each promotes the other ; while the contrition of tears flows from the love of God, through tears again our soul burns more fervidly toward the love of God. In this reciprocal and alternating action, the soul is purged of the filth of its offence."

Elsewhere Damiani suggests how the hermit may acquire the " grace of tears " :

" Seclude thyself from the turmoil of secular affairs and often even from talk with thy brethren. Cut off the cares and anxieties of mundane action ; clear them away as a heap of rubbish which stops the fountain's flow. As water in a cavern of the earth wells up from the abyss, but hindered by obstacles cannot flow forth, so sadness (*tristitia*) wells in a human heart from contemplation of the profundity of God's Judgment, and yet will not flow forth in tears if checked by the clog of earthly acts. Sadness is the material of tears. But in order that the veins of this fount may flow more abundantly, do thou clear away all obstacles of secular business : and not to omit what I have frequently experienced, even spiritual zeal, the punishment of delinquents and the labour of preaching, holy as they are and commanded by divine authority, nevertheless are certainly obstacles to tears.

" So if you would attain the grace of tears, you must even curb the exercise of spiritual duties, eliminate malice, anger, and hatred,

---

the day would close before my task were ended. For it is they that purify the sinner's soul, confirm his inconstant heart, prepare joy out of grief, and, breaking forth from our eyes of flesh, raise us to the hope of supernal beatitude. For their petition may not be set aside, so mighty are their voices in the Creator's ears. . . . Before the pious Judge they hesitate at nothing, but vindicate their claim to mercy as a right, and exult confident of having obtained what they implore.

" O ye tears, joys of the spirit, sweeter than honey, sweeter than nectar ! which with a sweet and pleasant taste refresh minds lifted up to God, and water consumed and arid hearts with a flood of penetrating grace from heaven. Weeping eyes terrify the devil ; he fears the onslaught of tears bursting forth, as one would flee a tempest of hail driven by the fury of all the winds. As the torrent's rush cleanses the river-bed, the flowing tears purge the weeper's mind from the devil's tares and every pest of sin."

and the other pests from your heart. And do not let your own accusing conscience dry up the dew of tears with the aridity of fear.   Indeed the confidence of holiness (*sanctitatis fiducia*) and a conscience bearing witness to its own innocence, waters the pure soul with the celestial rivulets of grace, softens the hardness of the impure heart, and opens the floodgates of weeping." [1]

" Many are the ways," says Damiani in words sounding like a final reflection upon the solitary life—" many are the ways by which one comes to God ; diverse are the orders in the society of the faithful ; but among them all there is no way so straight, so sure, so unimpeded, so free from obstacles which trip one's feet, as this holy life. It eliminates occasions for sin ; it cultivates the greatest number of virtues by which God may be pleased ; and thus, as it removes the opportunities of delinquency, it adds the strength of necessity's insistence upon good works." [2]

Peter Damiani, exiled from solitude, found no task more grateful than that of writing the Life of his older contemporary, St. Romualdus, the founder of Camaldoli and other hermit communities in Italy. That man had completely lived the life from which the Church's exigencies dragged his biographer.   Peter put himself, as well as his best literary powers, into this *Vita Romualdi,* and made it one of the most vivid of mediaeval *Vitae sanctorum.* If Romuald was a hermit in the flesh, Damiani had the imagination to make the hermit spirit speak.[3]

" Against thee, unclean world, we cry, that thou hast an intolerable crowd of the foolish wise, eloquent as regards thee, mute as to God.   Wise are they to do evil ; they know not how to do good.   For behold almost three *lustra* [4] have passed since the blessed Romualdus, laying aside the burden of flesh, migrated to the heavenly realm, and no one has arisen from these wise people to place upon the page of history even a few of the lessons of that wonderful life."

The tone of this prologue suggests the kind of lessons found by the biographer in the Life of Romuald. He was

[1] *De inst. ord. eremitarum,* cap. 26 (Migne 145, col. 358). On the distraction from the *vita contemplativa* involved in an abbot's duties see Damiani's verses, *De abbatum miseria,* ante, Chapter XI. IV.
[2] *De inst. ord. er.* cap. 1 (Migne 145, col. 337).
[3] The *Vita Romualdi* is printed in Migne 144, col. 953-1008.
[4] Romuald died in 1027 ; *lustrum* here may mean four years, which would bring the time of writing to 1039.

born of an illustrious Ravenna family about the year 950. In youth his devout mind became conscious of the sinfulness of the flesh. Whenever he went hunting, as was his wont, and would come to a retired nook in the woods, the hermit yearning came over him—and in love, says Damiani, he was prescient of what he was later to fulfil in deed.

His father chanced to kill a neighbour in knightly brawl ; and for this homicide the son entered the monastery of St. Apollinaris in Classe, to do forty days' penance for his parent. This introduction to the cloister had its natural effect on such a temper. Goaded by a vision of the saint, Romuald became a monk. He soon showed himself no easy man. His harsh censure of the brethren's laxities caused a plot to murder him, the first of many attempts upon his life.

Three years he dwelt there. Then the yearning for perfection drove him forth, and, for a master, he sought out a hermit named Marinus, who lived in the Venetian territory, a man well meaning, but untaught as to the method of the hermit life. He and his disciple would issue from their cell and wander, singing together twenty psalms under one tree, and then thirty or forty under another. The disciple was unlettered, and the master rude. Romuald experienced intolerable tedium from straining his fixed eyes upon a psalter, which he could not read. He may have betrayed his *ennui*. At all events Marinus, grasping his rod in his right hand, and sitting on his disciple's left, continually beat him, and always on the left side of his head. At length Romuald said humbly : " Master, if you please, would you henceforth beat me on the right side, as I have lost the hearing of my left ear."

In the neighbourhood there dwelt a duke whose rapacity had brought him into peril. It happened that the abbot of a monastery situated not far from Chalons-sur-Marne in France came pilgrimaging that way, and the duke took counsel of him. The two hermits were also called ; and the advice to the duke was to flee the world. So the whole party set forth, crossed the Alps, and travelled to the abbot's monastery. There the duke became a monk, while Romuald and Marinus dwelt as solitaries a little way off.

From this time Romuald increased in virtue, far outstripping all the brethren. He supplied his wants by tilling the soil, and fasted exceedingly. He sustained continual conflicts with the devil, who was always bringing into his mind the loves and hates of his former life in the world.

" The devil would come striking on his cell, just as Romuald was falling asleep, and then no sleep for him. Every night for nearly five years the devil lay on his feet and legs, and weighted them with the likeness of a phantom weight, so that Romuald could scarcely turn on his couch. How often did the devil let loose the raging beasts of the vices ! and how often did Romuald put them to flight by his dire threats ! Hence if any of the brethren came in the silence, knocking at his door, the soldier of Christ, always ready for battle, taking him for the devil, would threaten and cry out : ' What now, wretch ! what is there for thee in the hermitage, outcast of heaven ! Back, unclean dog ! Vanish, old snake ! ' He declared that with such words as these he gave battle to malignant spirits ; and with the arms of faith would go out and meet the challenge of the foe."

Marvellously Romuald increased his fasts and austerities after the manner of the old anchorites of Egypt.[1] Miraculous powers became his. But news came of his father which drew him back to Italy. That noble but sinful parent had entered a monastery where, under the persuasion of the devil, he was soon sorry for his conversion, and sought to return to the world. Romuald decided to go to his perishing father's aid. But the people of the region hearing of it, were distressed to lose a man of such spiritual might. They took counsel how to prevent his departure, and with impious

---

[1] *Vita Romualdi*, caps. 8, 9. Damiani does not say this here, but quite definitely suggests it in cap. 64. The lives of these eastern hermits were known to Romuald ; hermits in Italy had imitated them ; and the connection with the knowledge of the Orient was not severed. See Sackur, *Die Cluniacenser*, etc., i. 324 *sqq.* Thus for their models these Italian hermits go behind the *Regula Benedicti* to the anchorite examples of Cassian and the East. Cf. Taylor, *Classical Heritage*, p. 160. A good example was St. Nilus, a Calabrian, perhaps of Greek stock. As Abbot of Crypta-Ferrata in Agro-Tusculano, he did not cease from his austerities, and still dwelt in a cave. He died in 1005 at the alleged age of ninety-five. His days are thus described : from dawn to the third hour he copied rapidly, filling a $\tau\epsilon\tau\rho\alpha\delta\epsilon\hat{\iota}o\nu$ (quaternion) each day. From the third to the sixth hour he stood before the Cross of the Lord, reciting psalms and making genuflections ; from the sixth to the ninth, he sat and read—no profane book we may be sure. When the ninth hour was come, he addressed his evening hymn to God and went out to walk and study Him in His works. See his *Vita*, from the Greek, in *Acta sanctorum* Sept. t. vii. pp. 279-343, especially page 293.

piety (*impia pietate*) decided to send men to kill him, thinking that since they could not retain him alive, they would
have his corpse as a protection for the land (*pro patrocinio
terrae*). Knowing of this, Romuald shaved his head, and
as the murderers approached his cell in the dusk of morning,
he began to eat ravenously. Thinking him demented, they
did him no injury. He then set forth, staff in hand, and
walked from the centre of Gaul, even to Ravenna. There
finding his father still seeking to return to the world, he tied
the old sinner's feet to a beam, fettered him with chains,
flogged him, and at length by pious severity so subjugated
his flesh that with God's aid he brought his mind back to a
state of salvation.[1]

Thus far Romuald's life affords striking illustration of
the fact that prodigious austerities and the consequent repute
for miracles were the chief elements in mediaeval sainthood ;
also of the fact that the saint's dead body might be as good
as he. But while he lived, Romuald was much more than
a miracle-working relic. He was a strong, domineering
personality. It was soon after he brought his father back
to the way of holiness that the old man saw a vision, and
happily yielded up the ghost. The son continued to
advance in his chosen way of life and in the elements of
character which it fostered. He became a prodigious
solitary ; one to whom men and their ways were intolerable,
and who himself was sometimes found intolerable by men.
Even his appearance might be exceptional :

" The venerable man dwelt for a while in a swamp (near
Ferrara). At length the poisonous air and the stench of the
marsh drove him out ; and he emerged hairless, with his flesh
puffed and swollen (*tumefactus et depilatus*), not looking as if
belonging to the *genus homo* ; for he was as green as a newt." [2]

Such a story displays the very extravagance of fleshly
mortification. It has also its local colour. But one should
seek its explanation in the grounds of the hermit life as set
forth by Peter Damiani. Then the incidents of Romuald's
life will appear to spring from these hermit motives and
from the hermit temperament, which became of terrible

[1] *Vita Romualdi*, cap. 13.   [2] *Ibid.* cap. 20.

intensity with him. Also the egotism, so frequently an
element of that temperament, rose with him to spiritual
megalomania :

" One day (apparently in the latter part of his life) some
disciples asked him, ' Master, of what age does the soul appear,
and in what form is it presented for judgment ? ' He replied, ' I
know a man in Christ, whose soul is brought before God shining
like snow, and indeed in human form, with the stature of the
perfect time of life.' Asked again who that man might be, he
would not speak for indignation. And then the disciples talked
it over, and recognized that he was certainly the man." [1]

In another part of the *Vita*, Damiani, having told of
his hero's sojourn with a company of hermits who preferred
their will to his, thus continues : " Romuald, therefore,
impatient of sterility, began to search with anxious eager-
ness where he might find a soil fit to bear a fruitage of
souls." It was his passion to change men to anchorites :
he yearned to convert the whole world to the solitary life.
Many were the hermit communities which he established.
But he could not endure his hermit sons for long, nor they
him. His intolerant soul revolted from the give-and-take
of intercourse. Such intolerance and his passion to make
more converts drove him from place to place. He seemed
inspired with a superhuman power of drawing men from
the world. Now

" therefore he sent messengers to the Counts of Camerino. When
these heard the name of Romuald they were beside themselves
with joy, and placed their possessions, mountains, woods, and
fields at his disposal, to select from. He chose a spot suited to
the hermit way of living, intrenched amid forests and mountains,
and affording an ample space of level fruitful ground, watered with
crystal streams. The place was called of old the Valley of the
Camp (Vallis de Castro), and a little church was there with a
convent of women who had turned from the world. Here having
built their cells, the venerable man and his disciples took up
their abode.

" And what fruitage of souls the Lord there won through him,
pen cannot describe nor tongue relate. From all directions men
began to pour in for penance, and in pity to give away their goods
to the poor, while others utterly forsook the world and with fervent

---

[1] *Vita Romualdi,* cap. 51.

spirit hastened to the holy way of life.   For this most blessed man
was as one of the Seraphim, himself burning with the flame of
divine love, and kindling others, wherever he went, with the fires
of his holy preaching.   Often, while speaking, a vast contrition
brought him to such floods of tears that, breaking off his sermon,
he would flee anywhere for refuge, like one demented.   And also
when travelling on horseback with the brethren, he followed far
behind them, always singing psalms, as if he were in his cell, and
never ceasing to shed tears." [1]

In that age, the hopes and fears and wonderment of
men looked to the recluse as the perfected saint.   No wonder
that those Italian lands, so blithely sinful and so grievously
penitent, were moved by this volcanic tempest of a man,
fierce, merciless to the flesh, convulsed with scorching tears,
famed for austerities and miracles.   He lashed men from
their sins ;   men feared before one whose presence was a
threat of hell.   Said the Marquis of Tuscany :   " Not the
emperor nor any mortal man, can put such fear in me as
Romuald's look.   Before his face I know not what to say,
nor how to defend myself or find excuses."   And the
biographer adds that " of a truth the holy man had this
grace from the divine favour, that sinners, and especially the
great of this world, quaked in their bowels before him as if
before the majesty of God." [2]

But some men hated, and especially those of his own
persuasion who could not endure his harshness.   From
such came attempts at murder ;   from such also came
milder outbreaks of detestation and revolt.   No other
founder of ascetic communities seems to have been so
rebelled against.   He went from the Valley of the Camp
to Classe, where a simoniac abbot attempted to strangle
him ;   then he returned, but not for long, for the abbot
established in his place rejected his reproofs, and maligned
him with the lords of the land.   " And in that way," says
Damiani, " the tall cedar of Paradise was cast forth from the
forest of earthly men." [3]

His next sojourn was Vallombrosa, where after his
decease one of his disciples was to found a famous cloister.
From that nest in the Tuscan Apennines, he went to dwell

[1] *Vita Romualdi*, cap. 35.   [2] *Ibid.* cap. 40.
[3] *Ibid.* cap. 45.

permanently on the Umbrian mount of Sytrio. At this point his biographer proceeds :

" Whoever hears that the holy man so often changed his habitation, must not ascribe this to the vice of levity. For the cause of these changes was that wherever he stayed, an almost countless crowd assembled, and when he saw one place filled with converts he very properly would appoint a prior and at once hasten to fill another.

" In Sytrio what insults and what indignities he endured from his disciples ! We will set down one instance, and omit the rest for brevity. There was a disciple named Romanus, noble by birth, but ignoble by deed. Him the holy man for his carnal impurity not only chided by word but corrected with heavy beatings. That diabolic man dared to retort with the fabrication of the same charge, and to bark with sacrilegious mouth against this temple of the Holy Spirit, saying forsooth that the holy man was spotted with this same infection. The rage of the disciples broke out immediately against Romuald. All were his enemies : some declared that the wicked old man ought to be hanged from a gallows, others that he should be burned in his cell.

" One cannot understand how spiritual men could have believed such wickedness of a decrepit old man, whose frigid blood and aridity of attenuated frame would have forbade him, had he had the will. But doubtless it is to be deemed that this scourge of adversity came upon the holy man by the will of Heaven, to augment his merit. For he said himself that he had foreknown it with certainty in the solitude which he had left just before, and had come with alacrity to undergo this shame. But that false monkish reprobate who brought the charge against the holy man, afterwards became Bishop of Noceria through simony, and in the first year of his occupancy, saw, as he deserved, his house with his books and bells and the rest of his sacred paraphernalia burned ; and in the second year, the divine sentence struck him and he wretchedly lost both his dignity and his life.

" In the meanwhile the disciples put a penance on the holy man as if he had been guilty, and deprived him of the right to celebrate the holy mysteries. He willingly accepted this false judgment, and took his penance like a culprit, not presuming to approach the altar for well-nigh six months. At length, as he afterwards told his disciples, he was divinely commanded to celebrate mass. On the next day, when proceeding with the sacrifice, he became rapt in ecstasy, and continued speechless for so long a time that all present marvelled. When afterwards asked the reason of his delay, he replied : ' Carried into heaven, I was borne before God ; and the divine voice commanded me, that with

such intelligence as God had set in me, I should write and commend for use a Commentary on the Psalms.   Overcome with
terror, I could only respond : so let it be, so let it be.'   For this
reason the holy man made a Commentary on the whole Psalter ;
and although its grammar was bad, its sense was sound and
clear." [1]

Various attempts were made in the Middle Ages to
render the hermit life practicable, through permitting a
limited intercourse among a cluster of like-minded ascetics,
as well as to regulate it under the direction of a superior.
In Italy, in the tenth and eleventh centuries, the picturesque
energy of the individual hermit is prodigious, while in the
north, as in the establishment of the Carthusian Order, the
organization is better, the result more permanent, but the
imaginative and consistent extravagance of personality is
not there.   In the hermit communities founded by Romuald
there was a prior or abbot, invested with some authority.
Yet the organization was less complete than in coenobitic
monasteries ; for Romuald's hermit methods sought to
minimize the intercourse among the brethren, to an extent
which was scarcely compatible with effective organization.
An idea of these communities may be had from Damiani's
description of one of them :

" Such was the mode of life in Sytrio, that not only in name but
in fact it was as another Nytria.[2]   The brethren went barefoot ;
unkempt and haggard ; they were content with the barest neces-
saries.   Some were shut in with doomed doors (*damnatis januis*),
seemingly as dead to the world as if in a tomb.   Wine was unknown, even in extreme illness.   Even the attendants of the
monks (*famuli monachorum*) and those who kept the cattle,
fasted and preserved silence.   They made regulations among
themselves, and laid penances for speaking." [3]

For seven years Romuald lived at Sytrio as an *inclusus*,
shut up in his cell, and preserving unbroken silence.   Yet
though his tongue was dumb his life was eloquent.   He
lived on, setting a shining example of squalor and austerity,
eating only vile food, and handing back untouched any
savoury morsel.   His conflicts with the devil continued ; nor

---

[1] *Vita*, caps. 49, 50.
[2] The Syrian region famous for its early anchorites.
[3] *Vita Romualdi*, cap. 64.

was he ever vanquished. Advancing years intensified his aversion to human society and his passion for solitude. In proportion as he made his ways displeasing to men, his self-approval was enhanced.[1] A solitary death kept tally with the temper of a recluse life.

" When he saw his end draw near he returned to the Valley of the Camp, and had a cell with an oratory prepared, in which to immure himself and keep silence until death. Twenty years before, he had foretold to his disciples that there he should attain his peace ; and had declared his wish to breathe forth his spirit with no one standing by or bestowing the last rites. When this cell of immurement (reclusorium) was ready, his mind was set upon immediate inclusion. But his body grew heavy with the increasing ills of extreme age, and the hard breathing of tussis. Yet not for this would the holy man lie on a bed or relax his fasts. One day his strength gradually forsook him, and he found himself sinking with fatigue. So as the sun was setting he directed two brothers who stood by to go out and shut the door of his cell after them. He told them that when the time came for them to celebrate the matin hymns at dawn, they might return. Un- willingly they went out, but did not go at once to rest ; and waited anxiously, concealing themselves by the master's cell. After a while, as they listened intent and could hear no movement of his body nor any sound of his voice, correctly conjecturing what had happened, they broke open the door, rushed in and lighted the light ; and there, the blessed soul having been transported to heaven, they found the holy corpse supine. It lay as a celestial pearl neglected, but hereafter to be placed with honour in the treasury of the King." [2]

The spiritual unity which lies beneath the actions of Romuald should be sought in the reasons and temper of the hermit life. To perfect the soul for its passage to eternity is the fundamental motive. Monastic logic con- vinces the man that this can best be accomplished through withdrawal from the temptations of the world ; and the hermit temper draws irresistibly to solitude. The only consistent social function left to such a man is that of turning the steps of his fellows to his own recluse path of perfection. Romuald's life manifests such motives and such temper, and also this one function passionately performed.

[1] Cf. Sackur, *Die Cluniacenser*, i. 328 note.
[2] *Vita Romualdi*, 69.

We see in him no love of kind, but only a fiery passion for their salvation. Also we see the absorption of self in self with God, the harsh intolerance of other men, the fierce aversions and the passionate cravings which are germane to the hermit life.

Physical self-mortification is the element of the hermit life most difficult for modern people to understand. Yet nothing in Romuald extorted more entire admiration from his biographer than his austerities. And if there was one man on earth whom Peter admired as much as he did Romuald, it was a certain mail-coated Dominicus, a virtuoso in self-mortification. He exhibits its purging and penitential motives. Scourging purifies the body from carnality ; that is one motive. It also atones for sins, and lessens the purgatorial period after death ; this is another. There is a third which is rooted rather in temperament than in reason. This is contrition ; the contrite heart may love to flagellate itself in love of Him who suffered sinless.

Dominicus was surnamed Loricatus because he wore a coat of mail against the attacks of the devil through the frailties of the too-comfortable flesh. In his youth, family influence had installed him in a snug ecclesiastic berth. As he reached maturity and bethought himself, the sense of this involuntary simoniacal contamination filled him with remorse. He abjured the world and became a member of the hermit community of Fonte Avellana, where Damiani exercised the authority of prior. Yet the latter looked on Dominic as his master, whom he admired to the pitch of marvel, while regretting that he lacked himself the strength and leisure to equal his flagellations. So Peter was enraptured with this wonder of a Dominic, and wrote his biography, which deserved telling if, as Peter says, his entire life, his *tota quippe vita*, was a preaching and an edification, instruction and discipline (*praedicatio, aedificatio, doctrina, disciplina*).

One descriptive passage from it will suffice :

" I am speaking of Dominic, my teacher and my master, whose tongue indeed is rustic, but whose life is polished and accomplished (*artificiosa satis et lepida*). His life indeed preaches more effectively by its living actions (*vivis operibus*) than a barren tongue which inanely weighs out the balanced phrases of a be-spangled urbanity (*phaleratae urbanitatis*).   Through a long course of gliding years, girt with iron mail, he has waged truceless war against the wicked spirits ; with cuirassed body and heart always ready for battle, he marches eager warrior against the hostile array.

" Likewise it is his regular and unremitting habit, with a rod in each hand every day to beat time upon his naked body, and thus scourge out two psalters.   And this even in the slacker season.   For in Lent or when he has a penance to perform (and he often undertakes a penance of a hundred years), each day, while he plies himself with his rods, he pays off at least three psalters repeating them mentally (*meditando*).

" The penance of a hundred years is performed thus : With us three thousand blows satisfies a year of penance ; and the chanting (*modulatio*) of ten psalms, as has often been tested, admits one thousand blows.   Now, clearly, as the Psalter consists of one hundred and fifty psalms, any one computing correctly will see that five years of penance lie in chanting one psalter, with this discipline.   Now, whether you take five times twenty or twenty times five you have a hundred.   Consequently whoever chants twenty psalters, with this accompanying discipline, may be con-fident of having performed a hundred years of penance.   Herein our Dominic outdoes those who struck with only one hand ; for he, a true son of Benjamin, wars indefatigably with both hands against the rebellious allurements of the flesh.   He has told me himself that he easily accomplishes a penance of a hundred years in six days." [1]

This loricated Dominic was conscious of his virtuosity. We find him at the beginning of a certain Lent, requesting the imposition of a penance of a thousand years !   Again, he comes after vespers to Damiani's cell to tell him that between morning and evening he has broken his record by " doing " eight psalters !   And once more we read of his coming troubled to his master, saying : " You have written, as I have just heard, that in one day I chanted nine psalters with corporeal discipline.   When I heard it, I turned pale and groaned.   ' Woe is me,' I said ; ' without my knowledge, this has been written of me, and yet I do not know whether I could do it.'   So I am going to try again, and I shall certainly find out." [2]

[1] Peter Damiani, *Vitae SS. Rodulphi et Dominici loricati*, cap. 8 (Migne 144 col. 1015).
[2] *Ibid.* cap. 10 (Migne 144, col. 1015).

Dominic probably derived more pleasure than pain from his scourgings.   For besides the vanity of achievement, and some ecstasy of contrition, the flesh itself turns morbid and rejoices in its laceration.   Yet such austerity is pre-eminently penal, and is initially impelled by fear.   With Dominic, with Romuald, with Damiani, the fear of hell entered the motives of the secluded life.   To observe this fear writ large in panic terror, we turn to the old legend regarding the conversion of Bruno of Cologne, the founder of the Carthusian Order.   The scene is laid in Paris, where (with much improbability) Bruno is supposed to be studying in the year 1082.   One of the most learned and pious of the doctors of theology died.   His funeral had been celebrated, and his body was about to be carried to the grave, when the corpse raised its head and cried aloud with a dreadful voice : " Justo Dei judicio accusatus sum."   Then the head fell back.   The people, terror-stricken, postponed the interment to the following day, when again, as before, with a grievous and terrible voice the corpse raised its head and cried : " Justo Dei judicio judicatus sum."   Amid general terror the interment was again postponed to the next day, when, as before, with a horrible cry the corpse shrieked : " Justo Dei judicio condemnatus sum."

At this, Bruno, impressed and terrified, said to his friends : " Beloved, what shall we do ?   Unless we fly we shall all perish utterly.   Let us renounce the world, and, like Anthony and John the Baptist, seek the caves of the desert, that we may escape the wrath of the Judge, and reach the port of salvation."   So they flee, and the Carthusian Order, with its terrific asceticism, begins.[1]

This story, aside from its marvellous character, does not harmonize with the more authentic facts of Bruno's life.   It

---

[1] This story is told in all the early lives of Bruno, the *Vita antiquior*, the *Vita altera*, and the *Vita tertia* (Migne, *Pat. Lat.* 152, col. 482, 493, and 525).   These lives, especially the *Vita altera*, are interesting illustrations of the ascetic spirit, which, as might be expected, also moulds Bruno's thoughts and his understanding of Scripture.   All of which appears in his long *Expositio in Psalmos* (Migne, *Pat. Lat.* 152).   To us, for example, the note of the twenty-third (in the Vulgate the twenty-second) psalm is love ; to Bruno it is disciplinary guidance : the Lord guides me in the place of pasture, that is, He is my guide lest I go astray in the Scriptures, where the souls of the faithful are fed ; I shall not want, that is, an understanding of them shall not fail me.   Thy rod, that is the lesser tribulation, thy staff, that is the greater tribulation, correct and chastise me.

is, however, a striking expression of the ascetic fear ; it also
reflects psychologic truth.   Who but the man himself knows
the naughtiness of his own heart ? its never-to-be-disclosed
vile and morbid thoughts ?   The modern may realize this.
Hamlet did.   And it was just such a phase of self-conscious-
ness as the mediaeval imagination would transform into a
tale of horror.   Bruno himself had been a learned doctor, a
teacher, and the head of the cathedral school at Rheims ;
he had been a zealous soldier of the Church.   In all this
he had not found peace.   The profession of a doctor of
theology, even when coupled with more active belligerency
for the Church, afforded no certain salvation.   The story of
the Paris doctor may have symbolized the anxieties which
dwelt in Bruno's breast, until under their stimulus the
yearnings of a solitary temper gathered head and at last
brought him with six followers to Carthusia (*la grande
Chartreuse*), which lies to the north of Grenoble.   1084
is the year of its beginning.

It was a hermit community, the brethren living two by
two in isolated cells, but meeting for divine service in a little
chapel.   Camaldoli may have been the model.   Bruno
wrote no *regula* for his followers, and the practices of the
Order were first formulated by Guigo, the fifth prior, in
his *Consuetudines Cartusiae*, about the year 1130.[1]   These
permit a limited intercourse among the brethren, for the
service of God and the regulation of their own lives.   Yet
the broader object was seclusion.   Not only severance from
the world, but the seclusion of the brethren from each other,
in solitary labour and contemplation, was their ideal.   The
asceticism of these *Consuetudines* is of the strictest.   And
somehow it would seem as if in the Carthusian Order the
frailties of the spirit and the lust of the flesh were to be
permanently vanquished by this set life of labour, meditation,
and rigid asceticism.   *Carthusia nunquam reformata, quia
nunquam deformata*, remained true century after century.
This long freedom from corruption was partly due to the
lofty and somewhat exclusive character of the brotherhood.

___

[1] Guigo was born in 1083 at St. Romain near Valence, of noble family (like
most monks of prominence).   There was close sympathy between him and St.
Bernard, as their letters show.   Cf. *post*, Chapter XVIII.

Carthusia was no broad way for the monastic multitude. Its monks were relatively few and holy, the select of God. Men of devout piety, they must be. It was also needful that they should be possessed of such intellectual endowment and meditative capacity as would with God's grace yield provision for a life of solitary thought.

The intellectual piety of Carthusia finds its loftiest expression in the *Meditationes* of this same prior Guigo,[1] the form of which calls to mind the Reflections of Marcus Aurelius or Epictetus. In substance they reflect Augustine's intellectual devoutness and many of his thoughts. But they seem Guigo's very own, fruit of his own reflection ; and thus incidentally they afford an illustration of the general principle that by the twelfth century the Middle Ages had made over into themselves what they had drawn from the Fathers or from the pagan antique. Guigo's *Meditationes* possess spiritual calm ; their logic is unhesitating ; it is remorselessly correct, however incomplete may be its premises or its comprehension of life's data. Whoever wishes to know the high contemplative mind of monastic seclusion in the twelfth century may learn it from this work. A number of its precepts are given here for the sake of their illustrative pertinency and intrinsic merit, and because our author is not very widely known. He begins with general reflections upon Veritas and Pax :

" Truth should be set in the middle, as something beautiful. Nor, if any one abhors it, do thou condemn, but pity. Thou indeed, who desirest to come to it, why dost thou spurn it when it chides thy faults ?

" Without form and comeliness and fastened to the cross, truth is to be worshipped.

" If thou speakest truth not from love of truth but from wish to injure another, thou wilt not gain the reward of a truthspeaker but the punishment of a defamer.

" Truth is life and eternal salvation. Therefore you ought to pity any one whom it displeases. For to that extent he is dead and lost. But you, perverse one, would not tell him the truth unless you thought it bitter and intolerable to him. You do still worse when in order to please men you speak a truth which delights them as much as if it were lies and flattery. Not

---

[1] Migne 153, col. 601-631.

because it displeases or pleases should truth be spoken, but as it profits. Yet be silent when it would do harm, as light to weak eyes.

" Blessed is he whose mind is moved or affected only by the perception and love of truth, and whose body is moved only by his mind. Thus the body, like the mind, is moved by truth alone. For if there is no stirring in the mind save that of truth, and none in the body save that from the mind, then also there is no stirring in the body save from truth, that is from God.

" Thou dost all things for the sake of peace, toward which the way lies through truth alone, which is thine adversary in this life. Therefore either subject thee to it or it to thee. For nothing else is left thee.

" The lake does not boast because it abounds in water ; for that is from the source. So as to thy peace. Its cause is always something else. Therefore thy peace is shifting and inconstant in proportion to the instability of its cause. How worthless is it when it arises from the pleasingness of a human face !

" Let not temporal things be the cause of thy peace ; for then wilt thou be as worthless and fragile as they. You would have such a peace in common with the brutes ; let thine be that of the angels, which proceeds from truth.

" The beginning of the return to truth is to be displeased with falsity. Blame precedes correction.

" In the cares which engage thee for thy salvation, no service or medicine is more useful than to blame and despise thyself. Whoever does this for thee is thy helper.

" Easy is the way to God, since it advances by laying down burdens. So far then unburden thyself that, all things laid aside, thou mayest deny thyself.

" When anything good is said of thee, it is but as a rumour regarding which thou knowest better.

" Consider the two experiences of filling and emptying (*ingestionis et egestionis*) ; which blesses thee more ? That burdens thee with useless matters ; this disburdens thee. To have had that is to have devoured it altogether. Nothing remains for hope. So in all things of sense. They perish all. And what of thee after these ? Set thy love and hope on what will not pass.

" Bestial pleasure comes from the senses of the flesh ; it is diabolic, a thing of arrogance, envy, and deceit ; philosophic pleasure is to know the creature ; the angelic pleasure is to know and love God.

" When we take our pleasure from that from which brutes draw pleasure—from lust like dogs, or from gluttony like swine—our souls become like theirs. Yet we do not shudder. I had rather have a dog's body than his soul. It would be more tolerable if our body changed to bestial shape, while our soul remained in its dignity, that is, in the likeness of God.

" Readily man entangles himself in love of bodies and of vanity; but, willy, nilly, he is torn with fear and grief at their dissolution. For the love of perishable things is as a fountain of useless fears and sorrows.   The Lord frees the poor man from the mighty, by loosing him from the fetter of earthly love.

" The human soul is tortured in itself as long as it can be tortured, that is, as long as it loves anything besides God.

" Thou hast been clinging to one syllable of a great song, and art troubled when that wisest Singer proceeds in His singing. For the syllable which alone thou wast loving is withdrawn from thee, and others succeed in order.   He does not sing to thee alone, nor to thy will, but His.   The syllables which succeed are distasteful to thee because they drive on that one which thou wast loving evilly.

" All matters which are called adverse are adverse only to the wicked, that is, those who love the creature instead of the Creator.

" If in any way thou art tormented by fear, or anger or hate or pain of any kind, lay it to thyself, that is, to thy concupiscence, ignorance, or sloth.   And if any one wishes to injure thee, lay that to his concupiscence.   Thy distress is evidence of thy sin in loving anything destructible, having dismissed God.   Thou dost grieve over the ruined show ; lay it to thee and thine error because thou hast been cleaving to things that may be broken.

" He seeks a long temptation who seeks a long life.

" What God has not loved in His friends—power, rank, riches, dignities—do not thou love in thine.

" Snares thou eatest, drinkest, wearest, sleepest in ; all things are snares.

" We are exiles through love and wantonness and inclination, not through locality ; exiles in the country of defilement, of dark passions, of ignorance, of wicked loves and hates.

" In so far as thou lovest thyself—that is, this temporal life— so far dost thou love what is transitory.

" Adverse matters do not make thee wretched, but rather show thee to have been so ; prosperity blinds the soul by covering and increasing misery, not by removing it.

" Every one ought to love all men.   Whoever wishes another to show special love toward him is a robber, and an offender against all.

" Mixed through this body, thou wast wretched enough ; for thou wast subject to all its corruptions, even to the bite of the flea or the sorunculus.   This did not suffice thee.   Thou hast mixed thyself up with other quasi bodies, the opinion of men, admiration, love, honour, fear and the like.   When these are harmed, pain comes to thee, as from bodily hurt. Thy honour is hurt when contempt is shown thee ; and so with the rest. Think also thus regarding bodily forms.

" Unless thou hast despised whatever men can do to thwart or aid thee, thou wilt not be able to contemn their disposition toward thee, their hate and love, their opinions, good or bad.

" Why dost thou wish to be loved by men ?

" Who rejoices in praise, loses praise.

" Who is pained or angered by the loss of any temporal thing, shows himself worth what he has lost.

" No thing ought to wish to be loved as good, unless it blesses its lover for the very reason that it is loved. But no thing does this if it needs its lover, or is helped by loving or being loved by another. Most cruel, then, is the thing which wishes another to place affection and hope on it when it cannot benefit that other. The devils do this, who wish men to be engrossed in their service instead of God's. So cry to thy lovers, Cease, ye wretched, to admire or respect or honour me ; for I, miserable wretch, can neither aid myself nor you, but rather need your aid.

" So far as in thee is, thou hast destroyed all men, for thou hast put thyself between them and God, so that gazing on thee and ignoring God, they might admire and praise thee alone. This is utterly profitless to thee and them, not to say destructive.

" Whatever form thou dost enjoy is as the male to thy mind. For thy mind yields and lies down to it. Thou dost not assimilate it, but it thee. Its image endures, like an idol in its temple, to which thou dost sacrifice neither ox nor goat, but thy rational soul and thy body, to wit, thy whole self, when thou enjoyest it.

" See how, as in a wine-shop, thou dost prostitute thine as a venal love, and to the measure of pay weighest thyself out to men. In this wine-shop he receives nothing who gives nothing. And yet thou wouldst not have that which thou dost sell, unless freely from above it had been given to thee who gave nothing. There- fore thou hast received thy pay.

" To be empty and removed from God is to make ready for lust.

" Who wishes to enjoy thee in thyself, deserves from thee the thanks of flies and fleas who suck thy blood.

" This is the very sum of human depravity to forsake the better, which is God, and to regard the lesser and cleave to them by delighting in them—these temporalities !

" The beetle as it flies sees everything, and then selects nothing that is beautiful or wholesome or durable, but settles down upon dung. So thy soul in mental flight (*intuitu pervolans*) surveying heaven and earth and whatever is great and precious therein, cleaves to none of these, but embraces the cheap and dirty things occurring to its thought. Blush for this.

" When thou pleadest with God not to take from thee something to which thou cleavest by desire, it is as if an adulteress
caught by her husband in the act, should not ask pardon for her
crime, but beg him not to interrupt her pleasure.   It is not enough
for thee to go wantoning from God, but thou must incline Him to
save and approve the things in which thou takest delight to thy
undoing—the forms of bodies, their savours and their colours.

" The poverty of thine inner vision of God, purblind as thou
art, although He is there, makes thee willing to go out of doors
from thine own hearth, refusing to linger within thyself, as in the
dark.   So thou hast nothing to do but go gaping after the external
forms of bodies and the opinions of men.   Thou dost carry thyself
in this world as if thou hadst come hither to gaze and wonder at
the forms of bodies.

" May God be gracious to thee, that the feet of thy mind may
find no resting-place, so that somehow, O soul, thou mayest return
to the Ark, like Noah's dove.

" Prosperity is a snare, adversity the knife that cuts it ;
prosperity imprisons us from the love of God ; adversity is the
battering-ram which breaks the dungeon in pieces.

" Since you are taken only by pleasure, you should shun
whatever gives it.   The Christian soul is safe only in adversity.
From what thou cherishest God makes thee rods.

" The only medicine for every pain and torment is contempt
for whatever in thee is hurt by them, and the turning of the
mind to God.

" As many carnal pleasures as thou spurnest, just so many
snares of the devil dost thou escape.   As many tribulations—
especially those for truth's sake—as thou dost flee, so many
salutary remedies thou spurnest.

" In hope thou mayest cherish the unripened grain ; thus love
those who are not yet good.   Be such toward all as the Truth
has shown itself toward thee.   Just as it has sustained and loved
thee for thy betterment, so do thou sustain and love men in order
to better them.

" You are set as a standard to blunt the darts of the enemy,
that is, to destroy evil by opposing good to it.   You should never
return evil for evil, except perhaps medicinally ;   which is not to
return evil but good.

" If to cleave to God is thine whole and only good, thine whole
and only evil is separation from Him.

" Who loves all will be saved without doubt ; but who is loved
by men will not for that reason be saved."

The unity of these *Meditationes* lies in the absolute
manner in which the meditating soul attaches itself to God

as its whole and only good.   Herein Guigo's thoughts are
Augustinian.   One notes their clear intellectual tone.
Nothing lures the thinker from his aim and goal of God.
He abhors whatever might distract him ; and as to all
except God and God's commands, he is indifferent.   Guigo
detests impermanence as keenly as did the Brahmin and
Buddhist meditators of India.   He has as high regard as
any Indian or Greek philosopher for a life of thought.   But
there are differences between the Carthusian prior and the
Greek or Indian sage.   Guigo's renunciation does not (from
his standpoint) penetrate life as deeply as Gotama's ; for
Guigo renounces only things comparatively insignificant, so
utterly transient are they, so completely they pale before
the light of his goal of God.   Therein shall lie clearer
attainment than lay at the end of any Indian chain of
reasoning.   So note well, that Guigo, like other Christians,
is not essentially a renouncer, but one who attains and
receives.

The difference between him and the Greek is also
patent.   The source of his blue lake of thought is not
himself, but God.   Although calm and sustained by reason,
he is rationally the opposite of self-reliant, and so the
opposite of the ideal Stoic or Aristotelian.   God is his
Creator, the source of his thoughts, the loadstar of his
meditations, the all-comprehending object of his desire.

We find in Guigo further specific elements of Christian
asceticism, which sharpen his repugnances for the world of
transient phenomena.   Those phenomena mostly contain
elements of sin : all pleasure is temptation and a snare ;
adversity keeps the soul's wings trimmed true.   So the
main content of passing mortal life, while not evil in itself,
is so charged with temptation and allure, that it is worthy
only of avoidance.   The transient, the physical, the brutal,
the diabolic—one shades into the next, and leads on to the
last.   Have none of them, O Soul !   They are snares all.

Of course, Guigo has the specific monkish horror of
sexual lust, that chief of fleshly snares.   But he goes further.
With him all particular, disproportionate love is wrong ;
love no one, and desire not to be loved, out of the proportionment of the common love which God has for all His

creatures : so love you, and not otherwise. Others, even
women, attained this standard.   In the legend, St. Elizabeth
of Hungary gives thanks that she loves her own children no
more than others'. She is no mother, but a saint. So
Guigo will love all—love indeed ? one queries. Thus also
will he have others hold themselves toward him, lest he
be a stumbling-block in their or his salvation.

Yea, salvation ! If indeed this monk shall not have
attained that, of a truth he would be of all men most miserable—save for the quiet, thought-filled calm which is his
inner and his veritable life. It is a calm not riven by the
storms which drove the soul of Peter Damiani. God was
not less to Guigo ; but the temperaments of the two men
differed. Not beyond or out of one's nature can one love
or yearn, or even know the stress of storm.

CHAPTER XVIII

THE QUALITY OF LOVE IN SAINT BERNARD

THROUGH the prodigious power of his personality, St. Bernard gave new life to monasticism, promoted the reform of the secular clergy and the suppression of heresy, ended a papal schism, set on foot the Second Crusade, and for a quarter of a century swayed Christendom as never holy man before or after him. An adequate account of his career would embrace the entire history of the first half of the twelfth century.[1]

The man who was to move men with his love, and quell the proud with fear, had, as a youth, a graceful figure, a sweet countenance, and the most winning manners. Later in life he is spoken of as cheerfully bearing reproaches, but shamefaced at praise, and his gentle manners are again mentioned.

" As a helpmeet for his holy spirit, God made his body to conform. In his flesh there was visible a certain grace, but spiritual rather than of the flesh. A brightness not of earth shone in his look ; there was an angelic purity in his eyes, and a dove-like simplicity. The beauty of the inner man was so great that it would burst forth in visible tokens, and the outer man would seem bathed from the store of inward purity and copious grace. His frame was of the slightest (*tenuissimum*), and most spare of flesh ; a blush often tinged the delicate skin of his cheeks. And a certain natural heat (*quidquid caloris naturalis*) was in him, arising from assiduous meditation and penitent zeal. His hair was bright

---

[1] A bibliography of what has been written on Bernard would make a volume. His own writings and the *Vitae* and *Acta* (as edited by Mabillon) are printed in Migne, tomes 182-185. The *Vie de Saint Bernard*, by the abbé Vacandard, in two volumes, is to be recommended (2nd ed., Paris, 1897).

yellow, his beard reddish with some white hairs toward the end of
his life.   Actually of medium stature, he looked taller." [1]

This same biography says :

" He who had set him apart, from his mother's womb, for the
work of a preacher, had given him, with a weak body, a voice
sufficiently strong and clear.   His speech, whatever persons he
spoke to for the edifying of souls, was adapted to his audience ;
for he knew the intelligence, the habits and occupations of each
and all.   To country folk he spoke as if born and bred in the
country ;   and so to other classes, as if he had been always occupied with their business.   He was learned with the erudite, and
simple with the simple, and with spiritual men rich in illustrations
of perfection and wisdom.   He adapted himself to all, desiring to
gain all for Christ." [2]

Bernard was born of noble parents at the Château of
Fontaines, near Dijon, in the year 1090, and was educated
in a church school at Chatillon on the Seine.   It is an oft-
told story, how, when little more than twenty years of age,
he drew together a band formed of his own brothers, his
uncle, and his friends, and led them to Citeaux,[3] his ardent
soul unsatisfied so long as one held back.   Three years
later, in 1115, the Abbot, Stephen Harding, entrusted him
with the headship of the new monastery, to be founded in
the domains of the Count of Troyes.   Bernard set forth
with twelve companions, came to Clara Vallis on the river
Aube, and placed his convent in that austere solitude.

Great were the attractions of Clairvaux (Clara Vallis)
under Bernard's vigorous and loving rule.   Its monks
increased so rapidly and so constantly that during its
founder's life sixty-five bands were sent forth to rear new
convents.   Meanwhile, Bernard's activities and influence
widened, till they seemed to compass western Christendom.

---

[1] *Vita prima*, iii. cap. 1 (Migne, *Pat. Lat.* 185).   This *Vita* was written by
contemporaries of the saint who knew him intimately.   But one must be on one's
guard as to these apparently close descriptions of the saints in their *vitae* ;   for
they are commonly conventionalized.   This description of Bernard, excepting
perhaps the colour of his hair, would have fitted Francis of Assisi.

[2] *Vita prima*, iii. 3.   Bernard himself said that his aim in preaching was not
so much to expound the words (of Scripture) as to move his hearers' hearts (*Sermo
xvi. in Cantica canticorum*).   That his preaching was resistless is universally
attested.

[3] See, *e.g.*, Vacandard, *o.c.* chap. i.

He had become a power in the politics of Church and State. In 1130 he was summoned by Louis le Gros practically to determine the claims of the rival Popes Innocent II. and Anacletus II. He decided for the former, and was the chief instrument of his eventual reinstatement at Rome. Before this Bernard's health had been broken by his extreme austerities. Yet even the lamentable failure of the Second Crusade, zealously promoted by him, did not break his power over Europe, which continued unimpaired until his death in 1153.

This active and masterful man was impelled by those elements of the *vita contemplativa* which formed his inner self. First and last and always he was a monk. Had he not been the very monk he was, he would not have been the dominator of men and situations that he proved himself to be. Temperament fashions the objects of contemplation, and shapes the yearning and aversions, of great monks. The temperamental element of love—the love of God and man, with its appurtenant detestations — made the heart of Bernard's *vita contemplativa*, and impassioned and empowered his active faculties. It was the keynote of his life : in his letters it speaks in words of fire, while other writings of the saint analyse this great human quality with profundity and truth. In these he renders explicit the modes of affection which man may have for man and above all for God ; he sets them forth as the path as well as goal of life on earth, and then as the rapt summit of attainment in the life to come. Through all its stages, as it flows from self to fellow, as it rises from man to God, love still is love, and forms the unifying principle among men and between them and God.

Let us trace in his letters the nature and the power of Bernard's love, and see with what yearning he loved his fellows, seeking to withdraw them from the world ; and how his love strove to be as sword and armour against the flesh and the devil. By easy transition we shall pass to Bernard's warning wrath, flung against those who would turn the struggling soul aside, or threaten the Church's peace ; then by more arduous, but still unbroken stages, we may rise to the love of Jesus, and through love of the God-man to love of God. We shall realize at the close why that last mediaeval

assessor of destinies, whose name was Dante Alighieri,
selected St. Bernard as the exponent of the blessed vision
which is salvation's crown in the paradise of God.[1]

The way of life at Clara Vallis might discourage monks
of feeble zeal. Among the brethren of these early days was
one named Robert, a cousin of the Abbot, seemingly of weak
and petulant disposition. Soon he fled, to seek a softer cell
in Cluny, the great and rich monastery to which his parents
appear to have dedicated him in childhood. For a while
Bernard suppressed his grief ; but the day came when he
could endure no longer Robert's abandonment of his soul's
safety and of the friend who yearned for him. He stole out
of the monastery, accompanied by a monk named William.
There, in the open (*sub dio*), Bernard dictated a long letter to
be sent to the deserter. While the two were busy, the one
dictating, the other writing, a rainstorm broke upon them.
William wished to stop. " It is God's work ; write and fear
not," said Bernard. So William wrote on, in the midst of
the rain ; but no drop fell on him or the parchment ; for
the power of love which dictated the letter preserved the
parchment on which it was being written.[2]

Whoever has read this letter in its own fervent Latin
will not care to dispute this miracle, for which it stands first
in the collection of Bernard's correspondence. Bernard does
not recriminate or argue in it ; his love shall bring the young
monk back to him. Yes, yes, he says to all that the other
has urged regarding fancied slights and persecution :

" Quite right ; I admit it. I am not writing in order to contend, but to end contention. To flee persecution is no fault in
him who flees, but in him who pursues ; I do not deny it. I pass
over what has happened ; I do not ask why or how it happened.
I do not discuss faults, I do not dispute as to the circumstances,
I have no memory for injuries. I speak only what is in my heart.
Wretched me, that I lack thee, that I do not see thee, that I am
living without thee, for whom to die would be to live ; without
whom to live, is to die. I ask not why thou hast gone away ; I
complain only that thou dost not return. Come, and there shall
be peace ; return, and all shall be made good.

---

[1] *Post*, Chapter XLIV.
[2] *Vita prima*, i. cap. 11. This William became Abbot of St. Thierry and one
of Bernard's biographers.

" It was certainly my fault that thou didst go away. I was too austere with thy young years, and treated thee inhumanly. So thou saidst when here, and so I hear thou dost still reproach me. But that shall not be imputed to thee. I never meant it harshly ; I was only indiscreet. Now thou wilt find me different, and I thee. Where before thou didst fear the master, thou shalt now embrace the companion. Do not think that I will not excuse any fault of thine. Dost thou wish to be quite free from fault ? then return. If thou wilt forget thy fault I will pardon it ; also pardon thou me, and I too will forget my fault."

Bernard then argues long and passionately against those who had led the young man away and received him with such blandishments at Cluny ; and passionately he argues against the insidious softening of monastic principles.

" Arise, soldier of Christ, arise, shake off the dust, return to the battle whence thou hast fled, and more bravely shalt thou fight and more gloriously triumph. Christ has many soldiers who bravely began, stood fast and conquered ; He has few who have turned from flight and renewed the combat. Everything rare is precious ; and thou among that rare company shalt the more radiantly shine.

" Thou art fearful ? so be it ; but why dost thou fear where there is no fear, and why dost thou not fear where everything is to be feared ?   Because thou hast fled from the battle-line, dost thou think to have escaped the foe ?   It is easier for the Adversary to pursue a fugitive than to bear himself against manful defence. Secure, arms cast aside, thou takest thy morning slumbers, the hour when Christ will have arisen ! The multitude of enemies beset the house, and thou sleepest. Is it safer to be caught alone and sleeping, than armed with others in the field ?   Arouse thee, seize thy arms, and escape to thy fellow-soldiers. Dost thou recoil at the weight of thy arms, O delicate soldier ! Before the enemy's darts the shield is no burden, nor the helmet heavy. The bravest soldiers tremble when the trumpet is heard before the battle is joined ; but then hope of victory and fear of defeat make them brave. How canst thou tremble, walled round with the zeal of thy armed brethren, angels bearing aid at thy right hand, and thy leader Christ ? There shalt thou safely fight, secure of victory. O battle, safe with Christ and for Christ ! In which there is no wound or defeat or circumvention so long as thou fleest not. Only flight loses the victory, which death does not lose. Blessed art thou, and quickly to be crowned, dying in battle. Woe for thee, if recoiling, thou losest at once the victory and the crown—which may He avert, my beloved son, who in the Judgment will award thee deeper damnation because of this letter of mine if He finds thee to have taken no amendment from it."

" It is God's work," said Bernard to the hesitating scribe. These words suggest the character of the love which inspired this letter. He loved Robert as man yearns for man ; but his motive was to do God's will, and win the young man back to salvation. In after years this young man returned to Clara Vallis.

It was Bernard's lot to write many letters urging procrastinators to fulfil their vows,[1] or appealing to those who had laid aside the arms of austerity, perhaps betaking themselves to the more worldly life of the secular clergy. This seems to have been the case with a young canon Fulco, whom an ambitious uncle sought to draw back to the world, or at least to a career of sacerdotal emolument. In fact, Fulco at last became an archdeacon ; from which it may be inferred that in his case Bernard's appeal was not successful. He had poured forth his arguments in an ardent letter.[2] Love compels him to use words to make the recipient grieve ; for love would have him feel grief, that he might no longer have true cause for grief—good mother love, who can cherish the weak, exercise those who have entered upon their course, or quell the restless, and so show herself differently toward her sons, all of whom she loves. This letter, like the one to Robert, concludes with a burning peroration :

" What dost thou in the city, dainty soldier ? Thy fellows whom thou hast deserted, fight and conquer ; they storm heaven (*coelum rapiunt*) and reign, and thou, sitting on thy palfrey (*ambulatorem*), clothed in purple and fine linen, goest ambling about the highways ! "

Bernard also wrote letters of consolation to parents whose sons had become monks, or letters of warning to those who sought to withdraw a monk from his good fight. In one instance, his influence had made a monk of a youth of gentle birth named Godfrey, to his parents' grief. So Bernard writes to them :

" If God makes your son His also, what have you lost, or

---

[1] E.g. *Ep.* 107.   [2] *Ep.* 2.

he ? He, from rich, becomes richer, from being noble. still more illustrious, and what is more than all, from a sinner he becomes a saint. It behoved him to be made ready for the Kingdom prepared for him from the foundation of the world, and for this reason it is well for him to spend with us his short span of days, so that clean from the filth of living in the world, earth's dust shaken off, he may become fit for the heavenly mansion. If you love him you will rejoice that he goes to his Father, and such a Father ! He goes to God, but you do not lose him ; rather through him you gain many sons. For all of us who belong to Clara Vallis have taken him to be our brother and you for our parents.

" Perhaps you fear this hard life for his tender body—that were to fear where there is nothing to fear. Have faith and be comforted. I will be a father to him and he shall be my son until from my hands the Father of Mercies and God of all consolation shall receive him. Do not grieve ; do not weep ; your Godfrey is hastening to joy, not to sorrow. A father to him will I be, a mother too, a brother and a sister. I will make the crooked ways straight, and the steep places plain. I will so temper and provide for him that as his spirit profits, his body shall not want. So shall he serve the Lord in joy and gladness, and shall sing before Him, How great is the glory of the Lord." [1]

Young Godfrey was a daintily nurtured plant. For all the Abbot's eloquence he did not stay in Clara Vallis. The world drew him back. It was now for the saint to weep :

" I grieve over thee, my son Godfrey ; I grieve over thee. And with reason. For who would not lament that the flower of thy youth which, to the joy of angels, thou didst offer unsullied to God in the odour of sweetness, is now trampled on by demons, defiled with sins, and contaminated by the world. How could you, who were called by God, follow the devil recalling thee ? How could you, whom Christ had begun to draw to Himself, withdraw your foot from the very entry upon glory ? In thee I see the truth of those words : ' A man's foes are they of his own household.' Thy friends and neighbours drew near and stood up against thee. They called thee back into the jaws of the lion and have set thee again in the gates of death. They have set thee in darkness, like the dead ; and thou art nigh to go down into the belly of hell, which now is ravening to swallow thee.

" Turn back, I say, turn back, before the abyss swallows you and the pit closes its mouth, before you are engulfed whence you

---

[1] *Ep.* 110 (this is the whole letter).

shall not escape, before, bound hand and foot, you are cast into
outer darkness where there is weeping and gnashing of teeth,
before you are thrust into darkness, shut in with the gloom of
death.

" Perhaps you blush to return, where you have only now fallen
away.   Blush for flight, and not for turning to renew the combat.
The conflict is not ended ; the hostile arrays have not withdrawn
from each other.   The victory still awaits you.   If you are ready,
we would not conquer without you, nor do we envy you your share
of the glory.   Joyful we will run to thee, and receive thee in our
arms, crying : ' It is meet to make merry and be glad ; for this our
son was dead and is alive again, was lost and is found.' " [1]

Who knows whether this letter brought back the little
monk ?   Bernard wrote so lovingly to him, so gently to
his parents.   He could write otherwise, and show himself
insensible to this world's pestering tears.   To the importunate
parents of a monk named Elias, who would drag him away
from Clara Vallis, Bernard writes in their son's name
thus :

" To his dear parents, Ingorranus and Iveta, Elias, monk but
sinner, sends daily prayers.

" The only cause for which it is permitted not to obey parents
is God ; for He said : ' Whoso loveth father or mother more than
me is not worthy of me.'   If you truly love me as good and faithful parents, why do you molest my endeavour to please the Father
of all, and attempt to withdraw me from the service of Him, to
serve whom is to reign ?   For this I ought not to obey you as
parents, but regard you as enemies.   If you loved me, you would
rejoice, because I go to my Father and yours.   But what is there
between you and me ?   What have I from you save sin and
misery ?   And indeed the corruptible body which I carry I admit
I have from you.   Is it not enough that you brought miserable
me into the misery of this hateful world ? that you, sinners, in
your sin produced a sinner ? and that him born in sin, in sin you
nourished ?   Envying the mercy which I have obtained from
Him who desireth not the death of a sinner, would you make me
a child of hell ?

" O harsh father ! savage mother ! parents cruel and impious
—parents ! rather destroyers, whose grief is the safety of the
child, whose consolation is the death of their son ! who would
drag me back to the shipwreck which I, naked, escaped ; who

---

[1] *Ep.* 112 (the entire letter).   The Latin of this letter is given *post*, Chapter
XXXII.

would give me again to the robbers when through the good Samaritan I am a little recovering from my wounds.

" Cease then, my parents," concludes the letter after many other reproofs, " cease to afflict yourselves with vain weeping and to disquiet me. No messengers you send will force me to leave. Clara Vallis will I never forsake. This is my rest, and here shall be my habitation. Here will I pray without ceasing for my sins and yours ; here with constant prayer will I implore that He whose love has separated us for a little while, will join us in another life happy and inseparable,—in whose love we may live forever and ever. Amen." [1]

If Bernard was severe toward those who threatened some loved person's weal, his anger burned more fiercely against those whom he deemed enemies of God. Heavy was his hand upon the evils of the Church : " The insolence of the clergy—to which the bishop's neglect is mother— troubles the earth and molests the Church. The bishops give what is holy to the dogs, and pearls to swine." [2]

Likewise, fearlessly but with restraint arising from his respect for all power ordained of God, Bernard opposes kings. Thus he writes to Louis the Fat, in regard to the election of a bishop, with many protests, however, that he would not oppose the royal power—for which we note his reason : " If the whole world conspired to force me to do aught against kingly majesty, yet would I fear God, and would not dare to offend the king ordained by Him. For neither do I forget where I read that whosoever resisteth power, resisteth the ordinance of God." But—but—but— continues the letter, through many qualifyings which are also admonitions. At last come the words : " It is a fearful thing to fall into the hands of the living God, even for thee, O king." Thereupon the saint does not fail to speak his mind.[3]

Bernard's fiercest denunciations were reserved for heretics and schismatics, for Abaelard, for Arnold of Brescia, for the Antipope Anacletus—were they not enemies of God ? Clearly the saint saw and understood these men from his point of view. Thus in a letter to Innocent II.[4] he sums up his attitude towards Abaelard : " Peter Abaelard is

<hr/>

[1] *Ep.* 111.   [2] *Ep.* 152, *ad Innocentium papam*, A.D. 1135.
[3] *Ep.* 170, *ad Ludovicum.* Written in 1138.   [4] *Ep.* 191.

trying to make void the merit of Christian faith, when he
deems himself able by human reason to comprehend God
altogether. He ascends to the heavens and descends even
to the abyss ! Nothing may hide from him in the depths of
hell or in the heights above ! The man is great in his own
eyes—this scrutinizer of Majesty and fabricator of heresies."
Here was the gist of the matter. That a man should be great
in his own eyes, apart from God, and teach others so, stirred
Bernard's bowels.[1]

Of Arnold, the impetuous clerical revolutionist and pupil
of Abaelard, Bernard writes with fury : " Arnold of Brescia,
whose speech is honey and whose teaching poison, whose is
the head of a dove and the tail of a scorpion, whom Brescia
vomited forth, Rome abhorred, France repelled, Germany
abominates, Italy will not receive, is said to be with you." [2]
Again, Bernard rejoices with great joy when he hears that
the anti-pope who divided Christendom was dead.[3]

It is pleasant to turn back to Bernard's lovingness and
mercy. His God would not condemn those who repented ;
and the saint can be gentle toward sinners possibly repentant.
He urges certain monks to receive back an erring brother :
" Take him back then, you who are spiritual, in the spirit of
gentleness ; let love be confirmed in him, and let good
intention excuse the evil done. Receive back with joy him
whom you wept as lost." [4] In another letter he urges a
countess to be more lenient with her children ; [5] and there
is a story of his begging a robber from the hands of the
executioners, and leading him to Clara Vallis, where he
became at length a holy man.[6]

So one sees Bernard's severity, his gentle mercy, and the
love burning within him for his fellows' good. Such were
the emotions of Bernard the saint. The man's human heart

---

[1] Cf. post, Chapter XXXVII. I., regarding this instance of Bernard's zeal.
His position is critically set out in Wilhelm Meyer's " Die Anklagesätze des h.
Bernard gegen Abaelard," Göttingische gelehrte Nachrichten, philol. hist. Klasse,
1898, pp. 397-468.

[2] Ep. 196, ad Guidonen ; cf. Ep. 195 (A.D. 1140). See for the Latin of this
letter post, Chapter XXXII.

[3] Ep. 147, to Peter the Venerable, Abbot of Cluny (A.D. 1138).

[4] Ep. 101, ad religiosos ; cf. also Ep. 136.

[5] Ep. 300.

[6] Vita prima, lib. vii. cap. 15.

could also yearn, and feel bereavement in spite of faith.   As his zeal draws him from land to land, he is home-sick for Clara Vallis.   From Italy, in 1137, fighting to crush the anti-pope, a letter carries his yearning love to his dear ones there :

" Sad is my soul, and not to be consoled, until I may return. For what consolation save you in the Lord have I in an evil time and in the place of my pilgrimage ?   Wherever I go, your sweet recollection does not leave me ; but the sweeter the memory the more vexing is the absence.   Alas ! my wandering not only is prolonged but aggravated.   Hard enough is exile from the Lord, which is common to us all while we are pilgrims in the body. But I endure a special exile also, compelled to live away from you.

" For a third time my bowels are torn from me.[1]   Those little children are weaned before the time ; the very ones whom I begot through the Gospel I may not educate.   I am forced to abandon my own, and care for the affairs of others ; and it is not easy to say whether to be dragged from the former, or to be involved in the latter is harder to bear.   Thus, O good Jesus, my whole life is spent in grief and my years in groaning !   It is good for me, O Lord, to die, rather than to live and not among my brothers, my own household, my own dearest ones." [2]

Bernard had a younger brother, Gerard, whom he deeply loved.   In 1138 he died while still young, and having recently returned with Bernard from Italy.   Bernard, dry-eyed, read the burial-service over his body ; so says his biographer wondering, for the saint was not wont to bury even strangers without tears.[3]   No other eyes were dry at that funeral.   Afterwards he preached a sermon ;[4] it began with restraint, then became a long cry of grief.

The saint took the text from Canticles where he had left off in his previous sermon—" I am black, but comely, as the tents of Kedar."   He proceeded to expound its meaning : the tents are our bodies, in which we pilgrims dwell and carry on our war.   Then he spoke of other portions of the text—and suddenly deferred the whole subject till his next sermon : Grief ordains an end, " and the calamity which I suffer."

[1] It was Bernard's third absence in Italy.
[2] Ep. 144, *ad suos Clarae-Vallenses.*
[3] *Vita prima*, lib. iii. cap. 7.   [4] *Sermo xxvi. in Cantica.*

" For why dissemble, or conceal the fire which is scorching my sad breast ? What have I to do with this Song, I who am in bitterness ? The power of grief turns my intent, and the anger of the Lord has parched my spirit. I did violence to my soul and dissembled till now, lest sorrow should seem to conquer faith. Others wept, but with dry eyes I followed the hateful funeral, and dry-eyed stood at the tomb, until all the solemnities were performed. In my priestly robes I finished the prayers, and sprinkled the earth over the body of my loved one about to become earth. Those who looked on, weeping, wondered that I did not. With such strength as I could command, I resisted and struggled not to be moved at nature's due, at the fiat of the Powerful, at the decree of the Just, at the scourge of the Terrible, at the will of the Lord. But though tears were pressed back, I could not command my sadness ; and grief, suppressed, roots deeper. I confess I am beaten. My sorrow will out before the eyes of my children who understand and will console.

" You know, my sons, how just is my grief. You know what a comrade has left me in the path wherein I was walking. He was my brother in blood and still closer by religion. I was weak in body, and he carried me ; faint-hearted, and he comforted me ; lazy, and he spurred me ; thoughtless, and he admonished me. Whither art thou snatched away, snatched from my hands ! O bitter separation, which only death could bring ; for living, thou wouldst never leave me. Why did we so love, and now have lost each other ! Hard state, but my fortune, not his, is to be pitied. For thou, dear brother, if thou hast lost dear ones, hast gained those who are dearer. Me only this separation wounds. Sweet was our presence to each other, sweet our consorting, sweet our colloquy ; I have lost these joys ; thou hast but changed them. Now, instead of such a worm as me, thou hast the presence of Christ. But what have I in place of thee ? And perhaps though thou knewest us in the flesh, now that thou hast entered into the power of the Lord, thou art mindful only of His righteousness, forgetting us.

" I seem to hear my brother saying : ' Can a woman forget her sucking child ; even so, yet will I not forget thee.' That does not help, where no hand is stretched out.'

Bernard speaks of Gerard's unfailing helpfulness to him and every one, and of his piety and religious life. He feels the cares of his life and station closing around him, and his brother gone. Then he justifies his grief, and pours it forth unrestrained. Would any one bid him not to weep ? as well tell him not to feel when his bowels were torn from him ; he

feels, for his flesh is not brass ; he grieves, and his grief is
ever before him :

" I confess my sorrow. Will some one call me carnal ?
Certainly I am human, since I am a man. Nor do I deny being
carnal, for I am, and sold under sin, adjudged to death and
punishment. I am not insensible to punishments ; I shudder at
death, my own or others'. Mine was Gerard, mine ! He is gone,
and I feel, and am wounded, grievously !

" Pardon me, my sons ; or rather lament your father's state.
Pity me, and think how grievously I have been requited for my
sins by the hand of God. Though I feel the punishment, I do not
impugn the sentence. This is human ; that would be impious.
Man must needs be affected towards those dear to him, with gladness at their presence, with sorrow at their absence. I grieve over
thee, Gerard, my beloved, not because thou art to be pitied, but
because thou art taken away. May it be that I have not lost thee,
but sent thee on before ! Be it granted me some time to follow
whither thou art gone ; for thou hast joined the company of those
heavenly ones on whom in thy last hours thou didst call exultingly
to praise the Lord. For thee death had no sting, nor any fear.
Through his jaws Gerard passed to his Fatherland safe and glad
and exulting. When I reached his side, and he had finished the
psalm, looking up to heaven, he said in a clear voice : ' Father,
into thy hands I commend my spirit.' Then saying over again
and again the word, ' Father, Father,' he turned his joyful face to
me, and said : ' What great condescension that God should be
father to men ! What glory for men to be sons of God and heirs
of God ! ' So he rejoiced, till my grief was almost turned to a
song of gladness.

" But the pang of sorrow calls me back from that lovely vision,
as care wakens one from light slumber. I grieve, but only over
myself ; I lament his loss to this household, to the poor, to all our
Order ; whom did he not comfort with deed and word and example ? Grievously am I afflicted, because I love vehemently.
And let no one blame my tears ; for Jesus wept at Lazarus's
tomb. His tears bore witness to His nature, not to His lack of
faith. So these tears of mine ; they show my sorrow, not my
faithlessness. I grieve, but do not murmur. Lord, I will sing
of thy mercy and righteousness. Thou gavest Gerard ; thou
hast taken him. Though we grieve that he is gone, we thank
thee for the gift.

" I bear in mind, O Lord, my pact and thy commiseration,
that thou mightest the more be justified in thy word. For when
last year we were in Viterbo, and he fell sick, and I was afflicted
at the thought of losing him in a strange land and not bringing

him back to those who loved him, I prayed to thee with groans and tears : ' Wait, O Lord, until our return.   When he is restored to his friends, take him, if thou wilt, and I will not complain.'   Thou heardest me, God ; he recovered ; we finished the work thou hadst laid on us, and returned in gladness bringing our sheaves of peace.   Then I was near to forget my pact, but not so thou.   I shame me of these sobs, which convict me of prevarication.   Thou hast recalled thy loan, thou hast taken again what was thine. Tears set an end to words ; thou, O Lord, wilt set to them limit and measure." [1]

We may now turn to Bernard's love of God, and rise with him from the fleshly to the spiritual, from the conditioned to the absolute.   There is no break ; love is always love. More especially the love of Christ, the God-man, is the mediating term : He presents the Godhead in human form ; to love Him is to know a love attaching to both God and man.

Guigo, Prior of the "Grande Chartreuse," whose *Meditations* have been given,[2] was Bernard's friend, and wrote to him upon love.   Bernard replies : " While I was reading it, I felt sparks in my breast, from which my heart glowed within me as from that fire which the Lord sent upon the earth ! "   He hesitates to suggest anything to Guigo's fervent spirit, as he would hesitate to rouse a bride quiet in the bridegroom's arms.   Yet " what I do not dare, love dares ; it boldly knocks at a friend's door, fearing no repulse, and quite careless of disturbing your delightful ease with its affairs."   Bernard is here speaking of love's importunate devotion ; his words characterize the soul's importuning of God :

" I should call love undefiled because it keeps nothing of its own.   Indeed it has nothing of its own, for everything which it has is God's.   The undefiled law of the Lord is love, which seeks not what profits itself but what profits many.   It is called the law of the Lord, either because He lives by it, or because no one possesses it save by His gift.   It is not irrational to speak of God as living by law, that law being love.   Indeed in the blessed highest Trinity what preserves that highest ineffable unity, except love ? "

---

[1] " Finem verborum indicunt lacrymae ; tu illis, Domine, finem modumque indixeris."   [2] *Ante*, Chapter XVII.

So far, Bernard has been using the word *charitas*. Now, in order to indicate love's desire, he begins to use the words *cupiditas* and *amor*.[1] When these yearning qualities are rightly guided by God's grace, what is good will be cherished for the sake of what is better, the body will be loved for the soul's sake, the soul for God's sake, and God for His own sake.

" Yet because we are of the flesh (*carnales*) and are begotten through the flesh's concupiscence, our yearning love (*cupiditas vel amor noster*) must begin from the flesh ; yet if rightly directed, advancing under the leadership of grace, it will be consummated in spirit. For that which is first is not spiritual, but that which is natural (*animale*) ; then that which is spiritual. First man loves (*diligit*) himself for his own sake. For he is flesh, and is able to understand nothing beyond himself. When he sees that he cannot live (*subsistere*) by himself alone, he begins, as it were from necessity, to seek and love God. Thus, in this second stage, he loves God, but only for his own sake. Yet as his necessities lead him to cultivate and dwell with God in thinking, reading, praying, and obeying, God little by little becomes known and becomes sweet. Having thus tasted how sweet is the Lord, he passes to the third stage, where he loves God for God's sake. Whether any man in this life has perfectly attained the fourth stage, where he loves himself for God's sake, I do not know. Let those say who have knowledge ; for myself, I confess it seems impossible. Doubtless it will be so when the good and faithful servant shall have entered into the joy of his Lord, and shall be drunk with the flowing richness of God's house. Then oblivious to himself, he will pass to God and become one spirit with Him." [2]

So one sees the stages through which love of self and lust of fellow become love of God. A responsive emotion attends each ascending step in the saint's intellectual apprehension of love—as one should bear in mind while following the larger exposition of the theme in Bernard's *De diligendo Deo*.[3]

The cause and reason for loving God is God ; the *mode*

[1] As Augustine before him. Cf. Taylor, *The Classical Heritage, etc.*, pp. 129-131.
[2] *Ep.* 11, *ad Guigonem*. Bernard adds that when Paul says that flesh and blood shall not inherit the kingdom of God, it is not to be understood that the substance of flesh will not be there, but that every carnal necessity will have ceased ; the love of flesh will be absorbed in the love of the spirit, and our weak human affections transformed into divine energies.
[3] Migne, *Pat. Lat.* 182, col. 973-1000.

is to love without measure : " Causa diligendi Deum, Deus est ; modus, sine modo diligere." Should we love God because of His desert, or our advantage ? For both reasons. On the score of His desert, because He first loved us. What stint shall there be to my love of Him who is my life's free giver, its bounteous administrator, its kind consoler, its solicitous ruler, its redeemer, eternal preserver and glorifier ? On the other hand, " God is not loved without reward ; but He should be loved without regard to the reward. *Charitas* seeks not its own. It is affection and not a contract ; it is not bought, nor does it buy. *Amor* is satisfied with itself. It has the reward, which is what is loved. True love demands no reward, but merits one. The reward, although not sought by the lover, is due him, and will be rendered if he perseveres."

Bernard proceeds to expound the four stages or grades (*gradus*) of love :

" Love is a natural affection, one of the four.[1] As it exists by nature, it should diligently serve the Author of nature first of all. But as nature is frail and weak, love is compelled by necessity first to serve itself. This is carnal love, whereby, above everything, man loves himself for his own sake. It is not set forth by precept, but is rooted in nature ; for who hates his own flesh ? As love becomes more ready and profuse, it is not content with the channel of necessity, but will pour forth and overspread the broad fields of pleasure. At once the overflow is bridled by the command, ' Thou shalt love thy neighbour as thyself.' This is just and needful, lest what is part of nature should have no part in grace. A man may concede to himself what he will, so long as he is mindful to provide the same for his neighbour. The bridle of temperance is imposed on thee, O man, out of the law of life and discipline, in order that thou shouldst not follow thy desires, nor with the good things of nature serve the enemy of the soul, which is lust. If thou wilt turn away from thy pleasures, and be content with food and raiment, little by little it will not so burden thee to keep thy love from carnal desires, which war against the soul. Thy love will be temperate and righteous when what is withdrawn from its own pleasures is not denied to its brother's needs. Thus carnal love becomes social when extended to one's kind.

" Yet in order that perfect justice should exist in the love of neighbour, God must be regarded (*Deum in causa haberi necesse*

---

[1] Love, fear, joy, sorrow.

est). How can one love his neighbour purely who does not love in God ? God makes Himself loved, He who makes all things good. He who founded nature so made it that it should always need to be sustained by Him. In order that no creature might be ignorant of this, and arrogate for himself the good deeds of the Creator, the Founder wisely decreed that man should be tried in tribulations. By this means, when he shall have failed and God have aided, God shall be honoured by him whom He has delivered. The result is that man, animal and carnal, who knew not how to love any one beside himself, begins for his own sake to love God ; because he has found out that in God he can accomplish everything profitable, and without Him can do nothing.

"So now for his own interest, he loves God—love's second grade ; but does not yet love God for God's sake. If, however, tribulation keeps assailing him, and he continually turns to God for aid, and God delivers him, will not the man so oft delivered, though he have a breast of iron and a heart of stone, be drawn to cherish his deliverer, and love Him not only for His aid but for Himself ? Frequent necessities compel man to come to God incessantly ; repeatedly he tastes and, by tasting, proves how sweet is the Lord. At length God's sweetness, rather than human need, draws the man to love Him. Thereafter it will not be hard for the man to fulfil the command to love his neighbour. Truly loving God, he loves for this reason those who are God's. He loves chastely, and is not oppressed through obeying the chaste command ; he loves justly, and willingly embraces the just command. That is the third grade of love, when God is loved for Himself.

"Happy is he who attains to the fourth grade, where man loves himself only on account of God. Thy righteousness, O God, is as the mountain of God ; love is that mountain, that high mountain of God. Who shall ascend into the mountain of the Lord ? Who will give me the wings of a dove and I will fly away and be at rest. Alas ! for my long-drawn sojourning ! When shall I gain that habitation in Zion, and my soul become one spirit with God ? Blessed and holy will I call him to whom in this mortal life such has been given though but once. For to be lost to self and not to feel thyself, and to be emptied of thyself and almost to be made nothing, that pertains to heavenly intercourse, not to human affection. And if any one among mortals here gain admission for an instant, at once the wicked world is envious, the day's evil disturbs, the body of death drags down, fleshly necessity solicits, corruption's debility does not sustain, and, fiercest of all, brotherly love calls back ! Alas ! he is dragged back to himself, and forced to cry : 'O Lord, I suffer violence, answer thou for me' (Isa. xxxviii. 14) ; 'Who will deliver me from the body of this death ?' (Rom. vii. 24).

" Yet Scripture says that God made all things for His own
sake ; that will come to pass when the creation is in full accord
with its Author.   Therefore we must sometime pass into that
state wherein we do not wish to be ourselves or anything else,
except for His sake and by reason of His will, not ours.   Then
not our need or happiness, but His will, will be fulfilled in us.   O
holy love and chaste !   O sweet affection !   O pure and purged
intention of the will, in which nothing of its own is mingled !
This is it to be made God (*deificari*).   As the drop of water is
diffused in a jar of wine, taking its taste and colour, and as
molten iron becomes like to fire and casts off its form, and as the
air transfused with sunlight is transformed into that same brightness of light, so that it seems not illumined, but itself to be the
light, thus in the saints every human affection must in some
ineffable mode be liquefied of itself and transfused into the will
of God.   How could God be all in all if in man anything of man
remained ?   A certain substance will remain, but in another form,
another glory, another power."

Hereupon St. Bernard considers how this fourth grade of
love will be attained in the resurrection, and " perpetually
possessed, when God only is loved and we love ourselves
only for His sake, that He may be the recompense and aim
(*praemium*) of those who love themselves, the eternal
recompense of those who love eternally."

Christ is the universal Mediator between God and man,
not only because reconciling them, but as forming the
intervening term, the concrete instance of the One suited
to the comprehension of the other.   When certain thoughts
and sentiments commonly applying to man are applied
to Christ, they become fit to apply to God.   Herein
especially may be perceived the continuing identity of love,
whether relating to human beings or to God.   The soul's
love of Christ is mediatorial, and symbolic of its love of
God.   All of which Bernard has demonstrated with
a mighty power of argument and feeling in his famous
Sermons on Canticles.[1]

The human personality of Christ draws men to love Him,
till their love is purged of carnality and exalted to a perfect
love of God :

" Observe that the heart's love is partly carnal ; it is affected

---

[1] Migne 183, col. 785-1198.

through the flesh of Christ and what He said and did while in the flesh. Filled with this love, the heart is readily touched by discourse upon His words and acts. It hears of nothing more willingly, reads nothing more carefully, recalls nothing more frequently, and meditates upon nothing more sweetly. When man prays, the sacred image of the God-man is with him, as He was born or suckled, as He taught or died, rose from the dead or ascended to heaven. This image never fails to nerve man's mind with the love of virtue, cast out the vices of the flesh and quell its lusts. I deem the principal reason why the invisible God wished to be seen in the flesh, and, as man, hold intercourse with men, was that He might draw the affections of carnal men, who could only love carnally, to a salutary love of His flesh, and then on to a spiritual love."

Conversely, the Saviour's example teaches men how they should love Him :

" He loved sweetly, wisely, and bravely : sweetly, in that He put on flesh ; wisely, in that He avoided fault ; bravely, in that He bore death. Those, however, with whom He sojourned in the flesh, He did not love carnally, but in prudence of spirit. Learn then, Christian, from Christ how to love Christ."

Bernard shows how even the Apostles failed sometimes to love Him according to His perfect teaching and example :

" Good, indeed, is this carnal love," he concludes, " through which a carnal life is shut out ; and the world is despised and conquered. This love progresses as it becomes rational, and perfected as it becomes spiritual." [1]

From his own experiences Bernard could have spoken much of the winning power of Jesus, and could have told how sweetly it drew him to love his Saviour's steps from Bethlehem to Calvary. The fifteenth sermon upon Canticles is on the healing power of Jesus' name.

" Dry is all food for the soul unless anointed with that oil. Whatever you write is not to my taste unless I read Jesus there. Your talk and disputation is nothing unless that name is rung. Jesus is honey in the mouth, melody in the ear, joy in the heart. He is medicine as well. Is any one troubled, let Jesus come into the heart and thence leap to the lips, and behold ! at the rising of that bright name the clouds scatter and the air is again serene. If any one slips in crime, and then desponds amid the snares of

---

[1] *Sermo xx. in Cantica.*

death, will he not, invoking that name of life, regain the breath of
life ?   In whom can hardness of heart, sloth, rancour, languish-
ment stand before that name ?   In whom at its invocation will
not the dried fount of tears burst forth more abundantly and
sweetly ?   To what fearful trembler did the power of that name
ever fail to bring back confidence ?   To what man struggling
amid doubts did not the clear assurance of that name, invoked,
shine forth ?   Who despairing in adversity lacked fortitude if
that name sounded ?   These are the languors and sickness of the
soul, and that the medicine.   Nothing is as potent to restrain
the attack of wrath, or quell the tumour of pride, or heal envy's
wound, or put out the fire of lust, or temper avarice.   When I
name Jesus, I see before me a man meek and humble of heart,
benignant, sober, chaste, pitying, holy, who heals me with His
example and strengthens me with aid.   I take example from the
Man, and draw aid from the Mighty One.   Here hast thou, O
my soul, an herb of price, hidden in the vessel of that name
which is Jesus, bringing thee health surely and in thy sickness
failing thee never."

This is a little illustration of Bernard's love of the
Christ-man, a love which is ever taking on spiritual hues and
changing to a love of the Christ-God.   Christians, from the
time of Origen, had recognized the many offices of Christ,
the many saving potencies in which He ministered unto
each soul according to its need.   And so Bernard preaches
that the sick soul needs Christ as the physician, but that
the saintly soul has other yearnings for a more perfect
communion.

This perfect communion, this most complete relationship
which in this mortal life a soul can have with Christ, with
God, had been symbolized, likewise ever since the time of
Origen, by the words Bride and Bridegroom, and the Song
of Songs had furnished the burning phrases.   With sur-
passing spirituality Bernard uses the texts of Canticles to set
forth the relationship of the soul to Christ, of man to God.
The texts are what they are, burning, sensuous, fleshly,
intense, and beautiful—every one knows them ; but in
Bernard's sermons flesh fades before the spirit's whiter glow.

" O love (*amor*), headlong, vehement, burning, impetuous, that
canst think of nothing beyond thyself, detesting all else, despising
all else, satisfied with thyself !   Thou dost confound ranks, carest
for no usage, knowest no measure.   In thyself dost thou triumph

over apparent opportuneness, reason, shame, council and judgment, and leadest them into captivity. Everything which the
soul-bride utters resounds of thee and nothing else ; so hast thou
possessed her heart and tongue." [1]

What Bernard here ejaculates as to the overwhelming
sufficiency of love, he sets forth finally in a sustained and
reasoned passage, in which man's ways of loving God are
cast together in a sequence of ardent thought and image.
He has been explaining the soul's likeness to the Word.
Although it be afflicted and defiled by sin, it may yet
venture to come to Him whose likeness it retains, however
obscured. The soul does not leave God by change of place,
but, in the manner of spiritual substance, by becoming
depraved. The return of the soul is its conversion, in which
it is made conformable to God.

" Such conformity marries the soul to the Word, whom it is
like by nature, and may show itself like in will, loving as it is loved.
If it loves perfectly it weds. What more delightful than this
conformity, what more desirable than this love, through which
thou, O soul, faithfully drawest near to the Word, with constancy
cleavest to the Word, consulting Him in everything, as capable
in intellect as audacious in desire. Spiritual is the contracting
of these holy nuptials, wherein always to will the same makes
one spirit out of two. No fear lest the disparity of persons make
but a lame concurrence of wills : for love does not know respect.
The name love comes from loving and not from honouring. He
may honour who dreads, who is struck dumb with fear and
wonder. Not so the lover. Love aboundeth in itself, and derides
and imprisons the other emotions. Wherefore she who loves,
loves, and knows nothing else. And He who is to be honoured
and marvelled at, still loves rather to be loved. Bridegroom
and Bride they are. And what necessity or bond is there between
spouses except to be loved and love ?
" Think also, that the Bridegroom is not only loving but very
love. Is He also honour ? I have not so read. I have read that
God is love ; not that He is honour, or dignity. God indeed
demands to be feared as Lord, to be honoured as Father, and as
Bridegroom to be loved. Which excels the rest ? Love, surely.
Without it, fear is penal, and honour graceless. Fear is slavish
till manumitted by love ; and the honour which does not rise
from love is adulation. To God alone belong honour and glory ;
but He will accept neither unless it is flavoured with love's honey.

---

[1] *Sermo lxxix. in Cantica.*

" Love asks neither cause nor fruit beyond itself. I love
because I love ; I love that I may love. A great thing is love.
Among all the movements, sensations, and affections of the soul,
it is the only one wherein the creature can make a return to its
Author. If God be angry with me, shall I likewise be angry with
Him ? Nay, I will fear and tremble and beseech. If He accuse
me, I will make no counter-charge, but plead before Him. If He
judge me, I will not judge but worship. And when He saves me,
He asks not to be saved by me ; nor does He who frees all ask
to be freed of any one. Likewise if He commands, I obey, and do
not order Him. Now see how different it is with love. For when
God loves, He wishes only to be loved ; He loves with no other end
than to be loved, knowing that those who love are blessed with
love itself.

" A great thing is love ; but there are grades in it. The Bride
stands at the summit. Sons love, but they are thinking of their
inheritance. Fearing to lose that, they honour, rather than love,
him from whom they expect it. Love is suspect when its suffrage
appears to be won by hope of gain. Weak is it, if it cease or
lessen with that hope withdrawn. It is impure if it desires
anything else. Pure love is not mercenary : it gains no strength
from hope, nor weakens with lack of trust. This love is the
Bride's, because she is what she is by love. Love is the Bride's
sole hope and interest. In it the Bride abounds and the Bridegroom is content. He seeks nothing else, nor has she ought beside.
Hence he is Bridegroom and she Bride. This belongs to spouses
which none else, not even a son, can attain. Man is commanded
to honour his father and mother ; but there is silence as to love.
Which is not because parents are not to be loved by their sons ;
but because sons are rather moved to honour them. The honour
of the King loves judgment ; but the Bridegroom's love—for He
is love—asks only love's return and faith.

" Rightly renouncing all other affections, the Bride reposes on
love alone, and returns a love reciprocal. And when she has
poured her whole self out in love, what is that compared with the
perennial flood of that fountain ? Not equals in abundance are
this loving one and Love, the soul and the Word, the Bride and
Bridegroom, creature and Creator—no more than thirst equals
the fount. What then ? shall she therefore despair, and the vow
of the would-be Bride be rendered empty ? Shall the desire of
this panting one, the ardour of this loving one, the trust of this
confiding one be baffled because she cannot keep pace with the
giant's course, in sweetness contend with honey, in mildness with
the Lamb, in whiteness with the Lily, in brightness with the Sun,
in love with Him who is love ? No. For although the creature
loves less, because she is less, yet if she loves with her whole self,

nothing lacks where there is all.   Wherefore, as I have said, so to love is to have wedded ; for no one can so love and yet be loved but little, and in mutual consent stands the entire and perfect marriage." [1]

Who has not marvelled that the relationship of marriage should make so large a part of the symbolism through which monks and nuns expressed the soul's love of God ? Historically it might be traced to Paul's precept, " Husbands love your wives, as Christ loved the Church " ; still more potently it was derived from the Song of Songs.   But beyond these almost adventitious influences, did not the holy priest, the monk, the nun, feel and know that marriage was the great human relationship ?   So they drew from it the most adequate allegory of the soul's communion with its Maker : differently according to their sex, with much emotion, and even with unseemly imaginings, they thought and felt the love of God along the ways of wedded union or even bridal passion.[2]

[1] *Sermo lxxxiii. in Cantica.*   This is nearly the whole of this sermon.   Bernard's sermons were not long.   See *post*, Chapter XXXVII. II., as to Bernard's use of the symbolism of the kiss.

[2] *Post*, Chapter XX.

CHAPTER XIX

ST. FRANCIS OF ASSISI [1]

TWENTY-NINE years after the death of St. Bernard, Francis was born in the Umbrian hill town of Assisi. The year was 1182. On the fourth of October 1226, in the forty-fifth year of his age, this most loving and best beloved of mediaeval saints breathed his last, in the little church of the Portiuncula, within the shadows of that same hill town.

Of all mediaeval saints, Bernard and Francis impressed themselves most strongly upon their times. Neither of them was pre-eminently an intellectual force—Francis especially would not have been what he was but for certain childlike qualities of mind which never fell away from him.

[1] The present chapter is intended as an appreciation of the personality of Francis ; incidents of his life are used for illustration. I have endeavoured to confine myself to such as are generally accepted as authentic, and to those parts of the sources which are confirmed by corroborative testimony. The reader doubtless is aware that the sources of Franciscan history are abundant, but that there is still much critical and even polemic controversy touching their trustworthiness. Of the *Speculum perfectionis*, edited by Sabatier, I would make this remark : many of its narratives contain such wisdom and human truth as seem to me to bring them very close to the acts and words of some great personality, *i.e.* Francis. This is no sure proof of their authenticity, and yet is a fair reason for following their form of statement of some of the incidents in Francis's life, the human value of which perhaps appears narrowed and deflected in other accounts.

The chief sources for the life of St. Francis of Assisi are first his own compositions, edited conveniently under the title of *Opuscula sancti patris Francisci Assisiensis*, by the Franciscans of Quarrachi (1904). They have been translated by P. Robinson (Philadelphia, The Dolphin Press, 1906). Next in certainty of authenticity come the two Lives by Celano, i.e. *Vita prima S. Francisci Assisiensis*, auctore B. Thoma de Celano, ejus discipulo, Bollandi *Acta sanctorum*, tome 46 (Oct. tome 2), pp. 683-723 ; also edited by Canon Amoni (Rome, 1880) ; *Vita secunda seu appendix ad Vitam primam*, ed. by Amoni (Rome, 1880). Better editions than Amoni's are those of Edouard d'Alençon (Rome, 1906), and H. G. Rosedale (Dent, London, 1904). Of great importance also is the *Legenda trium sociorum* (*Leo, Rufinus, Angelus*), Bollandi *Acta sanctorum*, t. 46 (Oct. t. 2), pp.

The power of these men sprang from their personalities and the *vivida vis* (their contemporaries would have said, the grace of God) realizing itself in every word and act. Bernard's power was more directly dependent upon the conditions of his epoch, and his influence was more limited in duration.

The reason is not far to seek. Both men were of the Middle Ages, even of those decades in which they lived. But Bernard's strength was part of the medium wherein he worked and the evil against which he fought—the clerical corruptions, the heresies, the schisms and political controversies, the warfare of Christ with Mahomet—all matters of vital import for his time, but which were to change and pass.

Francis, on the other hand, was occupied with none of these. He was no scourge of clerical corruptions, no scourge of anything ; he knew nought of heresy or schism, nothing of politics or war ; into the story of his life there comes not even a far-off echo of the Albigensian Crusade or the conflict between pope and emperor. His life appears detached from the special conditions of his time ; it is neither held within them nor compelled by them, but only by its inner impulse. For it was not occupied with the exigencies of Italy and Germany, or Southern France, during that first quarter of the thirteenth century, when De Montfort was hurling the orthodox and brutal north upon the fair but heretical provinces of Languedoc, and when Innocent III. was excommunicating Otho IV., and

723-742 ; also ed. by Amoni (Rome, 1880). (Amoni's texts differ somewhat from those of the Bollandist.) It is also edited by Pulignani (Foligno, 1898), and edited and hypothetically completed from the problematical Italian version, by Marcellino da Civezza and Teofilo Domenichelli (Rome, 1899). Perhaps most vivid of all the early sources is the so-called *Speculum perfectionis seu S. Francisci Assisiensis legenda antiquissima auctore fratre Leone*, as edited by Paul Sabatier (Paris, 1898). It has been translated into English several times. Its date and authenticity are still under violent discussion. One may conveniently refer to the article " Franciscan Literature " in the *Edinburgh Review* for January 1904, and to P. Robinson's *Short Introduction to Franciscan Literature* (New York, 1907) for further references, which the student must supplement for himself from the mass of recent literature in books and periodicals touching the life of Francis and its sources. See also Fierens, *La Question franciscaine, etc.* (Louvain, 1909). Among modern Lives, that by Sabatier is probably known to all readers of this note. The Lives by Bonghi and Le Monnier may be referred to. Gebhard's *Italie mystique* is interesting in connection with Francis.

Frederick II. was disclosing himself as the most dangerous foe the papacy had yet known. The passing turmoil and danger of the time did not touch this life ; the man knew naught of all these things. He was not considering thirteenth century Italians, Frenchmen, and Germans ; he was fascinated with men as men, with the dumb brutes as fellow-creatures, and even with plants and stones as vessels of God's loveliness or symbols of His Word ; above all he was absorbed in Christ, who had taken on humanity for him, had suffered for him, died for him, and who now around, above, within him, inspired and directed his life.

So Francis's life was not compassed by its circumstances ; nor was its effect limited to the thirteenth century. His life partook of the eternal and the universal, and might move men in times to come as simply and directly as it turned men's hearts to love in the years when Francis was treading the rough stones of Assisi.

On the other hand, Francis was mediaeval and in a way to give concrete form and colour to the elements of universal manhood that were his. He was mediaeval in complete and finished mode ; among mediaeval men he offers perhaps the most distinct and most perfectly consistent individuality. He is Francis of Assisi, born in 1182 and dying in 1226, and no one else who ever lived either there and then or elsewhere at some other time. He is Francis of Assisi perfectly and always, a man presenting a complete artistic unity, never exhibiting act or word or motive out of character with himself.

From a slightly different point of view we may perceive how he was a perfect individual and at the same time a perfect mediaeval type. There was no element in his character which was not assimilated and made into Francis of Assisi. Anterior and external influences contributed to make this Francis. But in entering him they ceased to be what they had been ; they changed and became Francis. For example, nothing of the antique, no distinct bit of classical inheritance, appears in him ; if, in any way, he was touched by it—as in his joyous love of life and the world about him—the influence had ceased to be anything distinct in him ; it had become himself. Likewise, whatever he may have known of the Fathers and of all the dogmatic possession and ecclesiastical tradition of the Church, this also was remade in Francis. Evidently such an all-assimilating and transforming individuality could not have existed in those earlier centuries when the immature mediaeval world was taking over its great inheritance from the pagan and Christian antique—those centuries when men could but turn their heritage of thought and knowledge this way and that, disturb and distort and rearrange it. Such an individuality as Francis could exist only at the climax of the Middle Age, at the period of its fullest strength and greatest distinction, when it had masterfully changed after its own heart whatever it had received from the past, and had made its transformed acquisitions into itself.

Francis is of this grand mediaeval climacteric. The Middle Ages were no longer in a stage of transition from the antique ; they had attained ; they were themselves. Sides of this distinctive mediaeval development and temper express themselves in Francis—are Francis verily. The spirit of romance is incarnate in him. Roland, Oliver, Charlemagne (he of the *Chansons de geste*), and the knights of the Round Table, are part of Francis ;—his first disciples are his paladins. Again, instead of emperor or paladin, he is himself the *jongleour,* the *joculator Dei* (God's minstrel).

And of all that had become Francis the greatest was Christ. He had not taken the theology of Augustine ; he had not taken the Christ handed over by the transition centuries to the early Middle Ages ; he had not adopted the Christ of the ecclesiastical hierarchy. He took Jesus from the Gospel, or at least such elements of Jesus' life and teaching as he felt and understood. Francis modelled his life on his understanding of Christ and His teaching. So many another saint had done ; in fact, so must all Christians try to do. Francis accomplished it with completeness and power ; he created a new Christ life ; a Christ life partial and reduced from the breadth and balance of the original, yet veritable and living. Francis himself felt that his whole life was Christ-directed and inspired, and that even because of his own special insignificance Christ

had chosen him to show forth the true Gospel life again—
but chosen him indeed.[1]

Although the life of Francis appears as if detached from
the larger political and ecclesiastical movements of the time,
it yields glimpses of the ways and doings of the people of
Assisi. We see their jealousies and quarrels, their war with
Perugia, also their rustic readiness to jeer at the unusual
and incomprehensible ; or we are struck with instances of
the stupid obstinacy and intolerance often characterizing a
small community. Again, we see in some of those citizens
an open and quick impulsiveness, which, at the sight of love,
may turn to love. It would seem as if the harshest, most
impossible man of all the town was Peter Bernardone, a
well-to-do merchant whose affairs took him often from
Assisi, and not infrequently to France.

Bernardone had a predilection for things French, and the
child born to his wife while he was absent in France, he called
Francis upon his return, although the mother had given it
the name of John. The mother, whose name was Pica, may
have been of Provençal or French blood. Apparently such
education as Francis received in his boyhood was as much
French as Italian. Through all his life he never lost the
habit of singing French songs which he composed himself.[2]

[1] Consciousness of direct authority from God speaks in the saint's unquestionably authentic Testament : " And after the Lord gave me some brothers, no one
showed me what I ought to do, but the Most High himself revealed to me that
I ought to live according to the model of the holy Gospel." It is also rendered
with picturesque vehemence in a scene (*Speculum perfectionis*, ed. Sabatier, ch.
68) which may or may not be authentic. At a general meeting of the Order,
certain wise brethren had persuaded the Cardinal-Bishop of Ostia to advise
Francis to follow their counsel, and had adduced certain examples from the
monastic rule of Benedict and others. " When the Cardinal had related these
matters to the blessed Francis, in the way of admonition, the blessed Francis
answered nothing, but took him by the hand and led him before the assembled
brothers, and spoke to the brothers in the fervour and power of the Holy Spirit,
thus : ' My brothers, my brothers, the Lord called me in the way of simplicity
and humility, and showed me in truth this way for myself and for those who
wish to believe and imitate me. And therefore I desire that you will not name
any rule to me, neither the rule of St. Benedict, nor that of St. Augustine or St.
Bernard, or any other rule or model of living except that which was mercifully
shown and given me by the Lord. And the Lord said that He wished me to be
a new covenant (*pactum*) in the world, and did not wish us to live by any other
way save by that knowledge.' "

[2] These songs (none of which survive) were apparently in the *langue d'oïl*
and not in the *langue d'oc*. The phrases used by the biographers are *lingua
francigena* (1 Cel. i. 7) and *lingua gallica* (*III. Soc.* iii.) or *gallice cantabat* (*Spec.
perf.* vii. 93).

The biographers assert that Francis was nourished in worldly vanity and insolence. His temperament drew him to the former, but kept him from the latter. For while he delighted in making merry with his friends, he was always distinguished by a winning courtesy of manner toward poor and rich. An innate generosity was also his, and he loved to spend money as he roamed with his companions about Assisi singing jovial choruses and himself the leader of the frolic. Bernardone did not object to his son's squandering some money in a way which led others to admire him and think his parents rich ; while Pica would keep saying that some day he would be God's son through grace. A vein of sprightly fantasy runs through these gaieties of Francis's, which we may be sure were unstained by any gross dissipation. Francis's life as a saint is peculiarly free from monkish impudicity, free, that is, from morbid dwelling upon things sensual ; which shows that in him there was no reaction or need of reaction against any youthful dissoluteness, and bears testimony to the purity of his unconverted years.[1]

In those days Francis loved to be admired and praised. He was possessed with a romantic and imaginative vanity. Costly clothes delighted him as he dreamed of still more royal entertainment, and fancied great things to come. His mind was filled with the figures of Romance ; a knight would he be at least ; why not a paladin, whom all the world should wonder at ? So he dreamed, and so he acted out his whim as best he might on the little stage of Assisi ; for Francis was a poet, and a poet even more in deed than in words. He was endowed with exquisite fancy, and he did its dictates never doubting. His life was to prove an almost unexampled inspiration to art, because it was itself a poem by reason of its unfailing realization of the conceptions of a fervent and beautiful imagination.

There came war with Perugia, a very hard-hitting town ; and the Assisi cavaliers, Francis among them, found themselves in their neighbours' dungeons. There some desponded ; but not Francis. For in these careless days he was always gleeful and jocular, even as afterwards his entire saintly life

---

[1] In fact this is vouched for in *III. Soc.* i.

was glad with an invincible gaiety of spirit. So Francis
laughed and joked in prison till his fellow-prisoners thought
him crazy, which no whit worried him, as he answered with
the glad boast that some day he would be adored by
all the world. He showed another side of his inborn
nature when he was kind to a certain one of the captives
whom the rest detested, and tried to reconcile his fellows
with him.

It was soon after his release from this twelvemonth
captivity that the sails of Francis's spirit began to fill with
still more topping hopes, and then to waver strangely. He
naturally fell sick after the privations of a Perugia prison.
As he recovered and went about with the aid of a staff, the
loveliness of field and vineyard failed to please him. He
wondered at himself, and suspected that his former pleasures
were follies. But it was not so easy to leave off his previous
life, and Francis's thoughts were lured back again to this
world's glory ; for a certain nobleman of Assisi was about
to set out on an expedition to Apulia to win gain and fame,
and Francis was inflamed to go with him. In the night he
dreamed that his father's house with its heaps of cloth and
other wares was filled instead with swords and lances, with
glittering shields, helmets and breastplates. He awoke in
an ecstasy of joy at the great glory portended by this dream.
Then he fitted himself out sumptuously, with splendid garb,
bright weapons, new armour and accoutrements, and in due
time set forth with his fellow-adventurers.

Once more he wavered. Before reaching Spoleto he
stopped, left the company, turned back on his steps, this
time impelled more strongly to seek those things which he
was to love through life. He was about twenty-three years
old. It was his nature to love everything, fame and
applause, power perhaps, and joy ; but he had not yet
loved worthily. Now his Lord was calling him, the voice at
first not very certain, and yet becoming stronger. Francis
seems to have seen a vision, in which the vanity of his
attachments was made clear, and he learned that he was
following a servant instead of the Lord. So his heart
replied," Lord, what wouldst thou have me to do ? " and then
the vision showed him that he should return, for he had

misunderstood his former dream of arms. When Francis awoke he thought diligently on these matters.

Such spiritual experiences are incommunicable, even though the man should try to tell them. But we know that as Francis had set out joyfully expecting worldly glory, he now returned with exultation, to await the will of the Lord, as it might be shown him. The facts and also their sequence are somewhat confused in the biographies.

On his return to Assisi, his comrades seem to have chosen him as lord of their revels ; again he ordained a merry feast ; but as they set forth singing gleefully, Francis walked behind them, holding his marshal's staff, in silence. Thoughts of the Lord had come again, and withdrawn his attention : he was thinking sweetly of the Lord, and vilely of himself. Soon after he is found providing destitute chapels with the requisites for a decent service ; already— in his father's absence—he is filling his table with beggars ; and already he has overcome his fastidious temper, has forced himself to exchange the kiss of peace with lepers, and has kissed the livid hands in which he presses alms.[1] He appears to have made a trip to St. Peter's at Rome, where, standing before the altar, it struck him that the Prince of the Apostles was being honoured with mean offerings. So in his own princely way he flung down the contents of his purse, to the wonder of all. Then going without the church, he put on the clothes of a beggar and asked alms.

In such conduct Francis showed himself a poet and a saint. Imagination was required to conceive these extreme, these perfect acts, acts perfect in their carrying out of a lovely thought to its fulfilment, and suffering nothing to impede its perfect realization. So Francis flings down all he has, and not a measure of his goods ; he puts on beggars' clothes, and begs ; he kisses lepers' hands, eats from the same bowl with them—acts which were perfect in the single-ness of their fulfilment of a saintly motive, acts which were likewise beautiful. They are instances of obsession with a saintly idea of great spiritual beauty, obsession so complete that the ridiculous or hideous concomitants of the realiza-

---

[1] St. Martin of Tours had done the same.

tion serve only to enhance the beauty of the holy thought perfectly fulfilled.

One day at Assisi, passing by the church of St. Damian, Francis was moved to enter for prayer. As he prayed before the Crucifix, the image seemed to say, " Francis, dost thou not see my house in ruins ? Rebuild it for me." And he answered, " Gladly, Lord," thinking that the little chapel of St. Damian was intended. Filled with joy, having felt the Crucified in his soul, he sought the priest and gave him money to buy oil for the lamp before the Crucifix. This day was ever memorable in Francis's walk with God. His way had lost its turnings ; he saw his life before him clear, glad, and full of tears of love. " From that hour his heart was so wounded and melted at the memory of his Lord's passion that henceforth while he lived he carried in his heart the marks of the Lord Jesus. Again he was seen walking near the Portiuncula, wailing aloud. And in response to the inquiries of a priest, he answered : ' I bewail the passion of my Lord Jesus Christ, which it should not shame me to go weeping through the world ! ' Often as he rose from prayer his eyes were full of blood, because he had wept so bitterly." [1]

It appears to have been after this vision in St. Damian's Church that Francis went on horseback to Foligno, carrying pieces of cloth, which he sold there, and his horse as well. He travelled back on foot, and seeking out St. Damian's astonished little priest, he kissed his hands devoutly and offered him the money. When, for fear of Bernardone, the priest would not receive it, Francis threw it into a box. He prevailed on the priest, however, to let him stay there.

What Bernardone thought of this son of his is better only guessing. The St. Damian episode brought matters to a crisis between the two. He came looking for his son, and Francis escaped to a cave, where he spent a month in tears and prayer to the Lord, that he might be freed from his father's pursuit, so that he might fulfil his vows. Gradually courage and joy returned, and he issued from his cave and took his way to the town. Former acquaintances of his pursued him with jeers and stones, as one demented, so

[1] *III. Soc.* v. par. 13, 14.

wretched was he to look upon after his sojourn in the cave. He made no reply, save to give thanks to God. The hubbub reached the father, who rushed out and seized his son, beat him, and locked him up in the house. From this captivity he was released by his mother, in her husband's absence, and again betook himself to St. Damian's.

Shortly afterward Bernardone returned, and would have haled Francis before the magistrates of the town for squandering his patrimony; but his son repudiated their jurisdiction, as being the servant of God. They were glad enough to turn the matter over to the bishop, who counselled Francis to give back the money which was his father's. The scene which followed has been made famous by the brush of Giotto. The *Three Companions* narrate it thus:

" Then arose the man of God glad and comforted by the bishop's words, and fetching the money said, ' My lord, not only the money which is his I wish to return to him, but my clothes as well, and gladly.' Then entering the bishop's chamber, he took off his clothes, and placing the money upon them, went out again naked before them, and said : ' Hear ye all and know. Until now I have called Pietro Bernardone my father ; but because I have determined to serve God, I return him the money about which he was disturbed, and these clothes which I had from him, wishing only to say, " Our Father who art in heaven " and not " Father Pietro Bernardone." ' The man of God was found even then to have worn haircloth beneath his gay garments. His father rising, incensed, took the money and the clothes. As he carried them away to his house, those who had seen the sight were indignant that he had left not a single garment for his son, and they shed tears of pity over Francis. The bishop was moved to admiration at the constancy of the man of God, and embraced him and covered him with his cloak." [1]

Thus Francis was indeed made naked of the world. With joy he hastened back to St. Damian's ; and there prepared himself a hermit garb, in which he again set forth through the streets of the city, praising God and soliciting stones to rebuild the Church. As he went he cried that whoever gave one stone should have one reward, and he who gave two, two rewards, and he who gave more as many rewards as he gave stones. Many laughed at him, thinking

[1] *III. Soc.* vi. par. 20.

him crazy ; but others were moved to tears at the sight of one who from such frivolity and vanity had so quickly become drunken with divine love.

Francis became a beggar for the love of Christ, seeking to imitate Him who, born poor, lived poor, and had no place to lay His head. Not only did he beg stones to rebuild St. Damian's, but he began to go from house to house with a bowl to beg his food. Naked before them all, he had chosen " holy poverty," " lady poverty " [1] for his bride. He was filled with the desire to copy Christ and obey His words to the letter. According to the *Three Companions*, when the blessed Francis completed the church of St. Damian, his wont was to wear a hermit garb and carry a staff ; he wore shoes on his feet and a girdle about him. But listening one day to Jesus' words to His disciples, as He sent them out to preach, not to take with them gold, or silver, or a wallet, or bread, or a staff, or shoes, nor have two cloaks, Francis said with joy : " This is what I desire to fulfil with my whole strength." [2]

The literal imitation of certain particular Gospel instances, and the unconditional carrying out of certain of Christ's specially intended precepts, mark Francis's understanding of his Lord. It is exemplified in the account of the conversion of Francis's first disciple, as told by the *Three Companions* :

" As the truth of the blessed Francis's simple life and doctrine became manifest to many, two years after his own conversion, certain men were moved to penitence by his example, and were drawn to give up everything and join with him in life and garb. Of these the first was Bernard of saintly memory, who reflecting upon the constancy and fervour of the blessed Francis in serving God, and with what labour he was repairing ruined churches and leading a hard life, although delicately nurtured, he determined to distribute his property among the poor and cling to Francis. Accordingly one day in secret he approached the man of God and disclosed his purpose, at the same time requesting that on such an evening he would come to him. Having no companion hitherto, the blessed Francis gave thanks to God, and rejoiced greatly, especially as Messer (*dominus*) Bernard was a man of exemplary life.

---

[1] " Sancta paupertas," " domina paupertas " are the phrases. The first is used by St. Bernard.

[2] *III. Soc.* viii. ; I Cel. ix.

" So with exulting heart the blessed Francis went to his house
on the appointed evening and stayed all night with him.   Messer
Bernard said among other things : ' If a person should have much
or a little from his lord, and have held it many years, how could he
do with the same what would be the best ? '   The blessed Francis
replied that he should return it to his lord from whom he had
received it.

" And Messer Bernard said : ' Therefore, brother, I wish to
distribute, in the way that may seem best to thee, all my worldly
goods for love of my Lord, who conferred them on me.'

" To whom the saint said : ' In the morning we will go to the
Church, and will learn from the copy (*codex*) of the Gospels there
how the Lord taught His disciples.'

" So rising in the morning, with a certain other named Peter,
who also desired to become a brother, they went to the church of
St. Nicholas close to the piazza of the city Assisi.   And commencing to pray (because they were simple men and did not know where
to find the Gospel text relating to the renouncing of the world)
they asked the Lord devoutly, that He would deign to show them
His will at the first opening of the Book.

" When they had prayed, the blessed Francis taking in his
hands the closed book, kneeling before the altar opened it, and his
eye fell first upon this precept of the Lord : ' If thou wouldst be
perfect, go, sell all that thou hast, and give to the poor, and thou
shalt have treasure in heaven.'   At which the blessed Francis was
very glad and gave thanks to God.   But because this true observer
of the Trinity wished to be assured with threefold witness, he
opened the Book for the second and third time.   The second time
he read, ' Carry nothing for the journey,' and the third time, ' Who
wishes to come after me, let him deny himself.'

" At each opening of the Book, the blessed Francis gave thanks
to God for the divine confirmation of his purpose and long-con-
ceived desire, and then said to Bernard and Peter : ' Brothers, this
is our life and this is our rule, and the life and rule of all who shall
wish to join our society.   Go, then, and as you have heard, so do.'

" Messer Bernard went away (he was very rich) and, having
sold his possessions and got together much money, he distributed
it to the poor of the town.   Peter also complied with the divine
admonition as best he could.   They both assumed the habit which
Francis had adopted, and from that hour lived with him after the
model (*formam*) of the holy Gospel shown them by the Lord.
Therefore the blessed Francis has said in his Testament : ' The
Lord himself revealed to me that I should live according to the
model (*formam*) of the holy Gospel.' " [1]

---

[1] *III. Soc.* viii. ; see 1 Cel. x. and 2 Cel. x.

The words which met the eyes of Francis on first opening this Gospel-book, had nearly a thousand years before his
time driven the holy Anthony to the desert of the Thebaid.
Still one need not think the later tale a fruit of imitative
legend.   The accounts of Francis afford other instances of
his literal acceptance of the Gospels.[1]

After the step taken by Bernard and Peter, others
quickly joined themselves to Francis, and in short time the
small company took up its abode in an abandoned cabin at
Rivo-torto, near Assisi.   In a twelvemonth or more they
removed to the little church of Santa Maria de Portiuncula
(Saint Mary of the little portion).[2]   In the meanwhile
Francis had been to Rome and gained papal authorization
from the great Innocent III. for his lowly way of life.   It
would be hard to describe the joyfulness of these first Gospel
days of the brethren : they come and go, and pray and
labour ; all are filled with joy ; *gaudium, jucunditas, laeta-
bantur*, such words crowd each other in accounts of the early
days.   Their love was complete ; they would gladly give
their bodies to pain or death not only for the love of Christ,
but for the love of each other ; they were founded and rooted
in humility and love ; Francis's own life was a song of joy,
as he went singing (always *gallice*) and abounding in love
and its joyful prayers and tears.   What joy indeed could be

---

[1] *Spec. per.* 3, 9, 19, 122.   How truly he also felt their spirit is seen in the
story of his words, at a somewhat later period, to a certain Dominican : " While
he was staying at Siena, a certain doctor of theology, of the order of the Preachers,
himself an humble and spiritual man, came to him.   When they had spoken for
a while about the words of the Lord, this master interrogated him concerning this
text of Ezekiel : ' If thou dost not declare to the wicked man his wickedness,
I will require his soul of thy hand ' (Ezek. iii. 18).   And he added : ' I know
many indeed, good father, in mortal sin, to whom I do not declare their wickedness.
Will their souls be required at my hand ? '

" To whom the blessed Francis humbly said that it was fitting that an ignorant
person like himself should be taught by him rather than give answer upon the
meaning of Scripture.   Then that humble master replied : ' Brother, albeit I
have heard the exposition of this text from a number of the wise, still would I
willingly make note of your understanding of it.'

" So the blessed Francis said : ' If the text is to be understood generally, I
take it to mean that the servant of God ought by his life and holiness so to burn
and shine in himself, that the light of his example and the tenor of his holy conversation would reprove all wicked men.   Thus I say will his splendour and the
odour of his reputation declare their iniquities to all,' " *Spec. perf.* 53 ; also
2 Cel. iii. 46.

[2] As to the acquisition of the Portiuncula see *Spec. perf.* 55, and on Francis's
love of it see *Spec. perf.* 82-84, 124.

greater than his ; he had given himself to his Lord, and had been accepted. One day he had retired for contemplation, and as he prayed, " God be merciful to me a sinner," an ineffable joy and sweetness was shed in his heart. He began to fall away from himself ; the anxieties and fears which a sense of sin had set in his heart were dispelled, and a certitude of the remission of his sins took possession of him. His mind dilated and a joyful vision made him seem another man when he returned and said in gladness to the brethren : " Be comforted, my best beloved, and rejoice in the Lord. Do not feel sad because you seem so few. Let neither my simplicity nor yours abash you, for it has been shown me of the Lord that God will make of you a great multitude, and multiply you to the confines of the earth. I saw a great multitude of men coming to us, desiring to assume the habit and rule of our blessed religion ; and the sound of them is in my ears as they come and go according to the command of holy obedience ; and I saw the ways filled with them from every nation. Frenchmen come, and Spaniards hurry, Germans and English run, and a multitude speaking other tongues." [1]

Thus far the life of Francis was a poem, even as it was to be unto the end ; for, although the saint's plans might be thwarted by the wisdom and frailty of men, his words and actions did not cease to realize the exquisite conceptions of his soul. But the volume of his life, from this time on, becomes too large for us to follow, embracing as it does the far from simple history of the first decades of his Order. Our object is still to observe his personality, and his love of God and man and creature-kind.

Francis's mind was as simple as his heart was single. He had no distinctly intellectual interests, as nothing appealed to his mentality alone.[2] In his consciousness, everything related itself to his way of life, its yearnings and aversions. Whatever was unsuited to enter into this catholic relationship repelled rather than interested him. Hence he was averse to studies which had nothing to do with the man's closer walk with God, and love of fellow. " My brothers who are led by the curiosity of knowledge will find

---

[1] 1 Cel. xi.   [2] This seems to be true of Francis's great Exemplar.

their hands empty in the day of tribulation. I would wish
them rather to be strengthened by virtues, that when the
time of tribulation comes they may have the Lord with
them in their straits—for such a time will come when they
will throw their good-for-nothing books into holes and
corners." [1]

The moral temper of Francis was childlike in its simple
truth. He could not endure in the smallest matter to seem
other than as he was before God : " As much as a man is
before God so much is he, and no more." [2] Once in Lent
he ate of cakes cooked in lard, because everything cooked
in oil violently disagreed with him. When Lent was over,
he thus began his first sermon to a concourse of people :
" You have come to me with great devotion, believing me to
be a holy man, but I confess to God and to you that in this
Lent I have eaten cakes cooked in lard." [3] At another
time, when in severe sickness he had somewhat exceeded
the pittance of food which he allowed himself, he rose, still
shaking with fever, and went and preached to the people.
When the sermon was over, he retired a moment, and
having first exacted a promise of obedience from the monks
accompanying him, he threw off his cloak, tied a rope around
his waist, and commanded them to drag him naked before
the people, and there cast ashes in his face ; all which was
done by the weeping monks. And then he confessed his
fault to all.[4]

Francis took joy in obedience and humility. One of
his motives in resigning the headship of the Order was that
he might have a superior to obey.[5] However pained by the
shortcomings and corruptions of the Church, he was always
obedient and reverent. He had no thought of revolution,
but the hope of purifying all. One day certain brothers
said to him : " Father, do you not see that the bishops do
not let us preach, and keep us for days standing idle, before
we are able to declare the word of God ? Would it not be
better to obtain the privilege from the Pope, that there
might be a salvation of souls ? "

---

[1] *Spec. perf.* 69 ; 2 Cel. iii. 124; *III. Soc.* 25.
[2] *Francisci admonitiones,* xx.   [3] *Spec. perf.* 62 ; 2 Cel. iii. 71.
[4] *Spec. perf.* 61 ; see 1 Cel. 19.   [5] 2 Cel. iii. 81 ; *Spec. perf.* 39.

" You, brothers Minorites," answered Francis, " know
not the will of God, and do not permit me to convert the
whole world, which is God's will ; for I wish first through
holy obedience and reverence to convert the prelates, who.
when they see our holy life and humble reverence for them,
will beg you to preach and convert the people, and will
call the people to hear you far better than your privileges,
which draw you to pride. For me, I desire this privilege
from the Lord that I may never have any privilege from
man except to do reverence to all, and through obedience
to our holy rule of life convert mankind more by example
than by word." [1]

And again he said to the brothers : " We are sent to
aid the clergy in the salvation of souls, and what is found
lacking in them should be supplied by us. Know, brothers,
that the gain of souls is most pleasing to God, and this we
may win better by peace with the clergy, than by discord.
If they hinder the salvation of the people, vengeance is
God's and He will repay in time. So be ye subject to the
prelates and take heed on your part that no jealousy arise.
If ye are sons of peace ye shall gain both clergy and people,
and this will be more acceptable to God than to gain the
people alone by scandalizing the clergy. Cover their slips,
and supply their deficiencies ; and when ye shall have done
this be ye the more humble." [2]

So Francis loved *sancta obedientia* as he called it. As
a wise builder he set himself upon a rock, to wit, the perfect
humility and poverty of the Son of God ; and because of his
own humility he called his company the Minorites (the
" lesser " brethren).[3] For himself, he deemed that he should
most rejoice when men should revile him and cast him forth
in shame, and not when they revered and honoured him.[4]

Above all he loved his " lady poverty " and could not
say enough to impress his followers with her high worth
and beauty, and with the dignity and nobility of begging
alms for the love of the Lord.[5] As a high-born lady, poor
and beautiful, he had seen her in a vision, in the midst of

[1] *Spec. perf.* 50.   [2] *Spec. perf.* 54 ; 2 Cel. iii. 84.   [3] *Spec. perf.* 44.
[4] *Spec. perf.* 64 ; *III. Soc.* 39 ; 2 Cel. iii. 83 ; cf. *Admon.* iii.
[5] Cf. *Spec. perf.* 22 and 23 ; 2 Cel. iii. 23.

a desert, and worthy to be wooed by the King.[1] In the early days when the brothers were a little band, Francis had gone about and begged for all. He loved them so that he dreaded to require what might shame them. But when the labour was too great for one man, so delicate and weak, he said to them : " Best beloved brothers and my children, do not be ashamed to go for alms, because the Lord made Himself poor for us in this world after whose example we have chosen the truest poverty. For this is our heritage, which our Lord Jesus Christ achieved and left to us and to all who, after His example, wish to live in holy poverty. I tell you of a truth that many wise and noble of this world shall join that congregation and hold it for an honour and a grace to go out for alms. Therefore boldly and with glad heart seek alms with God's blessing ; and more freely and gladly should you seek alms than he who offers a hundred pieces of money for one coin, since to those from whom you ask alms you offer the love of God, saying, ' Do us an alms for the love of the Lord God,' in comparison with which heaven and earth are nothing." [2]

With Francis all virtues were holy (*sancta obedientia, sancta paupertas*). Righteousness, goodness, piety, lay in imitating and obeying his Lord. What joy was there in loving Christ, and being loved by Him ! and what an eternity of bliss awaited the Christian soul ! To do right, to imitate Christ and obey and love Him, is a privilege. Can it be other than a joy ? Indeed, this following of Christ is so blessed, that not to rejoice continually in it, betokens some failure in obedience and love. Many have approved this Christian logic ; but to realize it in one's heart and manifest it in one's life, was the more singular grace of Francis of Assisi. His heart sang always unto the Lord ; his love flowed out in gladness to his fellows ; his enchanted spirit rejoiced in every creature. The gospel of this new evangelist awoke the hearts of men to love and joy. Nothing rejoiced him more than to see his sons rejoice in the Lord ; and nothing was more certain to draw forth his tender reproof than a sad countenance.

[1] *III. Soc.* xii. 50, 51.
[2] *Spec. perf.* 18 ; cf. 2 Cel. iii. 20.

" Once while the blessed Francis was at the Portiuncula, a certain good beggar came along the way, returning from alms-begging in Assisi, and he went along praising God with a high voice and great jocundity.   As he approached, Francis heard him, and ran out and met him in the way, and joyfully kissed his shoulder where he bore the wallet containing the gifts.   Then he lifted the wallet, and set it on his own shoulder, and so carried it within, and said to the brothers : ' Thus I wish to have my brothers go and return with alms, joyful and glad and praising God.' " [1]

" Aside from prayer and the divine service, the blessed Francis was most zealous in preserving continually an inward and outward spiritual gladness.   And this he especially cherished in the brothers, and would reprove them for sadness and depression. For he said that if the servant of God would study to preserve, inwardly and outwardly, the spiritual joy which rises from purity of heart, and is acquired through the devotion of prayer, the devils could not harm him, for they say : So long as the servant of God is joyful in tribulation and prosperity, we cannot enter into him or harm him. . . . To our enemy and his members it pertains to be sad, but to us always to rejoice and be glad in the Lord." [2]

Thus the glad temper of his young unconverted days passed into his saintly life, of which Christ was the primal source of rapture.

" Drunken with the love and pity of Christ, the blessed Francis would sometimes act like this, for the sweetest melody of spirit within him often boiling outward gave sound in French, and the strain of the divine whisper which his ear had taken secretly, broke forth in a glad French song.   He would pick up a stick and, holding it over his left arm, would with another stick in his right hand make as if drawing a bow across a violin (viellam), and with fitting gestures would sing in French of the Lord Jesus Christ. At last this dancing would end in tears, and the jubilee turn to pity for the Passion of Christ.   Thereupon sighing continuously with redoubled groans, forgetting what he held in his hand, he would be drawn up to heaven." [3]

Francis had been a lover from his youth ; naturally and always he had loved his kind.   But from the time when Christ held his heart and mind, his love of fellow-man was moulded by his thought and love of Christ.   Henceforth the loving acts of Francis moving among his fellows become

[1] Spec. perf. 25 ; 2 Cel. iii. 22.
[2] Spec. perf. 95 ; 2 Cel. iii. 65.   But Francis condemned all vain and foolish words which move to laughter (Admon. xxi. ; Spec. perf. 96).
[3] Spec. perf. 93 ; 2 Cel. iii. 67.

a loving following of Christ. He sees in every man the character and person of his Lord, soliciting his love, commanding what he should do. He never refused, or permitted his followers to refuse, what was asked in Christ's name ; but it displeased him when he heard the brothers ask lightly for the love of God, and he would reprove them, saying : " So high and precious is God's love that it never should be invoked save with great reverence and under pressing need." [1]

Such a man felt strong personal affection. Pure and wise was his love for Santa Clara ; [2] and a deep affection for one of his earliest and closest followers touches us in his letter to brother Leo. Not all of the writings ascribed to Francis breathe his spirit ; but we hear his voice in this letter as it closes : " And if it is needful for thy soul or for thy consolation, and thou dost wish, my Leo, to come to me, come. Farewell in Christ."

Francis's love was unfailing in compassionate word and deed. Although cold and sick, he would give his cloak away at the first demand, till his own appointed minister-general commanded him on his obedience not to do so without permission ; and he saw that the brothers did not injure themselves with fasting, though he took slight care of himself. On one occasion he had them all partake of a meal, in order that one delicate brother, who needed food, might not be put to shame eating while the rest fasted. And once, early in the morning, he led an old and feeble brother secretly to a certain vineyard, and there ate grapes before him, that he might not be ashamed to do likewise, for his health.[3]

The effect of his sweet example melted the hearts of angry men, reconciling such as had been wronged to those who had wronged them, and leading ruffians back to ways of gentleness. His conduct on learning of certain dissensions in Assisi illustrates his method of restoring peace and amity.

" After the blessed Francis had composed the Lauds of the creatures, which he called the Canticle of Brother Sun, it happened

---

[1] *Spec. perf.* 34.   [2] Cf. *Spec. perf.* 108 ; 2 Cel. 132.
[3] *Spec. perf.* 27, 28, 33 ; cf. 2 Cel. i. 15 ; *ibid.* iii. 30 and 36.

that great dissension arose between the bishop and the podestà of the City of Assisi, so that the bishop excommunicated the podestà, and the podestà made proclamation that no person should sell anything to the bishop or buy from him or make any contract with him.

" When the blessed Francis (who was now so very sick) heard this, he was greatly moved with pity, since no one interposed between them to make peace. And he said to his companions : ' It is a great shame for us servants of God that the bishop and the podestà hate each other so, and none interposes to make peace.'

" And so for this occasion he at once made a verse in the Lauds above mentioned and said :

' Praised be thou, O my Lord, for those who forgive from love of thee,
And endure sickness and tribulation.
Blessed are those who shall endure in peace,
For by thee, Most High, shall they be crowned.'

" Then he called one of his companions and said to him : ' Go to the podestà, and on my behalf tell him to come to the bishop's palace with the magnates of the city and others that he may bring with him.'

" And as that brother went, he said to two other of his companions : ' Go before the bishop and podestà and the others who may be with them, and sing the Canticle of Brother Sun, and I trust in the Lord that He will straightway humble their hearts, and they will return to their former affection and friendship.'

" When all were assembled in the piazza of the episcopate, the two brothers arose, and one of them said : ' The blessed Francis in his sickness made a Lauds of the Lord from His creatures in praise of the Lord and for the edification of our neighbour. Wherefore he begs that you would listen to it with great devoutness.' And then they began to say and sing them.

" At once the podestà rose, and with folded hands listened intently, as if it were the Lord's gospel ; this he did with the greatest devoutness and with many tears, for he had great trust and devotion toward the blessed Francis.

" When the Lauds of the Lord were finished, the podestà said before them all : ' Truly I say to you that not only my lord-bishop, whom I wish and ought to hold as my lord, but if any one had slain my brother or son I would forgive him.' And so saying, he threw himself at the bishop's feet, and said to him : ' Look, I am ready in all things to make satisfaction to you as shall please you, for the love of our Lord Jesus Christ and His servant the blessed Francis.'

" The bishop accepting him, raised him with his hands and said: 'Because of my office it became me to be humble, and since I am naturally quick-tempered you ought to pardon me.' And so with great kindness and love they embraced and kissed each other.

" The brothers were astounded and made glad when they saw fulfilled to the letter the concord predicted by the blessed Francis. And all others present ascribed it as a great miracle to the merits of the blessed Francis, that the Lord suddenly had visited them, and out of such dissension and scandal had brought such concord."[1]

It would be mistaken to refer to any single pious sentiment, the saint's blithe love of animals and birds and flowers, and his regard even for senseless things. It is right, however, for Thomas of Celano, as a proper monkish biographer, to say :

" While hastening through this world of pilgrimage and exile that traveller (Francis) rejoiced in those things which are in the world, and not a little. As toward the princes of darkness he used the world as a field for battle, but as toward the Lord he treated it as the brightest mirror of goodness ; in the fabric he commended the Artificer, and what he found in created things, he referred to the Maker ; he exulted over all the works of the hands of the Lord, and in the pleasing spectacle beheld the life-giving reason and the cause. In beautiful things he perceived that which was most beautiful, as all good things acclaim, He who made us is best. Through vestiges impressed on things he followed his chosen, and made of all a ladder by which to reach the throne. He embraced all things in a feeling of unheard-of devotion, speaking to them concerning the Lord and exhorting them in His praise."[2]

This was true, even if it was not all the truth. Living creatures spoke to Francis of their Maker, while things insensible aroused his reverence through their suggestiveness, their scriptural associations, or their symbolism. But beyond these motives there was in this poet Francis a happy love of nature. If nature always spoke to him of God, its loveliness needed no stimulation of devotion in order to be loved by him. His feeling for it found everywhere sensibility and responsiveness. He was as if possessed by an imaginative animism, wherein every object had a soul. His acts and words may appear fantastic; they never lack loveliness and beauty.[3]

---

[1] *Spec. perf.* 101. This is one of the apparently unsupported stories of the *Speculum*, that none would like to doubt.

[2] 2 Cel. iii. cap. 101.

[3] One is tempted to amuse oneself with paradox, and say : Not he of Vaucluse, who ascended a mountain for the view and left a record of his sentiments, but he

" Wrapped in the love of God, the blessed Francis perfectly discerned the goodness of God not only in his own soul but in every creature.   Wherefore he was affected with a singular and yearning (*viscerosa*) love toward creatures, and especially toward those in which was figured something of God or something pertaining to religion.

" Whence above all birds he loved a little bird called the lark (the *lodola capellata* of the vulgar tongue) and would say of her : ' Sister lark has a hood like a Religious and is a humble bird, because she goes willingly along the road to find for herself some grains of corn.   Even if she find them in dung she picks them out and eats them.   In flying she praises the Lord very sweetly, as the good Religious look down upon earthly things, whose conversation is always in the heavens and whose intent is always upon the praise of God.   Her garments are like earth, that is, her feathers, and set an example to the Religious that they should not have delicate and gaudy garments, but such as are vile in price and colour, as earth is viler than other elements.' " [1]

The unquestionably true story of Francis preaching to the birds is known to all, especially to readers of the *Fioretti*.   Thus Thomas of Celano tells it : As the blessed Father Francis was journeying through the Spoleto Valley, he reached a place near Mevanium, where there was a multitude of birds—doves, crows, and other kinds.   When he saw them, for the love and sweet affection which he bore toward the lower creatures, he quickly ran to them, leaving his companions.   As he came near and saw that they were waiting for him, he saluted them in his accustomed way.   Then wondering that they did not take flight, he was very glad, and humbly begged them to listen to the word of God ; among other things he said to them : " My brothers who fly, verily you should praise the Lord your Maker and love Him always, who gave you feathers to clothe you and wings to fly with and whatever was necessary to you.   God made you noble among creatures, prepared your mansion in the purity of air ; and though you neither sow nor reap, nevertheless without any solicitude on your part, He protects and guides you."

of Assisi, who loved the sheep, the birds, the flowers, the stones, and fire and water, was " the first modern man."   But such statements are foolish ; there was no " first modern man."

[1] *Spec. perf.* **113.**

At this, those little birds as he was speaking, marvellously exulting, began to stretch out their necks and spread their wings and open their beaks, looking at him. He passed through their midst, sweeping their heads and bodies with his mantle. At length he blessed them, and with the sign of the cross gave them leave to fly away. Then returning gladdened to his companions, he yet blamed himself for his neglect to preach to the birds before, since they so reverently heard the word of God. And from that day he ceased not to exhort all flying and creeping things, and even things insensible, to the praise and love of their Creator.[1]

Thomas also says that above all animals Francis loved the lambs, because so frequently in Scripture the humility of our Lord is likened unto a lamb. One day, as Francis was making his way through the March of Ancona he met a goat-herd pasturing his flock of goats. Among them, humbly and quietly, a little lamb was feeding. Francis stopped as he saw it, and, deeply touched, said to the brother accompanying him : " Dost thou see this sheep walking so gently among the goats ? I tell you, thus our Lord Jesus Christ used to walk mild and humble among Pharisees and chief priests. For love of Him, then, I beg thee, my son, to buy this little sheep with me and lead it out from among these goats."

The brother was also moved with pity. They had nothing with them save their wretched cloaks, but a merchant chancing to come along the way, the money was obtained from him. Giving thanks to God and leading the sheep they had bought, they reached the town of Osimo whither they were going ; and entering the house of the bishop, were honourably received by him. Yet my lord bishop wondered at the sheep which Francis was leading with such tender love. But when Francis had set forth the parable of his sermon, the bishop too was touched and gave thanks to God.

The following day they considered what to do with the sheep, and it was given over to the nuns of the cloister of St. Severinus, who received it as a great boon given them

[1] Cel. xxi. 58.

from God.   Long while they cared for it, and in the course
of time wove a cloak from its wool, which they sent to the
blessed Francis at the Portiuncula at the time of a Chapter
meeting.   The saint accepted it with joy, and kissed it,
and begged all the brothers to be glad with him.[1]

Celano also tells how Francis loved the grass and vines
and stones and woods, and all comely things in the fields,
also the streams, and earth and fire and air, and called
every creature " brother " ;[2] also how he would not put
out the flame of a lamp or candle, how he walked reverently upon stones, and was careful to injure no living
thing.[3]

[1] 1 Cel. cap. xxviii.   [2] 1 Cel. cap. xxix.

[3] 2 Cel. iii. 101.   These matters are set forth more picturesquely in the *Speculum
perfectionis* ; if authentic, they throw a vivid light on this wonderful person.
Here are examples :

" Francis had come to the hermitage of Fonte Palumbo, near Riete, to cure
the infirmity of his eyes, as he was ordered on his obedience by the lord-cardinal
of Ostia and by Brother Elias, minister-general.   There the doctor advised a
cautery over the cheek as far as the eyebrow of the eye that was in worse state.
Francis wished to wait till brother Elias came, but when he was kept from coming
Francis prepared himself.   And when the iron was set in the fire to heat it, Francis,
wishing to comfort his spirit, lest he be afraid, spoke to the fire : ' My Brother
Fire, noble and useful among other creatures, be courteous to me in this hour,
since I have loved and will love thee for the love of Him who made thee.   I also
beseech our Creator, who made us both, that He may temper thy heat so that I
may bear it.'   And when his prayer was finished he made the sign of the cross over
the fire.

" We indeed who were with him then fled for pity and compassion, and the
doctor remained alone with him.   When the cautery was finished, we returned,
and he said to us : ' Fearful and of little faith, why did you flee ?   I tell you
truly I felt no pain, nor any heat of the fire.   If it is not well seared he may sear
it better.'

" The astonished doctor assured them all that the cautery was so severe that
a strong man, let alone one so weak, could hardly have endured it, while Francis
showed no sign of pain " (*Spec. perf.* 115).   " Thus fire treated Francis courteously ;
for he had never failed to treat it reverently and respect its rights.   Once his
clothes caught fire, and he would not put it out, and forbade a brother, saying :
' Nay, dearest brother, do no harm to the fire.'   He would never put out fire,
and did not wish any brother to throw away a fire or push a smoking log away,
but wished that it should be just set on the ground, out of reverence to Him whose
creature it is " (*ibid.* 116).

" Next to fire he had a peculiar love for water, wherein is figured holy penitence
and the tribulation with which the soul's uncleanness is washed away, and because
the first washing of the soul is through the water of baptism.   So when he washed
his hands he would choose a place where the water which fell would not be trodden
on.   Also when he walked over rocks, he walked with trembling and reverence
for the love of Him who is called the ' Rock ' ; and whenever he repeated that
psalm, ' Thou hast exalted me upon a rock,' he would say with great reverence
and devotion : ' Under the foot of the rock thou hast exalted me.' "

" He directed the brother who cut and fetched the fire-wood never to cut

There are two documents which are both (the one with much reason and the other with certainty) ascribed to Francis. Utterly different as they are, each still remains a clear expression of his spirit. The one is the Lauds commonly called the Canticle of the Brother Sun, and the other is the saint's last Testament. One may think of the Canticle as the closing stanza of a life which was an enacted poem :

Most High, omnipotent, good Lord, thine is the praise, the glory, the honour and every benediction ;
To thee alone, Most High, these do belong, and no man is worthy to name thee.
Praised be thou, my Lord, with all thy creatures, especially milord Brother Sun that dawns and lightens us ;
And he, beautiful and radiant with great splendour, signifies thee, Most High.
Be praised, my Lord, for Sister Moon and the stars that thou hast made bright and precious and beautiful.
Be praised, my Lord, for Brother Wind, and for the air and cloud and the clear sky and for all weathers through which thou givest sustenance to thy creatures.
Be praised, my Lord, for Sister Water, that is very useful and humble and precious and chaste.
Be praised, my Lord, for Brother Fire, through whom thou dost illumine the night, and comely is he and glad and bold and strong.
Be praised, my Lord, for Sister, Our Mother Earth, that doth

---

a whole tree, so that some part of it might remain untouched for the love of Him who was willing to work out our salvation upon the wood of the cross.

" Likewise he told the brother who made the garden, not to devote all of it to vegetables, but to have some part for flowering plants, which in their seasons produce Brother Flowers for love of Him who is called the ' Flower of the field and the Lily of the valley.' He said indeed that Brother Gardener always ought to make a beautiful patch in some part of the garden, and plant it with all sorts of sweet-smelling herbs and herbs that produce beautiful flowers, so that in their season they may invite men seeing them to praise the Lord. For every creature cries aloud, ' God made me for thy sake, O man.' We that were with him saw that inwardly and outwardly he did so greatly rejoice in all created things, that touching or seeing them his spirit seemed not to be upon the earth, but in heaven " (*ibid.* 113).

" Above all things lacking reason he loved the sun and fire most affectionately, for he would say : ' In the morning when the sun rises every man ought to praise God who created it for our use, because by day our eyes are illumined by it ; in the evening, when night comes, every man ought to give praise on account of Brother Fire, because by it our eyes are illumined by night. For all of us are blind, and the Lord through those two brothers lightens our eyes ; and therefore for these, and for other creatures which we daily use, we ought to praise the Creator.' Which indeed he did himself up to the day of his death " (*ibid.* 119).

cherish and keep us, and produces various fruits with coloured flowers and the grass.

Be praised, my Lord, for those who forgive for love of thee, and endure sickness and tribulation ; blessed are they who endure in peace ; for by thee, Most High, shall they be crowned.

Be praised, my Lord, for our bodily death, from which no living man can escape ; woe unto those who die in mortal sin.

Blessed are they that have found thy most holy will, for the second death shall do them no hurt.

Praise and bless my Lord, and render thanks, and serve Him with great humility.[1]

The self-expression of the more personal parts of the Testament supplement these utterances :

" Thus the Lord gave to me, Brother Francis, to begin to do penance : because while I was in sins, it seemed too bitter to me to see lepers ; and the Lord himself led me among them, and I did mercy with them. And departing from them, that which seemed to me bitter, was turned for me into sweetness of soul and body. And a little afterwards I went out of the world.

" And the Lord gave me such faith in churches, that thus simply I should pray and say : ' We adore thee, Lord Jesus Christ, and in all thy churches which are in the whole world, and we bless thee, because through thy holy cross thou hast redeemed the world.'

" Afterwards the Lord gave and gives me so great faith in priests who live after the model of the holy Roman Church according to their order, that if they should persecute me I will still turn to them. And if I should have as great wisdom as Solomon had, and should have found the lowliest secular priests in the parishes where they dwell, I do not wish to preach contrary to their wish. And them and all others I wish to fear and honour as my lords ; and I do not wish to consider sin in them, because I see the Son of God in them and they are my lords.

" And the reason I do this is because corporeally I see nothing in this world of that most high Son of God except His most holy body and most holy blood, which they receive and which they alone administer. And I wish these most holy mysteries to be honoured above all and revered, and to be placed together in precious places. Wherever I shall find His most holy names and His written words in unfit places, I wish to collect them, and I ask that they be collected and placed in a proper place ; and all theologians and those who administer the most holy divine words,

---

[1] Translated from the text as given in E. Monaci's *Crestomazia italiana dei primi secoli.* Substantially the same text is given in *Spec. perf.* 120.

we ought to honour and venerate, as those who administer to us spirit and life.

"And after the Lord gave me brothers, no one showed me what I ought to do, but the Most High himself revealed to me that I ought to live according to the model of the holy Gospel. And I in a few words and simply had this written, and the lord Pope confirmed it to me. And they who were coming to receive life, all that they were able to have they gave to the poor ; and they were content with one patched cloak, with the cord and breeches ; and we did not wish to have more. We who were of the clergy said our office as other clergy ; the lay members said ' Our Father.' And willingly we remained in churches ; and we were simple (*idiotae*) and subject to all. And I laboured with my hands, and I wish to labour ; and I wish all other brothers to labour. Who do not know how, let them learn, not from the cupidity of receiving the price of labour, but on account of the example, and to repel slothfulness. And when the price of labour is not given to us, we resort to the table of the Lord by seeking alms from door to door.

"The Lord revealed to me a salutation that we should say : The Lord give thee peace."

Francis's precepts for the brothers follow here. The last paragraph of the Will is : "And whoever shall have observed these principles, in heaven may he be filled with the benediction of the most high Father, and on earth may he be filled with the benediction of His beloved Son, with the most holy spirit Paraclete, and with all the virtues of the heavens and with everything holy. And I, Brother Francis, your very little servant, so far as I am able, confirm to you within and without that most holy benediction."

CHAPTER XX

MYSTIC VISIONS OF ASCETIC WOMEN

ELIZABETH OF SCHÖNAU; HILDEGARD OF BINGEN; MARY OF OGNIES; LIUTGARD OF TONGERN; MECHTHILD OF MAGDEBURG

WE pass to matters of a different colour. Thus far, besides Bernard and Francis, matchless examples of monastic ideals there have been instances of contemplation and piety, with much emotion, and a sufficiency of experience having small part in reason ; also hallucinations and fantastic conduct, as in the case of Romuald. The last class of phenomena, however, have not been prominent. Now for a while we shall be wrapt in visions, rational, imitative, fashioned with intent and plan ; or, again, directly experienced, passionate, hallucinative. They will range from those climaxes of the constructive or intuitive imagination,[1] which are of the whole man, to passionate or morbid delusions representing but a partial and passing phase of the subject's personality. Moreover, we have been occupied with hermits and monks, that is to say, with men. The present chapter has to do with nuns ; who are more prone to visions, and are occasionally subject to those passionate hallucinations which are prompted by the circumstance that the Christian God was incarnate in the likeness of a man.

Besides the conclusions which the mind draws from the data of sense, or reaches through reflection, there are other modes of conviction whose distinguishing mark is their apparent immediacy and spontaneity. They are not elicited from antecedent processes of thought, as inferences or

---

[1] The mediaeval term *apex mentis* is not inapt.

deductions ; rather they loom upon the consciousness, and are experienced. Yet they are far from simple, and may contain a multiplicity of submerged reasonings, and bear relation to countless previous inferences. They are usually connected with emotion or neural excitement, and may even take the guise of sense-manifestations. Through such convictions, religious minds are assured of God and the soul's communion with Him.[1] While not issuing from argument, this assurance may be informed with reason and involve the total sum of conclusions which the reasoner has drawn from life.

In devout mediaeval circles, the consciousness of communion with God, with the Virgin, with angels and saints, and with the devil, often took on the semblance of sense-perception. The senses seemed to be experiencing : stenches of hell, odours of heaven, might be smelled, or a taste infect the mouth ; the divine or angelic touch was felt, or the pain of blows ; most frequently voices were heard, and forms were seen in a vision. In these apparent testimonies of sight and hearing, the entire spiritual nature of the man or woman might set the vision, dramatize it with his or her desires and aversions, and complete it from the store of knowledge at command.

The visions of an eleventh-century monk named Othloh have been observed at some length.[2] Intimate and trying, they were also, so to speak, in and of the whole man : his tastes, his solicitudes, his acquired knowledge and ways of reasoning, joined in these vivid experiences of God's truth and the devil's onslaughts. One may be mindful of Othloh in turning to the more impersonal visions of certain German nuns, which likewise issued from the entire nature and intellectual equipment of these women.[3]

---

[1] Assurance of the soul's communion, and even union, with God is the chief element of what is termed mysticism, which will be discussed briefly in connection with scholastic philosophy, *post*, Chapter XXXVII. II. In the twelfth and thirteenth centuries those who experienced the divine through visions, ecstasies, and rapt contemplation, were not as analytically and autobiographically self-conscious as later mystics. Yet St. Theresa's (sixteenth century) mystical analysis of self and God (for which see H. Delacroix, *Études d'histoire et de psychologie du mysticisme*, Paris, 1908) might be applied to the experiences of St. Elizabeth of Schönau or St. Hildegard of Bingen.

[2] *Ante*, Chapter XIII. II.

[3] Neither Othloh's visions, nor those to be recounted, were narratives of

On the Rhine, fifteen miles north-east of Bingen, lies the village of Schönau, where in the twelfth century flourished a Benedictine monastery, and near it a cloister for nuns. At the latter a girl of twelve named Elizabeth was received in the year 1141. She lived there as nun, and finally as abbess, till her death in 1165. Like many other lofty souls dwelling in the ideal, she was a stern censor of the evils in the world and in the Church. The bodily infirmities from which she was never free, were aggravated by austerities, and usually became most painful just before the trances that brought her visions. Masses and penances, prayer and meditation, made her manner of approach to these direct disclosures of eternity, wherein the whole contents of her faith and her reflection were unrolled. Frequently she beheld the Saints in the nights following their festivals; her larger visions were moulded by the Apocalypse. These experiences were usually beatific, though sometimes she suffered insult from malignant shapes. What humility bade her conceal, the importunities of admirers compelled her to disclose : and so her visions have been preserved, and may be read in the *Vita* written by her brother Eckbert, Abbot of Schönau.[1] Here is an example of how the saint and seeress spoke :

" On the Sunday night following the festival of St. James (in the year 1153), drawn from the body, I was borne into an ecstasy (*avocata a corpore rapta sum in exstasim*). And a great flaming wheel flared in the heaven. Then it disappeared, and I saw a light more splendid than I was accustomed to see ; and thousands of saints stood in it, forming an immense circle ; in front were some glorious men, having palms and shining crowns and the titles of their martyrdoms inscribed upon their foreheads. From these titles, as well as from their pre-eminent splendour, I knew them to be the Apostles. At their right was a great company having the same shining titles ; and behind these were others, who lacked the signs of martyrdom. At the left of the Apostles shone the holy order of virgins, also adorned with the signs of martyrdom, and behind them another splendid band of maidens, some crowned, but without these signs. Still back of these, a

voyages to the other world. The name of these is legion. They begin in *Bede's Ecclesiastical History*, and continue through the Middle Ages—until they reach their apotheosis in the *Divina Commedia*. See *post*, Chapter XLIV.

[1] Migne, *Pat. Lat.* 195.

company of venerable women in white completed the circle.
Below it was another circle of great brilliancy, which I knew to be
of the holy angels.

" In the midst of all was a Glory of Supreme Majesty, and its
throne was encircled by a rainbow. At the right of that Majesty
I saw one like unto the Son of Man, seated in glory ; at the left
was a radiant sign of the Cross. . . . At the right of the Son of
Man sat the Queen of Kings and Angels on a starry throne cir-
cumfused with immense light. At the left of the Cross four-and-
twenty honourable men sat facing it. And not far from them I
saw two rams sustaining on their shoulders a great shining wheel.
The morning after this, at tierce, one of the brothers came to the
window of my cell, and I asked that the mass for the Holy Trinity
might be celebrated.

" The next Sunday I saw the same vision, and more : for I saw
the Lamb of God standing before the throne, very lovable, and
with a gold cross, as if implanted in its back. And I saw the four
Evangelists in those forms which Holy Scripture ascribes to them.
They were at the right of the Blessed Virgin, and their faces were
turned toward her."

And Elizabeth saw the Virgin arise and advance from
out the great light into the lower ether, followed by a multitude of women saints, and then return amid great praise.

In another vision she saw the events of the Saviour's last
days on earth : saw Him riding into Jerusalem, and the
multitude throwing down branches ; saw Him washing the
disciples' feet, then the agony in the garden, the betrayal,
the crowning with thorns, the spitting, the Lord upon the
Cross, and the Mother of God full of grief ; she saw the pierc-
ing of His side, the dreadful darkness,—all as in Scripture,
and then the Scriptural incidents following the Resurrection.
Upon this, her vision took another turn, and words were put
in her mouth to chastise the people for their sins.

Apparently more original was Elizabeth's vision of the
Paths of God (the *Viae Dei*). In it three paths went straight
up a mountain from opposite sides, the first having the
hyacinthine hue of the deep heaven ; the second green, the
third purple. At the top of the mountain was a man, clad
with a hyacinthine tunic, his reins bound with a white girdle ;
his face was splendid as the sun, his eyes shone as stars, and
his hair was white ; from his mouth issued a two-edged
sword ; in his right hand he held a key and in his left a

sceptre. Elizabeth interprets : the man is Christ ; and the mountain represents the loftiness of celestial beatitude ; the light at the top is the brightness of eternal life ; the three paths are the diverse ways in which the elect ascend. The hyacinthine path is that of the *vita contemplativa* ; the green path is that of the religious *vita activa* ; and the purple path is the way of the blessed martyrs.

There were also other paths up the mountain, one beset with brambles until half way up, where they gave place to flowers. This is the way of married folk, who pass from brambles to flowers when they abandon the pleasures of the flesh ; for the flowers are the virtues which adorn a life of continence. Still other ways there were, for prelates, for widows, and for solitaries. And Elizabeth turns her visions into texts, and preaches vigorous sermons, denouncing the vices of the clergy as well as laity. In other visions she had seen prelates and monks and nuns in hell.

The visions of this nun appear to have been the fruit of the constructive imagination working upon data of the mind. Yet she is said to have seen them in trances, a statement explicitly made in the account of those last days when life had almost left her body. Praying devoutly in the middle of the night before she died, she seemed much troubled ; then she passed into a trance (*exstasim*). Returning to herself, she murmured to the sister who held her in her arms : " I know not how it is with me ; that light which I have been wont to see in the heavens is dividing." Again she passed into a trance, and afterwards, when the sisters begged her to disclose what she had seen, she said her end was at hand, for she had seen holy visions which, many years before, God's angel had told her she should not see again until she came to die. On being asked whether the Lord had comforted her, she answered, " Oh! what excellent comfort have I received! "

A more imposing personality than Elizabeth was Hildegard of Bingen,[1] whose career extends through nearly

[1] The works of St. Hildegard of Bingen are published in vol. 197 of Migne's *Pat. Lat.* and in vol. viii. of Pitra's *Analecta sacra*, under the title *Analecta Sanctae Hildegardis opera Spicilegio Solesmensi parata* (1882). Certain supplementary

the whole of the twelfth century ; for she was born in 1099 and died in 1179. Her parents were of the lesser nobility, holding lands in the diocese of Mainz. A certain holy woman, one Jutta, daughter of the Count of Spanheim, had secluded herself in a solitary cell at Disenberg—the mount of St. Disibodus—near a monastery of Benedictine monks. Drawn by her reputation, Hildegard's parents brought their daughter to Jutta, who received her to a life like her own. The ceremony, which took place in the presence of a number of persons, was that of the last rites of the dead, performed with funeral torches. Hildegard was buried to the world. She was eight years old. At the same time a niece of Jutta also became a recluse, and afterwards others joined them.

On the death of Jutta in 1136, Hildegard was compelled to take the office of Prioress. But when the fame of the dead Jutta began to draw many people to her shrine, and cause a concourse of pilgrims, Hildegard decided to seek greater quiet, and possibly more complete independence ; for the authority of the new abbot at the monastery may

passages to the latter volume are published in *Analecta Bollandiana*, i. (Paris, 1882). These publications are completed by F. W. E. Roth's *Lieder und die unbekannte Sprache der h. Hildegardis* (Wiesbaden, 1880). The same author has a valuable article on Hildegard in *Zeitschrift für kirchliche Wissenschaft, etc.*, 1888, pp. 453-471. See also an article by Battandier, *Revue des questions historiques*, 33 (1883), pp. 395-425. Other literature on Hildegard in Chevalier's *Répertoire des sources historiques du moyen âge*, under her name.

Her two most interesting works, for our purposes at least, are the *Scivias* (meaning *Scito vias Domini*), completed in 1151 after ten years of labour, and the *Liber vitae meritorum per simplicem hominem a vivente luce revelatorum* (Pitra, o.c. pp. 1-244), begun in 1159, and finished some five years later. Extracts from these are given in the text. Other works show her extraordinary intellectual range. Of these the *Liber divinorum operum simplicis hominis* (Migne 197, col. 741-1038) is a vision of the mysteries of creation, followed by a voluminous commentary upon the world and all therein, including natural phenomena, human affairs, the nature of man, and the functions of his mind and body. It closes with a discussion of Antichrist and the Last Times. The work was begun about 1164, when Hildegard finished the *Liber vitae meritorum*, and was completed after seven years of labour. She also wrote a Commentary on the Gospels, and sundry lives of saints, and there is ascribed to her quite a prodigious work upon natural history and the virtues of plants, the whole entitled : *Subtilitatum diversarum naturarum creaturarum libri IX*. (Migne 197, col. 1118-1351) ; and probably she composed another work on medicine, *i.e.* the unpublished *Liber de causis et curis* (see Pitra, o.c., prooemium, p. xi.). On the psychological and scientific knowledge of Hildegard, see the illustrated essay by Charles Singer in *Studies in the History and Method of Science*, vol. i. (Oxford, 1917) ; also Lynn Thorndike, *History of Magic and Experimental Science*, vol. ii. chap. 40 (1923).

not have been to her liking. She was ever a masterful woman, better fitted to command than to obey. So in 1147 she and her nuns moved to Bingen, and established themselves permanently near the tomb of St. Rupert. From this centre the energies and influence of Hildegard, and rumours of her visions, soon began to radiate. Her advice was widely sought, and often given unasked. She corresponded with the great and influential, admonishing dukes and kings and emperors, monks, abbots, and popes. Her epistolary manner sometimes reminds one of Bernard, who was himself among her correspondents. The following letter to Frederick Barbarossa would match some of his :

" O King, it is very needful that thou be foreseeing in thy affairs. For, in mystic vision, I see thee living, small and insensate, beneath the Living Eyes (of God). Thou hast still some time to reign over earthly matters. Therefore beware lest the Supreme King cast thee down for the blindness of thine eyes, which do not rightly see how thou holdest the rod of right government in thy hand. See also to it that thou art such that the grace of God may not be lacking in thee." [1]

This is the whole letter. Hildegard's communications were not wont to stammer. They were frequently announced as from God, and began with the words " Lux vivens dicit."

Hildegard was a woman of intellectual power. She was also learned in theology, and versed in the medicine and scanty natural science of an epoch which preceded the reopening of the great volume of Aristotelian knowledge in the thirteenth century. Yet she asserts her illiteracy, and seems always to have employed learned monks to help her express, in awkward Latin, the thoughts and flashing words which, as she says, were given her in visions. Her many gifts of grace, if not her learning, impressed contemporaries, who wrote to her for enlightenment upon points of doctrine and biblical interpretation ; they would wait patiently until she should be enabled to answer, since her answers were not in the power of her own reflection, but had to be seen or heard. For instance, a monk named Guibert, who afterwards became the saint's amanu-

<hr>

[1] *Analecta Sanctae Hildegardis opera Spicilegio Solesmensi parata*, p. 523 ; cf. *ibid.* p. 561 ; also *Ep.* 27 of Hildegard in Migne 197, col. 186.

ensis and biographer, propounded thirty-eight questions of
biblical interpretation on behalf of the monks of the monastery of Villars.   In the course of time Hildegard replies: "In
visione animae meae, haec verba vidi et audivi," and thereupon she gives a text from Canticles with an exposition of it,
which neither she nor the monks regarded quite as hers, but
as divinely revealed.   At the end of the letter she says that
she, insignificant and untaught creature, has looked to the
" true light," and through the grace of God has laboured
upon their questions and has completed the solutions of
fourteen of them.[1]

In some of Hildegard's voluminous writings, visions
were apparently a form of composition; again, more veritable
visions, deemed by her and by her friends to have been
divinely given, made the nucleus of the work at length produced by the labour of her mind.   Guibert recognized both
elements, the God-given visions of the seeress and her con-
tributory labour.   In letters which had elicited the answers
above mentioned, he calls her *speculativa anima*, and urges
her to direct her talents (*ingenium*) to the solution of the
questions.   But he also addresses her in words just varied
from Gabriel's and Elizabeth's to the Virgin :

" Hail—after Mary—full of grace ; the Lord is with thee ;
blessed art thou among women, and blessed is the word of thy
mouth. . . . In the character of thy visions, the logic of thy
expositions, the orthodoxy of thy opinions, the Holy Spirit has
marvellously illuminated thee, and revealed to babes divers
secrets of His wisdom." [2]

In answer to more personal inquiries from the deeply
interested Guibert, Hildegard (who at the time was venerable in years and in repute for sanctity) explains how she
saw her visions, and how her knowledge of Scripture came
to her :

" From infancy, even to the present time when I am more
than seventy years old, my soul has always beheld this *visio*,[3] and

---

[1] These questions and Hildegard's solutions are given in Migne 197, col. 1038-
1054, and the letter in Pitra, *o.c.* 399-400.

[2] Pitra, *o.c.* 394, 395.

[3] By *visio* as used here, Hildegard refers to the general undefined light—the
umbra viventis lucis, in which she saw her special visions.

in it my soul, as God may will, soars to the summit of the firmament and into a different air, and diffuses itself among divers
peoples, however remote they may be.   Therefore I perceive
these matters in my soul, as if I saw them through dissolving views
of clouds and other objects.   I do not hear them with my outer
ears, nor do I perceive them by the cogitations of my heart, or by
any collaboration of my five senses ; but only in my soul, my eyes
open, and not sightless as in a trance ; wide awake, whether by
day or night, I see these things.   And I am perpetually bound by
my infirmities and with pains so severe as to threaten death, but
hitherto God has raised me up.

" The brightness which I see is not limited in space, and is
more brilliant than the luminous air around the sun, nor can I
estimate its height or length or breadth.   Its name, which has
been given me, is Shade of the living light (*umbra viventis luminis*).
Just as sun, moon, or stars appear reflected in the water, I see
Scripture, discourses, virtues and human actions shining in it.

" Whatever I see or learn in this vision, I retain in my memory ;
and as I may have seen or heard it, I recall it to mind, and at
once see, hear, know ; in an instant I learn whatever I know.
On the other hand, what I do not see, that I do not know, because
I am unlearned ; but I have had some simple instruction in
letters.   I write whatever I see and hear in the vision, nor do I
set down any other words, but tell my message in the rude Latin
words which I read in the vision.   For I am not instructed in the
vision to write as the learned write ; and the words in the vision
are not as words sounding from a human mouth, but as flashing
flame and as a cloud moving in clear air.

" Nor have I been able to perceive the form of this brightness,
just as I cannot perfectly see the disk of the Sun.   In that brightness I sometimes see another light, for which the name *Lux vivens*
has been given me.   When and how I see it I cannot tell ; but
sometimes when I see it, all sadness and pain is lifted from me,
and then I have the ways of a simple girl and not those of an
old woman." [1]

The obscure Latin of this letter gives the impression
of one trying to put in words what was unintelligible to
the writer.   And the same sense of struggle with the in-
adequacies of speech comes from the prologue of a work
written many years before :

" Lo, in the forty-third year of my temporal course, while I, in
fear and trembling, was intent upon the celestial vision, I saw a

---

[1] Pitra, *o.c.* 332.

great splendour in which was a voice speaking to me from heaven :
Frail creature, dust of the dust, speak and write what thou seest
and hearest.   But because that thou art timid of speech and
unskilled in writing, speak and write these things not according to
human utterance nor human understanding of composition ; but
as thou seest and hearest in the heavens above, in the marvels of
God, so declare, as a hearer sets forth the words of his preceptor,
preserving the fashion of his speech, under his will, his guidance
and his command.   Thus thou, O man (*homo*), tell those things
which thou seest and hearest, and write, not according to thyself
or other human being, but according to the will of Him who knows
and sees and disposes all things in the secrets of His mysteries.

" And again, I heard a voice saying to me from heaven : Tell
these marvels and write them, taught in this way, and say : It
happened in the year one thousand one hundred and forty-one of
the incarnation of Jesus Christ the Son of God, when I was forty-
two years old, that a flashing fire of light from the clear sky transfused my brain, my heart, and my whole breast as with flame ;
yet it did not burn but only warmed me, as the sun warms an
object upon which it sheds its rays.   And suddenly I had intelligence of the full meaning of the Psalter, the Gospels, and
the other books of the Old and New Testaments, although I did
not have the exact interpretation of the words of their text, nor
the division of syllables nor knowledge of cases and moods."

The writer continues with the statement :

" The visions which I saw, I did not perceive in dreams or
sleeping, nor in delirium, nor with the corporeal ears and eyes of
the outer man ; but watchful and intent in mind I received them
according to the will of God." [1]

Hildegard spoke as truthfully as she could about her
visions and the source of her knowledge, matters hard for
her to put in words, and by no means easy for others to
classify in categories of seeming explanation.   Guibert may
have read the work in question.   At all events, his interesting correspondence with her, and her great repute, led him
to come to see for himself and investigate her visions ; for
he realized that deceptions were common, and wished to
follow the advice of Scripture to prove all things.   So he

---

[1] This is from the prologue to the *Scivias*, Pitra, *o.c.* 503, 504 (Migne 197,
483, 484). Guibert in his *Vita* speaks of Hildegard as *indocta* and unable to
penetrate the meaning of Scripture *nisi cum vis internae aspirationis illuminans
eam juvaret* (Pitra, *o.c.* 413). Compare Hildegard's prooemium to her *Life of
St. Disibodus* (Pitra, *o.c.* 357) and the preface to her *Liber divinorum operum*
(Migne 197, 741, 742).

made the journey to Bingen, and stayed four days with Hildegard. This was in 1178, about a year before her death. " So far as was possible in this short space of time, I observed her attentively ; and I could not perceive in her any invention or untruth or hypocrisy, or indeed anything that could offend either us or other men who follow reason." [1]

Springing from her rapt faith, the visions of this seeress and *anima speculativa* disclose the range of her knowledge and the power of her mind. All her visions were allegories ; but while some appear as sheer spontaneous visions, in others the mind of Hildegard, aware of the intended allegorical significance, constructs the vision, and fashions its details to suit the spiritual meaning. This woman, fit sister to her contemporaries Hugo of St. Victor and Bernard of Clairvaux, was ancestress of him who saw his *Commedia* both as fact and allegory, and with intended mind laboured upon that inspiration which kept him lean for twenty years.

Let us now follow these visions for ourselves, and begin with the *Book of the Rewards of Life* revealed by the Living Light through a simple person.[2]

" When I was sixty years old, I saw the strong and wonderful vision wherein I toiled for five years. And I saw a Man of such size that he reached from the summit of the clouds of heaven even to the Abyss. From his shoulders upward he was above the clouds in the serenest ether. From his shoulders down to his hips he was in a white cloud ; from his hips to his knees he was in the air of earth ; from the knees to the calves he was in the earth ; and from his calves to the soles of his feet he was in the waters of the Abyss, so that he stood upon the Abyss. And he turned to the East. The brightness of his countenance dazzled me. At his mouth was a white cloud like a trumpet, which was full of all sounds sounding quickly. When he blew in it, it sent forth three winds, of which one sustained above itself a fiery cloud, and one a storm-cloud, and one a cloud of light. But the wind with the fiery cloud above it hovered before the Man's face, while the two others descended to his breast and blew there.

" And in the fiery cloud there was a living fiery multitude all one in will and life. Before them was spread a tablet covered

---

[1] Guibertus to Radilfus, a monk of Villars (Pitra, *o.c.* 577) apparently written in 1180.

[2] Pitra, *o.c.* pp. 1-244.

with quills (*pennae*) which flew in the precepts of God.   And when
the precepts of God lifted up that tablet where God's knowledge
had written certain of its secrets, this multitude with one impulse
gazed on it.   And as they saw the writing, God's virtue was so
bestowed upon them that as a mighty trumpet they gave forth in
one note a music manifold.

" The wind having the storm-cloud over it, spread, with that
cloud, from the south to the west.   In it was a multitude of the
blessed, who possessed the spirit of life ; and their voice was as the
noise of many waters as they cried : We have our habitations
from Him who made this wind, and when shall we receive them ?
But the multitude that was in the fiery cloud chanted responding :
When God shall grasp His trumpet, lightning and thunder and
burning fire shall He send upon the earth, and then in that trumpet
shall ye have your habitation.

" And the wind which had over it the cloud of light spread with
that cloud from the east to the north.   But masses of darkness
and thick horror coming from the west, extended themselves to the
light cloud, yet could not pass beyond it.   In that darkness was
a countless crowd of lost souls ; and these swerved in their
course whenever they heard the song of those singing in the storm-
cloud, as if they shunned their company.

" Then I saw coming from the north, a cloud barren of delight,
untouched by the Sun's rays.   It reached towards the darkness
aforesaid, and was full of malignant spirits, who go about devising
snares for men.   And I heard the old serpent saying, ' I will
prepare my men of might and will make war upon mine enemies.'
And he spat forth among men a spume of things impure, and
inflated them with derision.   Then he blew up a foul mist which
filled the whole earth as with black smoke, out of which was heard
a groaning ; and in that mist I saw the images of every sin." [1]

These images now speak in their own defence, and are
answered by the virtues, speaking from the storm-cloud,
Heavenly Love replying to Love of this World, Discipline
answering Petulance, Shame answering Ribaldry (the vice of
the *jongleours*) after the fashion of such mediaeval allegorical
debates.   The virtues are simply voices ; but the monstrous
or bestial image of each sin is described :

" Ignavia (cowardly sloth) had a human head, but its left ear
was like the ear of a hare, and so large as to cover the head.   Its
body and limbs were worm-like, apparently without bones ; and
it spoke trembling." [2]

Hildegard explains the general features of her vision : God with secret inquisition, reviewing the profound disposal of His will, made three ways of righteousness, which should advance in the three orders of the blessed. These are the three winds with the three clouds above them. The first wind bears over it the fiery cloud, which is the glory of angels burning with love of God, willing only what He wills ; the wind bearing over it the storm-cloud represents the works of men, stormy and various, done in straits and tribulations ; the third way of righteousness, through the Incarnation of our Lord, bears above it a white and untouched virginity, as a cloud of light.[1]

Then Hildegard sees the punishments of those who die in their sins impenitent. They were in a pit having a bottom of burning pitch, out of which crawled fiery worms ; and sharp nails were driven about in that pit as by a wind.

" I saw a well deep and broad, full of boiling pitch and sulphur, and around it were wasps and scorpions, who scared but did not injure the souls of those therein ; which were the souls of those who had slain in order not to be slain.

" Near a pond of clear water I saw a great fire. In this some souls were burned and others were girdled with snakes, and others drew in and again exhaled the fire like a breath, while malignant spirits cast lighted stones at them. And all of them beheld their punishments reflected in the water, and thereat were the more afflicted. These were the souls of those who had extinguished the substance of the human form within them, or had slain their infants.

" And I saw a great swamp, over which hung a black cloud of smoke, which was issuing from it. And in the swamp there swarmed a mass of little worms. Here were the souls of those who in the world had delighted in foolish merriment (*inepta laetitia*).[2]

" And I saw a great fire, black, red, and white, and in it horrible fiery vipers spitting flame ; and there the vipers tortured the souls of those who had been slaves of the sin of uncharitableness (*acerbitas*).

" And I saw a fire burning in a blackness, in which were dragons, who blew up the fire with their breath. And near was an icy river ; and the dragons passed into it from time to time and disturbed it. And a fiery air was over both river and fire. Here were punished the souls of liars ; and for relief from the heat, they

---

[1] Pitra, *o.c.* p. 24.   [2] *Ibid.* p. 51 *sqq.*

pass into the river, and again, for the cold, they return to the fire, and the dragons torment them. But the fiery air afflicts only those who have sworn falsely.[1]

" I saw a hollow mountain full of fire and vipers, with a little opening ; and near it a horrible cold place crawling with scorpions. The souls of those guilty of envy and malice suffer here, passing for relief from one place of torment to the other.

" And I saw a thickest darkness, in which the souls of the disobedient lay on a fiery pavement and were bitten by sharp-toothed worms. For blind were they in life, and the fiery pavement is for their wilful disobedience, and the worms because they disobeyed their prelates.

" And I beheld at great height in the air a hail of ice and fire descending. And from that height, the souls of those who had broken their vows of chastity were falling, and then as by a wind were whirled aloft again wrapped in a ligature of darkness, so that they could not move ; and the hail of cold and fire fell upon them.

" And I saw demons with fiery scourges beating hither and thither, through fires shaped like thorns and sharpened flails, the souls of those who on earth had been guilty bestially." [2]

After the vision of the punishment, Hildegard states the penance which would have averted it, and usually follows with pious discourse and quotations from Scripture. Apparently she would have the punishments seen by her to be taken not as allegories, but literally as those actually in store for the wicked.

It is different with her visions of Paradise. In Hildegard, as in Dante, descriptions of heaven's blessedness are pale in comparison with the highly-coloured happenings in hell. And naturally, since Paradise is won by those in whom spirit has triumphed over carnality. But flesh triumphed in the wicked on earth, and hell is of the flesh, though the spirit also be agonized. Hildegard sees many blessed folk in Paradise, but all is much the same with them : they are clad in splendid clothes, they breathe an air fragrant with sweetest flowers, they are adorned with jewels, and many of them wear crowns. For example, she sees the blessed virgins standing in purest light and limpid splendour, sur-

[1] Pitra, *o.c.* p. 92 *sqq.*

[2] *Ibid.* p. 131 *sqq.* Of course, one at once thinks of the punishments in Dante's *Inferno*, which in no instance are identical with those of Hildegard, and yet offer common elements. Dante is not known to have read the work of Hildegard.

passing that of the sun. They are clad " quasi candidissima
veste velut auro intexta, et quasi pretiosissimis lapidibus
a pectore usque ad pedes, in modum dependentis zonae,
ornata induebantur, quae etiam maximum odorem velut
aromatum de se emittebat. Sed et cingulis, quasi auro et
gemmis ac margaritis supra humanum intellectum ornatis,
circumcingebantur."

This seems a description of heavenly millinery. Are
these virgins rewarded in the life to come with what they
spurned in this ? What would the saint have thought of
virgins had she seen them in the flesh clad in the whitest
vestment ornamented with interwoven gold and gems, falling
in alluring folds from their breasts to their feet, giving out
aromatic odours, and belted with girdles of pearls beyond
human conception ? Could it be possible that the woman
surviving in the nun took delight in contemplating the
blissful things forbidden here below ? However this
may be, the quasi-s and velut-s suggest the symbolical
character of these marvels. This indication becomes stronger
as Hildegard, in language wavering between the literal
and the symbolical, explains the appropriateness of ornaments and perfumes as rewards for the virtues shown
by saints on earth. At last all is made clear : the *Lux
vivens* declares that these ornaments are spiritual and eternal;
gold and gems, which are of the dust, are not for the eternal
life of celestial beings ; but the elect are spiritually adorned
by their righteous works as people are bodily adorned with
costly ornaments. So one gains the lesson that the bliss of
heaven can only be shown in allegories, since it surpasses
the understanding of men while held in mortal flesh.[1]

[1] Pitra, *o.c.* pp. 230-240. I am not clear as to Hildegard's ideas of Purgatory,
for which she seems to have no separate region. In the case of sinners who have
begun, but not completed, their penances on earth, the punishments described
work *purgationem,* and the souls are loosed (*ibid.* p. 42). In Part III. of the work
we are considering, the paragraphs describing the punishments are entitled *De
superbiae, invidiae, inobedientiae, infidelitatis,* etc., *poenis purgatoriis* (*ibid.* p.
130). But each paragraph is followed by one entitled *De poenitentia superbiae,*
etc., and the *poenitentia* referred to is worked out with penance in this life. Consequently it is not quite clear that the word *purgatoriis* attached to *poenis* signifies
temporary punishment to be followed by release.
In a vision of the Last Times (*ibid.* p. 225) Hildegard sees " black burning
darkness," in which was *gehenna,* containing every kind of horrible punishment.
She did not then see *gehenna* itself, because of the darkness surrounding it ; but
heard the frightful cries. Cf. *Aeneid,* vi. 548 *sqq.*

These visions from Hildegard's *Book of the Rewards of Life* may be supplemented by one or two selected from the curious and lengthy work which she named *Scivias*, signifying *Scito vias domini* (know the ways of the Lord). In this work, on which she laboured for nine years, the seeress shows forth the Church, in images seen in visions, and the whole dogmatic scheme of Christian polity. The allegories form the texts of expository sermons. For example, the first vision in the first Book is of an iron-coloured mountain, which is at once explained as an image of the stability of God's eternal kingdom. The third vision is of a fiery, egg-shaped object, very complicated in construction, and devised to illustrate the truth that things visible and temporal shadow forth the invisible and eternal, in the polity of God.[1] In the fourth vision, globes of fire are seen to enter the human form at birth, and are then attacked by many whirlwinds rushing in upon them. This is an allegory of human souls and their temptations, and forms the text for a long discourse on the nature of the soul.

The fifth vision is of the Synagogue, the *Mater incarnationis Filii Dei* :

" Then I saw as it were the image of a woman, pale from the top to the navel, and black from the navel to the feet, and its feet were blood-colour, and had about them a very white cloud. This image lacked eyes, and kept its hands under its arm-pits. It stood by the Altar that is before the eyes of God, but did not touch it."

The pale upper part of this image represents the prescience of the patriarchs and prophets, who had not the strong light of the Gospel ; the black lower portion represents Israel's later backslidings ; and the bloody feet surrounded by a white cloud, the slaying of Christ, and the Church arising from that consummation. The image is sightless— blind to Christ—and stands before His altar, but will have none of it : and its slothful hands keep from the work of righteousness.[2]

[1] This is the view expounded so grandly by Hugo of St. Victor in his *De sacramentis, post*, Chapter XXIX.

[2] Migne 197, col. 433. All this is interesting in view of the many figures of the Church and Synagogue carved on the cathedrals, most of them later than Hildegard's time. The " Synagogue " of sculpture has her eyes bound, the sculpturesque expression of eyelessness. The rest of Hildegard's symbolism was not followed in sculpture.

The sixth vision is of the orders of celestial spirits, and harks back to the *Celestial Hierarchy* of Dionysius the Areopagite. In the height of the celestial secrets Hildegard sees a shining company of supernal spirits having as it were wings (*pennas*) across their breasts, and bearing before them a face like the human countenance, in which the look of man was mirrored. These are angels spreading as wings the desires of their profound intelligence ; not that they have wings, like birds ; but they quickly do the will of God in their desires, as a man flees quickly in his thoughts.[1] They manifest the beauty of rationality through their faces, wherein God scrutinizes the works of men. For these angels see to the accomplishment of the will of God in men ; and then in themselves they show the actions of men.

Another celestial company was seen, also having as it were wings over their breasts, and bearing before them a face like the human countenance in which the image of the Son of Man shone as in a mirror. These are archangels contemplating the will of God in the desires of their own intelligences, and displaying the grace of rationality ; they glorify the incarnate Word by figuring in their attributes the mysteries of the Incarnation. This vision, symbolizing the angelic intelligence, is consciously and rationally constructed.

Perhaps the same may be said of the second vision of the second Book : [2]

" Then I saw a most glorious light and in it a human form of sapphire hue, all aflame with a most gentle glowing fire ; and that glorious light was infused in the glowing fire, and the fire was infused in the glorious light ; and both light and fire transfused that human form—all inter-existent as one light, one virtue, and one power."

This vision of the Trinity, in which the glorious light is the Father, the human form is the Son, and the fire is the Holy Spirit, may remind the reader of the closing " vision " of the thirty-third canto of Dante's *Paradiso*.

The third Book contains manifold visions of a four-sided edifice set upon a mountain, and built with a double (*biformis*) wall. Here an infinitude of symbolic detail illustrates the

---

[1] Migne 197, col. 437 *sqq.* Cf. St. Bernard, *Sermo xix. in Cantica.*
[2] Migne 197, col. 449.

entire Christian Faith.   Observe a part of the symbolism of
the twofold wall :   the wall is double (*in duabus formis*).   One
of its formae[1] is speculative knowledge, which man possesses
through careful and penetrating investigation of the speculation
of his mind ;   so that he may be circumspect in all his ways.
The other forma of the wall represents the *homo operans*.

" This speculative knowledge shines in the brightness of the
light of day, that through it men may see and consider their acts.
This brightness is of the human mind carefully looking about
itself ;   and this glorious knowledge appears as a white mist
permeating the minds of the peoples, as quickly as mist is scattered
through the air ;   it is light as the light of day, after the brightness
of that most glorious work which God benignly works in men,
to wit, that they shun evil and do the good which shines in them
as the light of day. . . .   This knowledge is speculative, for it is
like a mirror (*speculum*) in which a man sees whether his face
be fair or blotched ;   thus this knowledge views the good and evil
in the deed done." [2]

The *Scivias* closes with visions of the Last Judgment,
splendid, ordered, tremendous, and rendered audible in
hymns rising to the Virgin and to Christ.   Apostles, martyrs,
saints chant the refrains of victory which echo the past
militancy of this faithful choir.

The visions of Elizabeth of Schönau and Hildegard of
Bingen set forth universal dogmas and convictions.   They
show the action of the imaginative and rational faculties and
the full use of the acquired knowledge possessed by the
women to whom they came.   Such visions spring from
the mind :   quite different are those born of love.   Emotion
dominates the latter ;   their motives are subjective ;   they are
personal experiences having no clear pertinency to the lives
of others.   If the visions of Hildegard were object lessons, the
blissful ecstasies of Mary of Ognies and Liutgard of Tongern
were specifically their own, very nearly as the intimate consolation of a wife from a husband, or a lady from her
faithful knight, would be that woman's and none other's.
One cannot say that there was no love of God before

[1] Notice the supra-terrestrial term, which can hardly be translated so as to fit
an actual wall.
[2] Migne 197, col. 583.   Compare this vision with the symbolic interpretation
of the cathedral edifice, *post*, Chapter XXX., I.

Jesus was born; still less that men had not conceived of God as loving them. Nevertheless in Jesus' words God became lovable as never before, and God's love of man was shown anew, and was anew set forth as the perfect pattern of human love. In Christ, God offered the sacrifice which afore He had demanded of Abraham: for "God so loved the world that He gave His only-begotten Son." That Son carried out the Father's act: "Greater love hath no man than this, that a man lay down his life for his friend." So men learned the final teaching: "God is love."

A new love also was aroused by the personality of Jesus. Was this the love of God or love of man? Rather, it was such as to reveal the two as one. In Jesus' teachings, love of God and love of man might not be severed: "As ye have done it unto one of the least of these, my brethren, ye have done it unto me." And the love which He inspired for himself was at once a love of man and love of God.[1] Think of that love, new in the world, with which, more than with her ointment or her tears, the woman who had been a sinner bathed the Master's feet.

This woman saw the Master in the flesh; but the love which was hers was born again in those who never looked upon His face. Through the Middle Ages the love of Christ with which saintly women were possessed was as impulsive as this sinner's, and also held much resembling human passion. Their burning faith tended to melt into ecstatic experiences. They had renounced the passionate love of man in order to devote themselves to the love of Christ; and as their thoughts leapt toward the Bridegroom, the Church's Spouse and Lord, their visions sometimes kept at least the colour of the love for knight or husband which they had abjured.[2]

[1] Cf. St. Bernard's treatment of this matter, ante, Chapter XVIII.

[2] In a Middle High German Marienleben, by Bruder Phillips (13th century) the young virgin is made herself to say to God:

"Du bist min lieber priutegam (bridegroom),
Dir gib ich minen magetuom (maidenhood),
Du bist min vil schoener man.

"Du bist min vriedel (lover) und min vriunt (ami);
Ich bin von diner minne entzundt."

Bobertag, Erzählende Dichtungen des späteren Mittelalters, p. 46 (Deutsche Nat. Litt.).

At the height of the horrors of the Albigensian Crusade, in the year 1212, Fulco, Bishop of Toulouse, was driven from his diocese by the incensed but heretical populace. He travelled northward through France, seeking aid against these foes of Christ, and came to the diocese of Liége. There he observed with joy the faith and humility of those who were leading a religious life, and was struck by the devotion of certain saintly women whose ardour knew no bounds. It was all very different from Toulouse. " Indeed I have heard you declare that you had gone out of Egypt— your own diocese—and having passed through the desert, had reached the promised land—in Liége."

Jacques de Vitry is speaking. His friend the bishop had asked him to write of these holy women, who brought such glory to the Church in troubled times. Jacques was himself a clever Churchman, zealous for the Church's interests and his own. He afterwards became Bishop and Cardinal of Tusculum ; and as papal legate consecrated the holy bones of her whom the Church had decided to canonize, the blessed Mary of Ognies, the paragon of all these other women who rejoiced the ecclesiastical hearts of himself and Fulco. Jacques had known her and had been present at her pious death ; and also had witnessed many of the matters of which he is speaking at the commencement of his *Vita* of this saint.[1]

Many of these women, continues Jacques, had for Christ spurned carnal joys, and for Him had despised the riches of this world, in poverty and humility clinging to their heavenly Spouse.

" You saw," says Jacques, again addressing Fulco, " some of these women dissolved with such a particular and marvellous love toward God (*tam speciali et mirabili in Deum amoris affectione resolutas*) that they languished with desire, and for years had rarely been able to rise from their cots. They had no other infirmity, save that their souls were melted with desire of Him, and, sweetly resting with the Lord, as they were comforted in spirit they were weakened in body. They cried in their hearts,

---

[1] *Vita B. Mariae Ogniacensis*, per Jacobum de Vitreaco, Bollandi, *Acta sanctorum* t. 21 (June t. iv. pp. 636-666). Jacques had good reason to canonize her bones, since one of them, in his saddle-bags, had saved his mule from drowning while crossing a river in Tuscany.

though from modesty their lips dissimulated: " Fulcite me floribus, stipate me malis, quia amore langueo." [1] The cheeks of one were seen to waste away, while her soul was melted with the greatness of her love. Another's flow of tears had made visible furrows down her face. Others were drawn with such intoxication of spirit that in sacred silence they would remain quiet a whole day, ' while the King was on His couch ' (*i.e.* at meat),[2] with no sense or feeling for things without them, so that they could not be roused by clamour or feel a blow. I saw another whom for thirty years her Spouse had so zealously guarded in her cell, that she could not leave it herself, nor could the hands of others drag her out. I saw another who sometimes was seized with ecstasy five-and-twenty times a day, in which state she was motionless, and on returning to herself was so enraptured that she could not keep from displaying her inner joy with movements of the body, like David leaping before the Ark. And I saw still another who after she had lain for some time dead, before burial was permitted by the Lord to return to the flesh, that she might on earth do purgatorial penance ; and long was she thus afflicted of the Lord, sometimes rolling herself in the fire, and in the winter standing in frozen water." [3]

But what need to say more of these, as all their graces are found in one precious and pre-excellent pearl—and Jacques proceeds to tell the life of Mary of Ognies. She was born in a village near Namur in Belgium, about the year 1177. She never took part in games or foolishness with other girls ; but kept her soul free from vanity. Married at fourteen to a young man, she burned the more to afflict her body, passing the nights in austerities and prayer. Her husband soon was willing to dwell with her in continence, himself sustaining her in her holy life, and giving his goods to the poor for Christ's sake.

There was nothing more marvellous with Mary than her

---

[1] Cant. ii. 5. The translation in the English Revised Version is : " Stay me with cakes of raisins, comfort me with apples ; for I am sick of love." The phrases of Canticles, always in the words of the Latin Vulgate, come continually into the minds of these ecstatic women and their biographers. The sonorous language of the Vulgate is not always close to the meaning of the Hebrew. But it was the Vulgate and not the Hebrew that formed the mediaeval Bible, and its language should be observed in discussing mediaeval applications of Scripture.

[2] " Dum esset Rex in accubitu suo," Cant. i. 11, in Vulgate ; Cant. i. 12, in the English version, which renders it : " While the King sitteth at His table."

[3] *Vita B. Mariae, etc.*, par. 2-8. Since we are seeing these mediaeval religious phenomena as they impressed contemporaries, it would be irrelevant to subject them to the analyses which pathological psychology applies to not dissimilar phenomena.

gift of tears, as her soul dwelt in the passion of her Lord. Her tears—so says her biographer—wetted the pavement of the Church or the cloth of the altar. Her life was one of body-destroying austerities : she went barefoot in the ice of the winter ; often she took no food through the day, and then watched out the night in prayer. Her body was afflicted and wasted ; her soul was comforted. She had frequent visions, the gift of second sight, and great power over devils. Once for thirty-five days in silent trance she rested sweetly with the Lord, only occasionally uttering these words : " I desire the body of our Lord Jesus Christ " (*i.e.* the Eucharist) ; and when she had received it, she turned again to silence.[1] Always she sought after her Lord : He was her meditation, and example in speech and deed. She died in the year 1213, at the age of thirty-six. She was called Mary of Ognies, from the name of the town where a church was dedicated to her, and where her relics were laid to rest.

Emotionally, another very interesting personality was the blessed virgin, Liutgard of Tongern, a younger contemporary of Mary of Ognies. In accordance with her heart's desire, she was providentially protected from the forceful importunities of her wooers, and became a Benedictine nun. After some years, however, seeking a more strenuous rule of life, she entered the Cistercian convent at Aquiria, near Cambray.[2]

Liutgard's experiences were sense-realizations of her faith, but chiefly of her love of Christ. Sometimes her senses realized the imagery of the Apocalypse ; as when singing in Church she had a vision of Christ as a white lamb. The lamb rests a foot on each of her shoulders, sets his mouth to hers, and draws out sweetest song. Far more frequently she realized within her heart the burning words of Canticles. Her whole being yearned continually for the Lord, and sought no other comfort. For five years she received almost daily visits from the Mother of Christ, as

---

[1] It is reported of St. Catharine of Siena that she would go for weeks with no other food than the Eucharist.

[2] I am drawing from her *Vita* by her contemporary, Thomas of Cantimpré, *Acta SS.*, Bollandi, t. 21 (t. 3 of June), p. 234 *sqq.*

well as from the Apostles and other saints ; the angels were continually with her. Yet in all these she did not find perfect rest for her spirit, till she found the Saint of saints, who is ineffably sweeter than them all, even as He is their sanctifier. Smitten as the bride in Canticles, she is wounded, she languishes, she pants, she arises ; " in the streets " she seeks the Saints of the New Dispensation, and through " the broad places " the Patriarchs of the Old Testament. Little by little she passes by them ; " because He is not far from every one of us," she finds Him whom her soul cherishes. She finds, she holds Him, because He does not send her away ; she holds Him by faith, happy in the seeking, more happy in the holding fast.[1]

There are three couches in Canticles : [2] the first signifies the soul's state of penitence ; the second its state of warfare ; the third the state of those made perfect in the *vita contemplativa*. On the first couch the soul is wounded, on the second it is wearied, on the third it is made glad. The saintly Liutgard sought her Beloved perfectly on the couch of penitence, and watered it with her tears, although she never had been stung by mortal sin. On the second couch she sought her Beloved, battling against the flesh with fasting and endeavour ; with poverty and humility she overcame the world, and cast down the devil with prayer and remedial tears. On the third couch, which is the couch of quiet, she perfectly sought her Beloved, since she did not lean upon the angels or saints, but through contemplation rested sweetly only upon the couch of the Spouse. This couch is called flowery (*floridus*) from the vernal quality of its virtues ; and it is called " ours " because common to husband and wife : in it she may say, " My Beloved is mine and I am His," and, " I am my Beloved's, and His desire is towards me." Why not say that ? exclaims the biographer, quoting the lines :

" Nescit amor Dominum ; non novit amor dominari,
    Quamlibet altus amet, non amat absque pari."

Thenceforth her spirit was absorbed in God, as drops of water in a jar of wine. When asked how she was wont to

---

[1] Cf. Canticles iii. 2 ; *Vita*, lib. iii. par. 42.
[2] Cant. iii. 1, 7 ; i. 16.

see the visage of Christ in contemplation, she answered :
" In a moment there appears to me a splendour incon-
ceivable, and as lightning I see the ineffable beauty of His
glorification ; the sight of which I could not endure in this
present life, did it not instantly pass from my view. A
mental splendour remains, and when I seek in that what I
saw for an instant, I do not find it."

A little more than a year before her death the Lord
Jesus Christ appeared to her, with the look as of one who
applauds, and said : " The end of thy labour is at hand : I
do not wish thee longer to be separated from me. This
year I require three things of thee : first, that thou shouldst
render thanks for all thy benefits received ; secondly, that
thou pour thyself out in prayer to the Father for my
sinners ; and thirdly, that, without any other solicitude, thou
burn to come to me, panting with desire." [1]

The religious yearning which with Liutgard touches
sense-realization, seems transformed completely into the
latter in the extraordinary German book of one Sister
Mechthild, called of Magdeburg.[2] The authoress probably
was born not far from that town about the year 1212. To

---

[1] *Vita*, lib. iii. pars. 9, 11. It is well known how great a love of her Lord
possessed St. Elizabeth of Hungary, and how she sent her children away from
her, that she might not be distracted from loving Him alone. The vision which
came to her upon her expulsion from the Wartburg, after the death of her husband,
King Louis of Thuringia, is given as follows, in her own words, according to the
sworn statement of her waiting-women : " I saw the heaven open, and that sweet
Jesus, my Lord, bending toward me and consoling me in my tribulation ; and
when I saw Him I was glad, and laughed ; but when He turned His face, as if to
go away, I cried. Pitying me, He turned His serene countenance to me a second
time, saying : ' If thou wishest to be with me, I wish to be with thee.' I responded : ' Thou, Lord, thou dost wish to be with me, and I wish to be with thee,
and I wish never to be separated from thee ' " (*Libellus de dictis quatuor ancillarum*,
Mencken, *Scriptores Rerum Germ.* ii. 2020 A-C, Leipzig, 1728). The German
sermon of Hermann von Fritzlar (cir. 1340) tells this vision in nearly the same
words, putting, however, this phrase in Elizabeth's mouth : " Our Lord Jesus
Christ appeared to me, and when He turned from me, I cried, and then He turned
to me, and I became red (blushed ?), and before I was pale " (Hildebrand, *Didaktik
aus der Zeit der Kreuzzüge*, p. 36, Deutsche Nat. Lit.).

[2] *Offenbarungen der Schwester Mechthild von Magdeburg oder das fliessende
Licht der Gottheit*, ed. by P. G. Morel, Regensburg, 1869. See Preger, *Gesch.
der deutschen Mystik*, i. 70, 91 *sqq.* Preger points out that the High-German
version of this work, which we possess, was made from the Low-German original
in the year 1344. Extracts from Mechthild's book are given by Vetter, *Lehrhafte
Literatur des 14. und 15. Jahrhunderts*, pp. 192-199 ; and by Hildebrand, *Didaktik
aus der Zeit der Kreuzzüge*, pp. 6-10 (Deutsche Nat. Lit.).

judge from her work, she belonged to a good family and was acquainted with the courtly literature of the time. She speaks of her loving parents, from whom she tore herself away at the age of twenty-three, and entered the town of Magdeburg, there to begin a life of rapt religious mendicancy, for which Francis had set the resistless example. Sustained by love for her Lord, she led a despised and homeless life of hardship and austerity for thirty years. At length bodily infirmities brought her to rest in a Cistercian cloister for nuns at Helfta, near Eisleben, where ruled a wise and holy abbess, the noble Gertrude of Hackeborn. Here Mechthild remained until her death in 1277. For many years it had been her custom to write down her experiences of the divine love in a book which she called *The Flowing Light of God*, in which she also wrote the prophetic denunciations, revealed to her to be pronounced before men, especially in the presence of those who were great in what should be God's holy Church.[1]

" Frau Minne (Lady Love) you have taken from me the world's riches and honour," cries Mechthild.[2] Love's ecstasy came upon her when she abandoned the world and cast herself upon God alone. Then first her soul's eyes beheld the beautiful manhood of her Lord Jesus Christ, also the Holy Trinity, her own guardian angel, and the devil who tempted her through the vainglory of her visions and through unchaste desire. She defended herself with the agony of our Lord. For Mechthild, hell is the " city whose name is eternal hate." With her all blessedness is love, as her book will now disclose.

Cries the Soul to Love (*Minne*) her guardian : " Thou hast hunted and taken, bound and wounded me ; never shall I be healed."

Love answers : " It was my pleasure to hunt thee ; to take thee captive was my desire ; to bind thee was my joy. I drove Almighty God from His throne in heaven, and took His human life from Him, and then with honour gave Him

[1] We pass over these portions of Mechthild's book which exemplify the close connection between ecstatic contemplation and the denunciation of evil in the world.

[1] Mechthild constantly uses phrases from the courtly love poetry of her time.

back to His Father; how couldst thou, poor worm, save thyself from me!"[1]

What then will love's omnipotence exact from this poor Soul? Merely all. Drawn by yearning, the Soul comes flying, like an eagle toward the sun. "See, how she mounts to us, she who wounded me"—it is the Lord that is speaking. "She has thrown away the ashes of the world, overcome lust, and trodden the lion of pride beneath her feet— thou eager huntress of love, what bringest thou to me?"

"Lord, I bring thee my treasure, which is greater than mountains, wider than the world, deeper than the sea, higher than the clouds, more beautiful than the sun, more manifold than the stars, and outweighs the riches of the earth."

"Image of my Divinity, ennobled by my manhood, adorned by my Holy Spirit, how is thy treasure called?"

"Lord, it is called my heart's desire: I have withdrawn it from the world, withheld it from myself, forbidden it all creatures. I can carry it no farther; Lord, where shall I lay it?"

"Thou shalt lay thy heart's desire nowhere else than in my divine heart and on my human breast. There only wilt thou be comforted and kissed with my spirit."

Love casts out fear and difference, and lifts the Soul to equality with the divine Lover. Through the passion of love the Soul may pass into the Beloved's being, and become one with Him: "He, thy life, died from love for thy sake; now love Him so that thou mayest long to die for His sake. Then shalt thou burn for evermore unquenched, like a shining spark in the great fire of the Living Majesty."

These are passion's vision-flights. But God himself points out the way by which the Soul that loves shall come to Him: she—the Soul—shall come, surmounting the need of penitence and penance, surmounting love of the world, conflicts with the devil, carnal appetite, and the promptings

---

[1] *Das fliessende Licht, etc.*, i. cap. 3. Hildebrand, *o.c.* p. 6, cites this apposite verse from the thoughtful and knightly Minnesinger, Reimar von Zweter:

> "Got herre unuberwundenlich,
> Wie uberwant die Minne dich!
> Getorste ich, so spraech ich:
> Si wart an dir so sigerich."

of her own will. Thereupon, exhausted, she shall yearn resistlessly for that beautiful Youth (Christ). He will be moved to come to meet her. Now her guardians (the Senses) bid her attire herself. " Love, whither shall I hence ? " she cries. The Senses make answer : " We hear the murmur ; the Prince will come to meet you in the dew and the sweet-bird song. Courage, Lady, He will not tarry."

The Soul clothes herself in a garment of humility, and over it draws the white robe of chastity, and goes into the wood. There nightingales sing of union with God, and strains of divine knowledge meet her ears. She then strives to follow in festal dance (i.e. to imitate) the example of the prophets, the chaste humility of the Virgin, the virtues of Jesus, and the piety of His saints. Then comes the Youth and says : " Maiden, thou hast danced holily, even as my saints."

The Soul answers : " I cannot dance unless thou leadest. If thou wouldst have me spring aloft, sing thou : and I will spring—into love, and from love to knowledge, and from knowledge to ecstasy, above all human sense."

The Youth speaks : " Maiden, thy dance of praise is well performed. Since now thou art tired, thou shalt have thy will with the Virgin's Son. Come to the brown shades at midday, to the couch of love, and there shalt thou cool thyself with Him."

Then the Soul speaks to her guardians, the Senses : " I am tired with the dance ; leave me, for I must go where I may cool myself." The Senses bid her cool herself in the tears of love shed by St. Mary Magdalen.

" Hush, good sirs : ye know not what I mean. Unhindered, for a little I would drink the unmixed wine."

" Lady, in the Virgin's chastity the great love is reached."

" That may be—with me it is not the highest."

" You, Lady, might cool yourself in martyr-blood."

" I have been martyred many a day."

" In the counsel of Father Confessors, the pure live gladly."

" Good is their counsel, but it helps not here."

" Great safety would you find in the Apostles' wisdom."

" Wisdom I have myself—to choose the best."

" Lady, bright are the angels, and lovely in love's hue ;
to cool yourself, be lifted up with them."

" The bliss of angels brings me love's woe, unless I see
their lord, my Bridegroom."

" Then cool you in the hard, holy life that John the
Baptist showed."

" I have tried that painful toil ; my love passes beyond
that."

" Lady, would you with love cool yourself, approach the
Child in the Virgin's lap."

" That is a childish love, to quiet children with.   I am a
full-grown bride and will have my Bridegroom."

" Lady, there we should be smitten blind.   The Godhead is so fiery hot.   Heaven's glow and all the holy lights
flow from His divine breath and human mouth by the
counsel of the Holy Spirit."

But the Soul feeling its nature and its affinity with God,
through love, makes answer boldly : " The fish cannot
drown in the water, nor the bird sink in the air, nor gold
perish in the flame, where it gains its bright clarity and
colour.   God has granted to all creatures to follow their
natures ; how can I withstand mine ?   To God will I go,
who is my Father by nature, my Brother through His humility,
my Bridegroom through love, and I am His forever." [1]   Not
long after this the Soul's rapture bursts forth in song :

> " Ich sturbe gern von minnen, moehte es mir geschehen,
> Denn jenen den ich minnen, den han ich gesehen
> Mit minen liehten ougen in miner sele stehen." [2]

Mechthild's book is heavy with passion—with God's
passionate love for the Soul, and the Soul's passionate
response.   No speech between lovers could outdo the converse between them.   God calls the Soul, sweet dove, dear
heart, my queen ; and with like phrase the quivering Soul
responds upward, as it were, to the great countenance
glowing above it.   Throughout, there is passion and impatient yearning—or satisfaction.   The pain of the Soul

---

[1] *Das fliessende Licht, etc.,* i. 38-44.

[2] " I would gladly die of love, might that be my lot ; for Him whom I love
I have seen with my bright eyes standing in my soul " (*ibid.* ii. cap. 2).

severed, not yet a bride, is deeper than the abyss, bitterer than the world ; but her joy shall exceed that of seraphs, she, Bride of the Trinity.[1]

The Soul must surrender herself, and become sheer desire for God.[2] God's own yearning has begotten this desire. As glorious prince, as knight, as emperor, God comes ; also in other forms :

> " I come to my Beloved
> As dew upon the flowers." [3]

For each other are these lovers wounded, for each other these lovers bleed, and each to the other is joy unspeakable and unforgettable. From the wafer of the holy Eucharist, the Lamb looks out upon me " with such sweet eyes that I never can forget."

> " His eyes in my eyes ; His heart in my heart,
> His soul in my soul,
> Embraced and untroubled." [4]

No need to say that in the end love draws the Soul to heaven's gate, which the Lord opens to her. All is marvellous ; but, far more, all is love : the Lord kisses her —what else than love can the soul thereafter know or feel.[5]

Mechthild, of course, is what is called a " mystic," and a forerunner indeed of many another—Eckhart, Suso, Tauler —of German blood. With direct and utter passion she realizes God's love ; also she feels and thinks in symbols, which, with her, never cease to be the things they literally are. They remain flesh and blood, while also signifying the mysteries of God. Jesus was a man, Mechthild a woman. Her love not only uses lovers' speech, but actually holds affinity with a maid's love for her betrothed. If it is the Soul's love of God, it is also the woman's love of Him who overhung her from the Cross.

[1] Cf. ii. 22.
[2] i. 13.
[3] See i. 10 ; ii. 23.
[4] ii. 4.
[5] iii. 1, 10.

CHAPTER XXI

THE SPOTTED ACTUALITY

THE TESTIMONY OF INVECTIVE AND SATIRE ; ARCHBISHOP RIGAUD'S
REGISTER ; ENGELBERT OF COLOGNE ; POPULAR CREDENCES

THE preceding sketches of monastic qualities and personalities illustrate the ideals of monasticism. That monastic
practices should fall away, corruptions enter, and when
expelled inevitably return, was to be expected. The cause
lay in those qualities of human nature which may be either
power or frailty. The acquisitive, self-seeking, lusting
qualities of men lie at the base of life, and may be essential
to achievement and advance. Yet a higher interpretation of
values will set the spiritual above the earthly, and beatify the
self-denial through which man ultimately attains his highest
self, under the prompting of his vision of the divine. The
sight of this far goal is given to few men steadily, and the
multitude, whether cowled or clad in fashions of the world,
pursue more immediate desires.

So human nature saw to it that monasticism should
constantly exhibit frivolity instead of earnestness, gluttony
instead of fasting, avarice instead of alms-giving, anger and
malice instead of charity and love, lustfulness instead of
chastity, and, instead of meekness, pride and vain-glory.
The particular forms assumed by these corruptions depended
on the conditions of mediaeval life and the position in it
occupied by monks.

It has already been said that the standard of conduct for
the secular clergy was the same in principle as that for
monks, though with allowance made for the stress of a life of

487

service in the cure of souls.[1]   But always the cloister and the
hermitage were looked upon as the abiding-places where one
stood the best chance to save one's soul : the life of the layman—merchant, usurer, knight—was fraught with instant
peril ; that of the secular clergy was also perilous. especially
when they held high office.   Dread of ecclesiastical pre-
ferment might be well founded ; the reluctance to be a
bishop was often real.   This sentiment, like all feelings in
the Middle Ages, took the form of a story, with the usual
vision to certify the moral of the tale :

" It is told of a certain prior of Clairvaux, Geoffrey by name,
that when he had been elected Bishop of Tournai, and Pope
Eugene as well as the blessed Bernard, his own abbot, was urging
him to take the office, he cast himself down at the feet of the
blessed Bernard and his clergy, and lay prone in the form of a
cross, and said : ' An expelled monk I may be, if you drive me
out ; but I will never be a bishop.'   At a later time, as this same
prior lay breathing his last, a monk who loved him well adjured
him in the name of God to bring him news of his state beyond the
grave, if God would permit it.   Some time after, as the monk was
praying prostrate before the altar, his friend appeared and said
that it was he.   When the monk asked him how he was faring,
' Well,' he replied, ' by the grace of God.   Yet verily it has been
revealed to me by the blessed Trinity, that had I been in the
number of bishops I should have been in the number of the reprobate and damned.' " [2]

Through the Middle Ages, Church dignities everywhere
were secularized through the vast possessions and corresponding responsibilities attaching to them.   The clerical
situation varied in different lands, yet with a like result.
The Italian clergy were secularized through participation in
civic and papal business, the German through their estates
and principalities.   In France clerical secularization was
most typically mediaeval, because there the functions and
fortunes of the higher clergy were most inextricably involved

[1] It is quite true that in the earliest Christian times the marriage of priests was
recognized, and continued to be at least connived at until, say, the time of Hildebrand.   Yet the best thoughtfulness and piety from the Patristic period onward
had disapproved of priestly marriages, which consequently tended to sink to
the level of concubinage, until they were absolutely condemned by the Church.

[2] *Anecdotes, etc., d'Étienne de Bourbon*, ed. by Lecoy de la Marche, p. 249
(Soc. de l'Histoire de France, t. 185, Paris, 1877).   This story refers to the years
1166-1171.

in feudalism. Monasteries and bishoprics were as feudal fiefs : abbots as well as bishops commonly held lands from an over-lord, and were themselves lords of their sub-vassals who held lands from them. To the former they owed rent, or aid, or service ; to the latter they owed protection. In either case they might have to go or send their men to war. They also managed and guarded their own lands, like feudal nobles, *vi et armis*. When the estates of a monastery, for example, lay in different places, the abbot might exercise authority over them through a local potentate, and might also have such a protector (*vîdame, avoué, advocatus*) for the home abbey. There was always a general feeling, often embodied in law or custom, that a Church dignitary should fight by another's sword and spear. But this did not prevent bishop and abbot in countless instances in France, England, Germany, and Spain, from riding mail-clad under their seignorial banner at the head of their forces.[1]

Episcopal lands and offices were not inherited : [2] yet with rare exceptions the bishops came from the noble, fighting, hunting class. They were noblemen first and ecclesiastics afterwards. The same was true of the abbots. Noble-born, they became dignitaries of the world through investiture with the broad lands of the monastery, and then administrators by reason of the temporal functions involved. As with the episcopal or monastic heads, so with canons and monks. They, too, for the most part were well-born. They also were good, bad, or indifferent, warlike or clerkly, devoted to study, abandoned to pleasure, or following the one and the other sparingly. Many a holy meditative monk there was ; and many a saintly parish priest, the stay of piety and justice in his village. The rude times, the ceaseless murder and harrying, uncertainty and danger everywhere, seemed to beget such holy lives.

[1] Many bishops and abbots held definite secular rank ; the Archbishop of Rheims was a duke, and so was the Bishop of Langres and Laon ; while the bishops of Beauvais and Noyon were counts. In Germany, the archiepiscopal dukes of Cologne and Mainz were among the chief princes of the land.

[2] There were, however, some (naturally shocking) instances of inheritance, as where the Bishop of Nantes in 1049 admitted that he had been invested with the bishopric during the lifetime of his father, the preceding bishop. See Luchaire, in vol. ii. (2), pp. 107-117 of Lavisse's *Hist. de France,* for this and other examples of episcopal feudalism.

Invectives, satires, histories, and records, bear witness to
the state of the clergy. All diatribes are to be taken with
allowance. Whoever, for example, reads Peter Damiani's
Liber Gomorrhianus against the foulness of the clergy, must
bear in mind the writer's fiercely ascetic temper, the warfare
which the stricter element in the Church was then waging
against simony and priestly concubinage, and the monkish
phraseology so common to ecclesiastical indictment of
frivolity and vice.

One cannot quote comfortably from the *Gomorrhianus*.
St. Bernard furnishes more decorous denunciation :

" Woe unto this generation, for its leaven of the Pharisees
which is hypocrisy !—if that should be called hypocrisy which
cannot be hidden because of its abundance, and through impudence does not seek to hide ! To-day, foul rottenness crawls
through the whole body of the Church. If a heretic foe should
arise openly, he would be cast out and withered ; or if the enemy
raged madly, the Church might hide herself from him. But
now whom shall she cast out, or from whom hide herself ? All
are friends and all are foes ; all necessary and all adverse ; all
of her own household and none pacific ; all are her neighbours
and all seek their own interest. Ministers of Christ, they serve
Antichrist. They go clothed in the good things of the Lord and
render Him no honour. Hence that *éclat* of the courtesan which
you daily see, that theatric garb, that regal state. Hence the
gold-trapped reins and saddles and spurs—for the spurs shine
brighter than the altars. Hence the splendid tables laden with
food and goblets ; hence the feastings and drunkenness, the
guitars, the lyres and the flutes ; hence the swollen wine-presses
and the storehouses heaped and running over from this one into
that, and the jars of perfumes, and the stuffed purses. 'Tis for
such matters that they wish to be and are the over-seers of
churches, deacons, archdeacons, bishops, and archbishops. For
neither do these offices come by merit, but through that sort of
business which walketh in darkness ! " [1]

Such rhetoric gives glimpses of the times, but also springs
from that temper which is always crying *hora novissima,
tempora pessima*. Invectives of this nature have their deepest

[1] *Sermo in Cantica*, 33, par. 15 (Migne 183, col. 958-959). With this passage
from St. Bernard, one may compare the far more detailed picture of the luxury
and dissolute ways of the secular clergy in France given in the *Apologia of Guido
of Bazoches* (latter part of the twelfth century). W. Wattenbach, " Die Apologie
des Guido von Bazoches." *Sitzungsberichte Preussichen Akad.*, 1893 (1), pp. 395-420.

source in the religious sense of the ineradicable opposition
between this world and the kingdom of heaven.   Yet luxury
did in fact pervade the Church of Bernard's time, and simony
was as wide as western Europe.   This crime was the offspring of the entire social state ; it was part and parcel of
the feudal system and the whole matter of lay investitures.
One sees that simony was no extraneous stain to be washed
off from the body ecclesiastic, but rather an element of its
actual constitution.   The eradication had to come through
social and ecclesiastical evolution, rather than spasmodic
reformation.

One may turn from the invectives of the great saint to
forms of satire more frankly literary.   The Latin poems
" commonly attributed to Walter Mapes " [1] satirize with
biting ridicule, through the mouth of " Bishop Golias," the
avarice and venality, the gluttony and lubricity of the
Church, secular and monastic.   In a quite different kind of
poem the satire directs itself against the rapacity of Rome.
She, head of the Church and Caput Mundi, is shown to be
like Scylla and Charybdis and the Sirens.[2]   These powerful
verses anticipate the denunciation of the Roman papacy
by the good Germans Walther von der Vogelweide and
Freidank,[3] and, a century later, in the *Vision of Piers
Ploughman.*

In this outcry against papal rapacity France was not
silent.   Most extreme is the " Bible " of Guiot de Provens :
it satirizes the entire age, " siècle puant et orrible."   As it
turns toward the papacy it cries :

> " Ha I Rome, Rome,
>   Encor ociras tu maint home I "

The cardinals are stuffed with avarice and simony and evil
living ; without faith or religion, they sell God and His
Mother, and betray us and their fathers.   Rome sucks and
devours us ; Rome kills and destroys all.   Guiot's voice is
raised against the entire Church ; neither the monks nor the
seculars escape—bishops, priests, canons, the black monks

[1] Ed. by T. Wright (Camden Society, London, 1841).
[2] The poem called *De ruina Romae.*   It begins, " Propter Syon non tacebo."
[3] *Post,* Chapter XXVII.

and the white, Templars and Hospitallers, nuns and abbesses, all bad.[1]

One might extend indefinitely the list of these invectives, which, like the corruptions denounced by them, were common to all mediaeval centuries. From the testimony of more definite accounts one perceives the rudeness and cruelty of mediaeval life, in which the Church likewise was involved. In order to rise, it had to lift the social fabric. To this end many of its children struggled nobly, devoting themselves and sometimes yielding up their lives for the betterment of the society in which their lots were cast.

One of these capable children of the Church who did his duty in the high ecclesiastical station to which he was called was Eude Rigaud, or Odo Rigaldus, Archbishop of Rouen from 1248 to 1275, the year of his death. He was a scion of a noble house whose fiefs lay in the neighbourhood of Brie-Comte-Robert (Seine-et-Marne). In 1236 he joined the Franciscans, and then studied at Paris under Alexander of Hales, one of the Order's great theologians. His first fame came from his preaching. As archbishop, he was a reformer, and abetted the endeavours of Pope Gregory IX. He was also a counsellor of Saint Louis, and followed him upon that last crusade from which the king did not return alive.[2]

The good archbishop was a man of method, and kept a record of his official acts. This monumental document exists, the *Register* of Rigaud's visitations among the monks and secular clergy within his wide jurisdiction, between the years 1248 and 1269.[3] Consisting of entries made at the time, it is a mirror of actual conditions, presumably similar to those existing in other parts of France. Rigaud visited many monasteries and parishes where he found nothing to reform, and merely made a memorandum of having been

---

[1] The " Bible " of Guiot is published in Barbazan's *Fabliaux*, t. ii. (Paris, 1808). It is conveniently given with other satirical or moralizing compositions in Ch.-V. Langlois, *La Vie en France au moyen âge d'après quelques moralistes du temps* (Paris, 1908).

[2] Salimbene gives an amusing picture of our worthy Rigaud hurrying to catch sight of the king at a Franciscan Chapter. *Post*, Chapter XXII.

[3] *Regestrum visitationum archiepiscopi Rothomagensis*, ed. Bonnin (Rouen, 1852). It is analysed by L. V. Delisle, in an article entitled " Le Clergé normand " (*Bib. de l'École des Chartes*, 2nd ser. vol. iii.).

there ; wherever abuses were found, the entry expands to a statement of them and the measures taken for their remedy. Consequently one may not infer that the blameworthy or abominable conditions recorded in the particular instance obtained universally in Normandy. Occasionally Rigaud records in more detail the good condition of some monastery. A few instructive extracts may be given.

" Calends of October (1248). We were again at Ouville (Ovilla). We found that the prior wanders about when he ought to stay in the cloister ; he is not in the cloister one day in five. Item, he is a drunkard, and of such vile drunkenness that he sometimes lies out in the fields because of it. Item, he frequents feasts and drinking-bouts with laymen. Item, he is incontinent, and is accused in respect to a certain woman of Grainville, and also with the wife of Robertot, and also with a woman of Rouen named Agnes. Item, brother Geoffrey was publicly accused with respect to the wife of Walter of Esquaquelon who recently had a child from him. Item, they do not keep proper accounts of their revenues. We ordered that they should keep better accounts." [1]

Such an entry needs no comment. But it is illuminating to observe the strictness or leniency with which Rigaud treats offences. Doubtless he was guided by what he thought he could enforce.

Apparently near the Ouville priory, the archbishop was scandalized by the priest of St. Vedasti de Depedale, who was convicted of taking part in the rough ball-play, common in Normandy, in which game, as might easily happen, he had injured some one. " He took oath before us that if again convicted he would hold himself to have resigned from his church." [2] Rigaud did not approve of these somewhat too merry games for his parish priests, who were not angels. The archbishop finds of the priest of Lortiey " that he but rarely wears his capa, that he does not confess to the *penitentiarius*, that he is gravely accused concerning two women, by whom he has had many children, and he is drunken." [3]

Rigaud enters the cases of other parish priests as follows :

" We found that the priest of Nigella was accused as to a woman, and of being engaged in trade and of treating his father despitefully, who is patron of the church which he holds, and that

---

[1] *Reg. vis.* p. 9.   [2] *R.V.* p. 10.   [3] *R.V.* p. 18.

with drawn sword he fought with a certain knight, with a riotous following of relatives and friends. Item, the priest of Basinval is accused as to a woman whom he takes about with him to the market-places and taverns. Likewise the priest of Vieux-Rouen is accused of incontinency, and goes about wearing a sword in shameless garb. Likewise the priest of Cotigines is a dicer and plays at quoits and frequents taverns, and is incontinent, and although corrected as to these matters, perseveres." [1]

Sometimes accusations were brought to the archbishop by the suffering parishioners :

" Calends of August (1255). Passing through the village of Brai, the parishioners of the church there accused the rector of the church in our presence. They said that he went about in the night through the village with arms, that he was quarrelsome and scurrilous and abusive to his parishioners, and was incontinent."

Summoning this priest before his ecclesiastical tribunal, the archbishop says, " We admonished him to abstain from such ill-conduct ; or that otherwise we should proceed against him." [2]

Either this priest or another of " Brayo subtus Baudemont," named Walter, was subsequently deprived of his priesthood on his own confession as follows :

" He confessed that the accusation against him concerning a woman of his parish, which he had denied under oath, was supported by truth ; item, he confessed in regard to a waxen image made to be used in divining ; he confessed (various other incontinencies and his fatherhood of various children) ; item, he confessed his ill-repute for usury and base gain ; he admitted that he had led the dances at the nuptials of a certain prostitute whom he had married." [3]

Rigaud continually records accusations against parish priests, commonly for incontinency and drunkenness and generally unbecoming conduct, and sometimes for homicide.[4] But his own examinations kept out many a turbulent and ignorant clerk, presented by the lay patron for the benefice ; and so he prevented improper inductions as he might. The *Register* gives a number of instances of crass illiteracy in these candidates, a matter to cause no surprise, for the feudal patrons of the living naturally presented their

[1] *R.V.* pp. 19-20.
[3] *R.V.* p. 379.
[2] *R.V.* p. 222.
[4] *R.V.* p. 154.

relatives. Some of these candidates appealed to Rome from the archbishop's refusal, probably without success.[1]

A monk might be as bad as any parish priest :

" Brother Thomas . . . wore gold rings. He went about in armour, by night, and without any monastic habit, and kept bad company. He wounded many clergy and laity at night, and was himself wounded, losing a thumb. We commanded the abbot to expel him ; or that otherwise we should seize the place and expel the monks." [2]

Life in a nunnery was the feminine counterpart of life in a monastery. There were good and bad nunneries, and nuns good and bad, serious and frivolous. Many had the foibles, and were addicted to the diversions, comforts, or fancies of their sex : they were always wanting to keep dogs and birds, and have locks to their chests !

" Nones of May (1250). We visited the Benedictine convent of nuns of St. Sauveur at Evreux. There were sixty-one nuns there. Sometimes they drank, not in the refectory or infirmary, but in their chambers. They kept little dogs, squirrels, and birds. We ordered that all such things be removed. They do not observe the *regula*. They eat flesh needlessly. They have locked chests. We directed the abbess to inspect their chests often and unexpectedly, or to take off the locks. We directed the abbess to take away their girdles ornamented with ironwork and their fancy pouches, and the silk cushions they were working." [3]

Again, the picture is more terrible :

" Nones of July (1249). We visited the priory of Villa Arcelli. Thirty-three nuns are there and three lay sisters. They confess and communicate six times a year. Only four of the nuns have taken the vows according to the *regula*. Many of them had cloaks of rabbit-fur, or made from the fur of hares and foxes. In the infirmary they eat flesh needlessly. Silence is not observed ; nor do they keep within the cloister. Johanna of Aululari once went out and lived with some one, by whom she had a child ; and sometimes she goes out to see that child : she is also suspected with a certain man named Gaillard. Isabella la Treiche (?) is a fault-finder, murmuring against the prioress and others. The stewardess is suspected with a man named Philip de Vilarceau. The prioress is too remiss ; she does not reprove. Johanna de

---

[1] See *e.g. R.V.* pp. 159, 162, 395-396.
[2] *R.V.* p. 109.   [3] *R.V.* p. 73.

Alto Villari kept going out alone with a man named Gayllard, and within a year had a child by him. The subprioress is suspected with Thomas the carter ; Idonia, her sister, with Crispinatus ; and the Prior of Gisorcium is always coming to the house for Idonia. Philippa of Rouen is suspected with a priest of Suentre, of the diocese of Chartres ; Marguarita, the treasuress, with Richard de Genville, a clerk. Agnes de Fontenei, with a priest of Guerrevile, diocese of Chartres. The Tooliere (?) with Sir Andrew de Monciac, a knight. All wear their hair improperly and perfume their veils. Jacqueline came back pregnant from visiting a certain chaplain, who was expelled from his house on account of this. Agnes de Monsec was suspected with the same. Emengarde and Johanna of Alto Villari beat each other. The prioress is drunk almost any night ; she does not rise for matins, nor eat in the refectory or correct excesses."

The archbishop thereupon issues an order, regulating this extraordinary convent, and prescribing a better way of living. He threatens to lay a heavier hand on them if they do not obey.[1] This was what a loosely regulated nunnery might come to. We close with the sketch of a good monastery which had an evil abbot :

" Nones of August (1258). Through God's grace we visited the monastery of Jumiéges. Forty-three monks were there, and twenty-one outside. All of these who dwelt there, except eleven, were priests (*sacerdotes*). We found, by God's grace, the convent well-ordered in its services and observances, yet greatly troubled by what was said of the abbot within and without its walls. For opinion was sinister regarding him, and there, in full chapter, brother Peter of Neubourg, a monk of the monastery, leaping up, made shameful charges against him. And he read the following schedule : I, brother Peter of Neubourg, a monk of Jumiéges, in my name and in the name of the monastery and for the benefit of the monastery, bring before you, Reverend Father, Archbishop of Rouen, for an accusation against Richard, Abbot of Jumiéges, that he is a forger (*falsarius*) because he wrote or caused to be written certain letters in the name of our convent, falsely alleging our approval of them although we were absent and ignorant ; and secretly by night he sealed them with the convent's seal. . . ."

The letters related to an important controversy in which the monastery was involved. Monk Peter offers to prove his case. A day is set for the hearing. But, instead, the

[1] *R.V.* pp. 43-45.

very next day, in order to avoid scandal, the archbishop
called the abbot before him and his counsellors ; and

" We admonished him specially regarding the following matters :
To wit : that he should not keep dogs and birds of chase ; that
he should send strolling players away from his premises ; that he
should abstain from extravagant expenses ; that he should not eat
in his own chambers ; that he should keep from consorting with
women altogether ; that he should order his household decently ;
that he should lease out the farms as well as might be ; that he
should not burden the monks unduly ; that he should be more
in the convent with them, and bear himself more soberly. He
made promises in the presence of all and took oath upon holy
relics that if he failed to obey our admonition he should be held
to do whatever we should decree in the premises." [1]

Rigaud seems to have been lenient here, but may have
known the wisest course to take.

A peaceful death terminated Rigaud's long career. We
may leave his diocese of Rouen, and travel north-easterly
to the German archiepiscopal dukedom of Cologne for a
very different example of a brave prelate who brought
death upon himself.

The man who was chosen Archbishop of Cologne in
1216 was of the highest birth. It was Engelbert, son of
Count Engelbert of Berg. A young nobleman, related by
blood to the local powers, lay and ecclesiastic, and destined
for Church dignities, would be quickly given benefices.
Engelbert received such, and also was appointed Provost of
the Cathedral. Strong of body, rich, he led a boisterous
martial life, and took a truculent part in the political
dissensions which were undoing the German realm. With
his cousin, the Archbishop Adolph, he went over to the
side of Philip of Suavia. For this the archbishop and
his provost were deposed and excommunicated by Pope
Innocent III. There ensued years of turbulence and
fighting, during which Engelbert's hand followed his passions.
But with the turning of events in 1208 he was reconciled
to the Pope, restored to his offices, and went crusading
against the Albigenses in atonement for his sins. He stood
by the young Frederick, then favoured by Innocent, and

[1] *R.V.* p. 607.

after some intervening years of proof, was, with general approval, elected Archbishop of Cologne. He was about thirty-one years old.

There had been power and bravery in the man from the beginning; and his faculties gained poise and gathered purpose through the stormy springtime of his life. Now he stood forth prince-bishop, feudal duke; a man strong of arm and clear of vision, steadfast against the violence of his brother nobles who oppressed the churches and cloisters within their lordships. The weak found him a rock of defence. Says his biographer, Caesar of Heisterbach:

" He was a defender of the afflicted and a hammer of tyrants, magnanimous and meek, lofty and affable, stern and gentle, dissembling for a time, and when least expected girding himself for vengeance. With the bishopric he had received the spiritual sword, and the material sword with the dukedom. He used either weapon against the rebellious, excommunicating some and crushing some by war."

Under him archbishopric and dukedom prospered, their well-managed revenues increased, palaces and churches rose. No mightier prince of the Church, no stronger, juster ruler could be found. Said Pope Honorius after Engelbert's death : " All men in Germany feared me from fear of him." From the lay and German side is heard the hearty voice of Walther von der Vogelweide, no friend of priests ! "Worthy Bishop of Cologne, happy should you be ! You have well served the realm, and served it so that your praise rises and waves on high. Master of princes ! if your might weighs hard on evil cowards, deem that as nothing ! King's guardian, high is your state, unequalled Chancellor ! " [1]

Archbishop of Cologne, duke of its double dukedom, and Regent of the German realm, Engelbert was well-nigh Germany's greatest figure during these years. If his arm was strong, his also was the spirit of counsel and wisdom. And although bearing himself as prince and ruler, he had within him the devotion and humility of a true bishop. Said one of Engelbert's chaplains, speaking to the Abbot of Heisterbach : " Although my lord seems as of the world,

[1] In Pfeiffer's ed. No. 159. See also *ibid.* 162.

within he is not as he appears outwardly. Know that he
has many secret comfortings from God."

The iron course of Engelbert's life brought queryings
to the monkish mind of his biographer. Caesar felt that it
was not easy for any bishop to be saved ; how much harder
was it for a statesman-warrior-prelate so to conduct himself
in the warfare of this world as to attain at last " the peace
of divine contemplation." Not thither did such a career
seem to lead ! But there was a way, or at least an exit,
which surely opened upon heaven's gate. This was the
purple steep, the *purpureum ascensum*, of martyrdom. Caesar
was not alone in thinking thus as to the saving close of
Engelbert's career ; for a devout and learned priest, who in
earlier years had been co-canon with Engelbert, said to
Caesar after the archbishop's murder : " I do not think
there was another way through which a man so placed (*in
statu tali positus*) could have entered the door of the
kingdom of heaven, which is narrow."

Caesar tells the story of this martyrdom in all its causes
and details of plot. That plot succeeded because it was the
envenomed culmination of the hatred for the archbishop felt
by the nobles—bishops among them too—whom he restrained with his authority and unhesitating hand. Frederic,
Count of Isenburg, a kinsman of Engelbert as well as of the
former archbishop, was the feudal warden of the nunnery of
Essen, which he greedily oppressed. The abbess turned to
Engelbert, as she had to his predecessor. The archbishop
hesitated to proceed against a relative. So the abbess
appealed to Rome. Papal letters came back causing
Engelbert to take the matter up. He acted with forbearance
and generosity ; for he even offered to make up from his
own revenues any loss the count might sustain from acting
justly toward the nunnery. In vain. Frederic, so we read,
would have none of his interference. The devil hardened
his heart ; and he began to incite his friends and kinsmen
(who were also the kin of Engelbert) to a treacherous
attack upon the man they could not openly withstand.

Rumours of the plot were in the air. Said a monk of
Heisterbach to his abbot : " Lord, if you have any business
with the archbishop, do it quickly, for his death is near."

Engelbert himself was not unwarned. A letter came to
him revealing the matter. Upon reading it, he threw it in
the fire. Yet he told its contents to his friend the Bishop
of Minden, who was present. Said the latter : " Have a
care for thyself, my lord, for God's sake, and not for thyself
alone, but for the welfare of your church and the safety of
the whole land."

The archbishop answered : " Dangers are all about me,
and what I should do the Lord knows and not I. Woe is
me, if I keep quiet ! Yet if I should accuse them of this
matter, they would complain to every one that I was fastening
the crime of parricide on them. From this hour I commit
my body and soul to the divine care."

" Then taking the bishop alone into his chapel, he began to
confess all his sins from his very youth, with a shower of tears
that wetted all his breast, and, as we hope, washed the stains from
his heart. And when the Lord of Minden said : ' I fear there is
still something on thy conscience which thou hast not told me,' he
answered : ' The Lord knows that I have concealed nothing
consciously.' But thinking over his sins more fully, the next
morning he took his confessor again into the same chapel and
with meek and contrite soul and floods of tears confessed everything that had recurred to his mind. Then his conscience being
clear, he said fearlessly : ' Now let God's will regarding me be
done.'

" In the meanwhile some one was knocking at the door of the
chapel. The archbishop would not let it be opened because his
eyes were wet with tears. But the knocking continued, and it was
announced that the bishops of Osnabrück and Münster (brothers
of Count Frederic) were there. After he had dried his eyes and
wiped his face, he allowed them to be shown in, and said when
they had entered : ' You lords both are kin of mine, and I have
injured you in nothing, as you know well, but have advanced your
interests, as I might, and your brother's also. And look you,
from all sides by word and letter I hear that your brother Count
Frederic, whom I have loved heartily and never harmed, is
devising ill to me and seeks to kill me.'

" They protested, trembling in their deceit : ' Lord, may this
never, never, be ! You need have no fear ; such a thought has
never entered his heart. We all have been honoured and enriched and lifted up by you.' Which last was true."

This was after the festival of All Saints in the first days
of November 1225 ; and Count Frederic, the better to

conceal his purpose, came and accepted the archbishop's terms. Together they set out from Cologne, the count knowing that the now unsuspecting Engelbert would stop the next day to dedicate a church at Swelm. So it turned out, and the count took that opportunity to excuse himself, and rode off to set his men in ambush. Just then a widow rose up from the roadside, and demanded judgment as to a fief withheld from her. At once the archbishop dismounted, and took his seat as duke to hear the cause. It went against the widow, and in favour of him who sat as judge. But he said : " Lady, this fief which you demand is taken from you by decree and adjudged to me. But for the sake of God, pitying your distress, I relinquish it to you."

The archbishop rode on. About midday Frederic came up again to see which way he was taking. Engelbert invited the count to pass the night with him. But he declined on some pretext, and rode away. The archbishop and his company proceeded on their road until the hour of vespers. Vespers were said, and again the count appeared. Observing him, a nobleman in Engelbert's train said : " My lord, this coming and going of the count looks suspicious. For the third time he is approaching, and now not as before on his palfrey but on his war-horse. I advise you to mount your war-horse too."

But the archbishop said that would be too noticeable, and there was nothing to fear. As the count drew near, they saw that the colour had left his face. The archbishop spoke to him : " Now, kinsman, I am sure you will stay with me." He answered nothing, and they went on together. Suspicious and alarmed, some of the clergy and some of the knights withdrew, so that but a small company remained ; for a good part of the episcopal household with the cooks had gone ahead to prepare the night's lodgings.

It was dusk as they drew near the place of ambush. The count grew agitated, and was blaming himself to his followers for planning to kill his lord and kinsman, but they egged him on. Now the foot of the Gevelberg was reached, and the count said as they began to ascend, " My lord, this is our path." " May the Lord protect us," replied Engelbert, for he was not without suspicion.

The company was entering the hollow way leading over the summit of the mountain, when suddenly the followers of Frederic, who were ahead, turned on them, and others leaped from hiding, while a shrill whistle sounded, startling the horses. " My lord, mount your war-horse ; death is at the door," cried a knight. It was indeed. The archbishop's company made no resistance, except the faithful noble who first had scented danger. The rest fled while the murderers rushed upon Engelbert, unable to turn in the narrow way, and struck at him with swords and daggers. One seized him by the cloak and the two rolled together on the ground ; but the strong and active prelate dragged himself and his antagonist out of the roadway into a thicket. There he was again set upon by the mad crew, urged on by the count, and was hacked and stabbed to death. He breathed his last beneath an oak ten paces from the roadway.

There is no need to recount the finding of the gashed and stripped body, its solemn interment in the Cathedral Church of St. Peter's at Cologne, the canonization of Engelbert, and the building of a chapel, succeeded by a cloister, to mark the place of his martyrdom. Nor need one follow with Caesar the banning of the murderers, and the unhappy ways in which their deaths made part atonement for the injury which their wicked deed had done the German realm.[1]

The ideals and shortcomings of monasticism were closely connected with popular beliefs. The monastic ideal had its inception in the thought of sin as entailing either purgatorial or everlasting punishment, and in the thought of holiness as ensuring eternal bliss. Whatever other motives participated, the knot of the monastic purpose was held in the jaws of this antithesis, which for itself drew form, colour, picturesqueness, from popular beliefs, and was made tangible in countless stories telling of purity and love and meekness impaired by lust and cruelty and pride, and of retribution

---

[1] The above is drawn from the " Vita Sancti Engelberti," by Caesar of Heisterbach, in Boehmer, *Fontes rerum Germanicarum*, ii. 294-329 (Stuttgart, 1845). E. Michael, *Culturzustände des deutschen Volkes während des 13ⁿ Jahrhunderts*, ii. 30 *sqq.* (Freiburg im Breisgau, 1899), has an excellent account drawn mainly from the same source.

avoided by some shifty supernatural adjustment of the sin. Such stories might be accepted as well by the learned as by the illiterate. The brooding soul of the Middle Ages, with its knowledge of humanity and its reaches of spiritual insight, was undisturbed by the crass superstitions so queerly at odds with its deeper inspiration—a remark specifically applicable to thoughtful or spiritually-minded individuals in the mediaeval centuries.

As we descend the spiritual scale, the crude superstitious elements become more prominent or apparently the whole matter. Likewise as we descend the moral scale ; for the more vicious the individual, the more utterly will he omit the spiritual from his working faith, and the more mechanical will be his methods of squaring his conduct with his fears of the supernatural. Nevertheless, in estimating the ethical shortcomings of mediaeval superstitions, one must remember how easily in a simple mind all sorts of superstition may co-exist with a sweet religious and moral tone.

Sins unatoned for and uncondoned bring purgatorial or perpetual torment after death, even as holiness brings eternal bliss. But how were sins thought to come to men and women in the Middle Ages, and especially to those who were earnestly striving to escape them ? Rather than fruit of the naughtiness of the human heart, they came through the malicious suggestions, the temptations, of a Tempter. They were in fine the machinations of the devil. This was the popular view, and also the authoritative doctrine, expressed, re-expressed, and enforced in myriad examples, by all the saints and magnates of the Church who had lived since the time when Athanasius wrote the life of Anthony in devil-fighting heroics.

Against the devil, every man had staunch allies ; the readiest were the Virgin Mary and the saints, for Christ was very high above the conflict, and at the Judgment Day must be its final umpire. The object of the cunning enemy was to trip man into hell, an object hostile alike to God and man. Saintly aid enabled man to overcome the devil, or if he succumbed to temptation and committed mortal sin, there was still a chance to frustrate the devil's plot, and save the soul by wiles or force. The sinner may use every stratagem

to defeat the devil and escape the results of sins committed
by himself, but prompted by his enemy.   This was war and
the ethics of war, in which man was the central struggling
figure, attacked by the devil and defended by the saints.
The latter also help man's earthly fortunes, and devotion to
them may ensure one's welfare in this very palpable and
pressing life of earth.

This popular and yet authoritative view of mortal peril
and saintly aid is illustrated in the tales from sermons and
other pious writings.   In them any uncanny or untoward
experience was ascribed to the devil.   So it was in monkish
Chronicles, *Vitae sanctorum, Dialogi miraculorum,* or indeed
in any edifying writing couched in narrative form or containing illustrative tales.   Throughout this literature the
devil inspires evil thoughts, instigates crimes, and causes any
unhappy or immoral happening.   It is just as much a matter
of course as if one should say to-day, I have a cold, or John
stole a ring, or James misbehaved with So-and-so.[1]   Any man
might meet the devil, and if sinful, suffer physical violence
from him.   If any one disappeared the devil might be
supposed to have carried him off.   Details of the abduction
might be given, or the whole matter take place before
witnesses.

" A rich usurer, with little fear of God in him, had dined well
one evening, and was in bed with his wife, when he suddenly
leaped up.   She asked what ailed him.   He replied : ' I was just
snatched away to God's judgment seat, where I heard so many
accusations that I did not know what to answer.   And while
I waited for something to happen, I heard the final sentence given
against me, that I should be handed over to demons, who were
to come and get me to-day.'   Saying this, he flung on a coat,

---

[1] The *Dialogi miraculorum* of Caesar of Heisterbach, and the *Exempla* of
Étienne de Bourbon (d. 1262) and Jacques de Vitry (d. 1240) present a huge
collection of such stories.   For the early Middle Ages, in the decades just before
and after the year one thousand, the mechanically supernatural view of any
occurrence is illustrated in the five books of *Histories* of Radulphus Glaber, an
incontinent and wandering, but observing monk, native of Burgundy.   Best
edition by M. Prou, in *Collection des textes, etc.* (Paris, Picard, 1886) ; also in Migne,
Pat. Lat. 142.   An interesting study of his work by Gebhart, entitled, " Un Moine
de l'an 1000," is to be found in the *Revue des deux mondes*, for October 1, 1891.
Glaber's fifth book opens with some excellent devil stories.   As there was a progressive enlightenment through the mediaeval centuries, such tales gradually
became less common and less crude.

and ran out of the house, for all his wife could do to stop him. His servants, following, discovered him almost crazed in a church where monks were saying their matins.   There they kept him in custody for some hours.   But he made no sign of willingness to confess or make restitution or repent.   So after mass they led him back toward his house, and as they came by a river, a boat was seen coming rapidly up against the current, manned apparently by no one.   But the usurer said that it was full of demons, who had come to take him.   The words were no sooner uttered, than he was seized by them, and put in the boat, which suddenly turned on its course and disappeared with its prey." [1]

One observes that this usurer had received sentence at God's tribunal, and the devils carried it out : the sentence gave them power.   Any man may be tempted ; but falls into his enemy's power only by sinning.   His yielding is an act of acquiescence in the devil's will, and may be the commencement of a state of permanent consent.   With this we reach the notion of a formal pact with the devil, of which there were many instances.   But still the pact is with the Enemy ; the man is not bound beyond the letter, and may escape by any trick.   It is still the ethics of war ; we are very close to the principle that a man by stratagem or narrow observance of the letter may escape the eternal retribution which God decrees conditionally and the devil delights in.

The sacraments prescribed by the Church were the common means of escaping future punishment.   Confession is an example.   The correct doctrine was that without penitence it was ineffective.   But popularly the confession represented the whole fact.   It was efficacious of itself, and kept the soul from hell.   It might even prevent retribution in this life.   Caesar of Heisterbach has a number of illustrative stories, rather immoral as they seem to us. There was, for instance, a person possessed (*obsessus*) of a devil who dwelt in him, and through his lips would make known the *unconfessed* sins of any one brought before him ; but the devil could not remember sins which had been confessed.   A certain knight suspected (quite correctly) a

[1] *Anecdotes historiques d'Étienne de Bourbon*, par. 422, ed. by Lecoy de la Marche (vol. 185 of Société de l'Histoire de France), Paris, 1877 ; cf. *ibid.* par. 383.

priest of sinning with his wife. So he haled him before this *obsessus*. On the way the priest managed to elude his persecutor for an instant, and, darting into a barn, confessed his sin to a layman he found there. Returning, he went along with the knight, and, behold, the sin was obliterated from the memory of the devil in the *obsessus*, and the priest remained undetected.[1]

Men and women sometimes escaped the wages of sin by the aid of a saint, but more often through the incarnate pity of the Virgin Mary. The Virgin and the saints were ready to take up any cause, however desperate, against the devil; which means that they were ready to intervene between the sinner and the impending punishment. People took kindly to these thoughts of irregular intervention, since everlasting torment for transient sin was so extreme; but a surer source of their approval lay in the incomplete spiritualization of the popular religion and its ethics.

To thwart the devil was the office of the Virgin and the saints. Their aid was given when it was besought. Sometimes they intervened voluntarily to protect a votary whose devotions had won their favour. The stories of the pitying intervention of the Virgin to save the sinner from the wages of his sin, and frustrate the devil, are among the fragrant flowers of the mediaeval spirit. Ethically some of them leave much to ask for; but others are tales of sweet forgiveness upon heart-felt repentance.

Jacques of Vitry has a story (scarcely fit to repeat) of a certain very religious Roman widow-lady, who had an only son, with whom she sinned at the devil's instigation. She was a devoted worshipper of the Virgin; and the devil, fearing that she would repent, plotted to bring her to trial and immediate condemnation before the emperor's tribunal, for her incest. When the widow knew of her impending ruin, she went with tears to the confessional, and then day and night besought the Virgin to deliver her from infamy and death. The day of trial came. Suddenly the accuser, who was the devil in disguise, began to quake and groan, and could not answer when the emperor asked what ailed him. But as the woman drew near the judgment seat, he uttered

---

[1] *Dialogus miraculorum*, iii. 2. Similar stories are told in *ibid*. iii. 3, 15, 19.

a horrid howl, exclaiming : " See ! Mary is coming with
the woman, holding her hand." And in a fetid whirlwind
he disappeared. " And thus," says Jacques of Vitry, " the
widow was set free through confession and the Virgin's aid,
and afterwards persevered in the service of God more
cautiously." [1]

Such a tale sounds immoral ; yet there is some good
in saving any soul from hell ; and here there was repentance.
Caesar of Heisterbach has another, of the Virgin taking
the place of a sinning nun in the convent until she repented
and returned. Again repentance and forgiveness make the
sinner whole. [2]

The *Miracles de Nostre Dame* [3] are an interesting
repertory of the Virgin's interventions. These " Mysteries "
or miracle plays in Old French verse are naïve enough in
their kindly stratagems, by which the votary is saved from
punishment in this life and his soul from torment in the
next. The first " Miracle " in this collection runs thus :
A pious dame and her knightly husband, from devotion to
the Virgin Mary took the not unusual vow of married continence. But under diabolic incitement, the knight over-
persuaded his lady, who in her chagrin at the broken vow
devoted the offspring to the devil. A son was born, and in
due time the devil came to claim it. Thereupon a huge
machinery, of pope and cardinals, hermits and archangels,
is set in motion. At last the case is brought before God,
where the devils show cause on one side, and " Nostre
Dame " pleads on the other. Our Lady wins on the
ground that the mother could not devote her offspring to
the devil without the father's consent, which was not
shown.

There is surely no harm in this pleasant drama ; for
the devil ought not to have had the boy. But there follow
quite different " Miracles " of Our Lady. The next one is
typical. An abbess sins with her clerk. Her condition is

---

[1] *Exempla* of Jacques de Vitry, ed. by T. F. Crane, pp. 110-111, vol. 26 (Folk-
lore Society, London, 1890).

[2] *Dialogus miraculorum*, vii. 34. Caesar's seventh book has many similar
tales.

[3] Ed. in eight volumes by Gaston Paris and U. Robert for the Société des
Anciens Textes Français.

observed by the nuns, and the bishop is informed. The
abbess casts herself on the mercy of Mary, who miraculously
delivers her of the child and gives it into the care of a
holy hermit. An examination of the abbess takes place,
after which she is declared innocent by the bishop. But
she is at once moved to repentance, and confesses all to him.
In the bishop's mind, however, the Virgin's intervention
is sufficient proof of the abbess's holiness. He absolves
her, and goes to the hermitage and takes charge of the
child.[1]

Such is an example of the kindly but peculiar miracles,
in which the Virgin saves her friends who turn to her and
repent. Many other tales, quite lovely and unobjectionable,
are told of her: how she keeps her tempted votaries from
sinning, or helps them to repent:[2] or blesses and leads on
to joy those who need no forgiveness. Such a one was the
monk-scribe who illuminated Mary's blessed name in three
lovely colours whenever it occurred in the works he copied,
and then kissed it devoutly. As he lay very ill, having
received the sacraments, another brother saw in vision the
Virgin hover above his couch and heard her say: " Fear
not, son, thou shalt rejoice with the dwellers in heaven,
because thou didst honour my name with such care. Thine
own name is written in the book of life. Arise and come
with me." Running to the infirmary the brother found his
brother dying blissfully.[3]

There are lovely stories too of passionate repentance,
coming unmiraculously to those devoutly thinking on the
Virgin and her infant Son. " For there was once a nun who
forsook her convent and became a prostitute, but returned
after many years. As she thought of God's judgment and
the pains of hell, she despaired of ever gaining pardon ; as
she thought of Paradise, she deemed that she, impure, could
never enter there ; and when she thought upon the Passion,
and how great ills Christ had borne for her and how great
sins she had committed, she still was without hope. But
on the Day of the Nativity she began to think that unto

[1] Étienne de Bourbon tells this same story in his Latin ; *Anecdotes historiques,*
etc., p. 114.
[2] See Étienne de Bourbon, *o.c.* pp. 109-110, 120.
[3] Étienne de Bourbon, *o.c.* p. 119.

us a Child is born, and that children are appeased easily. Before the image of the Virgin she began to think of the Saviour's infancy, and, with floods of passionate tears, besought the Child through the benignity of His childhood to have mercy upon her. She heard a voice saying to her that through the benignity of that childhood which she had invoked, her sins were forgiven." [1]

But enough of these stories. Nor is there need to enlarge upon the relic-worship and other superstitions of the Middle Ages. One sees such matters on every side. It was all a matter of course, and disapprovals were rare. Such conceptions of sin and the devil's part in it affected the morality of clergy as well as laity. The morals of the latter could not rise above those of their instructors ; and the layman's religion of masses, veneration of relics, pilgrimages, almsgiving and endowment of monasteries, scarcely interfered with the cruelty and rapine to which he might be addicted.

[1] Étienne de Bourbon, *o.c.* p. 83.

CHAPTER XXII

THE WORLD OF SALIMBENE

At the close of this long survey of the saintly ideals and actualities of the Middle Ages, it will be illuminating to look abroad over mediaeval life through the half mystic but most observant eyes of a certain Italian Franciscan. The Middle Ages were not characterized by the open eye. Mediaeval Chronicles and *Vitae* rarely afford a broad and variegated picture of the world. As they were so largely the work of monks, obviously they would set forth only what would strike the monastic eye, an eye often intense with its inner vision, but not wide open to the occurrences of life. The monk was not a good observer, commonly from lack of sympathy and understanding. Of course there were exceptions ; one of them was the Franciscan Salimbene, an undeniable if not too loving son of an alert north Italian city, Parma.

Humanism springs from cities ; and it began in Italy long before Petrarch. North of the Alps there was nothing like the city life of Italy, so quick and voluble, so unreticent and unrestrained, open and neighbourly—neighbours hate as well as love ! From Cicero's time, from Numa's if one will, Italian life was what it never ceased to be, urban. The city was the centre and the bound of human intercourse, almost of human sympathy. This was always true ; as true in those devastated seventh, eighth, and ninth centuries as before or after ; certainly true of the tenth and eleventh centuries when the Lombards and other Teuton children of the waste and forest had become good urban Italians. It was still more abundantly true of the following centuries when life was burgeoning with power. Whatever other cause or source of

parentage it had, humanism was a city child.   And as city
life never ceased in Italy, that land had no unhumanistic
period.   There humanism always existed, whether we take
it in the narrower sense of love of humanistic, that is, antique
literature, or take it broadly as in the words of old Menander-
Terence : " homo sum, humani nil a me alienum."

Now turn to the close of the twelfth century, and look at
Francis of Assisi.   It is his humanism and his naturalism,
his interest in men and women, and in bird and beast as well,
that fills this sweet lover of Christ with tender sympathy
for them all.   Through him human interest and love of man
drew monasticism from its cloister, and sent it forth upon
an unhampered ministry of love.   Francis (God bless him !)
had not been Francis, had he not been Francis *of Assisi*.

A certain gifted well-born city child was five years old
when Francis died.   It was to be his lot to paint for
posterity a picture of his world such as no man had painted
before ;   and in all his work no line suggests so many
reasons for the differences between Italy and the lands north
of the Alps, and also so many why Salimbene happened to
be what he was, as this remark, relating to his French tour :
" In France *only the townspeople* dwell in the towns ; the
knights and noble ladies stay in their villas and on their
own domains." [1]

Only the townspeople live in the towns, merchants,
craftsmen, artisans—the unleavened bourgeoisie !   In Lombardy how different !   There knights and nobles, and their
lovely ladies, have their strong dwellings in the towns ;   jostle

---

[1] In *Mon. Germ. Hist. Scriptores*, tome xxxii., Holder - Egger has edited
Salimbene's *Chronica*, with excellent indices (the above citation is from p. 222).
The greater part of the *Chronica* was printed in 1857 in the *Monumenta Historica
ad provincias Parmensem, etc.* The manner of its truncated editing has been a grief
to scholars.   The portions, omitted from the Parma edition, covering years before
Salimbene's time, are printed by Clédat, as an appendix to his Thesis, *De Fr.
Salimbene, etc.* (Paris, 1878).   Novati's article, "La Cronaca di Salimbene" in vol. i.
(1883) of the *Giornale Storico della Letteratura Italiana*, pp. 383-423, will be found
enlightening as to the faults of the Parma editor.   A good consideration of the man
and his chronicle is Emil Michael's *Salimbene und seine Chronik* (Innsbruck, 1889) ;
but Holder-Egger's "Zur Lebensgeschichte des Bruders Salimbene de Adam"
(*Neues Archiv für deutsche Geschichtskunde*, Bd. 37, pp. 163 *sqq.*, 1911, with continuations to follow) may supplant other sources of information.   A short translation
of parts of Salimbene's narrative, by T. L. K. Olyphant, may be found in vol. i. of
the *Translations of the Historical Society*, pp. 449-478 (London, 1872) ; and much
of Salimbene is translated in Coulton's *From St. Francis to Dante* (London, 1907).

with the townspeople, converse with them, intermarry sometimes, lord it over them when they can, hate them, murder
them.   But there they are, and what variety and colour and
picturesqueness and illumination do they not add to city
life ?   If a Lombardy town was thronged with merchants and
craftsmen, it was also gay and voluptuous with knights and
ladies.   How rich and fascinating its life compared with the
grey towns beyond the Alps.   In France the townspeople
made an audience for the Fabliaux !   The Italian town had
also its courtly audience of knight and dame for the love
lyrics of the troubadour, and for the romances of chivalry.
In fact, the whole world was there, and not just workaday,
sorry, parts of it.

Had it not been for the full and varied city life in which
he was born and bred, the quick-eyed youth would not have
had that fund of human interest and intuition which makes
him so pleasant and so different from any one north of the
Alps in the thirteenth century.   A city boy indeed, and
what a full personality !   He was to be a man of human
curiosity, a tireless sight-seer.   His interest is universal ; his
human love quick enough—for those he loved ; for he was
no saint, although a Minorite.   His detestation is vivid,
illuminating ; it brings the hated man before us.   And
Salimbene's wide-open eyes are his own.   He sees with a
fresh vision ; he is himself ; a man of temperament, which
lends its colours to the panorama.   His own interest or
curiosity is paramount with him ; so his narrative will naïvely
follow his sweet will and whim, and pass from topic to topic
in chase of the suggestions of his thoughts.

The result is for us a unique treasure-trove.   The story
presents the world and something more ; two worlds, if you
will, very co-related : *macrocosmos* and *microcosmos*, the
world without and the very eager ego, Salimbene.   There
he is unfailingly, the writer in his world.   Scarcely another
mediaeval penman so naïvely shows the world he moves
about in and himself.   Let us follow, for a little, his autobiographic chronicle, taking the liberty which he always
took, of selecting as we choose.

In the year 1221 Salimbene was born at Parma, into
the very centre of the world of strife between popes and

emperors—a world wherein also the renewed Gospel was
being preached by Francis of Assisi, who did not die till five
years later.   But St. Dominic died the year of Salimbene's
birth.   Innocent III., most powerful of popes, had breathed
his last five years before, leaving surviving him that viper-
nursling of the papacy, Frederick II., an able, much-
experienced youth of twenty-two.   Frederick was afterwards
crowned emperor by Honorius III., and soon showed
himself the most resourceful of his Hohenstaufen line of
arch-enemies to the papacy.   This Emperor Frederick, whom
Innocent III., says Salimbene, had exalted and named
" Son of the Church " . . . " was a man pestiferous and
accursed, a schismatic, heretic, and epicurean, who corrupted
the whole earth." [1]

Salimbene's family was in high regard at Parma, and
the boy naturally saw and perhaps met the interesting
strangers coming to the town.   He tells us that when he
was baptized the lord Balianus of Sydon, a great baron of
France, a retainer of the Emperor Frederick's, " lifted me
from the sacred font."   The mother was a pious dame, whom
Salimbene loved none too well, because once she snatched up
his infant sisters to flee from the danger of the Baptistery
toppling over upon their house during an earthquake, and
left Salimbene himself lying in his cradle !   The father had
been a crusader, and was a man of wealth and influence.

So the youth was born into a stirring swirl of life.
These vigorous northern Italian cities hated each other
shrewdly in the thirteenth century.   When the boy was
eight years old a great fight took place between the folk
of Parma, Modena, and Cremona on the one side, and that
big blustering Bologna.   Hot was the battle.   On the
Carrocio of Parma only one man remained ; for it was
stripped of its defenders by the stones from those novel war-
engines of the Bolognese, called *manganellae*.   Nevertheless
the three towns won the battle, and the Bolognese turned
their backs and abandoned their own *Carrocio*.   The
Cremona people wanted to drag it within their walls ; but
the prudent Parma leaders prevented it, because such action
would have been an insult forever, and a lasting cause of

[1] Parma edition, p. 3 ; *Mon. Germ.* xxxii. p. 31.

war with a strong enemy.   But Salimbene saw the captured
manginellae brought as trophies into his city.

Other scenes of more peaceful rejoicing came before his
eyes ; as in the year 1233, he being twelve years old.
That was a year of alleluia, as it was afterwards called,

" to wit a time of peace and quiet, of joy, jollity and merry-
making, of praise and jubilee ; because wars were over.   Horse
and foot, townsfolk and rustics, youths and virgins, old and young,
sang songs and hymns.   There was such devotion in all the cities
of Italy.   And I saw that each quarter of the city would have its
banner in the procession, a banner on which was painted the
figure of its martyr-saint.   And men and women, boys and girls,
thronged from the villages to the city with their flags, to hear the
preaching, and praise God.   They had branches of trees and
lighted candles.   There was preaching morning, noon, and evening, and *stationes* arranged in churches and squares ; and they
lifted their hands to God to praise and bless Him forever.   Nor
could they cease, so drunk were they with love divine.   There
was no wrath among them, or disquiet or rancour.   Everything
was peaceful and benign ; I saw it with my eyes." [1]

And then Salimbene tells of all the famous preachers, and
the lovely hymns, and Ave Marias ; Frater So-and-so, from
Bologna ; Frater So-and-so from somewhere else ; Minorite
and Preaching friar.

One might almost fancy himself in the Florence of
Savonarola.   Like enough this season of soul outpour and
tears and songs of joy first stirred the religious temper of
this quickly moved youth.   These were also the great days
of dawning for the Friars.   Dominic was not yet sainted ;
yet his Order of the Preaching Friars was growing.   The
blessed Francis had been canonized ;—sainted had he been
indeed before his death !   And the world was turning to
these novel, open, sympathetic brethren who were pouring
themselves through Europe.   Love's mendicancy, envied but
not yet discredited, was before men's eyes and in men's
thoughts ; and what opportunity it offered of helping people,
of saving one's own soul, and of seeing the world !   We can
guess how Salimbene's temper was drawn by it.   We know
at least that one of these friars, Brother Girard of Modena,
who preached at this jubilee in Parma, was the man who

[1] P. 31 ; *Mon. Germ.* p. 70.

made petition five years later for Salimbene, so that the
Minister-General of the Minorites, Brother Elias, being then
at Parma, received the seventeen-year-old boy into the
Order, in the year 1238.

Salimbene's father was frantic at the loss of his heir.
Never while he lived did he cease to lament it. He at once
began strenuous appeals to have his son returned to him.
Salimbene's account of this, exhibits himself, his father, and
the situation.

" He complained to the emperor (Frederick II.), who had come
to Parma, that the brothers Minorites had taken his son from him.
The emperor wrote to Brother Elias that if he held his favour dear,
he should listen to him and return me to my father. Then my
father went to Assisi, where Brother Elias was, and placed in his
hands the emperor's letter, which began : ' In order to mitigate
the sighs of our faithful Guido de Adam,' and so forth. Brother
Illuminatus, Brother Elias's scribe, showed me this letter long
afterwards, when I was with him in the convent at Siena.

" When the imperial letter had been read, Brother Elias wrote
at once to the brethren of the convent at Fano, where I dwelt, that
if I wished it, they should return me to my father without delay ;
but that if I did not wish to go with my father, they should guard
and keep me as the pupil of his eye.

" A number of knights came with my father to Fano, to see the
end of my affair. There was I and my salvation made the centre
of the spectacle. The brethren were assembled, with them of the
world ; and there was much talk. My father produced the letter
of the minister-general, and showed it to the brothers. When it
was read, Brother Jeremiah, who was in charge of me, answered
my father in the hearing of all : ' Lord Guido, we sympathize with
your distress, and are prepared to obey the letter of our father.
Behold, here is your son ; he is old enough ; let him speak for
himself. Ask him ; if he wishes to go with you, let him in God's
name ; if not, we cannot force him.'

" My father asked me whether I wished to go with him or not.
I replied, No ; because the Lord says, ' No one putting his hand to
the plow and looking back is fit for the kingdom of God.'

" And father said to me : ' Thou carest not for thy father and
mother, who are afflicted with many griefs for thee.'

" I replied : ' Truly I do not care, because the Lord says, Who
loveth father or mother more than me is not worthy of me. But
of thee He also says : Who loveth son or daughter more than me
is not worthy of me. Thou oughtest to care, father, for Him who
hung on the cross for us, that He might give us eternal life. For

it is himself who says : I am come to set a man against his father, and the daughter against her mother, and the daughter-in-law against her mother-in-law. And a man's foes are they of his household.'

"The brethren wondered and rejoiced that I said such things to my father. And then my father said : ' You have bewitched and deceived my son, so that he will not mind me. I will complain again of you to the emperor and to the minister-general. Now let me speak with my son apart from you ; and you will see him follow me without delay.'

"So the brothers allowed me to talk with him alone ; for they began to have a little confidence in me, because of my words. Yet they listened behind the wall to what we should say. For they trembled as a reed in water, lest my father should alter my mind with his blandishments. And not for me alone they feared, but lest my return should hinder others from entering the Order.

"Then my father said to me : ' Dear son, don't believe those nasty tunics [1] who have deceived you ; but come with me, and I will give you all I have.'

"And I replied : ' Go away, father. As the Wise Man says in Proverbs, Thou shall not hinder him to do right, who is able.'

"And my father answered with tears, and said to me : ' What then, son, shall I say to thy mother, who is afflicted because of thee ? '

"And I say to him : ' Thou shalt tell her from me ; thus says thy son : My father and mother have forsaken me, and the Lord hath taken me up ; also (Jer. iii.) : Thou shalt call me Father, and walk after me in my steps. . . . It is good for a man when he has borne the yoke from his youth.'

"Hearing all these things my father, despairing of my coming out, threw himself down in the presence of the brethren and the secular folk who had come with him, and said : ' I give thee to a thousand devils, cursed son, thee and thy brother here who has deceived thee. My curse be on you forever, and may it commend you to the spirits of hell.' And he went away excited beyond measure ; while we remained greatly comforted and giving thanks to our God, and saying to each other, ' They shall curse, and thou shalt bless.' Likewise the seculars retired edified at my constancy. The brethren also rejoiced seeing what the Lord had wrought through me, His little boy."

This whole scene presents such a conflict as the thirteenth century witnessed daily, and the twelfth, and other mediaeval centuries as well. The letters of St.

---

[1] The Latin is a little strong : " Non credas istis pissintunicis, idest qui in tunicis mingunt."

Bernard set forth situations quite as extreme or outrageous, from modern points of view. And Bernard can apply (or shall we say, distort ?) Scripture in the same drastic fashion. But these monks meant it deeply ; and from their standpoint they were in the right with their quotations. The attitude goes back to Jerome : that a man's father and mother, and they of his own household, may be his worst enemies, if they seek to hinder his feet set toward God. Of course we can see the sensible, worldly, martial father of the youth leap in the air and roll on the ground in rage ; flesh and blood could not stand such turn of Scripture : Tell my weeping mother (who so longs for me) that I say my father and mother have forsaken me, and the Lord hath taken me up ! This came to the Lord Guido as a maddening gibe ; but Salimbene meant simply that his parents did not care for his highest welfare, and the Lord had received him into the path of salvation. It is all a scene, which should evoke our serious reflections—after which it may be permitted us to enjoy it as we will.

In his conscience Salimbene felt justified ; for a dream set the seal of divine approval on his conduct.

" The Blessed Virgin rewarded me that very night. For it seemed to me that I was lying prostrate in prayer before her altar, as the brothers are wont when they rise for matins. And I heard the voice of the Blessed Virgin calling me. Lifting my face, I saw her sitting above the altar in that place where is set the host and the chalice. She had her little boy in her lap, and she held him out to me, saying : ' Approach without fear and kiss my son, whom yesterday thou didst confess before men.' And when I was afraid, I saw that the little boy gladly stretched out his arms. Trusting his innocence and the graciousness of his mother, I drew near, embraced and kissed him ; and the benign mother gave him to me for a long while. And when I could not have enough of it, the Blessed Virgin blessed me and said : ' Go, beloved son, and lie down, lest the brothers rising from matins find thee here with us.' I obeyed, and the vision disappeared ; but unspeakable sweetness remained in my heart. Never in the world have I had such bliss."

From this we see that Salimbene had sufficient mystic ardour to keep him a happy Franciscan. It made the otherworldly part of one who also was a merry gossip among his fellows. An inner power of spiritual enthusiasm and fantasy accompanied him through his life, giving him a double point of view : he looks at things as they are, with curiosity and interest, and ever and anon loses himself in transcendental dreams of Paradise and all at last made perfect.[1]

Although the father had devoted his son to a thousand devils, he did not cease from attempts, by persuasion and even violence, to draw him back into his own civic and martial world. So the young man got permission from the minister-general to go and live in Tuscany, where he might be beyond the reach of parental activities. " Thereupon I went and lived in Tuscany for eight years, two of them at Lucca, two at Siena, and four at Pisa." He gained great comfort from converse and gossip of an edifying mind, as he fell in with those loving enthusiasts who had received their cloaks from the hand of the blessed Francis himself. At Siena he saw much of Brother Bernard of Quintavalle who had been the very first to receive the dress of the Order from the hand of its founder. Salimbene gladly listened to his recollections of Francis, who in this venerable disciple's words might seem once more to walk the earth.

Yet Salimbene, still young in heart and years, could readily take up with the companionship of the ne'er-do-well vagabonds who frequently attached themselves, as lay brothers, to the Franciscan Order. He tells of a day's outing with one of whose character he is outspoken but without personal repugnance :

" I was a young man when I dwelt at Pisa. One day I went out begging with a certain lay brother, a good-for-nothing. He was a Pisan, and the same who afterwards went and lived with the brothers at Fixulus, where they had to drag him out of a well which he had jumped into from some foolishness or desperation. Then he disappeared, and could not be found. The brothers thought the devil had carried him off. However that may have been, this day at Pisa he and I went with our baskets to beg bread, and chanced to enter a courtyard. Above, all about, hung a thick, leafy vine, its freshness lovely to see and its shade sweet for resting in. There were leopards there and other beasts from over the sea, at which we gazed long, transfixed with delight, as one will at the

[1] These qualities led Salimbene to accept the teachings of Joachim and the *Evangelium eternum* (*post*, pp. 526 *sqq.*).

sight of the novel and beautiful. Girls were there also and boys at their sweetest age, handsome and lovely, and ten times as alluring for their beautiful clothes. The boys and girls held violas and cytharas and other musical instruments in their hands, on which they made sweet melodies, accompanied with gestures. There was no hub-bub, nor did any one talk ; but all listened in silence. And the song which they chanted was so new and lovely in words and melody as to gladden the heart exceedingly. None spoke to us, nor did we say a word to any one. They did not stop singing and playing so long as we were there—and long indeed we lingered and could scarcely take ourselves away. God knows, I do not, who set this joyful entertainment ; for we had never seen anything like it before nor could we ever find its like again."

From the witchery of this cloud-dropped entertainment Salimbene was rudely roused as he went out upon the public way.

" A man met me, whom I did not know, and said he was from Parma. He seized upon me, and began to chide and revile : ' Away scamp, away,' he cried. ' A crowd of servants in your father's house have bread enough and meat ; and you go from door to door begging bread from those without it, when you have enough to give to any number of beggars ! You ought to be riding on a war-horse through Parma, and delighting people with your skill with the lance, so that there might be a sight for the ladies, and comfort for the players. Now your father is worn with grief and your mother from love of you, so she despairs of God.' "

Salimbene fended off this attack of carnal wisdom with many texts of Scripture. Yet the other's words set him to thinking that perhaps it would be hard to lead a beggar's life year after year until old age. And he lay awake that night, until God comforted him as before with a reassuring dream.

Pretty dreamer as he was, Salimbene can often tell a ribald tale. There was rivalry, as may be imagined, between the Dominicans (*solemnes praedicatores*) and the Minorites. The former seem occasionally to have concerted together so as to have knowledge of what their friends in other places were about. Then, when preaching, they would exhibit marvels of second sight, which on investigation proved true ! A certain Brother John of Vicenza was a Dominican famed for preaching and miracles perhaps, and with such overtopping sense of himself that he went at least a little mad. Bologna was his tarrying-place. There a certain Florentine grammarian, Boncompagnus, tired of the foolery, made gibing rhymes about him and his admirers, and said he would do a miracle himself, and at a certain hour would fly with wings from the pinnacle of Sta. Maria in Monte. All came together at that hour to see.   There he stood aloft, with his wings, ready, and the folk expectant, for a long time —and then he bade them disperse with God's blessing, for it was enough for them to have seen him.   They then knew that they had been fooled !

None the less the *dementia* of Brother John increased, so that one day at the Dominican convent in Bologna he fell in a rage because when his beard was cut the brothers did not preserve the hairs as relics.   There came along a Minorite, Brother God-save-you, a Florentine like Boncompagnus, and like him a great buffoon and joker.   To this convent he came, but refused all invitation to stay and eat unless a piece of the cloak of Brother John were given him, which was kept to hold relics.   So they gave him a piece of the cloak, and after dinner he went off and befouled it, folded it up, and called for all to come and see the precious relics of the sainted John, which he had lost in the latrina.   So they flocked to see, and were somewhat more than satisfied.[1]

No need to say that this Salimbene had a quick eye for beauty in both men and women ; he is always speaking of so-and-so as a handsome man, and such and such a lady as " pulcherrima domina," of pleasing ways and moderate stature, neither too tall nor too short.   But one may win a more amusing side-light on the " eternal womanly " in his Chronicle, from the following : " Like other popes, Nicholas III. made cardinals of many of his relatives.   He made a cardinal of one, Lord Latinus, of the Order of Preachers (which we note with a smile, and expect something funny). He appointed him legate to Lombardy and Tuscany and Romagnola."   Note the enactments of this cardinal-legate :

" He disturbed all the women with a ' Constitution ' which he promulgated, to wit, that the women should wear short dresses

---

[1] Parma ed. pp. 37-41. This coarse story is given for illustration's sake ; there are many worse than it in Salimbene. Novati prints some in his article in the *Giornale Storico* that are amusing, but altogether beyond the pale of modern decency.

reaching to the ground, and only so much more as a palm's breadth. Formerly they wore trains, sweeping the earth for several feet (*per brachium et dimidium*).   A rhymer dubs them :

> ' Et drappi longhi, ke la polver menna.'
> (' The long cloaks that gather up the dust.')

"And he had this to be proclaimed in the churches, and imposed it on the women by command ; and ordered that no priest should absolve them unless they complied.   The which was bitterer to the women than any kind of death !   For as a woman said to me familiarly, that train was dearer to her than all the other clothes she wore.   And further, Cardinal Latinus decreed that all women, girls and young ladies, matrons and widows, should wear veils.   Which was again a horror for them.   But they found a remedy for that tribulation, as they could not for their trains.   For they made veils of linen and silk inwoven with gold, with which they looked ten times as well, and drew the eyes of men to lust all the more." [1]

Thus did the cardinal-legate, the Pope's relative.   And plenty of gossip has Salimbene to tell of such creatures of nepotism.   "Flesh and blood *had* revealed " to the Pope that he should make cardinals of them ; says he with a sort of giant sneer ; "for he built up Zion *in sanguinibus*," that is, through his blood-relatives !   "There are a thousand brothers Minorites, more fit, on the score of knowledge and holiness, to be cardinals than they."   Had not another pope, Urban IV., made chief among the cardinals a relation whose only use as a student had been to fetch the other students' meat from market ?

It was a few years after this that Salimbene returned to his native town of Parma, near the time when that city passed from the side of the Emperor to that of the Pope. This was a fatal defection for Frederick, which he set about to repair, by laying siege to the turn-coat city.   And the war went on with great devastation, and the wolves and other wild beasts increased and grew bold.   Salimbene throws Eccelino da Romano on the scene, that regent of the emperor, and monster of cruelty, "who was feared more than the devil," and had once burned to death "eleven thousand Paduans in Verona.   The building holding them was set on fire ; and while they burned, Eccelino and his knights held

---

[1] *Mon. Germ. Hist.* xxxii. p. 169.

a tournament about them (*circa eos*). . . . I verily believe
that as the Son of God desired to have one special friend,
whom He made like to himself, to wit the blessed Francis,
so the devil fashioned Eccelino in his likeness." [1]

Salimbene tells of the siege of Parma at much length,
and of the final defeat of the emperor, with the destruction
of the stronghold which he had built to menace the city,
and of all his curious treasures, with the imperial crown itself
taken by the men of Parma and their allies. But before
this, while the turmoil of the siege was at its height, in 1247,
he received orders to leave Parma and set out for Lyons,
where Innocent IV. at that time held his papal court, having
fled from Italy, from the emperor, three years before.
Setting out, he reached Lyons on All Saints Day.

" At once the Pope sent for me, and talked with me familiarly
in his chamber. For since my leaving Parma he had received
neither messenger nor letters. And he thanked me warmly and
listened to my prayers, for he was a courtly and liberal man ; . . .
and he absolved me from my sins and appointed me preacher ! "

Our autobiographic chronicler was at this time twenty-
six years old ; his personality bespoke a kind reception
everywhere. He soon left Lyons, and went on through the
towns of Champagne to Troyes, where he found plenty of
merchants from Lombardy and Tuscany, for there were
fairs there, lasting two months. So was it also in
Provins, the next halting-place ; from which Salimbene went
on to Paris. There he stayed eight days and saw much
which pleased him ; and then, going back upon his tracks,
he took up his journey to Sens, where he dwelt in the
Franciscan convent, " and the French brethren entertained
me gladly, because I was a friendly, cheerful youth, and
spoke them fair." From Sens he went south to Auxerre,
the place which had been named as his destination when he
left Parma. It was in the year 1248, and as he writes
(how many years after ?) there comes back to him the
memory of the grand wines of Auxerre :

" I remember when at Cremona (in 1245) Brother Gabriel of
that place, a Minorite, a great teacher and a man of holy life, told

---

[1] This in fact became the later legend of Eccelino.

me that Auxerre had more vines and wine than Cremona and Parma and Reggio and Modena together. I wouldn't believe him. But when I came to live at Auxerre, I saw that he spoke the truth. It is a large district, or bishopric, and the mountains, hills, and plains are covered with vines. There they neither sow nor reap nor gather into barns ; but they send their wine by river to Paris, where they sell it nobly ; and live and clothe themselves from the proceeds. Three times I went all about the district with one or another of the brothers ; once with one who was preaching and affixing crosses for the Crusade of the French king (St. Louis) ; then with another who preached to the Cistercians in a most beautiful monastery ; and the third time we spent Easter with a countess, who set before the whole company twelve courses of food, all different. And had the count been at home, there would have been a still greater abundance and variety. Now in four parts of France they drink beer, and in four, wine. And the three lands where the wine is most abundant are La Rochelle, Beaune, and Auxerre. In Auxerre the red wine is least regarded and is not as good as the Italian. But Auxerre has its white or golden wines, which are fragrant and comforting and good, and make every one drinking them feel happy. Some of the Auxerre wine is so strong that when put in a jug, drops appear on the outside (*lacrymantur exterius*). The French laugh and say that three b's and seven f's go with the best wine :

> ' Le vin bon et bel et blanc,
> Fort et fer et fin et franc,
> Freit et fres et fourmijant.'

" The French delight in good wine—no wonder ! since it ' gladdens God and men.' Both French and English are very diligent with their drinking-cups. Indeed the French have blear eyes from drinking overmuch ; and in the morning after a bout, they go to the priest who has celebrated mass and ask him to drop a little of the water in which he has washed his hands into their eyes. But Brother Bartholomew at Provins has a way of saying it would be better for them if they would put their water in their wine instead of in their eyes. As for the English, they take a measure of wine, drink it out, and say : ' I have drunk ; now you '—meaning that you should drink as much. And this is their idea of politeness ; and any one will take it very ill if the other does not follow his precept and example." [1]

---

[1] Parma ed. pp. 90-93 ; *Mon. Germ.* p. 218. In the *Mon. Germ.* edition the verse runs thus :

> " El vin bons e bels et blance,
> Forte e fer e fin e franble,
> Fredo e fras e formigant."

While Salimbene was living at Auxerre, in the year 1248, a provincial Chapter of the Franciscan Order was held at Sens, with the Minister-General, John of Parma, presiding. Thither went Salimbene.

" The King of France, St. Louis, was expected. And the brothers all went out from the house to receive him. And Brother Rigaud,[1] of the Order, Archbishop of Rouen, having put on his pontifical trappings, left the house and hurried toward the king, asking all the time, ' Where is the king ? where is the king ? ' And I followed him ; for he went alone and frantically, his mitre on his head and pastoral staff in hand. He had been tardy in dressing himself, so that the other brothers had gone ahead, and now lined the street, with faces turned from the town, straining to see the king coming. And I wondered, saying to myself, that I had read that these Senonian Gauls once, under Brennus, captured Rome ; now their women seemed a lot of servant girls. If the King of France had made a progress through Pisa or Bologna, the whole élite of the ladies of the city would have met him. Then I remembered the Gallic way, for the mere townsfolk to dwell in the towns, while the knights and noble ladies live in their castles and possessions.

" The king was slender and graceful, rather lean, of fair height, with an angelic look and gracious face. And he came to the church of the brothers Minorites not in regal pomp, but on foot in the habit of a pilgrim, with wallet and staff, which well adorned his royal shoulder. His own brothers, who were counts, followed in like humility and garb. Nor did the king care as much for the society of nobles as for the prayers and suffrages of the poor. Indeed he was one to be held a monk, both on the score of devotion and for his knightly deeds of arms.

" Thus he entered the church of the brethren, with most devout genuflections, and prayed before the altar. And when he left the church and paused at the threshold, I was next to him. And there, on behalf of the church at Sens, the warden presented him with a huge live pike swimming in water in a tub made of firwood, such as they bathe babies in. The pike is dear and highly prized in France. The king returned thanks to the sender as well as to the presenter of the gift. Then he requested audibly that no one, unless he were a knight, should enter the Chapter House, except the brethren, with whom he wished to speak. When we were met in Chapter, the king began to speak of his actions and, devoutly kneeling, begged the prayers and suffrages of the brethren for him-

---

[1] He whose *Regesta* we have read, *ante*, Chapter XXI.

self, his brothers, his lady mother the queen, and all his companions. And certain French brothers, next to me, from devotion and piety wept as if unconsolable. After the king, Lord Oddo, a Roman cardinal, who once was chancellor at Paris, and now was to cross the sea with the king, arose and said a few words. Then on behalf of the Order, John of Parma, the Minister - General, spoke fittingly, promising the prayers of the brethren, and ordaining masses for the king ; which, thereupon, at the king's request he confirmed by a letter under his seal.

" Afterwards, on that day, the king distributed alms and dined with the brethren in the refectory. There were at table his three brothers, a cardinal of the Roman curia, the minister-general, and Brother Rigaud, Archbishop of Rouen, and many brethren. The minister-general, knowing what a noble company was with the king, had no mind to thrust himself forward, although he was asked to sit next the king. So to set an example of courtliness and humility, he sat among the lowest. On that day first we had cherries and then the very whitest bread ; there was wine in abundance and of the best, as befitted the regal magnificence. And after the Gallic custom many reluctant ones were invited and forced to drink. After that we had fresh beans cooked in milk, fish and crabs, eel-pies, rice with milk of almonds and powdered cinnamon, broiled eels with excellent sauce ; and plenty of cakes and herbs, and fruit. Everything was well served, and the service at table excellent.

" The following day the king resumed his journey, and I followed him, as the Chapter was over ; for I had permission to go and stay in Provincia. It was easy for me to find him, as he frequently turned aside to go to the hermitages of the brothers Minorites or some other religious Order, to gain their prayers. And he kept this up continually until he reached the sea and took ship for the Holy Land.

" I remember that one day I went to a noble castle in Burgundy, where the body of the Magdalene was then believed to be. The next day was Sunday ; and early in the morning came the king to ask the suffrages of the brethren. He dismissed his retinue in the castle, from which the house of the brothers was but a little way. The king took his own three brothers, as was his wont, and some servants to take care of the horses. And when genuflections and reverences were duly made, the brothers sought benches to sit on. But the king sat on the earth in the dust, as I saw with my eyes. For that church had no pavement. And he called us, saying : ' Come to me, my sweetest brothers, and hear my words.' And we made a circle about him, sitting with him on the earth ; and his own brothers likewise. And he asked our prayers, as I have been saying. And when promise had been given him, he rose and went his way." [1]

Is not this a picture of St. Louis, pilgrimaging from convent to convent to make sure of the divine aid, and trusting, so far as concerned the business of the Holy Land, quite as much in the prayers of monks as in the deeds of knights ? We have hardly such a vivid sight of him in Joinville or Geoffrey of Beaulieu.[2]

After this scene, the king proceeded on his way, to make ready for his voyage, and Salimbene went to Lyons, then down the Rhone to Arles, then around by sea to Marseilles, and thence to Areae, the present Hyères, which lies near the coast. Here to his joy he met with Brother Hugo of Montpellier whom he was seeking, the great " Joachite," the great clerk, the mighty preacher and resistless disputer, whom he had not forgotten since the days, long before, when he had been in Hugo's company and listened to his preaching at Siena. Even then, Minorites, Dominicans, and all men, had flocked to hear this small dark man, who seemed another Paul, as he descanted on the marvels of Paradise and the contempt one should feel for this world ; but especially those Franciscans delighted in his preaching who were of the " spiritual " party, which sought to follow strictly the injunctions of the blessed Francis, and also cherished the prophesies of Joachim, abbot of Fiore in Calabria, who held to an eternal gospel of the Holy Spirit, which should supplement and finally supplant the letter of the New Testament.

Joachim died in 1202 a devoted adherent of the Church and papacy ; and although there was much loose heresy in his writings, they were not condemned until a storm was blown up by a certain *Introductorius ad Evangelium Aeternum* written by a " spiritual " Franciscan fifty years after the prophet's death. Joachim's genuine writings, as well as those falsely ascribed to him, contained striking prophecies and denunciations of the pride and worldliness of ecclesiastics. Thus they fell in with the enthusiasms of the " spiritual " Franciscans, who still lived in an ecstasy of love

[1] Parma ed. pp. 93-97 ; *Mon. Germ.* pp. 222 *sqq.*
[2] *Post,* Chapter XXIII.

and anticipation ;—in the coming time some of them were
to be dubbed Fratricelli, and under that name be held as
heretics.[1]

John of Parma was, of course, a " Joachite " ; and " I
was intimate with him," says Salimbene, " from love and
because I seemed to believe the writings of Abbot Joachim."
John was likewise a friend (so strong a bond was the belief
in the holy but over-prophetic Joachim) of Hugo of Montpellier, of whose manner and arguments we shall now let
Salimbene speak.

" Once Hugo came from Pisa to Lucca, where the brothers had
invited him to come and preach. He arrived at the hour for
setting out for the cathedral service. And there the whole
convent was assembled to accompany him and do him honour,
and from desire to hear him too. And he wondered, seeing the
brothers assembled outside of the convent door, and said : ' Ah
God ! what are they going to do ? ' The reply was, that they
were there to do him honour, and to hear him. But he said :
' I do not need such honour, for I am not pope. If they wish to
hear, let them come after we have got there. I will go ahead
with one companion, and I will not go with that band.' '

Hugo was worshipped by his admirers, and hated by
those whom he disagreed with or denounced. Aside from
his disputations in defence of Joachim, a sample of which
will be given shortly, one can see what hate must have
sprung from such invective as Salimbene reports him once to
have addressed to a consistory of cardinals at Lyons, where
the Pope then held court. Here is the story, quite too
harsh for the respectable editors of the Parma edition of the
Chronaca :

" The cardinals inquired of Brother Hugo for news (*rumores*).
So he reviled them, as asses, saying : ' I have no news, but a
plenitude of peace in my conscience and before my God, who surpasses sense and keeps my heart and mind in Christ Jesus my
Lord. I know that ye seek after news, and wait idle the live-long

---

[1] In the thirteenth century the spurious writings ascribed to Joachim were
more in vogue than his own compositions. On this much-discussed matter, see
Tocco, *L' Eresia nel medio evo*, pp. 449-483 (Florence, 1884) ; Denifle, " Das Evangelium aeternum," etc., *Archiv für Lit. und Kirchengesch.* i. p. 48 *sqq.* ; Fournier,
" Joachim de Flore," etc., *Revue des questions historiques*, lxvii. (1900), pp. 457
sqq. ; also an article in the *Church Quarterly Review*, vol. lxv. pp. 17-48 ; and the
article by Alphandery in the *Encyclopaedia Britannica*.

day. For ye are Athenians and not disciples of Christ. Of whom
Luke says in the Acts : For all the Athenians and the strangers
which were there had time for nothing else but to tell or hear some
new thing. The disciples of Christ were fishers and weak men
according to the world, but they converted the whole earth
because the hand of the Lord was with them. They set forth
and preached everywhere, the Lord working with them. But ye
are those who build up Zion in blood (*i.e.* consanguinity) and
Jerusalem in iniquity. For you choose your little nephews and
relations for the benefices and dignities of the Church, and you
exalt and make rich your clan, and shut out men good and fit
who would be useful to the Church, and you prebendate children
in their cradles. As a certain mountebank well has said : If
with an accusàtive you would go to the Curia, you'll take nothing
if you don't start with the dative ! And another says, the Roman
Curia cares not for a sheep without wool.' "

And with such like, Hugo continues a considerable space.

" Hearing these things the cardinals were cut to the heart and
gnashed their teeth at him. But they had not the hardihood to
reply ; for the fear of the Lord came over them and the hand of
the Lord was with him. Yet they wondered that he spoke to
them so boldly ; and finally it seemed best to them to slip out and
leave him, nor did they question him, saying, as the Athenians
to Paul : ' We will hear thee again of this matter.' " [1]

Hugo's invective is outdone by Salimbene's closing scorn.

And now (to return to Salimbene's journey) here at
Hyères in the year 1248 many notaries and judges, and
physicians and other men of learning, were assembled to
hear Brother Hugo speak of the Abbot Joachim's doctrines,
and expound Holy Scripture, and predict the future. " And
I was there to hear him ; for long before I had been instructed
in these teachings." But there came two Preaching friars,
and abode at the Franciscan house, since the Dominicans
had no convent at Hyères. One was Brother Peter of
Apulia, a learned man and a great speaker. After dinner a
brother asked him what he thought of Abbot Joachim. He
answered : " I care as much for Joachim as for the fifth
wheel of a coach."

Thereupon this brother hurried to Hugo's chamber, and
exclaimed in the presence of all the notables there : " Here

[1] From Novati, *o.c.* pp. 415, 416 ; *Mon. Germ.* pp. 226 *sqq.* Cf. pp. 97 *sqq.* of
the Parma ed.

is a brother Preacher who does not believe that doctrine at all."

To whom Brother Hugo: " And what is it to me if he does not believe ? Be it laid at his door ; he will see it when trouble shall enlighten him. Yet call him to debate ; let us hear of what he doubts."

So, called, he came, very unwillingly, because he held Joachim so cheaply, and besides thought there was no one in that house fit to dispute with him. When Brother Hugo saw him he said : " Art thou he who doubts the doctrine of Joachim ? "

Brother Peter replied : " Indeed I am."

Then said Brother Hugo: " Hast thou ever read Joachim ? "

Replied Brother Peter : " I have read and well read."

To whom Hugo : " I believe thou hast read as a woman reads the Psalter, who does not remember at the end what she read at the beginning. Thus many read and do not understand, either because they despise what they read, or because their foolish heart is darkened. Now, therefore, tell me what thou wouldst hear as to Joachim, so that we may better know thy doubts."

Thereupon there is question back and forth regarding the Scripture proofs of Joachim's prophecies, for instance, those supposed to relate to Frederick's reign. Brother Hugo dilates on Joachim's holiness ; explains the dark Scripture references, and brings in the prophecies of Merlin, *anglicus vates,* and talks of the allegorical, anagogical, tropological, moral and mystical, senses of Scripture. The discussion waxes hot. Peter begins to beat about the bush (*discurrere per ambages*), and declares it to be heretical to quote an infidel like Merlin. At which Hugo answers : " Thou liest, as I will prove *multipliciter* ; for the writings of Balaam, Caiaphas, Merlin, and the Sybil are not spurned by the Church : ' The rose gives forth no thorn, although the thorn's daughter.' " [1]

Peter then turns to the sayings of the saints and the philosophers. But as Hugo was *doctissimus* in these, he at

---

[1] For further interesting allusions to the prophecies of Merlin, see pp. 303, 309 *sqq.* Parma ed. and the index to the *Mon. Germ.* volume.

once twists him up and finishes him (*statim involvit eum et conclusit ei*). Hereupon Peter's brother Preacher, an old priest and a good, sought to come to his aid. But Peter said, " Peace, be still." For Peter knew himself vanquished, and began to praise Brother Hugo for his manifold wisdom.

" At this moment came a messenger from the ship's captain, bidding the brothers Preachers hurry, and go aboard. When they had left, Brother Hugo said to the learned men remaining, who had heard the debate : ' Take it not for evil, if we have said some things which ought not to have been said ; for disputants often roam the fields of licence. Those good men glory in their knowledge, and say that in their Order is found the fount of wisdom, which is the Word of God. They also say that they travel among simple folk when they pass through the places of the brothers Minorites, where they are ministered to with loving charity. But by the grace of God these two shall no longer be able to say they have walked among the simple.'

" His auditors dispersed, edified and comforted, saying, We have heard wonderful things to-day. Later, that same day, the brothers Preachers returned, to our delight, for the weather proved unfit for sailing. After dinner, Brother Hugo conversed with them familiarly, and Brother Peter sat himself on the earth at Brother Hugo's feet ; nor was any one able to make him rise and sit on the bench on the same level with him, not even when Brother Hugo himself besought him. So Brother Peter, no longer disputing or contradicting, but meekly listening, heard honied words spoken by Brother Hugo, and worthy to be set down, but omitted here for brevity's sake, as I hasten to record other things." [1]

So Salimbene passes on, both in his Chronicle and in his journey, but though his steps lead deviously through the cities of Provence, they bring him back once more to Hyères and Hugo, at whose feet he sits and listens for a season in rapt admiration.

After this happy season, Salimbene returned to Genoa, and from that time on spent his life among the Franciscan brotherhoods of Italy. Henceforth his Chronicle is chiefly occupied with those wretched unceasing wars of northern Italy, Imperialists against Papists, and city against city— and with the affairs of the Franciscan Order. The story is

---

[1] Pp. 104-109, Parma ed. ; *Mon. Germ.* pp. 239 *sqq.*

now less varied, yet not lacking in picturesque qualities ; and
through it all we still see the man himself, although the
man, as life goes on, seems to become more of a Franciscan
monk, and less of an observer of human life.   But he continues naïve.   Thus he tells that one time, with some
companions, he came to Bobbio, that famous book-lovers'
foundation of St. Columban, in the mountains north of
Genoa : " and there we saw one of those water-pots of the
Lord, in which the Lord made wine from water at the
marriage at Cana, for it is said to be one of those : whether
it is, God knows, to whom all things are known and open
and naked."

And again, some one brings him news of the state of
France in the year 1251, when King Louis was a captive in
Africa ; [1] and thus he tells it :

" In this year a countless crowd of shepherds came together in
France, saying that they would cross the sea to kill the Saracens
and free the King of France.   Many followed from divers cities of
France, and no one dared stop them.   For their leader said it
was revealed to him of God that he must lead that multitude
across the sea to avenge the King of France.   The common folk
believed him, and were enraged against the religious, especially
the Preachers, because they had preached the Crusade and had
' crossed ' men who were sailing with the king.   And the people
were angry at Christ, so that they dared blaspheme His blessed
name.   And when the Minorites and Preachers came seeking
alms in His name, they gnashed their teeth at them and in their
sight turned and gave the sou to some other beggar, saying, ' Take
this in Mahomet's name, who is stronger than Christ.' " [2]

Of those Italian wars—rather feuds, vengeances, and
monstrosities of hate—Salimbene can tell enough.   He
gives a ghastly picture of the fate of Alberic da Romano,
brother of Eccelino, and tyrant indeed of Treviso.

" There he lorded it for many years ; and cruel and hard was
his rule, as those know who experienced it.   He was a limb of the
devil and a son of iniquity, but he perished by an evil death with
his wife and sons and daughters.   For those who slew them tore
off the legs and arms from their living bodies, in their parents'
sight, and with them struck the parents' faces.   Then they bound
the wife and daughters to stakes, and burned them ; they were

---

[1] Cf. Joinville's account, *post*, p. 562.   [2] P. 225, Parma ed.

noble, beautiful virgins, nor in any way in fault. But their innocence and beauty did not save them, because of the hatred for the father and mother. Terribly had these afflicted the people of Treviso. So they came upon Alberic with tongs and ——"—

the sentence is too horrid for translation. But the chronicler goes on to tell that they destroyed his body amid gibes and insults and torments.

" For he had killed a blood-relative of this one, and that one's father, son or daughter. And he had laid such taxes and exactions on them, that they had to destroy their houses. The very walls and beams and chests and cupboards and wine-vats they put in boats and sent to Ferrara to sell them and redeem themselves. I saw those with my eyes. Alberic pretended to be at war with his brother Eccelino, so as to do his evil deeds more safely ; and he did not hold his hand from the slaughter of citizens and subjects. One day he hanged twenty-five prominent men of Treviso, who had done him no ill ; because he feared they would ! And thirty noble women, mothers, wives and daughters of these, were brought there to see them hanging ; and he had these women stripped half naked, that those who were hanging might see them so. The men were hanged quite close to the ground ; and he forced these women to go so close that their faces were struck by the legs and feet of those who were dying in anguish." [1]

Such was the kind of devil-madness that might walk abroad in Italy in the Middle Ages. Let us relieve our minds by a story our friend tells of a certain boy placed in a Franciscan convent in Bologna, to become a monk.

" When asleep he snored so mightily, that no one could have peace in the same house with him, so horribly did he disturb those who slept as well as those who were at their vigils. And they made him sleep in the shed where wood and staves were stored, but even then the brothers could not escape, so did that voice of malediction resound through the whole place. And all the priests and wise-acres among the brothers met in the director's chamber, to eject him from the Order because of his insupportable offence : I was there. It was decided to return him to his mother, who had deceived the Order, since she had known his defect before letting him go. But he was not returned to his mother, for the Lord performed a miracle through Brother Nicolas [a holy brother through whom God had worked other miracles as well]. This

---

[1] Pp. 179, 180, Parma ed. ; *Mon. Germ.* pp. 363 *sqq.*

brother seeing that the boy was to be expelled for no fault, but for a natural defect, called him at daybreak to assist at mass. When the mass was finished, the boy as commanded knelt before him, back of the altar, hoping to receive some grace. Brother Nicolas touched his face and nose with his hands, in the wish to confer health upon him, if the Lord would grant it, and commanded him to keep this secret. What more ? The boy at once was cured, and after that slept as quietly as a dormouse without annoying any brother." [1]

Thus we have this Chronicle, rambling, incoherent, picturesque, with its glimpses of all this pretty world, for which our Salimbene, despite his cowl, has an uncloistered eye—its keenness for incident and circumstance undeflected by the inner sight with which it could also look on the invisible world. When Brother Salimbene was young and an enthusiastic Joachite, a strong motive of his wish to live on in the flesh was to see whether those prophecies regarding Frederick came true. Alas ! for this purpose he lived too long : Frederick died before the prophecies were fulfilled, and with his death honest Salimbene had to put from him his darling trust in the words of Abbot Joachim.

[1] P. 324, Parma ed.; p. 558, *Mon. Germ.*

BOOK IV

THE IDEAL AND THE ACTUAL: SOCIETY

CHAPTER XXIII

FEUDALISM AND KNIGHTHOOD

FEUDAL AND CHRISTIAN ORIGIN OF KNIGHTLY VIRTUE; THE ORDER OF THE TEMPLE; GODFREY OF BOUILLON; ST. LOUIS; FROISSART'S *CHRONICLES*

THE world is evil! the clergy corrupt, the laity depraved! none denounces them! Awake! arise! be mindful! Such ceaseless cry rises more shrilly in times of reform and progress. It was the cry of the preacher in the twelfth and thirteenth centuries, when preaching was reviving with the general advance of life.[1]

Satire and pious invective struck at all classes : kings, counts and knights, merchants, tradesmen, artisans, even villain-serfs, came under its lash.[2] And properly, since every class is touched with universal human vices, besides those which are more peculiar to its special way of life. All men fall below the standards of the time ; and each

---

[1] See Bourgain, *La Chaire française au XII⁶ siècle*; Lecoy de la Marche, *La Chaire française au XIII⁶ siècle.*

[2] Certain kinds of literature, in nature satirical or merely gross, portray, doubtless with grotesque exaggeration, the ways and manners of clerks and merchants, craftsmen and vile serfs, as well as those of monks and bishops, lords and ladies. A notable example is offered by the old French *fabliaux*, which with coarse and heartless laughter, rather than with any definite satirical intent, display the harshness, brutality, the degradation and hardship of the ways of living coming within their range of interest. In them we see the brutal and deceived husband, the wily clerk, the merchant with his tricks of trade, the *vilain*, raised above the brute, not by a better way of life as much as by a certain native wit. The women were reviled as coarsely as in monkish writings ; but a Rabelaisian quality takes the place of doctrinal prurience. In weighing the evidence of these fabliaux their satirical nature should be allowed for. Cf. Langlois, *La Vie en France au moyen âge d'après quelques moralistes du temps* (Paris, 1908) ; also the *Sermons* of Jacques de Vitry ; Pitra, *Analecta novissima spicilegii Solesmensis*, t. ii., and generally J. Bedier, *Les Fabliaux* (Paris, 1895).

class fails with respect to its own ideals. The special shortcomings are most apparent with those classes whose ideals
are most definitely formulated.

Among the laity the gap between the ideal and the
actual may best be observed in the warrior class whose
ideals accorded with the feudal situation and tended to
express themselves in chivalry. Not that knights and
ladies were better or worse than other mediaeval men and
women. But literature contains clearer statements of their
ideals. The knightly virtues range before us as distinctly
as the monastic; and harsh is the contrast between the
character they outline and the feudal actuality of cruelty
and greed and lust. Feudalism itself presents everywhere
a state of contrast between its principles of mutual fidelity
and protection, and its actuality of oppression, revolt, and
private war.

The feudal system was a sprawling conglomerate fact.
The actual usages of chivalry (the term is loose and must
be allowed gradually to define itself) were one expression of
it, and varied with the period and country. But chivalry
had its home also in the imagination, and its most interesting
media are legend and romantic fiction. Still, much that
was romantic in it sprang from the aggregate of law,
custom, and sentiment, which held feudal society together.
Chivalry was the fine flower of honour growing from this
soil, embosomed in an abundant leafage of imagination.

The feudal system was founded on relations and
sentiments arising from a state of turbulence where every
man needed the protection of a lord: it could not fail to
foster sentiments of fealty. The fief itself, the feudal unit
of land held on condition of homage and service, symbolized
the principle of mutual troth between lord and vassal. The
land was part of mother earth; the troth, the elemental
personal tie, existed from of yore. In this instance it came
from the German forests. But the feudal system of land
tenure also stretched its roots back into the rural institutions
of the disintegrating Roman Empire. In the fifth century,
for example, when what was left of the imperial rule could
no longer enforce order, and provincial governments were
decaying with the decay of the central power from which

they drew their life, men had to look about them for protection. It became customary for men to hand over land and liberty to some near lord, and enter into a relationship akin to serfage in return for protection. Thus the Gallo-Roman population were becoming accustomed to personal dependence even while the Merovingians were establishing their kingdom.

On their side the Franks and other Teutons had inherited the institution of the *comitatus*, which bound the young warrior to his chief. They were familiar with exacting modes of personal retainership, which merged the follower's freedom in his lord's will. If during the reigns of Pepin and his prodigious son the development of local dominion and dependence was held in some abeyance, on the death of Charlemagne it would proceed apace. All the factors which tend to make institutions out of abuses and the infractions of earlier custom, sprang at once into activity in the renewed confusion. Everything served to increase the lesser man's need of defence, weld his dependence on his lord, and augment the latter's power. Moreover, long before Charlemagne's time, not only for protection in this life, but for the sake of their souls, men had been granting their lands to monasteries and receiving back the use thereof—such usufruct being known as a *beneficium*. This custom lent the force of its example and manifest utility to the relations between lay lords and tenants. And finally one notes the frequent grant to monasteries and individuals of immunity from governmental visitation, a grant preventing the king's officers from entering lands in order to exercise the king's justice, or exact fines and requisitions.[1]

From out of such conditions the feudal system gradually took form. Its central feature was the tenure of a fief by a vassal from his lord on condition of rendering faithful military and other not ignoble service. By the tenth century fiefs had become hereditary. So long as the vassal fulfilled his duty to his lord, the rights of the lord over the land were nominal ; more substantial was the mutual obligation— on the part of the lord to protect his vassal against the

---

[1] Such immunities were common before Charlemagne. **Cf.** Brunner, *Deutsche Rechtsgeschichte*, ii. 243-302.

violence of others, and on the vassal's part to make good the
homage pledged by him when he knelt and placed his hands
within his lord's hands and vowed himself his lord's man
for the fief he held. His duty was to aid his lord against
enemies, yield him counsel and assistance in the judgment
of causes, and pay money to ransom him from captivity,
knight his eldest son, or portion his daughter. The
ramifications of these feudal tenures and obligations extended, with all manner of complications, from king and
duke down to such as held the meagre fief that barely kept
man and war-horse from degrading labour. All these made
up the feudal class whose members might expect to become
knights on reaching manhood.

Neither this system of land tenure, nor the sentiments
and relations sustaining it, drew their origin from Christianity.
But the Church was mighty in its influence over the secular
relationships of those who came under its spiritual guidance.
Feudal troth was to become Christianized. The old regard
for war-chief and war-comrade was to be broadened through
the Faith's solicitude for all believers ; then it was raised
above the human sphere to fealty toward God and His
Church ; and thereupon it was gentled through Christian
meekness and mercy.

This Christianized spirit of fealty, broadening to
courtesy and pity, was to take visible form in a universal
Order into which members of the feudal class were admitted
when their valour had been proved, and into which brave
deeds might bring even a low-born man. Gradually, as the
Order's *regula*, a code of knighthood's honour was developed,
valid in its fundamentals throughout western Christendom ;
but varying details and changing fancies from time to time
intruded, just as subsequent phases of monastic development were grafted on the common Benedictine rule.

Investing a young warrior with the arms of manhood
has always in fighting communities been the normal
ceremony of the youth's coming of age and his recognition
as a member of the clan. The binding on of the young
Teuton's sword in the assembly of his people was an
historical antecedent of the making of a knight. In all the
lands of western Europe—France, Germany, Anglo-Saxon

England, Lombard Italy, and Visigothic Spain—this ceremony appears to have remained a simple one through the ninth and tenth centuries. As for the eleventh, one may note the following passages : William of Malmesbury (d. 1142 cir.) speaks of William of Normandy receiving the insignia of knighthood (*militiae insignia*) from the King of France as soon as his years permitted.[1] Henry of Huntington (d. 1155) says that this same William the Conqueror, in the nineteenth year of his reign, invested his younger son Henry with the arms of manhood (*virilibus induit armis*) ; while another chronicler says that Prince Henry : " sumpsit arma in Pentecostem "—a festival at which it was customary to make knights. And again, Ordericus Vitalis says of the armour-bearer of Duke William that after five years' service he was by that same duke regularly invested with his arms and made a knight (*decenter est armis adornatus et miles effectus*).

These short references [2] do not indicate the nature of the ceremony. But one notes the use of the Latin words *miles* and *militia* as meaning knight and knighthood. Like so many other classical words, *miles* took various meanings in the Middle Ages. But it came commonly to signify knight, chevalier, or ritter.[3] And whatever other meanings *militia* and *militare* retained or acquired, they signified knighthood and the performance of its duties. Frequently they suggested the relationship of vassal to a lord : and in this sense *miles* meant one who held a fief under the obligation to do knightly service in return.

But how did this word *miles* (which in classical Latin meant a soldier and sometimes specifically a foot-soldier as contrasted with an *eques*) come to mean a knight ? It was first applied to the warriors of the various Teutonic peoples, who for the most part fought on foot. But the wars with the Saracens in the eighth century appear to have made clear the need of a large and efficient corps of horse. From the time of Charles Martel the warrior class began to fight

---

[1] *Gesta regum Anglorum*, iii. (Migne 179, col 1213).

[2] Taken from the note to p. 274 of Gautier's *Chevalerie*.

[3] See Du Cange, *Glossarium*, under " Miles," etc. ; where much information may be found uncritically put together.

regularly on horseback ; [1] and thus, apparently, the term *miles* began to signify primarily one of these tried and well-armed riders.[2] Such were the very ones who would regularly be invested with their arms on reaching manhood. Many of them had inherited the sentiments of fealty to a chief, and probably were vassals of some lord from whom they had received lands to be held on military tenure. They were not all noble (an utterly loose term with reference to these early confused centuries) nor were they necessarily free (another inappropriate term with respect to these incipiently mediaeval social conditions).[3] But their mainly military duties would naturally develop into a retainer's relationship of fealty.

The ninth century passes into the tenth, the tenth into the eleventh, the eleventh into the twelfth. Classes and orders of society become more distinct. The old warrior groups have become lords and vassals, and compose the feudal class whose members upon maturity are formally girt with the arms of manhood, and thereupon become knights. The ceremony of their investiture has been gradually made more impressive ; it has also been imbued with religious sentiment and elaborated with religious rite. It now constitutes the initiation to a universally recognized fighting Order which has its knightly code of honour, if not its knightly duties. In a word, along with the clearer determination of its membership, and the elaboration of the ceremonies of entry or " adoubement," knighthood has become a distinct conception and has attained existence as an Order. And an Order it remains, into which one is

---

[1] Cf. Brunner, *Deutsche Rechtsgeschichte*, ii. 202-216.

[2] The way that *miles* came to mean knight has its analogy in the etymological history of the word " knight " itself. In German and French the words " Ritter " and " chevalier " indicate one who fought on horseback. Not so with the English word " knight," which in its original Anglo-Saxon and Old-German forms (see Murray's *Dictionary*) as *cniht* and *kneht* might mean any armed follower. It lost its servile sense slowly. " In 1086 we read that the Conqueror *dubbade his sunu Henric to ridere* ; this . . . is the next year Englished by *cniht* " (Kington-Oliphant, *Old and Middle English*, p. 130 ; Macmillan, 1878).

[3] We naturally use the term " free " with reference to modern conditions, where law and its sanctions emanate, in fact as well as theory, from a stable government. But in these early feudal periods where a man's life and property were in fact and theory protected by the power of his immediate lord, to whom he was bound by the strongest ties then recognized, to be " free " might be very close to being an unprotected outlaw.

admitted, but into which no one is born, though he be hereditary king or duke or count. Moreover, although the candidates normally would be of the feudal class, the Order is not closed against knightly merit in whomsoever found.[1] Of course there was no written *regula* or charter, except of certain special Orders. Yet there was no uncertainty as to who was or was not a knight.

A knight could be " made " or " dubbed " at any time, for example, on the field of battle or before the fight. But certain festivals of the Church, Christmas, Easter, and Pentecost, came to be regarded as peculiarly appropriate for the ceremony. Any knight, but no unknighted person however high his rank, could " dub " another knight.[2] This appears to have been the universal rule, and yet it suffered infringements. For example, at a late period a king might claim the right to *confirm* the bestowal of knighthood, which in fact commonly was bestowed by a great lord or sovereign prince. On its negative side, the general rule may be said to have been infringed when Church dignitaries, no longer content with blessing the arms of the young warrior, usurped the secular privilege of investing him with them and dubbing him a knight.[3]

The ceremony itself probably originated in the girding on of the sword. As these warriors in time changed to mounted riders with elaborate arms and armour, it became more of an affair to invest them fully with their equipment. There would be the putting on of helm and coat of mail, and there would be the binding on of spurs ; and at some time it became customary for the youth to prepare himself by a bath. But girding on the sword was still the important point, although perhaps the somewhat enigmatical blow, given by him who conferred the dignity, and not to be returned (*non repercutiendus*), became the finish to the ceremony. That blow existed (we find it in the *Chansons de geste*) in the twelfth century as a thwack with the fist on

---

[1] In these respects it exhibits analogies to monkhood, which likewise was recruited commonly from the upper classes of society.

[2] See Gautier, *La Chevalerie*, p. 256 *sqq.* ; Du Cange, under the word " Miles."

[3] Cf. Gautier, *o.c.* 296-308. It must be remembered that an abbot or a bishop might also be a knight and so could make knights. See Du Cange, *Glossarium*, " Abbas " (*abbates miletes*).

the young man's bare neck; then in course of years it refined itself into a gentle sword-tap on the mailed shoulder.[1]

At an early period the Church sought to sanctify the ceremony through religious rites; for it could not remain unconcerned with the consecration of the warriors of Christendom, whose services were needed and whose souls were to be saved. What time so apt for inculcating obedience and other Christian virtues as this solemn hour when the young warrior's nature was stirred with the pride and hopes of knighthood? And the young knight needed the Church's blessing. Heathen peoples sought in every enterprise the protection of their gods, usually obtained through priestly magic. And when converted to the faith of Christ, should they not call on Him who was mightier than Odin? Should not His power be invoked to shield the Christian knight? Will not the sword which the priest has blessed and has laid upon Christ's miracle-working altar, more surely guard the wearer's life? Better still if there be blessed relics in its hilt. The dying Roland speaks to his great sword :

"O Durendel cum ies bele et seintisme ! "

"O Durendel how art thou fair and holy! In thy hilt what store of relics : tooth of St. Peter, blood of St. Basil, hairs of my lord St. Denis, cloth worn by the Holy Mary." [2] These relics made the " holiness " of that sword, not in the way of sentiment, but through their magic power. And we shall not be thinking in mediaeval categories if we lose sight of the magic-religious effect of the priest's blessing on the novice's sword : it is a protection for the future knight.

Doubtless the religious features of the " adoubement " revert to various epochs. The ancient watch-nights preceding Easter and Pentecost, followed at daybreak by the baptism of white-robed catechumens, may have been the original of the novice's night vigil over his arms laid by the altar. His bath had become a symbol of purification from

---

[1] On this blow, called in Latin *alapa*, in French *accolée*, in English *accolade*, see Du Cange under " Alapa," and Gautier, *o.c.* pp. 246-247, and 270 *sqq.*

[2] *Chanson de Roland*, 2344 *sqq.* Lines 2500-2510 speak of Charlemagne's sword, named *Joiuse* because of the honour it had in having in its hilt the iron of the lance which pierced the Saviour.

sin. He heard Mass in the early morning, and then came the blessing of the sword, the *benedictio ensis*, of which the oldest extant formula is found in a Roman manuscript of the early eleventh century : " Exaudi, quaeso, Domine, preces nostras, et hunc ensem quo hic famulus N. se circumcingi desiderat, majestatis tuae dextera benedicere dignare." [1]

Through the Middle Ages the fashions of feudalism did not remain unchanged ; likewise its quintessential spirit, chivalry, was modified, and one may say, between the ninth and the fourteenth centuries, passed from barbarism to preciosity. Nevertheless the main ideals of chivalry endured, springing as they did from the fundamental and but slowly-changing conditions of feudal society. Since that society was constantly at war,[2] the first virtue of the knight was valour. Next, since life and property hung on mutual aid and troth, and a larger safety was ensured if one lord could rely upon his neighbour's word, the virtues of truth-speaking and troth-keeping took their places in the chivalric ideal. Another useful quality, and means of winning men, was generosity (*largesse*). When coin is scarce, and stipulations for fixed pay unusual, he who serves looks for liberality, which, in accordance with feudal conditions, made the third of the chief knightly virtues.

Valour, troth, largesse, had no necessary connection with Christianity. It was otherwise with certain of the

---

[1] Gautier, *Chevalerie*, pp. 290, 297. Examples of these ceremonies may be found as follows : the actual one of the knighting of Geoffrey Plantagenet of Anjou by Henry I. of England, at Rouen in 1129, in the Chronicle of Johannis Turonensis, *Historiens de France*, xii. p. 520 ; Gautier, *Chevalerie*, p. 275. Gautier gives many examples, and puts together a typical ceremony, as of the twelfth century, in *Chev.* p. 309 *sqq.* Perhaps the most famous account of all is that of the poem entitled *Ordene de Chevalerie* (thirteenth century), published by Barbazan, *Fabliaux, etc.*, i. 59-82 (Paris, 1808). It relates how a captive Christian knight bestowed the order of chivalry, *i.e.* knighthood, upon Saladin. See other accounts cited in Du Cange under " Miles."

[2] Not war as we understand it, where with some large purpose one great cohesive state directs its total military power against another ; but neighbourhood war, never permanently ended. When not actually attacking or defending, men were anticipating attack, or expecting to make a raid. Perhaps nothing better suggests the local and neighbourly character of these feudal hostilities than the most famous means devised by the Church to mitigate them. This was the " Truce of God," promulgated in the eleventh century. It forbade hostilities from Thursday to Monday and in certain holy seasons of the year. Whether this ordinance was effective or not, it indicates the nature of the wars that could stop from Thursday to Monday !

remaining qualities of a knight. According to Christian
teaching, pride was the deadliest of sins. So haughtiness,
boasting, and vain-glory were to be held vices by the
Christian knight. He should show a humble demeanour,
save toward the mortal enemies of God ; and far from
boasting, he should rather depreciate himself and his
exploits, though never lowering the standard of his purpose
to achieve. Humility entered knighthood's ideal from
Christianity ; and so perhaps did courtesy, its kin, a virtue
which was not among the earliest to enter knighthood's
ideal, and yet reached universal recognition.

Christianity also meant active charity, beneficence, and
love of neighbour. These are virtues hard to import into a
state of war. Fighting means harm-doing to an enemy ;
and only indirectly makes for some one's good. Let there
be some vindication of good in the fighting of a Christian
knight : he shall be quick to right the wrong, succour
distress, and quickest to bear help where no reward can
come. Since knighthood's ideals took form in crusading
times, the slaughter of the Paynim became the supreme act
of knightly warfare.

If such elements of the knightly ideal were of Christian
origin, others still were even more closely part of mediaeval
Christianity. First of these was faith, orthodox faith,
heresy-uprooting, infidel-destroying, *fides* in the full Church
sense. Without faith's sacramental credentials—baptism,
participation in the mass—no one could be a knight : and
heresy degrades the recreant even before the scullion's
cleaver hacks off his spurs.

From faith knighthood advances to obedience to the
Church, a vow expressly made by every knight on taking
the Cross, and also incorporated in the Constitutions of the
crusading Orders of Templars and Hospitallers. But does
the knight pass on from obedience to chastity ? This virtue
might or might not enter knighthood's ideal. It scarcely
could exist with courtly or chivalric love ; [1] and, in fact,
knights commonly were either lovers or married men—or

[1] Courtly, chivalric, or romantic, love as an element of knightly excellence
is so inseverably connected with its romantic literature that I have kept it for
the next chapter.

both. Yet even in the Arthurian literature there is the monkish Galahad, and many a sinful knight becomes a hermit in the end ; and among real and living knights, the Templars and Hospitallers were vowed to celibacy. In these crusading orders the orbits of knighthood and monasticism cross ; and it will not be altogether a digression to review the foundation and constitution of one of them.

The Order of the Temple was founded in the year 1118 by Hugh of Payns (Champagne) and other French knights ; who placed their hands within those of the Patriarch of Jerusalem, and vowed to devote themselves to the protection of pilgrims in the Holy Land. Probably they also bestowed their lands for the support of the nascent Order. Ten years afterwards Hugh passed through France and England, winning new recruits and appearing at the Council of Troyes. With the authority of that Council and of Pope Honorius II. the *Regula pauperum commilitonum Christi Templique Salomonici* was promulgated. St. Bernard, to whom it is ascribed, was in large part its inspiration and its author. It still exists in some seventy-two chapters ; but one cannot distinguish between those belonging to the original document of 1128 and those added somewhat later.[1]

This *regula* with its amendments and additions was translated from Latin into Old French (*par excellence* the tongue of the Crusades), and became apparently the earliest form of the *Regle dou Temple*, upon which was grafted a mass of ordinances (*retrais et establissemens*). Apparently the whole of the extant Latin *regula* was prior to everything contained in the French *regle* ; and accordingly we shall simply regard the Latin as containing the earliest regulations of the Temple, and the French as exhibiting the modifications of tone and interest which came in the course of years.

The hand of St. Bernard ensured the dominance of the monastic temper in the original *regula* ; and Hugo, the first Master of the Temple, could not have been the Saint's close

[1] The following remarks upon the *regula* of the Templars, and the extracts which are given, are based on the introduction and text of *La Règle du Temple*, edited by Henri de Curzon for the Société de l'Histoire de France (Paris, 1886).

friend without sharing his enthusiasms. So the prologue opens with a true monastic note :

" Our word is directed primarily to all who despise their own wills, and with purity of mind desire to serve under the supreme and veritable King ; and with minds intent choose the noble warfare of obedience, and persevere therein. We therefore exhort you who until now have embraced secular knighthood (*miliciam secularem*) where Christ was not the cause, and whom God in His mercy has chosen out of the mass of perdition for the defence of the holy Church, to hasten to associate yourselves perpetually."

This phraseology would suit the constitution of a sheer monastic order. And the first chapter exhorts these *venerabiles fratres* who renounce their own wills and serve the King (Christ) with horses and arms, zealously to observe all the religious services regularly prescribed for monks. The *regula* contains the usual monastic commands. For example, obedience to the Master of the Order is enjoined *sine mora* as if God were commanding, which recalls the language of St. Benedict.[1] Clothes are regulated, and diet ; habitual silence is recommended ; the brethren are not to go alone, nor at their own will, but as directed by the Master, so as to imitate Him who said, I came not to do mine own will, but His who sent me.[2] Again, chests with locks are forbidden the brothers, except under special permission ; nor may any brother, without like permission, receive letters from parents or friends ; and then they should be read in the Master's presence.[3] Let the brethren shun idle speech, and above all let no brother talk with another of military exploits, " follies rather," achieved by him while " in the world," or of his doings with miserable women.[4] Let no brother hunt with hawks ; such mundane delectations do not befit the religious, who should be rather hearing God's precepts, and at prayer, or confessing their sins with tears. Yet the lion may always be hunted ; for he goes seeking whom he may devour.[5]

The *religio* professed by the Templars is called, in the Latin rule, *religio militaris*, which the French translates

---

[1] The phraseology of the Latin *regula* often follows that of the Benedictine rule.   [2] Chaps. 33, 35.
[3] Chaps. 40, 41.   [4] Chap. 42.   [5] Chaps. 46, 48.

" religion de chevalerie," not incorrectly, but with somewhat different flavour.[1]

" This new *genus religionis*, as we believe, by divine providence began with you in the Holy Land, a *religio* in which you mingle chivalry (*milicia*). Thus this armed religion may advance through chivalry, and smite the enemy without incurring sin. Rightfully then we decree that you shall be called knights of the Temple (*milites Templi*) and may hold houses, lands and men, and possess serfs and justly rule them." [2]

The pomp of the last sentence seems to remove from the tone of the earlier chapters, and suggests a later date. Another, possibly late, chapter (66) permits the knights to receive tithes, since they have abandoned their riches for *spontaneae paupertati*. Still another accords to married men a qualified admission to the brotherhood, but they may not wear the white robe and mantle (55). The next forbids the admission of *sorores* ; and the last chapter of all (72) warns against the sight of women, and forbids the brethren to kiss one, be she widow, virgin, mother, sister or friend.

Thus the Latin *regula* formulates an order of monasticism with only the modifications imperatively demanded by the exigencies of holy warfare. The French *regle* elaborates the military organization and enhances the chivalric element. This begins to appear in the portions which are a translation (usually quite close) of the Latin rule. But even that translation makes changes, for example, omitting the period of probation required in the Latin text, before admitting a brother to the Order.[3] A striking change was made by the later French ordinances in the interrogations and proceedings for admission. The Latin formula begins in Cistercian phrase :

" Vis abrenunciare seculo ?
" Volo.
" Vis profiteri obedientiam secundum canonicam institutionem et secundum preceptum domini papae ?

---

[1] Chap. 62 Latin *regula* and chap. 14 of French *regle*.
[2] Chap. 51.
[3] Chap. 58 of the Latin, chap. 11 of the French. The chapters of the French translation do not follow the order of the Latin.

" Volo.

" Vis assumere tibi conversationem (the monastic mode and change of life) fratrum nostrorum ?

" Volo." [1]

And so forth.

The substance of these and other questions was retained in the far longer French formula, which exacted specific promises of compliance with all the Order's ordinances. But far removed from the original are such questions as the following : " Biau dous amis " (the ordinary phrase of the chivalric romance) have you, or has any one for you, made any promise to any one in return for his aid in procuring your admission, which would be simony ? " Estes vos chevalier et fis de chevalier ? "

Is the candidate a knight, and son of knight and lady, and are his " peres . . . de lignage de chevaliers " ? This means chivalry and gentle blood ; and if the candidate answers in the negative, he cannot be admitted as a knight of the Temple, although he may be as " sergent," or in some other character. Most noble and courtly is the phrasing of these statutes. Their frequent " Beaus seignors freres " is the address proper for knights rather than monks.[2]

Usually wherever the translation of the Latin *regula* ends, the *Regle dou Temple* passes on to provisions meeting the requirements of a military, rather than a monastic order. We enter upon such in the chapters governing the powers and privileges of the (Grand) Master, of the Seneschal, of the Marshal, of the " Comandeor de la terre de Jerusalem." Many sections have to do with military discipline, with the ordering of the knights and their followers on the march and in the battle ; they forbid the knights to joust or leave the squadron without orders.[3] Horses, armour, and accoutrements are regulated, and, in short, full provision is made for everything conducing to make the army efficient in war. There is also a long list of faults and crimes for which a knight may be disciplined or expelled ; the latter shall be

---

[1] Page 167 of de Curzon's edition.

[2] See in de Curzon's edition, sections 431, 436, 448, 454, and 657 *sqq.*

[3] It would seem as if military discipline, as moderns understand it, took its rise in these Templars and Hospitallers.

his punishment if he flee before the Saracens and forsake his standard in battle.[1]

The history of the Templars, significantly epitomized in the amendments to their *regula*, shows the necessary as well as inevitable secularization of a military monastic order ; an order which for the purposes of this chapter may be placed among the chief historical examples of chivalry. For in this chapter we are not straying through the pleasant mazes of romantic literature, but are keeping close to history, with the intention of drawing from it illustrations of chivalry's ideals. We shall not, however, enter further upon the story of the Order of the Temple, with its valorous and rapacious achievements and most tragic end ; but will rather look to the careers of historic individuals for the illumination of our theme.

Reaching form and consciousness in the eleventh and twelfth centuries, chivalry became part of the crusading ardour of those times. All true knights were or might be Crusaders ; and of a truth there was no purer incarnation of the crusading spirit than Godfrey of Bouillon, that figure of veritable if somewhat slender historicity, upon whom in time chronicler and trouvère alike were to fasten as the true hero of the enterprise that won Jerusalem. And so he was. Not that Godfrey was commander of the host. He was not even its most energetic or most capable leader. Boemund of Tarentum and Raymond of Toulouse were his superiors in power and military energy. But neither Boemund, nor Tancred, nor Raymond, nor any other of those princes of Christendom, was what Godfrey appears to us, the type and symbol of the perfect, single-hearted, crusading knight, fighting solely for the Faith, with Christian devotion and humility, and, like them all, with more than Christian wrath. The First Crusade (1096–1099) was stamped with hatred and slaughter : on the dreadful march, at the more dreadful siege and final sack of Antioch, and finally when the holy sepulchre's defilement was washed out in Saracen blood. And there was no slaughterer more eager than Godfrey.

The cruelty and religious fervour of the Crusade are

[1] See *e.g.* de Curzon's edition, sections 419, 420, 574.

rendered in the words of Raymond of Agiles, one of the clergy in the train of Count Raymond of Toulouse, and an eye-witness of the capture of Jerusalem. After days of despairing struggle to effect a breach, success came as by the mercy of God :

" Among the first to enter was Tancred and the Duke of Lothringia (Godfrey), who on that day shed quantities of blood almost beyond belief. After them the host mounted the walls, and now the Saracens suffered. Yet although the city was all but in the hands of the Franks, the Saracens resisted the party of Count Raymond as if they were never going to be taken. But when our men had mastered the walls of the city and the towers, then wonderful things were to be seen. Numbers of the Saracens were beheaded—which was the easiest for them ; others were shot with arrows, or forced to jump from the towers ; others were slowly tortured and were burned in flames. In the streets and open places of the town were seen piles of heads and hands and feet. One rode about everywhere amid the corpses of men and horses. But these were small matters ! Let us go to Solomon's temple, where they were wont to chant their rites and solemnities. What had been done there ? If we speak the truth we exceed belief : let this suffice. In the temple and porch of Solomon one rode in blood up to the knees and even to the horses' bridles by the just and marvellous Judgment of God, in order that the same place which so long had endured their blasphemies against Him should receive their blood."

So the Crusaders wrought ; and what joy did they feel ! Raymond continues :

" When the city was taken it was worth the whole long labour to witness the devotion of the pilgrims to the sepulchre of the Lord, how they clapped their hands, exulted, and sang a new song unto the Lord. For their hearts presented to God, victor and triumphant, vows of praise which they were unable to explain. A new day, new joy and exultation, new and perpetual gladness, the consummation of toil and devotion drew forth from all new words, new songs. This day, I say, glorious in every age to come, turned all our griefs and toils into joy and exultation." [1]

So new songs of gladness burst from the hearts of the soldiers of the Cross. In a few days the princes made an election, and offered the kingdom to Count Raymond : he declined. Then Godfrey was made, not king, but

[1] Raimundus de Agiles, *Hist. Francorum qui ceperunt Jerusalem*, cap. 38-39. (Migne 155, col. 659).

Advocatus of the Holy Sepulchre ; he would never wear a crown where his Lord had worn a crown of thorns. As a servant of Christ and of His Church he fought and ruled some short months till his death. His fame has grown because his heart was pure, and because, among the knights, he represented most perfectly the religious impulse of this crusade which fought its way through blood, until it poured out its new song of joy over the blood-drenched city. He errs who thinks to find the source and power of the First Crusade elsewhere than in the flaming zeal of feudal Christianity. There was doubtless much divergence of motive, secular and religious ; but over-mastering and unifying all was the passion to wrest the sepulchre of Christ from paynim defilement, and thus win salvation for the Crusader. Greed went with the host, but it did not inspire the enterprise.[1]

Doubtless the stories of returning knights awakened a spirit of romantic adventure, which stirred in later crusading generations. It was not so in the eleventh century when the First Crusade was gathering. The romantic imagination was then scarcely quickened ; adventure was still inarticulate, and the literature of adventure for the venture's sake was yet to be created. So the First Crusade, with its motive of religious zeal, is in some degree distinguishable from those which followed when knighthood was in different flower. If not the Crusades themselves, at least the *Chansons* of the trouvères who sang of them, follow a change corresponding with the changing taste of chivalry : they begin with serious matters, and are occupied with the great enterprise ; then they become adventurous in theme, romantic, till at last even romantic love is infelicitously grafted upon the religious rage that won Jerusalem.

This process of change may be traced in the growth of the legends of the First Crusade and Godfrey of Bouillon. Something was added to his career even by the Latin Chronicles of fifty years later. But his most venturesome development is to be found in those French *Chansons de geste* which have been made into the " Cycle " of the First Crusade. Two of these, the *Chansons* of *Antioche* and *Jerusalem*, were originally composed by a contemporary, if

[1] Cf. *ante*, Chap. XIV.

not a participant in the expedition.   They were refashioned
perhaps seventy-five or a hundred years later, in the reign
of Philip Augustus, by another trouvère, who still kept their
old tone and substance.   They remained poetic narratives of
the holy war.   In them the knights are fierce and bloody,
cruel and sometimes greedy ; but their whole emprise makes
onward to the end in view, the winning of the holy
city.   These poems are epic and not romantic : they may
even be called historical.   The character of Godfrey is
developed with legendary or epic propriety, through a
heightening of his historic qualities.   He equals or excels
the other barons in fierce valour, and yet a touch of courtesy
tempers his wrath.   In Christian meekness and in modesty
he surpasses all, and he refuses the throne of Jerusalem
until he has been commanded from on high.   At that he
accepts the kingdom as a sacred charge in defence of which
he is to die.

It is otherwise with a number of other *chansons*
composed in the latter part of the twelfth and through
the thirteenth century.   Some of them (the *Chanson des
chétifs*, for example) had probably to do with the First
Crusade.   Others, like the various poems which tell of the
Chevalier au Cygne, were inaptly forced into connection with
the family of Godfrey.   They have become adventurous,
and are studded with irrelevant marvels, rather than assisted
to their denouements by serious supernatural intervention.
Monsters appear, and incongruous romantic episodes ;
Godfrey's ancestor has become the Swan-knight, and he
himself duplicates the exploits previously ascribed to that
half-fairy person.   Knightly manners, from brutal have
become courteous.   Women throng these poems, and the
romantic love of women enters, although not in the finished
guise in which it plays so dominant a rôle in the Arthurian
Cycle.   Such themes, unknown to the earlier crusading
chansons, would have fitted ill with a martial theme driving
on through war and carnage (not through " adventures ")
to the holy end in view.[1]

---

[1] On these poems see Pigeonneau, *Le Cycle de la Croisade* (St. Cloud, 1877) ;
Paulin Paris, in *Histoire littéraire de la France*, vol. 22, pp. 350-402, and *ibid.*
vol. 25, p. 507 *sqq.* ; Gaston Paris, " La Naissance du chevalier au Cygne,"
Romania, 19, p. 314 *sqq.* (1890).

The Crusades open with the form of Godfrey of Bouillon.
A century and a half elapses and they deaden to a close
beneath the futile radiance of a saintlike and perfect
knightly personality. St. Louis of France is as clear a
figure as any in the Middle Ages. From all sides his life is
known. We see him as a painstaking sovereign meting out
even justice, and maintaining his royal rights against feudal
turbulence and also against ecclesiastical encroachment.
During his reign the monarchy of France continues to
advance in power and repute. And yet there was no jot of
worldly wisdom, and scant consideration of a realm sorely
needing its ruler, in the fanatical religious devotion which
drew him twice across the sea on crusades unparalleled
in their foolishness. For the world was growing wiser
politically ; and what was glorious feudal enthusiasm in the
year 1099, was deliberate disregard of experience in the
years 1248 and 1270.

Yet who would have had St. Louis wiser in his
generation ? The loss to France was mankind's gain, from
the example of saintly king and perfect knight, kept bright
in the narratives of men equal to the task. Louis was
happy in his biographers. Two among them knew him
intimately and in ways affording special opportunities to
observe the sides of his character congenial to their respective
tempers. One was his confessor for twenty years, the
Dominican Geoffrey of Beaulieu ; the other was the Sire
de Joinville. Geoffrey's *Vita* records Louis' devotions ;
Joinville's *Histoire* notes the king's piety ; but the qualities
which it illuminates are those of a French gentleman and
knight and grand seigneur, like Joinville himself.

The book of the Dominican [1] is not picturesque. It
opens with an edifying comparison between King Josiah
and King Louis. Then it praises the king's mother, Queen
Blanche of pious memory. As for Louis, the confessor has
been unable to discover that he ever committed a mortal
sin : he sought faithful and wise counsellors ; he was careful
and gracious in speech, never using an oath or any
scurrilous expression. In earlier years, when under the

---

[1] " Vita Ludovici noni auctore Gaufrido de Belloloco " (*Recueil des historiens
des Gaules et de la France*, t. xx. pp. 3-26).

necessity of taking oath, he would say, " In nomine mei " ;
but afterwards, hearing that some religious man had objected
to this, he restricted his asseverations to the " est, est " and
" non, non " of the Gospel.

From the time he first crossed the sea, he wore no
scarlet raiment, but clothed himself in sober garments.
And as such were of less value to give to the poor than
those which he had formerly worn, he added sixty pounds a
year to his almsgiving ; for he did not wish the poor to
suffer because of his humble dress.   Geoffrey gives the long
tale of his charities to the poor and to the mendicant
Orders.   On the Sabbaths it was the king's secret custom
to wash the feet of three beggars, dry them, and kiss them
humbly.   He commanded in his will that no stately monument should be erected over his grave.   He treated his
confessors with great respect, and, while confessing, if
perchance a window was to be closed or opened, he quickly
rose and shut or opened it, and would not hear of his
confessor doing it.   In Advent season and Lent he
abstained from marital intercourse.   Some years before his
death, if he had had his will, he would have resigned his
kingdom to his son and entered the Order of the Franciscans or Dominicans.   He brought up his children most
religiously, and wished some of them to take the vows.[1]

He confessed every Friday and also between times, if
something occurred to him ; and if he thought of anything
in the night, he would send for his confessor and confess
before matins.[2]   After confession he always took his
discipline from his confessor, whom he furnished with a
scourge of five little braided iron chains, attached to an
ivory handle.   This he would afterwards put back into a
little case, which he carried hanging to his belt, but out
of sight.   Such little cases he sometimes presented to
his children or friends in secret, that they might have a

[1] The Testament of St. Louis, written for his eldest son, is a complete rule of
conduct for a Christian prince, and indicates St. Louis' mind on the education of
one.   It has been printed and translated many times.   Geoffrey of Beaulieu
gives it in Latin (chap. xv.) and in French at the end of the *Vita*.   It is also in
Joinville.

[2] One sees here the same religious anxiety which is so well brought out by
Salimbene's account of St. Louis, *ante*, pp. 524 *sqq*.

convenient instrument of discipline. He wore haircloth next his flesh in the holy seasons, a habit distressing to his tender skin, until his confessor persuaded him to abandon this form of penance as ill comporting with his station. He replaced it by increasing his charities. His fasts were regular and frequent, till he lessened them upon prudent advice ; for he was not strong. He would have liked to hear all the canonical hours chanted ; and twice a day he heard Mass, and daily the Office for the Dead. Sometimes, soon after midnight, he would rise to hear matins, and then would take a quiet time for prayer by his bed. Likewise he loved to hear sermons. On returning over the sea, when the ships suffered a long delay, he had preaching three times a week, with the sermon specially adapted to the sailors, a class of men who rarely hear the Word of God. He prevailed on many of them to confess, and declared himself ready at any time to put his hand to a rope, if necessary, so that a sailor while confessing might not be called away by any exigency of the sea.

While beyond the sea, this good king, hearing that a Saracen Sultan had collected the books of their philosophy at his own expense for his subjects' use, determined not to be outdone whenever he should return to Paris, a purpose which he amply carried out, diligently and generously supplying money for copying and renewing the writings of the Doctors. At enormous expense he obtained the Saviour's crown of thorns and a good part of the true cross, from the emperor at Constantinople, with many other precious relics ; all of which the king barefooted helped to carry in holy procession when they were received by the clergy of Paris.

The king was very careful in the distribution of ecclesiastical patronage, always seeing to it that the candidate was not already enjoying another benefice. His heart exulted when it came to him to bestow a benefice upon some especially holy man. He was most zealous in the suppression of swearing and blasphemy, and with the advice of the papal legate then in France issued an edict, providing that the lips of those guilty of this sin should be seared with hot irons ; and when certain ones murmured, he declared that he would willingly suffer his own lips to be branded if that would purge his realm of this vice.

Such were the acts and qualities of Louis which impressed his Dominican confessor. They were the qualities of a saint, and would have brought their possessor to a monastery, had not his royal station held him in the world. The Dominican could not know the knightly nature of his royal penitent, and still less reflect it in his Latin of the confessional. For this there was needed the pen of a great gentleman, whose nature enabled him to picture his lord in a book of such high breeding that it were hard to find its fellow. This book is stately with the Sire de Joinville's consciousness of his position and blood, and stately through the respect he bore his lord—a book with which no one would take a liberty. Yet it is simple in thought and phrase, as written by one who lived through what he tells, and closely knew and dearly loved the king. From it one learns that he who was a saint in his confessor's eyes was also a monarch from his soul out to his royal manners and occasional royal insistence upon acts which others thought unwise. We also learn to know him as a knightly, hapless soldier of the Cross, who would not waver from his word plighted even to an infidel.

That St. Louis was a veritable knight is the first thing one learns from Joinville. The first part of my book, says that gentleman, tells how the king conducted his life after the way of God and the Church, and to the profit of his realm ; the second tells of his " granz chevaleries et de ses granz faiz d'armes." " The first deed (*faiz*) whereby ' il mist son cors en avanture de mort ' was at our arrival before Damietta, where his council was of the opinion, as I have understood, that he ought to remain in his ship until he saw what his knights (*sa chevalerie*) should do, who made a landing. The reason why they so counselled him was that if he disembarked, and his people should be killed and he with them, the whole affair was lost ; while if he remained in his ship he could in his own person renew the attempt to conquer Egypt. And he would credit no one, but leaped into the sea, all armed, his shield hanging from his neck, his lance in hand, and was one of the first upon the beach."

This is from Joinville's Introduction. He recommences formally :

" In the name of God the all powerful, I, John, Sire of Joinville, Seneschal of Champagne, cause to be written the life of our sainted king Louis, as I saw and heard of it for the space of six years while I was in his company on the pilgrimage beyond the sea, and since we returned. And before I tell you his great deeds and prowess (*chevalerie*), I will recount what I saw and heard of his holy words and good precepts, so that they may be found one after the other for the improvement of those who hear.

" This holy man loved God with all his heart, and imitated His works : which was evident in this, that as God died for the love which He bore His people, so he (Louis) put his body in peril several times for the love which he bore his people. The great love which he had for his people appeared in what he said to his eldest son, Louis, when very sick at Fontainebleau : ' Fair son,' said he, ' I beg thee to make thyself loved by the people of thy kingdom ; for indeed I should prefer that a Scot from Scotland came and ruled the people of the kingdom well and faithfully, rather than that thou shouldst rule them ill in the sight of all.' "

Joinville continues relating the virtues of the king, and recording his conversations with himself :

" He called me once and said, ' Seneschal, what is God ? ' And I said to him, ' Sire, it is a being so good that there can be no better.'

" ' Now I ask you,' said he, ' which would you choose, to be a leper, or to have committed a mortal sin ? ' And I who never lied to him replied that I had rather have committed thirty than be a leper. Afterwards he called me apart and made me sit at his feet and said : ' Why did you say that to me yesterday ? ' And I told him that I would say it again. And he : ' You speak like a thoughtless trifler ; for you should know there is no leprosy so ugly as to be in mortal sin, because the soul in mortal sin is like the devil. This is why there can be no leprosy so ugly. And then, of a truth, when a man dies, he is cured of the leprosy of the body ; but when the man who has committed a mortal sin dies, he does not know, nor is it certain, that he has so repented while living, that God has pardoned him ; this is why he should have great fear that this leprosy will last as long as God shall be in paradise. So I pray you earnestly that you will train your heart, for the love of God and of me, to wish rather for leprosy or any other bodily evil, rather than that mortal sin should come into your soul.' He asked me whether I washed the feet of the poor on Holy Tuesday. ' Sire,' said I, ' *quel malheur !* I will not wash those villains' feet.' ' Truly that was ill said,' said he ; ' for you should not hold in contempt what God did for our instruction. So I pray you, for the love of God first, and for the love of me, to accustom yourself to wash them.' "

Joinville was some years younger than his king, who loved him well and wished to help him. The king also esteemed Master Robert de Sorbon [1] for the high respect as a *preudom* in which he was held, and had him eat at his table. One day Master Robert was seated next to Joinville.

" ' Seneschal,' said the king, smiling, ' tell me the reasons why a man of wisdom and valour (*preudom, prud'homme*) is accounted better than a fool.' Then began the argument between me and Master Robert ; and when we had disputed for a time, the king rendered his decision, saying : ' Master Robert, I should like to have the name of *preudom*, so be it that I was one, and all the rest I would leave to you ; for *preudom* is such a grand and good thing that it fills the mouth just to pronounce it.' "

Master Robert plays a not altogether happy part in another scene, varicoloured and delightful :

" The holy king was at Corbeil one Pentecost, and twenty-four knights with him. The king went down after dinner into the courtyard back of the chapel, and was talking at the entrance with the Count of Brittany, the father of the present duke, whom God preserve. Master Robert de Sorbon came to seek me there, and took me by the cloak, and led me to the king, and all the other gentlemen came after us. Then I asked Master Robert : ' Master Robert, what would you ? ' And he said to me : ' If the king should sit down here, and you should seat yourself above him, I ask you whether you would not be to blame ? ' And I said, Yes.

" And he said to me : ' Yet you lay yourself open to blame, since you are more nobly clad than the king : for you wear squirrel's fur and cloth of green, which the king does not.'

" And I said to him : ' Master Robert, saving your grace, I do nothing worthy of blame when I wear squirrel's fur and cloth of green ; for it is the clothing which my father and mother left me. But you do what is to blame ; for you are the son of a *vilain* and *vilaine*, and have abandoned the clothes of your father and your mother, and are clad in richer cloth than the king.' And then I took the lappet of his surcoat and that of the king's, and said to him : ' See whether I do not speak truly.' And the king set himself to defend Master Robert with all his might."

---

[1] The founder of the College of the Sorbonne.

" Afterwards Messire the king called to him Monseigneur Philippe his son, the father of the present king, and the king Thibaut (of Navarre), and laid his hand on the earth and said : ' Sit close to me, so that they may not hear.'

" ' Ah Sire,' say they, ' we dare not sit so close to you.'

" And he said to me, ' Seneschal, sit down here.' And so I did, so close that our clothes touched. And he made them sit down by me, and said to them : ' You have done ill, you who are my sons, who have not obeyed at once all that I bade you : and see to it that this does not happen with you again.' And they promised. And then he said to me, that he had called us in order to confess to me that he was in the wrong in defending Master Robert against me. ' But,' said he, ' I saw him so dumbfounded that there was good need I should defend him. And do none of you attach any importance to all I said defending Master Robert ; for, as the seneschal said to him, you ought to dress well and becomingly, so that your wives may love you better, and your people hold you in higher esteem. For the sage says that one should appear in such clothes and arms that the wise of this world may not say you have done too much, nor the young people say you have done too little.' "

The hopelessly worthy *parvenu* was quite outside this charmed circle of blood and manners.

Another story of Joinville opens our eyes to Louis' views on Jews and infidels. The king was telling him of a grand argument between Jews and Christian clergy which was to have been held at Cluny. And a certain poverty-stricken knight was there, who obtained leave to speak the first word ; and he asked the head Jew whether he believed that Mary was the mother of God and still a virgin. And the Jew answered that he did not believe it at all. The knight replied that in that case the Jew had acted like a fool to enter her monastery, and should pay for it ; and with that he knocked him down with his staff, and all the other Jews ran off. When the abbot reproached him for his folly, he replied that the abbot's folly was greater in having the argument at all. " So I tell you," said the king on finishing his story, " that only a skilled clerk should dispute with misbelievers ; but a layman, when he hears any one speak ill of the Christian law, should defend that law with nothing but his sword, which he should plunge into the defamer's belly, to the hilt if possible."

Well known is the hapless outcome of St. Louis' Crusades : the first one leading to defeat and captivity in Egypt, the second ending in the king's death by disease at Tunis. Yet in what he sought to do in his Lord's cause, St. Louis was a true knight and soldier of the Cross. The spirit was willing ; but the flesh accomplished little. Let us take from Joinville's story of that first crusade a wonderfully illustrative chapter, giving the confused scenes occurring after the capture of Damietta, when the French king and his feudal host had advanced southerly through the Delta, along the eastern branch of the Nile. Joinville was making a reconnaissance with his own knights, when they came suddenly upon a large body of Saracens. The Christians were hard pressed ; here and there a knight falls in the melée, among them

" Monseigneur Hugues de Trichatel, the lord of Conflans, who carried my banner. I and my knights spurred to deliver Monseigneur Raoul de Wanou, who was thrown to the ground. As I was making my way back, the Turks struck at me with their lances ; my horse fell on his knees under the blows, and I went over his head. I recovered myself as I might, shield on neck and sword in hand ; and Monseigneur Erard de Siverey (whom God absolve !), who was of my people, came to my aid, and said that we had better retreat to a ruined house, and there wait for the king who was approaching."

One notes the high-born courtesy with which the Sire de Joinville speaks of the gentlemen who had the honour of serving him. The fight goes on.

" Monseigneur Erard de Siverey was struck by a sword-blow in his face, so that his nose hung down over his lips. And then I was minded of Monseigneur Saint Jacques, whom I thus invoked : ' Beau Sire Saint Jacques, help and succour me in this need.'

" When I had made my prayer, Monseigneur Erard de Siverey said to me : ' Sire, if you think that neither I nor my heirs would suffer reproof, I would go for aid to the Count of Anjou, whom I see over there in the fields.' And I said to him : ' Messire Erard, I think you would do yourself great honour, if you now went for aid to save our lives ; for your own is in jeopardy.' And indeed I spoke truly, for he died of that wound. He asked the advice of all our knights who were there, and all approved as I had approved. And when he heard that, he requested me to let him have his horse, which I was holding by the bridle with the rest. And so I did."

The knightliness of this scene is perfect, with its liege fealty and its carefulness as to the point of honour, its carefulness also that the vassal knight shall fail in no duty to his lord whereby the descent of his fief may be jeopardized. Monseigneur Erard (whom God absolve, we say with Joinville !) is very careful to have his lord's assent and the approval of his fellows, before he will leave his lord in peril, and undergo still greater risk to bring him succour.

Well, the Count of Anjou brought such aid as created a diversion, and the Saracens turned to the new foe. But now the king arrives on the scene :

" There where I was on foot with my knights, wounded as already said, comes the king with his whole array, and a great sound of trumpets and drums. And he halted on the road on the dyke. Never saw I one so bravely armed : for he showed above all his people from his shoulders up, a gilded casque upon his head and a German sword in his hand."

Then the king's good knights charge into the battle, and fine feats of arms are done. The fighting is fierce and general. At length the king is counselled to bear back along the river, keeping close to it on his right hand, so as to reunite with the Duke of Burgundy who had been left to guard the camp. The knights are recalled from the melée, and with a great noise of trumpets and drums, and Saracen horns, the army is set in motion.

" And now up comes the constable, Messire Imbert de Beaujeu, and tells the king that the Count of Artois, his brother, was defending himself in a house in Mansourah, and needed aid. And the king said to him : ' Constable, go before and I will follow you.' And I said to the constable that I would be his knight, at which he thanked me greatly."

Again one feels the feudal chivalry. Now the affair becomes rather distraught. They set out to succour the Count of Artois, but are checked, and it is rumoured that the king is taken ; and in fact six Saracens had rushed upon him and seized his horse by the bridle ; but he had freed himself with such great strokes that all his people took courage. Yet the host is driven back upon the river, and is in desperate straits. Joinville and his knights defend a bridge over a tributary, which helps to check the Saracen advance, and affords an uncertain means of safety to the French. But there is no cessation of the Saracen attack with bows and spears. The knights seemed full of arrows. Joinville saved his life with an arrow-proof Saracen vest, " so that I was wounded by their arrows only in five places "! One of Joinville's own stout burgesses, bearing his lord's banner on a lance, helped in the charges upon the enemy. In the melée up speaks the good Count of Soissons, whose cousin Joinville had married. " He joked with me and said : ' Seneschal, let us whoop after this canaille ; for by God's coif (his favourite oath) we shall be talking, you and I, about this day in the chambers of the ladies.' "

At last, the arbalests were brought out from the camp, and the Saracens drew off—fled, says the Sire de Joinville. And the king was there, and

" I took off his casque, and gave him my iron cap, so that he might get some air. And then comes brother Henry de Ronnay, Prevost of the Hospital, to the king when he had passed the river, and kisses his mailed hand. And the king asked him whether he had news of the Count of Artois, his brother ; and he said that he had indeed news of him, for he was sure that his brother the Count of Artois was in Paradise. ' Ha ! sire,' said the Prevost, ' be of good cheer ; for no such honour ever came to a king of France as is come to you. For to fight your enemies you have crossed a river by swimming, have discomfited your enemies and driven them from the field, and taken their engines and tents, where you will sleep this night.' And the king replied that God be adored for all that He gave ; and then the great tears fell from his eyes."

One need not follow on to the ill ending of the campaign, when king and knights all had to yield themselves prisoners, in most uncertain captivity. The Saracen Emirs conspired and slew their Sultan ; the prisoners' lives hung on a thread ; and when the terms were arranging for the delivery and ransom of the king, his own scruples nearly proved fatal. For the Emirs, after they had made their oath, wished the king to swear, and put his seal to a parchment,

" that if he the king did not hold to his agreements, might he
be as shamed as the Christian who denied God and His Mother,
and was cut off from the company of the twelve Companions
(apostles) and of all the saints, male and female. To this the king
consented. The last point of the oath was this : That if the
king did not keep his agreements, might he be as shamed as the
Christian who denied God and His law, and in contempt of God
spat on the Cross and trod on it. When the king heard that,
he said, please God, he would not make that oath."

Then the trouble began, and the Emirs tortured the
venerable patriarch of Jerusalem till he besought the king to
swear. How the oath was arranged I do not know, says
Joinville, but finally the Emirs professed themselves satisfied.
And after that, when the ransom was paid, the Saracens by
a mistake accepted a sum ten thousand livres short, and
Louis, in spite of the protest of his counsellors, refused to
permit advantage to be taken and insisted on full payment.

Many years afterwards, when Louis was dead and
canonized, a dream came to his faithful Joinville who was
then an old man.

" It seemed to me in my dream that I saw the king in front of
my chapel at Joinville ; and he was, so he seemed to me, wonderfully happy and glad at heart ; and I also was glad at heart,
because I saw him in my chateau. And I said to him : ' Sire,
when you go hence, I will prepare lodging for you at my house in
my village of Chevillon.' And he replied, smiling, and said to me :
' Sire de Joinville, by the troth I owe you, I do not wish so soon
to go from here.' When I awoke I bethought me ; and it seemed
to me that it would please God and the king that I should provide
a lodging for him in my chapel. So I have placed an altar in
honour of God and of him there, where there shall be always
chanting in his honour. And I have established a fund in per-
petuity to do this."

Godfrey of Bouillon and St. Louis of France show
knighthood as inspired by serious and religious motives.
We pass on a hundred years after St. Louis, to a famous
Chronicle concerning men whose knightly lives exhibit no
such religious, and possibly no such serious, purpose, so far
at least as they are set forth by this delightful chronicler.
His name of course is Sir John Froissart, and his chief work
goes under the name of *The Chronicles of England, France,
Spain, and the adjoining Countries*. It covers the period

from the reign of Edward II. to the coronation of Henry IV. of England. Have we not all known his book as one to delight youth and age ?

Let us, however, open it seriously, and first of all notice the Preface, with its initial sentence giving the note of the entire work : " That the *grans merveilles* and the *biau fait d'armes* achieved in the great wars between England and France, and the neighbouring realms may be worthily recorded, and known in the present and in the time to come, I purpose to order and put the same in prose, according to the true information which I have obtained from valiant knights, squires, and marshals at arms, who are and rightly should be the investigators and reporters of such matters." [1]

" Marvels " and " deeds of arms "—soon he will use the equivalent phrase *belles aventures*. With delicious garrulity, but never wavering from his point of view, the good Sir John repeats and enlarges as he enters on his work in which "to encourage all valorous hearts, and to show them honourable examples " he proposes to " point out and speak of each adventure from the nativity of the noble King Edward (III.) of England, who so potently reigned, and who was engaged in so many battles and perilous adventures and other feats of arms and great prowess, from the year of grace 1326, when he was crowned in England."

Of course Froissart says that the occasion of these wars was King Edward's enterprise to recover his inheritance of France, which the twelve peers and barons of that realm had awarded to Lord Philip of Valois, from whom it had passed on to his son, King Charles. This enterprise was the woof whereon should hang an hundred years of knightly and romantic feats of arms, which incidentally wrought desolation to the fair realm of France. Yet the full opening of these matters was not yet ; and Froissart begins with the story of the troubles brought on Queen Isabella and the

---

[1] *Chroniques de J. Froissart,* ed. S. Luce (Société de l'Histoire de France). The opening of the Prologue. It seemed desirable to render this sentence literally. The rest of my extracts are from Thomas Johnes's translation, for which I plead a boyhood's affection. For a brief account of Froissart's chief source (Jean le Bel), with excellent criticism, see W. P. Ker, " Froissart " (*Essays on Medieval Literature,* Macmillan and Co., 1905).

nobles of England through the overbearing insolence of Sir Hugh Spencer, the favourite of her husband Edward II.

The Queen left England secretly, to seek aid at Paris from her brother King Charles, that she might regain her rights against the upstart and her own weak estranged husband. King Charles received her graciously, as a great lord should receive a great dame ; and richly provided for her and her young son Edward. Then he took counsel of the " great lords and barons of his kingdom " ; and their advice was that he should permit her to enlist assistance in his realm, and yet himself appear ignorant of the matter. Of this, Sir Hugh hears, and his gold is busy with these counsellors ; so that the Court becomes a cold place for the self-exiled queen. On she fares in her distress, and, as advised, seeks the aid of the great Earl of Hainault, then at Valenciennes. But before the queen can reach that city, the earl's young brother, Sir John, Lord of Beaumont, rides to meet her, ardent to succour a great lady in distress, " being at that time very young, and panting for glory like a knight-errant." In the evening he reached the house of Sir Eustace d'Ambreticourt, where the queen was lodged. She made her lamentable complaint, at which Sir John was affected even to tears, and said, " Lady, see here your knight, who will not fail to die for you, though every one else should desert you ; therefore will I do everything in my power to conduct you and your son, and to restore you to your rank in England, by the grace of God, and the assistance of your friends in those parts ; and I, and all those whom I can influence, will risk our lives on the adventure for your sake."

Is not this a chivalric beginning ? And so the Chronicle goes on. King Edward III. is crowned, marries the Lady Philippa, daughter of the Earl of Hainault, and afterwards sends his defiance to Philip, King of France, for not yielding up to him his rightful inheritance, and this after the same King Edward had, as Duke of Aquitaine, done homage to King Philip for that great duchy.

So the challenge of King Edward, and of sundry other lords, was delivered to the King of France ; and thereupon the first bold raid is made by the knightliest figure of the first generation of the war, Sir Walter Manny, a young Hainaulter who had remained in the train of Queen Philippa. The war is carried on by incursions and deeds of derring-do, the larger armies of the kings of England and France circumspectly refraining from battle, which might have checked the martial jollity of the affair. It is all beautifully pointless and adventurous, and carried out in the spirit of a knighthood that loves fighting and seeks honour and adventure, while steadying itself with a hope of plunder and reward. There are likewise ladies to be succoured and defended.

One of these was the lion-hearted Countess of Montfort, who with her husband had become possessed of the disputed dukedom of Brittany. The Earl of Montfort did homage to the King of England ; the rival claimant, Charles of Blois, sought the aid of France. He came with an army, and Montfort was taken and died in prison ; the duchess was left to carry on the war. She was at last shut up and besieged in Hennebon on the coast ; the burghers were falling away, the knights discouraged ; emissaries from Lord Charles were working among them. His ally, Lord Lewis of Spain, and Sir Hervé de Leon were the leaders of the besiegers. Sir Hervé had an uncle, a bishop, Sir Guy de Leon, who was on the side of the Countess of Montfort. The nephew won the uncle over in a conference without the walls ; and the latter assumed the task of persuading the Lords of Brittany who were with the countess to abandon the apparently hopeless struggle. Re-entering the town, the bishop was eloquent against the countess's cause, and promised free pardon to the lords if they would give up the town. Now listen to Froissart, how he tells the story :

"The countess had strong suspicions of what was going forward, and begged of the lords of Brittany, for the love of God, that they would not doubt but she should receive succours before three days were over. But the bishop spoke so eloquently, and made use of such good arguments, that these lords were in much suspense all that night. On the morrow he continued the subject, and succeeded so far as to gain them over, or very nearly so, to his opinion ; insomuch that Sir Hervé de Leon had advanced close to the town to take possession of it, with their free consent, when the countess looking out from a window of the castle toward the sea, cried out most joyfully, ' I see the succours I have so long expected and wished for coming.' She repeated this twice ; and the town's people ran to the ramparts and to the windows of the castle, and saw a numerous fleet of great and small vessels, well trimmed, making all the sail they could toward Hennebon. They rightly imagined it must be the fleet from England, so long detained at sea by tempests and contrary winds.

" When the governor of Guingamp, Sir Yves de Tresiquidi, Sir Galeran de Landreman, and the other knights, perceived this succour coming to them, they told the bishop that he might break up his conference, for they were not now inclined to follow his advice. The bishop, Sir Guy de Leon, replied, ' My lords, then our company shall separate ; for I will go to him who seems to me to have the clearest right.' Upon which he sent his defiance to the lady, and to all her party, and left the town to inform Sir Hervé de Leon how matters stood. Sir Hervé was much vexed at it, and immediately ordered the largest machine that was with the army to be placed as near the castle as possible, strictly commanding that it should never cease working day nor night. He then presented his uncle to the Lord Lewis of Spain, and to the Lord Charles of Blois, who both received him most courteously. The countess, in the meantime, prepared and hung with tapestry halls and chambers to lodge handsomely the lords and barons of England, whom she saw coming, and sent out a noble company to meet them. When they were landed, she went herself to give them welcome, respectfully thanking each knight and squire, and led them into the town and castle that they might have convenient lodging : on the morrow, she gave them a magnificent entertainment. All that night, and the following day, the large machine never ceased from casting stones into the town.

" After the entertainment, Sir Walter Manny, who was captain of the English, inquired of the countess the state of the town and the enemy's army. Upon looking out of the window, he said, he had a great inclination to destroy that large machine which was placed so near, and much annoyed them, if any would help him. Sir Yves de Tresiquidi replied, that he would not fail him in this his first expedition ; as did also the lord of Landreman. They went to arm themselves, and then sallied quietly out of one of the gates, taking with them three hundred archers, who shot so well, that those who guarded the machine fled, and the men at arms, who followed the archers, falling upon them, slew the greater part, and broke down and cut in pieces this large machine. They then dashed in among the tents and huts, set fire to them, and killed and wounded many of their enemies before the army was in motion. After this they made a handsome retreat. When the enemy were mounted and armed they galloped after them like madmen.

" Sir Walter Manny, seeing this, exclaimed, ' May I never be embraced by my mistress and dear friend, if I enter castle or fortress before I have unhorsed one of these gallopers.' He then turned round, and pointed his spear toward the enemy, as did the two brothers of Lande-Halle, le Haze de Brabant, Sir Yves de Tresiquidi, Sir Galeran de Landreman, and many others, and spitted the first coursers. Many legs were made to kick the air. Some of their own party were also unhorsed. The conflict became very serious, for reinforcements were perpetually coming from the camp ; and the English were obliged to retreat towards the castle, which they did in good order until they came to the castle ditch ; there the knights made a stand, until all their men were safely returned. Many brilliant actions, captures, and rescues might have been seen. Those of the town who had not been of the party to destroy the large machine now issued forth, and, ranging themselves upon the banks of the ditch, made such good use of their bows, that they forced the enemy to withdraw, killing many men and horses. The chiefs of the army, perceiving they had the worst of it, and that they were losing men to no purpose, sounded a retreat, and made their men retire to the camp. As soon as they were gone, the townsmen re-entered, and went each to his quarters. The Countess of Montfort came down from the castle to meet them, and with a most cheerful countenance, kissed Sir Walter Manny, and all his companions, one after the other like a noble and valiant dame."

In this manner the genial chronicler goes on through his long delightful ramble. After a while the chief combatants close. Cressy is fought and Poictiers. The Black Prince, that extremest bit of knightly royalty, fills the page. The place of Sir Walter Manny is taken by the larger figure of Sir John Chandos, and, on the other side, the usually unfortunate but unconquerable Bertrand du Guesclin. Froissart is at his best when he tells of the great expedition of the Black Prince to restore the cruel Don Pedro of Castille to the throne from which he had been expelled by that picturesque bastard brother Henry, who had a poorer title but a better right, by virtue of being fit to rule.

This whole expedition was—as we see it in Froissart— neither politics nor war, but chivalry. What interest had England, or Edward III., or the Prince of Wales in Don Pedro ? None. He was a cruel tyrant, rightfully expelled.

The Prince of Wales would set him back upon his throne in the interest of royal legitimacy, and because there offered a brilliant opportunity for fame and plunder : the Black Prince thought less of the latter than the Free Companies enlisted under his banner, and less than his own rapacious knights.

So in three divisions, headed by the most famous knights and in a way generalled by Sir John Chandos, the host passes through the kingdom of Navarre, and crosses the Pyrenees. Then begin a series of exploits. Sir Thomas Felton and a company set out just to dare and beard the Castillian army, and after entrancing feats of knight-errantry, are all captured or slain. Much is the prince annoyed at this ; but bears on, gladdened with the thought, often expressed, that the bastard Henry is a bold and hardy knight, and is advancing to give battle.

And true it was. One of Henry's counsellors explains to him how easy it were to hem in the Black Prince in the defiles, and starve him into a disastrous retreat. Perish the thought ! " By the soul of my father," answers King Henry, " I have such a desire to see this prince, and to try my strength with him, that we will never part without a battle."

So the unnecessary and resultless battle of Navaretta took place. Don Pedro, the cruel rightful king, was knighted, with others, by the Prince of Wales before the fight. The tried unflinching chivalry of England and Aquitaine conquered, although one division of King Henry's host had du Guesclin at its head. That knight was captured ; somehow his star had a way of sinking before the steadier fortune of Sir John Chandos, who was here du Guesclin's captor for a second time. King Henry, after valiant fighting, escaped. Don Pedro was re-set upon his throne ; and played false with the Black Prince and his army, in the matter of pay. The whole expedition turned back across the Pyrenees. And not so long after, Henry bestirred himself, and the tardily freed du Guesclin hurried again to aid him. This time there was no Black Prince and Sir John Chandos ; and Don Pedro was conquered and slain, and Henry was at last firm upon his throne.

Could anything have been more chivalric, more objectless, and more absolutely lacking in result ? It is a beautiful story ; every one should refresh his childhood's memory of it by reading Froissart's delightful pages. And then let him also read at least the subsequent story of the death of Sir John Chandos in a knightly brush at arms ; he, the really wise and great leader, perishes through his personal rash knighthood ! It is a fine tale of the ending of an old and mighty knight, the very flower of chivalry, as he was called.

So matters fare on through these Chronicles. All is charming and interesting and picturesque ; charming also for the knights : great fame is won and fat ransoms paid to recoup knightly fortunes. Now and then—all too frequently, alas ! and the only pity of it all !—some brave knight has the mishap to lose his life ! That is to say, the only pity of it from the point of view of good Sir John. But we can see further horrors in this picture of chivalry's actualities : we see King Edward pillage, devastate, destroy France ; [1] we see the awful outcome of the general ruin in the rising of the vile, unhappy peasants, the Jacquerie ; then in the indiscriminate slaughter and pillaging by the Free Companies, no longer well employed by royalties ; and then we see the cruel treachery of many an incident wrought out by such a flower of chivalry even as du Guesclin.[2] Indeed all the horrors of ceaseless interminable war are everywhere, and no more dreadful horror through the whole story than the bloody sack of Limoges commanded by that perfect knight, the Black Prince, himself stricken with disease, and carried in a litter through the breach of the walls into the town, and there reposing, assuaging his cruel soul, while his men run hither and thither " slaying men, women and children according to their orders." [3]

But when King Edward was old, and the Prince of Wales dying with disease, the French and their partisans gathered heart, and pressed back the English party with successful captures and reprisals. Du Guesclin was made Constable of France ; and there remained no English leader who was his match. From this second period onwards, the wars and slaughters and pillagings become more embittered, more horrid and less relieved. The tone of everything

[1] Froissart, i. 210.   [2] Froissart, i. 220.   [3] Froissart, i. 290.

is brutalized, and the good chronicler himself frequently animadverts on the wanton destruction wrought, and the frightful ruin. All is not as in the opening of the story, which was so fascinating, so knightly and almost as purely adventurous as the Arthurian romances—only that there was less love of ladies and a disturbing dearth of forests perilous and enchanted castles. It was then that the reader had ever and anon to remind himself that Froissart is not romance or legend, but a contemporary chronicle ; and that in spite of heightened colours and expanded (if not invented) dialogues, his narrative does not belong to the imaginative or fictitious side of chivalry, but to its actualities.[1]

Froissart's pictures of the depravity and devastation caused by the wars of England and France, disclose the unhappy actuality in which chivalry might move and have its being. And the knights were part of the cruelty, treachery, and lust. One may remark besides in Froissart a certain shallowness, a certain emptying, of the spirit of chivalry. One phase of this lay in the expansion of form and ceremony, while life was departing ;—as, for example, in the hypertrophe of heraldry, and in the pageantry of the later tournaments, where such care was taken to prevent injury to the combatants. A subtler phase of chivalry's emptying lay in its preciosity and in the excessive growth of fantasy and utter romance—of which enough will be said in the next chapter.

[1] Yet the matter was fit for legend and romance ; and a late impotent *chanson de geste* was formed out of the career of du Guesclin.

CHAPTER XXIV

ROMANTIC CHIVALRY AND COURTLY LOVE

FROM ROLAND TO TRISTAN AND LANCELOT

THE instance of Godfrey of Bouillon showed how easy was the passage from knighthood in history to knighthood in legend and romance : legend springing from fact, out of which it makes a story framed in a picture of the time ; romance unhistorical in origin, borrowing, devising, imagining according to the taste of an audience and the faculty of the trouvère. A boundless mediaeval literature of poetic legend and romantic fiction sets forth the ways of chivalry. Our attention may be confined to the Old French, the source from which German, English, and Italian literatures never ceased to draw. Three branches may be selected : the *chansons de geste* ; the *romans d'aventure* ; and the Arthurian romances. The subjects of the three are distinct, and likewise the tone and manner of treatment. Yet they were not unaffected by each other ; for instance, the hard feudal spirit of the *chansons de geste* became touched with the tastes which moulded the two other groups, and there was even a borrowing of topic. This was natural, as the periods of their composition over-lapped, and doubtless their audiences were in part the same.

The *chansons de geste* (*gesta* = deeds) were epic narratives with historical facts for subjects, and commonly were composed in ten-syllable assonanced or (later) rhyming couplets, *laisses* so called, the same final assonance or rhyme extending through a dozen or so lines. They told the deeds of Charlemagne and his barons, or the feuds of the barons among themselves, especially those of the time following the emperor's death. So the subject might be national, for instance the war against the Saracens in Spain ; or it might be more provincially feudal in every sense of the latter word.[1] It is not to our purpose to discuss how these poems grew through successive generations, nor how much of Teutonic spirit they put in Romance forms of verse. They were composed by trouvères or *jongleurs*. The *Roland* is the earliest of them, and in its extant form belongs to the last part of the eleventh century. One or two others are nearly as early ; but the vast majority, as we have them, are the creations, or rather the *remaniements*, of the twelfth and thirteenth centuries.

These *chansons* present the feudal system in epic action. They blazon forth its virtues and its horrors. The heroes are called barons (*ber*) and also chevaliers ;[2] *vassalage* and prowess (*proecce*) are closely joined ; the *Roland* speaks of the *vassalage* of Charles *le ber* (Charlemagne). The usages of chivalry are found :[3] a baron begins as *enfant*, and does his youthful feats (*enfances*) ; then he is girt with manhood's sword and given the thwack which dubs him *chevalier*. Naturally, the chivalry of the *chansons* is feudal rather than romantic. It is chivalry, sometimes crusading against " felun paien," sometimes making war against emperors or rivals ; always truculent, yet fighting for an object and not for pure adventure's sake or the love of ladies. The motives of action are quite tangible, and the tales reflect actual situations and conditions. They tell what knights (the chevaliers and barons) really did, though, of course, the particular incidents related may not be historical. Naturally they speak from the time of their composition. The *Roland*,

---

[1] On the *chansons de geste* see Gaston Paris, *Littérature française au moyen âge* ; Leon Gautier in Petit de Julleville's *Histoire de la langue et de la littérature française*, vol. i. ; more at length, J. Bedier, *Les Légendes Épiques*, 4 vols. (1908) ; P. Paris in vol. 22 of *L'Histoire littéraire de France* ; also Nyrop, *Storia dell' epopea francese nel medio evo*. Ample bibliographies will be found in these works.

[2] On the field of Roncesvalles, Roland folds the hands of the dead Archbishop Turpin, and grieves over him, beginning :

" E ! gentilz hum chevaliers de bon aire, . . ."

(*Roland*, line 2252).

[3] Leon Gautier, in his *Chevalerie*, makes the *chansons de geste* his chief source.

for example, throbs with the crusading wrath of the eleventh century—a new fervour, and no passionate memory of the old obscure disaster of Roncesvalles. It does not speak from the time of the great emperor. For when Charlemagne lived there was neither a " dulce France " nor the sentiment which enshrined it ; nor was there a sharply deliminated feudal Christianity set over against a world of " felun paien " —those false paynim, who should be trusted by no Christian baron. The whole poem revolves around a treason plotted by a renegade among vile infidels.

In this rude poem which carries the noblest spirit of the *chansons de geste,* the soul of feudal chivalry climbs to its height of loyal expiation for overweening bravery. The battle-note is given in Roland's words, as Oliver descries the masses of paynim closing in around that valiant rear-guard.

Said Oliver : " Sir comrade, I think we shall have battle with these Saracens."

Replied Roland : " God grant it ! Here must we hold for our king. A man should suffer for his lord, endure heat and cold, though he lose his hair and hide. Let each one strike his best, that no evil song be sung of us. The paynim are in the wrong, Christians in the right ! " [1]

Then follows Oliver's prudent solicitation, and Roland's fatal refusal to sound his horn and recall Charles and his host : " Please God and His holy angels, France shall not be so shamed through me ; better death than such dishonour. The harder we strike, the more the emperor will love us." Oliver can be stubborn too ; for when the fight is close to its fell end, he swears that Roland shall never wed his sister Aude, if, beaten, he sound that horn.[2]

The paynim host is shattered and riven ; but nearly all the Franks have fallen. Roland looks upon the mountains and the plain. Of those of France he sees so many lying dead, and he laments them like a high-born knight (*chevaliers gentilz*). " *Seigneurs barons,* may God have pity on you and grant Paradise to your souls, and give them to repose on holy flowers ! Better vassals shall I never see ; long are the years that you have served me, and conquered wide countries for Charles—the emperor has nurtured you for an

---

[1] 1006-1016.   [2] 1051 *sqq.* and 1700 *sqq.*

ill end! Land of France, sweet land, to-day bereft of barons of high prize! Barons of France! for me I see you dying. I cannot save or defend you! God be your aid, who never lies! Oliver, brother, you I must not fail. I shall die of grief, if no one slay me! Sir comrade, let us strike again." [1]

Roland and Oliver are almost alone, and Oliver receives a death-stroke. With his last strength he slays his slayer, shouts his defiance, and calls Roland to his aid. He strikes on blindly as Roland comes and looks into his face;—and then might you have seen Roland swoon on his horse, and Oliver wounded to death. " He had bled so much, that his eyes were troubled, and he could not see to recognize any mortal man. As he met his comrade, he struck him on his helmet a blow that cut it shear in twain, though the sword did not touch the head. At this Roland looked at him, and asked him soft and low : ' Sir comrade, did you mean that ? It is Roland, who loves you well. You have not defied me.'

" Says Oliver, ' Now I hear you speak ; I did not see you ; may the Lord God see you! I have struck you ; for which pardon me.' "

Roland replied : " I was not hurt. I pardon you here and before God."

" At this word they bent over each other, and in such love they parted." Oliver feels his death-anguish at hand ; sight and hearing fail him : he sinks from his horse and lies on the earth ; he confesses his sins, with his two hands joined toward heaven. He prays God to grant him Paradise, and blesses Charles and sweet France, and his comrade Roland above all men. Stretched on the ground the count lies dead. [2]

A little after, when Roland and Turpin the stout archbishop have made their last charge, and the paynim have withdrawn, and the archbishop too lies on the ground, just breathing ; then it is that Roland gathers the bodies of the peers and carries them one by one to lay them before the archbishop for his absolution. He finds Oliver's body, and tightly straining it to his heart, lays it with the rest before the archbishop, whose dying breath is blessing and absolving

---

[1] 1851-1868.　　　　　[2] 1940-2023.

his companions. And with tears Roland's voice breaks :
" Sweet comrade, Oliver, son of the good count Renier, who
held the March of Geneva ; to break spear and pierce shield,
and counsel loyally the good, and discomfit and vanquish
villains, in no land was there better knight." [1] Knowing his
own death near, Roland tries to shatter his great sword, and
then lies down upon it with his face toward Spain ; he holds
up his glove toward God in token of fealty ; Gabriel accepts
his glove and the angels receive his soul.

This was the best of knighthood in the best of the
chansons : and we see how close it was to what was best
in life. As the fight moves on to Oliver's blow and Roland's
pardon, to Roland's last deeds of Christian comradeship, and
to his death, the eyes are critical indeed that do not swell
with tears. The heroic pathos of this rough poem is great
because the qualities which perished at Roncesvalles were so
noble and so knightly.

The poem passes on to the vengeance taken by the
emperor upon the Saracens, then to his return to Aix, and
the short great scene between him and Aude, Roland's
betrothed :

" Where is Roland, the chief, who vowed to take me for
his wife ? "

Charles weeps, and tears his white beard as he answers :
" Sister, dear friend, you are asking about a dead man.
But I will make it good to thee—there is Louis my son,
who holds the Marches. . . . "

Aude replies : " Strange words ! God forbid, and His
saints and angels, that I should live after Roland." And
she falls dead at the emperor's feet.

As was fitting, the poem closes with the trial of the
traitor Ganelon, by combat. His defence is feudal : he had
defied Roland and all his companions ; his treachery was
proper vengeance and not treason. But his champion is
defeated, and Ganelon himself is torn in pieces by horses,
while his relatives, pledged as hostages, are hanged. All of
which is feudalism, and can be matched for savagery in
many a scene from the Arthurian romances of chivalry—
not always reproduced in modern versions.

[1] 2164 *sqq.*

So the *chansons de geste* are a mirror of the ways and customs of feudal society in the twelfth century. The feudal virtues are there, troth to one's liege, orthodox crusading ardour, limitless valour, truth-speaking. There is also enormous brutality ; and the recognized feudal vices, cruelty, impiousness, and treason. In the *Raoul de Cambrai*, for example, the nominal hero is a paroxysm of ferocity and impiety. All crimes rejoice him as he rages along his ruthless way to establish his seignorial rights over a fief unjustly awarded him by Louis, the weak son of Charlemagne. His foil is Bernier, the natural son of one of the rightful heirs against whom Raoul carries on raging feudal war. But Bernier is also Raoul's squire and vassal, who had received knighthood from him, and so is bound to the monster by the strongest feudal tie. He is a pattern of knighthood and of every feudal virtue. On the day of his knighting he implored his lord not to enter on that fell war against his (Bernier's) family. In vain. The war is begun with fire and sword. Bernier must support his lord ; says he : " Raoul, my lord, is worse (*plu fel*) than Judas ; he is my lord ; he has given me horse and clothes, my arms and cloth of gold. I would not fail him for the riches of Damascus " : and all cried, " Bernier, thou art right." [1]

But there is a limit. Raoul is ferociously wasting the land, and committing every impiety. He would desecrate the abbey of Origni, and set his tent in the middle of the church, stabling his horse in its porch and making his bed before the altar. Bernier's mother is there as a nun ; Raoul pauses at her entreaties and those of his uncle. Then his rage breaks out afresh at the death of two of his men ; he burns the town and abbey, and Bernier's mother perishes with the other nuns in the flames.

Now the monster is feasting on the scene of desolation —and it is Lent besides ! After dining, he plays chess : enter Bernier. Raoul asks for wine. Bernier takes the cup and, kneeling, hands it to him. Raoul is surprised to see him, but at once renews his oath to disinherit all of Bernier's family—his father and uncles. Bernier speaks and re-proaches Raoul with his mother's death : " I cannot bring

[1] *Raoul de Cambrai*, cited by Gautier, *Chevalerie*, p. 75.

her back to life, but I can aid my father whom you unjustly follow up with war. I am your man no longer. Your cruelty has released me from my duties ; and you will find me on the side of my father and uncles when you attack them." For reply, Raoul breaks his head open with the butt of his spear ; but then at once asks pardon and humiliates himself strangely. Bernier answers that there shall be no peace between them till the blood which flowed from his head returns back whence it came. Yet in the final battle he still seeks to turn Raoul back before attacking him who had been his liege lord. Again in vain ; and Raoul falls beneath Bernier's sword. Here are the two sides of the picture, the monster of a lord, the vassal vainly seeking to be true : a situation utterly tragic from the standpoint of feudal chivalry.

It is not to be supposed that a huge body of poetic narrative could remain utterly truculent. Other motives had to enter ;—the love of women, of which the *Roland* has its one great flash. The ladies of the *chansons* are not coy, and often make the first advances. Such natural lusty love is not romantic ; it is not *l'amour courtois* ; and marriage is its obvious end. The *chansons* also tend to become adventurous and to fill with romantic episode. An interesting example of this is the *Renaud de Montauban* where Renaud and his three brothers are aided by the enchanter, Maugis, against the pursuing hate of Charlemagne, and where the marvellous horse, Bayard, is a fascinating personality. This diversified and romantic tale long held its own in many tongues. In the somewhat later *Huon de Bordeaux* we are at last in fairyland—verily at the Court of Oberon—his first known entry into literature.[1] Thus the *chansons* tend toward the tone and temper of the *romans d'aventure*.

The latter have the courtly love and the purely adventurous motives of the Arthurian romances, with which the men who fashioned them probably were acquainted, as were the *jongleurs* who recast certain of the *chansons de geste* to suit a more courtly taste. Of the *romans*

---

[1] Unless indeed Oberon, the fairy king, be a romantic form of the Alberich of the *Nibelungen* (Gaston Paris).

d'aventure, so called, the *Blancandrin* or the *Amadas* or the *Flamenca* may be taken as the type ; or, if one will, *Flore et Blanchefleur* and *Aucassin et Nicolette*, those two enduring lovers' tales.[1]   Courtly love and knightly ventures are the themes of these *romans* so illustrative of noble French society in the thirteenth century.   They differ from the Arthurian romances in having a somewhat broader origin ; and their heroes and heroines are sometimes of more easily imagined historicity than the knights and ladies of the Round Table.   But they never approached the universal vogue of the Arthurian Cycle.

It goes without saying that tastes in reading (or rather listening) diverged in the twelfth century, just as in the twentieth.   One cannot read the old *chansons de geste* in which fighting, and not love, is the absorbing topic, without feeling that the audience before whom they were chanted was predominantly male.   One cannot but feel the contrary to have been the fact with the romances in verse and prose which constitute that immense mass of literature vaguely termed Arthurian.   These two huge groups, the *chansons de geste* and the Arthurian romances, overlap chronologically and geographically.   Although the development of the *chansons* was somewhat earlier, the Arthurian stories were flourishing before the *chansons* were past their prime ; and both were in vogue through central and northern France. But the Arthurian stories won adoptive homes in England, Germany, Italy, and elsewhere.   Indeed their earlier stages scarcely seem attached to real localities : nor were their manners and interests rooted in the special traditions of any definite place.

The tone and topics of these romances suggest an audience chiefly of women, and possibly feminine authorship. Doubtless, with a few exceptions, men composed and recited them.   But the male authors were influenced by the taste, the favour and patronage, and the sympathetic suggestive interest of the ladies.   Prominent among the first known

[1] See Gaston Paris, *Lit. française, etc.*, chaps. iii. and v. ; and Émile Littré in vol. 22 of the *Histoire littéraire de la France*. For examples of these *romans*, see Langlois, *La société française au XIIe siècle d'après dix romans d'aventure* (2nd ed., Paris, 1904).

composers of these " Breton " poems was a woman, Marie de France as she is called, who lived in England in the reign of Henry II. (1154-1189). Her younger contemporary was the facile trouvère Chrétien de Troies, of whose life little is actually known. But we know that the subject of his famous Lancelot romance, called the *Conte de la charrette*, was suggested to him (about 1170) by the Countess Marie de Champagne, daughter of Louis VII. Surely then he wrote to please the taste of that royal dame, whose queenly mother, Eleanor of Aquitaine, was also a patroness of this courtly poetry.

These are instances proving the feminine influence upon the composition of these romances. And the growth of this great Arthurian Cycle represents, *par excellence*, the entry of womanhood into the literature of chivalry. Men love, as well as women ; but the topic engrosses them less, and they talk less about it. Likewise men appreciate courtesy ; but in fact it is woman's influence that softens manners. And while the masculine fancy may be drawn by what is fanciful and romantic, women abandon themselves to its charm.

Of course the origin or *provenance* of these romances was different from that of the *chansons de geste*. It was Breton—it was Welsh, it was *walhisch* (the Old-German word for the same) which means that it was *foreign*. In fact, the beginnings of these stories floated beautifully in from a *weiss-nicht-wo* which in the twelfth century was already hidden in the clouds. When the names of known localities are mentioned, they have misty import. Arthurian geography is more elusive than Homeric.

In the twelfth and thirteenth centuries these stories took form in the verse and prose compositions in which they still exist. Sometimes the poet's name is known, Chrétien de Troies, for instance ; but the source from which he drew is doubtful. It probably was Breton, and Artus once in Great Britain fought the Saxons like as not. But the growth, the development, the further composition, of the *matière de Bretagne* is predominantly French. In France it grows ; from France it passes on across the Rhine, across the Alps, then back to what may have been its old

home across the British Channel. With equal ease on the
wings of universal human interest it surmounts the Pyrenees.
It would have crossed the ocean, had the New World been
discovered.

Far be it from our purpose to enter the bottomless
swamp of critical discussion of the source and history of the
Arthurian romances. Two or three statements—general
and probably rather incorrect—may be made. Marie de
France, soon after the middle of the twelfth century, wrote
a number of shortish narrative poems of chivalric manners
and romantic love, which, as it were, touch the hem of
Arthur's cloak. Chrétien de Troies between 1160 and
1175 composed his *Tristan* (a story originally having
nothing to do with Arthur), and then his *Erec* (Geraint), then
Cligés ; then his (unfinished) *Lancelot* or the *Conte de la
charrette* ; then *Ivain* or the *Chevalier au lion*, and at last
Perceval or the *Conte du Graal*. How much of the matter
of these poems came from Brittany—or indirectly from
Great Britain ? This is a large unsolved question ! Another
is the relation of Chrétien's poems to the subsequent
Arthurian romances in verse and prose. And perhaps
most disputed of all is the authorship (Beroul ? Robert
de Boron ? Walter Mapes ?) of this mass of Arthurian Old
French literature which was not the work of Chrétien.
Without lengthy *prolegomena* it would be fruitless to attempt
to order and name these compositions. The Arthurian
matters were taken up by German poets of excellence—
Heinrich von Veldeke, Hartmann von Aue, Gottfried von
Strassburg, Wolfram von Eschenbach,—and sometimes the
best existing versions are the work of the latter ; for instance,
Wolfram's *Parzival* and Gottfried's *Tristan*. And again the
relation of these German versions to their French originals
becomes still another problem.

For the chivalry of these romances, one may look to the
poems of Chrétien and to passages in the Old French prose
(presumably of the early thirteenth century), to which the
name of Robert de Boron or Walter Mapes is attached.
Chrétien enumerates knightly excellences in his *Cligés*, and,
speaking from the natural point of view of the *jongleur*, he
puts *largesce* (generosity) at their head. This, says he,

makes one a *prodome* more than *hautesce* (high station) or *corteisie* or *savoirs* or *jantillesce* (noble birth) or *chevalerie*, or *hardemanz* (hardihood) or *seignorie*, or *biautez* (beauty).[1]

Such are the knightly virtues, which, however, reach their full worth only through the aid of that which makes perfect the Arthurian knight, the high love of ladies, shortly to be spoken of. In the meanwhile let us turn from Chrétien to the broader tableau of the Old French prose, and note the beginning of *Artus*, as he is there called. The lineage of the royal boy remains romantically undiscovered, till the time when he is declared to be the king. It is then that he receives all kinds of riches from the lords of his realm. He keeps nothing for himself ; but makes inquiry as to the character and circumstances of his future knights, and distributes all among them according to their worth. This is the virtue of *largesce*.

Now comes the ceremony of making him a knight, and then of investing him with, as it were, the supreme knighthood of kingship. The archbishop, it is told, " fist (made) Artu chevalier, et celle nuit veilla Artus a la mestre Eglise (the cathedral) jusques au jour." Then follows the ceremony of swearing allegiance to him ; but Arthur has not yet finally taken his great sword. When he is arrayed for the mass, the archbishop says to him : " Allez querre (seek) l'espee et la jostise dont vos devez defendre Saincte Eglise et la crestiante sauver."

" Lors alla la procession au perron, et la demanda li arcevesques a Artu, se il est tiels que il osast jurer et creanter Dieu et madame Sainte Marie et a tous Sains et toutes Saintes, Sainte Eglise a sauver et a maintenir, et a tous povres homes et toutes povres femmes pais et loiaute tenir, et conseiller tous desconseillies, et avoier (guide) tous desvoies (erring), et maintenir toutes droitures et droite justice a tenir, si alast avant et priest l'espee dont nostre sire avoit fait de lui election. Et Artus plora et dist : ' Ensi voirement com Dieus est sire de toutes les choses, me donit-il force et povoir de ce maintenir que vous avez dit.'

" Il fu a genols et prit l'espee a jointes mains et la leva de l'enclume (anvil) ausi voirement come se ele ne tenist a riens ; et lors, l'espee toute droite, l'enmenerent a l'autel et la mist sus ;

---

[1] Chrétien, *Cligés*, line 201 *sqq.*

et lors il le pristrent et sacrerent et l'enoindrent, et li firent toutes iceles choses que l'en doit faire a roi." [1]

All this is good chivalry as well as proper feudalism. And there are other instances of genuine feudalism in these Romances. Such is the scene between the good knight Pharien and the bad king Claudas, where the former renounces his allegiance to the latter (*je declare renoncer a vostre fief*) and then declares himself to be Claudas's enemy, and claims the right to fight or slay him ; since Claudas has not kept troth with him.[2]

There is perhaps nothing lovelier in all these Romances than the story of the young Lancelot, reared by the tender care of the Lady of the Lake. His training supplements the genial instincts of his nature, and the result is the mirror of all knighthood's qualities. He is noble, he is true, he is perfect in bravery, in courtesy, in modesty, the Lady imparting the precepts of these virtues to his ready spirit.[3] There is no knightly virtue that is not perfect in this peerless youth, as he sets forth to Arthur's Court, there to receive knighthood and prove himself the peerless knight and perfect lover. In this Old French prose his career is set forth most completely, and most correctly, so to speak. One or two points may be adverted to.

Lancelot is not strictly Arthur's knight. Originally he owed no fealty to him ; and he avoided receiving his sword from the king, in order that he might receive it from Guinever, as he did. And so, from the first, Lancelot was Guinever's knight, as he was afterwards her accepted lover. Consequently his relations to her broke no fealty of his to Arthur.

Again, one notices that the absolute character of Lancelot's love and troth to Guinever is paralleled by the friendship of the high prince Galahaut to him. That has the same *précieuse* logic ; it is absolute. No act or thought

[1] The Old French from vol. ii. of P. Paris, *Romans de la Table Ronde*, p. 96. One sees that the coronation is a larger knighting, and kingship a larger knighthood.
[2] *Romans de la Table Ronde*, iii. 96. This scene closely parallels that between Bernier and Raoul de Cambrai, instanced above.
[3] See the first part of vol. iii. of *Romans de la Table Ronde*, especially pp. 113-117.

of Galahaut infringes friendship's least conceived require-
ment , while conversely that marvellous high prince leaves
undone no act, however extreme, which can carry out the
logic of this absolute single-souled devotion. At last he
dies on thinking that Lancelot is dead ; just as the latter
could not have survived the death of Guinever. In spite of
the beauty of Galahaut's devotion, its logic and preciosity
scarcely throb with manhood's blood. It will not cause our
eyes to swell with human tears, as did the blind blow and
the true words which passed between Oliver and Roland at
Roncesvalles.[1]

Chivalry—the institution and the whole knightly
character—began in the rough and veritable, and progressed
to courtlier idealizations. Likewise that knightly virtue,
love of woman, displays a parallel evolution, being part of
the chivalric whole. Beginning in natural qualities, its
progress is romantic, logical, fantastic, even mystical.

Feudal life in the earlier mediaeval centuries did not
foster tender sentiments between betrothed or wedded
couples. The chief object of every landholder was by
force or policy to secure his own safety and increase his

---

[1] It would be easy to go on drawing illustrations of the actual and imaginative elements in chivalry, until this chapter should grow into an encyclopaedia.
They could so easily be taken from many kinds of mediaeval literature in all the
mediaeval tongues. The French has barely been touched upon. It affords an
exhaustless store. Then in the German we might draw upon the courtly epics,
Gottfried of Strassburg's *Tristan* or the *Parzival* of Wolfram von Eschenbach ;
or on the *Nibelungenlied*, wherein Siegfried is a very knight. Or we might draw
upon the knightly precepts (the Ritterlehre) of the Winsbeke and the Winsbekin
(printed in Hildebrand's *Didaktik aus der Zeit der Kreuzzüge*, Deutsche Nat.
Litt.). And we might delve in the great store of Latin Chronicles which relate
the mediaeval history of German kings and nobles. In Spanish, there would
be the *Cid*, and how much more besides. In Italian we should have latter-day
romantic chivalry ; Pulci's *Rotta di Roncisvalle* ; Boiardo's *Orlando innamorato* ;
Ariosto's *Orlando furioso* ; still later, Tasso's *Gerusalemme liberata*, which takes
us well out of the Middle Ages.   And in English there is much Arthurian romance ;
there is *Chevy Chace* ; and we may come down through Chaucer's *Knight's Tale*
to the sunset beauty of Spenser's *Fairie Queen*. This glorious poem should
serve to fix in our minds the principle that chivalry, knighthood, was not merely
a material fact, a ceremony and an institution ; but that it also was that ultra-
reality, a spirit. And this spirit's ideal creations—the ideal creations of the
many phases of this spirit—accorded with actual deeds which may be read of
in the old Chronicles. For final exemplification of the actual and the ideally
real in chivalry, the reader may look within himself, and observe the inextricable
mingling of the imaginative and the real. He will recognize that what at one
time seems part of his imagination, at another will prove itself the veriest reality
of his life. Even such wavering verity of spirit was chivalry.

retainers and possessions. A ready means was for him to marry lands and serfs in the robust person of the daughter, or widow, of some other baron. The marriage was prefaced by scant courtship ; and little love was likely to ensue between the rough-handed husband and high-tempered wife. Such conditions, whether in Languedoc, Aquitaine, or Champagne, made it likely that high-blooded men and women would satisfy their amorous cravings outside the bonds of matrimony. For these reasons, among others, the Provençal and Old French literature, which was the medium of development for the sentiment of love, did not commonly concern itself with bringing lovers to the altar.

In literature, as in life, marriage is usually the goal of bliss and silence for love-song and love-story : attainment quells the fictile elements of fear and hope. Entire classes of mediaeval poetry like the *aube* (dawn) and the *pastorelle* had no thought of marriage. The former *genre* of Provençal and Old French, as well as Old German, poetry, is a lyric dialogue wherein the sentiments of lover and mistress become more tender with the approach of the envious dawn.[1] The latter is the song of the merry encounter of some clerk or cavalier with a mocking or complaisant shepherdess. Yet one must beware of speaking too categorically. For in mediaeval love-literature, marriage is looked forward to or excluded according to circumstances ; and there are instances of romantic love where the lovers are blessed securely by the priest at the beginning of their adventures. But whether the lover look to wed his lady, or whether he have wedded her, or whether she be but his paramour, is all a thing of incident, dependent on the traditional or devised plot of the story.[2]

Like all other periods that have been articulate in

[1] See Gaston Paris in *Journal des savants*, 1892, pp. 161-163. Of course the English reader cannot but think of the brief secret marriage between Romeo and Juliet.

[2] Marriage or no marriage depends on the plot ; but occasionally a certain respect for marriage is shown, as in the *Eliduc* of Marie de France, and of course far more strongly in Wolfram's *Parzival*. In Chrétien's *Ivain* the hero marries early in the story ; and thereafter his wife acts towards him with the haughty caprice of an *amie* ; Ivain, at her displeasure, goes mad, like an *ami*. The *romans d'aventure* afford other instances of this courtly love, sometimes illicit, sometimes looking to marriage. See Langlois, *La Société française au XIIIᵉ siècle d'après dix romans d'aventure.*

literature—and those that have not been, so far as one may guess—the Middle Ages experienced and expressed the usual ways of love. These need not detain us. For they were included as elements within those interesting forms of romantic love, which were presented in the lyrics of the Troubadours and their more or less conscious imitators, and in the romantic narratives of chivalry. This literature elaborately expresses mediaeval sentiments and also love's passion. Its ideals drew inspiration from Christianity and many a suggestion from the antique. More especially, in its growth, at last two currents seem to meet. The one sprang from the fashions of Languedoc and the courtly centres of the north ; the other was the strain of fantasy and passion constituting the *matière de Bretagne*.

Languedoc had been Romanized before the Christian era, and thereafter did not cease to be the home of the surviving Latin culture. By the eleventh century, castles and towns held a gay and aristocratic society, on which Christianity, honeycombed with heresy, sat lightly, or at least joyfully. This society was inclined to luxury, and the gentle relationships between men and women interested it exceedingly. Out of it as the eleventh century closes, songs of the Troubadours begin to rise and give utterance to thoughts and feelings of chivalric love. These songs flourished during the whole of the twelfth century, and then their notes were crushed by the Albigensian Crusade, which destroyed the pretty life from which they sprang.

She whom such songs were meant to adulate or win, frequently was the wife of the Troubadour's lord. The song might intend nothing beyond such worship as the lady's spouse would sanction ; or it might give subtle voice to a real passion, which offered and sought all. To separate the sincere and passionate from the fanciful in such songs is neither easy nor apt, since fancy may enhance the expression of passion, or present a pleasing substitute. At all events, in this very personal poetry, passion and imaginative enhancings blended in verses that might move a lady's heart or vanity.

Love, with the Troubadours and their ladies, was a source of joy. Its commands and exigencies made life's

supreme law. Love was knighthood's service ; it was
loyalty and devotion ; it was the noblest human giving. It
was also the spring of excellence, the inspiration of high
deeds. This love was courteous, delicately ceremonial,
precise, and on the lady's part exacting and whimsical. A
moderate knowledge of the poems and lives of the Troubadours and their ladies will show that love with its joys and
pains, its passion, its fancies and subtle conclusions, made
the life and business of these men and dames.[1]

In culture and the love of pleasure the great feudal
courts of Aquitaine, Champagne, and even Flanders, were
scarcely behind the society of Languedoc. And at these
courts, rather than in Languedoc, courtly love encountered
a new passionate current, and found the tales which
were to form its chief vehicle. These were the poems
and stories, as of Tristan and of Arthur and his knights,
which from Great Britain had come to Brittany and Normandy. They were now attracting many listeners who had
no part with Arthur or Tristan, save the love of love and
adventure. Marie de France had put certain Breton lays
into Old French verse. And one or two decades later, a
request from the great Countess Marie de Champagne led
Chrétien de Troies, as we have seen, to recast other Breton
tales in a manner somewhat transformed with thoughts of
courtly love. These northern poems of love and chivalry
were written to please the taste of high-born dames, just as
the Troubadours had sung and still were singing to please
their sisters in the south. The southern poems influenced
the northern.[2]

In the courtly society of Champagne and Aquitaine
diverse racial elements had long been blending, and acquirements, once foreign, had turned into personal qualities.
Views of life had been evolved, along with faculties to
express them. Likewise modes of feeling had developed.

[1] On Provençal poetry see Diez, *Poesie der Troubadours* (2nd ed. by Bartsch,
Leipzig, 1883) ; *id., Leben und Werke der Troubadours* ; Justin H. Smith, *The
Troubadours at Home* (New York and London, 1899) ; Ida Farnell, *Lives of the
Troubadours* (London).

[2] Cf. Gaston Paris, t. 30, pp. 1-18, *Hist. lit. de la France* ; Paul Meyer, *Romania*,
v. 257-268 ; xix. 1-62. "Trouvère" is the Old French word corresponding to
Provençal "Troubadour."

This society had become what it was within the influence of Christianity and the antique educational tradition. It knew the Song of Songs, as well as Ovid's stories, and likewise his *Ars amatoria*, which Chrétien was the first to translate into Old French. Possibly its Christianity had learned of a boundless love of God, and its mortal nature might feel mortal loves equally resistless. And now, in the early twelfth century, there came from lands which were or had been Breton, an abundance of moving and catching stories of adventure and of passion which broke through restraint, or knew none. Dames and knights and their rhymers would eagerly receive such tales, and not as barren vessels ; for they refashioned and reinspired them with their own thoughts of the joy of life and love, and with thoughts of love's high service and its uplifting virtue for the lover, and again of its ways and the laws which should direct and guide, but never stem, it.

Thus it came that French trouvères enlarged the matter of these Breton poems. Their romances reflected the loftiest thoughts and the most eloquent emotion pertaining to the earthly side of mediaeval life. In these rhyming and prose compositions, love was resistless in power ; it absorbed the lover's nature ; it became his sole source of joy and pain. So it sought nothing but its own fulfilment ; it knew no honour save its own demands. It was unimpeachable, for in ecstasy and grief it was accountable to no law except that of its being. This resistless love was also life's highest worth, and the spring of inspiration and strength for doing valorously and living nobly. The trouvère of the twelfth century created new conceptions of love's service, and therewith the impassioned thought that beyond what men might do in the hope of love's fruition or at the dictates of its affection, love was itself a power strengthening and ennobling him who loved. Thought and feeling joined in this conviction, each helping the other on, in interchanging rôles of inspirer and inspired. And finally the two are one :

> "Oltre la spera, che più larga gira,
>   Passa il sospiro ch' esce del mio core:
> Intelligenza nuova, che l' Amore
>   Piangendo mette in lui, pur su lo tira."

No one can separate the thought and feeling in this verse.
But they were not always fused. The mediaeval fancy
sported with this love ; the mediaeval mind delighted in it as
a theme of argument. And the fancy might be as fantastic
as the reasoning was finely spun.

The literature of this love draws no sharp lines between
love as resistless passion and love as enabling virtue ; yet
these two aspects are distinguishable. The first was less
an original creation of the Middle Ages than the second.
Antiquity had known the passion which overwhelmed the
stricken mortal, and had treated it as something put upon
the man and woman, a convulsive joy, also a bane.
Antiquity had analyzed it too, and had shown its effects,
especially its physical symptoms. Much had been written
of its fatal nature ; songs had sung how it overthrew the
strong and brought men and women to their death. Looking
upon this love as something put on man and woman,
antiquity pictured it mainly as an insanity cast like a spell
upon some one who otherwise would have been sane. But
the Middle Ages saw love transformed into the man and
woman, saw it constitute their will as well as passion, and
perceived that it was their being. If the lover could not
avoid or resist it, the reason was because it was his mightiest
self, and not because it was a compulsion from without ; it
was his nature, not his disease.

The nature, ways, and laws of this high and ennobling
love were much pondered on and talked of. They were
expounded in pedantic treatises, as well as set forth in tales
which sometimes have the breath of universal life. Ovid's
Ars amatoria furnished the idea that love was an art to be
learned and practised. Mediaeval clerks and rhymers took
his light art seriously, and certain of them made manuals
of the rules and precepts of love, devised by themselves
and others interested in such fancies. An example is the
Flos amoris or *Ars amatoria* of Andrew the Chaplain, who
compiled his book not far from the year 1200.[1] He wrote
with his obsequious head filled with a sense of the authority

---

[1] On this work see Gaston Paris, *Romania*, xii. 524 *sqq*. (1883) ; *id.* in *Journal
des savants*, 1888, pp. 664 *sqq*. and 727 *sqq*. ; also (for extracts) Raynouard, *Choix
des poésies des Troubadours*, ii. lxxx. *sqq*.

in love matters of Marie de Champagne, and other great ladies. His book contains a number of curious questions which had been laid before one or the other of those reigning dames, and which they solved boldly in love's favour. Thus on solicitation Countess Marie decided that there could be no true love between a husband and wife ; and that the possession of an honoured husband or beautiful wife did not bar the proffer or acceptance of love from another. The living literature of love was never constrained by the foolishness of the first proposition, but was freely to exemplify the further conclusion which others besides the countess drew.

Andrew gives a code of love's rules. He would have no one think that he composed them ; but that he saw them written on a parchment attached to the hawk's perch, and won at Arthur's Court by the valour of a certain Breton knight. They read like proverbs, and undoubtedly represent the ideas of courtly society upon courtly love. There are thirty-one of them—for example :

(1) Marriage is not a good excuse for rejecting love.
(2) Who does not conceal, cannot love.
(3) None can love two at once. There is no reason why a woman should not be loved by two men, or a man by two women.
(4) It is love's way always to increase or lessen.
(9) None can love except one who is moved by love's suasion.
(12) The true lover has no desire to embrace any one except his (or her) co-lover (co-amans).
(13) Love when published rarely endures.
(14) Easy winning makes love despicable ; the difficult is held dear.
(15) Every lover turns pale in the sight of the co-lover.
(16) The lover's heart trembles at the sudden sight of the co-lover.
(18) Prowess (probitas) alone makes one worthy of love.
(20) The lover is always fearful.
(23) The one whom the thought of love disturbs, eats and sleeps little.
(25) The true lover finds happiness only in what he deems will please his co-lover.
(28) A slight fault in the lover awakens the co-lover's suspicion.
(30) The true lover constantly, without intermission, is engrossed with the image of the co-lover.

These rules were exemplified in the imaginative litera-

ture of courtly love. Such love and the feats inspired by
it made the chief matter of the Arthurian romances, which
became the literary property of western Europe ; and the
supreme examples of their darling theme are the careers and
fortunes of the two most famous pairs of lovers in all this
gallant cycle, Tristan and Iseult, Lancelot and Guinevere.
In the former story love is resistless passion ; in the latter
its virtue- and valour-bestowing qualities appear.   In both,
the laws forbidding its fruition are shattered : in the Tristan
story blindly, madly, without further thought ; while in the
tale of Lancelot this conflict sometimes rises to consciousness even in the lovers' hearts.   How chivalric love may
reach accord with Christian precept will be shown hereafter
in the progress of the white and scarlet soul of Parzival, the
brave man proving himself slowly wise.

Probably there never was a better version of the story of
Tristan and Iseult than that of Gottfried of Strassburg, who
transformed French originals into his Middle High German
poem about the year 1210.[1] The poet-adapter sets forth
his ideas of love in an elaborate prologue.   Very anti-
thetically he shows its bitter sweet, its dear sorrow,
its yearning need ; indeed to love is to yearn—an idea
not strange to Plato—and Gottfried uses the words
sene, senelich, senedaere (all of which are related to *sehn-
sucht*, which is yearning) to signify love, a lover, and his
pain.   His poem shall be of two noble lovers :

> " Ein senedaere, eine senedaerin."

The more love's fire burns the heart, the more one
loves ; this pain is full of love, an ill so good for the heart
that no noble nature once roused by it would wish to lose
part therein.   Who never felt love's pain has never felt love :

> " Liep unde leit diu waren ie
> An minnen ungescheiden."

It is good for men to hear a tale of noble love, yes, a
deep good.   It sweetens love and raises the hearer's mood ;
it strengthens troth, enriches life.   Love, troth, a constant

---

[1] On origins and sources see, generally, Gaston Paris, *Tristan and Iseult* (Paris,
1894), reprinted from *Revue de Paris* of April 15, 1894 ; W. Golther, *Die Sage von
Tristan und Isolde* (Munich, 1887).

spirit, honour, and whatever else is good, are never so
precious as when set in a tale of love's joy and pain. Love
is such a blessed thing, such a blessed striving, that no one
without its teaching has worth or honour. These lovers
died long ago ; yet their love and troth, their life, their
death, will still give troth and honour to seekers after these.
Their death lives and is ever new, as we listen to the tale.
Evidently, in Gottfried's mind the Tristan tale of love's
almighty passion carried the thought of love as the inspiration of a noble life.   Yet that thought was not native to the
legend, and finds scant exemplification in Gottfried's poem.

The tragic passion of the main narrative is presaged by
the story of Tristan's parents. His mother was Blancheflur,
King Mark's sister, and his father Prince Riwalin. She saw
him in the May-court tourney held near Tintajoel. She
took him into her thoughts ; he entered her heart, and
there wore crown and sceptre.

She greeted him ; he her. She bashfully began :—" My
lord, may God enrich your heart and courage ; but I harbour
something against you."

" Sweet one, what have I done ? "

" You have done violence to my best friend "—it was
her heart, she meant.

" Beauty, bear me no hate for that ; command, and I
will do your bidding."

" Then I will not hate you bitterly. I will see what
atonement you will make."

He bowed, and carried with him her image. Love's
will mastered his heart, as he thought of Blancheflur, of her
hair, her brow, her cheek, her mouth, her chin, and the glad
Easter day that smiling lay in her eyes. Love the heart-
burner set his heart aflame, and lo ! he entered upon another
life ; purpose and habit changed, he was another man.

Sad is the short tale of these lovers. Riwalin is killed
in battle, and at the news of his death Blancheflur expires,
giving birth to a son. Rual the Faithful names the child
Tristan, to symbolize the sorrow of its birth.

The story of Tristan's early years draws the reader to
the accomplished, happy youth. He is the delight of all ;
for his young manhood is courtliness itself, and valour and

generosity. He is loved, and afterwards recognized and knighted, by his uncle Mark. Then he sets out and avenges his father's death ; after which he returns to Mark's Court, and vanquishes the Irish champion Morold. A fragment of Tristan's sword remained in Morold's head ; Tristan himself received a poisoned wound, which could be healed, as the dying Morold told him, only by Ireland's queen, Iseult. Very charming is the story of Tristan's first visit to Ireland, disguised as a harper, under the name of Tantris. The queen hearing of his skill, has him brought to the palace, where she heals him, and he in return becomes the teacher of her daughter, the younger Iseult, whom he instructs in letters, music and singing, French and Latin, ethics, courtly arts and manners, till the girl became as accomplished as she was beautiful, and could write and read, and compose and sing *pastorelles* and *rondeaux* and other songs.

On his return to Cornwall he told Mark of the young Iseult, and then, at Mark's request, set forth again to woo her for him. The Irish king has promised his daughter to whoever shall slay the dragon. Tristan does the deed, cuts out the dragon's tongue as proof, and then falls overcome and fainting. The king's cupbearer comes by, breaks his lance on the dead dragon, and, riding on, announces that he has slain the monster ; he has the great head brought to the Court upon a wagon. Iseult is in despair at the thought of marrying the cupbearer ; her mother doubts his story, and bids Iseult ride out and search for the real slayer. The ladies discover Tristan, with him the dragon's tongue. They carry him to the palace to heal him, and the young Iseult recognizes him as the harper Tantris, and redoubles her kind care. But after a while she noticed the notch in his sword, and saw that it fitted the fragment found in Morold's head—and is not Tantris just Tristan reversed ? This is the man who slew Morold, her mother's brother ! She seizes the sword and rushes in to kill him in his bath. Her mother checks her, and at last she is appeased, Tristan letting them see that an important mission has brought him to Ireland. There is truce between them, and Tristan goes to the king with Mark's demand for Iseult's hand. Then the cupbearer is discomfited, peace is made between the

Irish king and Mark, and the young Iseult, with Brangaene her cousin, makes ready to sail with Tristan. The queen secretly gave a love-drink into Brangaene's care, which Iseult and Mark should drink together. The people followed down to the haven, and all wept and lamented that with fair Iseult the sunshine had left Ireland.

Iseult is sad. She cannot forget that it is Tristan who slew her uncle and is now taking her from her home. Tristan fails to comfort her. They see land. Tristan calls for wine to pledge Iseult. A little maid brings—the love-drink! They drink together, not wine but that endless heart's pain which shall be their common death. Too late, Brangaene with a cry throws the goblet into the sea. Love stole into both their hearts; gone was Iseult's hate. They were no longer two, but one; the sinner, love, had done it. They were each other's joy and pain; doubt and shame seized them. Tristan bethought him of his loyalty and honour, struggling against love vainly. Iseult was like a bird caught with the fowler's lime; shame drove her eyes away from him; but love drew her heart. She gave over the contest as she looked on him, and he also began to yield. They thought each other fairer than before; love was conquering.

The ship sails on. Love's need conquered. They talk together of the past, how he had once come in a little boat, and of the lessons: " Fair Iseult, what is troubling you ? "

" What I know, that troubles me; what I see, the heaven and sea, that weighs on me; body and life are heavy."

They leaned toward each other; bright eyes began to fill from the heart's spring; her head sank, his arm sustained her ;—" Ah! sweet, tell me, what is it ? "

Answered love's feather-play, Iseult : " Love is my need, love is my pain."

He answered painfully : " Fair Iseult, it is the rude wind and sea."

" No, no, it is not wind or sea; love is my pain."

" Beauty, so with me! Love and you make my need. Heart's lady, dear Iseult, you and the love of you have seized me. I am dazed. I cannot find myself. All the world has become naught, save thee alone."

"Sir, so is it with me."

They loved, and in each other saw one mind, one heart, one will. Their silent kiss was long. In the night, love the physician brought their only balm. Sweet had the voyage become ; alas ! that it must end.

With their landing begins the trickery and falsehood compelled by the situation. The fearful Iseult plotted to murder the true Brangaene, who alone knew. After a while Mark's suspicion is aroused, to be lulled by guile. Plot and counterplot go on ; the lovers win and win again ; truth and honour, everything save love's joy and fear and all-sufficiency, are cast to the winds. Even the " Judgment of God " is tricked ; the hot iron does not burn Iseult swearing her false oath, literally true. Many a time Mark's jealousy has been fiercely stirred, only to be tricked to sleep again. Yet he knows that Tristan and Iseult are lovers. He calls them to him ; he tells them he will not avenge himself, they are too dear to him. But let them take each other by the hand and leave him. So, together, they disappear in the forest.

Then comes the wonderful, beautiful story of the love-grotto and the lovers' forest-life ; they had the forest and they had themselves, and needed no more. One morning they arose to the sweet birds' song of greeting ; but they heard a horn ; Mark must be hunting near. So they were very careful, and again prepared deception. Mark has been told of the love-grotto in the wood. In the night he came and found it, looked through its little rustic window as the day began to dawn. There lay the lovers, apart, a naked sword between them. A sunbeam, stealing through the window, touches Iseult's cheek, touches her sweet mouth. Mark loves her anew. Then fearful lest the sunlight should disturb her, he covered the window with grass and leaves and flowers, blessed her, and went away in tears. The lovers waken. They had no need to fear. The lie of the naked sword again had won. Mark sends and invites them to return.

Insatiable love knew no surcease or pause. The German poet is driven to a few reflections on the deceits of Eve's daughters, the anxieties of forbidden love, and the

crown of worth and joy that a true woman's love may be
At last the lovers are betrayed—in each other's arms.
They know that Mark has seen them.

"Heart's lady, fair Iseult, now we must part. Let me
not pass from your heart. Iseult must ever be in Tristan's
heart. Forget me not."

Says Iseult : " Our hearts have been too long one ever
to know forgetting. Whether you are near or far, nothing
but Tristan enters mine. See to it that no other woman
parts us. Take this ring and think of me. Iseult with
Tristan has been ever one heart, one troth, one body, one
life. Think of me as your life—Iseult."

The fateful turning of the story is not far off : Tristan
has met the other Iseult, her of the white hands. The poet
Gottfried did not complete his work. He died, leaving
Tristan's heart struggling between the old love and the new
—the new and weaker love, but the more present offering
to pain. The story was variously concluded by different
rhymers, in Gottfried's time and after. The best ending is
the extant fragment of the *Tristan* by Thomas of Brittany,
the master whom Gottfried followed. In it, the wounded
Tristan dies at the false news of the black sails—the
treachery of Iseult of the white hands. The true Iseult
finds him dead ; kisses him, takes him in her arms, and
dies.

From the time when on the ship Tristan and Iseult cast
shame and honour to the winds, the story tells of a love
which knows no law except itself, a love which is not
hindered or made to hesitate and doubt by any command
of righteousness or honour. Love is the theme ; the tale
has no sympathy or understanding for anything else. It is
therefore free from the consciously realized inconsistencies
present at least in some versions of the story of Lancelot
and Guinevere. In them two laws of life seem on the verge
of conflict. On the one—the feebler—side, honour, troth
to marriage vows, some sense of right and wrong ; on the
other, passionate love, which is law and right unto itself,
having its own commands and prohibitions ; a love which is
also an inspiration and uplifting power unto the lover ; a
love holy in itself and yet because of its high nature the

more fatally impeached by truth and honour trampled on.
In the conflict between the two laws of life in the Lancelot
story, the rights and needs and power of love maintain
themselves ; yet the end must come, and the lovers live out
love's palinode in separate convents. For this love to be
made perfect, must be crowned with repentance.

Who first created Lancelot, and who first made the
peerless knight love Arthur's queen ? This question has
not yet been answered.[1] Chrétien de Troies' poem, *Le
Conte de la charrette*, has for its subject an episode in
Lancelot's long love of Guinevere.[2] Here, as in his other
poems, Chrétien is a facile narrator, with little sense of the
significance that might be given to the stories which he
received and cleverly remade. But their significance is
shown in the Old French prose *Lancelot*, probably composed two or three decades after Chrétien wrote. It contains the lovely story of Lancelot's rearing, by the Lady of
the Lake, and of his glorious youth. It brings him to the
Court of Arthur, and tells how he was made a knight—it
was the queen and not the king from whom he received
his sword. And he loves her—loves her and her only from
the first until his death. He has no thought of serving any
other mistress. And he is aided in his love by the " haute
prince Galehaut," the most high-hearted friend that ever
gave himself to his friend's weal.

From the beginning Lancelot's love is worship, it is
holy ; and almost from the beginning it is unholy. From
the beginning, too, it is the man's inspiration, it is his
strength ; it makes him the peerless knight, peerless in
courtesy, peerless in emprise ; this love gives him the single
eye, the unswerving heart, the resistless valour to accomplish
those adventures wherein all other knights had found their
shame—they were not perfect lovers ! Only through his
perfect love could Lancelot have accomplished that greatest
adventure of the *Val des faux amants ;—Val sans retour* for
all other knights.[3] Lancelot alone had always been, and to

[1] Cf. generally, J. L. Weston, *The Legend of Sir Lancelot du Lac* (London,
1901, David Nutt).

[2] See Gaston Paris, *Romania*, xii. 459-534.

[3] Paulin Paris, *Romans de la Table Ronde*, iv. 280 *sqq.*

his death remained, a lover absolutely true in act and word and thought; incomparably more chastely loyal to Guinevere than her kingly spouse. Against the singleness of this perfect love enchantments fail, and swords and lances break. Yet this love, fraught with untruth and dishonour, must conceal itself from that king who, while breaking his own marriage vows as passion led him, trusted and honoured above all men the peerless knight whose peerlessness was rooted in his unholy holy love for Arthur's queen.

The first full sin between Lancelot and Guinevere was committed when Arthur was absent on a love-adventure, which brought him to a shameful prison. He was delivered by Lancelot, and recognizing his deliverer, he said in royal gratitude: " I yield you my land, my honour, and myself." Lancelot blushes! Thereafter, as towards Arthur, Lancelot and Guinevere are forced into stratagems almost as ignoble as those by which King Mark was tricked. And Guinevere —she too is peerless among women; perfect in beauty, perfect in courtliness, perfect in dutifulness to her husband —saving her love for Lancelot! Guinevere's dutifulness to Arthur is not shaken by his outrageous treatment of her because of the " false Guinevere," when he cast off and sought to burn his queen. She will continue to obey him though he has dishonoured her—and all the time, unknown to her outrageous, unjustly accusing lord, how had she cast her and his honour down with Lancelot. Only while she is put away from her lord, and under Lancelot's guard, for that time she will be true to marriage vows; and Lancelot assents.[1]

The latter part of the story, when asceticism enters with Galahad,[2] suggests that the peerless knight of " les temps

---

[1] See Paulin Paris, *Romans de la Table Ronde*, iv. Guinevere's woman-mind is shown in the following scene. On an occasion the lover's sophisticated friend, the Dame de Malehaut, laughs tauntingly at Lancelot :

" ' Ah ! Lancelot, Lancelot, dit-elle, je vois que le roi n'a plus d'autre avantage sur vous que la couronne de Logres ! '

" Et comme il ne trouvait rien à répondre de convenable, ' Ma chère Malehaut, dit la reine, si je suis fille de roi, il est fils de roi ; si je suis belle, il est beau ; de plus, il est le plus preux des preux. Je n'ai donc pas à rougir de l'avoir choisi pour mon chevalier ' " (Paulin Paris, *ibid*. iv. 58).

[2] Galahad's mother was Helene, daughter of King Pelles (*roi pêcheur*), the custodian of the Holy Grail. A love-philter makes Lancelot mistake her for Guinevere ; and so the knight's loyalty to his mistress is saved. The damsel

adventureux " was sinful. But the main body of the tale
put no reproach on Lancelot for his great love. It told of a
love as perfect and as absolute as the author or compiler
could conceive ; and the conduct of Lancelot was intended
to be that of a perfect lover, whose sentiments and actions
should accord with the idea of courtly love and exemplify its
rules. Their underlying principle was that love should
always be absolute, and that the lover's every thought and
act should on all occasions correspond with the most
extreme feelings or sentiments or fancies possible for a
lover. In the prose narrative, for example, Lancelot goes
mad three times because of his mistress's cruelty, a cruelty
which may seem to us absurd, but which represents the
adored lady's insistence, under all circumstances, upon the
most unhesitating and utter devotion from her lover.

Chrétien's *Conte de la charrette* is a clear rendering of the
idea that love shall be absolute, and hesitate at nothing ; it
is an example of courtly love carried to its furthest imagined
conclusions. It displays all the rules of Andrew the
Chaplain in operation. In it Lancelot will do anything for
Guinevere, will show himself a coward knight at her
command, or perform feats of arms ; he will desire the least
little bit of her—a tress of hair—more than all else which is
not she ; he will throw himself from the window to be near
her ; engaged in deadly combat, the sight of her makes him
forget his enemy ; at the news of her death he seeks at once
to die. Of course his heart loathes the thought of infringing
this great love by the slightest fancy for another woman.
On the other hand, when by marvels of valour Lancelot
rescues Guinevere from captivity, she will not speak to him
because for a single instant he had hesitated to mount a
charrette, in which no knight was carried save one who
was felon and condemned to death. This was logical on
Guinevere's part ; Lancelot's love should always have been
so absolute as never for one instant to hesitate. Much of
this is extreme, and yet hardly unreal. Heloïse's love for
Abaelard never hesitated.

---

herself was without passion, beyond the wish to bear a son begotten by the best
of knights (*Romans, etc.*, v. 308 *sqq.*).

Such love, imperious and absolute, shuts out all laws
and exigencies save its own ; [1] it must be virtue and honour
unto itself ; it is careless of what ill it may do so long as
that ill does not infringe love's laws. Evidently before it
the bonds of marriage break, or pale to insignificance. It is
its own sanction, nor needs the faint blessing of the priest.
The poet—as the actual lover likewise—may even deem
that love can best show itself to be the principle of its own
honour when unsustained by wedlock ; thus unsustained and
unobscured it stands alone, fairer, clearer, more interesting
and romantic. Again, since mediaeval marriage in high life
was more often a joining of fiefs than a union of hearts,
there would be high-born dames and courtly poets to
declare that love could only exist between knight and
mistress, and not between husband and wife. Marriage
shuts out love's doubts and fears ; there is no need of
further knightly services ; and husband and wife by law
are bound to render to each other what between lovers
is gracious favour ; this was the opinion of Marie de
Champagne, it also was the opinion of Heloïse. In
chivalric poetry the lovers, when at last duly married, may
continue to call each other *ami et amie* rather than wife and
lord ; [2] or a knight may shun marriage lest he settle down
and lose worship, doing no more adventurous feats of arms,
like Chrétien's Erec, till his wife Enide stung him by her
speech.[3] Some centuries later Malory has Lancelot utter a
like sentiment : " But to be a wedded man I think never
to be, for if I were, then should I be bound to tarry with
my wife, and leave arms and tournaments, battles and
adventures."

If allowance be made for the difference in topic and
treatment between the Arthurian romances and Guillaume
de Lorris's portion of the *Roman de la rose*, the latter will

[1] " For what is he that may yeve a lawe to lovers ? Love is a gretter lawe
and a strengere to himself than any lawe that men may yeven " (Chaucer, *Boece*,
book iii. metre 12).

[2] As in Chrétien's *Cligés*, 6751 *sqq.*, when Cligés is crowned emperor and Fenice
becomes his queen, then : *De s'amie a feite sa fame*—but he still calls her *amie et
dame*, that he may not cease to love her as one should an *amie*. Cf. also Chrétien's
Erec, 4689.

[3] See also Gawain's words to *Ivain* when the latter is married—in Chrétien's
Ivain, 2484 *sqq.*

be seen to illustrate similar love principles.   De Lorris's poem is fancy playing with thoughts of love which had inspired these tales of chivalry.   Every one knows its gentle idyllic character ; — how charming, for instance, is the conflict between the Lover-to-be and Love, who quickly overcomes the ready yielder.   So he surrenders unconditionally, gives himself over ; Love may slay him or gladden him—" le cuers est vostre, non pas miens," says the lover to Love, and you shall do with it as you will.   Then Love sweetly takes his little golden key, and locks the lover's heart, after which he safely may impart his rules and counsels : the lover must abjure *vilanie*, and foul and slanderous speech—the opposite of courtesy.   Pride also (*orgoil*) must be abandoned.   He should attire himself seemingly, and show cheerfulness ; he must be niggardly in nothing ; his heart must be given utterly to one ; he shall undergo toils and endure griefs without complaint ; in absence he will always think of the beloved, sighing for her, keeping his love aflame ; he will be shameful, confused and changing colour in her presence ; at night he will toss and weep for love of her, and dream dreams of passionate delight ; then wakeful, he will rise and wander near her dwelling, but will not be seen—nor will he forget to be generous to her waiting-maid.   All of this will make the lover pale and lean.   To aid him to endure these agonies, will come Hope with her gentle healings, and Fond-thought, and Sweet-speech of the beloved with a wise confidant, and Sweet-sight of her dwelling, maybe of herself.   The *Roman de la rose* is fancy, and the Arthurian romances are fiction. In the one or the other, imagination may take the place of passion, and the contents of the poem or romance afford a type and presentation of the theory of love.